A HISTORY OF CHINA

A HISTORY OF CHINA

BEING THE HISTORICAL CHAPTERS FROM "THE MIDDLE KINGDOM"

BY THE LATE

SAMUEL WELLS WILLIAMS

PROFESSOR OF THE CHINESE LANGUAGE AND LITERATURE IN YALE COLLEGE

WITH A CONCLUDING CHAPTER NARRATING RECENT EVENTS

By

FREDERICK WELLS WILLIAMS

INSTRUCTOR IN ORIENTAL HISTORY IN YALE UNIVERSITY

GYAN

ISBN : 978-81-212-1564-0(HB)

First Published, 1897

Published, 2018

Published by

Gyan Publishing House
5, Ansari Road
Daryaganj, New Delhi-110002
Phone: 011-47034999, 9811692060
www.gyanbooks.com
E-mail: books@gyanbooks.com

Printed at: G. Print Process, Delhi.

PREFACE.

The need for a good history of China remains as unsatisfied to-day as when "The Middle Kingdom" was first written half a century ago. This is intended neither as a reflection upon the times in which we live, nor as a reproach to the small band of learned men that deserve the name of Sinologues; for an age is competent to determine its own interests, and if educated Europe cares little for the Far East it but continues in the traditions of the past; nor have scholars yet been able to investigate the unexplored mass of Chinese printed books which must supply authorities for the story of China's long career. The statement that the history of this nation has yet to be written is only made here in explanation of the reappearance in this volume of an inadequate sketch originally designed to form part of a comprehensive study of the country and its inhabitants. In view of an awakening interest in the affairs of Asia manifest throughout Europe and the United States, it has seemed advisable to provide—at least temporarily—for the wants of many readers by re-issuing the historical chapters of "The Middle Kingdom," adding thereto a summary of the more important occurrences that have marked the dozen years of Chinese history since that work was last revised. No attempt has been made to amend the portion already in type, since it is hoped that the lessened cost of the volume secured by using the old plates would compensate for any advantages to be expected from its revision within the limited time at the editor's command. Such accounts of political and social China as have appeared in our language within the past half-century have for the most part suffered from the bias, national, religious or otherwise, of their authors. While absolute impartiality is not a quality to be found here or elsewhere among human annalists, a true conception of eastern Asiatic politics is only to be obtained by forsaking so far as possible our prejudices of race and creed and approaching them with unselfish and sympathetic interest. An endeavor is made in these pages to comprehend the stand-point of the Chinese instead of either condemning or excusing their acts.

Events so recent as those detailed in the last chapter of this book must needs be arranged in the form of a rather colorless chronicle, the perspective being too small as yet to develop them into a philosophic history. In her present distress and indecision, it is still more difficult to discuss the future than the present of the Chinese Empire. She has now had nearly three generations of intercourse and experience with Western nations, and yet with few exceptions her statesmen to-day exhibit the same hopeless incapacity in dealing with questions involving the fate of the nation that marked the advisers of Taukwang and Hienfung. Apparently their lessons at the hands of hardier peoples have taught them nothing; they show since their discomfiture by Japan the same abject fear that has in times past driven or drifted them into spasms of abasement, which to the merely superficial observer seem closely bordering upon imbecility. The dread inspired by defeat is not an unaccustomed phenomenon to students of Asiatic nations. In the simple structure of an oriental despotism a disastrous campaign means, usually, the supplanting of the reigning family by a new house, native or foreign. This event has more than once during this century been confidently awaited in the East as the normal outcome of Chinese reverses. At each catastrophe the mandarinate—which is but a ruling clique—has, as it were, bent its head for the *coup de grace*, involving, of course, the extinction of the dynasty, only to arise to renewed life and a lengthened lease of corrupt control.

In a very real sense the government and the nation of China are two different things. The former has just escaped, thanks in part to European interference, from peril of its life; the latter feels no sense of escape whatever, only a renewal of the unjust rule under which it has repined since the present dynasty became effete. In some degree we may account, therefore, for the prostration of the governing minority in the Empire, its weakness and ineptness in war and in peace; with characteristic oriental stoicism it has not thought seriously of guaranteeing the future, being still confident of its inevitable doom. Meanwhile, the nation itself, conscious of new forces on every side, has shown by rebellions cropping out everywhere, by the machinations of secret societies and by the more open and laudable efforts of a few individuals, its discontent with the old régime and its desire to participate in the profits of industrial life with modern appliances and under modern conditions. This is the New China, that the Old; the one has insisted upon the adoption of railroads and telegraphs, the circulation of newspapers, and the introduction of Western science into the curriculum of official education; the other has excited the hatred of the ignorant people against foreigners and thwarted or ridiculed every attempt to re-establish the Empire by the adoption of European institutions.

Whether the one party or the other will eventually succeed in obtaining permanent control is now rendered doubly uncertain by the active and apparently unresisted interference of Russia in Chinese affairs. While this new political factor, and the still newer phenomenon of militant Japan, introduce elements into the problem of the Far East as yet too undefined to discuss, it may be observed in conclusion that the proposed network of railroads in Manchuria to be built, equipped and guarded by Russian money and troops, shows who is the chief gainer by the late war. This is what British diplomatists have uniformly expected as a result of a contest which involved China with any other power, and for this reason they tried to prevent the war. Having failed to do so they not unnaturally declined to join their continental rival and humiliate Japan by interfering in the treaty which gave her the rewards of victory. The hopes of political prophets as to the military value of China's millions being for the present in abeyance, it is still possible for Great Britain—the representative of what is best in Christian civilization in Asia—to count upon an ally that is imbued with a dislike as intense as her own for Russia, and that is willing to join her in rescuing from the Adversary the country which each in turn has invaded and vanquished.

A word ought to be said as to the spelling of proper names in this volume. Had a thorough revision been practicable the editor might have conformed to the Wade system, not because of its intrinsic superiority to others, but because of its general use in a matter where a clear majority ought to be law. While endeavoring to preserve the same forms throughout the volume, he has in the final chapter yielded to common usage in some familiar names like Foochow, Kelung, etc., and has for the sake of simplicity abandoned the accent employed to mark the Italian *i*. In Korean names any scientific consistency in spelling is excessively difficult to attain, since with the nomenclature of three languages to choose from foreign writers naturally vary widely in their selections. The place called in the text Ping yang, for example, is written *P'ing jang* (or *yang*) in Chinese, *Phyöng yang* in Korean, and *Hei jō* in Japanese, and so with every spot in that unblest and stricken peninsula. In general the consonants have their English values here while the vowels are sounded approximately as in Italian or Spanish, with the exception of *ŭ* which corresponds with *ê* in the Wade system and represents the short *u* in such words as *fun*, *tun*, etc.

F. W. W.

NEW HAVEN, CONN., February, 1897.

CONTENTS.

CHAPTER I.

PAGE

CHRONOLOGY AND EARLY HISTORY, ... 1–53

General doubts and ignorance concerning the subject, 2; The mythological period, 3; Chinese notions of cosmogony, 4; The god Pwanku, 5; Chu Hí's cosmogony, 7; The legendary period, Fuh-hí, 9; The eight monarchs, 11; Hwangtí and the sexagenary cycle, 12; The deluge of Yao, 13; The historical period: The Hia dynasty, 14; Yu the Great, his inscription on the rocks of Kau-lau shan, 15; Records of the Hia, 18; The Shang dynasty, 20; Chau-sin, 22; Rise of the house of Chau, 23; Credibility of these early annals, 25; The Tsin dynasties. Tsin Chí Hwangtí, 26; The dynasty of Han, 28; From the Han to the Sui, 31; The great Tang dynasty, 33; Taitsung and the Empress Wu, 35; The Five Dynasties, 38; The Sung dynasty, 39; The Mongol conquest, Kublai Khan, 41; The Mings, 43; The Manchus, or Tsing dynasty, 45; Kanghí, 46; Yungching and Kienlung, 47; Kiaking and Taukwang, 49; Tables of the monarchs and dynasties, 52.

CHAPTER II.

FOREIGN INTERCOURSE WITH CHINA, ... 54-110

Limited conception of the Chinese as to embassies, 54; Earliest mention of China or Cathay, 56; Acquaintance between Rome and Seres, or Sinæ, 57; Knowledge of China under the Greek Empire, 60; Narratives of Buddhist pilgrims, 61; Notices of Arab travellers, 62; Plano Carpini's mission from the Pope to Kuyuk Khan, 63; Rubruquis sent by Louis XI. to Mangu Khan, 66; Travels of Marco Polo and King Hayton of Armenia, 68; Of the Moor, Ibn Batuta, 69; Of Friar Odoric, 70; Of Benedict Goës, 72; Of Ibn Wahab, 73; The Manchus

PAGE

confine foreign trade to Canton, 74; Character of early Portuguese traders, 75; Their settlement at Macao and embassies to Peking, 76; Relations of Spain with China, 79; The Dutch come to China, 81; They occupy Formosa, 82; Koxinga expels them from the island, 85; Van Hoorn's embassy to Peking, 86; Van Braam's mission to Kienlung, 87; France and China, 88; Russian embassies to the court at Peking, 89; Intercourse of the English with China, 91; Attempts of the East India Company to establish trade, 93; The Co-hong, 95; Treatment of Mr. Flint, 96; Anomalous position of foreigners in China during the eighteenth century, 98; Chinese action in sundry cases of homicide among foreigners, 99; Lord Macartney's embassy to Peking, 102; Attitude of the Chinese regarding Macao, 104; Regarding English and American "squabbles," 105; Embassy of Lord Amherst, 106; Close of the East India Company monopoly, 107; American trade with China, 108; Chinese terms for foreigners, 109.

CHAPTER III.

ORIGIN OF THE FIRST WAR WITH ENGLAND, . . . 111–161

Features of the war with England, 111; Lord Napier appointed superintendent of British trade, 112; He goes to Canton, 115; His contest with the governor, 116; Chinese notions of supremacy, 120; Lord Napier retires from Canton, his sudden death, 122; Petition of the British merchants to the king, 124; Trade continued as before, 126; Sir B. G Robinson the superintendent at Lintin, 127; Is succeeded by Captain Elliot, 129; Hü Nai-tsí proposes to legalize the opium trade, 130; Countermemorials to the Emperor. 131; Discussion of the matter among foreigners, 135; Canton officers enforce the prohibitory laws, 138; Elliot ordered to drive the opium ships from Lintin, 139; Arrival of Admiral Sir F. Maitland, 140; Smuggling increases, 141; A mob before the factories, 143; Captain Elliot's papers and actions regarding the opium traffic 144; Commissioner Lin sent to Canton, 145; He demands a surrender of opium held by foreigners, 147; Imprisons them in the factories, 148; The opium given up and destroyed, 150; Homicide of Lin Wei-hí at Hongkong, 153; Motives and position of Governor Lin, 156; The war an opium war, 158; Debate in Parliament upon the question, 160.

CHAPTER IV.

PAGE

THE OPIUM WAR, ... 162–222

Arrival of the British fleet and commencement of hostilities, 162; Fall of Tinghai, 163: Lin recalled to Peking, 164; Kíshen sent to Canton, negotiates a treaty with Captain Elliot at the Bogue, 165; The negotiations fail, 167; Capture of the Canton River defences, 169; The city ransomed, 171; Amoy and Tinghai taken, 173; Fall of Chinhai and Ningpo, 175; The Emperor determines to resist, 177; Attempt to recapture Ningpo, 179; The British reduce the neighboring towns, 181; The fleet enters the Yangtsz', capture of Wusung, 183; Shanghai taken, 184; Proclamations issued by both parties respecting the war, 185; Storming of Chinkiang, 188; Terrible carnage among its Manchu inhabitants, 190; Singular contrast at Íching, 192; Kíying communicates with Sir H. Pottinger, 194; The envoy and commissioners meet, 195; A treaty drawn up, 197; Conversation on the opium question, 198; The Treaty of Nanking signed, 201; Massacre of shipwrecked crews on Formosa, 202; Losses and rewards on both sides after the war, 204: Settlement of a tariff and commercial relations, 205; Deaths of Howqua and John R. Morrison, 207; A supplementary treaty signed, 209; Renewal of opium vexations, 210; Trèaties arranged with other foreign powers, 213; The ambassador and letter from the United States to China, 214; Caleb Cushing negotiates a treaty with Kíying, 215; Homicide by an American at Canton, and subsequent correspondence, 216; A French treaty concluded by M. de Lagrené at Whampoa, 219; Position of England and China after the war, 220.

CHAPTER V.

THE TAI-PING REBELLION, ... 223–272

Attitude of the ruling classes in China toward foreigners, 223; Governor Sir J. Davis and Commissioner Kíying, 225; Killing of six Englishmen at Canton, 226; Chinese notions of treaties, *ibid.*; Causes of the Tai-ping Rebellion, 229; Life of Hung Siutsuen, its leader, 230; His wonderful vision, 231; He interprets it by Christian ideas, 233; Early phases

PAGE

of the movement, 235; Commencement of the insurrection, 238; Political and religious tenets of the rebels, 240; Rapid advance to the Yangtsz' and occupation of Nanking, 244; The expedition against Peking, 245; Its failure, 247; Dissensions among the rebel *wangs*, or leaders, 250; Rebel sortie from Nanking, 253; Assistance of foreigners sought by imperialists, 255; Achievements of the Chung Wang, 256; Colonel Gordon assumes control of the "Ever-Victorious force," 257; His successful campaigns, 259; Environment of Suchau, 261; The city surrenders, 262; Execution of its wangs by Governor Lí, 263; Gordon's responsibility in the matter, 264; Further operations against the insurgents, 265; The Ever-Victorious force disbanded, 266; Fall of Nanking and dispersion of the rebels, 269; Subsequent efforts of the Shí and Kan wangs, 270; Disastrous character of the rebellion, 271.

CHAPTER VI.

THE SECOND ANGLO-CHINESE WAR, ... 273–337

Relations between the Cantonese and foreigners after the first war, 274; Collecting of custom duties at Shanghai entrusted to foreigners, 275; Common measures of defence against the rebels there, 277; The insurrection in Kwangtung, 278; Frightful destruction of life, 281; Governor Yeh's policy of seclusion, 281; Smuggling lorchas at Hongkong and Macao, 282; The lorcha Arrow affair, 283; The initial acts of the war, 286; Collision with Americans at the Barrier forts, 287; View of the war in England, 289; Arrival of Lord Elgin and Baron Gros in China, 291; Bombardment and capture of Canton, *ibid.*; Problem of governing the city, 294; The allies repair to the Pei-ho, 297; Capture of the Taku forts, 299; Negotiations with Kweiliang and Hwashana at Tientsin, 300; Unexpected appearance of Kíying, 301; Difficulties of Lord Elgin's position at Tientsin, 302; The treaties signed and ratified, 304; Revision of the tariff undertaken at Shanghai, 305; Effect of treaty stipulations and foreign trade on the people of China, 306; Lord Elgin visits the Tai-ping rebels at Hankow, 307; Sentiment of officials and people in China regarding foreigners, 308; Coolie trade outrages, 311; The foreign ministers repair to Taku, 312; Repulse at the Taku forts, 314; The American minister conducted to Peking, 316; Discussion concerning the formalities of an audience, 317;

PAGE

He retires and ratifies the treaty at Pehtang, 318; Lord Elgin and Baron Gros sent back to China, 319; War resumed, the allies at Pehtang, 321; Capture of villages about Taku, 322; Fall of the Taku forts, 324; Lord Elgin declines to remain at Tientsin, 325; Interpreters Wade and Parkes sent to Tungchau, 326; Capture of Parkes and Loch, 328; Skirmish of Pa-lí-kiau, 330; Pillage of Yuen-ming Yuen, 331; Its destruction upon the return of the prisoners, 332; Entry into Peking and signing of the treaties, 334; Permanent settlement of foreign embassies at the capital, 336.

CHAPTER VII.

THE ADMINISTRATION OF THE EMPRESSES, ... 338-389

Palace conspiracy upon the death of Hienfung, 338; The regency established at Peking, 339; The Lay-Osborne flotilla, 341; Collapse of the scheme and dismissal of Lay, 343; The Burlingame mission to foreign countries, 344; Its treaty with the United States, 346; Outbreak at Tientsin, 348; Investigation into the riot, 351; Bitter feeling among foreigners, 353; Memorandum from the Tsung lí Yamun on the missionary question, 355; Conclusion of the Kansuh insurrection, 357; Marriage of the Emperor Tungchí, 358; The foreign ministers demand an audience, 360; Reception of the ambassadors by Tungchí, 362; Stopping of the coolie trade, 363; Japanese descent upon Formosa, 365; English expedition to Yunnan, 367; Second mission, murder of Margary, 369; The Grosvenor mission of inquiry, 371; The Chifu Convention between Lí Hung-chang and Sir T. Wade, 373; Death of Tungchí and accession of Kwangsü, 375; The rebellion of Yakub Beg in Turkestan, 375; He overthrows the Dungani Confederation, 378; His forces conquered by Tso Tsung-tang, 379; Negotiations as to the cession of Kuldja, 380; The great famine of 1878, 382; Efforts of foreigners for its relief, 384; Chinese boys sent to America for education, 387; Grounds of hope for the future of China, 389.

CHAPTER VIII.

PAGE

NARRATIVE OF RECENT EVENTS, ... 390–462

Three important occurrences mark the close of the century, 390; Beginning of French interference in Indo China, 391; Chinese suzerainty over Annam, 392; The French raid on Tongking, 395; Death of Rivière at Hanoi, 396; The conquest of Tongking, 397; The Fournier convention and renewal of hostilities, 399; A War-no-war, 401; The Franco-Chinese treaty of 1885, 403; A spasm of progress in China, 405; Agreements as to Hongkong and Macao, 406; The English in Burma and Port Hamilton, 409; Kwangsü's accession and retirement of the Dowager-Empress Hi, 411; Audience negotiations, 413; Western science and railroads, 415; The Yellow River flood, 417; Reactionary tendencies, 420; Outrages committed on foreigners, 421; Riots at Wuhu, 422; At Wusueh, Icbang and Kirin, 425; At Sungpu, Chingtu and elsewhere, 426; The massacre at Hwashan, 429; Causes of Anti-foreign fanaticism, 430; Necessity of punishment rather than indemnity, 435; The rivalry of China and Japan over Korea, 437; Political demoralization of Korea, 441; The *Kowshing* affair, 443; The Battle of Ping yang, 444; The Battle of Hai yang, 447; The fall of Port Arthur, 451; The Japanese in Manchuria, 454; The capture of Wei hai wei, 456; The treaty of Shimonoseki, 461.

CHAPTER I.

CHRONOLOGY AND EARLY HISTORY.

The history of the Chinese people has excited less attention among western scholars than it deserves, though in some respects no nation offers more claims to have its chronicles carefully and fairly examined. The belief is generally entertained that their pretensions to antiquity are extravagant and ridiculous, and incompatible with the Mosaic chronology; that they not only make the world to have existed myriads of years, but reckon the succession of their monarchs far beyond the creation, and ascribe to them a longevity that carries its own confutation on its face. In consequence of this opinion, some have denied the credibility of native historians altogether, and the whole subject of the settlement and early progress of this ancient race has been considered beyond the reach, and almost unworthy the attempt, of sober investigation. This erroneous and hasty conclusion is gradually giving way to a careful inquiry into those histories which show that the early records of the sons of Han contain much which is worthy of credence, and much more that is highly probable. A wide field is here opened for the researches of a Gibbon or a Niebuhr; for as long as we are destitute of a good history of China and its connections with other Asiatic nations, we shall not only be unable to form a correct opinion respecting the people, but shall lack many important data for a full illustration of the early history of the human race. It is easy to laud the early records of the Chinese to the skies, as French writers have done; and it is quite as easy to cry them down as worthless—manufactured in after-ages to please the variety of their writers. The reputation both people and records have received is owing, in some measure, to this undue laudation and depreciation, as well as to the intrinsic merits and defects of their histories. These, however, still mostly remain in their originals, and will require the united labors of many scholars to be fully brought to light and made a part of the world's library.

The enormous difficulties arising from the extent and tedious minuteness of native historians, coupled with the scarcity of translators competent or willing to undertake the labor of even such a *résumé* of these works as will satisfy rational curiosity, are now being slowly overcome, both by Chinese and foreign students. These researches, it is to be earnestly hoped, will be rewarded by promoting a juster estimate in the minds of both classes of their relative positions among the nations of the earth.

China, like other countries, has her mythological history, and it should be separated from the more recent and received, as her own historians regard it, as the fabrication of subsequent times. She also has her ancient history, whose earliest dates and events blend confusedly with the mythological, but gradually grow more credible and distinct as they come down the stream of time to the beginning of modern history. The early accounts of every nation whose founding was anterior to the practice of making and preserving authentic records must necessarily be obscure and doubtful. What is applicable to the Chinese has been true of other ancient people: "national vanity and a love of the marvellous have influenced them all, and furnished materials for many tales, as soon as the spirit of investigation has supplanted that appetite for wonders which marks the infancy of nations as well as of individuals." The ignorance of the "art preservative of all arts" will greatly explain the subsequent record of the wonderful, without supposing that the infancy of nations partook of the same traits of weakness and credulity as that of individuals. There is neither space nor time in this work to give the details concerning the history and succession of dynasties that have swayed the Middle Kingdom, for to one not specially engaged in their examination their recital is proverbially dry; the array of uncouth names destitute of lasting interest, and the absence of the charm of association with western nations render them uninviting to the general reader. Some account of the leading events and changes is all that is necessary to explain what has been elsewhere incidentally referred to.[1]

Chinese historians have endeavored to explain the creation and origin of the world around them; but, ignorant of the sublime fact that there is one Creator who upholds his works by the word of his power, they have invented various modes to account for it, and wearied themselves in theorizing and disputing with each other. One of them, Yangtsz', remarks, in view of these conflicting suppositions: "Who knows the affairs of remote antiquity, since no authentic records have come down to us? He who examines these stories will find it difficult to believe them, and careful scrutiny will convince him that they are without foundation. In the primeval ages no historical records were kept. Why then, since the ancient books that described those times were burnt by Tsin, should we misrepresent those remote ages, and satisfy ourselves with vague fables? However, as everything except heaven and earth must have a cause, it is clear that they have always existed, and that cause produced all sorts of men and beings, and endowed them with their various qualities. But it must have been man who in the beginning produced all things on earth, and who may therefore be viewed as the lord, and from whom rulers derive their dignities."

This extract is not a bad example of Chinese writers and historians; a mixture of sense and nonsense, partially laying the foundation of a just argument, and ending with a tremendous non-sequitur, apparently satisfactory to themselves, but showing pretty conclusively how little pains they take to gather facts and discuss their bearings. Some of these writers imagine that the world owes its existence to the retroactive agency of the dual powers *yin* and *yang*, which first formed the outline of the universe, and were themselves influenced by

[1] Among the works which will repay perusal on this topic are Mailla's *Histoire de la Chine* and Pauthier's *Chine*, in French, and Du Halde's *History*, translated into English; besides the briefer compilations of Murray, Grosier, Gutzlaff, Davis, and more recently of Boulger and Richthofen, Band I.

their own creations. One of the most sensible of their authors says:

> Heaven was formless, an utter chaos; the whole mass was nothing but confusion. Order was first produced in the pure ether, and out of it the universe came forth; the universe produced air, and air the milky-way. When the pure male principle *yang* had been diluted, it formed the heavens; the heavy and thick parts coagulated, and formed the earth. The refined particles united very soon, but the union of the thick and heavy went on slowly; therefore the heavens came into existence first, and the earth afterward. From the subtle essence of heaven and earth, the dual principles *yin* and *yang* were formed; from their joint operation came the four seasons, and these putting forth their energies gave birth to all the products of the earth. The warm effluence of the *yang* being condensed, produced fire; and the finest parts of fire formed the sun. The cold exhalations of the *yin* being likewise condensed, produced water; and the finest parts of the watery substance formed the moon. By the seminal influence of the sun and moon, came the stars. Thus heaven was adorned with the sun, moon, and stars; the earth also received rain, rivers, and dust.[1]

But this acute explanation, like the notions of Hesiod among the Greeks, was too subtle for the common people; they also wanted to personify and deify these powers and operations, but lacking the imaginative genius and fine taste of the Greeks, their divine personages are outrageous and their ideal beings shapeless monsters. No creator is known or imagined who, like Brahm, lives in space, ineffable, formless; but the first being, Pwanku, had the herculean task to mould the chaos which produced him and chisel out the earth that was to contain him. One legend is that "the dual powers were fixed when the primeval chaos separated. Chaos is bubbling turbid water, which enclosed and mingled with the dual powers, like a chick *in ovo*, but when their offspring Pwanku appeared their distinctiveness and operations were apparent. *Pwan* means a 'basin,' referring to the shell of the egg; *ku* means 'solid,' 'to secure,' intending to show how the first man Pwanku was hatched from the chaos by the dual powers, and then settled and exhibited the arrangement of the causes which produced him."

The Rationalists have penetrated furthest into the Dædalian

---

[1] *Chinese Repository*, Vol. III., p. 55.

mystery of this cosmogony,[1] and they go on to show what Pwanku did and how he did it. They picture him holding a chisel and mallet in his hands, splitting and fashioning vast

Pwanku Chiselling Out the Universe.

masses of granite floating confusedly in space. Behind the openings his powerful hand has made are seen the sun, moon, and stars, monuments of his stupendous labors; at his right

[1] For the Buddhist notions of cosmography and creation, see Rémusat, *Mélanges Posthumes*, pp. 65–131.

hand, inseparable companions of his toils, but whose generation is left in obscurity, stand the dragon, the phœnix, and the tortoise, and sometimes the unicorn, divine types and progenitors with himself of the animal creation. His efforts were continued eighteen thousand years, and by small degrees he and his work increased; the heavens rose, the earth spread out and thickened, and Pwanku grew in stature, six feet every day, till, his labors done, he died for the benefit of his handiwork. His head became mountains, his breath wind and clouds, and his voice thunder; his limbs were changed into the four poles, his veins into rivers, his sinews into the undulations of the earth's surface, and his flesh into fields; his beard, like Berenice's hair, was turned into stars, his skin and hair into herbs and trees, and his teeth, bones, and marrow into metals, rocks, and precious stones; his dropping sweat increased to rain, and lastly (*nascitur ridiculus mus*) the insects which stuck to his body were transformed into people!

Such was Pwanku, and these were his works. But these grotesque myths afford none of the pleasing images and personifications of Greek fable or Egyptian symbols; they fatigue without entertaining, and only illustrate the childish imagination of their authors. Pwanku was succeeded by three rulers of monstrous forms called the Celestial, Terrestrial, and Human sovereigns, impersonations of a trinity of powers, whose traces and influences run through Chinese philosophy, religion, and politics; their acts and characters are detailed with the utmost gravity, and more than Methusalean longevity allowed them to complete their plans. Their reigns continued eighteen thousand years (more or less according to the author quoted), during which time good government commenced, men learned to eat and drink, the sexes united, sleep was invented, and other improvements adopted. One would think, if the subjects of these wonderful beings were as long-lived, great perfection might have been attained in these and other useful arts; but the mysterious tortoise, companion of Pwanku, on whose carapace was written, in tadpole-headed characters, the history of the anterior world, did not survive, and their record has not come down. After them flourished two other monarchs, one of them called

Yu-chau, which means 'having a nest,' and the other Sui-jin, or 'match-man.' Whether the former invented nests for the abodes of his subjects, such as the Indians on the Orinoco have, is not stated; but the latter brought down fire from heaven for them to cook with, and became a second, or rather the first, Prometheus.

These fancies are gathered from a popular summary of knowledge, called the *Coral Forest of Ancient Matters*, and from the opening chapters of *History Made Easy*. A higher style of philosophizing is found in Chu Hi's disquisition, from which an extract has been given in Chapter XII. Another on Cosmogony will show that he comes no nearer to the great fact of creation than ancient western writers.

In the beginning heaven and earth were just the light and dark air. This one air revolved, grinding round and round. When it ground quickly much sediment was compressed, which, having no means of exit, coagulated and formed the earth in the centre. The subtle portion of the air then became heaven and the sun, moon, and stars, which unceasingly revolve on the outside. The earth is in the centre and motionless; it is not below the centre.

Heaven revolving without ceasing, day and night also revolve, and hence the earth is exactly in the centre. If heaven should stand still for one moment, then the earth must fall down; but heaven revolves quickly, and hence much sediment is coagulated in the centre. The earth is the sediment of the air; and hence it is said, the light, pure air became heaven, the heavy, muddy air became earth. . . .

At the beginning of heaven and earth, before chaos was divided, I think there were only two things—fire and water; and the sediment of the water formed the earth. When one ascends a height and looks down, the crowd of hills resemble the waves of the sea in appearance: the water just flowed like this. I know not at what period it coagulated. At first it was very soft, but afterward it coagulated and became hard. One asked whether it resembled sand thrown up by the tide? He replied, Just so; the coarsest sediment of the water became earth, and the purest portion of the fire became wind, thunder, lightning, sun, and stars. . . .

Before chaos was divided, the *yin-yang*, or light-dark air, was mixed up and dark, and when it divided the centre formed an enormous and most brilliant opening, and the two *i* or principles were established. Shao Kang-tsieh considers one hundred and twenty-nine thousand six hundred years to be a *yuen*, or kalpa; then, before this period of one hundred and twenty-nine thousand six hundred years there was another opening and spreading out of the world; and before that again, there was another like the present; so that motion and rest, light and darkness, have no beginning. As little things shadow forth great things, this may be illustrated by the revolutions of day and night. . . .

Kang-tsieh says, Heaven rests upon form, and earth reclines upon air. The reason why he repeats this frequently, and does not deviate from the idea, is lest people should seek some other place beyond heaven and earth. There is nothing outside heaven and earth, and hence their form has limits, while their air has no limit. Because the air is extremely condensed, therefore it can support the earth; if it were not so the earth would fall down.[1]

A third belief respecting the position of the earth in the centre of the universe derives great strength in the opinion of intelligent natives from these speculations of Chu Hí. His theory considers the world to be a plane surface, straight, square, and large, measuring each way about 1,500 miles (5,600 *li*), and bounded on the four sides by the four seas. The sun is estimated to be about 4,000 miles from the earth. Another calculation made it 81,394 *li*, and a third 216,781½ *li*.

One thing is observable in these fictions, characteristic of the Chinese at the present day: there is no hierarchy of gods brought in to rule and inhabit the world they made, no conclave on Mt. Olympus, nor judgment of the mortal soul by Osiris; no transfer of human love and hate, passions and hopes, to the powers above; all here is ascribed to disembodied agencies or principles, and their works are represented as moving on in quiet order. There is no religion, no imagination; all is impassible, passionless, uninteresting. It may, perhaps, be considered of itself as sensible as the Greek or Egyptian mythology, if one looks for *sense* in such figments; but it has not, as in the latter countries, been explained in sublime poetry, shadowed forth in gorgeous ritual and magnificent festivals, represented in exquisite sculptures, nor preserved in faultless, imposing fanes and temples, filled with ideal creations. For this reason it appears more in its true colors, and, when compared with theirs, "loses discountenanced and like folly shows"—at least to us, who can examine both and compare them with the truth.

Their pure mythological history ends with the appearance of Fuh-hí, and their chronology has nothing to do with the long periods antecedent, varying from forty-five to five hundred

---

[1] Canon McClatchie's *Confucian Cosmogony*, pp. 53–59.

thousand years. These periods are, however, a mere twinkling compared with the kulpas of the Hindus, whose highest era, called the Unspeakably Inexpressible, requires four million four hundred and fifty-six thousand four hundred and forty-eight cyphers following a unit to represent it. If the epoch of Fuh-hí could be ascertained with any probability by comparison with the history of other nations, or with existing remains, it would tend not a little to settle some disputed chronological points in other countries; but the isolation of the Chinese throughout their whole existence makes it nearly impossible to weave in the events of their history with those of other nations, by comparing and verifying them with biblical, Egyptian, or Persian annals. Perhaps further investigations in the vast regions of Eastern and Central Asia may bring to light corroborative testimony as striking and unexpected as the explorations in Mosul, Persepolis, and Thebes.

The accession of Fuh-hí is placed in the Chinese annals B.C. 2852,[1] and with him commences the period known among them as the "highest antiquity." The weight of evidence which the later chronological examinations of Hales and Jackson have brought to bear against the common period of four thousand and four years prior to the Advent, is such as to cast great doubt over its authenticity, and lead to the adoption of a longer period in order to afford time for many occurrences, which otherwise would be crowded into too narrow a space. Chinese chronology, if it be allowed the least credit, strongly corroborates the results of Dr. Hales' researches, and particularly so in the date of Fuh-hí's accession. This is not the place to discuss the respective claims of the two eras, but by reckoning, as he does, the creation to be five thousand four hundred and eleven years, and the deluge three thousand one hundred and fifty-five years, before the Advent, we bring the commencement of ancient Chinese history three hundred and three years subsequent to the deluge, forty-seven before the death of Noah, and about three centuries before the confusion of tongues. If we suppose that the ante-

[1] Or 3322, according to Dr. Legge, whose date has been used elsewhere in this work, and has probably quite as much authority as the one above.

diluvians possessed a knowledge of the geography of the world, and that Noah, regarding himself as the monarch of the whole, divided it among his descendants before his death, there is nothing improbable in the further supposition that the progenitors of the black-haired race, and others of the house and lineage of Shem, found their way from the valley of the Euphrates across the defiles and steppes of Central Asia, to the fertile plains of China before the end of the third diluvian century. Whether the surface of the world was the same after the cataclysm as before does not affect this point; there was ample time for the multiplication of the species with the blessing promised by God, sufficient to form colonies, if there was time enough to increase to such a multitude as conspired to build the tower of Babel.

The views of Dr. Legge, that the present Chinese descend from settlers who came through Central Asia along the Tarim Valley and across the Desert into Kansuh, about B.C. 2200, and settled around the elbow of the Yellow River, under the leadership of Yao, Shun, Yu, and others, are very reasonable. These settlers found the land at that time occupied with tribes, whom they partly merged with themselves or drove into mountain recesses in Kweichau, where some of their descendants perhaps still remain. These earlier tribes may have furnished the names and reigns prior to Yao, and the later Chinese annalists incorporated them into their own histories, taking everything in early times as of course belonging to the *lí min*, or 'black-haired race.' The lapse of a millennium between the Deluge and Yao allows plenty of time for several successive emigrations from Western and Central Asia into the inviting plains of China, which, through the want of a written language or the destruction of records, have come down to us in misty, doubtful legends.

Fuh-hí and his seven successors are stated to have reigned seven hundred and forty-seven years, averaging ninety-three each. Those who follow Usher consider these monarchs to be Chinese travesties of the eight antediluvian patriarchs; and Marquis d'Urban has gone so far as to write what he calls the *Antediluvian History of China*, collecting all the notices history affords of their acts. The common chronology brings the deluge about thirteen years after the accession of Yao and the death of Shun (the last of the eight), B.C. 2205, or twenty-five years after the confusion of tongues. According to Hales, the last epoch is one hundred and twelve years before the call of Abraham, and these eight Chinese monarchs are therefore contemporaries of the patriarchs who lived between Shem and Abraham, commencing with Salah and ending with Nahor. The duration of their reigns, moreover, is such as would bear the same proportion to ages of five hundred years, which their contemporaries lived, as the present average of twenty and twenty-five years does to a life of sixty. The Assyrian tablets, deciphered by George Smith, contain a reference to the twenty-eighth century B.C., as the founding of that monarchy; which is a notice of more value as a chronological epoch than anything in Chinese annals, indeed, and may help to countenance a date that had before been regarded as mythological.

Supposing that the descendants of Shem, Ham, and Japheth, knowing from their fathers and grandfather, that the void world was before them, began to colonize almost as soon as they began to form families, three centuries would not be too long a time for some of them to settle in China, perhaps offsetting from Elam and Asshur, and other descendants of Shem in Persia. The capital of Fuh-hí slightly indicates, it may be thought, their route through Central Asia across the Desert to Kiayü kwan in Kansuh, and then down the Yellow River to the Great Plain near Kaifung. But these suppositions are only by the way, as is also the suggestion that teaching of fishing and grazing, the regulation of times and seasons, cultivation of music, and establishment of government, etc., compare well enough with the duties that might reasonably be supposed to belong to the founder of a colony and his successors, and subsequently ascribed to them as their own inventions. The long period allotted to human life at that date would allow these arts and sciences to take root and their memory to remain in popular legends until subsequent historians incorporated them into their writings. The Chinese annalists fill up the reigns of these chiefs, down to the time of Yao, with a series of inventions and improvements in the arts of life and good government, sufficient to bring society to that degree of comfort and order they suppose consonant with the character of the monarchs. The earliest records of the Chinese correspond much too closely with their present character to receive full belief; but they present an appearance of probability and naturalness not possessed by the early annals of Greece. No one contends for their credibility as history, but they are better than the Arabian Nights.

The commencement of the sexagenary cycle[1] in the sixty-first year of Hwangtí's reign (or B.C. 2637), five hundred and eighteen years after the deluge, eighty-two years after the death of Arphaxad, and about that time before the confusion of tongues, is worthy of notice. The use of the ten horary characters applied to days in order to denote their chronological sequence dates from the reign of Yu in the twentieth century B.C., and there are other passages in the *Shu King* showing similar application. Sz'ma Tsien's history now contains the first attempt to arrange the years in cycles of sixty; but he cannot fairly be claimed as the inventor of this system. He might almost as well be regarded as the inventor of his whole *annals*, for all the materials out of which he compiled them have now perished except the canonical books. The mention of the individual Nao the Great, who invented it, and the odd date of its adoption in the middle of a reign, do not weaken the alleged date of its origin in the minds of those who are inclined to take a statement of this kind on its own basis.

Three reigns, averaging eighty years' duration, intervened between that of Hwangtí and Yao, whose occupants were elected by the people, much as were Shemgar, Jephthah, and other judges in Israel, and probably exercised a similar sway. The reigns and characters of Yao and Shun have been immortalized by Confucius and Mencius; whatever was their real history, those sages showed great sagacity in going back to those remote times for models and fixing upon a period neither fabulous nor certain, one which prevented alike the cavils of scepticism and the appearance of complete fabrication.

---

[1] *Journal Asiatique*, Avril, 1836, p. 394.

A tremendous deluge occurred during the reign of Yao, B.C. 2293, caused, it is said, by the overflowing of the rivers in the north of China. Those who place the Noachic deluge B.C. 2348 regard this as only a different version of that event; Klaproth, who favors the Septuagint chronology, says that it is nearly synchronous with the deluge of Xisuthrus, B.C. 2297, a name derived, as is reasonably inferred by George Smith, from the Assyrian name Hasisadra, the ancient hero who survived the deluge. The record of this catastrophe in the *Shu King* is hardly applicable to an overwhelming flood: "The Emperor said, Oh! chief of the four mountains, destructive in their overthrow are the waters of the inundation. In their vast extent they embrace the mountains and overtop the hills, threatening the heavens with their floods, so that the inferior people groan and murmur. Is there a capable man to whom I can assign the correction of this calamity?"[1] They presented Kwăn as a proper man, but he showed his inefficiency in laboring nine years without success to drain off the waters. Yao was then advised to employ Shun, who called in Yu, a son of Kwăn, to his aid, and the floods were assuaged by deepening the beds of the rivers and opening new channels. These slight notices hardly comport with a flood like the Noachic deluge, and are with much greater probability referred to an overflow or a change in the bed of the Yellow River from its present course into the Gulf of Pechele through Chihlí northeast, to its recent one along the lowlands of Kiangsu. The weight of topographical evidence, combined with the strong chronological argument, the discussions in council said to have taken place regarding the disaster, and the time which elapsed before the region was drained, all pre-suppose and indicate a partial inundation, and strengthen the assumption that no traces of the Deluge exist in the histories of the Chinese. In our view of the chronology of the Bible, as compared with the Chinese, it requires a far greater constraint upon these records to bring them to refer to that event, than to suppose they allude to a local disaster not beyond the power of remedy.

[1] Legge's *Shu King*, p. 24, Hongkong, 1867.

The series of chieftains down to the accession of Yu may here be recapitulated. The entirely fabulous period ends with Sui-jin, and legendary history commences with Fuh-hí, who with four of his successors (Nos. 2, 3, 7, and 8) are commonly known as the Five Sovereigns. Their names and reigns are as follows:

	Names.	Years reigned.	Began B.C.	Other Events.
1	Fuh-hí........ ...	115	2852*	The Deluge, B.C. 3155.
2	Shinnung	140	2737	Death of Noah, B.C. 2805.
3	Hwangtí	100	2697	
4	Shauhau	84	2597	Death of Arphaxad, 2715.
5	Chwenhüh	78	2513	Death of Shem, 2555.
6	Kuh	78	2435	Rise of Egyptian monarchy, 2450.
7	Yao	102	2357	Rise of Babylonian " 2300.
8	Shun	50	2255	Abraham's birth, 2153.

The records in the *Shu King* of Yao, Shun, and Yu the Great (B.C. 2205) are longer than those of any other persons who lived prior to Abraham. The chronicle represents the merits of Yu to have been first exhibited in reducing the waters and dividing the country into nine regions, and as he had assisted Shun in his government during his lifetime, he was unanimously called to the vacant dignity, and became the founder of the Hia dynasty. Allowing that the records of these times and people are brief and disjointed, and many things in them impossible to reconcile, still they are superior to the absurd tales describing the formation of some other ancient States, and should not be ridiculed as trivial or rejected as fabulous. The great advances made in settling obscure points in early history, by the success in deciphering records brought to light in Western Asia, lead to more respect for what we possess in Eastern Asia, rather than to reject the fragmentary records remaining. No one regards them as trustworthy, like the clay tablets exhumed at Nineveh, but if Abraham found the Egyptians to be living under a regular government not one hundred and fifty years after this, and Damascus, Babylon, Erech, and other cities were then old, no one need be unwilling to give the Chinese a line of monarchs, and a population quite sufficient to have deepened the channel of a river or raised dikes to restrain it. The glorious reigns and spotless characters of these three sovereigns are looked upon by the Chinese with much the same feelings of veneration that the Jews regard their three patriarchs; and to have had, or to have imagined, such progenitors and heroes is, to say the least, as much to their credit as the Achilles, Ulysses, and Romulus of the Greeks and Romans. A curious analogy can also be traced between the scheming Ulysses, warlike Romulus, and methodical Yao, and the subsequent character of the three great nations they represent.

Chinese historians supply many details regarding the conduct of Yu and Kieh Kwei, the first and last princes of the house of Hia, all the credible particulars of which are taken from the *Book of Records* and the *Bamboo Annals*. Dr. Legge candidly weighs the arguments in respect to the eclipse mentioned in the *Yuh Ching*, and gives his opinion as to its authenticity, even if it cannot yet be certainly referred to the year B.C. 2154. One such authentic notice lends strength to the reception of many vague statements, which are more likely to be the relics of fuller documents long since lost than the fabrications of later writers, such as were the Decretals of Isidore in the Middle Ages. In giving a full translation of the *Bamboo Books* in the prolegomena of the *Shu King*, Dr. Legge has shown one of the sources of ancient Chinese history outside of that work. There were many other works accessible to Sz'ma Tsien, nearly four centuries before they were discovered (A.D. 279), when he wrote his *Annals*. Pan Ku gives a list of the various books recovered after the death of Tsin Chí Hwangtí, amounting in all to thirteen thousand two hundred and nineteen volumes or chapters contained in six hundred and twenty different works. Well does Pauthier speak of the inestimable value which a similar catalogue of the extant literature of Greece and Rome at that epoch (B.C. 100) would now be.

One of the alleged records of the reign of Yu is an inscription traced on the rocks of Kau-lau shan, one of the peaks of Mount Hăng in Hunan, relating to the inundation. It contains seventy-seven characters only, and Amiot, who regarded it as genuine, has given its sense as follows:

The venerable Emperor said, Oh! aid and councillor! Who will help me in administering my affairs? The great and little islets (the inhabited places) even to their summits, the abodes of the beasts and birds, and all beings are widely inundated. Advise, send back the waters, and raise the dikes. For a long time, I have quite forgotten my family; I repose on the top of the mountain Yoh-lu. By prudence and my labors, I have moved the spirits; I know not the hours, but repose myself only in my incessant labors. The mountains Hwa, Yoh, Tai, and Hăng, have been the beginning and end of my enterprise; when my labors were completed, I offered a thanksgiving sacrifice at the solstice. My affliction has ceased; the confusion in nature has disappeared; the deep currents coming from the south flow into the sea; clothes can now be made, food can be prepared, all kingdoms will be at peace, and we can give ourselves to continual joy.[1]

Since Amiot's time, however, further opportunities have offered for more thorough inquiry into this relic by foreigners, and the results of their researches throw much doubt upon its authenticity, though they do not altogether destroy it. In the Introduction to the *Shu King*, Dr. Legge discusses the value of this tablet among other early records of that reign, and comes to the conclusion that it is a fabrication of the Han dynasty, if not later. The poet Han Yu (A.D. 800) gave it wide notoriety by his verses about its location and nature; but when he was there he could not find it on the peak, and cited only a Taoist priest as having seen it. More than three centuries afterward Chu Hí was equally unsuccessful, and his opinion that it was made by the priests of that sect has had much weight with his countrymen. It was not till one Ho Chí went to Mount Hăng, about A.D. 1210, and took a copy of the inscription from the stone then in a Taoist temple, that it was actually seen; and not till about 1510, that Chang Kí-wăn, another antiquary of Hunan province, published his copy in the form now generally accepted. In 1666 one Máo Tsăng-kien again found the tablet on the summit of Kau-lau, but reached it with much difficulty by the help of ladders and hooks, and found it so broken that the inscription could not be made out. A reduced *fac-simile* of Mao's copy is given by

[1] Pauthier, *La Chine*, p. 53; J. Hager's *Inscription of Yu*, Paris, 1802; Legge's *Shu King*, pp. 67–74; *Transactions of the N. C. Br. R. A. Soc.*, No. V., 1869, pp. 78–84; *Journal Asiatique*, 1867, Tome X., pp. 197–337.

Dr. Legge, whose translation differs from Amiot's in some particulars.

I received *the words of* the Emperor, saying, "Ah! Associate helper, aiding noble! The islands and islets may now be ascended, *that were* doors for the birds and beasts. *You* devoted your person to the great overflowings, and with the daybreak you rose up. Long were *you* abroad, forgetting your family; *you* lodged at the mountain's foot as in a hall; *your* wisdom schemed; *your* body was broken; *your* heart was all in a tremble. *You* went and sought to produce order and settlement. At Hwa, Yoh, Tai, and Hăng, by adopting the principle of dividing *the waters*, *your* undertakings were completed. With the remains of a taper, *you* offered your pure sacrifice. There were entanglement and obstruction, being swamped, and removals. The southern river flows on its course; for ever is the provision of food made sure; the myriad States enjoy repose; the beasts and birds are for ever fled away."

The characters in which this tablet is written are of an ancient tadpole form, and so difficult to read that grave doubts exist as to their proper meaning—and even as to which of two or three forms is the correct one. Since the copy of Mao was taken, the Manchu scholar Kwan-wăn, when Governor-General of Liang Hu in 1868, erected a stone tablet at Wu-chang, in the Pavilion of the Yellow Stork, upon the eminence overlooking the Yangtsz'. This he regarded as a true copy of the authentic *Yu Pai*, or 'Tablet of Yu.' A *fac-simile* of this tablet, and of another rubbing from a stone now existing at the foot of Mount Hăng (which is alleged to be an exact reproduction of the original on its top), was published by W. H. Medhurst in the *N. C. Asiatic Society Journal* for 1869. A comparison of these three will give the reader an idea of the difficulties and doubts attending the settlement of the credibility of this inscription. A living native writer quoted by Mr. Medhurst says that the earliest notice of the tablet is by Tsin Yung of the Tăng dynasty, about A.D. 700, from which he infers that the people of the time of Tăng must have seen the rock and its inscription. He regards the latter as consisting of fairy characters, utterly unreadable, and therefore all attempts to decipher them as valueless and misleading.

Amid so many conflicting opinions among native scholars, the verdict of foreigners may safely await further discoveries, and the day when competent observers can examine these localities and tablets for themselves. Without exaggerating the importance and credibility of the *Shu King* and other ancient Chinese records, they can be received as the writings of a very remote period; and while their claims to trustworthiness would be fortified if more intimations had been given of the manner in which they were kept during the long period antecedent to the era of Confucius, they still deserve a more respectful consideration than some modern writers are disposed to allow them. For instance, Davis remarks: "Yu is described as nine cubits in height, and it is stated that the skies rained gold in those days, which certainly (as Dr. Morrison observes) lessens the credit of the history of this period." Now, without laying too much stress upon the record, or the objections against it, this height is but little more than that of Og of Bashan, even if we adopt the present length of the cubit fourteen and one-tenth inches, English; and if *kin*, here called *gold*, be translated *metal* (which it can just as well be), it may be a notice of a meteoric shower of extraordinary duration. Let these venerable writings be investigated in a candid, cautious manner, weighing their internal evidence, and comparing their notices of those remote periods as much as they can be with those of other nations, and they will illustrate ancient history and customs in no slight degree. Mr. Murray has given a synopsis from Mailla of what is recorded of the Hia dynasty, which will fairly exhibit the matter of Chinese history. It is here introduced somewhat abridged, with dates inserted.

The accession of Yu (B.C. 2205) forms a remarkable era in Chinese history. The throne, which hitherto had been more or less elective, became from this period hereditary in the eldest son, with only those occasional and violent interruptions to which every despotic government is liable. The national annals, too, assume a more regular and authentic shape, the reigns of the sovereigns being at the same time reduced to a probable duration.

Yu justly acquired a lasting veneration, but it was chiefly by his labors under his two predecessors. When he himself ascended the throne, age had already overtaken him; still the lustre of his government was supported by able councillors, till it closed with his life at the end of seven years. Many of the grandees wished, according to former practice, to raise to the throne Pi-yih, his first minister, and a person of distinguished merit; but regard for the father, in this case, was strengthened by the excellent qualities of his son

Kí, or Tí Kí (*i.e.*, the Emperor Kí), and even Pí-yih insisted that the prince should be preferred (2197). His reign of nine years was only disturbed by the rebellion of a turbulent subject, and he was succeeded (2188) by his son, Tai Kang. But this youth was devoted to pleasure; music, wine, and hunting entirely engrossed his attention. The Chinese, after enduring him for twenty-nine years, dethroned him (2159), and his brother, Chung Kang, was nominated to succeed, and held the reins of government for thirteen years with a vigorous hand. He was followed by his son, Siang (2146), who, destitute of the energy his situation required, gave himself up to the advice of his minister Yeh, and was by him, in connection with his accomplice, Hantsu, declared incapable of reigning. The usurper ruled for seven years, when he was killed; and the rightful monarch collected his adherents and gave battle to Hantsu and the son of Yeh in the endeavor to regain his throne. Siang was completely defeated, and lost both his crown and life; the victors immediately marched to the capital, and made so general a massacre of the family that they believed the name and race of Yu to be for ever extinguished.

The Empress Min, however, managed to escape, and fled to a remote city, where she brought forth a son, called Shau Kang; and the better to conceal his origin, she employed him as a shepherd boy to tend flocks. Reports of the existence of such a youth, and his occupation, at length reached the ears of Hantsu, who sent orders to bring him, dead or alive. The royal widow then placed her son as under-cook in the household of a neighboring governor, where the lad soon distinguished himself by a spirit and temper so superior to this humble station, that the master's suspicions were roused, and obliged him to disclose his name and birth. The officer, being devotedly attached to the house of Yu, not only kept the secret, but watched for an opportunity to reinstate him, and meanwhile gave him a small government in a secluded situation, which he prudently administered. Yet he was more than thirty years old before the governor, by engaging other chiefs in his interest, could assemble such a force as might justify the attempt to make head against the usurper. The latter hastily assembled his troops and led them to the attack, but was defeated and taken prisoner by the young prince Chu himself; and Shau Kang, with his mother, returned with acclamations to the capital. His reign is reckoned to have been sixty-one years' duration in the chronology of the time, which includes the usurpation of forty years of Hantsu.

The country was ably governed by Shau Kang, and also by his son, Chu (2057), who ruled for seventeen years; but the succeeding sovereigns, in many instances, abandoned themselves to indolence and pleasure, and brought the kingly name into contempt. From Hwai to Kieh Kwei, a space of two hundred and twenty-two years, between B.C. 2040 and 1818, few records remain of the nine sovereigns, whose bare names succeed each other in the annals. At length the throne was occupied by Kieh Kwei (1818), a prince who is represented as having, in connexion with his consort, Mei-hí, practised every kind of violence and extortion, in order to accumulate treasure, which they spent in unbridled voluptuousness. They formed a large pond of wine, deep enough to float a boat, at which three thousand men drank at once. It was surrounded, too, by pyramids of delicate viands, which no one, however, was allowed to taste, till he had first intoxicated himself out of the lake. The drunken quarrels which ensued were their favorite amusement. In the interior of the palace the vilest orgies were celebrated, and the venerable ministers, who attempted to remonstrate against these excesses, were either put to death or exiled. The people were at once indignant and grieved at such crimes, which threatened the downfall of the dynasty; and the discarded statesmen put themselves under the direction of the wise Í Yin, and advised Chingtang, the ablest of their number, and a descendant of Hwangtí, to assume the reins of government, assuring him of their support. He with reluctance yielded to their solicitations, and assembling a force marched against Kieh Kwei, who came out to meet him at the head of a numerous army, but fled from the contest on seeing the defection of his troops, and ended his days in despicable obscurity, after occupying the throne fifty-two years.[1]

Chinese annals are generally occupied in this way; the Emperor and his ministers fill the whole field of historic vision; little is recorded of the condition, habits, arts, or occupations of the people, who are merely considered as attendants of the monarch, which is, in truth, a feature of the ancient records of nearly all countries and people. Monarchs controlled the chronicles of their reigns, and their own vanity, as well as their ideas of government and authority led them to represent the people as a mere background to their own stately dignity and acts.

The Shang dynasty began B.C. 1766, or about one hundred and twenty years before the Exodus, and maintained an unequal sway over the feudal States composing the Empire for a period of six hundred and forty-four years. Its first monarch, Chingtang, or Tang the Successful, is described as having paid religious worship to Shangtí, under which name, perhaps, the true God was intended. On account of a severe drought of seven years' duration, this monarch is reported to have prayed, saying, "I the child Lí presume to use a dark colored victim, and announce to thee, O Shang-tien Hao ('High Heaven's Ruler'). Now there is a great drought, and it is right I should be held responsible for it. I do not know but that I have offended the powers above and below." With regard to his own conduct, he blamed himself in six particulars, and his words were not ended when the rain descended copiously.

The fragmentary records of this dynasty contained in the *Shu King* are not so valuable to the student who wishes merely

---

[1] Hugh Murray, *China*, Vol. I., pp. 51–55 (edition of 1843).

to learn the succession of monarchs in those days, as to one who inquires what were the principles on which they ruled, what were the polity, the religion, the jurisdiction, and the checks of the Chinese government in those remote times. The regular records of those days will never be recovered, but the preservation of the last two parts of the *Shu King* indicates their existence by fair inference, and encourages those who try to reconstruct the early annals of China to give full value even to slight fragments. But these parts have been of great service to the people since they were written, in teaching them by precept and example on what the prosperity of a State was founded, and how their rulers could bring it to ruin. In these respects there are no ancient works outside of the Bible with which they can at all be compared. The later system of examination has given them an unparalleled influence in molding the national character of the Chinese. Of the eleven chapters now remaining all are occupied more or less with the relative duties of the prince and rulers, enforcing on each that the welfare of all was bound up with their faithfulness. One quotation will give an idea of their instructions. "Order your affairs by righteousness, order your heart by propriety, so shall you transmit a grand example to posterity. I have heard the saying, He who finds instructors for himself comes to the supreme dominion; he who says that others are not equal to himself comes to ruin. He who likes to ask becomes enlarged; he who uses *only* himself becomes small. Oh! he who would take care for his end must be attentive to his beginning. There is establishment for the observers of propriety, and overthrow for the blinded and wantonly indifferent. To revere and honor the way of Heaven is the way ever to preserve the favoring regard of Heaven."[1]

The chronicles of the Shang dynasty, as gathered from the *Bamboo Books* and other later records, resemble those of the Hia in being little more than a mere succession of the names of the sovereigns, interspersed here and there with notices of some remarkable events in the natural and political world. Luxurious and despised princes alternate with vigorous and warlike ones

---

[1] Part IV., Book II., Chap. IV., 8–9.

who commanded respect, and the condition of the State measurably corresponds with the character of the monarchs, the feudal barons sometimes increasing in power and territory by encroaching on their neighbors, and then suffering a reduction from some new State. The names of twenty-eight princes are given, the accounts of whose reigns are indeed fuller than those of the dukes of Edom in Genesis, but their slight notices would be more interesting if the same confidence could be reposed in them.

The bad sovereigns occupy more room in these *fasti* than the good ones, the palm of wickedness being given to Chau-sin, with whom the dynasty ended. The wars which broke out during this dynasty were numerous, but other events also find a place, though hardly anything which throws light on society or civilization. Droughts, famines, and other calamities were frequent and attended by dreadful omens and fearful sights; this fancied correlation between natural casualties and political convulsions is a feature running through Chinese history, and grows out of the peculiar position of the monarch as the vicegerent of heaven. The people seem to have looked for control and protection more to their local masters than to their lord paramount, ranging themselves under their separate banners as they were bidden. The *History Made Easy* speaks of the twenty-fifth monarch, Wu-yih (B.C. 1198), as the most wicked of them all. "Having made his images of clay in the shape of human beings, dignified them with the name of gods, overcome them at gambling, and set them aside in disgrace, he then, in order to complete his folly, made leathern bags and filled them with blood, and sent them up into the air, exclaiming, when his arrows hit them and the blood poured down, 'I have shot heaven,' meaning, I have killed the gods."

The names of Chau-sin and Tan-kí are coupled with those of Kieh and Mí-hí of the Hia dynasty, all of them synonymous in the Chinese annals for the acme of cruelty and licentiousness —as are those of Nero and Messalina in Roman history. Chau-sin is said one winter's morning to have seen a few women walking barelegged on the banks of a stream collecting shellfish, and ordered their legs to be cut off, that he might see the marrow of persons who could resist cold so fearlessly. The heart of one of his reprovers was also brought him, in order to see wherein it differed from that of cowardly ministers. The last *Book of Shang* contains the vain remonstrance of another of them, who tells his sovereign that his dynasty is in the condition of one crossing a large stream who can find neither ford nor bank. Many acts of this nature alienated the hearts of the people, until Wăn wang, the leader of a State in the northwest of China, united the principal men against his misrule; but dying, bequeathed his crown and power to his son, Wu wang. He gradually gathered his forces and met Chau-sin at the head of a great army at Muh, near the junction of the rivers Kí and Wei, north of the Yellow River in Honan, where the defeat of the tyrant was complete. Feeling the contempt he was held in, and the hopeless struggle before him, he fled to his palace and burned himself with all his treasures, like another Sardanapalus, though his immolation (in B.C. 1122) preceded the Assyrian's by five centuries.

Wu wang, the martial king, the founder of the Chau dynasty, his father, Wăn wang, and his brother, Duke Chau, are among the most distinguished men of antiquity for their erudition, integrity, patriotism, and inventions. Wăn wang, Prince of Chau, was prime minister to Tai-ting, the grandfather of Chau-sin, but was imprisoned for his fidelity. His son obtained his liberation, and the sayings and acts of both occupy about twenty books in Part V. of the *Shu King*. Duke Chau survived his brother to become the director and support of his nephew; his counsels, occupying a large part of the history, are full of wisdom and equity. Book X. contains his warning advice about drunkenness, which has been remarkably influential among his countrymen ever since. No period of ancient Chinese history is more celebrated than that of the founding of this dynasty, chiefly because of the high character of its leading men, who were regarded by Confucius as the impersonations of everything wise and noble. Wu wang is represented as having invoked the assistance of Shangtí in his designs, and, when he was successful, returned thanks and offered prayers and sacrifices. He removed the capital from the province of Honan to the present

Sí-ngan, in Shensí, where it remained for a long period. This prince committed a great political blunder in dividing the Empire into petty states, thus destroying the ancient pure monarchy, and leaving himself only a small portion of territory and power, which were quite insufficient, in the hands of a weak prince, to maintain either the state or authority due the ruling sovereign. The number of States at one time was one hundred and twenty-five, at another forty-one, and, in the time of Confucius, about six hundred years after the establishment of the dynasty, fifty-two, some of them large kingdoms. From about B.C. 700 the imperial name and power lost the allegiance and respect of the feudal princes, and gradually became contemptible. Its nominal sway extended over the country lying north of the Yangtsz' kiang, the regions on the south being occupied by tribes of whom no intelligible record has been preserved.

The duration of the three dynasties, the Hia, Shang, and Chau, comprises a long and obscure period in the history of the world, extending from B.C. 2205 to 249, from the time when Terah dwelt in Charran, and the sixteenth dynasty of Theban kings ruled in Egypt, down to the reigns of Antiochus Soter and Ptolemy Philadelphus and the translation of the Septuagint.

I.—The Hia dynasty, founded by Yu the Great, existed four hundred and thirty-nine years, down to B.C. 1766, under seventeen monarchs, the records of whose reigns are very brief. Among contemporary events of importance are the call of Abraham, in the year B.C. 2093, Jacob's flight to Mesopotamia in 1916, Joseph's elevation in Egypt in 1885, and his father's arrival in 1863.

II.—The Shang dynasty began with Tang the Successful, and continued six hundred and forty-four years, under twenty-eight sovereigns, down to B.C. 1122. This period was characterized by wars among rival princes, and the power of the sovereign depended chiefly upon his personal character. The principal contemporary events were the Exodus of the Israelites in 1648, their settlement in Palestine in 1608, judgeship of Othniel, 1564; of Deborah, 1406; of Gideon, 1359; of Samson, 1202; and death of Samuel in 1122.

III.—The Chau dynasty began with Wu wang, and continued for eight hundred and seventy-three years, under thirty-five monarchs, down to B.C. 249, the longest of any recorded in history. The sway of many of these was little more than nominal, and the feudal States increased or diminished, according to the vigor of the monarch or the ambition of the princes. In B.C. 770 the capital was removed from Kao, near the River Wei in Shensí, to Lohyang, in the western part of Honan; this divides the house into the Western and Eastern Chau. The contemporary events of these eight centuries are too numerous to particularize. The accession of Saul in 1110; of David, 1070; of Rehoboam, 990; taking of Troy, 1084; of Samaria, 719; of Jerusalem, 586; death of Nebuchadnezzar, 561; accession of Cyrus and return of the Jews, 551; battle of Marathon, 490; accession of Alexander, 235; etc. The conquest of Egypt by Alexander in 322 brought the thirty-first and last dynasty of her native kings to an end, the first of which had begun under Menes about B.C. 2715, or twenty-two years after the supposed accession of Shinnung.

The absence of any great remains of human labor or art previous to the Great Wall, like the Pyramids, the Temple of Solomon, or the ruins and mounds in Syria, has led many to doubt the credibility of these early Chinese records. They ascribe them to the invention of the historians of the Han dynasty, working up the scattered relics of their ancient books into a readable narrative, and therefore try to bring every statement to a critical test for which there are few facts. The analogies between the records in the *Shu King* and the Aryan myths are skilfully explained by Mr. Kingsmill by reference to the meanings of the names of persons and places and titles, and a connection shown which has the merit at least of ingenuity and beauty. Almost the only actual known relic of these three dynasties is the series of ten stone drums (*shih ku*) now in the Confucian temple at Peking. They were discovered about A.D. 600, in the environs of the ancient capital of the Chau dynasty, and have been kept in Peking since the year 1126. They are irregularly shaped pillars, from eighteen to thirty-five inches high and about twenty-eight inches across; the inscriptions are much worn, but enough remains to show that they commemorate a great hunt of Süen wang (B.C. 827) in the region where they were found.[1]

Among the feudal States under the house of Chau, that of Tsin, on the northwest, had long been the most powerful, occupying nearly a fifth of the country, and its inhabitants forming a tenth of the whole population. One of the princes, called Chausiang wang, carried his encroachments into the acknowledged imperial possessions, and compelled its master, Tungchau kiun, the last monarch, to humble himself at his feet. Although, in fact, master of the whole Empire, he did not take the title, but left it to his son, Chwangsiang wang, who exterminated the blood royal and ended the Chau dynasty, yet lived only three years in possession of the supreme power.

The son carried on his father's successes until he had reduced all the petty States to his sway. He then took the name of Chí Hwangtí ('Emperor First') of the Tsin dynasty, and set himself to regulate his conquests and establish his authority by securing to his subjects a better government than had been experienced during the feudal times. He divided the country into thirty-six provinces, over which he placed governors, and went throughout them all to see that no injustice was practised.

This monarch, who has been called the Napoleon of China, was one of those extraordinary men who turn the course of events and give an impress to subsequent ages; Klaproth gives him a high character as a prince of energy and skill, but native historians detest his name and acts. It is recorded that at his new capital, Hienyang, on the banks of the Hwai, he constructed a palace exactly like those of all the kings who had submitted to him, and ordered that all the precious furniture of each and those persons who had inhabited them should be transported to it, and everything rearranged. The whole occupied an immense space, and the various parts communicated with each other by a magnificent colonnade and gallery. He made progresses through his dominions with a splendor hitherto unknown, accompanied by officials and troops from all parts, thus making

[1] *Journal of the N. C. Branch of R. A. Society*, Vols. VII., p. 137; VIII., pp. 23, 133. In the last paper, by Dr. Bushell, translations and fac-similes of the inscriptions are given, with many historical notices.

the people interested in each other and consenting to his sway. He also built public edifices, opened roads and canals to facilitate intercourse and trade between the various provinces, and repressed the incursions of the Huns, driving them into the wilds of Mongolia. In order to keep them out effectually, he conceived the idea of extending and uniting the short walls which the princes of some of the Northern States had erected on their frontier into one grand wall, stretching across the Empire from the sea to the Desert. This gigantic undertaking was completed in ten years (B.C. 204), at a vast expense in men and material, and not until the family of its builder had been destroyed. This mode of protecting the country, when once well begun, probably commended itself to the nation. It is impossible, indeed, to imagine otherwise how it could have been done, for the people were required to supply a quota of men from each place, feed and clothe them while at work, and continue this expense until their portion was built. No monarch could have maintained an army which could force his subjects against their will to do such a work or carry it on to completion after his death. It is one of the incidental proofs of a great population that so many laborers were found. However ineffectual it was to preserve his frontiers, it has made his name celebrated throughout the world, and his dynasty *Tsin* has given its name to China for all ages and nations.[1]

The vanity of the new monarch led him to endeavor to destroy all records written anterior to his own reign, that he might be by posterity regarded as the first Emperor of the Chinese race. Orders were issued that every book should be burned, and especially the writings of Confucius and Mencius, explanatory of the *Shu King* upon the feudal States of Chau, whose remembrance he wished to blot out. This strange command was executed to such an extent that many of the Chinese literati believe that not a perfect copy of the classical works escaped destruction, and the texts were only recovered by rewriting them from the memories of old scholars, a mode of reproduction

---

[1] Pauthier, *La Chine*, pp. 30, 221; *Mém. conc. les Chinois*, Tome III., p. 183.

that does not appear so singular to a Chinese as it does to us. If the same literary tragedy should be re-enacted to-day, thousands of persons might easily be found in China who could rewrite from memory the text and commentary of their nine classical works. "Nevertheless," as Klaproth remarks, "they were not in fact all lost; for in a country where writing is so common it was almost impossible that all the copies of works universally respected should be destroyed, especially at a time when the material on which they were written was very durable, being engraved with a stylet on bamboo tablets, or traced upon them with dark-colored varnish." The destruction was no doubt as nearly complete as possible, and not only were many works entirely destroyed, but a shade of doubt thereby thrown over the accuracy of others, and the records of the ancient dynasties rendered suspicious as well as incomplete. Not only were books sought after to be destroyed, but nearly five hundred literati were buried alive, in order that no one might remain to reproach, in their writings, the Emperor First with having committed so barbarous and insane an act.

The dynasty of Tsin, set up in such cruelty and blood, did not long survive the death of its founder; his son was unable to maintain his rule over the half-subdued feudal chieftains, and after a nominal reign of seven years he was overcome by Liu Pang, a soldier of fortune, who, having been employed by one of the chiefs as commander of his forces, used them to support his own authority when he had taken possession of the capital. Under the name of Kautsu he became the founder of the Han dynasty, and his accession is regarded as the commencement of modern Chinese history. The number and character of its heroes and literati are superior to most other periods, and to this day the term *Han-tsz'*, or 'Sons of Han,' is one of the favorite names by which the Chinese call themselves.

The first fourteen princes of this dynasty reigned in Shensí, but Kwangwu removed the capital from Chang-an to Lohyang, as was done in the Chau dynasty seven centuries before, the old one being ruined. During the reign of Ping tí (or the 'Emperor Peace') the Prince of Peace, our Lord Jesus Christ, was born in Judea, a remarkable coincidence which has often attracted notice. During the reign of Ming tí, A.D. 65, a deputation was sent to India to obtain the sacred books and authorized teachers of Buddhism, which the Emperor intended to publicly introduce into China. This faith had already widely spread among his subjects, but henceforth it became the popular belief of the Chinese and extended eastward into Japan. This monarch and his successor, Chang tí, penetrated with their armies as far westward as the Caspian Sea, dividing and overcoming the various tribes on the confines of the Desert and at the foot of the Tien shan, and extending the limits of the monarchy in that direction farther than they are at present. The Chinese sway was maintained with varied success until toward the third century, and seems to have had a mollifying effect upon the nomads of those regions. In these distant expeditions the Chinese heard of the Romans, of whom their authors speak in the highest terms: "Everything precious and admirable in all other countries," say they, "comes from this land. Gold and silver money is coined there; ten of silver are worth one of gold. Their merchants trade by sea with Persia and India, and gain ten for one in their traffic. They are simple and upright, and never have two prices for their goods; grain is sold among them very cheap, and large sums are embarked in trade. Whenever ambassadors come to the frontiers they are provided with carriages to travel to the capital, and after their arrival a certain number of pieces of gold are furnished them for their expenses." This description, so characteristic of the shop-keeping Chinese, may be compared to many accounts given of the Chinese themselves by western authors.

Continuing the *résumé* of dynasties in order—

IV.—The Tsin dynasty is computed to end with Chwangsiang by the authors of the *History Made Easy*, and to have existed only three years, from B.C. 249 to 246.

V.—The After Tsin dynasty is sometimes joined to the preceding, but Chí Hwangtí regarded himself as the first monarch, and began a new house, which, however, lasted only forty-four years, from B.C. 246 to 202. The commotions in the farthest East during this period were not less destructive of life than the wars in Europe between the Carthaginians and Romans, and the Syrians, Greeks, and Egyptians.

VI., VII. The HAN and EASTERN HAN dynasties.—Liu Pang took the title of Han for his dynasty, after the name of his principality, and his family swayed the Middle Kingdom from B.C. 202 to A.D. 221, under twenty-six monarchs. The Han dynasty was the formative period of Chinese polity and institutions, and an instructive parallel can be drawn between the character and acts of the Emperors who reigned four hundred years in China, and the numerous consuls, dictators, and emperors who governed the Roman Empire for the same period from the time of Scipio Africanus to Heliogabalus. The founder of the Han is honored for having begun the system of competitive examinations for office, and his successors, Wăn tí, Wu tí, and Kwang-wu, developed literature, commerce, arts, and good government to a degree unknown before anywhere in Asia. In the West the Romans became the great world power, and the advent of Christ and establishment of His church within its borders only, render this period the turning epoch of progress among mankind.

The period between the overthrow of the Han dynasty, A.D. 190, and the establishment of the Eastern Tsin, A.D. 317, is one of the most interesting in Chinese history, from the variety of characters which the troubles of the times developed. The distractions of this period are described in the *History of the Three States*, but this entertaining work cannot be regarded as much better than a historical novel. It has, however, like Scott's stories, impressed the events and actors of those days upon the popular mind more than any history in the language.

VIII.—The AFTER HAN dynasty began A.D. 211, and continued forty-four years, under two princes, to A.D. 265. The country was divided into three principalities, called Wei, Wu, and Shuh. The first, under the son of Tsao Tsao, ruled the whole northern country at Lohyang, and was the most powerful of them for about forty years. The second, under Siun Kien, occupied the eastern provinces, from Shantung and the Yellow River down to the mountains of Fuhkien, holding his court at Nanking. The third, under Liu Pí, is regarded as the legitimate dynasty from his affinity with the Han; he had his capital at Chingtu fu, in Sz'chuen.

IX.—The Tsin dynasty was founded by Sz'ma Chao, a general in the employ of Hau of the last house, who seated himself on the throne of his master A.D. 265, the year of the latter's death. His son, Sz'ma Yen, took his place and extended his power over the whole Empire by 280. The inroads of the Huns and internal commotions were fast reducing the people to barbarism. Four Emperors of this house held their sway at Lohyang during fifty-two years, till A.D. 317. The Huns maintained their sway in Shensí until A.D. 352, under the designations of the Han and Chau dynasties. It is related of Liu Tsung, one of this barbaric race, that he built a great palace at Chang-an, where he gathered a myriad of the first subjects of his kingdom and lived in luxury and magnificence quite unknown before in China. Among his attendants was a body-guard of elegantly dressed women, many of whom were good musicians, which accompanied him on his progresses.

X.—The Eastern Tsin is the same house as the last, but Yuen tí having moved his capital in 317 from Lohyang to Nanking, his successors are distinguished as the Eastern Tsin. Eleven princes reigned during a period of one hundred and three years, down to A.D. 420. Buddhism was the chief religion at this time, and the doctrines of Confucius were highly esteemed; "children of concubines, priests, old women, and nurses administered the government," says the indignant annalist. At this period twelve independent and opposing kings struggled for the ascendency in China, and held their ephemeral courts in the north and west. It was at this time that Constantine moved the capital of the Roman Empire in 328, and the nations of northern Europe under Attila invaded Italy in 410.

XI.—The Sung, or Northern Sung dynasty, as it is often called to distinguish it from the XXIId dynasty (A.D. 970), is the first of the four dynasties known as the *Nan-peh Chao*, or 'South-north dynasties,' which preceded the Sui. It was founded by Liu Yu, who commanded the armies of Tsin, and gradually subdued all the opposing States. Displeased at the weakness of his master, Ngan tí, he caused him to be strangled, and placed his brother, Kung tí, upon the throne, who, fearing a like fate, abdicated the empty crown, and Liu Yu became monarch under the name of Kautsu, A.D. 420. Eight princes held the throne till A.D. 479, many of them monsters of cruelty, and soon cut off, when Siau Tau-ching, Duke of Tsí, the prime minister, recompensed them as their ancestor had those of Tsin.

XII. Tsí dynasty.—The new monarch took the name of Kau tí, or 'High Emperor,' but enjoyed his dignity only four years. Four princes succeeded him at Nanking, the last of whom, Ho tí, was besieged in his capital by a faithless minister, assisted by the prince of Liang, who overthrew the dynasty A.D. 502, after a duration of twenty-three years.

XIII. Liang dynasty.—The first Emperor, Wu tí, reigned forty-eight years, and reduced most of his opponents; his dominions are described as being mostly south of the Yangtsz' River, the Wei ruling the regions north of it. Wu tí did much to restore literature and the study of Confucius; envoys from India and Persia also came to his court, and his just sway allowed the land to recruit. In his latter days he was so great a devotee of Buddhism that he retired to a monastery, like Charles V., but being persuaded to resume his crown, employed his time in teaching those doctrines to his assembled courtiers. Three successors occupied the throne, the last of whom, King tí, was killed A.D. 557, after surrendering himself, by the general of the troops, who then seized the crown.

XIV. Chin dynasty.—Three brothers reigned most of the time this house held its sway. During this period and that of the three preceding families, the Hunnish kingdom of Wei ruled the northern parts of China from A.D. 386 to 534, under eleven monarchs, when it was violently separated into the Eastern and Western Wei, and a third one called Chau, which ere long destroyed the last Wei at Chang-an and occupied northwest China. It is probable that the intercourse between China and other parts of Asia was more extensive and complete during the Wei dynasty than at any other period. Its sovereigns had preserved peaceful relations with their ancestral seats, and with the tribes beyond Lake Baikal and the Obi River to the North Sea. Trade seems to have flourished throughout the regions lying between the Caspian Sea and Corea, and the records of this period present accounts of the State in this vast tract to be found nowhere else. One of these works referred to by Rémusat is the report of officers sent by Tai-wu during his reign to travel through his dominions (424–451) and give full accounts of them.

One of the sovereigns of Chau, Wu tí (A.D. 561–572), had given his daughter in marriage to Yang Kien, the Prince of Sui, one of his ministers, who, gradually extending his influence, took possession of the throne of his master Tsing tí in 580. In a few years he restored order to a distracted land by bringing the several States under his sway and reuniting all China under his hand A.D. 589, after it had been divided nearly four centuries.

XV. Sui dynasty.—The founder of this house has left an enduring name in Chinese annals by a survey of his dominions and division of them into interdependent *chau*, *kiun*, and *hien*, with corresponding officers, an arrangement which has ever since existed. He patronized letters and commerce, and tried to introduce the system of caste from India. After a vigorous reign of twenty-four years he was killed by his son Yang tí, who carried on his father's plans, and during the fourteen years of his reign extended the frontiers through the Tarim Valley and down to the Southern Ocean. His murder by one of his generals was the signal for several ambitious men to rise, but the Prince of Tang aided the son to rule for a year or two till he was removed, thus bringing the Sui dynasty to an end after thirty-nine years, but not before its two sovereigns had taught their subjects the benefits of an undivided sway.

XVI. Tang dynasty.—This celebrated line of princes began its sway in peace, and during the two hundred and eighty-seven years (618 to 908) they held the throne China was probably the most civilized country on earth; the darkest days of the West, when Europe was wrapped in the ignorance and degradation of the Middle Ages, formed the brightest era of the East. They exercised a humanizing effect on all the surrounding countries, and led their inhabitants to see the benefits and understand the management of a government where the laws were above the officers. The people along the southern coast were completely civilized and incorporated into the Chinese race, and mark the change by always calling themselves *Tang Jin*, or 'Men of Tang.' An interesting work on the trade and condition of China at this time is the *Akhbar-al-Syn oual-Hind*, or 'Observations on China and India,' by two Arab travellers to those lands in the years 851 and 878, compiled by Abu Zaid and translated by Reinaud in 1845.[1] Lí Shí-min, the son of Lí Yuen the founder of this dynasty, may be regarded as the most accomplished monarch in the Chinese annals—famed alike for his wisdom and nobleness, his conquests and good government, his temperance, cultivated tastes, and patronage of literary men. While still Prince of Tang he contributed greatly to his father's elevation and to the extension of his sway over the regions of Central Asia. When the house of Tang was fully acknowledged, and the eleven rival States which had started up on the close of the house of Sui had been overcome, the capital was removed from Lohyang back to Chang-an, and everything done to compose the disordered country and reunite the distracted State under a regular and vigorous administration. Feeling himself unequal to all the cares of his great office, Lí Yuen, known as Kau-tsu Shin Yao tí (lit. 'High Progenitor, the Divine Yao Emperor'), resigned the yellow in favor of his son, who took the style of *Ching kwan* ('Pure Observer') for his reign, though his posthumous title is Tai-tsung Wăn-wu tí ('Our Exalted Ancestor, the Literary-Martial Emperor'), A.D. 627, and still further extended his victorious arms. One of his first acts was to establish schools and institute a system of literary examinations; he ordered a complete and accurate edition of all the classics to be published under the supervision of the most learned men in the Empire, and honored the memory of Confucius with special ceremonies of respect. Extraordinary pains were taken to prepare and preserve the historical records of former days and draw up full annals of the recent dynasties; these still await the examination of western scholars.

He constructed a code of laws for the direction of his high officers in their judicial functions, and made progresses through

---

[1] *Chinese Repository*, Vol. I., p. 6; Reinaud, *Relations des Voyages*, 2 Vols., Paris, 1845. Yule, *Cathay and the Way Thither*, Introd., p. cii.

his dominions to inspect the condition of the people. During his reign the limits of the Empire were extended over all the Turkish tribes lying west of Kansuh and south of the Tien shan as far as the Caspian Sea, which were placed under four satrapies or residences, those of Kuché, Pisha or Khoten, Harashar, and Kashgar, as their names are at present. West of the last many smaller tribes submitted and rendered a partial subjection to the Emperor, who arranged them into sixteen governments under the management of a governor-general over their own chieftains. His frontiers reached from the borders of Persia, the Caspian Sea, and the Altai of the Kirghís steppe, along those mountains to the north side of Gobi eastward to the Inner Hing-an. Sogdiana and part of Khorassan, and the regions around the Hindu-kush, also obeyed him. The rulers of Nipal and Magadha or Bahar in India sent their salutations by their ambassadors, and the Greek Emperor Theodosius sent an envoy to Sí-ngan in 643 carrying presents of rubies and emeralds, as did also the Persians. The Nestorian missionaries also presented themselves at court. Tai-tsung received them with respect, and heard them rehearse the leading tenets of their doctrine; he ordered a temple to be erected at his capital, and had some of their sacred books translated for his examination, though there is no evidence now remaining that any portion of the Bible was done into Chinese at this time.

Near the close of his life Tai-tsung undertook an expedition against Corea, but the conquest of that country was completed by his son after his death. A sentiment has been preserved at this time of his life which he uttered to his sons while sailing on the River Wei: "See, my children, the waves which float our fragile bark are able to submerge it in an instant; know assuredly that the people are like the waves, and the Emperor like this fragile bark." During his reign his life was attempted several times, once by his own son, but he was preserved from these attacks, and died after a reign of twenty-three years, deeply lamented by a grateful people. The Chinese accounts state that the foreign envoys resident at his court cut off their hair, some of them disfigured their faces, bled themselves, and sprinkled the blood around the bier in testimony of their grief.

Whatever may have been the truth in this respect, many proofs exist of the distinguished character of this monarch, and that the high reputation he enjoyed during his lifetime was a just tribute to his excellences. He will favorably compare with Akbar, Marcus Aurelius, and Kanghí, or with Charlemagne and Harun Al Raschid, who came to their thrones in the next century.

Tai-tsung was succeeded by his son Kau-tsung, whose indolent imbecility appeared the more despicable after his father's vigor, but his reign fills a large place in Chinese history, from the extraordinary career of his Empress, Wu Tsih-tien, or Wu hao ('Empress Wu') as she is called, who by her blandishments obtained entire control over him. The character of this woman has, no doubt, suffered much from the bad reputation native historians have given her, but enough can be gathered from their accounts to show that with all her cruelty she understood how to maintain the authority of the crown, repress foreign invasions, quell domestic sedition, and provide for the wants of the people. Introduced to the harem of Tai-tsung at the age of fourteen, she was sent at his death to the retreat where all his women were condemned for the rest of their days to honorable imprisonment. While a member of the palace Kau-tsung had been charmed with her appearance, and, having seen her at one of the state ceremonies connected with the ancestral worship, brought her back to the palace. His queen, Wang-shí, also favored his attentions in order to draw them off from another rival, but Wu Tsih-tien soon obtaining entire sway over the monarch, united both women against her; she managed to fill the principal offices with her friends, and by a series of manœuvres supplanted each in turn and became Empress. One means she took to excite suspicion against Wang-shí was, on occasion of the birth of her first child, after the Empress had visited it and before Kau-tsung came in to see his offspring, to strangle it and charge the crime upon her Majesty, which led to her trial, degradation, and imprisonment, and ere long to her death.

As soon as she became Empress (in 655), Wu began gradually to assume more and more authority, until, long before the Emperor's death in 684, she engrossed the whole management of affairs, and at his demise openly assumed the reins of government, which she wielded for twenty-one years with no weak hand. Her generals extended the limits of the Empire, and her officers carried into effect her orders to alleviate the miseries of the people. Her cruelty vented itself in the murder of all who opposed her will, even to her own sons and relatives; and her pride was rather exhibited than gratified by her assuming the titles of Queen of Heaven, Holy and Divine Ruler, Holy Mother, and Divine Sovereign. When she was disabled by age her son, Chung-sung, supported by some of the first men of the land, asserted his claim to the throne, and by a palace conspiracy succeeded in removing her to her own apartments, where she died aged eighty-one years. Her character has been blackened in native histories and popular tales, and her conduct held up as an additional evidence of the evil of allowing women to meddle with governments.[1]

A race of twenty monarchs swayed the sceptre of the house of Tang, but after the demise of the Empress Wu Tsih-tien none of them equalled Tai-tsung, and the Tang dynasty at last succumbed to ambitious ministers lording over its imbecile sovereigns. In the reign of Hiuen-tsung, about the year 722, the population of the Fifteen Provinces is said to have been 52,884,818. The last three or four Emperors exhibited the usual marks of a declining house—eunuchs or favorites promoted by them swayed the realm and dissipated its resources. At last, Lí Tsüen-chung, a general of Chau-tsung, whom he had aided in quelling the eunuchs in 904, rose against his master, destroyed him, and compelled his son, Chau-siuen tí, to abdicate, A.D. 907.

XVII. After Liang dynasty.—The destruction of the famous dynasty loosened the bonds of all government, and nine separate kings struggled for its provinces, some of whom, as Apkí over the Kítan in the north-east, succeeded in founding kingdoms. The Prince of Liang, the new Emperor, was unable to extend his sway beyond the provinces of Honan and Shantung. After

---

[1] *Chinese Repository*, Vol. III., p. 543; *Canton Miscellany*, No. 4, 1831, pp. 246 ff.

a short reign of six years he was killed by his brother, Liang Chu-tien, who, on his part, fell under the attack of a Turkish general, and ended this dynasty, A.D. 923, after a duration of sixteen years.

XVIII. AFTER TANG dynasty.—The conqueror called himself Chwang-tsung, and his dynasty Tang, as if in continuation of that line of princes, but this mode of securing popularity was unsuccessful. Like Pertinax, Aurelian, and others of the Roman emperors, he was killed by his troops, who chose a successor, and his grandson, unable to resist his enemies, burned himself in his palace, A.D. 936, thus ending the weak dynasty after thirteen years of struggle.

XIX. AFTER TSIN dynasty.—The Kítan or Tartars of Liautung, who had assisted in the overthrow of the last dynasty, compelled the new monarch to subsidize them at his accession, A.D. 936, by ceding to them sixteen cities in Chihlí, and promising an annual tribute of three hundred thousand pieces of silk. This disgraceful submission has ever since stigmatized Tien-fuh ('Heavenly Happiness') in the eyes of native historians. His nephew who succeeded him is known as Chuh tí (the 'Carried-away Emperor'), and was removed in 947 by those who put him on the throne, thus ending the meanest house which ever swayed the black-haired people.

XX. AFTER HAN dynasty.—The Tartars now endeavored to subdue the whole country, but were repulsed by Liu Chí-yuen, a loyal general who assumed the yellow in 947, and called his dynasty after the renowned house of Han; he and his son held sway four years, till A.D. 951, and then were cut off.

XXI. AFTER CHAU dynasty.—Ko Wei, the successful aspirant to the throne, maintained his seat, but died in three years, leaving his power to an adopted son, Shí-tsung, whose vigorous rule consolidated his still unsettled sway. His early death and the youth of his son decided his generals to bestow the sceptre upon the lately appointed tutor to the monarch, which closed the After Chau dynasty A.D. 960, after a brief duration of nine years. He was honored with a title, and, like Richard Cromwell, allowed to live in quiet till his death in 973, a fact creditable to the new monarch. These short-lived houses between A.D. 907–

960 are known in Chinese history as the *Wu tai*, or 'Five Dynasties.' While they struggled for supremacy in the valley of the Yellow River, the regions south and west were portioned among seven houses, who ruled them in a good degree of security. Fuhkien was held by the King of Min, and Kiangnan by the King of Wu; the regions of Sz'chuen, Nganhwui, and Kansuh were held by generals of note in the service of Tang; another general held Kwangtung at Canton through two or three reigns; and another exercised sway at Kingchau on the Yangtsz' River. It is needless to mention them all. During this period Europe was distracted by the wars of the Normans and Saracens, and learning there was at a low ebb.

XXII.—SUNG dynasty began A.D. 970, and maintained its power over the whole Empire for one hundred and fifty-seven years, till A.D. 1127. The mode in which its founder, Chau Kwang-yun, was made head of the State, reminds one of the way in which the Prætorian guards sometimes elevated their chiefs to the throne of the Cæsars. After the military leaders had decided upon their future sovereign they sent messengers to announce to him his new honor, who found him drunk, and "before he had time to reply the yellow robe was already thrown over his person." At the close of his reign of seventeen years the provinces had mostly submitted to his power at Kaifung, but the two Tartar kingdoms of Liau and Hia remained independent. This return to a centralized government proves the unity of the Chinese people at this time in their own limits, as well as their inability to induce their neighbors to adopt the same system of government. The successors of Tai-tsu of Sung had a constant struggle for existence with their adversaries on the north and west, the Liau and Hia, whose recent taste of power under the last two dynasties had shown them their opportunity. On the return of prosperity under his brother's reign of twenty-two years, the former institutions and political divisions were restored throughout the southern half of the Empire; good government was secured, aided by able generals and loyal ministers, and the rebels everywhere quelled. Chin-tsung was the third sovereign, and his reign of forty-one years is the brightest portion of the house of Sung. The kings of Hia in Kansuh acknowledged themselves to be his tributaries, but he bought a cowardly peace with the Liau on the north-east. During his reign and that of his son, Tin-tsung, a violent controversy arose among the literati and officials as to the best mode of conducting the government. Some of them, as Sz'ma Kwang the historian, contended for the maintenance of the old principles of the sages. Others, of whom Wang Ngan-shí was the distinguished leader, advocated reform and change to the entire overthrow of existing institutions. For the first time in the history of China, two political parties peacefully struggled for supremacy, each content to depend on argument and truth for the victory. The contest soon grew too bitter, however, and the accession of a new monarch, Shin-tsung, enabled Wang to dispossess his opponents and manage State affairs as he pleased. After a trial of eight or ten years the voice of the nation restored the conservatives to power, and the radicals were banished beyond the frontier. A discussion like this, involving all the cherished ideas of the Chinese, brought out deep and acute inquiry into the nature and uses of things generally, and the writers of this dynasty, at the head of whom was Chu Hí, made a lasting impression on the national mind.

The two sons of Shin-tsung were unable to oppose the northern hordes of Liau and Hia, except by setting a third aspirant against both. These were the Niu-chih or Kin,[1] the ancestors of the present Manchus, who carried away Hwui-tsung as a captive in 1125, and his son too the next year, pillaging Lohyang and possessing themselves of the region north of the Yellow River. This closed the Northern Sung. The Kin established themselves at Peking in 1118, whence they were driven in 1235 by Genghis Khan, and fled back to the ancestral haunts on the Songari and Liau Rivers.

XXIII.—SOUTHERN SUNG dynasty forms part of the preceding, for Kao-tsung, the brother of the last and ninth monarch of the weakened house of Northern Sung, seeing his capital in ruins, fled to Nanking, and soon after to the beautiful city of Hangchau on the eastern coast at the mouth of the Tsientang River.

[1] Two graves of the Kin monarchs exist on a hill west of Fangshan hien, fifty miles south-west of Peking; they were repaired by Kanghí. Dr. Bushell visited them in 1870.

Nanking was pillaged by the Kin, but Hangchau was too far for them. It gradually grew in size and strength, and became a famous capital. Kao-tsung resigned in 1162, after a reign of thirty-six years, and survived his abdication twenty-four years. The next Emperor was Hiao-tsung, who also resigned the yellow to Kwang-tsung, his son, and he again yielded it to his son Ning-tsung. This last, in his distress, called the rising Mongols into his service in 1228 to help against the Kin. The distance from the northern frontier, where the Mongols were flushed with their successes over the Tangouth of Hia at Ninghia in 1226, was too far for them to aid Ning-tsung at this time. He was, however, relieved from danger to himself, and the Mongols deferred their intentions for a few years. From this date for about fifty years the Sung grew weaker and weaker under the next five sovereigns, until the last scion, Tí Ping, was drowned with some of his courtiers, one of whom, clasping him in his arms, jumped from the vessel, and ended their life, dignity, and dynasty together. It had lasted one hundred and fifty-two years under nine monarchs, who showed less ability than those of Northern Sung, and were all much inferior as a whole to the house of Tang. Their patronage of letters and the arts of peace was unaccompanied by the vigor of their predecessors, for they were unwilling to leave the capital and risk all at the head of their troops. It is the genius and philosophy of its scholars that has made the Sung one of the great dynasties of the Middle Kingdom.

XXIV.—The Yuen dynasty was the first foreign sway to which the Sons of Han had submitted; their resistance to the army, which gradually overran the country, was weakened, however, by treachery and desultory tactics until the national spirit was frittered away. During the interval between the capture of Peking by Genghis and the final extinction of the Sung dynasty, the whole population had become somewhat accustomed to Mongol rule. Having no organized government of their own, these khans were content to allow the Chinese the full exercise of their own laws, if peace and taxation were duly upheld. Kublai had had ample opportunity to learn the character of his new subjects, and after the death of Mangu khan in 1260 and his own establishment at Peking in 1264, he in fifteen years brought his vast dominions under a methodical sway and developed their resources more than ever. Though failing in his attempt to conquer Japan, he enlarged elsewhere his vanishing frontiers during his life till they could neither be defined nor governed. His patronage of merit and scholarship proves the good results of his tutelage in China, while the short-lived glory of his administration in other hands chiefly proved what good material he had to work with in China in comparison with his own race.[1] He was a vigorous and magnificent prince, and had, moreover, the advantage of having his acts and splendor related by Marco Polo—a chronicler worthy of his subject. The Grand Canal, which was deepened and lengthened during his reign, is a lasting token of his sagacity and enlightened policy. An interesting monument of this dynasty, erected in 1345, is the gateway in the Kü-yung kwan (pass) of the Great Wall north of Peking. Upon the interior of this arch is cut a Buddhist charm in six different kinds of character—Mongolian, Chinese, Oigour, antique Devanagari, Niu-chih, and Tibetan.[2]

After the Grand Khan's death the Mongols retained their power under the reign of Ching-tsung, or Timur khan, a grandson of Kublai, and Wu-tsung, or Genesek khan,[3] a nephew of the former, but their successors met with opposition, or were destroyed by treachery. The offices were also filled with Mongols, without any regard to the former mode of conferring rank according to literary qualifications, and the native Chinese began to be thoroughly dissatisfied with a sway in which they had no part. The last and eleventh, named Ching-tsung, or Tohan-Timur, came to the throne at the age of thirteen, and gave himself up to pleasure, his eunuchs and ministers dividing the possessions and offices of the Chinese among themselves and their adherents. This conduct aroused his subjects, and Chu Yuen-chang, a plebeian by birth, and formerly a priest, raised the standard of

---

[1] See Rémusat, *Nouveaux Mélanges*, Tomes I., p. 427; II., pp. 64, 88, and 89–97, for a series of notices concerning the Mongol generals and history.

[2] Compare Wylie in the *R. A. Soc. Jour.*, Vol. V. (N.S.), p. 14; Fergusson, *Hist. Ind. and East. Architecture*, p. 708; Yule's *Polo*, I., pp. 28, 409.

[3] This should be Kaishau-kulluk khan, called *Kai-sang* in Chinese. Rémusat, *Nouveaux Mélanges*, Tome II., pp. 1–4.

revolt, and finally expelled the Mongols, A.D. 1368, after a duration of eighty-nine years.[1]

Like most of the preceding dynasties, the new one established itself on the misrule, luxury, and weakness of its predecessors; the people submitted to a vigorous rule, as one which exhibited the true exposition of the decrees of Heaven, and upheld its laws and the harmony of the universe; while a weak sovereign plainly evinced his usurpation of the "divine utensil" and unfitness for the post by the disorders, famines, piracies, and insurrections which afflicted the mismanaged State, and which were all taken by ambitious leaders as evidences of a change in the choice of Heaven, and reasons for their carrying out the new selection which had fallen on them. Amid all the revolutions in China, none have been founded on principle; they were mere mutations of masters, attended with more or less destruction of life, and no better appreciation of the rights of the subject or the powers of the rulers. Nor without some knowledge of the high obligations man owes his Maker and himself is it easy to see whence the sustaining motive of free religious and political institutions can be derived.

XXV. The Ming, *i.e.*, 'Bright dynasty.'—The character of Hungwu, as Chu Yuen-chang called his reign on his accession, has been well drawn by Rémusat, who accords him a high rank for the vigor and talents manifested in overcoming his enemies and cementing his power. He established his capital at Nanking, or the 'Southern Capital,' and after a reign of thirty years transmitted the sceptre to his grandson, Kienwăn, a youth of sixteen. Yungloh, his son, dissatisfied with this arrangement, overcame his nephew and seized the crown after five years, and moved the capital back to Peking in 1403. This prince is distinguished for the code of laws framed under his auspices, which has, with some modifications and additions, ever since remained as the basis of the administration. During the reign of Kiahtsing the Portuguese came to China, and in that of Wanleih, about 1580, the Jesuits gained an entrance into the

[1] One of the causes of their easy overthrow is stated to have been the enormous robbery of the people by the lavish issue of paper money, which at last became worthless.

country. In his time, too, the Niu-chih, or Kin, whom Genghis had driven away in 1235, again became numerous and troublesome, and took possession of the northern frontiers. The first chieftain of the Manchus who attained celebrity was Tienming, who in 1618 published a manifesto of his designs against the house of Ming, in which he announced to Heaven the seven things he was bound to revenge. These consisted of petty oppressions upon persons passing the frontiers, assisting his enemies, violating the oath and treaty of peace entered into between the two rulers, and killing his envoys. The fierce nomad had already assumed the title of Emperor, and "vowed to celebrate the funeral of his father with the slaughter of two hundred thousand Chinese." Tienming overran the north-eastern parts of China, and committed unsparing cruelties upon the people of Liautung, but died in 1627, before he had satisfied his revenge, leaving it and his army to his son Tientsung.

The Chinese army fought bravely, though unsuccessfully, against the warlike Manchus, whose chief not only strove to subdue, but endeavored, by promises and largesses, to win the troops from their allegiance. The apparently audacious attempt of this small force to subdue the Chinese was assisted by numerous bodies of rebels, who, like wasps, sprung up in various parts of the country, the leaders of each asserting his claims to the throne, and all of them rendering their common country an easier prey to the invader. One of them, called Lí Tsz'-ching, attacked Peking, and the last Emperor Hwai-tsung, feeling that he had little to hope for after the loss of his capital, and had already estranged the affections of his subjects by his ill conduct, first stabbed his daughter and then hung himself, in 1643, and ended the house of Ming, after two hundred and seventy-six years. The usurper received the submission of most of the eastern provinces, but the Chinese general, Wu San-kwei, in command of the army on the north, refused to acknowledge him, and, making peace with the Manchus, invoked the aid of Tsungteh in asserting the cause of the rightful claimant to the throne. This was willingly agreed to, and the united army marched to Peking and speedily entered the capital, which the rebel chief had left a heap of ruins when he took away his booty. The

Manchus now declared themselves the rulers of the Empire, but their chief dying, his son Shunchí, who at the age of six succeeded his father in 1644, is regarded as the first Emperor; his uncle, Aina-wang, ruled and reorganized the administration in his name.

XXVI. The Tsing,[1] *i.e.*, 'Pure dynasty.'—During the eighteen years he sat upon the throne Shunchí and his officers subdued most of the northern and central provinces, but the maritime regions of the south held out against the invaders, and one of the leaders, by means of his fleets, carried devastation along the whole coast. The spirit of resistance was in some parts crushed, and in others exasperated by an order for all Chinese to adopt as a sign of submission the Tartar mode of shaving the front of the head and braiding the hair in a long queue. Those who gave this order, as Davis remarks, must have felt themselves very strong before venturing so far upon the spirit of the conquered, and imposing an outward universal badge of surrender upon all classes of the people. "Many are the changes which may be made in despotic countries, without the notice or even the knowledge of the larger portion of the community; but an entire alteration in the national costume affects every individual equally, from the highest to the lowest, and is perhaps of all others the most open and degrading mark of conquest." This order was resisted by many, who chose to lose their heads rather than part with their hair, but the mandate was gradually enforced, and has now for about two centuries been one of the distinguishing marks of a Chinese, though to this day the natives of Fuhkien near the seaboard wear a kerchief around their head to conceal it. The inhabitants of this province and of Kwangtung held out the longest against the invaders, and a vivid account of their capture of Canton, November 26, 1650, where the adherents of the late dynasty had intrenched themselves, has been left us by Martini, an eyewitness. Some time after its subjugation a brave man, Ching Chí-lung, harassed them by his fleet; and his son, Ching

---

[1] For the origin of the Manchus see Klaproth, *Mémoires sur l'Asie*, Tome I., p. 441.

Ching-kung, or Koxinga, molested the coast to such a degree that the Emperor Kanghí, in 1665, ordered all the people to retire three leagues inland, in order to prevent this heroic man from reaching them. This command was generally obeyed, and affords an instance of the singular mixture of power and weakness seen in many parts of Chinese legislation; for it might be supposed that a government which could compel its maritime subjects to leave their houses and towns and go into the country at great loss, might have easily armed and equipped a fleet to have defended those towns and homes. Koxinga, finding himself unable to make any serious impression upon the stability of the new government, went to Formosa, drove the Dutch out of Zealandia, and made himself master of the island.[1]

Shunchí died in 1661 and was succeeded by his son Kanghí,[2] who was eight years old at his accession, and remained under guardians till he was fourteen, when he assumed the reins of government, and swayed the power vested in his hands with a prudence, vigor, and success that have rendered him more celebrated than almost any other Asiatic monarch. It was in 1661 that Louis XIV. had assumed the sovereignty of France at about the same age, and for fifty-four years the reigns of these two monarchs ran parallel. During Kanghí's unusually long reign of sixty-one years (the longest in Chinese annals, except Taimao of the Shang dynasty, B.C. 1637–1562), he extended his dominions to the borders of Kokand and Badakshan on the west, and to the confines of Tibet on the south-west, simplifying the administration and consolidating his power in every part of his vast dominions. To his regulations, perhaps, are mainly owing the unity and peace which the Empire has exhibited for more than a century, and which has produced the impression abroad of the unchangeableness of Chinese institutions and character. This may be ascribed, chiefly, to his indefatigable applica-

[1] Compare the interesting translation from a Chinese record of the capture of Fort Zealandia, by H. E. Hobson, *Journal of N. C. Br. R. A. Society*, No. XI., Art. I., 1876.

[2] Rémusat, *Nouveaux Mélanges*, Tome II., pp. 21–44; Bouvet, *Life of Kanghí*; Gutzlaff, *Life of Kanghí*.

tion to all affairs of State, to his judgment and penetration in the choice of officers, his economy in regard to himself and liberal magnificence in everything that tended to the good of his dominions, and his sincere desire to promote the happiness of his people by a steady and vigorous execution of the laws and a continual watchfulness over the conduct of his high officers. These qualities have perhaps been unduly extolled by his foreign friends and biographers, the Romish missionaries, and if their expressions are taken in their strictest sense, as we understand them, they do elevate him too high. He is to be compared not with Alfred or William III. of England, Louis IX. or Henry IV. of France, and other European kings, but with other Chinese and Asiatic princes, few of whom equal him. The principal events of his long reign are the conquest of the Eleuths, and subjugation of several tribes lying on the north and south of the Tien shan; an embassy across the Russian Possessions in 1713 to the khan of the Tourgouth Tartars, preparatory to their return to the Chinese territory; the settlement of the northern frontier between himself and the czar, of which Gerbillon has given a full account; the survey of the Empire by the Romish missionaries; and the publication of a great thesaurus of the language. In many things he showed himself liberal toward foreigners, and the country was thrown open to their commerce for many years.

His son Yungching succeeded in 1722, and is regarded by many natives as superior to his father. He endeavored to suppress Christianity and restore the ancient usages, which had somewhat fallen into desuetude during his father's sway, and generally seems to have held the sceptre to the benefit of his subjects. Yungching is regarded as an usurper, and is said to have changed the figure four to fourteen on the billet of nomination, himself being the fourteenth son, and the fourth being absent in Mongolia, where he was soon after arrested and imprisoned, and subsequently died in a palace near Peking; whether he was put to death or not is uncertain. Kienlung succeeded Yungching in 1736, and proved himself no unworthy descendant of his grandfather Kanghí; like him he had the singular fortune to reign sixty years, and for most of that period in peace.[1] Some local insurrections disturbed the general tranquillity, principally among the aborigines in Formosa and Kweichau, and in an unprovoked attack upon Birmah his armies sustained a signal defeat and were obliged to retreat. The incursions of the Nipalese into Tibet induced the Dalai Lama to apply to him for assistance, and in doing so he contrived to establish a guardianship over the whole country, and place bodies of troops in all the important positions, so that in effect he annexed that vast region to his Empire, but continued the lamas in the internal administration.

During his long reign Kienlung exhausted the resources of his Empire by building useless edifices and keeping up large armies. He received embassies from the Russians, Dutch, and English, by which the character of the Chinese and the nature of their country became better known to western nations. These embassies greatly strengthened the impression on the side of the Chinese of their superiority to all other nations, for they looked upon them as acknowledgments on the part of the governments who sent them of their allegiance to the court of Peking. The presents were regarded as tribute, the ambassadors as deputies from their masters to acknowledge the supremacy of the Emperor, and the requests they made for trade as rather another form of receiving presents in return than a mutual arrangement for a trade equally beneficial to both. Kienlung abdicated the throne in favor of his fifth son and retired with the title of *Supreme Emperor*, while his son, Kiaking, had that of Emperor.

The character of this prince was dissolute and superstitious, and his reign of twenty-five years was much disturbed by secret combinations against the government and by insurrections[2] and

---

[1] His character and enthusiasm for literary pursuits merit, on the whole, the lines inscribed by the Roman Catholic missionaries beneath his portrait in the *Mémoires conc. les Chinois:*

> Occupé sans relâche à touts les soins divers
> D'un gouvernement qu'on admire,
> Le plus grand potentat qui soit dans l'univers
> Et le meilleur lettré qui soit dans son Empire.

[2] Among the most serious of these was the revolt of the Peh lien kiao. *Lettres Édifiantes,* Tome III., pp. 291-298, 353, 379, etc. In 1789 the ladrones infested the southern coasts. *Ib.*, Tome II., p. 492.

pirates in and about the Empire. A conspiracy against him broke out in the palace in 1813, where he was for a time in some danger, but was rescued by the courage of his guard and family; one of his sons, Mien-ning, was designated as his successor for his bravery on this occasion. A fleet of about six hundred piratical junks, under Ching Yih and Chang Pau, infested the coasts of Kwangtung for several years, and were at last put down in 1810 by the provincial government taking advantage of internal dissensions between the leaders. The principal scene of the exploits of this fleet was the estuary of the Pearl River, whose numerous harbors and channels afforded shelter and escape to their vessels when pursued by the imperialists, while the towns upon the islands were plundered and the inhabitants killed if they resisted. The internal government of this audacious band was ascertained by two Englishmen, Mr. Turner and Mr. Glasspoole, who at different times fell into their hands and were obliged to accompany them in their marauding expeditions. To so great a height did they proceed that the governor of Canton went to Macao to reside, and entered into some arrangements with the Portuguese for assistance in suppressing them. The piratical fleet was attacked and blockaded for ten days by the combined forces, but without much damage; there was little prospect of overcoming them had not rivalry between the two leaders gone so far as to result in a severe engagement and loss on both sides. The conquered pirate soon after made his peace with the government, and the victor shortly afterward followed the same course. The story of those disturbed times to this day affords a frequent subject for the tales of old people in that region, and the same waters are still infested by the "foam of the sea," as the Chinese term these freebooters.

The reign of Kiaking ended in 1820; by the Emperor's will his second son was appointed to succeed him, and took the style Taukwang. He exhibited more energy and justice than his father, and his efforts purified the administration by the personal supervision taken of their leading members. His reign was marked by many local insurrections and disasters in one quarter or another of his vast dominions. A rebellion in Turkestan in 1828 was attended with great cruelty and treachery on the part of the Chinese, and its leader, Jehangír, was murdered, in violation of the most solemn promises. An insurrection in Formosa and a rising among the mountaineers of Kwangtung, in 1830–32, were put down more by money than by force, but as peace is both the end and evidence of good government in China, the authorities are not very particular how it is brought about.

The rapid increase of opium-smoking among his people led to many efforts to restrain this vice by prohibitions, penalties, executions, and other means, but all in vain. The Emperor's earnestness was stimulated by the death of his three eldest sons from its use, and the falling off of the revenue by smuggling the pernicious drug. In 1837–38 the collective opinion of the highest officials was taken after hearing their arguments for legalizing its importation; it was resolved to seize the dealers in it. The acts of Commissioner Lin resulted in the war with Great Britain and the opening of China to an extended intercourse with other nations. Defeated in his honest efforts to protect his people against their bane, the Emperor still fulfilled his treaty obligations, and died in 1850, just as the Tai-ping rebellion broke out.

His fourth son succeeded him under the style of Hienfung, but without his father's earnestness or vigor when the State required the highest qualities in its leader. The devastations of the rebels laid waste the southern half of the Empire, and their approach to Peking in 1853 was paralyzed by floods and want of supplies more than by the imperial troops. A second war with Great Britain, in 1858–60, completely broke down the seclusion of China, and at its conclusion an inglorious reign of eleven years ended at Jeh-ho in August, 1860. His only son succeeded to the throne at the age of five years, under the style of Tungchí; the government being under the control of two Empress-regents and Prince Kung, his uncle. During his reign of twelve years the vigor of the new authorities succeeded in completely quelling the Tai-ping rebellion, destroying the Mohammedan rising in Yunnan and Kansuh, and opening up diplomatic intercourse with the Treaty Powers. Just as the

Emperor began to exercise his authority, he died in January, 1875, without issue. The vacant "utensil" has been filled by the appointment of his cousin, a boy of four years, whose reign was styled Kwangsü. Affairs continue to be conducted by the same regency as before, now still more conversant with the new relations opening up with other lands. The real Empress-dowager, or *Tung Kung*, died April 18, 1881.

So far as can be judged from the imperfect data of native historians of former days, compared with the observations of foreigners at present, there is little doubt that this enormous population has been better governed by the Manchus than under the princes of the Ming dynasty; there has been more vigor in the administration of government and less palace favoritism and intrigue in the appointment of officers, more security of life and property from the exactions of local authorities, bands of robbers, or processes of law; in a word, the Manchu sway has well developed the industry and resources of the country, of which the population, loyalty, and content of the people are the best evidences.

The sovereigns of the Ming and Tsing dynasties, being more frequently mentioned in history than those of former princes, are here given, with the length of their reigns. For convenience of reference a table of the dynasties is appended, taken from the author's *Syllabic Dictionary of the Chinese Language*. In this list, compiled from a Chinese work (the *Digest of the Reigns of Emperors and Kings*), the Tsin and After Tsin dynasties are joined in one (No. 4), making a total of twenty-six dynasties.[1]

The whole number of acknowledged sovereigns in the twenty-six dynasties, according to the received Chinese chronology, from Yu the Great to Kwangsü, is 238, or 246 commencing with Fuh-hí; by including the names of some ursurpers and moribund claimants, the first number is increased to 250. From Yu the Great to the accession of Kwangsü (B.C. 2205 to A.D. 1875) is 4,080 years, which gives to each dynasty a duration of 157

---

[1] Compare the Chinese Chronological Tables by W. F. Mayers in *N. C. Br. R. A. S. Journal*, No. IV., Art. VIII., 1867.

Kwoh Hiao, or Reigning Title.	Miao Hiao, or Temple Title.	Began to Reign.	Length of Reign.	Contemporary Monarchs.
1. Hungwu....	Taitsu..........	1368	30	Tamerlane, Richard II., Robert II.
2. Kienwan....	Kienwan tí	1398	5	Manuel-Paleologus, Henry IV. of Eng.
3. Yungloh....	Taitsung.......	1403	22	James I., Henry V., Martin V.
4. Hunghi.....	Jintsung.......	1425	1	Amurath II., Henry VI., Charles VII.
5. Siuentih....	Siuentsung.....	1426	10	Albert II., Cosmo de Medicis.
6. Chingtung ..	Yingtsung	1436	21	James II., Fred. III. of Aus., Nich. V.
7. Kingtai.....	Kingti.........	1457	8	Mahomet II., Edward IV., Sixtus IV.
8. Chinghwa...	Hientsung	1465	23	James III., Ferd. and Isabella, Louis XI.
9. Hungchi....	Hiautsung	1488	18	Bajazet II., James IV., Henry VII.
10. Chingtih....	Wutsung.......	1506	16	James V., Henry VIII., Charles V.
11. Kiahtsing...	Shítsung.......	1522	45	Solyman II., Mary, Philip II., Henry II.
12. Lungking...	Muhtsung......	1567	6	Selim II., Elizabeth, Gregory III.
13. Wanleih	Shintsung......	1573	47	James I., Henry IV., Louis XIII.
14. Taichang ...	Kwangtsung ...	1620	1	Othman II., Philip IV., Gregory XV.
15. Tienki......	Hitsung	1621	7	Amurath IV., Charles I., Urban VIII.
16. Tsungching.	Hwaitsung.....	1628	16	Innocent X., Frederick the Great.
1. Shunchi[1] ...	Chang hwangti.	1644	18	Mahomet IV., Cromwell, Louis XIV.
2. Kanghi	Jin hwangtí ...	1662	61	Charles II., Clement IX., Sobiesky.
3. Yungching..	Hien hwangti..	1723	13	Mahomet V., George II., Louis XV.
4. Kienlung ...	Shun hwangtí..	1736	60	Osman III., George III., Clement XIV.
5. Kiaking	Jui hwangti....	1796	25	Selim III., Napoleon, Fred. Wm. II.
6. Taukwang ..	Ching hwangti .	1821	30	Mahmoud, George IV., Louis XVIII.
7. Hienfung ...	Hien hwangti ..	1851	11	Mahmoud, Victoria, Louis XVIII.
8. Tungchi	....	1862	12	Napoleon III., Alexander II.
9. Kwangsü[2] ..	....	1875		

Dynasty.	Number of Sovereigns.	Began.	Ended.	Duration.
1. Hia	Seventeen, averaging 26 years to each monarch's reign	B.C. 2205	B.C. 1766	439
2. Shang	Twenty-eight, averaging 23 years..........	1766	1122	644
3. Chau.......	Thirty-four, averaging 25½ years..........	1122	255	867
4. Tsin........	Two, one reigning 37 years, the second 3 years.	255	206	40
5. Han........	Fourteen, averaging 16½ years	206	A.D. 25	231
6. East Han...	Twelve, averaging 16⅓ years..........	A.D. 25	221	196
7. After Han..	Two, one reigning 2, the other 41 years......	221	264	43
8. Tsin........	Four, averaging 14¼ years..........	265	322	57
9. East Tsin ..	Eleven, averaging about 9⅔ years..........	323	419	106
10. Sung	Eight, averaging 7¼ years	420	478	58
11. Tsí.........	Five, averaging 4⅗ years	479	502	23
12. Liang.......	Four, one 48 years, and three together 7 years.	502	556	54
13. Chin	Five, averaging about 6⅖ years	557	589	32
14. Sui........	Three, one reigning 16, another 12, and another 2 years..........	589	619	30
15. Tang	Twenty, averaging 14⅓ years	620	907	287
16. After Liang.	Two, one 8 and one 7 years	907	923	16
17. After Tang .	Four, averaging 3¼ years..........	923	936	13
18. After Tsin..	Two, one 7 and one 3 years	936	946	10
19. After Han..	Two, one 3 years, another 1 year	947	951	4
20. After Chau .	Three, averaging 3 years..........	951	960	9
21. Sung	Nine, averaging 18½ years..........	960	1127	167
22. South Sung.	Nine, averaging 17 years	1127	1280	153
23. Yuen.......	Nine, averaging 9⅘ years	1280	1368	88
24. Ming.......	Sixteen, averaging 17 years..........	1368	1644	276
25. Tsing	Eight up to 1875, averaging nearly 30 years ..	1644		

[1] Shunchi and the four following monarchs are named in Manchu, Chidsuidimbukhé, Elkhe taifin, Khowaligasoun toh, Abkai wekhiyekhe, and Saichungs fengchen, respectively.

[2] Kwangsü was born August 14, 1871.

years, and to each monarch an average of $17\frac{1}{7}$ years. From Wu wang's accession to Kwangsü is 2,997 years, giving an average of 125 years to a dynasty and $15\frac{1}{2}$ to each sovereign. From the days of Menes in Egypt, B.C. 2719 to 331, Manetho reckons 31 dynasties and 378 kings, which is about 77 years to each family and $6\frac{1}{3}$ to each reign. In England the 34 sovereigns from William I. to Victoria (A.D. 1066 to 1837) averaged $22\frac{2}{3}$ years each; in Israel, the 23 kings from Saul to Zedekiah averaged 22 years during a monarchy of 507 years.

CHAPTER II.

FOREIGN INTERCOURSE WITH CHINA.

THE most important notices which the research of authors had collected respecting the intercourse between China and the West, and the principal facts of interest of a political and commercial nature down to the year 1834, are carefully arranged in the first three chapters of Sir John Davis' work.[1] In truth, the terms *intercourse* and *ambassies*, so often used with reference to the nations of Eastern Asia, indicate a peculiar state of relations with them; for while other courts send and receive resident ministers, those of China, Japan, Corea, and Cochinchina have until very recently kept themselves aloof from this national interchange of civilities, neither understanding its principles nor appreciating its advantages. Embassies have been sent by most European nations to the two first, which have tended rather to strengthen their assumptions of supremacy than to enlighten them as to the real objects and wishes of the courts proposing such courtesies. The commercial intercourse has, like the political, either been forced upon or begged of these governments, constantly subject to those vexatious restrictions and interruptions which might be expected from such ill-defined arrangements; and though mutually advantageous, has never been conducted on those principles of reciprocity and equality which characterize commerce at the West. As yet, the rulers and merchants of oriental nations are hardly well enough acquainted with their own and others' rights to be able or willing

---

[1] *The Chinese*, 2 Vols., Harper's Family Library, 1837. See also Murray's *China*, Vol. I., 1843. Montgomery Martin's *China*, passim, 1847. *Mémoires conc. les Chinois*, Tome V., pp. 1–23. T. W. Kingsmill in *N. C. Br. R. A. Soc. Journal*, N. S., No. XIV., 1879.

to enter into close relations with European powers. Both magistrates and people are ignorant and afraid of the resources, power, and designs of Christian nations, and consequently disinclined to admit them or their subjects to unrestrained intercourse. When western adventurers, as Pinto, Andrade, Weddell, and others came to the shores of China and Japan in the sixteenth and seventeenth centuries, they found the governments disposed to traffic, but the conquests subsequently made by Europeans in the neighboring regions of Luçonia, Java, and India, and their cruel treatment of the natives, led these two powers to apprehend like results for themselves if they did not soon take precautionary measures of exclusion and restriction. Nor can there be much doubt that this policy was the safest measure, in order to preserve their independence and maintain their authority over even their own subjects. Might made right more generally among nations then than it does now, and the belief entertained by most Europeans at that period, that all pagan lands belonged justly to the Pope, only wanted men and means to be everywhere carried into effect. Had the Chinese and Japanese governments allowed Portuguese, Spanish, French, and English colonists to settle and increase within their borders, they would, probably, long since have crumbled to pieces and their territories have been possessed by others.

The data brought together by Davis in 1838 on this subject has since been enlarged and illustrated by Col. Yule in his admirable "Preliminary Essay" of 1866, prefixed to *Cathay and the Way Thither*, and by Richthofen, the latter half of whose first volume on China is devoted to an exhaustive treatise upon the "Development of the Knowledge of China."[1] A digest of these elaborate works would be too long for our purpose here,

---

[1] *China, Ergebnisse eigener Reisen und darauf gegründeter Studien*, Berlin, 1877. This author's arrangement of the subject into "Periods" is as follows: I.—Legendary notices of intercourse before the year 1122 B.C. II.—From the accession of the Chaus to the building of the Great Wall (1122–212 B.C.). III.—From the building of the Great Wall to the accession of the Tangs (212 B.C.–619 A.D.). IV.—From the Tangs to the Mongols (619–1205). V.—From the rise of the Mongol power to the arrival of the Portuguese in China (1205–1517). VI.—From the arrival of the Portuguese to the present time.

where only the most interesting points can be noticed. The first recorded knowledge of China among the nations of the West does not date further back than the geographer Ptolemy, A.D. 150, who seems himself to have been indebted to the Tyrian author Marinus. The Periplus of the Erythræan Sea, however, refers to the same land under the name *Θὶν*, or *Thin*, at perhaps an earlier date. Previous to this time, moreover, accounts of the existence of the land of Confucius, and an appreciation and demand for the splendid silks made there, had reached Persia, judging from the legends found in its writers alluding to ancient wars and embassies with China, in which the country, the government, people, and fabrics are invested with a halo of power and wealth which has not yet entirely vanished. These legends strengthen the conclusion that the Prophet Isaiah has the first mention now extant of the Flowery Land under the name *Sinim*. The interchange of the initial in *China*, *Thina* or *Tina*, and *Sina* ought to give no trouble in identifying the land, for such changes in pronunciation are still common in it; *e.g.*, *Chau-chau fu* into *Tiè-chiu hu*.

The Periplus of Arrian places the city of Thina perhaps as far east as Sí-ngan, but too vaguely to be relied on; that great city must certainly have then been known, however, among the traders of Central Asia, who probably were better acquainted with its geography than the authors who have survived them. Under the term *Seres* the Chinese are more clearly referred to at even an earlier date than *Sina*, and among the Latin writers it was about the only term used, its association with the silks brought thence keeping it before them. The two names were used for different regions,[1] the Seres being understood as lying to the north. Mela places them between the Indians and Scythians; Ptolemy calls the country *Serice* and the capital *Sera*, but regarded them as distinct from the *Sinæ*, precisely as a Chinese geographer might confuse Britain and England. He says there

[1] The different appellations seem to have been employed according as it was regarded as the terminus of a southern sea route or a journey across the continent. In the former aspect the name has nearly always been some form of *Sin*, *Chin*, Sinæ, China; in the latter, to the ancients as the land of the *Seres*, to the middle ages as the Empire of *Cathay*.—Yule.

was a long and dangerous land route leading to Sera through Persia to Bactria, over mountain defiles and perilous paths, which occupied the largest part of a year. Besides Ptolemy, there are notices by Pliny of the Seres, and these two authors furnished their successors with most of their knowledge down to the reign of Justinian. Col. Yule concisely summarizes the knowledge of China down to that date among the Romans: "The region of the Seres is a vast and populous country, touching on the east the ocean and the limits of the habitable world; and extending west nearly to Imaus and the confines of Bactria. The people are civilized men, of mild, just, and frugal temper; eschewing collisions with their neighbors, and even shy of close intercourse, but not averse to dispose of their own products, of which raw silk is the staple, but which include also silk stuffs, furs, and iron of remarkable quality." He further explains how authors writing at Rome and Constantinople were quite unable to traverse and rectify what was said of the marts and nations spoken of in the farthest East, and place them with any precision. They were, in truth, in the same difficulty in coming to an accurate conclusion that the Chinese geographer Seu Kí-yu was when writing at Fuhchau in 1847; he could not explain the discrepancies he found between Rhodes and its colossus and Rhode Island in the United States.

Among the marts mentioned in the various authors, Greek, Roman, and Persian, only a few can be identified with even fair probability. The "Stone Tower" of Ptolemy seems to have denoted *Tashkend*, a name of the same meaning, and a town still resorted to for trade. His port of Cattigara may have been a mart at the mouth of the Meinam, the Meikon, the Chu Kiang, or some other large stream in that region, where seafaring people could exchange their wares with the natives, then quite independent of the Chinese in Shensí, who were known to him as Seres. Cattigara is more probably to be looked for near Canton, for its annals state that in the reign of Hwan tí (A.D. 147–168) "Tienchuh (India), Ta-tsin (Rome, Egypt or Arabia), and other nations came by the southern sea with tribute, and from this time trade was carried on at Canton with foreigners." During the same dynasty (the Eastern Han), foreigners came from Cantoo, Lu-hwang-chí, and other nations in the south. The nearest was about ten days' journey, and the farthest about five months'.[1]

On the land frontier, the Chinese annals of the Han dynasty record the efforts of Wu tí (B.C. 140–86) to open a communication with the Yuehchí, or Getæ, who had driven out the Greek rulers in Bactria and settled themselves north of the River Oxus, in order to get their help against his enemies the Huns. He sent an envoy, Chang Kiang, in 135, who was captured by the Huns and kept prisoner for ten years, when he escaped with some of his attendants and got to *Ta-wan*, or Ferghana, and thence reached the Yuehchí further south. He was unsuccessful in his mission, and attempted to return home through Tibet, but was re-taken by the Huns, and did not succeed in reporting himself at Chang-an till thirteen years had elapsed. The introduction of the vine into China is rather doubtfully ascribed to this brave envoy.

De Guignes concludes that this notice about trade at Canton refers to the embassy sent in A.D. 166 by the Emperor Marcus Aurelius (whom the Chinese call *An-tun*), which entered China by the south at Tongking, or Canton. The Latin author Florus, who lived in Trajan's reign, about fifty years before, has a passage showing, as proof of the universal awe and veneration in which the power of Rome was held under Augustus, that ambassadors from the remotest nations, the Seres and the Indians, came with presents of elephants, gems, and pearls—a rhetorical exaggeration quite on a par with the Chinese account of the tribute sent from An-tun, and not so well authenticated. Whether, indeed, the *Ta-tsin kwoh* mentioned by Chinese writers meant Judea, Rome, or Persia, cannot now be exactly ascertained, though Yule concludes that this name almost certainly means the Roman Empire, otherwise called the Kingdom of the Western Sea. The title was given to these regions because of the analogy of its people to those of the Middle King-

---

[1] *Chinese Repository*, I., p. 365. Heeren, *Asiatic Researches*, II., pp. 285–295. Murray's *China*, I., p. 141. Yule's *Cathay*, Vol. I., pp. xli–xlv. Smith, *Classical Dictionary*, Art. SERES.

dom.[1] The envoys sent to that country reported that "beyond the territory of the Tau-shi (perhaps the Persians) there was a great sea, by which, sailing due west, one might arrive at the country where the sun sets." Like most attempts of the kind in subsequent days, the mission of Antoninus appears to have been a failure, and to have returned without accomplishing any practical benefit to intercourse or trade between the two greatest empires in the world. It was received, no doubt, at Lohyang, then the capital, with ostentatious show and patronizing kindness, and its occurrence inscribed in the national records as another evidence of the glory and fame of the Son of Heaven. That a direct trade between Rome and China did not result at this period may have been largely due to the jealousy of the Parthian merchants, who reaped great profits as middle-men in the traffic, and disposed of their own woven and colored stuffs to the Romans, all of which gain they knew would have passed over their heads had the extreme East and West come into more intimate relations.

It is worthy of observation how, even from the earliest times, the traffic in the rich natural and artificial productions of India and China has been the great stimulus to urge adventurers to come from Europe, who on their part offered little in exchange besides precious metals. The *Serica vestis*, whether it was a silken or cotton fabric, and other rarities found in those regions, bore such a high price at Rome as to tempt the merchants to undertake the longest journeys and undergo the greatest hardships to procure them; and such was the case likewise during the long period before the discovery of the Cape of Good Hope. The existence of this trade early enabled the Nestorian missionaries to penetrate into those remote regions, and keep up a communication with their patrons at home; the more extended

[1] *Cathay and the Way Thither*, p. lvi. Klaproth, *Tableaux Historiques de l'Asie* (Paris, 1826), p. 68. So Richthofen (*China*, Bd. I., p. 470), who adds: "It is accepted now, by almost all those who have written on the subject, that the Chinese by *Ta-tsin* meant to denote 'Great-China,' and through this, on the other hand, we have a proof that the Chinese called their own country *Tsin*. It will hardly do, however, to suppose that so prejudiced a people as they would recognize another folk as greater. The appellation *Ta* (great) is given to every nation whose power the Chinese feel to be considerable."

voyages of modern commerce likewise assist benevolent persons in reaching the remotest tribes and carrying on their labors, through their patrons on the other side of the world, probably with less danger and delay than a mission at Cadiz could have been directed from Jerusalem in the days of the apostles.

The notices in Cosmas (a Greek monk who had been a merchant, and wrote his "Universal Christian Topography" between 530 and 550 A.D.) of China and its products refer to the maritime trade under the Byzantine emperors. This country he locates very correctly as occupying the extreme east of Asia, and calls *Tzinista*, a name probably picked up from the Persians or old Hindus, and nearly similar to the *Tzinisthan* of the tablet at Sí-ngan. Another Greek, Theophylact, in the next century describes the internal intercourse in Central Asia, and a great Turkish people, the *Taugas*, whom he was unaware were the Chinese. It may be that he miswrote *Tang* in a grecized form for the dynasty just about that time settling its power. The indirect commerce between China and the Greek Empire increased by sea and land until the rise of the Moslem power. The same indifference on the part of the Chinese respecting the power, resources, and position of other lands is seen through all their notices of those western kingdoms. The products carried west were silk in various forms, but the demand for this article diminished after the worms had been successfully taken to Greece about A.D. 550. Cotton fabrics, medicines, and spices went westward as well as silk, but it is impossible to distinguish the trade with China from that with India. The leaf called *malabathrum* in the Periplus was not a Chinese plant, but the *tamalapatra*, a kind of cassia (*Cinnamomum nitidum*, whose leaves were purchased in Rome for three hundred denarii per pound), and now called Malabar leaf; it was probably mixed or confounded with the Indian *nard* and with camphor. The people called *Sesatæ* in the Periplus are probably to be looked for in Assam or Sikkim, where wild cassia grows, and where the real tea plant is native; but neither tea nor betel-leaf can be regarded as the ancient malabathrum.[1]

---

[1] Heeren's *Asiatic Researches*, II., p. 294; Yule's *Cathay*, pp. xlvi, cxliv.

Within the last few years the translations of the travels of Buddhist pilgrims between China and India have furnished more satisfactory details of the peoples inhabiting the central and western parts of Asia than all the Greek and Latin authors. Those of Fahian (399–414), of Hiuen-tsang (628–645), and of Hwui-sing (518), are the most extensive. Further researches into conventual libraries in China and Tibet are encouraged by what has been found on their shelves, and from them enough has already been gained to reward the labor. Of greater worth than these, perhaps, are the official histories of the Han, Tsin, and Tang dynasties, reaching from B.C. 200 to A.D. 900, only portions of which have yet been made accessible in full. Their trivialties are so numerous that their entire translation into English would hardly repay the printing, as the experiment by Mailla, in 1785, of the *Tang Kien Kang-muh*, in thirteen volumes quarto, shows. These histories, on the whole, supply more accurate information about Syria, Persia, Greece, and Parthia, than the writers of those countries give about China;—for example, the notices of *Fulin*, or Constantinople, are more minute than any account of Chang-an in western writers. But as Yule well remarks, there is much analogy between the fragmentary views each party had, the same uncertainty as to exact position, and the same application of facts belonging to the nearer skirts of a half-seen empire to the whole land. It can well be paralleled by reading some of our own travellers who applied all that they saw and heard at Canton to the Eighteen Provinces. Only a few embassies from *Ta-tsin* and *Fulin* are enumerated by Pauthier in his *Chine* as coming down to the year 1091; but the tractate by Dr. E. Bretschneider, of the Russian Legation at Peking,[1] shows how constant were the visits of the Arabs down to the Sung (A.D. 1086), and especially during the Tang dynasty. During the Tsin and Wei dynasties the visits of envoys from Ceylon were frequent, all of them an outgrowth of Buddhism, but repaid in more ways than one by the trade and its results—as shown by Sir E. Tennent in his *History of Ceylon*. In 1266 the King of Ceylon had Chinese soldiers in

[1] *On the Knowledge of the Arabs and Arabian Colonies possessed by the Ancient Chinese*, London, 1871.

his service, and envoys came to him to buy Buddha's sacred alms-dish. In 1405 the Emperor Yungloh of the Ming dynasty, taking umbrage at the indignities offered to his representative by Wijayabahu IV., despatched Ching Ho with a fleet of sixty-two ships and a land force to cruise along the coasts of Cambodia, Siam, and other places, demanding tribute and conferring gifts as the successor of the throne held by the great Kublai. Going again the next year as far as Ceylon, Ching Ho evaded a snare set by the king, and captured him and his whole family and officials, carrying them all to Peking. In 1411 the latter were set free, but a new king was appointed to the vacant throne, who reigned fifty years and sent tribute till 1459; this was only thirty-eight years before Gama arrived at Calicut. It was the last attempt of the Chinese to assert their sway beyond the limits of the Middle Kingdom seaward.[1]

One intimation of a continuance of the intercourse with China from the time of Justinian to that of the Arab travellers Wahab and Abu Zaid, is the Nestorian inscription (page 277). The narratives of the Arabs (A.D. 850 and 877) are trustworthy in their general statements as to the course pursued in the voyage, the port to which they sailed in China, the customs of the people there, and the nature and mode of conducting the trade; they form, in fact, the first authentic accounts we have of the Chinese from western writers, and make us doubt a little whether others like them have not been lost, rather than suppose that such were never written. These interesting relics were translated by Reinaud in 1845, with the text and notes.[2] The second traveller speaks of the sack of the city of Canfu, then the port of all the Arabian merchants, in which one hundred and twenty thousand Mohammedans, Jews, Christians, and Magians, or Parsees, engaged in traffic, were destroyed. This shows the extent and value of the trade. Canfu was Kanpu, a fine port near the modern town of the same name, twenty-five miles from Hangchau, and near Chapu on the Bay of Hangchau; the

[1] Tennent's *Ceylon*, I., pp. 607–626. Yule's *Cathay*, pp. lxvi–lxxvi.

[2] *Relation des Voyages faits par les Arabes et les Persans dans l'Inde et à la Chine dans le IXme Siècle de l'ère Chrètienne*, 2 Vols., Paris, 1845.

Gates of China were probably in the Chusan Archipelago and its numerous channels. Much of the statement made by Abu Zaid respecting the wealth, extent, and splendor of Canfu really refers to the city of Hangchau. The bore in the Tsientang River makes it impossible for ships to lie off that place, and this had its effect in developing Kanpu. The destruction of the capital in 877 contributed to direct part of the trade to Canton, which even then and long after was comparatively a small place, and the people of that part of the country but little removed from gross barbarism. In Marco Polo's time Ganpu was frequented by all the ships that bring merchandise from India.[1]

Prior to the date when he reached the confines of the Pacific, the ravages of the Mongols, under Genghis and his successors, in the regions between the Mediterranean and Caspian, and their great victory near Lignitz, April 12, 1241, had aroused the fears of the Pope and other potentates for their own safety. After the sudden recall of the hosts of Okkodai, in the same year, at his death, and their retreat from Bohemia and Poland to the Dneiper, the Pope determined to send two missions to the Tartars to urge them to greater humanity. One was a Franciscan monk, John of Plano Carpini, who carried the following letter to Batu khan on the Wolga:

INNOCENT, BISHOP, SERVANT OF THE SERVANTS OF GOD, TO THE KING AND PEOPLE OF THE TARTARS.

Since not only men, but also irrational animals, and even the mechanical mundane elements, are united by some kind of alliance, after the example of superior spirits, whose hosts the Author of the universe has established in a perpetual and peaceful order, we are compelled to wonder, not without reason, how you, as we have heard, having entered many lands of Christians and others, have wasted them with horrible desolation, and still, with continued fury, not ceasing to extend further your destroying hands, dissolving every natural tie, neither sparing sex nor age, direct indifferently against all the fury of the sword. We therefore, after the example of the Prince of Peace, desiring to unite all mankind in unity and the fear of God, warn, beseech, and exhort you henceforth to desist wholly from such outrages, and especially from

---

[1] *Chinese Repository*, Vol. I., pp. 6, 42, 252; Vol. III., p. 115. Yule's *Marco Polo*, Vol. II., pp. 149, 156. *Cathay*, p. cxciii.

the persecution of Christians; and since, by so many and so great offences, you have doubtless grievously provoked the wrath of the Divine majesty, that you make satisfaction to him by suitable penitence; and that you be not so daring as to carry your rage further, because the omnipotent God has hitherto permitted the nations to be laid prostrate before your face. He sometimes thus passes by the proud men of the age; but if they do not humble themselves, he will not fail to inflict the severest temporal punishment on their guilt. And now, behold, we send our beloved brother John, and his companions, bearers of these presents, men conspicuous for religion and honesty, and endued with a knowledge of sacred Scripture, whom we hope you will kindly receive and honorably treat as if they were ourselves, placing confidence in what they may say from us, and specially treat with them on what relates to peace, and fully intimate what has moved you to this extermination of other nations, and what you further intend, providing them in going and returning with a safe conductor, and other things needful for returning to our presence. We have chosen to send to you the said friars, on account of their exemplary conduct and knowledge of the sacred Scriptures, and because they would be more useful to you as imitating the humility of our Saviour, and if we had thought they would be more grateful and useful to you, we would have sent other prelates or powerful men.[1]

M. D'Avezac's essay contains a full account of the travels and proceedings of Carpini and his companion, Benedict, in their hazardous journey of a hundred days from Kiev, across the plains of Russia and Bokhara, to the court of Kuyuk, who had succeeded Okkodai. They were first sent forward by the commanding officers of the several posts to Batu's camp, where the Pope's letter was translated; from hence they were again despatched at the most rapid rate, on horseback, to Kara-korum, where they arrived July 22, 1246, almost exhausted. After they had been there a few days the election was decided, and all ambassadors were introduced to an audience to the khan, when the Pope's envoys alone were without a present. The letter was read, and an answer returned in a few weeks in the same style. These two potentates, so singularly introduced to each other in their mutual ignorance by the letters carried by John, had much more in common in their pretensions to universal dominion by the command of God than they suspected. The khan's letter was as follows:

---

[1] Murray's *Marco Polo*, p. 49. Yule's *Cathay*, p. cxxiii ff. D'Avezac's essay in the *Recueil de Voyages*, IV., p. 399.

LETTER OF THE KING OF THE TARTARS TO THE LORD POPE.

The strength of God, Kuyuk khan, the ruler of all men, to the great Pope. You and all the Christian people who dwell in the West have sent by your messengers sure and certain letters for the purpose of making peace with us. This we have heard from them, and it is contained in your letter. Therefore, if you desire to have peace with us, you Pope, emperors, all kings, all men powerful in cities, by no means delay to come to us for the purpose of concluding peace, and you will hear our answer and our will. The series of your letters contained that we ought to be baptized and to become Christians; we briefly reply, that we do not understand why we ought to do so. As to what is mentioned in your letters, that you wonder at the slaughter of men, and chiefly of Christians, especially Hungarians, Poles, and Moravians, we shortly answer, that this too we do not understand. Nevertheless, lest we should seem to pass it over in silence, we think proper to reply as follows: It is because they have not obeyed the precept of God and of Genghis khan, and, holding bad counsel, have slain our messengers;[1] wherefore God has ordered them to be destroyed, and delivered them into our hands. But if God had not done it, what could man have done to man? But you, inhabitants of the West, believe that you only are Christians, and despise others; but how do you know on whom he may choose to bestow his favor? We adore God, and, in his strength, will overwhelm the whole earth from the east to the west. But if we men were not strengthened by God, what could we do?[2]

The khan took the precaution, which the Pope did not, of putting his reply into an intelligible language, and when it was written in Tartar he had it carefully explained to the friars, who translated it into Latin, and were soon after dismissed. They left the court on November 13, 1246, and "travelled all winter through a wide open country, being commonly obliged to sleep on the ground after clearing away the snow, with which in the morning they often found themselves covered." They reached Kiev the next June, and Carpini was rewarded for his hardships by being appointed Archbishop of Antivari in Dalmatia. As Yule remarks, "they were the first to bring to western Europe the revived knowledge of a great and civilized nation lying in the extreme East upon the shores of the ocean."

Louis XI. of France having heard that Sartach, the son of Batu, then commanding on the western frontier, was a Chris-

[1] Allusion is here made to Tartar ambassadors, whom the Russians murdered before the battle of Kalka.

[2] Murray's *Marco Polo*, p. 59.

tian, sent a mission to him, consisting of the friar William Rubruquis[1] and three companions. They left Constantinople May 7, 1253, and proceeded to the Crimea, from whence they set out with a present of wines, fruits, and biscuits intended for the khan. In three days they met the Tartars, who conducted them first to Scacatai, a chieftain by whom, after considerable delay and vexation, they were furnished with everything necessary for a journey across the plains of southern Russia to the Wolga and the camp of Sartach. The monks attempted to convert the rude nomads, but ignorance of the language and suspicions of their intentions interposed great obstacles on both sides. On arriving at the end of their journey, they were disappointed at finding the ruler of these warriors a besotted infidel, who expected all persons admitted into his presence to bring him costly presents. A Nestorian named Cojat, whom Rubruquis regarded as no better than a heretic, was high in authority, and the only medium of communication with the khan. He told the friar to bring his books and vestments and make himself ready to appear before the khan on the morrow; their elegance was such that at the close of the audience Cojat seized most of them under an idle pretext that it was improper to appear in them a second time before Batu khan, to whom Rubruquis and his companions were to be sent.

Their journey was soon after prosecuted by following up the Wolga some distance, and when they arrived at the encampment of Batu khan, he made many inquiries about the resources and power of the French king and the war he was waging with the Saracens. On his introduction, "the friar bent one knee, but finding this unsatisfactory did not choose to contend, and dropped on both. Misled by his position, instead of answering questions he began a prayer for the conversion of the khan, with warning of the dreadful consequences of unbelief. The prince merely smiled; but the derision which was loudly expressed by the surrounding chiefs threw him into a good deal of confusion." The interview was followed by an order to proceed to the court

---

[1] Or, more correctly, Rubruk, as D'Avezac has pointed out (*Bull. de la Soc. de Géogr.*, 1868), and in whose conclusions Yule joins (*Marco Polo*, second edition, p. 536).

of Mangu, who had succeeded Kuyuk as Grand khan. This long journey occupied four months, through the high land of Central Asia (farther eastward than where Carpini found Kuyuk's court), and subjected them to severe hardships. Mangu received the mission hardly with civility, but having been examined by some Nestorian priests, they were admitted to an audience. The same ceremonies were required as at Batu's court, and inquiries made as to the possessions of the French king, especially the number of rams, horses, and oxen he owned, which, the friar was amazed to learn, were soon to be attacked by the Tartars. No permission to remain could be obtained, but he was furnished with a house and allowed to tarry till the cold mitigated. In this remote region he found a European architect, William Bourchier, and his wife, from Mentz, besides many Armenians, Saracens, and Nestorians, all of whom the khan received. He accompanied the court to Kara-korum, where he nearly became involved in dangerous religious disputes, and on the approach of milder weather was compelled to return to Batu khan, by whom he was sent on, in a south-westerly direction, until he entered Armenia, and thence found his way to Iconium, having been absent nearly two years.

These ambassadors had not the aid of printing to diffuse their narratives, and it was perhaps chiefly owing to the high standing of those who sent them that their relations have been preserved. In the case of many travellers of humbler origin or pretensions, there was no inducement to write what they had seen; these therefore only told their stories, which were lost with the narrators. Even the travels of Marco Polo would perhaps never have been given to the world if the leisure of captivity had not induced him to adopt this method of relieving its tedium. Every examination of his record has added to its reputation for accuracy, both in the position of the cities he mentions or visited and in the events he details; and when it is considered that he dictated it several years after his return to a fellow-prisoner, Rusticiano of Pisa, who wrote it in French, his accuracy is wonderful. The edition by Marsden in 1818 remained for fifty years the chief authority, but the recent editions by Pauthier and Yule, with their full notes, have made the traveller's record vastly better understood, while adding much to our knowledge of mediæval Asia.

Ser Marco Polo, the Venetian, was the son of Nicolo Polo, who with his brother Matteo, nobles and merchants of Venice, first left that city about 1254, and Constantinople in 1260, on a mercantile voyage to the Crimea, from which point a series of events led them eastward as far as China, then lately conquered by Kublai, the Grand Khan and successor of Mangu khan, whom Rubruquis visited. They were favorably received, and when they left Kublai it was under a promise to return, which they did about December, 1274, bearing letters from Gregory X., and accompanied by young Marco, then about sixteen years old. He soon became a favorite with the Emperor, and was able to travel to many parts of the country, spending in all about twenty-one years in the East; the three Polos reached Venice again in 1295. Marco was prefect at Yangchau on the Grand Canal for three years, and this involves a knowledge of Mongolian and Chinese speech and writing, without which he could hardly have administered its official duties. His possession of these accomplishments was nearly indispensable to the post, though Col. Yule infers, from an easily explained mistake in Chapter LXXV., that he did not have them. On reaching Venice, by way of India and Persia, the long-lost travellers appeared so completely altered that their friends and countrymen did not recognize them. Their wealth and entertaining recitals, however, soon restored them to the highest ranks of society. The industry of recent editors has probably brought together all that can be learned of their subsequent history, which is now so well known as to require no further words here.

In the year 1254, Hethum, or Hayton, king of Little Armenia, undertook a journey to Mangu khan, to petition for an abatement of the tribute which he had been obliged to pay the Mongols. Having first sent forth his brother, Sempad, or Sinibald (in 1246), to Kuyuk khan, Hayton himself set out upon the accession to the throne of his successor. Passing through Kars and Armenia Proper to the Wolga, he was there received by Batu and forwarded by a route to the north of that traversed by Carpini to Kara-korum and the Grand khan. At the end of a six weeks' sojourn with the court, during which time he appears to have been kindly received, Hayton commenced his homeward journey via Bishbalig and Songaria to Samarkand, Bokhara, Khorasan, and thence to Tabriz. The accounts of these two embassies, wherein are described many wonderful things concerning the heathens of the East and barbarians upon the route, made up, doubtless, a large part of the "History" (written in 1307) by the king's relative, Hayton of Gorigos.[1] The different positions held by these men and the Polos naturally led each of them to look upon the same people and events with vastly different feelings. The efforts of John of Montecorvino to propagate Christianity in China were undertaken just as the Polos returned, but no detailed accounts of his labors (beyond what Col. Yule has gathered in his *Cathay*) have been preserved.

Among the most important mediæval travellers in Asia was the Moor, Ibn Batuta, who at the age of twenty-one set out (in 1325) upon his journeys, from which he did not return until thirty years later.[2] Abu-Abdullah Mahomed (nicknamed Ibn Batuta, "The Traveller") commenced his wanderings, which were contemporaneous with those of the more doubtful Englishman, Sir John Mandeville, by a series of pilgrimages to the sacred places of his religion; among other excursions, he found time at one period to continue three years in Mecca. Going from one city to another, along the shores of the Mediterranean, and in the countries between it and the Caspian, he at length reached Delhi, where he resided eight years, enjoying—until the latter end of his stay—high favor from the Sultan Mahomed. The versatile Moor occupied the position of judge, though there is good reason to doubt his serious attention to any business while at this magnificent court, other than that of spending his master's money. In the spring of 1342, having recovered

[1] The chapter concerning Cathay appears in Yule's *Cathay*, p. cxcv. A translation of the elder Hayton's narrative is given by Klaproth in the *Journal Asiatique*, IIe Séries, Tome XII., pp. 273 ff.

[2] His work has been very ably edited and translated into French by M. Defrémery and Dr. Sanguinetti (four volumes, Paris, 1858–59), under the patronage of the Asiatic Society of Paris. Several partial translations of the journal have appeared from time to time within the present century.

from a temporary disgrace, he was despatched on an ambassy to China by the Sultan. It seems that a Chinese envoy had arrived at Delhi to request permission for the natives to rebuild a temple in Butan, as they were poor and dependent upon the inhabitants of the plain, and had besought the Chinese government to intercede for them. Ibn Batuta was sent with lavish presents to the Emperor, but a refusal to assist in the building project unless that sovereign would go through the form of paying a poll-tax to the Sultan. This embassy was attacked by a body of Hindus when scarcely out of Delhi, and obliged to return. Again it was sent out, going to Calicut on the Malabar coast, where were found fifteen Chinese vessels or galleys at anchor, whose crews and guard amounted to a thousand men each. The envoy embarked his attendants on one of these ships, but while he remained on shore to pray for a prosperous voyage, a storm sunk the vessel and all on board. After this second mishap the luckless Moor was afraid to return to his master, and went to Sumatra, from whence he found his way to China, landing at Zayton, the present Chinchew, in Fuhkien.

Though it is doubtful if Ibn Batuta, notwithstanding his description of the place, ever reached Peking, his spirited accounts of Zayton, Sinkalan (Canton), Khansa (Hangchau), Kanjanfu, and other centres of trade in the south, are both entertaining and important. Spite of exaggerations, confusion of names and dates, and certain cases of positive fiction, one can hardly fail to put faith in the generality of his statements and conclude in favor of his veracity and genuine character. He mentions that the circulation of paper money, which Marco Polo thought so excellent a device for a king to raise funds, had entirely driven out the use of metallic currency. In every large town he found Mohammedans, ruled by officers of their own persuasion.

The journal of Friar Odoric (1286–1331) contains much of interest in connection with China of the middle ages. This worthy priest landed at "Censcalan" (Canton), after a long and tedious trip from Bagdad round by Sumatra and thence northeast by land to Zayton. Here, says he, "we friars minor have two houses, and there I deposited the bones of our friars who suffered martyrdom for the faith of Jesus Christ." He had brought these relics from Tana, near Bombay. Thence he journeyed to Fuhchau, Hangchau, and Nanking, going on northward to Peking, where the aged archbishop, Corvino, was still living, and remained there three years. His return journey as far as H'lassa was not very different from that of Huc and Gabet in 1843; from the Tibetan capital he probably continued on a westerly course to Cabul and Tabriz, reaching Venice in 1330, after an absence of thirteen years. His itinerary was taken down the following year by William of Solagna, a brother of the order, at Padua.

In this narrative there is mention of a number of characteristics of the Chinese, well known to all the world of to-day, but left wholly unnoticed by other travellers of his age. "His notices of the custom of fishing with cormorants, of the habits of letting the finger-nails grow long, and of compressing the women's feet, as well as of the divisions of the khan's Empire into twelve provinces, with four chief vizirs, are peculiar to him, I believe, among all the European travellers of the age. Polo mentions none of them. The names which he assigns to the Chinese post-stations, and to the provincial Boards of Administration, the technical Turki term which he uses for a sack of rice, etc., are all tokens of the reality of his experience."[1] On the other hand, the influence of superstition upon their own minds rendered most of the religious travellers into Central Asia—Odoric as well as the others—less trustworthy and observant than they would perhaps have been either centuries before or after that period. Everything of a religious sort they regarded as done under the direct agency of the powers of darkness, into whose dominions they were venturing. Too fearful, moreover, to examine candidly or record accurately what they beheld, these pious adventurers were constantly misled by endeavors to explain any uncommon experience by referring the same to their own imperfect or erroneous conceptions. This is true as well of the Romish priests connected with the Peking mission, a few of whose letters have been preserved and re-

---

[1] Yule, *Cathay and the Way Thither*, p. 21.

cently made known to the public by Col. Yule; among these are Friar Jordanus, Bishop Andrew of Zayton, Pascal of Vittoria, together with the Archbishop of Soltania, author of the "Book of the Estate and Governance of the Great Caan of Cathay."[1]

But much fairer than these missionaries, in his reputation for veracity, was the Jesuit Benedict Goës, who in the century preceding what may be termed the modern period of our knowledge of China, undertook a journey across the desert, to die on the threshold of the Empire. Born in one of the islands of the Azore group, Goës spent his youth in the profession of a soldier on board of the Portuguese fleet. Becoming suddenly converted, he entered the service of the Jesuits as a lay brother—which humble rank he resolutely held during the rest of his career—and was sent to the court of Akbar. His residence in India gained him a high reputation for courage, judgment, and skill in the Persian tongue, the *lingua franca* of Asia at that date. He was selected, therefore, to undertake a journey to the Cathay of Marco Polo, in the capital of which Jerome Xavier thought he had hopes of finding the Christian ruler and descendant of Prester John. Goës set out from Agra in 1602, joined a company of merchants, and with them took a route passing through Cabul, the Hindu kush, along the River Oxus to its head-waters on the Pamir table-land, and so to Yangi Hissar, Yarkand, Aksu, and Suh-chau, where he was detained seventeen months, and finally died, shortly after assistance had been sent him from the mission at Peking.

His journey was full of terrible hardships, and it was to these as well as to the careless treatment he suffered in Suh-chau that he owed his untimely end. Could we have Goës' own narrative of his experience, the information concerning the unknown regions of Central Asia over which he toiled would be of priceless worth. His journals, however, were either lost or destroyed during his miserable detention at the frontier town, and nothing remained save a few meagre notes

---

[1] About 1330. See ibid., pp. 238–250.

and his faithful Armenian servant Isaac, whose language no one at Peking could understand. Such as it was, an account was compiled from these sources by Ricci himself, and published soon after that missionary's death in the work of Trigautius, *De Christiana Expeditione apud Sinas.*[1] To Benedict Goës we may give the credit of the discovery that *Cathay* and *China* (*Sina*) were in reality one and the same land. It is a curious illustration of the condition of intercommunication between distant parts of the world in those days, that this fact must have been known to the earliest Jesuit missionaries in Peking, though the friars of the same order stationed in India held to a belief in Cambaluc and its Christian prince until far into the seventeenth century.

In many particulars the practical descriptions of Abu Zaid, Masudi,[2] Ibn Wahab, and Marco Polo stand in decided contrast to the details noted down by such as Rubruquis and Odoric. The accounts of all these writers convey the impression that China was in their time free to all travellers. Ibn Wahab, speaking of the regulations practised under the Tang dynasty, observes:

> If a man would travel from one province to another, he must take two passes with him, one from the governor, the other from the eunuch [or lieutenant]. The governor's pass permits him to set out on his journey and contains the names of the traveller and those also of his company, also the ages of the one and the other and the clan to which he belongs. For every traveller in China, whether a native or an Arab, or other foreigner, cannot avoid carrying a paper with him containing everything by which he can be verified. The eunuch's pass specifies the quantities of money or goods which the traveller and those with him take along; this is done for the information of officers at the frontier places where these two passes are examined. Whenever a traveller arrives at any of them, it is registered that "Such a one, son of such a one, of such a calling, passed here on such a day, month, and year, having

---

[1] A translation of this notice appears in Col. Yule's oft-quoted *Cathay and the Way Thither*, pp. 529–591. Trigautius' work appeared in 1615, and was subsequently translated into all the continental languages. Compare Purchas, *His Pilgrimes*, Vol. III., pp. 380, ff.—*A Discourse of the Kingdome of China, taken out of Riccivs and Trigavtivs, contayning the Countrey, People, Gouernment*, etc., etc.

[2] Reinaud, *Relation des Voyages*, etc. MM. Barbier de Meynard and Pavet de Courteille, *Les Praries d'Or*, Paris, 1861–66.

such things with him." The government resorts to this means to prevent danger to travellers in their money or goods; for should one suffer loss or die, everything about him is immediately known and he himself or his heirs after his death receive whatever is his.[1]

The same writer speaks of the Mabed, a nation dwelling in Yunnan, on the south-west, who sent ambassadors every year with presents to the Emperor; and in return he sent presents annually to them. These embassies, indeed, were simply trading companies in disguise, who came from the Persians, Arabs, and other nations, with every protestation of respect and humility, bearing presents to the Son of Heaven. The dignity of the Emperor demanded that these should be returned with gifts three or four times the value of this "tribute," and that the ambassadors should be royally entertained during their sojourn at the capital. It is needless to add that such missions were repeated by the merchants as often as circumstances would permit. Entrance into the country overland otherwise than by some such ruse seems to have been withheld after the fall of the Mongol dynasty.

It was, however, not until the subjugation of the Empire by the Manchus that foreign trade was limited to Canton, the jealous conduct of the present rulers being to a certain extent actuated by a fear of similar reprisals from some quarter, which the Mongols experienced. The outrageous behavior of foreign traders themselves must, moreover, be regarded as a chief cause of the watchful seclusion with which they were treated. "Their early conduct," says Sir John Davis, referring to the Portuguese, "was not calculated to impress the Chinese with any favorable idea of Europeans; and when in course of time they came to be competitors with the Dutch and the English, the contests of mercantile avarice tended to place them all in a still worse point of view. To this day the character of the Europeans is represented as that of a race of men intent alone on the gains of commercial traffic, and regardless altogether of the means of attainment. Struck by the perpetual hostilities which existed among these foreign adventurers, as-

[1] Reinaud, *Relation*, Tome I., p. 41.

similated in other respects by a close resemblance in their costumes and manners, the government of the country became disposed to treat them with a degree of jealousy and exclusion which it had not deemed necessary to be exercised toward the more peaceable and well ordered Arabs, their predecessors."[1]

These characteristics of avarice, lawlessness, and power have been the leading traits in the Chinese estimate of foreigners from their first acquaintance with them, and the latter have done little to effectually disabuse orientals upon these points. The following record of their first arrival, taken from a Chinese work, is still good authority in the general opinion of the natives:

> During the reign of Chingtih [1506], foreigners from the West, called Fah-lan-kí [Franks], who said that they had tribute, abruptly entered the Bogue, and by their tremendously loud guns, shook the place far and near. This was reported at court, and an order returned to drive them away immediately and stop their trade. At about this time also the Hollanders, who in ancient times inhabited a wild territory and had no intercourse with China, came to Macao in two or three large ships. Their clothes and their hair were red; their bodies tall; they had blue eyes, sunk deep in their heads. Their feet were one cubit and two-tenths long; and they frightened the people by their strange appearance.[2]

The Portuguese Rafael Perestrello sailed in a junk for China in 1516, five years after the conquest of Malacca, and was the first person who ever conducted a vessel to China under a European flag. Ferdinand Andrade came in the next year, in four Portuguese and four Malay ships, and gave great satisfaction to the authorities at Canton by his fair dealings; his galleons were allowed to anchor at Shangchuen, or St. John's Island. His brother Simon came the following year, and by his atrocious conduct entirely reversed the good opinion formed of his countrymen; the Chinese besieged him in port and drove him away in 1521. Others of his countrymen followed him, and one of the earliest ships accompanied some Chinese junks along the coast, and succeeded in establishing a factory

[1] *The Chinese*, Vol. I., p. 20.

[2] The term *Hung-mao*, or 'red-haired,' then applied to the Dutch, has since been transferred to the English.

at Ningpo; trade was also conducted at Amoy. In 1537 there were three Portuguese settlements near Canton, one at St. John's, one at a smaller island called Lampaçao (Lang-peh-kau), lying north-west of the Grand Ladrones, and the third just begun on Macao.[1] In 1542 traders had left St. John's for Lampaçao, and ten years afterward, at the time of Xavier's death, trade was concentrated at the latter, where five or six hundred Portuguese constantly resided in 1560. Macao was commenced under the pretext of erecting sheds for drying goods introduced under the appellation of tribute, and alleged to have been damaged in a storm. In 1573 the Chinese government erected a barrier wall across the isthmus joining Macao to the island of Hiangshan, and in 1587 established a civil magistracy to rule the Chinese. By their ill conduct at Ningpo the Portuguese drew upon them the vengeance of the people, who rose upon them and "destroyed twelve thousand Christians, including eight hundred Portuguese, and burned thirty-five ships and two junks." One of their provocative acts is stated to have been going out in large parties into the neighboring villages and seizing the women and virgins, by which they justly lost their privileges in one of the provinces and ports best adapted to European trade. Four years later, in 1549, they were also driven from their newly formed settlement at Chinchew.

The Portuguese have sent four embassies to the Emperor of China. The first envoy, Thomé Pires, was appointed by the Governor at Goa, and accompanied Ferdinand Andrade to Canton, in 1517, where he was received and treated in the usual style of foreign ambassadors. When his mission was reported at Peking the Emperor Chingtih was influenced against it by a subject of the Sultan of Malacca, and detained Pires at Canton three years; the flagitious conduct of Andrade's brother

[1] There stood originally on the site of this town an idol known as *Ama. Amau-gau*, or *Ama-kau*, then, meant the 'Harbor of Ama,' which in Portuguese was written *Amacao*, and afterward shortened to *Macao*. Comp. Trigautius, *De Christiana Expeditione apud Sinas*, 1615. Nieuwhof, *Nauwkeurige Beschryvinge van't Gesandschap*, etc., Amsterdam, 1664. Sir A. Ljungstedt, *Historical Sketch of the Portuguese Settlements in China*, Boston, 1836. *Chinese Commercial Guide*, fifth edition, p. 229.

and the character of the Portuguese induced the Emperor to appoint a court to examine whether the embassy was legitimate or spurious, and Pires and his companions were adjudged to be spies and sent back to Canton to be detained till Malacca was restored. This not being done, he and others suffered death in September, 1523; other accounts lead to the inference that he died in prison. Thus the innocent were made to suffer for the guilty. The next embassy was undertaken in 1552, at the suggestion of Xavier, by the Viceroy of Goa, but the mission proceeded no farther than Malacca, the governor of that town refusing to allow it to leave the place—a significant intimation of the degree of subordination and order maintained by the Portuguese in the administration of their new colonies. The third was also sent from Goa in 1667, in the name of Alfonso VI., on occasion of the suspension of the trade of Macao by Kanghí; the expense was defrayed by that colony (about forty thousand dollars), and "the result of it so little answered their expectations that the Senate solicited his Majesty not to intercede in behalf of his vassals at Macao with the government of China, were it not in an imperious and cogent case."

A good opportunity and necessity for this, it was thought, presented itself in 1723, when Magaillans returned to China carrying the answer of the Pope to Kanghí, to send an envoy, Alexander Metello, along with him to Peking. He arrived at court in May, 1727, and had his audience of leave in July, receiving in exchange for the thirty chests of presents which he offered, and which Yungching received with pleasure "as evidences of the affection of the King of Portugal," as many for his master, besides a cup of wine and some porcelain dishes, sent from the Emperor's table, and other presents for himself and his retinue, which were "valuable solely because they were the gifts of a monarch." No more advantage resulted from this than the embassy sent a century previous, though it cost the inhabitants of Macao a like heavy sum. Another and last Portuguese embassy reached Peking in 1753, conducted and ending in much the same manner as its predecessors; all of them exhibiting, in a greater or less degree, the spectacle of humiliating submission of independent nations through their envoys to a court which took pleasure in arrogantly exalting itself on the homage it received, and studiously avoided all reference to the real business of the embassy, that it might neither give nor deny anything. But in estimating its conduct in these respects, it must not be overlooked that the imperial court never associated commercial equality and regulations with embassies and tribute.

The influence and wealth of the Portuguese in China for the last century and a half have gradual decreased. A Swedish knight, Sir Andrew Ljungstedt, published a historical sketch of their doings down to 1833, including an account of the colony, which is still the fullest book on the subject. In 1820 the opium trade was removed to Lintin, and that being the principal source of income, the commerce of the place for many years was at a low ebb. The imperial commissioner Kiying granted some additional privileges to the settlement in 1844, among others, permitting the inhabitants to build and repair new houses, churches, and ships without a license, and to trade at the five ports open to foreign commerce on the same terms as other nations; it was just three centuries before this that the Portuguese were driven away from Ningpo. The anchorage of the Typa was included in the jurisdiction of Macao, but the application of the Portuguese commissioner to surcease payment of the annual ground-rent of five hundred taels to the Chinese met with a decided refusal. Its advantages as a summer resort and its accessibility to a densely peopled region west invite visitors and traders to some extent, but the proximity and wealth of Hongkong make it secondary to that. Its short-lived prosperity in 1839–50, during the opium war and early days of Hongkong, was followed by the enlargement of the coolie trade, which for twenty-five years was the only real business. The Chinese have never ceded the peninsula to the Portuguese crown, although they were powerless to prevent the export of coolies; the relations now between the two countries are not distinctly defined. In 1862 a treaty was negotiated at Peking by Governor Guimaraēs, in which the supremacy of the Portuguese authority over the territory within the Barrier was implied rather than declared in Article IX., wherein the equal appointment of consular officers was mutually agreed to. The Chinese found out, however, that this virtually acknowledged the independence of the colony, and refused to ratify the treaty without an express stipulation asserting their right of domain to the peninsula. It has never been ratified, therefore, but trade is unfettered, and the Chinese inhabitants continue to increase; no rental has been paid for the ground-tax since 1849. The cessation of the coolie trade in 1873 has reduced Macao lower than ever, and it now hardly pays its own officials; all the thrifty or wealthy foreign citizens have removed elsewhere.

The trade between the Spaniards and Chinese has been smaller, and their relations less important than most other European nations. The Spanish admiral Legaspi conquered the Philippines in 1543, and Chinese merchants soon began to trade with Manila; but the first attempt of the Spaniards to enter China was not made until 1575, when two Augustine friars accompanied a Chinese naval officer on his return home from the pursuit of a famous pirate named Li-ma-hon, whom the Spaniards had driven away from their new colony. The missionaries landed at Tansuso, a place on the coast of Kwangtung, and went up to Canton, where they were courteously received. The prefect sent them to the governor at Shauking, by whom they were examined; they stated that their chief object was to form a close alliance between the two nations for their mutual benefit, adding at the same time what their countrymen had done against Li-ma-hon; a second object was their wish to learn the language of China and teach its inhabitants their religion. The governor kept them in a sort of honorable bondage several weeks, and at last sent them back to Manila, doubtless by orders from court, though he alleged as a reason that the pirate Li-ma-hon was still at large. After the return of this mission the governor of the Philippines deemed it advisable to let the trade take its own course, and therefore refused the proposal of a body of Franciscans to enter the country. They, however, made the attempt in a small native vessel, and passed up the river to Tsiuenchau, where they were seized and examined as to their designs. Not being acquainted with the language, they were both themselves deluded and misrepresented to the prefect by a professed native friend who understood Portuguese; after many months' delay they were mortified to learn that no permission to remain would be given, and in 1580 they returned to Manila, not at all disposed to renew the enterprise.

Philip II., however, having received the suggestion made by the Chinese admiral that he should send an embassy to Peking, had already ordered the governor to undertake such an enterprise. He fitted out a mission, therefore, in 1580, at the head of which was Martin Ignatius. It gives one a low idea of the skill of navigators at that day to learn that in this short trip, the vessel being carried up the coast northward of Canton, the party thought it better to land than to try to beat back to their destination. The envoy and all with him were brought before the Chinese officers, who, probably entirely misunderstanding their object, imprisoned them; after considerable delay they were brought before a higher officer and sent on to Canton, where they were again imprisoned; the Portuguese governor of Macao subsequently obtained their liberation. This unlucky attempt, if Mendoza is right in calling it an embassy, was the only one ever made by the Spanish government to communicate with the court of Peking until the mission of Don Sinibaldo de Mas in 1847 and his treaty of 1864. The pecular feature of that treaty was the privilege, first granted to Spanish merchants, of engaging coolies as contract laborers for Cuba. The harsh treatment they received there led the Chinese to send a commission of inquiry in 1873, and to suspend the validity of this article until the truth could be ascertained. This procedure has resulted in a cessation of imported Chinese laborers at Havana.

The Chinese have carried on a valuable trade at Manila, but the Spaniards have treated them with peculiar severity. They are burdened with special taxes, and their immigration is rather restrained than encouraged. The harsh treatment of Chinese settlers there excited the attention and indignation of one of their countrymen many years ago, and on his return to Canton he exercised all his influence with officers of his own government, making what he had seen the model and the motive to induce them to treat all foreigners at Canton in the same way. It ended in perfecting the principal features of the system of espionage and restriction of the co-hong which existed for nearly a century, until the treaty of 1842;—another instance of the treatment requited upon foreigners for their own acts.

The Dutch commerce with the East commenced after their successful struggle against the Spanish yoke, and soon after completing their independence they turned their arms against the oriental possessions of their enemies, capturing Malacca, the Spice Islands, and other places. They appeared before Macao in 1622 with a squadron of seventeen vessels, but being repulsed with the loss of their admiral and about three hundred men, they retired and established themselves on the Pescadores in 1624. Their occupation of this position was a source of great annoyance both to the Spaniards and to the Chinese authorities in Fuhkien. According to the custom of those days, they began to build a fort, and forced the native Chinese to do their work, treating them with great severity. Many of the laborers were prisoners, whom the Dutch had taken in their attacks. Alternate hostilities and parleys succeeded, the Chinese declaring that the Dutch must send an envoy to the authorities on the mainland; they accordingly despatched Von Mildert to Amoy, and the sub-prefect forwarded him to Fuhchau to the governor. He decided to send a messenger to the Dutch to state to them that trade would be allowed if they would remove to Formosa, but this proposition was refused. However, after a series of attacks and negotiations, the Chinese constantly increasing their forces and the Dutch diminishing in their supplies, the latter acceded to the proposition, and removed to Formosa, where they erected Fort Zealandia in 1624. It is recorded that the Chinese landed five thousand troops on one of the Pescadore Islands; and their determined efforts in repelling the aggressions or occupation of their soil by the Dutch probably raised their reputation for courage, and prevented the repetition of similar acts by others. It was doubtless a good stroke of policy on their part to propose the occupation of Formosa to the Dutch in exchange for the Pescadores, for they had not the least title to it themselves, and hardly knew its exact size or the character of the inhabitants. The Dutch endeavored to extend their power over it, but with only partial success; in the villages around Fort Zealandia they introduced new laws among the inhabitants, and instead of their councils of elders, constituted one of their chief men supervisor in every village, to administer justice and report his acts to the governor of the island.

The moral interests of the natives were not neglected, and in 1626 George Candidius, a Protestant minister, was appointed to labor among them, and took great pains to introduce Christianity. The natives were ignorant of letters, their superstitions resting only on traditions or customs which were of recent origin; the prospects, therefore, of teaching them a better religion were favorable. In sixteen months he had instructed over a hundred in the leading truths of Christianity. The work was progressing favorably, churches and schools were multiplying, the intermarriages of the colonists and natives were bringing them into closer relationship with each other, and many thousands of the islanders had been baptized, when the Dutch governors in India, fearful of offending the Japanese, who were then persecuting the Christians in Japan—in which the Dutch helped them, to their lasting disgrace—restricted these benevolent labors, and discouraged the further conversion of the islanders. Thus, as often elsewhere in Asia, the interests of true religion were sacrificed upon the altar of mammon, and the trade thus bought died from inanition.

During the struggles ensuent upon the overthrow of the Ming dynasty, many thousands of families emigrated to Formosa, some of whom settled under the Dutch, while others planted separate colonies; their industry soon changed the desolate island into a cultivated country, and increased the produce of rice and sugar for exportation. The immigration went on so rapidly as to alarm the Dutch, who, instead of taking wise measures to conciliate and instruct the colonists, tried to prevent their landing, and thereby did much to irritate them and lead them to join in any likely attempt to expel the foreigners.

Meanwhile, their trade with China itself was trifling compared with that of their rivals, the Portuguese, and when the undoubted ascendancy of the Manchus was evident, the government of Batavia resolved to despatch a deputation to Canton to petition for trade. In January, 1653, Schedel was sent in a richly freighted ship, but the Portuguese succeeded in preventing any further traffic, even after the envoy had spent considerable sums in presents to the authorities, and obtained the governor's promise to allow his countrymen to build a factory. Schedel was informed, however, that his masters would do well to send an embassy to Peking, a suggestion favorably entertained by the Company, which, in 1655, appointed Goyer and Keyzer as its envoys. The narrative of this embassy by Nieuwhof, the steward of the mission, made Europeans better acquainted with the country than they had before been—almost the only practical benefit it produced, for as a mercantile speculation it proved nearly a total loss. Their presents were received and others given in return; they prostrated themselves not only before the Emperor in person, but made the *kotow* to his name, his letters, and his throne, doing everything in the way of humiliation and homage likely to please the new rulers. The only privilege their subserviency obtained was permission to send an embassy once in eight years, at which time they might come in four ships to trade.

This mission left China in 1657, and very soon after, the Chinese chieftain, Ching Ching-kung (Koshinga, or Koxinga as his name is written by the Portuguese), began to prepare an attack upon Formosa. The Dutch had foreseen the probability of this onset, and had been strengthening the garrison of Zealandia since 1650 while they were negotiating for trade; Koxinga, too, had confined himself to sending emissaries among his countrymen in Formosa, to inform them of his designs. He set about preparing an armament at Amoy, ostensibly to strengthen himself against the Manchus, meanwhile carrying on his ordinary traffic with the colony to lull all apprehensions until the council had sent away the admiral and force despatched from Java to protect them, when in June, 1661, he landed a force of twenty-five thousand troops, and took up a strong position. The communication between the forts being cut off, the governor sent two hundred and forty men to dislodge the enemy, only half of whom returned alive; one of the four ships in the harbor was burned by the Chinese, and another hastened to Batavia for reinforcements. Koxinga followed up these successes by cutting off all communication between the garrison and the surrounding country, and compelling the surrender of the garrison and cannon in the small fort. Fort Zealandia was now closely invested, but finding himself severely galled, he turned the siege into a blockade, and vented his rage against the Dutch living in the surrounding country, and such Chinese as abetted them. Some of the ministers and schoolmasters were seized and crucified, under the pretext that they encouraged their parishioners to resist; others were used as agents to treat concerning the surrender of the fort. Valentyn has given a clear history of the occupation of Formosa by his countrymen in his great work, and especially of their defeat at Zealandia. He narrates an incident of Rev. A. Hambroek, as does also Nieuwhof, from whose travels it is quoted.

Among the Dutch prisoners taken in the country, was one Mr. Hambroek, a minister. This man was sent by Koxinga to the governor, to propose terms for surrendering the fort; and that in case of refusal, vengeance would be taken on the Dutch prisoners. Mr. Hambroek came into the castle, being forced to leave his wife and children behind him as hostages, which sufficiently proved that if he failed in his negotiation, they had nothing but death to expect from the chieftain. Yet was he so far from persuading the garrison to surrender, that he encouraged them to a brave defence by hopes of relief, assuring them that Koxinga had lost many of his best ships and soldiers, and began to be weary of the siege. When he had ended, the council of war left it to his choice to stay with them or return to the camp, where he could expect nothing but present death; every one entreated him to stay. He had two daughters within the castle, who hung upon his neck, overwhelmed with grief and tears to see their father ready to go where they knew he must be sacrificed by the merciless enemy. But he represented to them that having left his wife and two other children as hostages, nothing but death could attend them if he returned not: so unlocking himself from his daughters' arms, and exhorting everybody to a resolute defence, he returned to the camp, telling them at parting that he hoped he might prove serviceable to his poor fellow-prisoners. Koxinga received his answer sternly; then causing it to be rumored that the prisoners excited the Formosans to rebel, he ordered all the Dutch male prisoners to be slain; some being beheaded, others killed in a more barbarous manner, to the number of five hundred, their bodies stripped quite naked and buried; nor were the women and children spared, many of them likewise being slain, though some of the best were preserved for the use of the commanders, and the rest sold to the common soldiers. Among the slain were Messrs. Hambroek, Mus, Winsam, Ampzingius, and Campius, clergymen, and many schoolmasters.

A force of ten ships and seven hundred men arriving from Batavia, the besieged began to act on the offensive, but were unable to drive Koxinga from the town, though they checked his operations and brought down the garrisons from Kilung and Tamsui to their aid. A letter from the governor of Fuhkien to Coyet, the Dutch governor, came soon after, suggesting a junction of their forces to drive Koxinga away from the coast, after which both could easily conquer him in Formosa. This proposal was followed, but no sooner had the five vessels gone than Koxinga made his advances so vigorously that the garrison was forced to surrender, after a siege of nine months and the loss of one thousand six hundred men. Thus ended the Dutch rule in Formosa, after twenty-eight years' duration.[1]

This loss induced the council at Batavia to prosecute their former enterprise against Amoy, where Koxinga still had a garrison. Twelve vessels were fitted out under Bort, who arrived, in 1662, at the mouth of the River Min, where he was visited by deputies from the governor, and induced to send two of his officers to arrange with him concerning operations. The governor was in the country, and the two officers, on reaching his camp, soon saw that there could be no cordiality between their leaders; this proposal of a foreign power to assist them against the Chinese was too much like that of Wu San-kwei to their chieftains in 1644 for the Manchus to entertain it. Bort, desirous of doing something, commenced a series of attacks on the fleet and garrisons of Koxinga, burning and destroying them

---

[1] *Chinese Repository*, Vols. I., p. 414, and XX., p. 543. *Journal N. C. Br. R. As. Soc.*, Vol. XI. (1876), Art. I. Moreau de St.-Mêry, *Voyage de l'Ambassade de la Compagnie des Indes orientales Hollandaises vers l'Empereur de la Chine, tiré du journal d'André Everard van Braam Houckgeest*, translated and published in London, 2 Vols., 1798. J. Nieuwhof, *Nauwkeurige Beschryvinge van't Gesandschap der Nederlandtsche Oost-Indische Compagnie van Batavia nar Peking in Sina, door de Heeren Pieter de Goyer en Jacob de Keyser*, Amsterdam, 1664.

in a piratical manner, that was not less ineffectual toward regaining Formosa and obtaining privilege of trade at Canton than harassing to the Chinese on the coast. He returned to Batavia in 1663, and was despatched to Fuhkien in a few months with a stronger force, and ordered to make reprisals on both Manchus and Chinese, if necessary, in order to get satisfaction for the loss of Formosa. The governor received him favorably, and after a number of skirmishes against the rebellious Chinese, Amoy was taken and its troops destroyed, which completed the subjugation of the province to the Manchus. As a reward for this assistance, the real value of which cannot, however, be easily ascertained, the governor lent *two junks* to the Dutch to retake Formosa, but Koxinga laughed at the pitiful force sent against him, and Bort sailed for Batavia.

These results so chagrined the council that they fitted out no more expeditions, preferring to despatch an embassy, under Van Hoorn, to Peking, to petition for trade and permission to erect factories. He landed at Fuhchau in 1664, where he was received in a polite manner. The imperial sanction had been already received, but he unwisely delayed his journey to the capital until his cargo was sold. While discussing this matter the Dutch seized a Chinese vessel bringing bullion from Java contrary to their colonial regulations, and the governor very properly intimated that until restitution was made no amicable arrangement could be completed; consequently Van Hoorn, in order to save his dignity and not contravene the orders of his own government, was obliged to allow the bullion to be carried off, as if by force, by a police officer.

These preliminary disputes were not settled till nearly a year had elapsed, when Van Hoorn and his suite left Fuhchau, and after a tedious journey up the River Min and across the mountains to Hangchau, they reached the canal and Peking, having been six months on the way, "during which they saw thirty-seven cities and three hundred and thirty-five villages." The same succession of prostrations before an empty throne, followed by state banquets, and accompanied by the presentation and conferring of presents, characterized the reception of this embassy as it had all its predecessors. It ended with a similar farce, alike pleasing to the haughty court which received it, and unworthy the Christian nation which gave it; and the "only result of this grand expedition was a sealed letter, of the contents of which they were wholly ignorant, but which did not, in fact, grant any of the privileges they so anxiously solicited." They had, by their performance of the act of prostration, caused their nation to be enrolled among the tributaries of the Grand khan, and then were dismissed as loyal subjects should be, at the will of their liege lord, with what he chose to give them. It was a fitting end to a career begun in rapine and aggression toward the Chinese, who had never provoked them.

The Dutch sent no more embassies to Peking for one hundred and thirty years, but carried on trade at Canton on the same footing as other nations. The ill success of Macartney's embassy in 1793 induced Van Braam, the consular agent at Canton, to propose a mission of salutation and respect from the government of Batavia, on the occasion of Kienlung reaching the sixtieth year of his reign. He hoped, by conforming to Chinese ceremonies, to obtain some privileges which would place Dutch trade on a better footing, but one would have supposed that the miscarriage of former attempts might have convinced him that nothing was to be gained by new humiliations before a court which had just dismissed a well-appointed embassy. The Company appointed Isaac Titsingh, late from Japan, as chief commissioner, giving Van Braam the second place, and making up their cortege with a number of clerks and interpreters, one of whom, De Guignes, wrote the results of his researches during a long residence in Canton, and his travels with the embassy to Peking, under the title of *Voyages à Peking*. It is needless to detail the annoyances, humiliations, and contemptuous treatment experienced by the embassy on its overland journey in midwinter, and the degrading manner in which the Emperor received the envoys: his hauteur was a befitting foil to their servility, at once exhibiting both his pride and their ignorance of their true position and rights. They were brought to the capital like malefactors, treated when there like beggars, and then sent back to Canton like mountebanks to perform the three-times-three prostration at all times and before everything their conductors saw fit; who on their part stood by and laughed at their embarrassment in making these evolutions in their tight clothes. They were not allowed a single opportunity to speak about business, which the Chinese never associate with an embassy, but were entertained with banquets and theatrical shows, and performed many skilful evolutions themselves upon their skates, greatly to the Emperor's gratification, and received, moreover, a present of broken victuals from him, which had not only been honored by coming from his Majesty's own table, but bore marks of his teeth and good appetite; "they were upon a dirty plate, and appeared rather destined to feed a dog than form the repast of a human creature." Van Braam's account of this embassy is one of the most humiliating records of ill-requited obsequiousness before insolent government lackeys which any European was ever called upon to pen. The mission returned to Canton in April, 1796, having attained no more noble end than that of saluting the Emperor, and this, indeed, was all the Chinese meant should be done when themselves suggesting the entire performance; for in order to understand much of their conduct toward their guests, the feelings they entertained toward them must not be lost sight of.

In 1843 the governor-general at Batavia sent T. Modderman to Canton to make inquiries respecting trade at the newly opened ports and establish consulates. The council there had, in 1839, forbidden Chinese to settle in any of their Indian colonies, owing to their skill in engrossing the native trade; but when this prohibition was removed about 1875, the Chinese showed no disposition to emigrate to Java. In 1863 a treaty was negotiated by M. Van der Hoeven at Tientsin, which placed the trade on the same footing as other nations.

The French Government has never sent a formal mission to the capital to petition for trade and make obeisance, though through their missionaries that nation has made Europeans better acquainted with China and given the Chinese more knowledge of western countries than all other Christian nations together. In the year 1289 Philip the Fair received a letter from Argun khan in Persia, and in 1305 another from Oljaitu, both of them proposing joint action against their enemies the Saracens. The originals are still to be seen in Paris. In 1688 Louis XIV. addressed a letter to Kanghí, whom he called "Most high, most excellent, most puissant, and most magnanimous prince, dearly beloved good friend;" and signed himself "Your most dear and good friend, Louis." In 1844 diplomatic relations were resumed by the appointment of a large mission, at the head of which was M. Lagrené, by whom a treaty was formed between France and China.[1]

The Russians have sent several embassies to Peking, and compelled the Chinese to treat them as equals. The first recorded visit of Russian agents at Peking is that of two Cossacks, Petroff and Yallysheff, in 1567, who, however, did not see the Emperor Lungking, who succeeded to the throne that year, because they had brought no presents. In 1619 Evashko Pettlin reached that city, having come across the desert from Tomsk; but he and his companion, having no presents, could not see the "dragon's face," and were dismissed with a letter, which all the learning at Tobolsk and Moscow could not decipher. Thirty-four years after, the Czar Alexis (1653) sent his envoy Baikoff, who refused to prostrate himself before the Emperor Shunchí, and was promptly dismissed. This repulse did not interfere with trade, for in the years 1658, 1672, and 1677 three several trading embassies reached Peking. During all this time Russian and Chinese subjects and soldiers frequently quarrelled, especially along the banks of the Amur, and the necessity of settling these disturbances and pretexts for trouble by fixing the boundary line being evident to both nations, commissioners were appointed and met at Nipchu, where, on August 27, 1689, they signed the first treaty ever agreed upon by the court of Peking. The principal points in it were the retirement of the Russians from Albazin and Manchuria, where they had held their own for thirty-eight years, the freedom of trade, and defining the frontier along the Daourian Mountains. The missionary Gerbillon was mainly instrumental

[1] *Chinese Repository*, Vol. XIX., pp. 526–535. Yule's *Cathay*, p. cxxx. Rémusat in *Mém. de l'Acad. Ins.*, Vol. VII., pp. 367, 391 ff.

in settling these disputes, and neither party would probably have lowered its arrogant claims if it had not been through his influence; the Chinese were far the most difficult to please.[1]

Peter sent Ysbrandt Ides in 1692 as his envoy to Peking to exchange the ratifications. His journey across the wilds and wastes of Central Asia took up more time than a voyage by sea, for it was not till a year and eight months that "he could return thanks to the great God, who had conducted them all safe and well to their desired place." Ides' own account of his mission contains very slight notices regarding its object or how he was received; but it is now credibly believed that he performed the *kotow* before the Emperor. About twenty years after his departure, Kanghí sent a Manchu envoy, Tulishen, through Russia to confer with the khan of the Tourgouth Tartars about their return to China, which a portion of them accomplished some years after. Tulishen executed his mission so well that he was sent again as envoy to the Czar about 1730, and reached Petersburg in the reign of Peter II. In 1719 Peter the Great despatched another embassy, under Ismailoff, to arrange the trade then conducted on a precarious footing—an account of which was drawn up by John Bell in 1763. Ismailoff refused to prostrate himself until it was agreed that a Chinese minister, whenever sent to Petersburg, should conform to the usages of the Russians; a safe stipulation, certainly, to a court which never demeans itself to send missions. The evident desirableness of keeping on good terms with the Russians led the Chinese to treat their envoys with unusual respect and attend to the business they came to settle. One of the most instructive books on the kind of intercourse carried on during this period is the *Journal* of Lange, who went first in 1716, and thrice afterward, and has left an account of his residence at Kanghí's capital.[2]

---

[1] *Chinese Repository*, Vol. VIII., pp. 417, 506. Du Halde, *Description géographique, historique, chronologique, politique et physique de l'Empire de la Chine et de la Tartarie chinoise*, 4 vols., Paris, 1735. G. Timkowski, *Travels of the Russian Mission through Mongolia to China*, etc., 2 vols., London, 1827. Klaproth, *Mémoires sur l'Asie*, Tome I., pp. 1–81.

[2] Published in one volume with Bell: *Journey from St. Petersburgh in Russia to Ispahan in Persia*, etc., London, 1715.

In 1727 a fifth mission was sent by the Empress Catherine under Count Vladislavitch, which succeeded in establishing the intercourse on a still better basis, viz., that a mission, consisting of six ecclesiastical and four lay members, should remain at Peking to study the Chinese and Manchu languages, so that interpreters could be prepared and communications carried on satisfactorily; the members were to be changed decennially. The caravans, which had been the vehicles of trade, were regulated about 1730 by the establishment, at Kiakhta and Maimaichin, of two marts on the frontier, where it could be brought under regulations; the last reached Peking in 1755. This embassy was the most successful of all, and partly owing to the Emperor Yungching's desire to counterbalance Jesuit intrigues by raising up other interpreters. This treaty, signed August 27, 1727, remained in force till June, 1858—the longest lived treaty on record. The narrative of George Timkowski, who conducted the relief sent in 1821, gives an account of his trip from Kiakhta across the desert, together with considerable information relating to the Kalkas and other Mongol tribes subject to China. The archimandrite, Hyacinth Batchourin, has given a description of Peking, but such works as the members of the Russian college have written are for the most part still in that language. Up to the present date there have been sixteen archimandrites (1736 to 1880) and many monks attached to the ecclesiastical mission in Peking.[1]

The intercourse of the English with China, though it commenced later than other maritime nations of Europe, has been far more important in its consequences, and their trade greater in amount than all other foreign nations combined. This intercourse has not been such as was calculated to impress the Chinese with a just idea of the character of the British nation as a leading Christian people; for the East India Company, which had the monopoly of the trade between the two countries for nearly two centuries, systematically opposed every effort to diffuse Christian doctrine and general knowledge among them down to the end of their control in 1834.

[1] Dudgeon's monograph on *Russian Intercourse with China* contains notices of all events of any importance between the two nations, digested with great care, pp. 80, Peking, 1872. Also, Martin's *China*, Vol. I., p. 386.

The first English vessels anchored off Macao in July, 1635, under the command of Weddell, who was sent to China in accordance with a "truce and free trade" which had been entered into between the English merchants and the viceroy of Goa, who gave letters to the governor of Macao. The fleet was coldly received and Weddell deluded with vain promises until the Portuguese fleet had sailed for Japan, when he was denied permission to trade. Two or three of his officers having visited Canton, he was very desirous to participate in the traffic, and proceeded with his whole fleet up to the Bogue forts, where this desire was made known to the commanders of the forts, who promised to return an answer in a week. Meanwhile the Portuguese so misrepresented them to the Chinese that the commander of the forts concluded to end the matter by driving them away. Having made every preparation during the period the fleet was waiting, an attack was first made upon a watering-boat by firing shot at it when passing near the forts.

"Herewith the whole fleet, being instantly incensed, did, on the sudden, display their bloody ensigns; and, weighing their anchors, fell up with the flood, and berthed themselves before the castle, from whence came many shot, yet not any that touched so much as hull or rope; whereupon, not being able to endure their bravadoes any longer, each ship began to play furiously upon them with their broadsides; and after two or three hours, perceiving their cowardly fainting, the boats were landed with about one hundred men: which sight occasioned them, with great distractions, instantly to abandon the castle and fly; the boats' crews, in the meantime, without let, entering the same and displaying his Majesty's colors of Great Britain upon the walls, having the same night put aboard all their ordnance, fired the council-house and demolished what they could. The boats of the fleet also seized a junk laden with boards and timber, and another with salt. Another vessel of small moment was surprised, by whose boat a letter was sent to the chief mandarins at Canton, expostulating their breach of truce, excusing the assailing of the castle, and withal in fair terms requiring the liberty of trade."[1] This letter was shortly answered,

[1] Staunton's *Embassy*, Vol. I., pp. 5–12.

and after a little explanatory negotiation, hastened to a favorable conclusion on the part of the Chinese by what they had seen, trade was allowed after the captured guns and vessels were restored and the ships supplied with cargoes.

No other attempt to open a trade was made till 1664, and during the change of dynasty which took place in the interim, the trade of all nations with China suffered. The East India Company had a factory at Bantam in Java, and one at Madras, but their trade with the East was seriously incommoded by the war with the Dutch; when it was renewed in 1664, only one ship was sent to Macao, but such were the exactions imposed upon the trade by the Chinese, and the effect of the misrepresentations of the Portuguese, that the ship returned without effecting sale. This did not discourage the Company, however, who ordered their agents at Bantam to make inquiries respecting the most favorable port and what commodities were most in demand. They mentioned "Fuhchau as a place of great resort, affording all China commodities, as raw and wrought silk, tutenague, gold, china-root, tea, etc." A trade had been opened with Koxinga's son in Formosa and at Amoy, but this rude chieftain had little other idea of traffic than a means of helping himself to every curious commodity the ships brought, and levying heavy imposts upon their cargoes. A treaty was indeed entered into with him, in which the supercargoes, as was the case subsequently in 1842, stipulated for far greater privileges and lighter duties than Chinese goods and vessels would have had in English ports. Besides freedom to go where they pleased without any one attending them, access at all times to the king, liberty to choose their own clerks and trade with whom they pleased, it was also agreed "that what goods the king buys shall pay no custom; that rice imported pay no custom; that all goods imported pay three per cent. *after sale*, and all goods exported be custom free." The trade at Amoy was more successful than at Zealandia, and a small vessel was sent there in 1677, which brought back a favorable report. In 1678 the investments for these two places were $30,000 in bullion and $20,000 in goods; the returns were chiefly in silk goods, tutenague, rhubarb, etc.;

the trade was continued for several years, apparently with considerable profit, though the Manchus continually increased the restrictions under which it labored. In 1681 the Company ordered their factories at Amoy and Formosa to be withdrawn, and one established at Canton or Fuhchau, but in 1685 the trade was renewed at Amoy.

The Portuguese managed to prevent the English obtaining a footing at Canton until about 1684; and, as Davis remarks, the stupid pertinacity with which they endeavored to exclude them from this port and trade is one of the most striking circumstances connected with these trials and rivalries. It is the more inexplicable in the case of the Portuguese, for they could carry nothing to England, nor could they force the English to trade with them at second hand; theirs was truly the "dog in the manger" policy, and they have subsequently starved upon it. In 1689 a duty of five shillings per pound was laid upon tea imported into England; and the principal articles of export are stated to have been wrought silks of every kind, porcelain, lacquered-ware, a good quantity of fine tea, some fans and screens. Ten years after, the court of directors sent out a consul's commission to the chief supercargo, Mr. Catchpoole, which constituted him king's minister or consul for the whole Empire of China and the adjacent islands. In 1701 an attempt was made by him to open a trade, and he obtained permission to send ships to Chusan or Ningpo; an investment in three vessels, worth £101,300, was accordingly made, but he found the exactions of the government so grievous, and the monopoly of the merchants so oppressive, that the adventure proved a great loss, and the traders were compelled to withdraw. The Company's hopes of trade at that port must, however, have been great, for their investment to Amoy that year was only £34,400, and to Canton £40,800. In 1702 Catchpoole also established a factory at Pulo Condore, an island near the coast of Cochinchina which had been taken by the English. The whole concern, however, experienced a tragical end in 1705, when the Malays rose upon the English, murdered them all, and burned the factory. The Cochinchinese are said to have instigated this treacherous attack to regain the island, which was claimed by them.

The extortions and grievances suffered by the traders at Canton were increased in 1702 by the appointment of an individual who alone had the right of trading with them and of farming it out to those who had the means of doing so. The trade seems hardly, even at this time, to have taken a regular form, but by 1720 the number and value of the annual commodities had so much increased that the Chinese established a uniform duty of four per cent. on all goods, and appointed a body of native merchants, who, for the privilege of trading with foreigners, became security for their payment of duties and good behavior. The duty on imports was also increased to about sixteen per cent. and an enormous fee demanded of purveyors before they could supply ships with provisions, besides a heavy measurement duty and cumshaw to the collector of customs. These exactions seemed likely to increase unless a stand was taken against them. This was done by a united appeal to the governor in person in 1728; yet the relief was only temporary, for the plan was so effectual and convenient for the government that the co-hong was ere long re-established as the only medium through which the foreign trade could be conducted. An additional duty of ten per cent. was laid upon all exports, which no efforts were effectual in removing until the accession of Kienlung in 1736. This apparently suicidal practice of levying export duties is, in China, really a continuation of the internal excise or transit duties paid upon goods exported in native vessels as well as foreign.

The Emperor, in taking off the newly imposed duty of ten per cent., required that the merchants should hear the act of grace read upon their knees; but the foreigners all met in a body, and each one agreed on his honor not to submit to this slavish posture, nor make any concession or proposal of accommodation without acquainting the rest. The Emperor also required the delivery of all the arms on board ship, a demand afterward waived on the payment of about ten thousand dollars. The hong merchants shortly became the only medium of communication with the government, themselves being the exactors of the duties and contrivers of the grievances, and when complaints were made, the judges of the equity of their own acts.

In 1734 only one English ship came to Canton, and one was sent to Amoy, but the extortions there were greater than at the other port, whereupon the latter vessel withdrew. In 1736 the number of ships at Canton was four English, two French, two Dutch, one Danish, and one Swedish vessel; the Portuguese ships had been restricted to Macao before this date.

Commodore Anson arrived at Macao in 1742, and as the Centurion was the first British man-of-war which had visited China, his decided conduct in refusing to leave the river until provisions were furnished, and his determination in seeking an interview with the governor, no doubt had a good effect. A mixture of decision and kindness, such as that exhibited by Anson when demanding only what was in itself right, and backed by an array of force not lightly to be trifled with or incensed, has always proved the most successful way of dealing with the Chinese, who on their part need instruction as well as intimidation. The constant presence of a ship of war on the coast of China would perhaps have saved foreigners much of the personal vexations, and prevented many of the imposts upon trade which the history of foreign intercourse exhibits, making it in fact little better than a recital of annoyances on the part of a government too ignorant and proud to understand its own true interests, and recriminations on the part of traders unable to do more than protest against them.

In consequence of the exactions of the government and the success of the co-hong in preventing all direct intercourse with the local authorities, the attempt was again made to trade at Amoy and Ningpo. The Hardwicke was sent to Amoy in 1744, and obliged to return without a cargo. Messrs. Flint and Harrison were despatched to Ningpo in 1755, and were well received; but when the Holderness subsequently came to trade, it was with difficulty that she procured a cargo, and an imperial edict was promulgated soon after restricting all foreign ships to Canton. In 1759 the factory at Ningpo was demolished, so that Mr. Flint, who repaired there that year, was unable to do anything toward restoring the trade. This gentleman was a person of uncommon perseverance and talents, and had mastered the difficulties of the Chinese language so as to act as interpreter at Canton twelve years before he was sent on his mission. "The ungrateful return which his energy and exertions in their service met with from his employers," justly observes Sir John Davis, "was such as tended in all probability, more than any other cause, to discourage his successors from undertaking so laborious, unprofitable, and even hazardous a work of supererogation."

On his arrival at Ningpo, Mr. Flint, finding it useless to attempt anything there, proceeded in a native vessel to Tientsin, from whence he succeeded in making his case known to the Emperor Kienlung. A commissioner was deputed to accompany him overland to Canton; Mr. Flint proceeded to the English factory soon after his arrival, and the foreigners of all nations assembled before the commissioner, who informed them that the hoppo had been superseded, and all duties remitted over six per cent. on goods and the cumshaw and tonnage dues on ships. The sequel of Mr. Flint's enterprise was unfortunate, and the mode the Chinese took to bring it about thoroughly characteristic.

It proved, however, that these fair appearances were destined only to be the prelude to a storm. Some days afterward the governor desired to see Mr. Flint for the purpose of communicating the Emperor's orders, and was accompanied by the council of his countrymen. When the party had reached the palace, the hong merchants proposed their going in one at a time, but they insisted on proceeding together; and on Mr. Flint being called for, they were received at the first gate and ushered through two courts with seeming complaisance by the officers in waiting; but on arriving at the gate of the inner court they were hurried, and even forced into the governor's presence, where a struggle ensued with their brutal conductors to force them to do homage after the Chinese fashion until they were overpowered and thrown down. Seeing their determination not to submit to these base humiliations, the governor ordered the people to desist; and then telling Mr. Flint to advance, he pointed to an order, which he called the Emperor's edict, for his banishment to Macao, and subsequent departure for England, on account of his endeavoring to open a trade at Ningpo contrary to orders from Peking. He added that the native who had written the petition in Chinese was to be beheaded that day for traitorously encouraging foreigners, which was performed on a man quite innocent of what these officers were pleased to call a crime. Mr. Flint was soon after conveyed to Tsienshan, a place near Macao, called Casa Branca by the Portuguese, where he was imprisoned two years and a half and then sent to England.[1]

---

[1] Davis, *Chinese*, Vol. I., p. 58.

Mr. Flint stated to the Company that a fee of one thousand two hundred and fifty dollars to the governor would set him at liberty, but they contented themselves with a petition. The punishment he received from the Chinese for this attempt to break their laws would not have been considered as unmerited or unjust in any other country, but the neglect of the Company to procure the liberation of one who had suffered so much to serve them reflects the greatest reproach upon that body.

The whole history of the foreign trade, as related by Auber in his chronological narrative, during the one hundred and fifty years up to 1842 is a melancholy and curious chapter in national intercourse. The grievances complained of were delay in loading ships and plunder of goods on their transit to Canton; the injurious proclamations annually put up by the government accusing foreigners of horrible crimes; the extortions of the underlings of office; and the difficulty of access to the high authorities. The hong merchants, from their position as traders and interpreters between the two parties, were able to delude both to a considerable extent, though their responsibility for the acts and payments of foreigners, over whom they could exercise no real restraint, rendered their situation by no means pleasant. The rule on which the Chinese government proceeded in its dealings with foreigners was this: "The barbarians are like beasts, and not to be ruled on the same principles as citizens. Were any one to attempt controlling them by the great maxims of reason, it would tend to nothing but confusion. The ancient kings well understood this, and accordingly ruled barbarians by misrule; therefore, to rule barbarians by misrule is the true and best way of ruling them." The same rule in regard to foreign traders was virtually acted on in England during the reign of Henry VII., and the ideas among the Chinese of their power over those who visit their shores are not unlike those which prevailed in Europe before the Reformation.

The entire ignorance of foreign traders of the spoken and written language of China brought them into contempt with all classes, and where all intercourse was carried on in a jargon which each party despised, the results were often misunderstanding, dislike, and hatred. Another fruitful source of difficulty was the turbulent conduct of sailors. The French and English seamen at Whampoa, in 1754, carried their national hatred to such a degree that they could not pursue their trade without quarrelling; and a Frenchman having killed an English sailor, the Chinese stopped the trade of the former nation until the guilty person was given up, though he was subsequently liberated. The Chinese allotted two different islands in the river at Whampoa for the recreation of the seamen of each nation, in order that such troubles might be avoided in future. A similar case occurred at Canton in 1780, when a Frenchman killed a Portuguese sailor at night in one of the merchants' houses and fled to the consul's for refuge. The Chinese demanded the criminal, and after some days he was given up to them and publicly strangled; this punishment he no doubt merited, although it was the first case in which they had interfered where the matter was altogether among foreigners. In 1784 a native was killed by a ball left in a gun when firing a salute, and the Chinese, on the principle of requiring life for life, demanded the man who had fired the gun. Knowing that the English were not likely to give him up, the police seized Mr. Smith, the supercargo of the vessel, and carried him a prisoner into the city. On the seizure of this gentleman the ships' boats were ordered up from Whampoa with armed crews to defend the factories. A messenger from the Chinese, however, declared that their purpose in seizing Smith was simply to examine him on the affair, to which statement the captive himself added a request that the gunner should be sent up to the authorities and submit to their questions. Trusting too much to their promises, the man was allowed to go alone before the officials within the city walls, when Mr. Smith was immediately liberated and the unhappy gunner strangled, after some six weeks' confinement, by direct orders of the Emperor. The man, probably, underwent no form of trial intelligible to himself, and his condemnation was the more unjust, as by Section CCXCII. of the Chinese code he was allowed to ransom himself by a fine of about twenty dollars. As a counterpart of this tragedy, the Chinese stated (and there was reason for believing them) that a native who had accidentally killed a British seaman about the same time was executed for the casualty.

The Chinese mode of operations, when it was impracticable to get possession of the guilty or accused party, was well exhibited in the case of a homicide occurring in 1807. A party of sailors had been drinking at Canton, when a scuffle ensued, and the sailors put the populace to flight, killing one of the natives in the onset. The trade was promptly stopped, and the hong merchant who had *secured* the ship held responsible for the delivery of the offender. Eleven men were arrested and a court instituted in the Company's hall before Chinese judges, Captain Rolles, of H. B. M. ship Lion, being present with the committee. The actual homicide could not be found, but one Edward Sheen was detained in custody, which satisfied the Chinese while he remained in Canton; but when the committee wished to take him to Macao with them they resisted, until Captain Rolles declared that otherwise he should take the prisoner on board his own ship, which he did. Being now beyond their reach, the authorities were fain to account for the affair to the supreme tribunal at the capital by inventing a tale, stating that the prisoner had caused the death of a native by raising an upper window and accidentally dropping a stick upon his head as he was passing in the street below. This statement was reported to his Majesty as having been concurred in by the English after a full examination of witnesses who attested to the circumstances; the imperial rescript affirmed the sentence of the Board of Punishments, which ordered that the prisoner should be set at liberty after paying the usual fine of twenty dollars provided by law to defray the funeral expenses. The trade was thereupon resumed.[1]

Another case of homicide occurred at Whampoa in 1820, when the authorities reported that the butcher of another ship, who had committed suicide the day of the inquest, was the guilty person. The court of directors very properly blamed their agents at Canton for their complicity in this subterfuge, and spoke of "the paramount advantages which must invari-

[1] Sir G. T. Staunton, *Penal Code of China*, p. 516.

ably be derived from a strict and inflexible adherence to truth as the foundation of all moral obligations."[1]

Other cases of murder and homicide have since occurred between foreigners and natives. In the instance of the British frigate Topaze at Lintin Island in 1822, whose crew had been attacked on shore, her captain successfully resisted the surrender of a British subject for the death of two natives in the affray. The dignified and united action of the British authorities on this occasion was a striking contrast to the weakness of the Americans the year before in the case of Terranova. It proved the beneficial results of a stand for the right, for no foreigner has since been executed by the Chinese. It also proved the necessity and advantages of competent interpreters and translators, inasmuch as the case owed much of its success to Dr. Morrison's aid, which had been rejected by the hong merchants the previous year.[2]

These cases are brought together to illustrate the anomalous position which foreigners once held in China. They constituted a community by themselves, subject chiefly to their own sense of honor in their mutual dealings, but their relations with the Chinese were like what lawyers call a "state of nature." The change of a governor-general, of a collector of customs, or senior hong merchant, involved a new course of policy according to the personal character of these functionaries. The committee of the East India Company had considerable power over British subjects, especially those living in Canton, and could deport them if they pleased; but the consuls of other nations had little or no authority over their countrymen. Trade was left at the same loose ends that politics were, and the want of an acknowledged tariff encouraged smuggling and kept up a constant spirit of resistance and dissatisfaction between the native and foreign merchants, each party endeavoring to get along as advantageously to itself as practicable. Nor was there any acknowledged medium of communication between them, for the

---

[1] Auber, *China: An Outline of its Government, Laws, Policy*, etc., p. 286, London, 1834.

[2] *Chinese Repository*, Vol. II., pp. 513–515. Morrison's *Memoirs*, Vol. II., App., p. 10. Auber, *China, its Government*, etc., pp. 288–309.

consuls, not being credited by the Chinese Government, came and went, hoisted or lowered their flags, without the slightest notice from the authorities. Trade could proceed, perhaps, without involving the nations in war, since if it was unprofitable it would cease; but while it continued on such a precarious footing national character suffered, and the misrepresentations produced thereby rendered explanations difficult, inasmuch as neither party understood or believed the other.

The death of the unfortunate gunner in 1784, and the large debts owed to the English by the hong merchants, which there seemed no probability of recovering, induced the British Government to turn its attention to the situation of the king's subjects in China with the purpose of placing their relations on a better footing. The flagitious conduct of a Captain M'Clary, who seized a Dutch vessel at Whampoa in 1781, which Davis narrates,[1] and the inability of the Company to restrain such proceedings, also had its weight in deciding the crown to send an embassy to Peking. Colonel Cathcart was appointed envoy in 1788, but his death in the Straits of Sunda temporarily deferred the mission, which was resumed on a larger scale in 1792, when the Earl of Macartney was sent as ambassador, with a large suite of able men, to place the relations between the two nations, if possible, on a well-understood and secure footing. Two ships were appointed as tenders to accompany his Majesty's ship Lion (64), and nothing was omitted, either in the composition of the mission or the presents to the Emperor, to insure its success. Little is known regarding its real impression upon the Chinese; they treated it with great consideration while it remained in the country, although at an estimated cost of $850,000, and probably dismissed it with the feeling that it was one of the most splendid testimonials of respect that a tributary nation had ever paid their court. The English were henceforth registered among the nations who had sent tribute-bearers, and were consequently only the more bound to obey the injunctions of their master.[2]

---

[1] *The Chinese*, Vol. I., p. 63.

[2] Sir G. L. Staunton, *Authentic Account of an Embassy from the King of Great Britain to the Emperor of China*, 3 vols., London, 1798.

To the European world, as well as to the British nation, however, this expedition may be said to have opened China, so great was the interest taken in it and so well calculated were the narratives of Staunton and Barrow to convey better ideas of that remote country. "Much of the lasting impression which the relations of Lord Macartney's embassy leave on the mind of his reader," to quote from a review of it, "must be ascribed, exclusive of the natural effect of clear, elegant, and able composition, to the number of persons engaged in that business, the variety of their characters, the reputation they already enjoyed or afterward acquired; the bustle and stir of a sea voyage: the placidity and success which finally characterized the intercourse of the English with the Chinese; the splendor of the reception the latter gave to their European guests; the walks in the magnificent gardens of the 'Son of Heaven;' the picturesque and almost romantic navigation upon the imperial canal; and perhaps, not less for the interest we feel for every grand enterprise, skilfully prepared, and which proves successful, partly in consequence of the happy choice of the persons and the means by which it was to be carried into effect." This impression of the grandeur and extent of the Chinese Empire has ever since more or less remained upon the minds of all readers of Staunton's narrative; but truer views were imparted than had before been entertained concerning its real civilization and its low rank among the nations.

That the embassy produced some good effect is undeniable. though it failed in most of the principal points. It also afforded the Chinese an opportunity of making arrangements concerning that future intercourse which they could not avoid, even if they would not negotiate, and of acquiring information concerning foreign nations which would have proved of great advantage to them. Their contemptuous rejection, ignorant though they decided to remain of the real character of these courtesies, of peaceful missions like those of Macartney, Titsingh, and others, takes away much of our sympathy for the calamities which subsequently came upon them. With characteristic shortsightedness they looked upon the very means taken to arrange existing ill-understood relations as a reason for considering those relations as settled to their liking, and a motive to still further exactions.

For many years subsequent to this embassy the trade went on without interruption, though the demands and duties were rather increased than diminished, and the personal liberty of foreigners more and more restricted. The government generally, down to the lowest underling, systematically endeavored to degrade and insult foreigners in the eyes of the populace and citizens of Canton, in order, in case of any disturbance, to have their co-operation and sympathy against the "barbarian devils." The dissolute and violent conduct of many foreigners toward the Chinese gave them, alas, too many arguments for their aspersions and exactions, and both parties too frequently considered the other fair subjects for imposition.

In 1802 the English troops occupied Macao by order of the governor-general of India, lest it should be attacked by the French, but the news of the treaty of peace arriving soon after, they re-embarked almost as soon as the Chinese remonstrated. The discussion was revived, however, in 1808, when the French again threatened the settlement; and the English, under Admiral Drury, landed a detachment to assist the Portuguese in defending it. The Chinese, who had previously asserted their complete jurisdiction over this territory, and which a little examination would have plainly shown, now protested against the armed occupation of their soil, and immediately stopped the trade and denied provisions to the ships. The English traders were ordered by the Committee to go aboard ship, and the governor refused to have the least communication with the admiral until the troops were withdrawn. He attempted to proceed to Canton in armed boats, but was repulsed, and finally, in order not to implicate the trade any further (a step not at all apprehended in protecting the Portuguese), he wisely withdrew his troops and sailed for India. The success of the native authorities greatly rejoiced them; a temple was built on the river's bank to commemorate their victory, and a fort, called "Howqua's Folly" by foreigners (since washed away), erected to guard the river at that point.

The Chinese, ignorant of the principles on which international intercourse is regulated among western powers, regarded every hostile demonstration between them in their waters as directed toward themselves, and demanding their interference. Though often powerless to defend themselves against their own piratical subjects, as has been manifested again and again—for example, in 1810, and also in 1660, when Koxinga ravaged the coast—they still assume that they are able to protect all foreigners who "range themselves under their sway." This was exhibited in 1814, when the British frigate Doris, against all the acknowledged rights of a nation over its own waters, and simply because it could be done with impunity, cruised off the port of Canton to seize American vessels. The provincial authorities ordered the Committee to send her away, saying that if the English and Americans had any petty squabbles they must settle them between themselves and not bring them to China. The Committee stated their inability to control the proceedings of men-of-war, whereupon the Chinese began a series of annoyances against the merchants and shipping, prohibiting the employment of native servants, entering their houses to seize natives, molesting and stopping ships' boats proceeding up and down the river on business, hindering the loading of the ships, and other like harassing acts so characteristic of Asiatic governments when they feel themselves powerless to cope with the real object of their fear or anger. These measures proceeded at last to such a length that the Committee determined to stop the British trade until the governor would allow it to go on, as before, without molestation, and they had actually left Canton for Whampoa, and proceeded down the river some distance, before he showed a sincere wish to arrange matters amicably. A deputation from each party accordingly met in Canton, and the principal points in dispute were at last gained. In this affair the Chinese would be adjudged to have been altogether in the right according to international law. At this time the governor-general conceded three important points to the Committee, viz., the right of corresponding with the government, under seal, in the Chinese language, the unmolested employment of native servants, and the assurance that the houses of foreigners should not be entered without permission; nor were these stipulations ever retracted or violated.

The proceedings in this affair were conducted with no little apprehension on both sides, for the value of the traffic was of such importance that neither party could really think of stopping it. Besides the revenue accruing to government from duties and presents, the preparation and shipment of the articles in demand for foreign countries give employment to millions of natives in different parts of the Empire, and had caused Canton to become one of the greatest marts in the world. The governor and his colleagues were responsible for the revenue and peaceful continuance of the trade; but through their ignorance of the true principles of a prosperous commerce, their fear of the consequences resulting from any innovation or change, or the least extension of privileges to the few half-imprisoned foreigners, they thought their security lay rather in restriction than in freedom, in a haughty bearing to intimidate, and not in conciliation to please their customers. On the other hand, the existence of the East India Company's charter depended in a good degree upon keeping a regular supply of tea in England, and therefore the success of the Committee's bold measure of stopping the trade depended not a little upon the ignorance of the Chinese of the great power a passive course of action would give them.

The government at home, on learning these proceedings, resolved to despatch another ambassy to Peking in order to state the facts of the case at court, and if possible agree upon some understood mode of conducting trade and communicating with the heads of government. Lord Amherst, who like Lord Macartney had been governor-general of India, was appointed ambassador to Peking, and Henry Ellis and Sir George T. Staunton associated with him as second and third commissioners. A large suite of able men, with Dr. Morrison as principal interpreter, accompanied the ambassy, and the usual quantity and variety of presents.[1] The mission reached the capital August 28, 1816, but was summarily dismissed without an audience, because the ambassador would not perform the kotow

[1] Ellis, *Embassy to China*, London, 1840. Sir J. F. Davis, *Sketches of China*, 2 Vols., London, 1841. Clarke Abel, *Narrative of a Journey in the Interior of China and a Voyage to and from that Country in* 1816 *and* 1817, London, 1818. R. Morrison, *A View of China*, etc., Macao, 1817.

or appear before his Majesty as soon as he arrived; the intrigues of the authorities at Canton with the high officers about the Emperor to defeat the ambassy by deceiving their master have also been adduced as reasons for its failure. Its real failure, as we can now see, was owing to the utter misconception of their true position by the Emperor and his officials, arising from their ignorance, pride, isolation, and mendacity, all combining to keep them so until resistless force should open them to meliorating influences. It was the last attempt of the kind, and three alternatives only remained: the resort to force to compel them to enter into some equitable arrangement, entire submission to whatever they ordered, or the withdrawal of all trade until they proposed its resumption. The course of events continued the second until the first was resorted to, and eventuated in laying open the whole coast to the enterprise of western nations.

At the close of the East India Company's exclusive rights in China, the prospect for the continuance of a peaceful trade was rather dubious. The enterprising Mr. Marjoribanks despatched a vessel to ascertain how far trade could be carried on along the coast, which resulted in satisfactorily proving that the authorities were able and determined to stop all traffic, however desirous the people might be for it. The contraband trade in opium was conducted in a manner that threatened ere long to involve the two nations, but the Company nominally kept itself aloof from it by bringing none in its ships: the same Company, however, did everything in India to encourage the growth and sale of the drug, and received from it at the time of its dissolution an annual revenue of nearly two millions sterling. During its whole existence in China the East India Company stood forward as the defenders of the rights of foreigners and humanity, in a manner which no community of isolated merchants could have done, and to some extent compelled the Chinese to treat all more civilly. As a body it did little for the encouragement of Chinese literature or the diffusion of Christian truth or of science among the Chinese, except the printing of Morrison's Dictionary and an annual grant to the Anglo-Chinese College; and although Dr. Morrison was their official translator for twenty-five years, the directors never gave him the empty compliment of enrolling him in the list of their servants, nor contributed one penny for carrying on his great work of translating and printing the Bible in Chinese. They set themselves against all such efforts, and during a long existence the natives of that country had no means put into their hands, by their agency, of learning that there was any great difference in the religion, science, or civilization of European nations and their own.

The trade of the Americans to China commenced in 1784, the first vessel having left New York February 22d of that year, and returned May 11, 1785; it was commanded by Captain Green, and the supercargo, Samuel Shaw, on his return, gave a lucid narrative of his voyage to Chief Justice Jay. His journal, published in 1847, contains the only record of this voyage, and furnishes many curious facts about the political and social relations existing between foreigners then in China. Our trade with China steadily increased after this date, and has been the second in amount for many years. The only political event in the American intercourse up to 1842 was the suspension of trade in October, 1821, in consequence of the homicide of a Chinese by a sailor at Whampoa. The American merchants were really helpless to carry the trial of Terranova to a just conclusion against the Chinese law, which peremptorily required life for life wherever foreigners were concerned, and gave him up on the assurance that his life was in no danger. They are stated, in a narrative published in the *North American Review*, to have told Howqua at the trial on board the Emily at Whampoa, "We are bound to submit to your laws while we are in your waters; be they ever so unjust, we will not resist them." The poor man was taken out of the ship by force, while all the Americans present protested against the unfair trial he had had; he was then promptly carried to Canton and strangled at the public execution ground (October 25); his body was given up next day, and the trade reopened.[1]

[1] Shaw's *Journal*, Boston, 1847. *North American Review*, January, 1835. *Chinese Repository*, September, 1836. Sir Geo. T. Staunton's *Notices of China*, second edition, pp. 409–432, 1850.

The American Government neither took notice of this affair nor made remonstrance against its injustice, but still left the commerce, lives, and property of its citizens wholly unprotected, and at the mercy of Chinese laws and rulers. The consuls at Canton were merely merchants, having no salary from their government, no funds to employ interpreters when necessary, or any power over their countrymen, and came and went without the least notice or acknowledgment from the Chinese.

The trade and intercourse of the Swedes, Danes, Prussians, Italians, Austrians, Peruvians, Mexicans, or Chilians, at Canton, have been attended with no peculiarities or events of any moment. None of these nations ever sent "tribute" to the court of the Son of Heaven, and their ships traded at Canton on the same footing with the English. The voyage of Peter Osbeck, chaplain to a Swedish East Indiaman, in 1753, contains considerable information relating to the mode of conducting the trade and the position of foreigners, who then enjoyed more liberty and suffered fewer extortions than in later years.[1]

The term *fan-kwei*, by which they were all alike called by the Cantonese, indicated the popular estimation, and this epithet of '*foreign devil*' did much, in the course of years, to increase the contempt and ill will which it expressed, not only there but throughout the Empire, for they were thereby maligned before they were known. Another term, *ǐ*, has been raised into notice by its condemnation in the British Treaty as an epithet for British subjects or countries. This word, there rendered '*barbarian*,' conveys to a native but little more than the idea that the people thus called do not understand the Chinese language and usages, and are consequently less civilized. This epithet *barbarian* meant to the Greeks those who could not speak Greek, as it did to Shakspeare those who were not English; likewise among the Chinese, under *ǐ* were included great masses of their own subjects. By translating *wai ǐ* as '*outside barbarians*,' foreigners have been misrepresented in the status they

---

[1] *A Voyage to China and the East Indies, translated from the German by* John R. Forster, 2 vols., London, 1771.

held among educated natives, which was not that of savages but of the illiteracy growing out of their ignorance of the language and writings of Confucius.

The ancient Chinese books speak of four wild nations on the four sides of the country, viz., the *fan*, *í*, *tih*, *man*; the first two seem to have been applied to traders from the south and west, and grew into more distinct expressions because these traders often acted so outrageously. Other terms, as "western ocean men," "far-travelled strangers," and "men from afar," have occasionally been substituted when *í* was objected to. When used as a general term, without an opprobrious addition, *í* is as well adapted as any to denote all foreigners; but the most recent usage gives prominence to the terms *wai kwoh* and *yang jăn* ('outside country' and 'ocean man'). Among educated natives the national names are becoming more and more common, as *Ying kwoh*, *Fah kwoh*, *Mei kwoh*, *Teh kwoh*, for England, France, America, Germany, etc.

CHAPTER III.

ORIGIN OF THE FIRST WAR WITH ENGLAND.

THE East India Company's commercial privileges ceased in 1834, and it is worthy of note that an association should have been continued in the providence of God as the principal representative of Christendom among the Chinese, which by its character, its pecuniary interests, and general inclination was bound in a manner to maintain peaceful relations with them, while every other important Asiatic kingdom and island, from Arabia to Japan, was at one time or another during that period the scene of collision, war, or conquest between the nations and their visitors. Its monopoly ceased when western nations no longer looked upon these regions as objects of desire, nor went to Rome to get a privilege to seize or claim such pagan lands as they might discover, and when, too, Christians began to learn and act upon their duty to evangelize these ignorant races. China and Japan were once open to such agencies as well as trade, but no effective measures were taken to translate or distribute the pure word of God in them.

Believing that the affairs of the kingdoms of this world are ordered by their Almighty Governor with regard to the fulfilment of his promises and the promulgation of his truth, the first war between England and China is not only one of great historical interest, but one whose future consequences cannot fail to exercise increasing influence upon many millions of mankind. This war was extraordinary in its origin as growing chiefly out of a commercial misunderstanding; remarkable in its course as being waged between strength and weakness, conscious superiority and ignorant pride; melancholy in its end as forcing the weaker to pay for the opium within its borders against all its laws, thus paralyzing the little moral power its feeble government could exert to protect its subjects; and momentous in its results as introducing, on a basis of acknowledged obligations, one-half of the world to the other, without any arrogant demands from the victors or humiliating concessions from the vanquished. It was a turning-point in the national life of the Chinese race, but the compulsory payment of six million dollars for the opium destroyed has left a stigma upon the English name.

In 1834 the select Committee of the East India Company repeated its notice given in 1831 to the authorities at Canton, that its ships would no longer come to China, and that a king's officer would be sent out as chief to manage the affairs of the British trade. The only "chief" whom the Chinese expected to receive was a commercial headman, qualified to communicate with their officers by petition, through the usual and legal medium of the hong merchants. The English Government justly deemed the change one of considerable importance, and concluded that the oversight of their subjects and the great trade they conducted required a commission of experienced men. The Rt. Hon. Lord Napier was consequently appointed as chief superintendent of British trade, and arrived at Macao July 15, 1834, where were associated with him in the commission John F. Davis and Sir G. B. Robinson, formerly servants of the Company, and a number of secretaries, surgeons, chaplains, interpreters, etc., whose united salaries amounted to $91,000. On arriving at Canton the tide-waiters officially reported that three "foreign devils" had landed. As soon as Governor Lu had learned that Lord Napier had reached Macao, he ordered the hong merchants to go down and intimate to him that he must remain there until he obtained legal permission to come to Canton; for, having received no orders from court as to the manner in which he should treat the English superintendent, he thought it the safest plan to adhere to the old regulations.

Lord Napier had been ordered to report himself to the governor at Canton *by letter*. A short extract from his instructions will show the intentions of the English Government in constituting the commission, and the entirely wrong views it had of the notions of the Chinese respecting foreign intercourse, and the character they gave to the English authorities. Lord Palmerston says:

In addition to the duty of protecting and fostering the trade of his Majesty's subjects with the port of Canton, it will be one of your principal objects to ascertain whether it may not be practicable to extend that trade to other parts of the Chinese dominions. . . . It is obvious that, with a view to the attainment of this object, the establishment of direct communications with the port of Peking would be desirable; and you will accordingly direct your attention to discover the best means of preparing the way for such communications, bearing constantly in mind, however, that peculiar caution and circumspection will be indispensable on this point, lest you should awaken the fears or offend the prejudices of the Chinese Government, and thus put to hazard even the existing opportunities of intercourse by a precipitate attempt to extend them. In conformity with this caution you will abstain from entering into any new relations or negotiations with the Chinese authorities, except under very urgent and unforeseen circumstances. But if any opportunity for such negotiations should appear to you to present itself, you will lose no time in reporting the circumstance to his Majesty's government, and in asking for instructions; but previously to the receipt of such instructions you will adopt no proceedings but such as may have a general tendency to convince the Chinese authorities of the sincere desire of the king to cultivate the most friendly relations with the Emperor of China, and to join with him in any measures likely to promote the happiness and prosperity of their respective subjects.

Governor Lu's messengers arrived too late to detain the British superintendent at Macao, and a military officer despatched to intercept him passed him on the way; so that the first intimation the latter received of the governor's disposition was in an edict addressed to the hong merchants, from which two paragraphs are extracted:

On this occasion the barbarian *eye*, Lord Napier, has come to Canton without having at all resided at Macao to wait for orders; nor has he requested or received a permit from the superintendent of customs, but has hastily come up to Canton—a great infringement of the established laws! The customhouse waiters and others who presumed to admit him to enter are sent with a communication requiring their trial. But in tender consideration for the said barbarian *eye* being a new-comer, and unacquainted with the statutes and laws of the Celestial Empire, I will not strictly investigate. . . . As to his object in coming to Canton, it is for commercial business. The Celestial Empire appoints officers, civil ones to rule the people, military ones to intimidate the wicked. The petty affairs of commerce are to be directed by the merchants themselves: the officers have nothing to hear on the subject. . . . If any affair is to be newly commenced, it is necessary to wait till a respectful memorial be made, clearly reporting it to the great Emperor, and his mandate be received; the great ministers of the Celestial Empire are not permitted to have intercourse by letters with outside barbarians. If the said barbarian eye *throws in* private letters, I, the governor, will not at all receive or look at them. With regard to the foreign factory of the Company without the walls of the city, it is a place of temporary residence for foreigners coming to Canton to trade; they are permitted only to eat, sleep, buy and sell in the factories; they are not allowed to go out to ramble about.[1]

How unlike were these two documents and the expectations of their writers! The governor felt that it was safest to wait for an imperial mandate before commencing a new affair, and refused to receive *a letter* from a foreign officer. Had he done so he would have laid himself open to reprimand and perhaps punishment from his superiors; and in saying that the superintendent should report himself and apply for a permit before coming to Canton, he only required what the members of the Company had always done when they returned from their summer vacation at Macao. Lord Napier thought he had the same liberty to come to Canton without announcing himself that other and private foreigners exercised; but an officer of his rank would have pleased the Chinese authorities better by observing their regulations. He had thought of this contingency before leaving England, and had requested "that in case of necessity he might have authority to treat with the government at Peking;" this request being denied, he desired that his appointment to Canton might be announced at the capital; this not being granted, he wished that a communication from the home authorities might be addressed to the governor of Canton; but this was deemed inexpedient, and he was directed to "go to Canton and report himself by letter." These reasonable requests involved no loss of dignity, but the court of St. James chose to send out a superintendent of trade, an officer partaking of both ministerial and consular powers, and ordered him to act in a certain manner, involving a violation of the regulations of the country where he was going, without providing for the alternative of his rejection.

---

[1] *Correspondence relating to China* (Blue Book), p. 4. *Chinese Repository*, Vol. III., p. 188; Vol. XI., p. 188.

To Canton, therefore, he came, and the next day reported himself by letter to the governor, sending it to the city gates. His lordship was directed to have nothing to do with the hong merchants; and therefore when they waited upon him the morning of his arrival, with the edict they had been sent down to Macao to "enjoin upon him," he courteously dismissed them, with an intimation that "he would communicate immediately with the viceroy in the manner befitting his Majesty's commission and the honor of the British nation." The account of the reception of his communication is taken from his correspondence:

On the arrival of the party at the city gates, the soldier on guard was despatched to report the circumstance to his superior. In less than a quarter of an hour an officer of inferior rank appeared, whereupon Mr. Astell offered my letter for transmission to the viceroy, which duty this officer declined, adding that his superior was on his way to the spot. In the course of an hour several officers of nearly equal rank arrived in succession, each refusing to deliver the letter on the plea that higher officers would shortly attend. After an hour's delay, during which time the party were treated with much indignity, not unusual on such occasions, the linguists and hong merchants arrived, who entreated to become the bearers of the letter to the viceroy. About this time an officer of rank higher than any of those who had preceded him joined the party, to whom the letter was in due form offered, and as formally refused. The officer having seen the superscription on the letter, argued, that "as it came from the superintendent of trade, the hong merchants were the proper channels of communication:" but this obstacle appeared of minor importance in their eyes, upon ascertaining that the document was styled a *letter*, and not a *petition*. The linguists requested to be allowed a copy of the address, which was of course refused.

About this time the *kwang-hieh*, a military officer of the rank of colonel, accompanied by an officer a little inferior to himself, arrived on the spot, to whom the letter was offered three several times and as often refused. The senior hong merchant, Howqua, after a private conversation with the colonel, requested to be allowed to carry the letter in company with him and ascertain whether it would be received. This being considered as an insidious attempt to circumvent the directions of the superintendents, a negative was made to this and other overtures of a similar tendency. Suddenly all the officers took their departure for the purpose, as it was afterward ascertained, of consulting with the viceroy. Nearly three hours having been thus lost within the city, Mr. Astell determined to wait a reasonable time for the return of the officers, who shortly afterward reassembled; whereupon Mr. Astell respectfully offered the letter in question three separate times to the colonel and afterward to the other officers, all of whom distinctly refused even to touch it; upon which the party returned to the factory.[1]

---

[1] *Chinese Repository*, Vol. XI., p. 27.

The governor reported this occurrence at court in a memorial, in which, after stating that his predecessor had instructed the Company's supercargoes to make arrangements that "a *taipan* [or supercargo, the word being applied to all foreign consuls] acquainted with affairs should still be appointed to come to Canton to control and direct the trade," he states what had occurred, and adds:

The said barbarian eye would not receive the hong merchants, but afterward repaired to the outside of the city to present a letter to me, your Majesty's minister, Lu. On the face of the envelope the forms and style of equality were used, and there were absurdly written the characters *Ta Ying kwoh* ['Great English nation']. Now it is plain on the least reflection, that in keeping the central and outside [people] apart, it is of the highest importance to maintain dignity and sovereignty. Whether the said barbarian eye has or has not official rank there are no means of thoroughly ascertaining. But though he be really an officer of the said nation, he yet cannot write letters on equality with the frontier officers of the Celestial Empire. As the thing concerned the national dignity, it was inexpedient in the least to allow a tendency to any approach or advance by which lightness of esteem might be occasioned. Accordingly orders were given to Han Shau-king, the colonel in command of the military forces of this department, to tell him authoritatively that, by the statutes and enactments of the Celestial Empire, there has never been intercourse by letters with outside barbarians; that, respecting commercial matters, petitions must be made through the medium of the hong merchants, and that it is not permitted to offer or present letters. . . . On humble examination it appears that the commerce of the English barbarians has hitherto been managed by the hong merchants and *taipans;* there has never been a barbarian eye to form a precedent. Now it is suddenly desired to appoint an officer, a superintendent, which is not in accordance with old regulations. Besides, if the said nation has formed this decision, it still should have stated in a petition the affairs which, and the way how, such superintendent is to manage, so that a memorial might be presented requesting your Majesty's mandate and pleasure as to what should be refused, in order that obedience might be paid to it and the same be acted on accordingly. But the said barbarian eye, Lord Napier, without having made any plain report, suddenly came to the barbarian factories outside the city to reside, and presumed to desire intercourse to and fro by official documents and letters with the officers of the Central Flowery Land; this was, indeed, far out of the bounds of reason.[1]

The governor here intimates that the intention of his government in requesting a *taipan* to come to Canton was only to have a responsible officer with whom to communicate. In refusing

[1] *Chinese Repository*, Vol. III., p. 327.

to receive an 'eye,' or superintendent, therefore, he did not, in his own view of the case, suppose that he was refusing, nor did he or the court of Peking intend to refuse, the residence of a supercargo, for they were desirous to have responsible heads appointed over the commerce and subjects of every nation trading at Canton. These occurrences were discussed by the Hon. John Quincy Adams in his lecture upon the war with China, delivered in 1841, in which he alleged that the rejection of Lord Napier's letter and mission was a sufficient reason for the subsequent contest. He showed the impolicy of allowing the Chinese ideas of supremacy over other nations, and exhibited their natural results in the degraded position of foreigners. He had, however, only an imperfect conception of the strength of this assumption, but it was not debated in this contest between Governor Lu and Lord Napier. The former was not blameworthy for endeavoring to carry the laws of his own country into execution, while the latter was doing his best to obey the instructions of his own sovereign. The question of the propriety of those laws, involving as they did the supremacy of the Emperor over the English, or the feasibility of those instructions, could only be discussed and settled by their principals. Whether this assumption was a proper ground of hostilities is altogether another question. When Lord Napier's letter was rejected he would probably have referred home to his government for further instructions if it had intended to settle the question of supremacy, but he did not do so, nor did the ministry refer to it or remonstrate against the unhandsome treatment their representative received.

The refusal of Lord Napier to confer with the hong merchants, and of the governor to receive any communication except a petition, placed the two parties in an awkward position. In his letter the former stated the object of his coming to Canton, and requested that his excellency would accord him an interview in order that their future intercourse might be arranged; and considering the desirableness of giving him accurate views, the party at the gate would have acted wisely in permitting the hong merchants to take it to him. The governor was irritated and alarmed, and vented his anger upon the unfortunate hong merchants. These had two or three interviews with Lord Napier after the rejection of the letter, but as they now said it would not be received unless superscribed *pin*, or 'petition.' they were dismissed. Having heard that there was a party among the British residents in Canton who disapproved of the proceedings of the superintendent, they vainly endeavored to call a meeting of the disaffected on the 10th of August, while his lordship assembled all of his countrymen next day, and found that they generally approved of his conduct. On the 14th he reviews his position in consequence of the rejection of his letter and the subsequent conduct of the governor. After recommending the renewal of the effort to open better understood relations with the court of Peking by a demand upon the Emperor to allow the same privileges to all foreigners residing in China which Chinese received in foreign countries, he goes on to say:

My present position is, in one point of view, a delicate one, because the trade is put in jeopardy on account of the difference existing between the viceroy and myself. I am ordered by his Majesty to "go to Canton and there report myself by letter to the viceroy." I use my best endeavors to do so; but the viceroy is a presumptuous savage, and will not grant the same privileges to me that have been exercised constantly by the chiefs of the committee. He rakes up obsolete orders, or perhaps makes them for the occasion; but the fact is, the chiefs used formerly to wait on the viceroy on their return from Macao, and continued to do it until the viceroy gave them an order to wait upon him, whereupon they gave the practice up. Had I even degraded the king's commission so far as to petition through the hong merchants for an interview, it is quite clear by the tenor of the edicts that it would have been refused. Were he to send an armed force and order me to the boat, I could then retreat with honor, and he would implicate himself; but they are afraid to attempt such a measure. What then remains but the stoppage of the trade or my retirement? If the trade is stopped for any length of time the consequences to the merchants are most serious, as they are also to the unoffending Chinese. But the viceroy cares no more for commerce, or for the comfort and happiness of the people as long as he receives his pay and plunder, than if he did not live among them. My situation is different; I cannot hazard millions of property for any length of time on the mere score of etiquette. If the trade shall be stopped, which is probable enough in the absence of the frigate, it is possible I may be obliged to retire to Macao to let it loose again. Then has the viceroy gained his point and the commission is degraded. Now, my lord, I argue that whether the commission retires by force of arms or by the injustice practised on the merchants, the viceroy has committed an outrage on the British crown which should be equally chastised. The whole system of government here is that of subterfuge and shifting the blame from the shoulders of the one to the other. . . . I shall not go, however, without publishing in Chinese and disseminating far and wide the base conduct of the viceroy in oppressing the merchants, native as well as foreign, and of my having taken the step out of pure compassion to them. I can only once more implore your lordship to force them to acknowledge my authority and the king's commission, and if you can do that you will have no difficulty in opening the ports at the same time.[1]

Such were the sentiments and desires which filled the mind of the English superintendent. He is in error in saying that the governor would not grant him the same privileges as had been accorded to the chiefs of the Company. The present question was not about having an interview, but regarding the superscription of his letter; for the chiefs of the Company sent their sealed communications through the hong merchants as petitions. The governor stopped the English trade on the 16th, and two days after issued an explanatory paper in reply to the report that his orders on that subject had been carried into effect. This document sets forth his determination to uphold the old regulations, and a few sentences from it are here introduced as a contrast with the preceding despatch. The conviction of the governor in the supremacy of his Emperor over all foreign nations which had sent embassies to his court, and his own official position making him responsible for successfully maintaining the laws over foreigners, must be borne in mind:

To refer to England: should an official personage from a foreign country proceed to the said nation for the arrangement of any business, how could he neglect to have the object of his coming announced in a memorial to the said nation's king, or how could he act contrary to the requirements of the said nation's dignity, doing his own will and pleasure? Since the said barbarian eye states that he is an official personage, he ought to be more thoroughly acquainted with these principles. Before, when he offered a letter, I, the governor, saw it inexpedient to receive it, because the established laws of the Celestial Empire do not permit ministers and those under authority to have private intercourse by letter with outside barbarians, but have, hitherto, in commercial affairs, held the merchants responsible; and if perchance any barbarian merchant should have any petition to make requesting the investigation of any affair, [the laws require] that by the said *taipan* a duly prepared petition should be in form presented, and an answer by proclamation awaited. There has never been such a thing as outside barbarians sending in a letter.

---

[1] *Chinese Repository*, Vol. XV., p. 68.

He then says that there had never been any official correspondence to and fro between the native officers and the barbarian merchants; by this he means a correspondence of equality, which the Chinese Government had indeed never yielded. The idea of supremacy never leaves him—witness, for example, the following strain, peculiarly Chinese:

The hong merchants, because the said barbarian eye will not adhere to the old regulations, have requested that a stop should be put to the said nation's commerce. This manifests a profound knowledge of the great principles of dignity. It is most highly praiseworthy. Lord Napier's perverse opposition necessarily demands such a mode of procedure, and it would be most right immediately to put a stop to buying and selling. But considering that the said nation's king has hitherto been in the highest degree reverently obedient, he cannot in sending Lord Napier at this time have desired him thus obstinately to resist. The some hundreds of thousands of commercial duties yearly coming from the said country concern not the Celestial Empire the extent of a hair or a feather's down. The possession or absence of them is utterly unworthy of one careful thought. Their broadcloths and camlets are still more unimportant, and of no regard. But the tea, the rhubarb, the raw silk of the Inner Land, are the sources by which the said nation's people live and maintain life. For the fault of one man, Lord Napier, must the livelihood of the whole nation be precipitately cut off? I, the governor, looking up and embodying the great Emperor's most sacred, most divine wish, to nurse and tenderly cherish as one all that are without, feel that I cannot bring my mind to bear it! Besides, all the merchants of the said nation dare dangers, crossing the seas myriads of miles to come from far. Their hopes rest wholly in the attainment of gain by buying and selling. That they did not attend when summoned by the hong merchants to a meeting for consultation, was because they were under the direction of Lord Napier; it assuredly did not proceed from the several merchants' own free will. Should the trade be wholly cut off in one morning, it would cause great distress to many persons, who, having travelled hither by land and sea, would by one man, Lord Napier, be ruined. They cannot in such case but be utterly depressed with grief. . . . I hear the said eye is a man of very solid and expansive mind and placid speech. If he consider, he can himself doubtless distinguish right and wrong: let him on no account permit himself to be deluded by men around him. . . . Hereafter, when the said nation's king hears respecting these repeated orders and official replies, [he will know] that the whole wrong lies on the barbarian eye; it is in nowise owing to any want on the part of the Celestial Empire of extreme consideration for the virtue of reverential obedience exercised by the said nation's king.[1]

He consequently sent a deputation of officials to Lord Napier to inquire why he had come to Canton, what business he

[1] *Chinese Repository*, Vol. III., p. 235.

was appointed to perform, and when he would retire to Macao. The letter was again handed them, but the superscription still remained, and they refused to touch it. They, however, learned enough to be able to inform their master what he wished to know: the real point of dispute between the two could only be settled between their sovereigns. The governor by this deputation showed a desire to make some arrangement, and the trade would probably have been shortly reopened had not Lord Napier carried out his idea, two days after, of appealing to the people in order to explain the reasons why the governor had stopped the trade and brought distress on them. The paper simply detailed the principal events which had occurred since his arrival, laying the blame upon the "ignorance and obstinacy" of the governor in refusing to receive his letter, and closing with—"The merchants of Great Britain wish to trade with all China on principles of mutual benefit; they will never relax in their exertions till they gain a point of equal importance to both countries; and the viceroy will find it as easy to stop the current of the Canton River as to carry into effect the insane determination of the hong."

In many of the former proceedings between the Chinese and foreigners, based as they were upon incorrect ideas, the rules of diplomacy elsewhere observed formed no guide; but the publication of this statement was unwise and dangerous. Not only did it jeopardize the lives and property of British subjects, but of all other foreigners residing at Canton, to whose safety and interests, as involved with his own dispute, Lord Napier makes no reference in his despatches. Happily, Governor Lu did not appease his irritation by letting loose the populace of Canton, which was highly excited, but by imprisoning members of the co-hong for allowing the superintendent to come to the city.

The governor and his colleagues stopped the English trade on September 2d, in a proclamation containing many inaccurate statements and absurd reasonings, in which he forbade either natives or foreigners to give aid or comfort to Lord Napier. Communication with the shipping at Whampoa was also interdicted, so that, in reality, the entire foreign trade was interrupted. A guard of Chinese troops was placed near the Company's factory, but no personal distress was felt on account of the interdict. H. B. M. frigates Andromache and Imogene were ordered up to protect the shipping and persons of British subjects, and the two vessels anchored at Whampoa on the 11th. In their passage through the Bogue they returned the fire from the forts, with little damage to either; and on anchoring, a lieutenant and boat's crew were despatched to Canton to protect the English factory. These decisive proceedings troubled the native authorities not a little, who, on their part, prepared for stronger measures by blocking up the river and stationing troops about Whampoa, but were relieved when they found that the ships remained at their anchorage.

Lord Napier sent a protest against the proceedings of the governor in stopping the trade, through the Chamber of Commerce and hong merchants; but at this juncture his health gave way so rapidly that three days after the frigates had anchored he decided to return to Macao and wait for instructions. The Chinese detained him on his passage down until the ships were out of the river; but he sank and died October 11th, a fortnight after reaching that city. As soon as he left Canton the trade was reopened. On hearing that the ships had reached Whampoa, the Emperor degraded or suspended all the officials who had been in any way responsible; but when he learned that "Lord Napier had been driven out, and the two ships of war dragged over the shallows and expelled," he restored most of those whom he had thus punished. The governor also vented his indignation upon ten of his subordinates, by subjecting them to torture in order to "ascertain if they were guilty of illicit connection with foreigners." The drama was closed on the part of the Chinese by an imperial mandate: "The English barbarians have an open market in the Inner Land, but there has hitherto been no interchange of official communications. Yet it is absolutely requisite that there should be a person possessing general control, to have the special direction of affairs: wherefore let the governor immediately order the hong merchants to command the said separate merchants, that they send a letter back to their country calling for the appointment of another person as *taipan*, to come for the control and direction of commercial affairs, in accordance with the old regulations."

The principles on which the Chinese acted in this affair are plainly seen. To have granted official intercourse by letter would have been to give up the whole question, to consider the king of England as no longer a tributary, and so release him and his subjects from their allegiance. To do so would not only permit them to come into their borders as equals, subject to no laws or customs, but would further open the door for resistance to their authority, armed opposition to their control, and ultimate in possession of their territory. The governor hints at this when speaking of the necessity of restraining the barbarian eye: "With regard to territory, it would also have its consequences." These would be the probable results of allowing such a mode of address from the Kalkas, or Tibetans, and the Emperor felt the importance of its concession in a way that Lord Napier himself could not appreciate. Nevertheless, with the inconsistency of children, the Son of Heaven and his courtiers, in the mandate just quoted, yield their obligations to justly govern the far-travelled strangers, by requiring them to get a countryman "to exercise general control" and live among them —thus establishing the principle of ex-territoriality within their borders which they now find so irksome.

It is pitiable, and natural too, that the Chinese should have had notions so incorrect and dangerous, for it led them to misinterpret every act of foreigners. Their entire intercourse with Europeans, since the Portuguese first came to their shores, had conspired to strengthen the opinion that all traders were crafty, domineering, avaricious, and contumacious, and must be kept down in every possible way to insure safety to the Chinese natives. The indignation of the Emperor on hearing of the entrance of the ships of war was mixed with great apprehension, "lest there were yet other ships staying at a distance ready to bring in aid to him" [Lord Napier]. Ignorant as he was of the true character of the embassies which had been received at Peking, he was still more likely to take alarm at any attempt to open an equal intercourse, and disposed to resist it as he would a forcible occupation of his territory, of which it was, in his view, only the precursor.

That these were the feelings of the rulers at Peking cannot be doubted; and we must know what views and fears actuated them in order to understand their proceedings. If the position of England in the eyes of the Chinese had been fully known in London, the unequal contest imposed upon Lord Napier would either have been avoided or directed against the imperial government. The offer of an amicable intercourse was given to the Chinese, but through the inapplicable instructions which his lordship received this offer was not made to the weaker and ignorant party in such a way as not to excite its fears, while it fully explained the real position and intentions of England, and through her all Christendom, in seeking intercourse with China. Yet so long as the court of Peking, in virtue of the Emperor's vicegerency over mankind, claimed supremacy over other nations, the struggle to maintain that assumption was sure to come. This false notion did, however, really continue among them for about forty years, till five foreign ministers had their first audience with the Emperor Tungchí, June, 1873, and stood before his throne as they presented their credentials.

The British residents at Canton saw the point of difficulty clearly, and in a petition to the king in council, dated December 4, 1834, recommended that a commissioner be sent to one of the northern ports with a small fleet to arrange the matter of future intercourse. In this petition they "trace the disabilities and restrictions under which British commerce now labors to a long acquiescence in the arrogant assumption of supremacy over the monarchs and people of other countries claimed by the Emperor of China for himself and his subjects," and conclude that "no essentially beneficial result can be expected to arise out of negotiations in which such pretensions are not decidedly repelled." The recommendations of the petitioners were disregarded in England. The cabinet disapproved of the spirit of Lord Napier's despatches, and intimated to him that it was "not by force and violence that his Majesty intended to establish a commercial intercourse between his subjects and China, but by conciliatory measures." After the events of 1834 if a commissioner, backed by a small fleet, had been immediately appointed to Peking to arrange the terms of future intercourse, the subsequent war might have been averted, though it is more likely that the imperial court would have rejected all overtures until compelled to treat by force.

As things were situated at Canton, it was really impossible for the Chinese Government to carry on a line of policy with respect to foreign intercourse which would at once maintain its assumptions, avoid the risk of a rupture, squeeze all the money possible out of the trade, and repress the complaints of the British merchants. The cessation of the Company's monopoly, as well as its control over all British subjects, had weakened the leverage of the local authorities to manage them, to a greater degree than they were aware.

The trade was conducted during the next season to the satisfaction of all parties. That of other nations had been practically stopped with that of the English, but the suspension was at a dull season of the year. Their consuls took no official part in the dispute, though they had some ground for complaint in the suspension of their trade and the imprisonment of their countrymen. The Chinese shopkeepers known as "outside merchants" having been interdicted trading at all with foreigners, went to the governor's palace in a large body and soon obtained a removal of the restriction. The hong merchants themselves instigated this decree, for these shopkeepers, while deriving large profits from their business, were almost free from the extortions which the monopolists suffered. All the extraordinary expenses incurred by the provincial exchequer in the late affair were required of these unfortunate men; and they *must* get it out of the trade in the best way they could. Amelioration could not be expected from such a system; for as soon as the foreigners began to complain, the hong merchants were impelled by every motive to misrepresent their complaints to the governor and quash every effort to obtain redress. The situation of foreigners there was aptly likened by a writer on the subject to the inmates of the Zoölogical Garden in Regent's Park: "They [the animals] have been free to play what pranks they pleased, so that they made no uproar nor escaped from confinement. The keepers looked sharply after them and tried to keep them quiet, because annoyed by the noise they made and responsible for the mischief they might commit if they got at liberty. They might do what was right in their own eyes with each other. The authorities of China do not expect from wild and restless barbarians the decorum and conduct exemplified in their own great family."

The peculiar position of the relations with the Chinese and the value of the trade, present and prospective, was so great that these events called out many pamphleteers both in England and the East. The servants of the Company naturally recommended a continuance of the peaceable system, urging that foreigners should obey the laws of the Empire where they lived and not interfere with the restrictions put upon them. Others counselled the occupation of an island on the coast, to which Chinese traders would immediately resort, and which was to be held only so long as the Emperor refused to open his ports and allow a fair traffic with his people. Others deprecated resort to force until a commissioner to Peking had explained the designs and wishes of his government, demanded the same privileges for foreigners in China that the Chinese enjoyed abroad, and then, in the event of a refusal, compel acquiescence. Some advised letting things take their own course and conducting trade as it could be at Canton until circumstances compelled the Chinese to act. "That which we now require is not to lose the enjoyment of what we have got," said the Duke of Wellington, and his advice was followed in most respects. A few thought it would be the wiser way to disseminate juster ideas of the position, power, and wishes of England and all foreign nations among the Chinese in their own language. They argued very properly that ignorance on these points would neutralize every attempt to bring about a better state of things; that although the Chinese were to blame for their uncompromising arrogance, it was also their great misfortune that they really had had little opportunity to learn the truth respecting their visitors. All these suggestions looked forward to no long continuance of the present undefined, anomalous relations, and all of them contained much pertinent advice and many valuable items of information; but it was a question not more difficult than important what course of procedure was the best. While the point of supremacy seemed to be settled in favor of the Son of Heaven, the virus of the contraband opium trade was working out its evil effects among his subjects and hastening on a new era.

The British superintendents now lived in Macao pending the action of their government, merely keeping a clerk at Canton to sign manifests. The foreign residents established the Society for the Diffusion of Useful Knowledge, and other benevolent projects mentioned in a previous chapter; they also sent two or three vessels along the coast to see what openings existed for entering the country, preaching the gospel, or living on shore. The results of the voyages fully proved the impossibility of entering the country in an open manner without the permission of the rulers, and the limited intercourse with the people also showed that the character of foreigners was generally associated with the opium trade. The dwellers immediately on the coast were eager for an extension of the traffic, because it brought them large gains, and the officers at the principal ports were desirous of participating in the emoluments of their fellows at Canton; but those who had the good of the country at heart (and there are many such in China) thought that the extension of foreign trade would bring with it unmitigated evil from the increased use of opium.

Sir G. B. Robinson, the superintendent, remained at Lintin on board a cutter among opium ships anchored there during the season of 1835-36, and was so well satisfied with his position that he recommended his government to purchase a small ship for the permanent accommodation of the commission there beyond the reach of the Chinese officers, and to vest its powers in a single individual. He also expressed his conviction that there was little hope of establishing a proper understanding with the Chinese Government, except by a resort to force and the occupation of an island off the mouth of the river:

I see no grounds to apprehend the occurrence of any fearful events on the north-east coast, nor can I learn what new danger exists. I am assured from the best authority that the scuffles between different parties of smugglers and mandarins, alike engaged and competing in the traffic, are not more serious or frequent than in this province. In no case have Europeans been engaged in any kind of conflict or affray: and while this increasing and lucrative trade is in the hands of the parties whose vital interests are so totally dependent on its safety and continuance, and by whose prudence and integrity it has been brought into its present increasing and flourishing condition, I think little apprehension may be entertained of dangers emanating from imprudence on their part. Should any unfortunate catastrophe take place, what would our position at Canton entail upon us but responsibility and jeopardy, from which we are now free? On the question of smuggling opium I will not enter in this place, though, indeed, smuggling carried on actively in the government boats can hardly be termed such. Whenever his Majesty's government directs us to prevent British vessels engaging in the traffic, we can enforce any order to that effect, but a more certain method would be to prohibit the growth of the poppy and the manufacture of opium in British India; and if British ships are in the habit of committing irregularities and crimes, it seems doubly necessary to exercise a salutary control over them by the presence of an authority at Lintin.

Taking all things into consideration, this is a remarkable despatch to be sent by the representative of a Christian government writing from the midst of a fleet of smugglers on the shores of a pagan country. "The scuffles caused by the introduction of opium are," he remarks, "*not more* serious or frequent on the coast than about Canton;" though even there, probably, not one-half which did occur were known; but Europeans never personally engaged in any of them. They only brought the cause and object of these collisions where the people could get it, and then quietly looked on to see them fight about it. The "prudence and integrity" of the merchants were engaged in cherishing it to a high degree of prosperity, and they were not likely to act imprudently. The orders of the supreme government for its officers on the coast to stop the traffic were utterly powerless, through the cupidity and venality of those officers and their underlings; yet their almost complete failure to execute them does not impugn the sincerity of the court in issuing them. There is not the least evidence to show that the court of Peking was not sincere in its desire to suppress the trade, from the first edict in 1800 till the war broke out in 1840. The excuse that the government smuggled because its revenue cruisers engaged in it and the helpless provincial authorities winked at it, is no more satisfactory than to make the successful bribery of custom-house officers in England or elsewhere a proof of the corruption of the treasury department. The temptation of an "increasing and lucrative" trade was as strong to the unenlightened pagan Chinese smuggler as it was to the Christian merchants and monopolists who placed the poisonous drug constantly within his reach. It would have been far more frank on the part of the British superintendent to have openly defended a traffic affording a revenue of more than two millions sterling to his own government, and suggested that such an "increasing and lucrative" business should not be impeded, than to say that he could stop British ships engaging in it as soon as he received orders to that effect.

The existence of the commission at the outer anchorages was fully known to the authorities at Canton, but no movement toward reopening the intercourse was made by either party. Lord Palmerston instructed the superintendent not to communicate with the governor-general through the hong merchants, nor to give his written communications the name of petitions. Captain Elliot succeeded Sir George in 1836, and immediately set about reopening the communication with the Chinese officers in the same way that the supercargoes of the Company had conducted it. He defended this course upon the grounds that he had no right to direct official communication with the governor, and that the remarkable movements of the Chinese and the state of uncertainty in respect to the whole foreign trade rendered it desirable to be at Canton. The successor of Lu, Tăng Ting-ching, willingly responded to this proposition by sending a deputation of three officers to Macao with the hong merchants to make some inquiries before memorializing the Emperor. In his report the governor avoided all reference to Lord Napier, and requested his Majesty's sanction to the present request as being in accordance with the orders that the English merchants should send home to have a supercargo come out to manage them. It was of course granted; and the British commission, having received a "red permit" from the collector of customs, returned to Canton April 12, 1837, after an absence of about thirty months. In his note to the governor upon receiving the imperial sanction, Captain Elliot says: "The undersigned respectfully assures his excellency that it is at once his duty and his anxious desire to conform in all things to the imperial pleasure; and he will therefore heedfully attend to the points adverted to in the papers now before him." This language was decided, and his excellency afterward called upon the superintendent to do as he had promised.

The remarkable movements of the supreme government here referred to grew out of a memorial from Hü Nai-tsí, formerly salt commissioner and judge at Canton, proposing the legalization of the opium trade. In this paper he acknowledges that it is impossible to stop the traffic or use of the drug; if the foreign vessels be driven from the coast, they will go to some island near by, where the native craft will go off to them; and if the laws be made too severe upon those who smoke the drug they will be disregarded. By legalizing it, he says, the drain of specie will be stopped, the regular trade rendered more profitable and manageable, and the consumption of the drug regulated. He proposes instant dismissal from office as the penalty for all functionaries convicted of smoking, while their present ineffectual attempts to suppress the trade, which resulted in general contempt for all law, would cease, and consequently the dignity of government be better maintained. The trade on the coast would be concentrated at Canton, and the fleet at Lintin broken up, thereby bringing all foreigners more completely under control.

This unexpected movement at the capital caused no little stir at Canton, and the hong merchants presently advertised the foreigners that soon there would no longer be any use for the receiving-ships at Lintin. Captain Elliot wrote that he thought legalization had come too late to stop the trade on the coast, and, with a prescient eye, adds that the "feeling of independence created among British subjects from the peculiar mode of conducting this branch of the trade," would ere long lead to graver difficulties and acts of violence requiring the armed interference of his government. The impression was general at Canton that the trade would be legalized, and increased preparations were accordingly made in India to extend the cultivation. The governor and his colleagues recommended its legalization on the grounds that "the tens of millions of precious money which now annually ooze out of the Empire will be saved," the duties be increased, the evil practices of transporting contraband goods by deceit and violence suppressed, numberless quarrels and litigations arising therefrom and the crimes of worthless vagrants diminished. They also deluded themselves with the idea that if the officers were dismissed as soon as convicted, the intelligent part of society would not indulge their depraved appetites, but let the "victims of their own self-sacrificing folly," the poor opium-smokers, be found only among the lower classes. In connection with this report, the hong merchants replied to various inquiries respecting the best mode of carrying on the opium trade in case it should be legalized, and their mode of conducting commerce generally; adding that it was beyond their power to control the smuggling traffic or restrain the exportation of sycee, and showed that the balance of trade would naturally leave the country in bullion. These papers are fairly drawn up, and their perusal cannot fail to elevate the character of the Chinese for consideration, carefulness, and business-like procedure.[1]

There were other statesmen, however, who regarded Hü Naitsí's memorial as a dangerous step in the downward path, and sounded the alarm. Among these the foremost was Chu Tsun, a cabinet minister, who sent in a counter-memorial couched in the strongest terms. He advised that the laws be more strictly maintained, and cited instances to show that when the provincial authorities earnestly set about it they could put the trade down; that the people would soon learn to despise all laws if those against opium-smoking were suspended; and that recreant officers should be superseded and punished. His indignation warms as he goes on: "It has been represented that advantage is taken of the laws against opium by extortionate underlings and worthless vagrants, to benefit themselves. Is it not known, then, that when government enacts a law, there is necessarily an infraction of that law? And though the law should sometimes be relaxed and become ineffectual, yet surely it should not on that account be abolished; any more than we

---

[1] *Chinese Repository*, Vol. V., pp. 139, 259, 385 ff.

should altogether cease to eat because of stoppage of the throat. The laws which forbid the people to do wrong may be likened to the dikes which prevent the overflowing of water. If any one urging, then, that the dikes are very old and therefore useless, we should have them thrown down, what words could express the consequences of the impetuous rush and all-destroying overflow! Yet the provincials, when discussing the subject of opium, being perplexed and bewildered by it, think that a prohibition which does not *utterly* prohibit is better than one which does not effectually prevent the importation of the drug. . . . If we can but prevent the importation of opium, the exportation of dollars will then cease of itself, and the two offences will both at once be stopped. Moreover, is it not better, by continuing the old enactments, to find even a partial remedy for the evil, than by a change of the laws to increase the importation still further?"

He then proceeds to show that the native article could not compete with the foreign, for it would not be as well manufactured, and moreover "all men prize what is strange and undervalue whatever is in ordinary use." Its cultivation would occupy rich and fertile land now used for nutritive grains: "To draw off in this way the waters of the great fountain requisite for the production of food and raiment, and to lavish them upon the root whence calamity and disaster spring forth, is an error like that of the physician who, when treating a mere external disease, drives it inward to the heart and centre of the body. Shall the fine fields of Kwangtung, which produce their three crops every year, be given up for the cultivation of this noxious weed?" He says the question does not concern property and duties, but the welfare and vigor of the people; and quotes from the *History of Formosa* a passage showing the way in which the natives there were enervated by using it, and adds that the purpose of the English in introducing opium into the country has been to weaken and enfeeble it. Kanghí long ago (1717) remarked, he observes, "There is cause for apprehension, lest in the centuries or millenniums to come China may be endangered by collisions with the various nations of the West who come hither from beyond the seas." And now, in less than two centuries, "we see the commencement of that danger which he apprehended."

The suggestion of Hü Nai-tsí, to allow it to the people and interdict the officers, is called bad casuistry, "like shutting a woman's ears before you steal her earrings." He shows that this distinction will be vain, for it will be impossible to say who is of the people and who are officers, for all the latter are taken from the body of the former. The permission will induce people to use it who now refrain from fear of the laws; for even the proposal has caused "thieves and villains on all hands to raise their heads and open their eyes, gazing about and pointing the finger under the notion that when once these prohibitions are repealed, thenceforth and forever they may regard themselves far from every restraint and cause of fear." He asserts that nothing but strong laws rigidly carried into effect will restrain them from their evil ways, and concludes by recommending increased stringency in their execution as the only hope of reformation.

This spirited paper was supported by another from a sub-censor, Hü Kiu, on the necessity of checking the exportation of silver, and recommending that a determined officer be sent to punish severely the native traitors, which would add dignity to the laws; and then the barbarians would be awed and consequently reform and be entirely defeated in their designs of conquering the country. He cites several instances of their outrageous violation of the laws, such as levelling graves in Macao for the purpose of making a road over them, landing goods there for entering them at Canton in order to evade the duties and port charges, and even riding in sedans with four bearers, like Chinese officers. Force needed only to be put forth a little and they would again be humbled to subjection; but if they still brought the pernicious drug, then inflict capital punishment upon them as well as upon natives. The sub-censor agrees with Chu Tsun regarding the designs of foreigners in doing so, that they wished first to debilitate and impoverish the land as a preparatory measure, for they never smoked the drug in their own country, but brought it all to China. This prevailing impression was derived mainly from the abstinence of foreign merchants and seamen.

Both these papers were transmitted to Canton for deliberation, although the local officers had already sent a memorial to the cabinet approving the suggestions of Hü Nai-tsí. At this time, however, it was properly remarked that "there had been a diversity of opinion in regard to it, some requesting a change in the policy hitherto adopted, and others recommending the continuance of the severe prohibitions. It is highly important to consider the subject carefully in all its bearings, surveying at once the whole field of action so that such measures may be adopted as shall continue forever in force, free from all failure." This subject, the most important, it cannot be doubted, which had ever been deliberated upon by the Emperor of China and his council, was now fairly brought before the whole nation: and if all the circumstances be taken into consideration, it was one of the most remarkable consultations of any age or country. A long experience of the baneful effects of opium-smoking upon the health, minds, and property of those who used it, had produced a deep conviction in the minds of well-wishers of their country of the necessity of some legal restraint over the people; while the annual drainage of specie at the rate of three or four million sterling for what brought misery and poverty in its train, alarmed those who cared only for the stability and prosperity of the country. The settlement or management of the question was one of equal difficulty and importance, and the result proved that it was quite beyond the reach of both their power and wisdom. Fully conscious of the weak moral principle in themselves and in their countrymen, they considered it right to restrain and deter the people by legislative enactments and severe penalties. Ignorant of the nature of commercial dealings, they thought it both practicable and necessary to limit the exportation of specie; for not having any substitute for coin or any system of national credit, there was serious hazard. otherwise, that the government would ultimately be bankrupted. It is unjust to the Chinese to say, as was argued by those who had never felt these sufferings, that all parties were insincere in their efforts to put down this trade, that it was a mere affectation of morality, and that no one would be more chagrined to see it stop than those apparently so strenuous against it. This assertion was made by Lord Palmerston in Parliament and re-echoed by the Indian officials; but those who have candidly examined the proceedings of the Chinese, or have lived among the people in a way to learn their real feelings, need not be told how incorrect is the remark. The highest statesman and the debilitated, victimized smoker alike agreed in their opinion of its bad effects, and both were pretty much in the position of a miserable lamb in the coil of a hungry anaconda.

The debate among the Chinese excited a discussion among foreigners, most of whom were engaged in the traffic. Here the gist of the question turned upon the points whether opium was really a noxious stimulant *per se*, and whether the Chinese government was sincere in its prohibitions in the face of the notorious connivance of the officers along the coast from Hainan to Tientsin. One writer conclusively proved its baneful effects upon the system when taken constantly, and that its habitual use in the smallest degree almost certainly led to intemperate or uncontrollable use; he then charges the crime of murder upon those who traffic in it, and asserts that "the perpetuating and encouraging and engaging in a trade which promotes disease, misery, crime, madness, despair, and death, is to be an accomplice with the guilty principals in that tremendous pursuit." He exposes the fallacy, hypocrisy, and guilt of the question whether it be less criminal for a man to engage in a pursuit which he knows to be injurious to his fellow-men, because if he does not do so some one else will. The Court of Directors, even, whom all the world knows to be chief managers of the cultivation, manufacture, and sale of the drug, says in one of its despatches that "so repugnant are their feelings to the opium trade, they would gladly, in compassion to mankind, put a total end to the consumption of opium if they could. But they cannot do this, and as opium will be grown somewhere or other, and will be largely consumed in spite of all their benevolent wishes, they can only do as they do"!

Another Englishman engaged in the traffic defended it on the ground that what is bad now was always bad; and the Emperor and his ministers had doubtless other grounds for their sudden opposition. He asserts that opium is "a useful soother, a harmless luxury, and a precious medicine, except to those who abuse it," and that while a few destroy themselves, the prudent many enjoy a pleasing solace, to get which tends to produce the persevering economy and the never-ceasing industry of the Chinese. He estimates that at a daily allowance of one and one-third ounce not more than one person in three hundred and twenty-six touches the pipe, and that there were not *more* than nine hundred and twelve thousand victimized smokers in the Empire. He also remarked that the present mode of conducting the trade by large capitalists kept it respectable, and that if their characters were held up to odium and infamy it would get into the hands of desperadoes, pirates, and maranders. He looked upon the efforts to put it down as utterly futile as the proclamations of Elizabeth were to put down hops, or the Counterblaste of James to stop tobacco.

This rejoinder was responded to by two writers, who clearly exhibited its unsoundness and ridiculed the plea that the trade should be kept in the hands of gentlemen and under the direction of a monopoly. The smuggler brought his vessel on the coast, and there waited till the people came off for his merchandise, disposing of it without the least risk to himself, "coolly commenting on the injustice of the Chinese government in refusing the practice of international law and reciprocity to countries whose subjects it only knows as engaged in constant and gross infraction of laws, the breaking of which affects the basis of all good government, the morals of the country." The true character of the smuggling trade is well set forth:

Reverse the picture. Suppose, by any chance, that Chinese junks were to import into England, as a foreign and fashionable luxury, so harmless a thing as arsenic or corrosive sublimate; that after a few years it became a rage; that thousands, yea, hundreds of thousands used it, and that its use was, in consequence of its bad effects, prohibited. Suppose that, in opposition to the prohibition, junks were stationed in St. George's Channel with a constant supply, taking occasional trips to the Isle of Wight and the mouth of the Thames when the officers were sufficiently attentive to their duty at the former station to prevent its introduction there. Suppose the consumption to increase annually, and to arouse the attention of the government and of those sound-thinking men who foresaw misery and destruction from the rapid spread of an insidious, unprofitable, and dangerous habit. Suppose, in fact, that, *mutato nomine*, all which has been achieved here had been practised there. Suppose some conservators of the public morals to be aroused at last, and to remonstrate against its use and increase; and that among the nation sending forth this destroyer to prey on private happiness and public virtue, one or two pious and well-meaning *bonzes* were to remonstrate with their countrymen on the enormity of their conduct:—how wonderfully consolatory to one party, and unanswerable to the other, must be the remark of the well-dressed and well-educated Chinese merchant: "Hai ya! my friend, do not you see my silk dress and the crystal knob on my cap; don't you know that I have read and can quote Confucius, Mencius, and all the Five Books; do you not see that the barbarians are passionately fond of arsenic, that they will have it, and even go so far as to pay for it; and can you, for one moment, doubt that it would not be much worse for them if, instead of my bringing it, it were left to the chance, needy, and uncertain supply which low men of no capital could afford to bring?"[1]

The writer shows that instead of only one person in every three hundred and twenty-six using the pipe, it was far more probable that at least one out of every one hundred and fifty (or about two million five hundred thousand in all) of the population was a victimized smoker. The assertion of its being a harmless luxury to the many, like wine or beer, is disputed, and the sophisticated argument of its use as a means of hospitality exploded. "What would a benevolent and sober-minded Chinese think," he asks, "were the sophistry of the defenders of this trade translated for him? Where would he find the high-principled and high-minded inhabitants of the far-off country? How could he be made to comprehend that the believers in and practisers of Christian morality advocated a trade so ruinous to his country? That the government of India compelled the growth of it by unwilling ryots; and that, instead of its being brought to China by 'desperadoes, pirates, and marauders,' it was purveyed by a body of capitalists, not participating certainly in what they carry, but supplying the Indian revenue safely and peaceably; that the British government and others encouraged it; and that the agents in the traffic were constantly residing at Canton, protected by the government whose laws they outraged, but monstrously indignant, and appealing to their governments, if No. 2 longcloths are classed as No. 1 through the desperate villany of some paltry custom-house servant?"

The other writer exposes the sinful fallacy of the argument

---

[1] *Chinese Repository*, Vol V., p. 409.

of expediency, and then proceeds to show how great an obstacle it is in the way of diffusing the gospel among the Chinese. We must refer to their own remarks[1] for the fuller development of the arguments, but this one showed the earnestness of his convictions by offering a premium of £100 for the best essay " showing the effects of the opium trade on the commercial, political, and moral interests of the nations and individuals connected therewith, and pointing out the course they ought to pursue in regard to it." There was, however, so little interest in the subject that this premium was never awarded, though the proposal was extensively advertised both in China and England.

The governor of Canton and his colleagues soon learned that the feeling at court was rather against legalizing the drug, though they were directed to report concerning the amount of duty proper to be levied on it; and to show their zeal, arrested several brokers and dealers. A-ming, one of the linguists, was severely tortured and exposed in the cangue for exporting sycee; others escaped similar treatment by absconding. The chief superintendent naïvely expressed his opinion that "the legalization of the trade in opium would afford his Majesty's government great satisfaction," but suggested that the gradual diversion of British capital into other channels would be attended with advantageous consequences. To one situated between his own government, which promoted the preparation and importation of opium, and the Chinese government, which was now making extraordinary efforts to regulate it, and deeply sensible of the injury resulting from its use to the people around him, and to the reputation of his own and all foreign nations from the constant infraction of the laws, the proposed step of legalization offered a timely relief. No one was more desirous of putting a stop to this destructive traffic than Captain Elliot, but knowing the impossibility of checking it by laws, he naturally wished to see the multitude of political and commercial evils growing out of smuggling done away with. There were, indeed, many things to urge in favor of this

---

[1] *Chinese Repository*, Vol. V., pp. 407, 413, and passim.

course; but the fact ought never to be lost sight of, and be mentioned to the lasting credit of the Emperor Taukwang and his advisers, in the midst of their perplexity and weakness, that he would not admit opium because it was detrimental to his people.

The conflict was now fairly begun; its issue between the parties, so unequally matched—one having almost nothing but the right on its side, the other assisted by every material and physical advantage—could easily be foreseen. Captain Elliot, as the recognized head of the British trade, received an order through the hong merchants from the provincial authorities to drive away the receiving-ships from Lintin, and send the Emperor's commands to his king, that henceforth they be prohibited coming. He replied that he could not transmit any orders to his own sovereign which did not come to him direct from the government, and quoted the recent instance of the governor-general of Fuhkien communicating directly with the captain of a British ship of war. The governor was therefore forced to send his orders to the prefect and colonel of the department to be enjoined on Captain Elliot. He replied by promising to send it to his country, and adds, in true diplomatic style, unworthy of himself and his nation: "He has already signified to your excellency, with truth and plainness, that his commission extends only to the regular trade with this Empire; and further, that the existence of any other than this trade has never yet been submitted to the knowledge of his own gracious sovereign." Captain Elliot transmitted with these "orders" a minute account of the condition of the opium trade, and a memorandum respecting the desirableness of opening communication with the court. Lord Palmerston, in reply, intimates that "her Majesty's government do not see their way in such a measure with sufficient clearness to justify them in adopting it at the present moment." He adds that no protection can be afforded to "enable British subjects to violate the laws of the country to which they trade. Any loss, therefore, which such persons may suffer in consequence of the more effectual execution of the Chinese laws on this subject, must be borne by the parties who have brought that loss on themselves by their own acts." A most paradoxical but convenient position for this "honorable" officer of the English government to assume, and worthy to be recorded in contrast to the utterances from Peking.

Near the close of 1837 the British flag was again hauled down at Canton, and the superintendent returned to Macao because he refused to superscribe the word *pin*, or 'petition,' upon his communications, according to his instructions, and the governor declined to receive them without it. In July, 1838, Sir Frederick Maitland arrived in the Wellesley (74), and was brought into correspondence with the Chinese Admiral Kwan, in consequence of the forts firing upon an English schooner passing the Bogue and stopping her to inquire whether he or any of his crew or women were on board. The Wellesley and her two consorts were anchored near the forts, and the Chinese admiral made a full apology for the mistake; his conduct in the affair was very creditable both to his judgment and temper. As soon as Sir Frederick arrived, Captain Elliot vainly endeavored to reopen correspondence with the governor by sending an open letter to the city gates, which was received and taken to him, but returned in the evening because it had not the required superscription.

Having now fully taken the sense of the Empire in the replies received from all its highest officials, the Emperor Taukwang increased his efforts to suppress the trade. In April, 1838, a native named Kwoh Sí-ping was publicly strangled at Macao by express command of the Emperor, as a warning to others not to engage in exporting sycee or introducing opium. The execution was conducted by the district magistrate and subprefect with dignity and order in the presence of a crowd of natives and foreigners. More than fifty small craft under the English or American flag were constantly plying off the port of Canton, most of them engaged in smuggling. Sometimes the government exerted its power; boats were destroyed, smugglers seized and tortured, and the sales checked; then it went on again as briskly as ever. These boats were easily caught, for the government could exercise entire control over its own subjects; but when the foreign schooners, heavily armed and manned, sailed up and down the river delivering the drug, the revenue cruisers were afraid to attack them. The hong merchants addressed a note to all foreign residents concerning them, the close of which vividly exhibits their unlucky position as the "responsible advisers" of the barbarians: "Lately we have repeatedly received edicts from the governor and hoppo severely reprimanding us; and we have also written to you, gentlemen of the different nations, several times, giving you full information of the orders and regulations, that you might perfectly obey them and manage accordingly; but you, gentlemen, continue wholly regardless."

Collisions became more and more frequent between the Chinese and their rulers, in consequence of the increased stringency of the orders from court. In September, in an affray near Whampoa between the military and villagers, several persons were killed and scores arrested. The retailers at Canton were imprisoned, and those found in other places brought there in chains. In Hupeh it was reported that the officers had punished arrested smokers by cutting out a portion of the upper lip to incapacitate them from using the pipe. Still, such was the venality of the officers that even at this time the son of Governor Tăng himself was engaged in the traffic, and many of the underlings only seized the drug from the smuggling-boats to retail it themselves. The memorial of Hwang Tsioh-tsz', advising the penalty of death, was promulgated in Canton; and the Emperor's rescript urged to stronger measures. In a rapid survey of the ill effects from the use of the drug, Hwang acknowledges that it had extended to Manchuria, and pervaded all ranks of official and humble life. The efflux of silver "into the insatiate depths of transmarine regions" had caused the rate of exchange for cash to rise until it was difficult to carry on the business of government. He then reviews the different plans proposed for checking the cause of all this evil, such as guarding the ports, stopping the entire foreign trade, arresting the smugglers, shutting up the shops, and, lastly, encouraging the home growth. He confesses that the bribes paid the coast-guard service and the maritime officers are so great as entirely to prevent their vigilance; and that the home-prepared drug does not yield the same stimulus as the foreign article. As a last resort, he proposes to increase the penalties upon the consumers, laying all the blame upon them, and advises death to be awarded all who smoke opium after a year's warning has been given them. The well-known subdivision of responsibility was to be made doubly strong by requiring bonds of every tithing and hundred that there were no smokers within their limits. Officers found guilty were not only to be executed, but their children deprived of the privilege of competing at the public examination. One cannot withhold a degree of sympathy for the helpless condition of the officers and statesmen of a great Empire sincerely desirous of doing their country service, and yet so sadly ignorant of their false position by their assumption of supremacy over the very nation whom they could not restrain, and whose officials they rejected for a formality. They might as well have tried to concert a measure to stop the Yangtsz' River in its impetuous flow, as to check the opium trade by laws and penalties.

On December 3, 1838, about two peculs of opium were seized while landing at the factories, and the coolies carried into the city. They declared that they had been sent to Whampoa by Mr. Innes, a British merchant, to obtain the opium from an American ship consigned to Mr. Talbot. The governor ordered the hong merchants to expel these two gentlemen and the ship within three days, on the garbled testimony of the two coolies. Mr. Talbot sent in a communication, stating that neither the ship nor himself had anything to do with the opium, and obtained a reversal of the order to leave. The hong merchants were justly irritated, and informed the Chamber of Commerce that they would not rent their houses to any who would not give a bond to abstain from such proceedings, and refusing to open the trade until such bonds were given; they furthermore declared their intention to pull Mr. Innes' house down if he refused to depart. The Chamber protested that "the inviolability of their personal dwellings was a point imperatively necessary" for their security; the hong merchants then resorted to entreaty, stating their difficult position between their own rulers on one side, who held them responsible for executing their orders, and the foreigners on the other, over whom they had little or no power. The Chamber could only express its regret at the unjust punishment inflicted on a hong merchant, Punhoyqua, for this, and reassert its inability to control the acts of any foreigner.

The governor had put himself in this helpless condition by refusing Captain Elliot's letters; and it is remarkable that he hesitated to arrest Mr. Innes, when one word would have set the populace on the factories and their tenants, and destroyed them all. As an alternative, he now resolved to show foreigners what consequences befel natives who dealt in opium; and while Mr. Innes still remained in Canton, he sent an officer with fifteen soldiers to execute Ho Lau-kin, a convicted dealer, in front of the factories. The officer was proceeding to carry his orders into effect near the American flag-staff, when the foreigners sallied out, pushed down the tent he was raising, and told him in loud tones not to execute the man there. Quite unprepared for this opposition, he hastily gathered up his implements and went into a neighboring street, where the man was strangled. Meanwhile a crowd collected to see these extraordinary proceedings, whom the foreigners endeavored to drive away, supposing that a little determination would soon scatter them. Blows, however, were returned, the foreigners driven into their factories, and the gates shut; the crowd had now become a mob, and under the impression that two natives had been seized, they began to batter the fronts and break the windows with stones and brickbats. They had had possession of the square about three hours, and the danger was becoming imminent, when the Pwanyu hien, or 'district magistrate,' came up, with three or four other officers, attended by a small body of police. Stepping out of his sedan he waved his hand over the crowd, the lictors pouncing upon three or four of the most active, whom they began to chastise upon the spot, and the storm was quelled. About twenty soldiers, armed with swords and spears, took their stand in a conspicuous quarter; the magistrate and his retinue seated themselves, leaving the hong merchants and the police to disperse the crowd. The foreigners were also assured that all should be kept quiet during the night, but not a word was said to them regarding their conduct in interfering with the execution or their folly in bringing this danger upon themselves. This occurrence tended to impress both the government and people with contempt and hatred for foreigners and their characters, fear of their designs, and the necessity of restraining them. The majority of them were engaged in the opium trade, and all stood before the Empire as violators of the laws, while the people themselves suffered the dreadful penalty.

There is no room for the details and correspondence connected with this remarkable incident.[1] Captain Elliot now reappeared in Canton, and at a general meeting expressed his conviction of the cause of these untoward events in the smuggling traffic on the river, declaring his intention of ordering all the British-owned vessels to leave it within three days; he moreover expressed the hope that the further step of opening communication with the provincial authorities to obtain their co-operation to drive them out would be prevented by their speedy departure. Injunctions and entreaties to his countrymen were, however, alike unavailing, and he accordingly addressed the governor, stating his wish to co-operate in driving them out. In a public notice he remarked that "this course of traffic was rapidly staining the British character with deep disgrace" and exposing the regular commerce to imminent jeopardy, and that he meant to shrink from no responsibility in drawing it to a conclusion. The governor, as was expected, praised the superintendent for his offer, but left him to do the whole work; remarking, in that peculiar strain of Chinese conceit which so effectually forestalls our sympathy for their difficulties, that "it may well be conceived that these boats trouble me not one iota:"—as if all he had to do was to arise in his majesty, and they were gone. The boats, however, gradually left the river. Mr. Innes retired, and the regular trade was resumed in January.

No British consular officer has been placed in a more difficult and humiliating dilemma, and Captain Elliot did himself honor in his efforts. The English newspapers ridiculed him as a tide-waiter of the Chinese custom-house, a man who aided the

---

[1] *Chinese Repository*, Vol. VII., pp. 437–456.

cowardly authorities to carry their orders into effect, thereby staining the honor of her Majesty's commission. Although he did not intend to draw a line between the heinousness of the opium trade inside of the Bogue and its harmlessness beyond that limit, still there were good reasons, under his peculiar position, for some action to show the Chinese government that British power would not protect British subjects in violating the laws of China.

At this period the Peking government had taken its course of action. Reports had been received from the provincial authorities almost unanimously recommending increased stringency to abolish the traffic. History, so far as we know, does not record a similar example of an arbitrary, despotic, pagan government taking the public sentiment of its own people before adopting a doubtful line of conduct. It was a far more momentous and difficult question than even the cabinet deemed it to be, while their conceit and ignorance incapacitated them from dealing with it prudently or successfully. There can be no reasonable doubt that the best part of his people and the moral power of the nation were with their sovereign in this attempt. Hü Nai-tsí was dismissed for proposing legalization, and three princes of the blood degraded for smoking opium ; arrests, fines, tortures, imprisonments, and executions were frequent in the provinces on the same grounds, all showing the determination to eradicate it. The governor of Hukwang, Lin Tseh-sü, was ordered to proceed to Canton, with unlimited powers to stop the traffic. The trade there was at this time almost suspended, the deliveries being small and at losing prices. Many underlings were convicted and summarily punished, and on February 26th Fung A-ngan was strangled in front of the factories for his connection with opium and participation in the affray at Whampoa. The foreign flags, English, American, Dutch, and French, were all hauled down in consequence. The entire stoppage of all trade was threatened, and the governor urged foreigners to send all opium ships from Chinese waters.

Commissioner Lin arrived in Canton March 10th. The Emperor sent him to inquire and act so as thoroughly to remove the source of the evil, for, says he, "if the source of the evil be not clearly ascertained, how can we hope that the stream of pernicious consequences shall be stayed? It is our full hope that the long-indulged habit will be forever laid aside, and every root and germ of it entirely eradicated; we would fain think that our ministers will be enabled to substantiate our wishes, and so remove from China the dire calamity." It was reported in Canton that the monarch, when recounting the evils which had long afflicted his people by means of opium, paused and wept, and turning to Lin, said: "How, alas! can I die and go to the shades of my imperial father and ancestors, until these direful evils are removed!" Such was the chief purpose of this movement on the part of the Chinese government, and Lin was invested with the fullest powers ever conferred on a subject. Although long experience of the ineffectiveness of Chinese edicts generally lead those residing in the country to regard them as mere verbiage, still, to say that they are all insincere and formal because they are ineffectual, is to misjudge and pervert the emotions of common humanity. Lin appears to have been well fitted for the mission; and if he had been half as enlightened as he was sincere, he would perhaps have averted the war which followed, and been convinced that legalization was the most judicious step he could recommend.

The commissioner spent a week making inquiries, during which time nothing was publicly heard from him; while natives and foreigners alike anxiously speculated as to his plans. It was not until March 18th that his first proclamations were issued to the hong merchants and foreigners; that to the latter required them to deliver up all the opium in the storeships, and to give bonds that they would bring no more, on penalty of death. The poor hong merchants were, as usual, instructed regarding their responsibility to admonish the foreigners, and strictly charged to procure these bonds, or they would be made examples of. Three days were allowed for compliance with these demands. The hoppo had already issued orders detaining all foreigners in Canton—in fact, making them prisoners in their own houses; communication with the shipping was suspended, troops were assembled about the factories, and armed cruisers stationed on the river. The Chamber of Commerce wrote to the hong merchants on the 20th, through their chairman, W. S. Wetmore, an American, stating that they would send a definite reply in four days, and adding that "there is an almost unanimous feeling in the community of the absolute necessity of the foreign residents of Canton having no connection with the opium traffic."

This paper was taken to the commissioner, and about ten o'clock P.M. the hong merchants again met the Chamber, and told them that if *some* opium was not given up two of their number would be beheaded in the morning. The merchants present, including British, Parsees, Americans, and others, acting as individuals, then subscribed one thousand and thirty-seven chests, to be tendered to the commissioner; but the hong merchants reported next morning that this amount was insufficient. In the afternoon Lin sent an invitation to Mr. Dent, a leading English merchant, to meet him at the city gates, who expressed his willingness to go if the commissioner would give him a safe-warrant guaranteeing his return within a day. The hong merchants returned without him; and the next morning two of them, Howqua and Mowqua, came again to his house with chains upon their necks, having been sent with an express order for him to appear. They repaired to the Chamber of Commerce then assembled, but all soon returned to Mr. Dent's house, where an animated debate took place, which resulted in the unanimous decision on the part of the foreign residents that he should not go into the city without the safe-warrant. This unexpected demand caused much discussion among foreigners, as it was doubtless a contrivance to secure a hostage; and the refusal of the former to give a written safe-warrant would probably have ended in seizing Mr. Dent and imprisoning him, if Howqua, the senior hong merchant, had not allowed everything to wait over one day till Monday. Mr. Dent's partner had that day seen the *an-chah sz'*, or 'provincial judge,' in the city to explain why he hesitated to go to Lin.

On the 22d Captain Elliot sent a note to the governor expressing his readiness to meet the Chinese officers, and use "his sincere efforts to fulfil the pleasure of the great Emperor as soon as it was made known to him." The Chinese could hardly draw any other conclusion from this admission than that he had the power, as well as the inclination to put down the opium trade, which he certainly could not do; it tended therefore to deceive them. This note was followed by a letter to Captain Blake, of the Larne, requesting his assistance in defending British property and life, and by a circular ordering all British ships, opium and others, to proceed to Hongkong and prepare themselves to resist every act of aggression. A second circular to British subjects detailed the reasons which compelled him to withdraw all confidence in the "justice and moderation of the provincial government," and demand passports for all his countrymen who wished to leave Canton, while counselling every one to make preparations to remove on board ship. Elliot now proceeded to Canton, which he safely reached about sunset Sunday evening, dressed in naval uniform and closely attended by cruisers watching his movements. The British flag was then hoisted, and Captain Elliot, conducting Mr. Dent to the consulate in the most conspicuous manner, summoned a public meeting, read his notice of the previous day, and told the hong merchants to inform the commissioner that he was willing to let Mr. Dent go into the city if he could accompany him.

His coming up the river had excited the apprehensions of the Chinese that he meant to force his way out again, and orders were issued to close every pass around the factories. By nine o'clock that evening the foreigners, about two hundred and seventy-five in number, were the only inmates of their houses. Patrols, sentinels, and officers, hastening hither and thither, with the blowing of trumpets and beating of gongs, added confusion to the darkness of the night.

On the 25th most of the foreign merchants of all nations signed a paper pledging themselves "not to deal in opium, nor to attempt to introduce it into the Chinese Empire:" how many of the individuals subsequently broke this pledge on the ground that it was forced from them cannot be stated, but part of the firms which signed it afterward actively engaged in the trade. Captain Elliot applied for passports for himself and countrymen, and requested the return of the servants, avoiding all reference to his promise of three days before, or mention of the cause of these stringent proceedings. His requests were refused; no native was allowed to bring food or water to the factories; letters could not be sent to Whampoa or Macao, except at imminent risk; the confinement was complete, and had been effected without the least personal harm. The heavy punishment which had fallen on Kwoh Sí-ping, Ho Lau-kin, and Fung A-ngan had now come near to the foreign agents of the traffic; but not an individual had been touched.

The commissioner next issued an exhortation to all foreigners, urging them to deliver the drug on four grounds, viz., because they were men and had reason; because the laws forbade its use, under severe penalties; because they should have feelings for those who suffered from using it; and because of their present duress, from which they would then be released. This paper, as were all those issued by Lin, was characterized by an unusual vigor of expression and cogency of reasoning, but betrayed the same arrogance and ignorance which had misled his predecessors. One extract will suffice. Under the first reason why the opium should be delivered up, he says that otherwise the retribution of heaven will follow them, and cites some cases to prove this:

> Now, our great Emperor, being actuated by the exalted virtue of heaven itself, wishes to cut off this deluge of opium, which is the plainest proof that such is the intention of high heaven! It is then a traffic on which heaven looks with disgust, and who is he that may oppose its will? Thus in the instance of the English chief Robarts, who violated our laws; he endeavored to get possession of Macao by force, and at Macao he died! Again, in 1834, Lord Napier bolted through the Bocca Tigris, but being overwhelmed with grief and fear he almost immediately died; and Morrison, who had been darkly deceiving him, died that very year also! Besides these, every one of those who have not observed our laws have either been overtaken with the judgments of heaven on returning to their country, or silently cut off ere they could return thither. Thus then it is manifest that the heavenly dynasty may not be opposed!

Two communications to Captain Elliot, from Lin through the prefect and district magistrates, accompanied this exhortation, stating his view of the superintendent's conduct in contumaciously resisting his commands and requiring him to give up the opium. For once in the history of foreign intercourse with China, these commands were obeyed, and after intimating his readiness to comply, Captain Elliot issued a circular on March 27th, which from its important results is quoted entire:

I, Charles Elliot, chief superintendent of the trade of British subjects in China, presently forcibly detained by the provincial government, together with all the merchants of my own and the other foreign nations settled here, without supplies of food, deprived of our servants, and cut off from all intercourse with our respective countries (notwithstanding my own official demand to be set at liberty that I might act without restraint), have now received the commands of the high commissioner, issued directly to me under the seals of the honorable officers, to deliver into his hand all the opium held by the people of my own country. Now I, the said chief superintendent, thus constrained by paramount motives affecting the safety of the lives and liberty of all the foreigners here present in Canton, and by other very weighty causes, do hereby, in the name and on the behalf of her Britannic Majesty's government, enjoin and require all her Majesty's subjects now present in Canton, forthwith to make a surrender to me for the service of her said Majesty's government, to be delivered over to the government of China, of all the opium under their respective control: and to hold the British ships and vessels engaged in the opium trade subject to my immediate direction: and to forward me without delay a sealed list of all the British-owned opium in their respective possession. And I, the said chief superintendent, do now, in the most full and unreserved manner, hold myself responsible for, and on the behalf of her Britannic Majesty's government, to all and each of her Majesty's subjects surrendering the said British-owned opium into my hands, to be delivered over to the Chinese government. And I, the said chief superintendent, do further especially caution all her Majesty's subjects here present in Canton, owners of or charged with the management of opium the property of British subjects, that failing the surrender of the said opium into my hands at or before six o'clock this day, I, the said superintendent, hereby declare her Majesty's government wholly free of all manner of responsibility in respect of the said British-owned opium. And it is specially to be understood that proof of British property and value of all British-owned opium surrendered to me agreeable to this notice, shall be determined upon principles, and in a manner hereafter to be defined by her Majesty's government.[1]

The guarantee offered in this notice was deemed sufficient by the merchants, though Captain Elliot had no authority to take such a responsibility, and exceeded his powers in giving it; being the authorized agent of the crown, however, his government was responsible for his acts, though the notice did not, nor could it, set any price upon the surrendered property.

At the time it was given it could not be honestly said that

[1] *Chinese Repository*, Vol. VII., p. 633.

the lives of foreigners were in jeopardy, and Lin had promised to reopen the trade as soon as the opium was delivered and the bonds given. What the other "very weighty causes" were must be guessed; but the requisition was promptly answered, and before night twenty thousand two hundred and eighty-three chests of opium had been surrendered, which Captain Elliot the next day tendered to the commissioner. Their market value at the time was not far from nine millions of dollars, and the cost price nearly eleven millions. Directions were sent to twenty-two vessels to anchor near the Bogue, to await orders for its delivery, the commissioner and the governor themselves going down forty miles to superintend the transfer. On April 2d the arrangements for delivering the opium were completed, and on May 21st it was all housed near the Bogue.

When the guard was placed about the factories, no native came near them for three days, but on the 29th a supply of sheep, pigs, poultry, and other provisions was "graciously bestowed" upon their inmates, most of whom refused them as gifts, which impressed Lin with the belief that they were not actually suffering for food. On May 5th the guards and boats were removed, and communication resumed with the shipping. Sixteen persons, English, Americans, and Parsees, named as principal agents in the opium trade, were ordered to leave the country and never return. On the 24th Captain Elliot left Canton, accompanied by the ten British subjects mentioned among the sixteen outlawed persons. In order still further to involve her Majesty's ministers in his acts, he forbade British ships entering the port, or any British subject living in Canton, on the ground that both life and property were insecure; there were, however, no serious apprehensions felt by other foreigners remaining there; and the propriety of the order was questioned by those who were serious sufferers from its action.

This success in getting the opium encouraged Lin to demand the bond, but although the captains of most of the ships signed it when the port was first opened, it was not required long after. The British merchants at Canton prepared a memorial to the foreign secretary of their government, recapitulating the aggressive acts of the Chinese government in stopping the legal trade, detaining all foreigners in Canton until the opium was surrendered, and requiring them to sign a bond not to bring it again, which involved their responsibility over those whom they could not control; but nothing was said in it of their own unlawful acts, no reference to their promises of a few months before, no allusion to the causes of these acts of aggression. Its burden was, however, to urge the government to issue a notice of its intentions respecting the pledge given them by the superintendent in his demand for the opium.

Lin referred to Peking for orders concerning the disposal of the opium, and his Majesty commanded the whole to be destroyed by him and his colleagues in the presence of the civil and military officers, the inhabitants of the coast, and the foreigners, "that they may know and tremble thereat." Captain Elliot, on the other hand, before it had all been delivered, wrote to his government, April 22d, his belief that the Chinese intended to sell it at a high price, remunerating the owners and pocketing the difference, preparatory to legalizing the traffic, and making some arrangements to limit the annual importation to a certain number of chests; consequently he recommended an "immediate and strong declaration to exact complete indemnity for all manner of loss" from the Chinese. He calls Lin "false and perfidious," though it is difficult to see why he applies these epithets to one who seems to have sincerely endeavored to carry out instructions, while his own communications certainly tended to mislead him. The sense of the responsibility he had assumed, and the irritating confinement under which it was written, account, in a measure, for this despatch, so different in its tenor from his previous declarations.

The opium was destroyed in the most thorough manner, by mixing it in parcels of two hundred chests, in trenches, with lime and salt water, and then drawing off the contents into the adjacent creek at low tide. Overseers were stationed to prevent the workmen or villagers from purloining the opium, and one man was summarily executed for attempting to carry away a small quantity. No doubt remained in the minds of persons who visited the place and examined the operation, that the entire quantity of twenty thousand two hundred and ninety-one chests received from the English (eight more having been sent from Macao) was completely destroyed:—a solitary instance in the history of the world of a pagan monarch preferring to destroy what would injure his subjects, rather than to fill his own pockets with its sale. The whole transaction will ever remain one of the most remarkable incidents in human history for its contrasts, and the great changes it introduced into China.[1]

The course of events during the remainder of the year 1839 presents a strange mixture of traffic and hostility. The British merchants were obliged to send their goods to Canton in ships sailing under other flags, which led the commissioner to issue placards exhorting British captains to bring their ships into port. This procedure brought out a rejoinder from Captain Elliot, giving the reasons why he had forbidden them to do so, and complaining of his own unjust imprisonment as unbecoming treatment to the "officer of a friendly nation, recognized by the Emperor, who had always performed his duty peacefully and irreproachably." Captain Elliot's own correspondence shows, however, that this is an unfair statement of the political relations between them.

While this matter of trade was pending, a drunken affray occurred at Hongkong with some English sailors, in which an inoffensive native named Lin Wei-hí lost his life. The commissioner ordered an inquest to be held, and demanded the murderer, according to Chinese law. The superintendent empanelled a regular court of criminal and admiralty jurisdiction at Hongkong, to try the seamen who had been arrested. He also offered

---

[1] Sir Robert Peel declared that this property was obtained by her Majesty's agent without any authority; but when the six millions of dollars were received from the Chinese as indemnity, the British government made its subjects receive their money in London, charged them with all expenses instead of paying it in China, and priced the opium at scarcely half what the East India Company had received from it, by taking the market rates when the trade at Canton was nominal. The merchants lost, with accruing interest, about two millions sterling, and "Sir R. Peel transferred a million sterling from their pockets to the public treasury."—*Chinese Repository*, Vol. XIII., p. 54 (from London paper).

a reward of $200 for such evidence as would lead to the conviction of the offenders; and advanced in all $2,000 to the friends of the deceased as some compensation for their heavy loss, and to the villagers for injuries done to them in the riot. Having formed the court, he politely invited the provincial officers to attend the trial; and when it was over, informed them that he had been unable to ascertain the perpetrator of the deed. Five sailors were convicted and punished for riotous conduct by fine and imprisonment, and sent to England under arrest, but to everybody's surprise were all liberated on their arrival. The proceedings in this matter were perfectly fair, and the commissioner should have been satisfied; but his subsequent violent conduct really placed the dispute on an entirely new ground, though he regarded his action as simply exercising the same prerogative of control over foreigners in both cases. Finding his demand for the murderer disregarded, he took measures against the English then in Macao which were calculated to bring serious loss upon the Portuguese population. His course was prompted by anger at losing the trade, and only injured his own cause. In order to relieve the unoffending and helpless people in Macao, Captain Elliot and all British subjects who could do so left the settlement August 26th, and went on board ship for a time. During this interval Lin and Governor Tăng visited Macao under an escort of Portuguese troops, but retired the same day. This move placed the English beyond his reach, but did not advance his efforts to drive the opium ships from the coast, or induce the regular traders to enter the port. The sales of opium had begun again even before the destruction of the drug, and rapidly increased when it was known that that immense quantity had really been destroyed. Lin now began to see that his plan of proceedings might not ultimately prove so successful as he had anticipated, for he was bound to remain at Canton until he could report the complete suppression of the contraband and safe continuance of the legal trade.

Finding that the British fleet at Hongkong was too strong to drive away, he forbade the inhabitants supplying the ships with provisions. This led to a collision between the British and three junks near Kowlung, which resulted, however, in no serious damage. On September 11th, Captain Elliot, having ordered all British vessels engaged in the opium trade to leave the harbor and coast, they mostly proceeded to Namoh. The Chinese burned the next day a Spanish vessel, the Bilbaino, in Macao waters, under the impression that she was English.

In unison with all the strange features of this struggle, while hostilities were going on, negotiations for continuing trade were entered into in October, when the commissioner signed the agreement, and Captain Elliot furnished security for its being conducted fairly. But the unauthorized entrance of the English ship Thomas Coutts, whose captain signed the bond, led to a rupture and the renewed demand for the murderer of Lin Wei-hí. Captain Elliot ordered all British ships to reassemble at Tungku under the protection of the ships of war Volage and Hyacinth. He also proceeded to the Bogue to request a withdrawal of the threats against the British until the two governments could arrange the difficulties, when an engagement ensued between Admiral Kwan, with a fleet of sixteen junks, and the two ships of war; three junks were sunk, one blown up, and the rest scattered. The commissioner had been foiled in all his efforts to destroy the opium trade and continue the legal commerce. As a last effort against the British, he declared their trade at an end after December 6, 1839, and issued an edict like that of Napoleon at Berlin, November 19, 1806, forbidding their goods to be imported in any vessels. An enormous amount of property now lay at Canton and on board ship waiting to be exchanged in the course of regular trade, but only the opium traffic flourished.

The close of the year 1839 saw the two nations involved in serious difficulties, and as the events here briefly recounted were the cause of the war, it will be proper to compare the opinions of the two parties, in order to arrive at a better judgment upon the character of that contest. The degree of authority to be exercised over persons who visit their shores is acknowledged by Christian nations among themselves to be nearly the same as that over their own subjects; but none of these nations have conceded this authority to unchristian powers, as Turkey, Persia, or China, mainly because of the little security and justice to be expected. The Chinese have looked upon foreigners resorting to their ports as doing so by sufferance; they entered into no treaty to settle the conditions of authority on either side, for the latter considered themselves as sojourners and aliens, and the natives were unaware of their rights in the matter. Their right to prohibit the introduction of any particular articles was acknowledged, and the propriety of making regulations as to duties allowed. But traders from western nations often set light by the fiscal regulations of such countries as China, Siam, etc., if they can do so without personal detriment or loss of character; and where there is a want of power in the government, joined to a lack of moral sense in the people, all laws are imperfectly executed. No one acquainted with these countries is surprised at frequent and flagrant violations of law, order, justice or courtesy, both among rulers and ruled; yet the obligation of foreigners to obey just laws made known to them surely is not to be measured solely by the degree of obedience paid by a portion of the people themselves.

The Chinese government discussed the measure of legalizing a trade it could not suppress, but before constructing a law to that effect, it determined to make a final and more vigorous effort to stamp it out. Might makes right, or at least enforces it; had the Chinese possessed the power to destroy every ship found violating their laws, although the loss of life would have been dreadful, no voice would have been raised against the proceeding. "Her Majesty's government," said Lord Palmerston, "cannot interfere for the purpose of enabling British subjects to violate the laws of the country to which they trade." But in that case this power would not have been dared; the known weakness of the government emboldened both sellers and buyers, until Captain Elliot told the Foreign Secretary that "it was a confusion of terms to call the opium trade a smuggling trade."

Lin probably wished to get Mr. Dent as a hostage for the delivery of the opium in the hands of his countrymen, not to punish him for disobedience to previous orders; expecting no opposition to this demand, he seems to have been unwilling to seize him immediately, preferring to try persuasion and command longer, and detain him and other foreigners until he was obeyed; Captain Elliot he viewed as a mere head merchant. When, therefore, the attempt was made, as he supposed, to take Mr. Dent out of his hands, he was apprehensive of a struggle, and instantly took the strongest precautionary measures to prevent the prey escaping. Considerate allowance should be granted for the serious mistake he made of imprisoning the innocent with the guilty; but when Captain Elliot took Mr. Dent thus under his protection, the commissioner felt that his purpose would be defeated, and no opium obtained, if he began to draw a distinction. Besides, conscious that he possessed unlimited power over a few defenceless foreigners, nearly all of whom were in his eyes guilty, he cared very little where his acts fell. There is no good evidence to show that *he* seriously meditated anything which would hazard their lives. When he had received this vast amount of property, success evidently made him careless as to his conduct, and judging the probity and good faith of foreigners by his own standard, he deemed it safest to detain them until the opium was actually in his possession. Concluding that Captain Elliot did attempt to abscond with Mr. Dent, it is less surprising, therefore, that he should have looked upon his offers to "carry out the will of the great Emperor," when set at liberty, as a lure rather than a sincere proposition. In imprisoning him he had no more idea he was imprisoning, insulting, threatening, and coercing the representative of a power like Great Britain, or violating rules western powers call *jus gentium*, than if he had been the envoy from Siam or Lewchew. Whether he should not have known this is another question, and had he candidly set himself, on his arrival at Canton, to ascertain the power, position, and commerce of western countries, he would have found Captain Elliot sincerely desirous of meeting him in his endeavors to fulfil his high commission. Let us deal fairly by the Chinese rulers in their desire to restrain a traffic of which they knew and felt vastly more of its evil than we have ever done, and give Lin his due, though his endeavors failed so signally.

The opium was now obtained; no lives had been lost, nor any

one endangered; but the British government felt bound to pay its own subjects for their chests. The only source Captain Elliot suggested was to make the Chinese refund. The Emperor ordered it to be destroyed, and the commissioner, after executing that order, next endeavored to separate the legal from the contraband trade by demanding bonds; they had been taken in vain from the hong merchants, but there was more hope if taken directly from foreigners. The bonds were not made a pretext for war by the English ministry; that, on the part of England, according to Lord John Russell, was "set afoot to obtain reparation for insults and injuries offered her Majesty's superintendent and subjects; to obtain indemnification for the losses the merchants had sustained under threats of violence; and, lastly, to get security that persons and property trading with China should in future be protected from insult and injury, and trade maintained upon a proper footing." Looking at the war, therefore, as growing out of this trade, and waged to recover the losses sustained by the surrendry to the British superintendent, it was an *unjust* one. It was, moreover, an *immoral* contest, when the standing of the two nations was examined, and the fact could not be concealed that Great Britain, the first Christian power, really waged this war against the pagan monarch who had vainly endeavored to put down a vice hurtful to his people. The war was looked upon in this light by the Chinese; it will always be so looked upon by the candid historian, and known as the Opium War.

On the other hand, the war was felt by every well-wisher to China to involve far higher principles than the mere recovery of the opium; and had it been really held to be so by the English ministry, they would have done well to have alluded to them. Lin's reiterated demands for the murderer of Lin Wei-hi, though told that he could not be found, was only one form of the supremacy the Chinese arrogantly assumed over other nations. In all their intercourse with their fellow-men they maintained a patronizing, unfair, and contemptuous position, which left no alternative but withdrawal from their shores or a humiliating submission that no one feeling the least independence could endure. Not unjustly proud of their country in comparison with those near it, her Emperor, her rulers, and her people all believed her to be impregnably strong, portentously awful, and immensely rich in learning, power, wealth, and territory. None of them imagined that aught could be learned or gained from other nations; for the "outside barbarians" were dependent for their health and food upon the rhubarb, tea, and silks of the Inner Land. They had seen, indeed, bad specimens of western power and people, but there were equal opportunities for them to have learned the truth on these points. The reception of the religion of the Bible, the varied useful branches of science, and the many mechanical arts known in western lands, with the free passage of their own people abroad, were all forbidden to the millions of China by their supercilious rulers; they thereby preferred to remain the slaves of debasing superstitions, ignorant of common science, and deprived of everything which Christian benevolence, philanthropy, and knowledge could and wished to impart to them. This assumption of supremacy, and a real impression of its propriety, was a higher wall around them than the long pile of stones north of Peking. Force seemed to be the only effectual destroyer of such a barrier, and in this view the war may be said to have been necessary to compel the Chinese government to receive western powers as its equals, or at least make it treat their subjects as well as it did its own people. There was little hope of an adjustment of difficulties until the Chinese were compelled to abandon this erroneous assumption; the conviction that it was unjust, unfounded, and foolish in itself could safely be left to the gradual influences of true religion, profitable commerce, and sound knowledge.

The report of the debate in the British Parliament on this momentous question hardly contains a single reference to this feature of the Chinese government. It turned almost wholly upon the opium trade, and whether the hostilities had not proceeded from the want of foresight and precaution on the part of her Majesty's ministers. The speeches all showed ignorance of both principles and facts: Sir James Graham asserted that the governors of Canton had sanctioned the trade; Sir George Staunton that it would not be safe for British power in India if these insults were not checked, and that the Chinese had far exceeded in their recent efforts the previous acknowledged laws of the land! Dr. Lushington maintained that the connivance of the local rulers acquitted the smugglers; Sir John Hobhouse truly stated that the reason why the government had done nothing to stop the opium trade was that it was profitable; and Lord Melbourne, with still more fairness, said: "We possess immense territories peculiarly fitted for raising opium, and though I would wish that the government were not so directly concerned in the traffic, I am not prepared to pledge myself to relinquish it." The Duke of Wellington thought the Chinese government was insincere in its efforts, and therefore deserved little sympathy; while Lord Ellenborough spoke of the million and a half sterling revenue "derived from foreigners," which, if the opium monopoly was given up and its cultivation abandoned, they must seek elsewhere. No one advocated war on the ground that the opium had been seized, but the majority were in favor of letting it go on because it was begun. This debate was, in fact, a remarkable instance of the way in which a moral question is blinked even by conscientious persons whenever politics or interest come athwart its course. No declaration of war was ever published by Queen Victoria, further than an order in council to the admiralty, in which it was recited that "satisfaction and reparation for the late injurious proceedings of certain officers of the Emperor of China against certain of our officers and subjects shall be demanded from the Chinese government;" the object of this order was, chiefly, to direct concerning the disposal of such ships, vessels, and cargoes belonging to the Chinese as might be seized. Perhaps the formality of a declaration of war against a nation which knew nothing of the law of nations was not necessary, but if a minister plenipotentiary from Peking had been present at the debate in Parliament in April, 1840, he would have declared the motives and proceedings of his government strangely misrepresented. It was time that better ideas of one another should find place in their councils, and that means should be afforded the rulers of each nation to learn the truth.

The Chinese apparently foresaw the coming struggle, and

began to collect troops and repair their forts; Lin, now governor-general of Kwangtung, purchased the Chesapeake, a large ship, and appointed an intendant of circuit near Macao, to guard the coasts. The English carried on their trade under neutral flags, and Lin made no further efforts to annoy them. He, however, wrote two official letters to Queen Victoria, desiring her assistance in putting down the opium trade, in which the peculiar ideas of his countrymen respecting their own importance and their position among the nations of the earth were singularly exhibited.[1] Notwithstanding the causes of complaint he had against the English, he behaved kindly to the surviving crew of the Sunda, an English vessel wrecked on Hainan, and sent them, on their arrival at Canton, to their countrymen.

[1] *Chinese Repository*, Vol. VIII., pp. 9–12, 497–503; Vol. IX., pp. 241–257.

CHAPTER IV.

THE OPIUM WAR.

On June 22, 1840, before the advance part of the British force reached China, Sir Gordon Bremer published a notice of the blockade of the port of Canton. The Americans living there had requested Lin to let all their ships arriving before it was laid on come directly up the river. He granted the application, but declared it "to be an egregious mistake, analogous to an audacious falsehood, that the English contemplated putting on a blockade." Captain Elliot also issued a manifesto to the people, which was widely dispersed, setting forth the grievances which had been suffered by the English at the hands of Lin, and assuring them that no harm would come while they pursued their peaceful occupations—for the quarrel was entirely between the two governments, and the Queen had deputed high officers to make known the truth to the Emperor.

Sir Gordon Bremer's force of five ships of war, three steamers, and twenty-one transports reached Tinghai harbor July 4th. In reply to a summons to surrender, the Chinese officers declared their determination to resist as far as their means allowed; but complained of the hardship of being made answerable for wrongs done at Canton, upon which place the blow should properly fall. The attack was made on Sunday, July 5th, when the Wellesley (74) opened her guns on the town, which were answered by the junks and batteries. A few minutes sufficed to silence the latter, and three thousand men landed and menaced Tinghai, whose walls were lined with soldiers. The town was evacuated during the night, most of the respectable inhabitants going to Ningpo; many of the Chinese high officials were killed, which, with the experience of the terrible foreign force brought against them, disheartened their troops beyond measure.

Two days after this attack the joint plenipotentiaries, Admiral G. Elliot and Captain Elliot, arrived in the Melville (74) at Chusan. To the authorities at Amoy and Ningpo they sent copies of Lord Palmerston's letter to the Emperor, with a request to forward them to Peking; the officials declined, however, undertaking any such responsibility.

The prefect of Ningpo took measures to prevent the people of Chusan from "aiding and comforting" their conquerors by sending police-runners to mark those who supplied them; a purveyor from Canton was seized and brought back. An idea that the Chinese people wished to throw off the Manchu yoke, and a desire to conciliate the islanders, led the British to take less decided measures for supplying themselves with provisions than they otherwise would. A small party was sent to recapture the purveyor, but its unsuccessful trip over the island showed the unwillingness of the people to have anything to do with their invaders, while their dread was increased by the arrest of several village elders. Mr. Gutzlaff was stationed at Chusan, doing his best to reassure the people; and as he went around exhorting them to act peaceably, some of them asked him, "If you are so desirous of peace, why did you come here at all?"

After arranging the government of the island, the stations of the troops, and blockading of Amoy, Ningpo, and the mouths of the Min and Yangtsz' Rivers, the two plenipotentiaries left Tinghai and anchored off the Pei ho August 11th. Captain Elliot went ashore, and finding that Kíshen, the governor-general of Chihlí, was at Taku, delivered the letter to his messenger, who returned with a request for ten days' delay in which to lay it before the Emperor. During this interval the ships visited the coast of Liautung to procure provisions, which they obtained with some difficulty. No message coming off, a strong boat-force was sent ashore on the 28th, with a menacing letter to Kíshen, when it was ascertained that the reply had in reality been awaiting the return of the ships during several days. Arrangements were now made for a personal interview at Taku between Kíshen and Captain Elliot, on Sunday, August 30th, in a large tent. Kíshen argued his side of the question with great tact and ability, sincerely urging the argument that his master had the most unquestionable right to treat the English as he had done, for they were and had enrolled themselves his tributary subjects. He could not treat definitely on all the points in dispute, and obtained a further delay of six days in order to refer again to Peking. The conclusion was the reasonable arrangement that Kíshen should meet the English plenipotentiaries at Canton, where the truth could be better ascertained; and on September 15th the squadron returned to Chusan.

While these things were taking place at Taku, there had occurred a few skirmishes elsewhere. A shipwrecked crew had fallen into Chinese hands and been carried to Ningpo, and some foraging parties were roughly handled. Lin tried to inspirit his troops by offering large rewards for British ships and subjects, and a force of about one thousand two hundred men was stationed in and around the Barrier at Macao. Captain Smith, however, moved two sloops and a steamer near their position, and soon drove the soldiers away, destroying their guns and barracks.

Lin was busy enlisting volunteers and preparing the defences of Canton, but in the summer he was ordered to return "with the speed of flames" to Peking. His Majesty was unnecessarily severe upon his servant: "You have not only proved yourself unable to cut off their trade," he says, "but you have also proved yourself unable to seize perverse natives. You have but dissembled with empty words, and so far from having been any help in the affair, you have caused the waves of confusion to arise, and a thousand interminable disorders are sprouting; in fact, you have been as if your arms were tied, without knowing what to do: it appears, then, you are no better than a wooden image. When I meditate on all these things, I am filled with anger and melancholy." Trade was carried on notwithstanding the blockade, by sending tea and goods through Macao; and many ships loaded for England and the United States.

Admiral Elliot entered into a truce with Ílípu, governor-general of Chehkiang, by which each party agreed to observe certain boundaries. Sickness and death had made sad inroads into the health and numbers of the troops at Tinghai, owing to their bad location, malaria, and improper food; more than four hundred out of the four thousand landed in July having died, and three times that number being in the hospitals. The people dared not reopen their shops until after the truce; the visits paid to various parts of the island better informed the inhabitants of the personal character of their temporary rulers, and a profitable trade in provisions encouraged them to farther acquaintance.

The two plenipotentiaries returned November 20th, and immediately sent a steamer bearing a despatch from Ílípu to Kíshen; the vessel was fired upon by an officer unacquainted with the meaning of a white flag—the intent and privileges of which were after this understood; Kíshen made an ample apology for this mishap. Negotiations were resumed during the month of December, but the determination of the Chinese to resist rather than grant full indemnity for the opium was more and more apparent. Kíshen probably found more zeal among the people for a fight than he had supposed, but his own desires were to settle the matter "more soon, more better." What demands were made as a last alternative are not known, but one of them, the cession of the island of Hongkong, he refused to grant, and broke off the discussion. Commodore Bremer thereupon attacked and took the forts at Chuenpí and Taikok-tau on January 7th, when the further progress of his forces was stayed by Kíshen, who was present and saw enough to convince him of the folly of resistance.

On January 20th the suspended negotiations had proceeded so far that Captain Elliot announced the conclusion of preliminary arrangements upon four points, viz., the cession of the island and harbor of Hongkong to the British crown, an indemnity of six millions of dollars in annual instalments, direct official intercourse upon an equal footing, and the immediate resumption of English trade at Canton. By these arrangements Chusan and Chuenpí were to be immediately restored to the Chinese, the prisoners at Ningpo released, and the English allowed to occupy Hongkong. One evidence of Kíshen's "scrupulous good faith," mentioned in Captain Elliot's notice, is the edict he put up on Hongkong, telling the inhabitants they were now under English authority. Two interviews took place after this, at the last of which it was plain that two of the four stipulations, viz., the first instalment of a million of dollars, and opening of trade by February 1st, would not be fulfilled. The intimations of the designs of the court were so evident that the treaty was probably never even presented to the Emperor for ratification.

Kíshen carried his negotiations thus far, with the hope perhaps that an adjustment of the difficulties on such terms would be accepted by his imperial master. On the other hand, Lin and his colleagues memorialized him as soon as Kíshen came to Canton against peaceful measures, and their recommendations as to the necessity of resistance were strongly backed by the mortifying loss of Chusan. The approach of a large force to the Pei ho alarmed his Majesty, and conciliatory measures were taken, and a reference to Canton proposed before settling the dispute; when the men-of-war left, he was inclined for peace, and issued orders not to attack the ships while the discussions were going on. But the memorials had already changed his mind, and war was determined on at the date of signing the treaty. It is probable if, instead of seizing Chusan, which had given no cause of provocation, the English had gone up the Yangtsz' kiang and Pei ho, and stationed themselves there until their demands were granted, peace would have been soon made. But, in that case, would the vain notion of their supremacy have left the Chinese?

Looking back forty years, one can recognize the benefit to both parties which resulted from the failure of this treaty. The great desire of Christian people, who believed that China was finally to receive the gospel, was that it might be opened to their benevolent efforts, but this treaty left the country as closed as ever to all good influences, commercial, political, social, and religious, while the evils of smuggling, law-breaking, and opium-smoking remained unmolested. The crisis which had brought out this expedition was not likely soon to recur, and if this failed to break down its seclusiveness, no other nation would attempt the task. Every well-wisher of China cherished the hope that, since this unfortunate conflict must needs be, its outcome would leave the entire land fully accessible to the regenerating, as well as shielded from the evil influences of Christian nations.

Captain Elliot appreciated the dilemma into which the Emperor had been brought by the acts of Lin, and knew that ignorance was much more the misfortune than the fault of both; he acted humanely, therefore, in pursuing a mild course at first, until the points at issue had been fairly brought before the people as well as the cabinet. However justly some parts of his conduct may have merited criticism, this praiseworthy feature of his policy by no means earned the torrent of abuse he received for consistently pursuing such a course. His countrymen would have had him burn, kill, and destroy, as soon as the expedition reached the coast, before even stating his demands at court; and during his negotiations with Kíshen, and when Chusan was restored, a smile of contempt at his supposed gullibility was everywhere seen. The treaty of the Bogue, though formed in good faith by both commissioners, was rejected by both sovereigns, though for opposite reasons; by Victoria, because it did not grant enough, by Taukwang, because it granted too much.

The Emperor issued orders to resume the war, collect troops from the provinces upon Canton and Tinghai, in order to "destroy and wipe clean away, to exterminate and root out the rebellious barbarians," and urged the people to regard them with the same bitterness they did their personal enemies. His mandate is couched in strong terms, saying that his enemies have been rebellious against heaven, opposing reason, one in spirit with the brute beasts, "beings that the overshadowing vault and all-containing earth can hardly suffer to live," obnoxious to angels and men, and that he must discharge his heaven-conferred trust by sweeping them from the face of the earth. This decree exhibited the true principles of action of this proud government, which deliberately rejected the offer of peace, and determined to uphold its fancied supremacy to the utmost. China must now win or break.

Hostile intentions had become so evident that Captain Elliot announced that Commodore Bremer would return to the Bogue with the force; the boats of the Nemesis were fired upon while sounding, and the battery near Anunghoy was attacked the same day that Chusan was evacuated. Rewards of $50,000 were offered for Elliot, Bremer, Morrison, and other ringleaders, and all the defences put in the best condition. On February 26th the Bogue forts were all taken, Admiral Kwan falling at his post. The British had nine ships, assisted by less than five hundred troops, and two steamers. The Chinese force was probably over three thousand, but it made no resistance after the batteries were taken; the total loss was supposed to be not far from a thousand. The forts were built so solidly that few were killed by the broadsides of the ships, and their magazines so well protected that no explosions took place; the powder found in them was used to demolish the walls. There were in all eight large forts on the sides of the river and Wangtong Island, forming altogether a line of batteries which would have been impregnable in the hands of European troops, and was not without reason deemed to be so by the Chinese themselves.

The next day the small ships moved up to the First Bar, where a long fortification on the river bank, and an intrenched camp of two thousand troops, defended by upward of a hundred cannon, with a strong raft thrown across the river, showed a resolution to make a stand. The ships and steamers opened a hot fire upon the batteries and camp, which returned it as well as they could, but the loss of life was greatest when the English landed. Many instances of personal bravery showed that the Chinese were not all destitute of courage, but without discipline and better weapons it was of no avail. Nearly one-fourth were killed, their camp burned, the Chesapeake and all her stores blown up, and most of the crew killed. The raft was easily removed by the steamers, to the mortification of the Chinese, who had trusted that this might prove a permanent barrier to the approach of ships to the city. From this point the way was open to within five miles of Canton, and when the forts at that place were taken, the prefect met Captain Elliot on March 3d with a flag of truce proposing a suspension of hostilities for three days.

Kíshen had already been ordered to return to Peking to await his trial; his memorial[1] on hearing of his degradation does him credit. Íliang was left in command of the province until four general officers, leading large bodies of troops, should arrive. The highest of these was Yihshan, a nephew of the Emperor, assisted by Yang Fang, Lungwăn, and Tsíshin. On the part of the English, Major-General Sir Hugh Gough arrived from India to take command of the land forces, and Sir Gordon Bremer sailed for Calcutta to procure recruits. Bodies of troops were gathering in and around Canton to the amount of five or six thousand, most of whom had come from the North-West Provinces, and were not less strange and formidable to the citizens than were their foreign enemies.

After the truce had expired the English moved toward Canton by both the channels leading to the city, the iron steamer Nemesis proceeding up the Inner Passage, subduing all obstacles in her way until every fort, raft, battery, camp, and stockade between the ocean and Canton had been taken or destroyed, and the city lay at their mercy. The factories had been kept safely, and were occupied by British troops just two years after Lin had imprisoned the foreigners there. A second truce was agreed upon March 20th, by which trade was allowed to proceed on the old mode; merchant ships accordingly advanced up the river, and for about six weeks trade went on uninterruptedly—one party getting their tea and the other their duties. The new governor, Ki Kung, together with the "rebel-quelling general" Yihshan, then arrived, and the people, thinking that a slight cause would disturb the truce, took advantage of it to remove their effects, well aware how much they would suffer from their own army in case of trouble.

Toward the middle of May the hostile intentions of the Chinese were manifest, though cloaked under professions of amity; and on the 21st Captain Elliot notified all foreigners to go

[1] *Chinese Repository*, Vol. X., p. 235.

aboard ship. The secret preparations for attack were very extensive. Large fire-boats and rafts were prepared, masked batteries erected along the river, troops quartered in the temples, and large cannon placed in the streets. The day before the notice of Captain Elliot was issued, the prefect had the impudence to publish a proclamation assuring all classes of the peaceful intentions of the commissioners. Finding their prey gone, a night attack was made by land and water on the ships, but none were seriously injured. As daylight advanced the Nemesis went in pursuit of the fire-boats and junks, and burned upward of sixty, while three men-of-war silenced the batteries along shore. Meantime the Chinese troops searched the factory buildings for arms and pillaged three of the hongs, to the consternation of the prefect, who told the commissioner that he would be forced to pay for losses thus sustained. On the 24th the land and naval forces under Sir Hugh Gough and Sir Fleming Senhouse arrived from Hongkong and prepared to invest the city. Most of the troops debarked above it, at Neishing, under the personal directions of Sir Fleming, who had provided many boats in which the force of two thousand six hundred men, besides followers, guns, and stores, were towed about twelve miles. A detachment landed and took possession of the factories. Sir Hugh Gough remained near the place of debarkation till the next morning, when the whole body moved onward to attack the forts and camps behind the city. As the English advanced the Chinese found that their shot did not reach them, so that after an hour's firing they began to collect outside of the forts, preparatory to retiring. The advance pushed on, and sent them scampering down the hills toward the city; the intrenched camp was carried with considerable loss to its defenders, who everywhere ran as soon as the fight came to close quarters; but in the forts there were many furious struggles.

On the 26th a driving rain stopped all operations; and a parley was also requested from the now deserted city walls by two officers, who agreed to send a deputation to make arrangements for surrender. Night came on before any heralds appeared, so that it was not till morning that the troops were in position, the guns loaded and primed, port-fires lighted, and everything in readiness to open fire, when a messenger arrived from Captain Elliot, desiring further operations to be delayed until he had concluded his negotiations. The terms were: that the forces should remain in position until a ransom of $6,000,000 was paid; that the three imperial commissioners and all their troops should march sixty miles from the city; that compensation for the loss of property in the factories and burning the Spanish brig Bilbaino should be at once handed over or secured; and that the Chinese troops, nearly fifty thousand in number, should evacuate the city. Captain Elliot ought indeed to have demanded a personal apology from Yihshan and his colleagues for their infamous treachery before letting them go. His acceptance of this ransom and sparing the city from capture were sharply criticised at the time, and the contemptuous bearing of the citizens during the sixteen ensuing years of their possession proved that it was an ill-timed mercy. How much influence the orders from home to be careful of the tea-trade had in this course cannot be learned.

While the English forces were occupying the heights the lawless soldiers from Kweichau and Kwangsí began to plunder the citizens, who retaliated till blood was shed and more than a thousand persons were killed in the streets; a patriot mob of villagers, numbering about fifteen thousand, attacked the few British troops left on the hills north of the city, but a prompt advance on the part of Sir Hugh drove this rabble a rout of some three miles. Upon their reappearance next day, the prefect was told that if they were not instantly dispersed the city would be bombarded; the threats and persuasions of the commissioners, aided by a British officer, finally induced the mob to retire. The superiority of discipline over mere numbers was probably never more remarkably exhibited; though the Chinese outnumbered the English more than forty to one, not a single foreigner was killed.

On the 31st the prefect furnished five hundred coolies to assist in transporting the guns and stores to the river side, and ten days after Captain Elliot's first notice everything was restored to the Chinese. The casualties among the British forces were fourteen killed and one hundred and twelve wounded, but about three hundred died from sickness. The losses of the Chinese from first to last could hardly have been much under five thousand men, besides thousands of cannon, ginjals, and matchlocks. In posting their forces, placing their masked batteries, and equipping their troops and forts, the Chinese showed considerable strategy and skill, but lack of discipline and confidence rendered every defence unavailing. Yihshan and his associates memorialized the Emperor, detailing their reasons for ransoming the city and requesting an inquiry into their conduct.[1]

The sickness of the troops compelled the British force to remain at Hongkong to recruit and wait for reinforcements. Commodore Bremer returned as joint plenipotentiary, bringing additional forces from Calcutta, and the expedition was on the point of sailing northward when both he and Captain Elliot were wrecked in a tyfoon, and this detained the ships a few days longer. Before they sailed Sir Henry Pottinger and Admiral Sir William Parker arrived direct from England to supersede them both. Sir Henry announced his appointment and duties, and also sent a communication to the governor of Canton, assuring him that the existing truce would be observed as long as the Chinese did not arm their forts, impede the regular trade, which had been lately reopened to British ships by imperial command, or trouble the merchants residing in the factories. The trade went on at Canton, after this, without any serious interruption during the war, the usual duties and charges being paid as if no hostilities existed.

The expedition moved northward, August 21st, under the joint command of Sir Hugh Gough and Admiral Parker, consisting of two seventy-fours and seven other ships of war, four steamers, twenty-three transports, and a surveying vessel, carrying in all about three thousand five hundred troops. Six ships and four or five hundred Indian troops remained off Canton and at Hongkong, to compel the observance of the truce. The force reached Amoy, and after a hasty reconnoissance attacked

[1] *Chinese Repository*, Vol. X. (p. 402), in which, and in Vols. VIII., IX., and XI., most of the official papers issued from the Chinese and English authorities during the war are contained.

all its defences, which were carried without much loss of life on either side. The city was taken on the 27th, and all the arms and public stores, wall-pieces, ginjals, matchlocks, shields, uniforms, bows, arrows, spears, and quantities of powder were destroyed; five hundred cannon were found in the forts. When H. M. S. Blonde came into this harbor, fourteen months previous, to deliver the letter for Peking, the fortifications consisted only of two or three forts near the city, but every island and protecting headland overlooking the harbor had since been occupied and armed, while a line of stone wall more than a mile long, with embrasures roofed by large slabs covered with earth to protect the guns, had been built, and batteries and bastions erected at well-chosen points. The broadsides of the ships had little effect here, and it was not until the troops landed and drove out the garrisons, who "stood right manfully to their guns," that the fire slackened, and the Chinese retreated. The city was completely pillaged by native robbers, who ran riot during several weeks until the craven authorities came back and resumed their functions. The island of Kulang su was garrisoned by a detachment of five hundred and fifty troops, and three ships left to protect them. The British found one two-decker among the war junks, built on a foreign model, launched and ready for sea, carrying twenty guns; all were burned.

The English fleet again entered the harbor of Tinghai, September 29th, and found the beach much altered since February: Stone walls and fortifications extended two miles in front of the suburbs, besides sand-bags and redoubts thrown up on well-selected positions. They were taken after a defence marked with unusual courage; the general commanding the battery and all his suite were killed at their posts, and many hand-to-hand conflicts took place. But bravery and numbers were alike unavailing, and in two hours their defences were cleared, the walls of the town escaladed, the whole force scattered, and the island subdued, with the estimated loss to the Chinese of a thousand men. Great quantities of ordnance, among which were forty brass guns made in imitation of foreign howitzers, with military stores and provisions in abundance, were seized. A detachment was sent throughout the island to drive off the enemy's troops, and announce to the inhabitants that they were now under English authority. They evinced none of the alarm they had done the year before; provisions came in, shops were opened, and confidence in these proclamations generally exhibited. A military government was appointed, and a garrison of four hundred men left to protect the island.

The military operations in Chehkiang were conducted by Yukien and Yu Pu-yun; both these men had urged war, and had done all they could to fortify Tinghai and Chinhai, whose batteries and magazines showed the vigor of their operations. The English fleet proceeded to Chinhai October 9th, and a force of about two thousand two hundred men, with twelve field pieces and mortars, landed next morning to attack the citadel and intrenched camp. There were nearly five thousand men in this position, who formed in good order as the English advanced, opening a well-directed fire upon the front column, but quite neglecting two detachments on their flanks; as the three opened upon them nearly simultaneously, their force was completely bewildered, and all soon broke and fled. Knowing nothing of the mode of asking for quarter, while some fled into the country, the greater part retreated toward the water, pursued by the three columns, hundreds being shot and hundreds drowned. Sir Hugh Gough sent out a flag with Chinese written upon it, to inform them that their lives would be spared if they yielded, but not more than five hundred either could or would throw down their arms. The water was soon covered with bodies, and fully fifteen hundred soldiers lost their lives. The town and its defences were bombarded, and the troops driven out. Yukien endeavored to drown himself on seeing the day was lost, but being prevented he retreated to Yüyau, where he committed suicide, as was said, by swallowing gold leaf. He was a Manchu, and could not brook his master's displeasure; but his atrocious cruelty to two Englishmen who fell into his hands, one of whom was flayed and then burnt to death, had aroused general detestation against him. About one hundred and fifty pieces of brass ordnance, with great quantities of gunpowder and other military stores, were destroyed. The guns and carriages in the fort and batteries were so well made and placed that in some cases the victors on entering turned them against the flying Chinese. The frame of a wheel vessel, intended to be moved by human power, was found near Chinhai, showing, as did the brass guns, traversing carriages, and frigate at Amoy, that the Chinese were already imitating the machinery of war from their foes.

Ningpo was taken without resistance on the 13th. Many of the people left the city, and those who remained shut themselves in their houses, writing *shun min*, 'submissive people,' on the doors. Captain Anstruther took possession of his old prison—where he found the identical cage he had been carried in—and released all the inmates to make way for his detachment of artillery. About $100,000 in sycee were found in this building, upward of $70,000 in the treasury, many tons of copper cash in the mint, and rice, silk, and porcelain in the public stores, forming altogether the most valuable prizes yet secured. Sir Henry Pottinger intended at first to burn the city, but, happily for his reputation, he decided to occupy it as winter quarters. Leaving a garrison at Chinhai, he returned to Hongkong in February, 1842, Sir Hugh and the admiral remaining at the north.

The fall of Amoy, Tinghai, Chinhai, and Ningpo, instead of disheartening the Emperor, served rather to inspirit him. His commissioners, generals, and high officers generally did the best their knowledge and means enabled them to do, and when defeated, endeavored to palliate the discomfiture they could not entirely conceal by misrepresenting the force brought against them, and laying the blame upon the common people, the elements, the native traitors who aided the British, or the inefficiency of the naval armaments. The troops sent home with tokens of victory from Canton stimulated the war spirit in the western provinces. After they had gone Yihshan concocted measures of defence, one of which was to enlist two or three thousand volunteers, or "village braves," near the city, and place them under their own officers. The people having been taught to despise foreigners were easily incensed against them, and several cases of insult and wantonness were repeated and magnified in order to stir up a spirit of revenge. These patriots supposed, moreover, that if the great Emperor had called on *them*, instead of entrusting the conduct of the quarrel to truckling traitorous poltroons like Kíshen and the prefect, they could have avenged him of his enemies.

Consequently the truce was soon broken in an underhand manner by sinking hundreds of tons of stones in the river. H. M. S. Royalist levelled the fortifications at the Bogue, and Captain Nias destroyed a number of boats at Whampoa. After the destruction of these forts and his retirement from the river, Yihshan directed his attention to erecting forts near the city, casting guns, and drilling the volunteers, who numbered nearly thirty thousand at the new year. He also gave a public dinner to the rich men of the city, in order to learn their willingness to contribute to the expenses of these measures. However, since no serious obstacles were placed in the way of shipping teas by the provincial officers, from the duties on which they chiefly derived the funds for these undertakings, the British officers deemed it advisable to let them alone.

The case was different at other points. The imperial government had supposed that Amoy would be attacked, because the visit of the Blonde showed that the barbarians, "sneaking in and out like rats," knew of its existence; but the people of that province, except near Amoy, took no particular interest in the dispute, and probably knew far less of it than was known in most parts of England and the United States; no newspapers, with "own correspondents" to write the "latest accounts from the seat of war," narrated the progress of this struggle, which to them was like the silent reflection of distant lightning in their own quiet firmament. The sack of Amoy was a heavy blow to its citizens, but the plunderers were mostly their countrymen; and when Captain Smith of the Druid had been there a short time in command, and his character became known, they returned to their houses and shops, supplied the garrison with provisions, and even brought back a deserter, and assisted in chasing some pirates. Rumors of attack were always brought to him, and his declarations allayed their fears, so that after the sub-prefect resumed his authority no disturbance occurred. The explanations of the missionaries on Kulang su, in diffusing a better understanding of the object in occupying that island, also contributed to this result.

The loss of Chinhai and Ningpo threw the eastern parts of Chehkiang open to the invaders, and alarmed the court far more than the destruction of Canton would have done. The Emperor appointed his nephew, Yihking, to be "majesty-bearing generalissimo," and with him Tih-í-shun and Wănwei, all Manchus, to command the grand army and arouse the dwellers on the seacoast to arm and defend themselves. "Ministers and people! Inhabitants of our dominions! Ye are all the children of our dynasty! For two centuries ye have trod our earth and eaten our food. Whoever among you has heavenly goodness must needs detest these rebellious and disorderly barbarians even as ye do your personal foes. On no account allow yourselves to be deceived by their wiles, and act or live abroad with them." Such was the closing exhortation of an imperial proclamation issued to encourage them. In order to raise funds for its operations, the government resorted to the sale of office and titles of nobility, and levied benevolences from rich individuals and contributions from the people; which, when large in amount, were noticed and rewarded. Kíshen, who had been tried at Peking and sentenced to lose his life, was for some reason reprieved to be associated with Yihking as an adviser, but never proceeded beyond Chihlí. Lin was also recalled from Ílí, if indeed he ever went beyond the Great Wall, and Ílípu, whose treatment and release of the prisoners at Ningpo had gained him the good-will of the English, was also sentenced to banishment, but neither did he go beyond the Desert.

Defences were thrown up at Tientsin and Taku to guard the passage to the capital, but the bar at the mouth of the Pei ho was its sufficient protection. Fearing that the English would advance upon the city of Hangchau, the troops of the province and all its available means were put into requisition. Sir Hugh Gough could only approach it by a land march from Ningpo, and deemed it advisable to wait for reinforcements, his available force being reduced to six hundred men on entering that city. The rewards given to the families of those who had fallen in battle, and the posthumous honors conferred by the Emperor, stimulated others to deeds of valor and a determination to accomplish their master's vengeance. Yukien, "who gave his life for his country, casting himself into the water," received high titular honors in the hall of worthies, and his brother was permitted to bring his corpse within the city of Peking. The names of humbler servants were not forgotten in the imperial rescripts, and a place was granted them among those whom the "king delighteth to honor." Thus did the Chinese endeavor to reassert their supremacy, though their counsels and efforts to chastise the rebellious barbarians were not unlike the deliberations of the rats upon "how to bell the cat."

The occupation of Ningpo was an eyesore to the Chinese generals, but the citizens had learned their best interests and generally kept quiet. They showed their genius in various contrivances to carry off plunder, such as putting valuable articles in coffins and ash-baskets, wrapping them around corpses, packing them under vegetables or rubbish. One party overtook two persons near Ningpo running off with a basket between them; on overtaking and recovering it, a well-dressed lady was found coiled up, who, however, did not scream when detected. Another was found in a locker on board a junk, and as the captain was desirous of examining the mode of bandaging her feet, he told his men to lift the body out of the closet, when a scream explained the trick; she was dismissed, and the money she had endeavored to hide put into her hands. Opium was found in most of the official residences; its sale received no serious check from the war, and no reference was made to it by either party.

Toward the end of the year 1841, information was received of the collection of a large force at Yüyau. Two iron steamers soon landed seven hundred men, who took up a position for the night, intending to escalade the walls in the morning; but their defenders evacuated the place. The marines and seamen took the circuit of the walls, and found the troops, about a thousand strong, drawn up in array; and the two, after exchanging their fire, started on the run. The public stores were destroyed, and the town left to the care of its citizens, without much loss of life on either side. On his return the general visited Tsz'kí, but the troops and the authorities had decamped. The rice found in the granaries was distributed to the townsmen, and the detachment returned to Ningpo December 31st. On a similar visit to Funghwa it was found that the authorities and troops had fled, so that to destroy the government stores and distribute the rice to the people was all that remained to be done. These two expeditions so terrified the "majesty-bearing generalissimo," Yihking, and his colleagues, that they fled to Suchau, in Kiangsu. With such leaders it is not strange that the villagers near Ningpo wished to enrol themselves under British rule; and the effect of the moderation of the English troops was seen in the people giving them little or no molestation after the first alarm was over, and supplying their wants as far as possible.

The force had fairly settled in its quarters at Ningpo, when the Chinese opened the campaign, March 10th, by a well-concerted night attack on the city. During the preceding day, many troops entered the city in citizen's clothes, and stationed themselves near the gates; and about three o'clock in the morning the western and southern gates were attacked and driven in. Colonel Morris ordered a party to retake the south gate, which was done, with considerable loss to the enemy; as usually happened, the moment the Chinese were opposed their main object was forgotten, and every man sought his own safety, thereby exposing himself more fully to destruction. On the approach of daylight the garrison assembled at the western gate, and dragging two or three howitzers through it, came upon the main force of the enemy drawn up in compact form, headed by an officer on horseback. The volleys poured into this dense mass mowed them down so that the street was choked with dead bodies, and the horse of the leader actually covered with corpses, from which he was seen vainly endeavoring to release himself. Those who escaped the fire in front were attacked in rear; at last about six hundred were killed, and the whole force of five thousand scattered by less than two hundred Europeans, with the loss of one man killed and six wounded.

The British then prepared to attack an intrenched camp of eight thousand troops near Tsz'ki, and about twelve hundred were embarked in the steamers. The Chinese had chosen their ground well, on the acclivity of two hills behind the town, and in order to confound and disperse their enemy completely, the attacking force was divided so as to fall upon them on three sides simultaneously, which was done with great slaughter. The Chinese did not run until they began to close in with their opponents, when they soon found that their intimidating gesticulations and cheers, their tiger-faced shields and two-edged swords, were of no avail in terrifying the barbarians or resisting their pistols, bayonets, and furious onset. In these cases, emulation among the different parties of English troops to distinguish themselves occasionally degenerated into unmanly slaughter of their flying enemy, who were looked upon rather as good game than fellow-men, and pursued in some instances several miles. Most of the Chinese troops in this engagement and in the attack on Ningpo were from the western provinces, and superior in size and bodily strength to those hitherto met. They had been encouraged to attack Ningpo by a bounty to each man of four or five dollars, and pieces of sycee were found on their bodies. The Chinese lost a thousand slain on the field, many by their own act; the English casualties were six killed and thirty-seven wounded.

The conquerors set fire to the Chinese camp in the morning, consuming all the houses used as arsenals, with arms and ammunition of every kind. The force then proceeded to the Changkí pass, a defile in the mountains, but the imperialists had abandoned their camp, leaving only "a considerable quantity of good bread." In his despatch Sir Hugh speaks of the forbearance shown by his men toward the inhabitants; and efforts were taken by the English, throughout the war, to spare the people and respect their property. The English thus dispersed that part of the Grand Army which had been called out by the Emperor and his "majesty-bearing generalissimo" to annihilate the rebels. The fugitives spread such dismay among their comrades near Hangchau that the troops began to desert and exhibit symptoms of disbanding altogether; the spirit of dissatisfaction was, moreover, increased by the people, who very naturally grumbled at being obliged to support their unsuccessful defenders, as well as submit to their tyrannous exactions.

The Chinese near Ningpo and Chinhai had so much confidence in the English, and were so greatly profited by their presence, that no disturbances took place. The rewards offered by the Chinese generals for prisoners induced the people to lay in wait for stragglers. One, Sergeant Campbell, was seized near Tinghai, put into a bag to be carried to the coast, where he was shipped in a junk and landed at Chapu, before being relieved of his hood. One of his ears was cut off with a pair of scissors, but after reaching Hangchau he was well treated. During his captivity there he was often questioned by the Chinese officers as to the movements, forces, and arms of his countrymen, and received a high idea of their intelligence from the character of their inquiries.

The entire strength with Sir Hugh Gough, in May, consisted of parts of four English regiments, a naval brigade of two hundred and fifty, and a few Indian troops, in all about two thousand five hundred men; the fleet comprised seven ships of war and four steamers. On the 17th the whole anchored in the harbor of Chapu, about forty miles above Chinhai. About six thousand three hundred Chinese troops and one thousand seven hundred Manchus were posted here in forts and intrenched camps. The English landed in three columns, as usual without opposition, and promptly turned the orderly arranged army and garrisons of their opponents into a mass of fugitives, each man throwing away his arms and uniform and flying *à pas de géant.* A body of three hundred Manchus, seeing their retreat cut off, retired into an enclosed temple, whose entrance was both narrow and dark. Every one who attempted to enter it was either killed or wounded, one of whom was Lieutenant-Colonel Tomlinson. At length a part of the wall was blown in, which exposed the inmates to the rifles of their foes, and a rocket or two set the building on fire, by which the inmates were driven from their position to the rooms below; when resistance ceased only fifty were taken prisoners, the others having been burned to death or suffocated. The total loss of the invaders was thirteen killed and fifty-two wounded.

The defences of Chapu being carried, with a loss to the enemy of about one thousand five hundred, the English moved on the city. This was the first time the Manchus had really come in contact with the English; and either fearing that indiscriminate slaughter would ensue on defeat, as it would have done had *they* been the victors, or else unable to brook their disgrace, they destroyed themselves in great numbers, first immolating their wives and children, and then cutting their own throats. Scores of bodies were found in their quarters, some not entirely dead; others were prevented from self-destruction, and in many instances, young children were found attending upon their aged or infirm parents, awaiting in dread suspense the visit of the conquerors, from whom they expected little less than instant destruction. The English surgeons endeavored to bind up the wounds of such Chinese as fell in their way, and these attentions had a good effect upon the high Chinese officers, Ílípu himself sending a letter in which he thanked the general and admiral for their kindness in giving the hungry rice to eat and caring for the wounded. The old man endeavored to requite it by making the condition of his prisoners as easy as he could, and paid them money on their release. When the English generals, having destroyed all the government stores, re-embarked, the prisoners were released with a small present, and on their return to Hangchau loudly proclaimed their praises of the foreigners.

The expedition proceeded northward to the mouth of the Yangtsz' kiang, and reached the embouchure of the Wusung, where the ships took their allotted positions, June 16th, before the well-built stone batteries, extending full three miles along the western banks of the river. One of these works enclosed the town of Paushan and mounted one hundred and thirty-four guns; the others counted altogether one hundred and seventy-five guns, forty-two of which were brass. These defences were manned by a well-selected force, under the command of Chin Hwa-ching. The ships had scarcely taken their stations when the batteries opened, and both sides kept up a cannonading for about two hours, the Chinese working their guns with much skill and effect. When the marines landed and entered, they bravely measured weapons with them, and died at their posts. Among the war-junks were several new wheel-boats, having two wooden paddle-wheels turned by a capstan, which interlocked its cogs into those upon the shaft, and was worked by men on the gun-deck. These were paddling out of danger, when the steamers overtook and silenced them. The number of Chinese killed was about one hundred, out of not less than five thousand men composing the garrison and army. The governor-general, Niu Kien, who was present, in reporting the loss of the forts and dispersion of the troops, says he braved the hottest of the fight, "where cannon-balls innumerable, flying in awful confusion through the expanse of heaven, fell before, behind, and on either side of him; while in the distance he saw the ships of the rebels standing erect, lofty as the mountains. The fierce daring of the rebels was inconceivable; officers and men fell at their posts. Every effort to resist and check the onset was in vain, and a retreat became inevitable."

Among the killed was General Chin, who had taken unwearied pains to drill his troops, appoint them to their places, and inspirit them with his own courageous self-devotion. In a memoir of him, it is said that on the morning of the attack "he arrayed himself in his robes of state, and having prayed to heaven and earth, ordered all his officers and soldiers to get their arms and ammunition ready." Niu Kien's conduct was not such as to cheer them on, and most of the officers "came forward and begged to retire" when they saw the dilapidated state of the batteries. Chin's second suggested a retreat when the marines entered the battery, but he drew his sword upon him, saying, "My confidence in you has been misplaced." He again inspirited his men, himself loading and firing the ginjals, and fell pierced with wounds on the walls of the fort, bowing his head as he died in the direction of the Emperor's palace. His Majesty paid him high honors, by erecting shrines to him in his native village and at the place where he fell; in the *Ching-hwang miao* at Shanghai there is a sitting image of him in his robes of state, before which incense is burned. A reward of a thousand taels was given his family, and his son was made a *kü-jin* by special patent. In this notice it is stated as a current rumor in Shanghai, that about a fortnight after his death Chin sent down the news through the divining altar at Sungkiang, that he had been promoted by the Supreme Ruler of

Heaven to the rank of second general-in-chief of the Board of Thunder, so that although he could not, while alive, repay the imperial favor by exterminating the rebels, he could still afford some aid to his country.

The stores of every kind were destroyed, except the brass pieces, among which were one Spanish gun of old date, and a Chinese piece more than three centuries old, both of them of singular shape, the latter being like a small-mouthed jar. The British landed on the 19th, two thousand in all, and proceeded to Shanghai by land. After the capture of Wusung, Mr. Gutzlaff, who accompanied the admiral as interpreter, succeeded in reassuring the people and inducing them to stay in their dwellings; he was also employed in procuring provisions. The ships silenced two small batteries near the city with a single broadside, and the troops entered it without resistance. The good effects of previous kindness shown the people in respecting their property were here seen. Captain Loch says that on the march along the banks he passed through two villages where the shops were open, with their owners in them, and that groups of people were assembled on the right and left to see them pass. The troops occupied the arsenals, the pawnbrokers' shops, and the temples, destroying all the government stores and distributing the rice in the granaries among the people. The total number of cannon taken was three hundred and eighty-eight, of which seventy-six were of brass; some of the latter were named "tamer and subduer of the barbarians;" others, "the robbers' judgment," and one piece twelve feet long was called the "Barbarian." The citizens voluntarily came forward to supply provisions, and stated that there had been a serious affray in the city a few days before between them and their officers, who wished to levy a subsidy for the defence of the city, which even then they were on the point of abandoning. The boats before the walls were crowded with inhabitants flying with their property, many of whom returned in a few days.

The troops retired from Shanghai June 23d, leaving it less injured than any city yet taken, owing chiefly to the efforts made by the people themselves to protect their property. The eight hundred junks and upward lying off the town were unharmed, but their owners no doubt were made to contribute toward the $300,000 exacted as a ransom. Sir Henry Pottinger now rejoined the expedition, accompanied by Lord Saltoun, with large reinforcements for both arms, and immediate preparations were made for proceeding up the Yangtsz', to interrupt the communication by the Grand Canal across that river. The Chinese officers, unable to read any European language, learned the designs of their enemy chiefly by rumors, which natives in the employ of the English brought them, and consequently not unfrequently misled his Majesty—unwittingly, in mentioning the wrong places likely to be attacked, but wilfully as to their numbers and conduct in the hour of victory. The fall of Shanghai and the probable march upon Sungkiang and Suchau greatly alarmed him, and he now began to think that the rebels really intended to proceed up to Nanking and the Grand Canal, which he had been assured was not their purpose.

He accordingly concentrated his troops at Chinkiang, Nanking, Suchau, and Tientsin, four places which he feared were in danger, and associated Kíying and Ílípu as commissioners with the governor-general, Niu Kien, to superintend civil affairs; military matters were still left under the management of the imbecile Yihking. Only a few places on the Yangtsz' kiang offered eligible positions for forts, and Niu Kien wisely declined to stake the Great River at Chinkiang, lest it should alarm the inhabitants. Fire-rafts and boats were, however, ordered for the defence of that city, and reinforcements of troops collected there and at Nanking, some of whom were encamped withuot the city, and part incorporated with the garrison. The tone of the documents which fell into the hands of the English showed the anxiety felt at court regarding the result of this movement up the river.

The British plenipotentiary published and circulated a manifesto at this date for "the information of the people of the country." In this paper he enumerated, in much the same manner as Captain Elliot had done, the grievances the English had suffered at Canton from the spoliations, insults, and imprisonment inflicted upon them by Lin in order to extort opium, which was given up by the English superintendent to rescue himself and his countrymen from death. The duplicity of the Chinese government in sending down Kíshen as a commissioner to Canton to arrange matters, and then, while he was negotiating, to break off the treaty and treacherously resort to war, was another "grand instance of offence against England." The bad treatment of kidnapped prisoners, the mendacious reports of victories gained over the English, which misled the Emperor and retarded the settlement of the war, was another cause of offence. The restriction of the trade to Canton, establishment of the monopoly of the hong merchants, the oppressive and unjust exactions imposed upon it through their scheming, and many other minor grievances which need not be enumerated, formed the last count in this indictment. Three things must be granted before peace could be made, viz., the cession of an island for commerce and the residence of merchants; compensation for losses and expenses; and allowing a friendly and becoming intercourse between the officers of the two countries on terms of equality. This proclamation, however, made no mention of the real cause of the war, the opium trade, and in that respect was far from being an ingenuous, fair statement of the question. It was much more like one of Napoleon's bulletins in the *Moniteur*, and considering the moral and intellectual condition of Great Britain and China, failed to uphold the high standing of the former.

While Sir Henry Pottinger knew that the use of this drug was one of the greatest evils which afflicted the people, he should have, in a document of this nature, left no room for the supposition, on the part of either ruler or subject, that the war was undertaken to uphold and countenance the opium trade. He could not have been ignorant that the Emperor and his ministers supposed the unequal contest they were waging was caused by their unsuccessful efforts to suppress the traffic; and that if they were defeated the opium trade must go on unchecked. The question of supremacy was set at rest in this proclamation; it must be given up; but no encouragement was held out to reassure the Chinese government in their lawful desire to restrain the tremendous scourge. Why should he? If he encouraged any action against the trade, he could expect little promotion or reward from his superiors in India or England, who looked to it for all the revenue it could be made to bring; or consideration from the merchants, who would not thank him for telling the Chinese they might attack the opium clippers wherever they found them, and seize all the opium they could, and English power would not interfere.

The Emperor issued a proclamation about the same time, recapitulating his conduct and efforts to put a stop to the war, stating what he had done to ward off calamity and repress the rebels. The opium trade, and his efforts for a long time to repress it, and especially the measures of Lin, are in this paper regarded as the causes of the war, which concludes by expressing his regrets for the sufferings and losses occasioned his subjects by the attacks of the English at Amoy, Chusan, Ningpo, and elsewhere, and exhorting them to renewed efforts. It is a matter of lasting regret that the impression has been left upon the minds of the Chinese people that the war was an opium war, and waged chiefly to uphold it. But nations, like individuals, must usually trust to might more than right to maintain their standing; and when conscious weakness leads them to adopt underhand measures to regain their rights, the temptation which led to these acts is rarely thought of in the day of retribution. The money demands of England were not deemed at the time to be exacting, but she should, and could at this time in an effectual manner, through her plenipotentiary, have cleared herself from all sanction of this traffic. If Lord Melbourne could wish it were a less objectionable traffic, Sir Henry Pottinger might surely have intimated, in as public a manner, his regret at its existence. He probably did not deem the use of opium very deleterious.

The number of ships, steamers, transports, and all in the expedition, when it left Wusung, July 6th, was seventy-two, most of them large vessels. They were arranged in five divisions, with an advance squadron of five small steamers and tenders to survey the river, each division having a frigate or seventy-four at its head. The world has seldom seen a more conspicuous instance of the superiority of a small body possessing science, skill, and discipline, over immense multitudes of undisciplined, ignorant, and distrustful soldiers, than was exhibited in this bold manœuvre. Not to speak alone of the great disparity in numbers, the distant quarters of the globe whence the ships were collected, the many languages and tribes found in the invading force, the magnitude of their ships, abundance of their supplies, and superiority of their weapons of war, the moral energy and confidence of power in this small troop over its ineffective adversary was not less conspicuous. The sight of such a fleet sailing up their Great River struck the inhabitants with mingled astonishment and dread.

Chinkiang lies half a mile from the southern bank of the Yangtsz', surrounded by a high wall four miles in circuit, and having hills of considerable elevation in its rear. The canal comes in from the south, close to the walls on its western side, and along the shores of both river and canal are extensive suburbs—at this time completely under the command of the guns of the ships, which could also bombard the city itself from some positions. A bluff hill on the north partly concealed the town from the ships, and it was not till this hill-top had been gained that the three Chinese encampments behind the city could be seen. The general divided his small force of seven thousand men into three brigades, under the command of Major-Generals Lord Saltoun, Schoedde, and Bartley, besides an artillery brigade of five hundred and seventy rank and file, under Lieutenant-Colonel Montgomerie. The Chinese encampments contained more than three thousand men, most of them soldiers from Hupeh and Chehkiang provinces. The Manchu garrison within the city consisted of one thousand two hundred regular troops and eight hundred Mongols from Koko-nor, together with eight hundred and thirty-five Chinese troops, making altogether from two thousand six hundred to two thousand eight hundred fighting men; the entire force was under the command of Hailing, who had made such a disposition of his troops and strengthened his means of defence as well as the time allowed. He closes his last communication to the Emperor with the assurance that "he cannot do otherwise than exert his whole heart and strength in endeavors to repay a small fraction of the favors he has enjoyed from his government."

The right brigade, under Lord Saltoun, soon drove the imperialists out of their camp, who did not wait for his near approach, but broke and dispersed after firing three or four distant volleys. Captain Loch says that while the party of volunteers were approaching the camp, they passed through a small hamlet on the hills; "the village had not been deserted; some of the houses were closed, while the inhabitants of others were standing in the streets staring at us in stupid wonder; and although they were viewing a contest between foreigners and their fellow-countrymen, and in danger themselves of being shot, were coolly eating their meals."

The centre brigade, under Major-General Schoedde, landed on the northern corner of the city, to escalade the walls on that side and prevent the troops from the camp entering the gates. He was received by a well-sustained fire, his men placing their ladders and mounting in the face of a determined resistance; as soon as they gained the parapet they drove the Tartars before them, though their passage was bravely disputed. While they were mounting the walls a fire was kept up on the city on the northern and eastern sides, under cover of which, after clearing the ramparts, they proceeded to the western gate, conquering all opposition in the northern part of the city, and driving the Tartars to the southern quarter.

The left brigade, under Major-General Bartley, did not reach the western side as soon as was expected, being delayed by the canal, here between seventy and eighty feet broad, which formed a deep ditch on this side. The western gate was blown in, the blast carrying before it a high pile of sand-bags heaped against the inside to strengthen the bars. While this work was going on, seven boats carrying artillerymen entered the canal to proceed up to the gate; but when nearly opposite they were repulsed by a severe fire from the walls, and the men compelled to abandon the three leading boats and take refuge in the houses along the banks; the others halted under cover of some houses until their comrades rejoined them, when all returned to the ships. Two hundred marines now landed, and with three hundred sepoys soon recovered the boats and carried back the wounded men. The party then planted their ladders in the face of a spirited fire from the walls, and succeeded in carrying them against all opposition.

All resistance at the three gateways having been overcome, it was supposed that the city was nearly subdued. Sir Hugh consequently ordered a halt for his men on account of the heat, and despatched a small force to proceed along the western ramparts to occupy the southern gate. This squad had proceeded about half a mile when it met a body of eight hundred or one thousand Tartars regularly drawn up in an open space. They fired with steadiness and regularity, but their bravery was of no avail, for the party, giving them one volley, charged down the bank and scattered them immediately, though not without some resistance. The dispersed Tartars, however, kept up a scattering fire along the streets and from the houses, which served chiefly to irritate their enemies and increase their own loss.

The heat of the day having passed, the commander-in-chief, guided by Mr. Gutzlaff and some Chinese, marched with two regiments into the southern quarter of the city. The scenes of desolation and woe which he met seem to have sickened the gray-haired warrior, for he says in his despatches, "finding dead bodies of Tartars in every house we entered, principally women and children, thrown into wells or otherwise murdered by their own people, I was glad to withdraw the troops from this frightful scene of destruction, and place them in the northern quarter." It was indeed a terrific scene. Captain Loch, who accompanied Sir Hugh, says they went to a large building thought to be the prefect's house, which was forced open and found entirely deserted, though completely furnished and of great extent; "we set fire to it and marched on." What the object or advantage of this barbarous act was he does not say. Leaving the general, he turned down a street and burst open the door of a large mansion; the objects which met his view were shocking.

After we had forced our way over piles of furniture placed to barricade the door, we entered an open court strewed with rich stuffs and covered with clotted blood; and upon the steps leading to the hall of ancestors there were two bodies of youthful Tartars, cold and stiff, who seemed to be brothers. Having gained the threshold of their abode, they had died where they had fallen from loss of blood. Stepping over these bodies we entered the hall, and met face to face three women seated, a mother and two daughters, and at their feet lay two bodies of elderly men, with their throats cut from ear to ear, their senseless heads resting upon the feet of their relations. To the right were two young girls, beautiful and delicate, crouching over and endeavoring to conceal a living soldier. In the heat of action, when the blood is up and the struggle is for life between man and man, the anguish of the wounded and the sight of misery and pain is unheeded; humanity is partially obscured by danger; but when excitement subsides with victory, a heart would be hardly human that could feel unaffected by the retrospection. And the hardest heart of the oldest man who ever lived a life of rapine and slaughter could not have gazed on this scene of woe unmoved. I stopped, horror-stricken at what I saw. The expression of cold, unutterable despair depicted on the mother's face changed to the violent workings of scorn and hate, which at last burst forth in a paroxysm of invective, afterward in floods of tears, which apparently, if anything could, relieved her. She came close to me and seized me by the arm, and with clenched teeth and deadly frown pointed to the bodies, to her daughters, to her yet splendid house, and to herself; then stepped back a pace, and with firmly closed hands and in a husky voice, I could see by her gestures, spoke of her misery, her hate, and, I doubt not, her revenge. I attempted by signs to explain, offered her my services, but was spurned. I endeavored to make her comprehend that, however great her present misery, it might be in her unprotected state a hundredfold increased; that if she would place herself under my guidance, I would pass her through the city gates in safety into the open country; but the poor woman would not listen to me, and the whole family was by this time in loud lamentation. All that remained for me to do was to prevent the soldiers bayoneting the man, who, since our entrance, had attempted to escape.[1]

The destruction of life was appalling. Some of the Manchus shut the doors of their houses, while through the crevices persons could be seen deliberately cutting the throats of their women, and destroying their children by throwing them into wells. In one house a man was shot while sawing his wife's throat as he held her over a well into which he had already thrown his children; her wound was sewed up and the lives of the children saved. In another house no less than fourteen dead bodies, principally women, were discovered; while such was their terror and hatred of the invaders, that every Manchu preferred resistance, death, suicide, or flight, to surrender. Out of a Manchu population of four thousand, it was estimated that not more than five hundred survived, the greater part having perished by their own hands.

---

[1] Capt. G. G. Loch, *Narrative of Events in China*, p. 109.

The public offices were ransacked and all arms and stores destroyed; only $60,000 in sycee were found in the treasury. The populace began to pillage, and in one instance, fearing a stop might be put to their rapacity, they set fire to the buildings at each end of a street in order to plunder a pawnbroker's shop without interference. The streets and lanes were strewed with silken, fur, and other rich dresses which the robbers had thrown away when they saw something more valuable, and the sepoys and camp-followers took what they could find. Parties were accordingly stationed at the gates to take everything from the natives as they went out, or which they threw over the walls, and in this way the thieves were in their turn stripped. Within twenty-four hours after the troops landed, the city and suburbs of Chinkiang were a mass of ruin and destruction; part of the eastern wall was subsequently blown in and all the gates dismantled to prevent any treachery. The total loss of the English was thirty-seven killed and one hundred and thirty-one wounded.

A curious contrast to the terrible scenes going on at Chinkiang was seen at Ĭching hien, on the northern side of the river. Four days before, the approach of the steamer Nemesis had caused no little consternation, and in the evening a Chinese gentleman came off to her with a few presents to learn if there was any intention of attacking the town. He was told that if he would send supplies of meat and provisions no harm would be done, and all he brought should be paid for. In the morning provisions were furnished, and he remained on board to see the steamer chase and bring junks to; being much amazed at these novel operations, which gave him a new idea of the energy of the invaders. In the evening commands were given him to bring provisions in larger quantities, and three boats went up to the town to procure them. The people showed no hostility, and through his assistance the English opened a market in the courtyard of a temple, at which supplies were purchased, put aboard small junks, and conveyed to the fleet. On the 21st the same person came, according to agreement, to accompany a large party of English from the ships to his house, where he had prepared an entertainment for them. Through the medium of a Chinese boy communication was easily carried on, and the alarms of the townspeople quieted; a proclamation was also issued stating that every peaceable person would be unharmed. This gentleman had invited a large company of his relatives and friends, and served up a collation for his guests; all this time the firing was heard from Chinkiang, where the countrymen of those so agreeably occupied were engaged in hostile encounter. On returning to their boats an additional mark of respect was shown by placing a well-dressed man each side of every officer to fan him as he walked. At the market-temple another entertainment was also served up. No injury was done by either side, and the forbearance of the English was not without good effect. Such queer contrasts as this have frequently characterized the contests between the Chinese and British.

Some of the large ships were towed up to Nanking, and the whole fleet reached it August 9th, at which time preparation had been made for the assault; but desirous of avoiding a repetition of the sad scenes of Chinkiang, the British leaders had also sent a communication to Niu Kien, offering to ransom the city for $3,000,000.

This celebrated city lies about three miles south of the river, but the north-east corner of an outer wall reaches within seven hundred paces of the water; the western face runs along the base of wooded hills for part of its distance, and is then continued through flat grounds around the southern side, both being defended by a deep ditch. The suburbs are on this low ground, where Sir Hugh Gough intended to bombard the place and make an entrance on the eastern side, while diversions at other points perplexed the garrison. His force consisted of only four thousand five hundred effective men; there were, as nearly as could be learned, six thousand Manchu and nine thousand Chinese troops within the city. On the 11th Lord Saltoun's brigade landed at a village from whence a paved road led to one of the eastern gates, and other detachments were stationed in the neighborhood. Everything was in readiness for the assault by daylight of August 15th, and the governor-general was told that it would assuredly be made unless the commissioners produced their authority for treating.

In the interval between the downfall of Chinkiang and investment of Nanking, several communications were received from the Chinese officers, and one from Kíying, couched in conciliatory language, and evincing a desire for peace. Sir Henry Pottinger replied in the same strain, deploring the war and calamities caused by its continuance, but stating that he could have no interview with any individual, however exalted, who was not properly commissioned to treat for peace. It is probable that the Emperor did not receive any suggestion from his ministers in regard to making peace until after the fall of Chinkiang, and it was a matter of some importance, therefore, for Ílípu and his colleague to delay the attack on Nanking until an answer could be received from the capital. The usual doubts in the minds of the English as to their sincerity led them to look upon the whole as a scheme to perfect the defences, and gain time for the people to retire; consequently the preparations for taking the city went on, in order to deepen the conviction that if one party was practising any deception, the other certainly was in earnest.

On the night of the 14th, scarcely three hours before the artillery was to open, Ílípu, Kíying, and Niu Kien addressed a joint letter to Sir Henry Pottinger requesting an interview in the morning, when they would produce their credentials and arrange for further proceedings. This request was granted with some reluctance, for the day before the *puching sz'* and Tartar commandant had behaved very unsatisfactorily, refusing to exhibit the credentials or discuss the terms of peace or ransom. The distress ensuent upon the blockade was becoming greater and greater; more than seven hundred vessels coming from the south had been stopped at Chinkiang, and a large fleet lay in the northern branch of the canal, so that some possibility existed of the whole province falling into anarchy if the pressure were not removed. The authorities of the city of Yangchau, on the canal, had already sent half a million dollars as the ransom of that place, while Niu Kien would only offer a third of a million to ransom the capital.

The Emperor's authority to treat with the English was, however, exhibited at this meeting, and in return Sir Henry's was fully explained to them. The delegates on the part of the commissioners were Hwang Ngăn-tung, secretary to Kíying, and Chin, the Manchu commandant, while Major Malcom, secretary of legation, and Mr. J. R. Morrison acted on the part of the plenipotentiary. Captain Loch, who was present, humorously describes the solemn manner in which the Emperor's commission was brought out from the box in which it was deposited, and the dismay of the lower attendants at seeing the foreigners irreverently handle it and examine its authenticity with so little awe. The skeleton of the treaty was immediately drafted for Hwang to take to his superiors. General Chin laughingly remarked that though the conditions were hard, they were no more so than the Chinese would have demanded if they had been the victors. The bearing of these officers was courteous, and Hwang especially found favor with all who were thrown into his company.

The utmost care being requisite in drawing up the articles, most of the work falling upon Mr. Morrison, it was not till late at night on the 17th that the final draft was sent to the Chinese. The plenipotentiary, on the 18th, desired the general and admiral to suspend hostilities, at which time arrangements were also made for an interview the next day between the representatives on both sides. The English officers meantime explored the vicinity of the city, and the demand for provisions to supply the force caused a brisk trade highly beneficial to the Chinese, and well calculated to please them.

On the 19th Kíying, Ílipu, and Niu Kien, accompanied by a large suite, paid their first visit to the English. The steamer Medusa brought them alongside the Cornwallis, and Sir Henry Pottinger, supported by the admiral and general, received them on the quarter-deck. The ship was decked with flags, and the crowd of gayly dressed officers in blue and scarlet contrasted well with the bright crapes and robes of the Chinese. This visit was one of ceremony, and after partaking of refreshments and examining the ship the commissioners retired, expressing their gratification at what they saw. They conducted themselves with decorum in their novel position, and Kíying and Ílipu, though both brought up in the full persuasion of the supremacy of their sovereign over the rulers of all other nations, and particularly over the English, manifested no ill-concealed chagrin. They had previously sent up a report of the progress of the expedition after the capture of Chinkiang, requesting in it that the demands of the invaders might be conceded; the inefficiency of their troops is acknowledged, and a candid statement of the impossibility of effectual resistance laid before his Majesty, with cogent reasons for acceding to the demands of the English as the wisest course of procedure. The further disasters which will ensue if the war is not brought to a close are hinted at, and the concession of the points at issue considered in a manner least humbling to imperial vanity. The sum of $21,000,000 to be paid is regarded by them as a present to the soldiers and sailors before sending them home; partly as the liquidation of just debts due from the hong merchants, whose insolvency made them chargeable to the government, and partly as indemnification for the opium. Trade at the five ports was to be allowed, because four of them had already been seized, and this was the only way to induce the invaders to withdraw, while Hongkong could be ceded inasmuch as they had already built houses there. The memorial is a curious effort to render the bitter pill somewhat palatable to themselves and their master.

The English plenipotentiary, accompanied by a large concourse of officers, returned the visit on shore in a few days, and were met at the entrance of a temple by the commissioners, who led them through a guard of newly uniformed and unarmed soldiers into the building, the bands of both nations striking up their music at the same time. This visit continued the good understanding which prevailed; the room had been carpeted and ornamented with lanterns and scrolls for the occasion, while the adjacent grounds accommodated a crowd of natives. On the 26th Sir Henry Pottinger and his suite, consisting of his secretary, Major Malcom, Messrs. Morrison, Thom, and Gutzlaff, the three interpreters, and three other gentlemen, proceeded about four miles to the landing-place on the canal, where they were met by a brigadier and two colonels; the banks of the canal were lined with troops. The party then took their horses, and, preceded by a mounted escort, were received at the city gate by the secretaries of Ílípu; the procession advanced to the place of meeting, guarded by a detachment of Manchu cavalry, whose shaggy ponies and flowing dresses presented a singular contrast to the envoy's escort and their beautiful Arabs. He himself was conducted through the outer gate, up the court and through the second gateway, ascending the steps into the third entrance, where he dismounted and entered the building with the commissioners and governor-general. The room had been elegantly fitted up, and a crowd of official attendants dressed in their ceremonial robes stood around. Sir Henry occupied the chief seat between Kíying and Ílípu, their respective attendants being seated in proper order, with small tables between every two persons, while dinner was served up in usual Chinese style.

These formalities being over, the thirteen articles of this most important treaty were discussed:

I.—Lasting peace between the two nations.

II.—The ports of Canton, Amoy, Fuhchau, Ningpo, and Shanghai to be opened to British trade and residence, and trade conducted according to a well-understood tariff.

III.—"It being obviously necessary and desirable that British subjects should have some port whereat they may careen and refit their ships when required," the island of Hongkong to be ceded to her Majesty.

IV.—Six millions of dollars to be paid as the value of the opium which was delivered up "as a ransom for the lives of H. B. M. Superintendent and subjects," in March, 1839.

V.—Three millions of dollars to be paid for the debts due to British merchants.

VI.—Twelve millions to be paid for the expenses incurred in the expedition sent out "to obtain redress for the violent and unjust proceedings of the Chinese high authorities."

VII.—The entire amount of $21,000,000 to be paid before December 31, 1845.

VIII.—All prisoners of war to be immediately released by the Chinese.

IX.—The Emperor to grant full and entire amnesty to those of his subjects who had aided the British.

X.—A regular and fair tariff of export and import customs and other dues to be established at the open ports, and a transit duty to be levied in addition which will give goods a free conveyance to all places in China.

XI.—Official correspondence to be hereafter conducted on terms of equality according to the standing of the parties.

XII.—Conditions for restoring the places held by British troops to be according to the payments of money.

XIII.—Time of exchanging ratifications and carrying the treaty into effect.

The official English and Chinese texts of this compact and a literal translation of the Chinese text are given in the *Chinese Repository*, Vols. XIII. and XIV.; in that serial is also to be found a full account of the struggle which was thus brought to a close. Looked at in any point of view, political, commercial, moral, or intellectual, it will always be considered as one of the turning points in the history of mankind, involving the welfare of all nations in its wide-reaching consequences.

When matters connected with the treaty had been arranged, Sir Henry proposed to say a few words upon "the great cause that produced the disturbances which led to the war, viz., the trade in opium." But upon hearing this (Captain Loch says) they unanimously declined entering upon the subject, until they were assured that he had introduced it merely as a topic for private conversation.

They then evinced much interest, and eagerly requested to know why we would not act fairly toward them by prohibiting the growth of the poppy in our dominions, and thus effectually stop a traffic so pernicious to the human race. This, he said, in consistency with our constitutional laws could not be done; and he added that even if England chose to exercise so arbitrary a power over her tillers of the soil, it would not check the evil, so far as the Chinese were concerned, while the cancer remained uneradicated among themselves, but that it would merely throw the market into other hands. It, in fact, he said, rests entirely with yourselves. If your people are virtuous, they will desist from the evil practice; and if your officers are incorruptible and obey your orders, no opium can enter your country. The discouragement of the growth of the poppy in our territories rests principally with you, for nearly the entire produce cultivated in India travels east to China; if, however, the habit has become a confirmed vice, and you feel that your power is at present inadequate to stay its indulgence, you may rest assured your people will procure the drug in spite of every enactment. Would it not, therefore, be better at once to legalize its importation, and by thus securing the co-operation of the rich and of your authorities, from whom it would thus be no longer debarred, thereby greatly limit the facilities which now exist for smuggling? They owned the plausibility of the argument, but expressed themselves persuaded that their imperial master would never listen to a word upon the subject.

To convince them that what he said was not introduced from any sinister wish to gain an end more advantageous for ourselves, he drew a rapid sketch of England's rise and progress from a barbarous state to a degree of wealth and civilization unparalleled in the history of the world; which rapid rise was principally attributable to benign and liberal laws, aided by commerce, which conferred power and consequence. He then casually mentioned instances of governments having failed to attain their ends by endeavoring to exclude any particular objects of popular desire; tobacco was one of those he alluded to, and now that it was legalized, not only did it produce a large revenue to the crown, but it was more moderately indulged in in Britain than elsewhere.[1]

To the well-wisher of his fellow-men this narrative suggests many melancholy reflections. On the one hand were four or five high Chinese officers, who, although pagans and unacquainted with the principles of true virtue, had evidently sympathized with and upheld their sovereign in his fruitless, misdirected endeavors to save his people from a vicious habit. "Why will you not act fairly toward us by prohibiting the growth of the poppy?" is their anxious inquiry; for they knew that there was no moral principle among themselves strong enough to resist the opium pipe. "Your people must become virtuous and your officers incorruptible, and then you can stop the opium coming into your borders," is the reply; precisely the words that the callous rumseller gives the broken-hearted wife of the besotted drunkard when she beseeches him not to sell liquor to her enslaved husband. "Other people will bring it to you if we should stop the cultivation of the poppy; if England chose to exercise so arbitrary a power over her tillers of the soil, it would not check the evil," adds the envoy; "you cannot do better than legalize it." Although nations are somewhat different from individuals in respect to their power of resisting and suppressing a vice.

---

[1] Loch's *Events in China*, p. 173, London, 1843. This same point is slightly referred to by Lieutenant Ouchterlony, on page 448 of his *Chinese War*, where he states that Sir Henry had prepared a paper for the information of the Chinese officials, proposing to them to permit the traffic in opium to be by barter.

and Sir Henry did right to speak of the legal difficulty in the way of restraining labor, yet how heartless was the excuse, "if we do not bring it to you others will." No suggestion was made to them as to the most judicious mode of restraining what they were told they could not prohibit; no hint of the farming system, which would have held out to them a medium path between absolute freedom and prohibition, and probably been seriously considered by the court; no frank explanation as to the real position the English government itself held in respect to the forced growth of this pernicious article in its Indian territories. How much nobler would that government have stood in the eyes of mankind if its head and ministers had instructed their plenipotentiary, that when their other demands were all paid and conceded no indemnity should have been asked for smuggled opium entirely destroyed by those who had seized it within their borders under threats of worse consequences. That government and ministry which had paid a hundred millions for the emancipation of slaves could surely afford to release a pagan nation from such an imposed obligation, instead of sending their armies to exact a few millions which the revenue of one year, derived from this very article alone, would amply discharge to their own subjects. For this pitiful sum must the great moral lesson to the Emperor of China and his subjects, which could have been taught them at this time, be lost.

Sir Henry inquired if an envoy would be received at Peking, should one be sent from England, which Kíying assured him would no doubt be a gratification to his master, though what ideas the latter connected with such a suggestion can only be inferred. The conference lasted three or four hours, and when the procession returned to the barges, through an immense crowd of people, nothing was heard from them to indicate dislike or dread; all other thoughts were merged in overpowering curiosity. It was remarkable that this was the anniversary of the day when English subjects, among whom were the three interpreters here present, left Macao in 1839, by order of Lin; on August 26, 1840, the plenipotentiaries entered the Pei ho to seek an interview with Kíshen; that day, the next year, Amoy and its extensive batteries fell; and now the three years' game is won and China is obliged to bend, her magnates come down from their eminences, and her wall of supremacy, isolation, and conceit is shattered beyond the possibility of restoration. Her rulers apparently submitted with good grace to the hard lesson, which seemed to be the only effectual means of compelling them to abandon their ridiculous pretensions; though it cannot be too often repeated that the effect of kindness, honorable dealing, and peaceful missions had not been fairly tried.

Arrangements were made on the 29th to sign the treaty on board the Cornwallis. After it was signed all sat down to table, and the admiral, as the host in his flagship, gave the healths of their Majesties, the Queen of England and the Emperor of China, which was announced to the fleet and army by a salute of twenty-one guns and hoisting the Union Jack and a yellow flag at the main and mizzen. The treaty was forwarded to Peking that evening. The embargo on the rivers and ports was at once taken off, the troops re-embarked, and preparations made to return to Wusung. The six millions were paid without much delay, and on September 15th the Emperor's ratification was received. The secretary of legation, Major Malcom, immediately left to obtain the Queen's ratification, going by steam the entire distance (except eighty miles in Egypt) from Nanking to London—an extraordinary feat in those days.

The imperial assent was also published in a rescript addressed to Kíying, in reply to his account of the settlement of affairs, in which he gives directions for disbanding the troops, rebuilding such forts as had been destroyed, and cultivating peace as well as providing for the fulfilment of the articles. It is, on the whole, a dignified approval of the treaty, and breathes nothing of a spirit of revenge or intention to prepare for future resistance.

The fleet of ships and transports returned down the river and reassembled at Tinghai, at the end of October, not a vessel having been lost. Even before leaving Nanking, and in the passage down the river, the troops and sailors, especially the Indian regiments, were reduced by cholera, fever, and other diseases, some of the transports being nearly disabled; the deaths amounted to more than a thousand before reaching Hongkong.

On arriving at Amoy the plenipotentiary was highly incensed on hearing of the melancholy fate of the captive crews of the Nerbudda and Ann, wrecked on Formosa. The first, a transport, contained two hundred and seventy-four souls, and when she went ashore all the Europeans abandoned two hundred and forty Hindus to their fate, most of whom fell into the hands of the Chinese. The Ann was an opium vessel, and her crew of fifty-seven souls were taken prisoners and carried to Taiwan fu. The prisoners were divided into small parties and had little communication with each other during their captivity, which was aggravated by want of food and clothing, filthy lodgings, and other hardships of a Chinese jail, so that many of the Indians died. The survivors, on August 13th, with the exception of ten persons, were carried out to a plain near the city, one of whom, Mr. Newman, a seacunnie on board the Ann and the last in the procession, gave the following account:

> On being taken out of his sedan, to have his hands shackled behind his back, he saw two of the prisoners with their irons off and refusing to have them put on. They had both been drinking and were making a great noise, crying out to him that they were all to have their heads cut off. He advised them to submit quietly, but they still refusing, he first wrenched off his own and then put them into theirs, to the great pleasure of the soldiers, but when the soldiers wished to replace his he declined. As they were on the point of securing him he accidentally saw the chief officer seated close to him. Going before him he threw himself on his head and commenced singing a few Chinese words which he had frequently heard repeated in a temple. The officer was so pleased with this procedure that he turned round to the soldiers and ordered them to carry him back to the city. All the rest, one hundred and ninety-seven in number, were placed at small distances from each other on their knees, their feet in irons and hands manacled behind their backs, thus waiting for the executioners, who went round and with a kind of two-handed sword cut off their heads without being laid on a block. Afterward their bodies were thrown into one grave and their heads stuck up in cages on the seashore.[1]

A journal was kept by Mr. Gully to within three days of his death, and another by Captain Denham of the Ann, one of the prisoners saved to send to Peking.[2] Both contain full accounts

---

[1] *Chinese Repository*, Vol. XII., p. 248.

[2] *Journals of Mr. Gully and Captain Denham during a Captivity in China in* 1842. London: Chapman & Hall, 1844.

of the treatment of the unhappy captives, and diminish the sympathy felt for the defeat of the government which allowed such slaughter. It was said to have been done by orders from court, grounded on a lying report sent up by the Manchu commandant, Tahungah. When their sad fate was learned Sir Henry Pottinger published two proclamations in Chinese, in which the principal facts were detailed, so that all might know the truth of the matter; a demand made for the degradation and punishment of the lying officers who had superintended it, and the confiscation of their property for the use of the families of the sufferers. Iliang, the governor-general, expressed his sincere regret to the English envoy at what had taken place, and examined into the facts himself, which led to the degradation and banishment of the commandant and intendant. While the prisoners were still at Taiwan fu, H. M. S. Serpent was sent over from Amoy to reclaim them, by which expedition the truth of the barbarous execution was first learned; this vessel afterward went there to receive the shipwrecked crew of the Herculaneum transport.

The citizens of Amoy, Ningpo, and Shanghai hailed the cessation of the war and the opening of their ports to foreign trade; but not so at Canton. The discharged volunteers still remained about the city, notwithstanding orders to return home and resume their usual employments, most of whom probably had neither. Scheming demagogues took advantage of a rumor that the English army intended to form a settlement opposite the city, and issued a paper in the name of the gentry, calling upon all to combine and resist the aggression. The enthusiasm it caused was worked up to a higher pitch by an inflammatory manifesto, in which desperate measures were plainly intimated: but the district magistrates took no steps against them. An invitation was circulated for the citizens and gentlemen from other provinces to meet at the public assembly hall to consult upon public affairs. A counter but less spirited manifesto was pasted up in the hall, which had the effect of inducing about half the people to disperse. The writers of this paper dissuaded their countrymen from hasty measures, by telling them that no land could be taken or dwellings occupied without permission from the provincial authorities, and urged upon them to live at peace with the English, in accordance with the injunctions of their wise sovereign.

A brawl occurred in Hog Lane on December 6th, between some hucksters and lascars, who were pursued into the Square, where the mob rapidly increased, and about two o'clock began pulling down a brick wall around the Company's garden and forcing open one of the factories, which was speedily pillaged, the inmates escaping through the back doors. The British flagstaff was fired by a party which kept guard around it, and the flames communicating to the verandah, other parts soon caught, and by midnight the three hongs east of Hog Lane were burning furiously. The ringleaders, satisfied with firing the British consulate, endeavored to prevent thieves carrying away the plunder; but they were forced to escape about midnight. These wretches soon began to quarrel among themselves for the dollars found in the ruins, and it was not till noon that the police and soldiers ventured to attack the knotted groups of struggling desperadoes and arrest the most conspicuous, and with the aid of boats' crews from the shipping recapture some of the specie. Full compensation was subsequently made to the foreigners for the losses sustained, amounting to $67,397, and some of the ringleaders were executed.

A large part of the officers in the army and navy engaged in the war received promotion or honorary titles. Sir Hugh was made a baronet, and, after more service in India, elevated to the peerage, with the title of Lord Gough, Baron of Chinkiang fu; the plenipotentiary and the admiral obtained Grand Crosses of the Bath. The three interpreters, Messrs. Morrison, Thom, and Gutzlaff, whose services had been arduous and important, received no distinctive reward from their government. The amount of prize money distributed among the soldiers and sailors was small. The losses of the English from shipwreck, sickness, and casualties during the war amounted to more than three thousand; the mortality was greatest among the Indian regiments and the European recruits, especially after the operations behind Canton and the capture of Chinkiang.

While the English government rewarded its officers, the Emperor expressed his displeasure at the conduct of the major part of his surviving generals, but distributed posthumous honors to those who had died at their posts. Hailing, with his wife and grandson, were honored with a fane, and his sons promoted. Kíying was appointed governor-general at Nanking. Though many civil and military officers were condemned to death, none actually lost their lives, except Yu Pu-yun, the governor of Chehkiang, who fled from Ningpo in October, 1841.

The settlement of the duties and regulations for carrying on foreign commerce immediately engaged the attention of the plenipotentiary. He called on the British merchants for information, but so utterly desultory was the manner in which the duties had been formerly levied, that they could give him little or no reliable information as to what was really done with the money. The whole matter was placed by both parties in the hands of Mr. Thom, who had been engaged in business at Canton, and Hwang Ngăn-tung, secretary to Kíying. To settle these multifarious affairs and restore quiet, Ílípu was sent to Canton as commissioner. On his arrival, he set about allaying the popular discontent at the treaty, and his edict[1] is a good instance of the mixture of flattery and instruction, coaxing and commanding, which Chinese officers frequently adopt when they are not sure of gaining their end by power alone, and do not wish to irritate. In this instance it did much to remove misapprehension and allay excitement, but its author had not long been engaged in these arduous duties before he "made a vacancy," aged seventy-two, having been more than half his life engaged in high employments in his country's service; his conduct and foresight in the last two years did credit to himself and elevated his nation. His associate, Kíying, took his place and exchanged the ratifications of the treaty of Nanking at Hongkong with Sir Henry Pottinger, ten months after it had been signed by the same persons. The island was then taken possession of on behalf of the Queen by proclamation, and the warrant read ap-

---

[1] *Chinese Repository*, Vol. XII., p. 106.

pointing Sir Henry governor of the colony. Its influence on the well-being of China since that period has been less than was anticipated by those who looked to the higher welfare and progress of a British colony so near to it as likely to be an example for good. A free port has encouraged smuggling to a degree that constantly irritates and baffles the native authorities on the mainland, and leads to armed resistance to their efforts toward collecting lawful revenue, especially on opium; while the influx of Chinese traders, attracted by its greater security, is gradually converting the island into a Chinese settlement protected by British rule. The peninsula of Kowlung, on the north side of the harbor, was added in 1860, to furnish ground for the commissary departments of the forces. The influence of a well-ordered Christian government exercising a beneficent rule over a less civilized race under its sway, is soon neutralized by licensing the opium farms and gambling saloons and lending its moral sanction to smuggling.

The tariff and commercial regulations were published July 22d. In this tariff, all emoluments and illegal exactions superimposed upon the imperial duties were prohibited, and a fixed duty put on each article, which seldom exceeded five per cent. on the cost; all kinds of breadstuffs were free. Commercial dealings were placed on a well-understood basis, instead of the former loose way of conducting business; the monopoly of the hong merchants was ended, the fees exacted on ships were abolished, and a tonnage duty of five mace per ton substituted; the charge for pilotage was reduced so much that the pilots were nearly stripped of all they received after paying the usual fees to the tidewaiters along the river. Disputes between English and Chinese were to be settled by the consuls, and in serious cases by a mixed court, when, upon conviction, each party was to punish its own criminals.

The proclamation giving effect to these regulations was one of the most important documents ever issued by the Chinese government; as an initiation of the new order of things, it was creditable to the people whose rulers were of themselves and could utter such words to them. After referring to the war and treaty of peace, Kíying goes on to say, respecting the tariff, that as soon as replies shall be received from the Board of Revenue, "it will then take effect with reference to the commerce with China of all countries, as well as of England. Henceforth, then, the weapons of war shall forever be laid aside, and joy and profit shall be the perpetual lot of all; neither slight nor few will be the advantages reaped by the merchants alike of China and of foreign countries. From this time forward, all must free themselves from prejudice and suspicions, pursuing each his proper avocation, and careful always to retain no inimical feelings from the recollection of the hostilities that have before taken place. For such feelings and recollections can have no other effect than to hinder the growth of a good understanding between the two peoples." It should be moreover added, as due praise to the imperial government, that none of the many hundreds who served the English on ship and shore against their country were afterward molested in any way for so doing. Many were apprehended, but the commissioner says he "has obtained from the good favor of his august sovereign, vast and boundless as that of heaven itself, the remission of their punishment for all past deeds; . . . they need entertain no apprehension of being hereafter dragged forward, nor yield in consequence to any fears or suspicions."[1]

These new arrangements pleased the leading Chinese merchants better than they did the hoppo and others who had lined their pockets and fed their friends with illegal exactions. The never-failing sponge of the co-hong could no longer be sucked, but for a last squeeze the authorities called upon the merchants for five millions of dollars, which they refused to pay, and withdrew from business with so much determination and union that the hoppo and his friends were foiled; they finally contributed among themselves about one million seven hundred thousand dollars, which was nearly or quite their last benevolence to their rulers. Howqua, the leading member of the body during thirty years, died about this time, aged seventy-five; he was, altogether, the most remarkable native known to foreigners, and while he filled the difficult station of senior merchant, exhibited

---

[1] *Chinese Repository*, Vol. XII., p. 443.

great shrewdness and ability in managing the delicate and difficult affairs constantly thrown upon him. He came from Amoy when a young man, and his property, probably over-estimated at four millions sterling, passed quietly into the hands of his children.[1]

The foreign community also suffered a great loss at this time in the death of John Robert Morrison, at the age of twenty-nine. He was born in China, and had identified himself with the best interests of her people and their advancement in knowledge and Christianity. At the age of twenty, on his father's decease, he was appointed Chinese secretary to the British superintendents, and filled that responsible situation with credit and efficiency during all the disputes with the provincial authorities and commissioner Lin, and of the war, until peace was declared. His intimate acquaintance with the policy of the Chinese government and the habits of thought of its officers eminently fitted him for successfully treating with them, and enlightening them upon the intentions and wishes of foreign powers; while his unaffected kindness to all natives assured them of the sincerity of his professions. The successful conduct of the negotiations at Nanking depended very much upon him, and the manner in which he performed the many translations to and from Chinese, connected with that event, was such as to secure the confidence of the imperial commissioners, in their ignorance of all foreign languages, that they were fairly dealt with.

He was eminently a Christian man, and whenever opportunity allowed, failed not to speak of the doctrines of the Bible to his native friends. The projected revision of the Chinese version of the Scriptures by the Protestant missionaries engaged his attention, and it was expected would receive his assistance. With his influence, his pen, his property, and his prayers, he contributed to the welfare of the people, and the confidence felt in him by natives who knew him was often strikingly exhibited

[1] Compare *The Fan Kwae at Canton before Treaty Days, by an Old Resident* (Mr. W. C. Hunter), London, 1882; a little volume which, besides many personal reminiscences of the characters mentioned in this narrative, furnishes an interesting picture of life in Canton a half century ago.

at Canton during the commotions of 1841 and the negotiations of 1843. He died at Macao August 29th, a year after the treaty of Nanking was signed, and was buried by the side of his parents in the Protestant burying-ground. Sir Henry Pottinger announced his death as a "positive national calamity," and it was so received by the government at home. He also justly added that "Mr. Morrison was so well known to every one, and so beloved, respected, and esteemed by all who had the pleasure and happiness of his acquaintance or friendship, that to attempt to pass any panegyric upon his private character would be a mere waste of words;" while his own sorrow was but a type of the universal feeling in which his memory and merit are embalmed. As a testimony of their sense of his worth, the foreign community, learning that he had died poor, leaving a maiden sister who had been dependent upon him, and that his official accounts were in some confusion, immediately came forward and contributed nearly fourteen thousand dollars to relieve his estate and relatives from all embarrassment.

The negotiations were concluded by the English and Chinese plenipotentiaries signing a supplementary treaty on October 8th (the day was a lucky one in the Chinese calendar), at the Bogue. This treaty provided, among other things, for the admission of all foreigners to the five open ports on the same terms as English subjects; it was inserted at the request of Kíying, that all might appreciate the intentions of his government; for neither he nor his master knew anything of that favorite phrase, "the most favored nation," and expected and wished to avoid all controversy by putting every ship and flag on the same footing.

It might have been expected that the Chinese government would have now taken some action upon the opium trade, which was still going on unchecked and unlicensed. Opium schooners were passing in and out of Hongkong harbor, though the drug sold by the Indian government at Calcutta was not allowed by the colonial British government at Hongkong to be stored on shore. Yet no edicts were issued, few or no seizures made, no notice taken of it; no proposition to repress, legalize, or manage it came from the imperial commissioner. The old laws denouncing its use, purchase, or sale under the penalty of death still remained on the statute book, but no one feared or cared for them. This conduct is fully explained by the supposition that, having undergone so much, the Emperor and his ministers thought safety from future trouble with the British lay in enduring what was past curing; they had already suffered greatly in attempting to suppress it, and another war might be caused by meddling with the dangerous subject, since too it was now guarded by well-armed British vessels. Public opinion was still too strong against it, or else consistency obliged the monarch to forbid legalization.[1]

Sir Henry Pottinger, hearing that persons were about sending opium to Canton under the pretense that unenumerated articles were admissible by the new tariff at a duty of five per cent., issued a proclamation in English and Chinese, to the intent that such proceedings were illegal. He also forbade British vessels going beyond lat. 32° N., and intimated to the Chinese that they might seize all persons and confiscate all vessels found above that line, or anywhere else on the coast besides the five ports; and, moreover, published an order in council which restricted, under penalty of $500 for each offence, all British vessels violating the stipulations of the treaty in this respect. All this was done chiefly to throw dust in their eyes, and put the onus of the contraband traffic on the Chinese government and the violation of law on those who came off to the smuggling vessels, and these proclamations and orders, like their edicts, were to be put "on record." This was shown when Captain Hope, of H.M.S. Thalia, for stopping two or three of the opium vessels proceeding above Shanghai, was recalled from his station and ordered to India, where he could not "interfere in such a manner with the undertakings of British subjects"—to quote Lord Palmerston's despatch to Captain Elliot. This effectually deterred other British officers from meddling with it.

Yet the commercial bearings of this trade were clearly seen in England, and a memorial to Sir Robert Peel, signed by two hundred and thirty-five merchants and manufacturers, was drawn

[1] Montgomery Martin, *China; Political, Commercial, and Social*, Vol. II., Chap. IV. (London, 1847)—a chapter containing some most suggestive reflections on this subject by a member of her Majesty's government at Hongkong.

up, in which they proved that the "commerce with China cannot be conducted on a permanently safe and satisfactory basis so long as the contraband trade in opium is permitted. Even if legalized, the trade would inevitably undermine the commerce of Great Britain with China, and prevent its being, as it otherwise might be, an advantageous market for our manufactures. It would operate for evil in a double way: first, by enervating and impoverishing the consumers of the drug, it would disable them from becoming purchasers of our productions; and second, as the Chinese would then be paid for their produce chiefly as now in opium, the quantity of that article imported by them having of late years exceeded in value the tea and silk we receive from them, our own manufactures would consequently be to a great extent precluded." The memorial shows that between 1803–08 the annual demand for woollens alone was nearly $750,000 more than it was for *all* products of British industry between 1834–39; while in that interval the opium trade had risen from three thousand to thirty thousand chests annually. Nothing in the annals of commerce ever showed more conclusively how heartless a thing trade is when it comes in contact with morality or humanity, than the discussions respecting the opium traffic. These memorialists plead for their manufactures, but the East India Company would have been sorry to have had their market spoiled: what could Sir Robert Peel, or even Wilberforce, if he had been premier, do against them in this matter? The question was which party of manufacturers should be patronized. But none of these "merchants and manufacturers of the highest standing and respectability" refer to the destruction of life, distress of families, waste of mind, body, and property, and the many other evils connected with the growth and use of opium, except as connected with the sale of their goods. One paper, in order to compound the matter, recommended the manufacture of morphine to tempt the Chinese, in order that, if they would smoke it, they might have a delicate preparation for fashionable smokers.

The conduct of the ministry in remunerating the merchants who had surrendered their property to Captain Elliot was appropriate to the character of the trade. The $6,000,000, instead of being divided in China among those who were to receive it —as could have been done without expense—was carried to England to be coined, which, with the freight, reduced it considerably. Then by the manner of ascertaining the market value at the time it was given up, and the holders of the opium script got their pay, they received scarcely one-half of what was originally paid to the East India Company, either directly or indirectly, thereby reducing it nearly a million sterling. Furthermore, by the form of payment they lost nearly one-fifth even of the promised sum, or about one million two hundred thousand dollars. Then they lost four years' interest on their whole capital, or about four million dollars more. What the merchants lost, the government profited. The Company gained during these four years at least a million sterling by the increased price of the drug, while Sir Robert Peel also transferred that amount from the pockets of the merchants to the public treasury. It was an undignified and pitiful haggling with the merchants and owners of the opium, whom that ministry had encouraged for many years in their trade along the Chinese coast, and then forced to take what was doled out.

Public opinion will ever characterize the contest thus brought to an end as an *opium war*, entered into and carried on to obtain indemnity for opium seized, and—setting aside the niceties of western international law, which the Chinese government knew nothing of—most justly seized. The British and American merchants who voluntarily subscribed one thousand and thirty-seven chests to Commissioner Lin, acknowledged themselves to be transgressors by this very act. Yet war seemed to be the only way to break down the intolerable assumptions of the court of Peking; that a war would do it was quite plain to every one acquainted with the character of that court and the genius of the people, and the result has shown the expectation to have been well based. Members of Parliament expressed their gratification at being at last out of a bad business; their desire, frequently uttered, that the light of the gospel and the blessings of Christian civilization might now be introduced among the millions of China, was a cheap peace-offering of good wishes, somewhat in the manner of the old Hebrews sacrificing a kid when they had committed a trespass. The short but pithy digest of the whole war by Justin McCarthy, in Chapter X. of the *History of Our Own Times*, brings out its leading features in a fairly candid manner.

The announcement of the treaty of Nanking caused considerable sensation in Europe and America, chiefly in commercial circles. M. Auguste Moxhet, the Belgian consul at Singapore, was sent on to China to make such inquiries for transmission to his government as would direct it in its efforts to open a trade. The Netherlands government sent orders to the authorities at Batavia, who despatched M. Tonco Modderman for the same purpose. The king of Prussia appointed M. Grube to proceed to China to prosecute researches as to the prospect of finding a market for German manufactures. The Spanish ministry, through the authorities at Manila, designated Don Sinibaldo de Mas in this new sphere. The governor of Macao, M. Pinto, before returning home, was appointed commissioner on behalf of H. M. F. Majesty, to treat respecting the rights and privileges of Macao under the new order of things, and succeeded in obtaining some stipulations favorable to the trade of the place, but could not get the Chinese to cede it to Portugal. These gentlemen arrived in China during the latter part of 1843, and most of them had interviews or communication with Kíying before he returned to court in December.

The governments of the United States and France early appointed ministers extraordinary to the court of Peking. Caleb Cushing, commissioner on behalf of the United States, brought a letter from the President to the Emperor, which is inserted in full as an instance of the singular mixture of patronizing and deprecatory address then deemed suitable for the Grand Khan by western nations:

LETTER TO THE EMPEROR OF CHINA FROM THE PRESIDENT OF THE UNITED STATES OF AMERICA.

I, John Tyler, President of the United States of America—which States are: Maine, New Hampshire, Massachusetts, Rhode Island, Connecticut, Vermont, New York, New Jersey, Pennsylvania, Delaware, Maryland, Virginia, North Carolina, South Carolina, Georgia, Kentucky, Tennessee, Ohio, Louisiana, Indiana, Mississippi, Illinois, Alabama, Missouri, Arkansas, and

Michigan—send you this letter of peace and friendship, signed by my own hand.

I hope your health is good. China is a great Empire, extending over a great part of the world. The Chinese are numerous. You have millions and millions of subjects. The twenty-six United States are as large as China, though our people are not so numerous. The rising sun looks upon the great mountains and great rivers of China. When he sets, he looks upon rivers and mountains equally large in the United States. Our territories extend from one great ocean to the other; and on the west we are divided from your dominions only by the sea. Leaving the mouth of one of our great rivers, and going constantly toward the setting sun, we sail to Japan and to the Yellow Sea.

Now, my words are that the governments of two such great countries should be at peace. It is proper, and according to the will of heaven, that they should respect each other, and act wisely. I therefore send to your court Caleb Cushing, one of the wise and learned men of this country. On his first arrival in China, he will inquire for your health. He has strict orders to go to your great city of Peking, and there to deliver this letter. He will have with him secretaries and interpreters.

The Chinese love to trade with our people, and to sell them tea and silk, for which our people pay silver, and sometimes other articles. But if the Chinese and the Americans will trade, there shall be rules, so that they shall not break your laws or our laws. Our minister, Caleb Cushing, is authorized to make a treaty to regulate trade. Let it be just. Let there be no unfair advantage on either side. Let the people trade not only at Canton, but also at Amoy, Ningpo, Shanghai, Fuhchau, and all such other places as may offer profitable exchanges both to China and the United States, provided they do not break your laws nor our laws. We shall not take the part of evil-doers. We shall not uphold them that break your laws. Therefore, we doubt not that you will be pleased that our messenger of peace, with this letter in his hand, shall come to Peking, and there deliver it; and that your great officers will, by your order, make a treaty with him to regulate affairs of trade—so that nothing may happen to disturb the peace between China and America. Let the treaty be signed by your own imperial hand. It shall be signed by mine, by the authority of our great council, the Senate.

And so may your health be good, and may peace reign.

Written at Washington, this twelfth day of July, in the year of our Lord one thousand eight hundred and forty-three. Your good friend.

Mr. Cushing arrived in China in the frigate Brandywine, Commodore Parker, February 24, 1844. The announcement of the general objects of his mission, and the directions he had to proceed to Peking, was made to Governor Ching, who instantly informed the court of his arrival; and with a promptitude indicative of the desire of the Emperor to give no cause of offence, Kíying was reappointed commissioner, with higher powers than before. The frigate had brought out a flagstaff and vane for the consulate at Canton; the vane was in the form of an arrow, and as it turned its barb to the four points of the compass, the superstitious people thought it conveyed destructive influences around, transfixing all the benign operations of heaven and earth, and thereby causing disease and calamity among them. An unusual degree of sickness prevailed at this time in the city and its environs, which the geomancers and doctors declared would not cease until the deadly arrow was removed. The people accordingly waited on the consul, Mr. Forbes, to request the removal of the arrow, which he acceded to, and substituted a vane of another shape. The gentry issued a placard the next day, commending its removal, and requesting the people to harbor no ill-will toward the Americans as the cause of the sickness.

Kíying having announced his appointment and powers to the people, proceeded to the Bogue to meet Sir Henry Pottinger, and be introduced to Governor Davis, from whence he went to Macao and took up his residence in the village of Wanghia, in the suburbs of that city. He had associated three assistants with himself, viz., Hwang Ngăn-tung, Pwan Sz'-shing, one of the late hong merchants, and Chau Chang-ling, a prefect. H. E. Hon. Caleb Cushing was sole commissioner and envoy extraordinary; Fletcher Webster, Esq., was secretary; Rev. E. C. Bridgman, D.D., and Rev. Peter Parker, M.D., were joint Chinese secretaries, and Dr. Bridgman, chaplain; Messrs. J. H. O'Donnell, R. McIntosh, S. Hernisz, T. R. West, and John R. Peters, Jr., were attached to the legation.

Mr. Cushing had already prepared the general outline of the treaty, which greatly abridged the negotiations, and the few disputed or doubtful points in the draft having been modified and settled, it was signed at Wanghia on July 3, 1844, by the two plenipotentiaries, Commodore Parker, and a few other Americans, a large company of Chinese being present. Its fulness of details and clear exhibition of the rights conceded by the Chinese government to foreigners dwelling within its borders, made it the leading authority in settling disputes among them until 1860.

Soon after Kiying left Canton the populace began to show signs of disturbance. A party of gentlemen were walking in the Company's garden, when the gate was burst open by a mob and they were obliged to escape by boats. On the next evening the mob again collected, with the intention of getting possession of the large garden, but were driven out of the passage without much opposition. Two or three Americans, in escorting one of their countrymen to his house, were attacked by missiles on their return; whereupon one of them fired low to drive the people back, but unhappily killed a native, named Sü A-mun. The case was investigated by the district magistrate, and a report made by the governor to Kíying; but Ching took no pains to send a sufficient force to repress the populace. In a communication to the American consul he says, after ordering him to deliver up the murderer: "It has been ascertained that the man who was killed was from the district of Tsingyuen, having no relatives in Canton. But if he had been a citizen, it would have become at the moment an occasion for attack, for it would have been told to the populace, and they would have revenged it by again setting fire to the factories and plundering their contents, or something of that sort. The people are highly irritated against the offender, and it is impossible but that they have constant debates among themselves until they are revenged."

A party of marines from the corvette St. Louis came up to Canton the next day, and quiet was restored. Kíying brought the case before Mr. Cushing, stating it to be his conviction that "the murderer ought to forfeit his life," and begging him to give orders for a speedy examination of the case. In his reply Mr. Cushing expressed his regret at what had occurred, his willingness to institute an inquiry, and added a few remarks upon the necessity of better protecting foreigners at Canton, in order to prevent the recurrence of such scenes, and embroiling the two countries. Kíying replied in a considerate manner, still upholding the authority of his government and laws: "It seems from this that, regarding our nations and their subjects, the people of our land may be peaceful, and the citizens of the United States may be peaceful, and yet, after their governments have become amicable, that then their people may become inimical; and albeit the authorities of the two governments may day after day deliberate upon friendship, it is all nothing but empty words. Thus, while we are deliberating and settling a treaty of peace, all at once the people of our two countries are at odds and taking lives." He also speaks of the overbearing and violent character of the people of Canton:

> Since the period when the English brought in soldiers, these ladrones have been banding together and forming societies; and while some, taking advantage of their strength, have plundered and robbed, others have called upon the able-bodied and valiant to get their living. Therefore, employing troops, which is the endangering of the authorities and [peaceable] people, is the profit of these miscreants; peace and good order which traders, both native and foreign, desire, is what these bad men do not at all wish. . . . I have heard that usually the citizens of Canton have respected and liked the officers and people of the United States, as they were peaceable and reasonable; that they would, even when there was a cause of difference, endeavor to settle it, which is very unlike the English. But unexpectedly, on the 16th instant, a cause for animosity was given in the shooting of Sü A-mun. I have heard different accounts of this affair; I judge reasonably in thinking that the merchants of your country causelessly and rashly took life. But the populace are determined to seek a quarrel, and I very much fear lest they will avail of this to raise commotion, perhaps under the pretence of avenging his death, but doubtless with other ideas too.

The American minister referred in a subsequent communication to the death of the boy Sherry, in May, 1841, when the boat's crew from the ship Morrison was captured. This affair had been already brought to the notice of the Chinese government by Commodore Kearny, and a sum of $7,800 paid for losses and damages sustained; but the present was a fitting opportunity for reviving it, since it and the case of Sü A-mun furnished a mutual commentary upon the necessity of securing better protection for foreigners. Kíying made an investigation of the case, and reported the successive actions of his predecessor, Kí Kung; so thoroughly indeed was his reply divested of all the rhodomontade usually seen in Chinese state papers, that one could hardly believe it was written by a governor-general of Canton. The exciting circumstances of the first casualty did indeed go far to extenuate it; though now both Kíying and his superiors could not but see that the time for demanding life for life had passed away. The commissioner was, however, in a dilemma. He could only appease the populace by stating in his proclamations that he was making every effort to ascertain who was the murderer and bring him to justice, and they must leave the management of the case in the hands of the regular authorities. On the other hand, the arguments of Mr. Cushing and the stipulations in the English treaty, both convinced him that foreign nations would not give up their treaty right of judging their own countrymen. He finally escaped the trouble by deferring the petitioners and relatives of the deceased awhile, and then appeasing them by a small donation.

In conducting these negotiations, and settling this treaty "between the youngest and oldest empires in the world," Mr. Cushing exhibited both ability and knowledge of his subject. In his instructions he was directed to deliver the President's letter to the Emperor in person, or to an officer of rank in his presence; and, therefore, on his arrival he informed the governor that he had been sent to the imperial court, and being under the necessity of remaining a few weeks at Macao, he improved the first opportunity to inquire after the health of his Majesty. Whether he regarded the mere going to court as important cannot be inferred from his correspondence, but if so, he should have gone directly to the mouth of the Pei ho and waited there for a commissioner to be sent to meet him. Yet the real advantages of such a proceeding at this time would have been trifling, and its risks and contingencies very serious; as the Emperor was not disposed to forego that homage required of all who appeared before him, however willing he might be to grant commercial privileges, it was undesirable to excite discussions on this point. Moreover, the appointment of Kíying with such unusual powers indicated a favorable disposition toward the Americans. It was fortunate that the two plenipotentiaries were at hand when the riot and homicide occurred, while the discussion which grew out of those events was no small benefit to the local government. The secret of much of the power of the Emperor of China consists in the acknowledgment by his subjects of his sacred character as the Son of Heaven; and although that lofty assumption must come down before the advance of western civilization, and will ere long crumble of itself, to have asked for an audience when this formality was known to be inadmissible would have irritated him, and put the foreign minister in an indefensible position. The subsequent discussions proved how deeply rooted in the Chinese mind was this attribute; the peaceful settlement of the question in 1873 could not have been anticipated in 1844.

The French ambassador, H. E. Th. de Lagrené, arrived in China August 14th. In addition to the two secretaries, MM. le Marquis de Ferrière le Voyer and le Comte d'Harcourt, five other gentlemen were sent out to make investigations into the commerce, arts, and industrial resources of the Chinese. M. de Lagrené took possession of the lodgings prepared for him at Macao, in the same building which Mr. Cushing had occupied. Kíying immediately made arrangements for opening the negotiations by sending his three associates to congratulate the French minister on his arrival; he himself reached Macao September 29th. The gratification of the Chinese statesmen at finding that the missions from the American and French governments were not sent, like the English expedition, to demand indemnity and the cession of an island, was great. Their arrival had been foreshadowed among the people of Canton, the number of ships of war had been exaggerated, and the design of the ambassadors strangely misrepresented as including the seizure of an island. These reports could hardly fail to reach and have some effect upon the highest officers in the land. The time, therefore, was favorable, not merely to obtain the same political and commercial advantages which had been granted to England, but further to explain to the Chinese officers something of the relations their nation should enter into with the other powers of the earth. The first interviews between Kíying and M. de Lagrené were held in October, and the treaty of Wanghia taken as the basis of agreement. The negotiations were amicably settled by the signing of the treaty at Whampoa on October 23d. This act may be said to have concluded the opening of China, so far as its government was prepared for the extension of this intercourse.

The instalments due according to the treaty of Nanking were

not yet all paid, but the Chinese had shown their desire to fulfil their engagements, and the $21,000,000 were received by the English within a short period of the specified time. This was a minor consideration, however, in comparison with the great advantages gained by England for herself and all Christendom over the seclusive and exclusive system of former days, which had now received such a shock that it could not only never recover from it, but was not likely even to maintain itself where the treaties had defined it. The intercourse begun by these treaties went on as fast as the two parties found it for their benefit. The war, though eminently unjust in its cause as an opium war—and even English officers and authors do not try to disguise that the seizure of the opium was the real reason for an appeal to arms, though the imprisonment of Captain Elliot and other acts was the pretext—was still, so far as human sagacity can perceive, a wholesome infliction upon a government which haughtily refused all equal intercourse with other nations, or explanations regarding its conduct, and forbade its subjects having free dealings with their fellow-men.

If in entering upon the conflict England had published to the world her declaration of the reasons for engaging in it, the merits of the case would have been better understood. If she had said at the outset that she commenced the struggle with the Emperor because he would not treat her subjects resorting to his shores by his permission with common humanity, allowing them no intercourse with his subjects, nor access to his officers; because he contemptuously discarded her ambassadors and consular agents, sent with friendly design; because he made foolish regulations (which his own subjects did not observe) an occasion of offence against others when it suited him, and had despoiled them of their property by strange and arbitrary proceedings, weakening all confidence in his equity; lastly, because he kept himself aloof from other sovereigns, and shut out his people from that intercourse with their fellow-men which was their privilege and right; her character in this war would have appeared far better. But it is the prerogative of the Governor of nations to educe good out of evil, and make the wrath, the avarice, and the ambition of men to serve his purposes and advance his own designs, although their intentions may be far otherwise.

The external and internal relations of the Chinese Empire at the close of the year 1844 were in a far better state than one would have supposed they could have become in so short a time after such a convulsion. The cities and provinces where the storm of war had beat most violently were reviving, the authority of the officers was becoming re-established, the bands of lawless desperadoes were gradually dispersing, and the people resuming their peaceful pursuits. No ill-will was manifested in Amoy on account of the losses its citizens had sustained, nor at Ningpo or Shanghai for their occupation by English troops. The English consuls at the five ports had all been received, and trade was commencing under favorable auspices. The opium trade—for this dark feature everywhere forces itself into the prospect—was also extending, and opium schooners plying up and down the coast, and anchoring on the outside limits of every port to deliver the drug.

The citizens of Canton, however, maintained their hereditary ill-will toward foreigners, and proceeded to such lengths that the local government became powerless to carry the stipulation of the British treaty, to enter its city gates, into effect. Governor Davis proceeded to Canton in May, 1847, with several vessels of war, capturing all the guns at the Bogue in his progress up the river, and compelled the authorities to grant a larger space for residences and warehouses on the south side of the Pearl River, to be occupied as soon as arrangements could be made. It was also agreed that the gates should be unconditionally opened within two years, so that foreigners might have the same access to this city as to the other four ports. When the time came for this to be carried out, the Emperor ordered Governor-General Sü to mind the voice of the people and disregard this engagement, which had probably never received his sanction. A careful examination of the Chinese text of all the treaties showed that an explicit permission to enter the citadel (*ching*), or walled portion of the marts opened to foreign commerce, was not given. In consequence of this vagueness the Hongkong authorities, acting under instructions from London, did not press the point, and the gates of Canton remained inviolate till January, 1858.[1]

---

[1] *Chinese Repository*, Vols. XVIII., pp. 216, 275; XV., p. 46 ff. Davis, *China during the War and since the Peace*, 1852, Vol. II., Chaps. V. and VI., *passim.* Among other authorities on the war may be mentioned Lord Jocelyin, *Six Months with the Chinese Expedition*, London, 1841; K. Stewart Mackenzie, *Narrative of the Second Campaign in China*, London, 1842; Col. Arthur Cunynghame, *Recollections of Service in China*, 1853; Lieut. John Ouchterlony, *The Chinese War*, 1844; *The Last Year in China to the Peace of Nanking*, by a Field Officer, London and Philadelphia, 1843; Auguste Haussmann, *La Chine, résumé historique*, etc., Paris, 1858; Ad. Barrot in the *Revue des Deux Mondes* for February 15, March 1, June 1, and July 1, 1842.

CHAPTER V.

THE TAI-PING REBELLION.

THE war, which was brought to an end by the treaty of Nanking, left the imperial government astonished and crippled, but not paralyzed or dejected. It had, moreover, the effect of arousing it from the old notions of absolutism and security; and though the actual heads of bureaus at Peking were unable, from their secluded position and imperfect education, to ascertain and appreciate the real nature of the contest, the maritime officials could see that its results were likely to be lasting and serious. A few thoughtful men among them, as Ílípu, Seu Kíyu, Kíying and his colleagues, understood better than their superiors at the capital that the advent of the 'Western Ocean people' at the five open ports introduced a permanent influence upon the Black-haired race. They could not, of course, estimate what this influence would become, but a sense of its power and vitality had the effect of preventing them from petty opposition in carrying out the treaty stipulations. With the major part of the officials, on the other hand, life-long prejudice, joined to utter ignorance as to the numbers, position, and resources of foreign nations, led them to withdraw from even such a measure of intercourse with consular and diplomatic officials as they could easily have held. The tone of official society was opposed to having any personal relations with their foreign colleagues, and after the old Emperor Taukwang had passed off the stage in 1850, his son showed—even eight years after the peace—that promotion was incompatible with cultivating a closer acquaintance with them.

It is not surprising that this reaction took on the form of doing as little as possible, and that its stringency was increased in reality by the device of making the governor-general at Canton the only channel of correspondence with foreign ministers. This magnate was surrounded in that city by subordinates whose training had been inimical to extending intercourse with foreigners, because they had reaped the advantages of the old system in their monopoly of the trade. The intendants at the other open ports were directed to refer difficult questions relating to foreigners to this high functionary, but as they were more disposed to let such disputes settle themselves, if possible, few cases were ever sent to him. The animus of the whole governing class gradually assumed a settled determination to keep aloof from those who had humbled them in the eyes of their subjects, and yet give no handle to these potent outsiders to repeat their descent on the coast. It was a poor policy in every point of view, only serving to hasten the evils they dreaded.

Sir John Davis was appointed governor of Hongkong in 1844, and during four years' service so soon after the war saw much of this proud and foolish spirit. His two volumes, published in 1852 (*China during the War and since the Peace*), contain a digest of the official records and acts of the Chinese government which is highly instructive. It is remarkable that he should show so much surprise at the mendacity, ill-will, and weakness of the officers in these reports to their master, or at the Emperor's persistency in wreaking his wrath on those whose poltroonery had done him so much harm. A residence of nearly thirty years in the country should have developed, in his case, an intimate acquaintance with native ideas of honor and mercy, and shown him how little of either are practised in time of war. If he blames the Chinese leaders for their ignorance and silly mistakes in its conduct, one can readily see that they never had an opportunity to learn the truth about their enemies. Their struggle against the impossible was not altogether in vain, therefore, if it prepared them for accepting the inevitable. Had Sir John manifested a little sympathy for their plight in such an unequal contest, and shown more humanity for their sufferings under the evils which afflicted them, his opinion of the best remedies would have carried much weight. As an instance of the result of his own training in the East India Company's school, he remarks respecting the imperial edicts against opium, that they fell into disuse, and that the subject had never been revived since the war; adding, "But at no time was the traffic deserving the full load of infamy with which many were disposed to heap it, for at most it only supplied the poison, which the Chinese were not obliged to take. The worst effect, perhaps, was the piracy it engendered, for this has told against the honest trade."[1] In his first interview with Kíying, in May, 1844, he proposed that the Chinese government should legalize the opium trade, for "such a wise and salutary measure would remove all chances of unpleasant occurrences between the two governments; it might provide an ample revenue for the Emperor, and check to the same extent the consumption of a commodity which was at present absolutely untaxed."[2] He, however, brought it more directly to his notice the next year in consequence of the revival of smuggling at Whampoa to as great a degree as in 1839, and the opium vessels all left the Reach.

Kíying was entirely indisposed to move, or even aid, in this matter, which he knew would be distasteful to the Emperor, other than by a truly Chinese device—that the officials of both nations should let it go on by mutual connivance. Sir John naïvely remarks on this: "The only thing wanting was that the Emperor should publicly sanction what he had once publicly condemned. . . . The trade, however, was practically tolerated, and to us this made a great difference. The Chinese government was not sufficiently honest to make a public avowal of this change in its system, but the position in which Great Britain stood became materially altered. China had distinctly declined a conventional arrangement for the remedy of the evil, and expressed a desire that we should not bring the existing abuse to its notice."[3] With two such men in command, of course nothing was ever done by either side to restrain the evils growing out of this contraband and demoralizing trade, until another war and new treaties changed the national relations.

[1] *China during the War*, etc., Vol. I., p. 19.

[2] *Ibid.*, Vol. II., p. 44.

[3] *Ibid.*, Vol. II., p. 203.

At Canton the long-cherished dislike to foreigners was fomented by demagogues and idlers. These worked upon the fears of the people by telling them that their lands were to be taken to build warehouses upon; and this rumor was so far believed that it soon became unsafe for foreigners to venture far into the suburbs. In December, 1847, not long after the arrangement with Sir John Davis respecting an entrance into Canton city was made, six Englishmen were attacked by a mob at Hwang-chuh-kí while on a ramble, and all killed, some of them with refined cruelty. Kíying took immediate measures—extremely creditable to his sense of what he owed to justice and maintenance of peace—to punish these villagers. A number of men whom their fellows indicated as leaders in the outrage were arrested; the prisoners were tried at Canton by the regular courts. Four were presently decapitated in the sight of a military deputation sent from Hongkong, and two others by orders from Peking. This well-timed justice secured the safety of foreigners peaceably going about the city and environs; but it was credibly stated afterward that there were numerous placards already posted in that region informing the people that foreigners would perhaps be coming thither to select sites for themselves. These unfortunate Englishmen, indeed, would perhaps have been allowed to return home, if they had been able to speak to the villagers and explain their object.

This incident makes it proper to notice a common misapprehension abroad in respect to the influence of the treaties which had been signed with China upon the people themselves. It was inferred that as soon as the three treaties with England, France, and America had been ratified, the great body of educated Chinese at least would inquire and learn what were their provisions, and a natural curiosity would be manifested to know something about the peoples of those lands. Nothing could be more likely—nothing was farther from the reality. No efforts were ever made by the imperial officers at the capital or in the provinces to promulgate these national compacts, whose original and ratified copies were never even transmitted to Peking. Consequently, the existence and nature of these *hwo yoh*, or 'peace contracts,' had to be continually taught to the natives, who on their part did not usually feel themselves under much obligation to obey them. In China, as elsewhere, just laws never execute themselves, and it is hardly surprising that not an officer of the Emperor should go out of his way to enforce their distasteful stipulations.

It was therefore uphill work to see that the treaties did not become a dead letter, and all the hardest part of this labor fell to the lot of the British consuls. They alone stood forth among foreign officials as invested with some power of their own; and being generally able to use the Chinese language, they came into personal relations with the local officers, and thus began the only effectual mode through which the treaties could become agencies for breaking down the hoary wall of prejudice, ignorance, and contempt which had so long kept China out of the pale of progress. In doing this, no fixed course could be laid down; though the constant tendency of the consuls was to encroach on the power of the mandarins, these latter were generally able to recur to the treaties, and thus learn the necessity and benefits of adherence to them. Their education was a colossal undertaking, and considering the enormous difficulties, its progress has been as rapid as was consistent with the welfare of themselves or their subjects. In this progress they bear the greatest share of the burden; its responsibilities and costs, its risks and results, almost wholly come upon them, while foreign nations, with the immense undefined rights of exterritoriality on their side, are interested on-lookers, ready to take advantage of every *faux pas* to compel them to conform to their interpretation of the treaties. Very little consideration is given to their ignorance of international law, to their full belief in the power of China, or to their consequent disinclination to accept the new order of things so suddenly forced on them. On the other hand, no one who knows all the features of this period will withhold the praise due to the British authorities in China for their conduct in relations with its functionaries; it might fairly be added that the improved state of international intercourse is mostly due to them.

The condition of the Empire at the close of the war was most discouraging to its rulers, who had not dreamed of receiving so crushing a defeat. It is creditable to them that they honorably paid up the $21,000,000 exacted of them by the British, who of course restored Chusan at the stipulated time. The name of R. Montgomery Martin, then treasurer of Hongkong colony, must be awarded due mention as being the only Queen's official who endeavored to resist its surrender, on the plea of its great benefit to her eastern empire and influence. Sir John Davis speaks of the "political and military considerations" which gave importance to it; but the proposal of Mr. Martin was promptly rejected by his superiors, and the whole archipelago has since been neglected. At the four northern ports opened by treaty, with the exception of Fuhchau, trade began without difficulty. This city having entirely escaped the ravages of the war, its proud gentry influenced the citizens against foreigners and their trade; the first European residents there met with some ill-usage, but this bitter feeling gradually wore off as the parties became better known.

At Canton the case was aggravated by the prejudices of race and the turbulence of the unemployed braves who had flocked into it on the invitation and inducements of Commissioner Lin to enlist against the English. They had been disbanded by Kiying, but had not returned to their homes; their lawlessness increased till it threatened the supremacy of the provincial government, and required the strongest measures of repression. The disorders spread rather than diminished under an impoverished treasury and ill-paid soldiery, and prepared the way for the rebellion which during the next twenty years tasked the utmost resources of the nation. The ignorance of one part of its people of what was taking place in another province—which during the foreign war so greatly crippled the Emperor's efforts to interest his subjects in this struggle—here did much to preserve them from uniting against him to his overthrow. It was plain to every candid observer that however weak, unprincipled, and tyrannical the Manchu rulers might be, they were as efficient sovereigns as the people could produce, and no substituted sway could possibly elevate and purify them until higher principles of social and political life had been adopted by the nation at large.

The protracted convulsion, known abroad as the Tai-ping

Rebellion, owed much of its duration as well to the exposure of the government's internal rottenness as to its weakness against foreign nations; but many other causes were at work. The body of the Chinese people are well aware that their rulers are no better than themselves in morals, honesty, or patriotism; but they are all ready to ascribe the evils they suffer from robbers, taxation, exactions, and unjust sentences to those in authority. The rulers are conscious that their countrymen consider it honorable to evade taxes, defy the police when they can safely do so, and oppose rather than aid in the maintenance of law and order. There is no basis of what in Christian lands is regarded as the foundation of social order and just government—the power of conscience and amenableness to law; nevertheless, from the habits of obedience taught in the family and in the schoolroom, the people have attained a good degree of security for themselves and show much regard to just rulers. The most serious evils and sufferings in Chinese society are caused by its disorderly members, not its rapacious rulers; and both can only be removed and reformed by the reception of a higher code which raises the standard of action from expediency to obligation.

In giving an account of the rise and overthrow of the Tai-ping Rebellion, it will be necessary to limit the narrative to the most important religious, political, and military events connected with it up to its suppression in 1867. The phrase "Tai-ping Rebellion" is wholly of foreign manufacture; at Peking and everywhere among those loyal to the government the insurgents were styled *Chang-mao tseh*, or 'Long-haired rebels,' while on their side, by a whimsical resemblance to English slang, the imperialists were dubbed *imps*. When the chiefs assumed to be aiming at independence in 1850, in order to identify their followers with their cause they took the term *Ping Chao*, or 'Peace Dynasty,' as the style of their sway, to distinguish it from the *Tsing Chao*, or 'Pure Dynasty,' of the Manchus. Each of them prefixed the adjective *Ta* (or *Tai*, in Cantonese), 'Great,' as is the Chinese custom with regard to dynasties and nations; thus the name *Tai-ping* became known to foreigners. The leader took the style *Tien-teh*, or 'Heavenly Virtue,' for his reign, thereby indicating his aim in seeking the throne. His own personal name, Hung Siu-tsuen, was regarded as too sacred to be used by his followers. The banners and edicts used at Nanking and in his army bore the inscription, *Tien-fu*, *Tien-hiung*, *Tien-wang Tai-ping Tien-kwoh*, or 'Heavenly Father, Heavenly Elder Brother, Heavenly King of the Great Peace [Dynasty] of the Heavenly Kingdom' (*i.e.*, China).

The incidents of this man's early life and education were ascertained in 1854, from his relative Hung Jin, by the Rev. Theodore Hamberg, whose narrative[1] bears the marks of a trustworthy recital. Hung Siu-tsuen was the youngest son of Hung Jang, a well-to-do farmer living in Hwa hien, a district situated on the North River, about thirty miles from Canton city, in a small village of which he was the headman. The family was from Kiaying prefecture, on the borders of Kiangsí, and the whole village was regarded as belonging to the Hakkas, or Squatters, and had little intercourse with the Pun-tis, or Indigenes, on that account. Siu-tsuen was born in 1813, and at the usual age of seven entered school, where he showed remarkable aptitude for study. His family being too poor to spare his services long, he had to struggle and deny himself, as many a poor aspirant for fame in all lands has done, in order to fit himself to enter the regular examinations. In 1826 his name appeared on the list of candidates in Hwa hien, but Hung Jin says: "Though his name was always among the first upon the board at the district examinations, yet he never succeeded in attaining the degree of Siu-tsai." In 1833 he was at Canton at the triennial examination, when he met with the native evangelist Liang A-fah, who was distributing and selling a number of his own writings near the Kung yuen to the candidates as they went in and out of the hall. Attracted by the venerable aspect of this man, he accepted a set of his tracts called *Kiuen Shí Liang Yen*, or 'Good Words to Exhort the Age.' He took them home with him, but threw them aside when he found that they advocated Christianity, then a proscribed doctrine.

In 1837 he was again in the provincial tripos, where his re-

---

[1] *Visions of Hung Siu-tshuen and Origin of the Kwang-sí Insurrection*, Hongkong, 1854. Mr. W. Sargent in the *North American Review* for July, 1854, Vol. LXXIX., p. 158.

peated disappointment and discontent aggravated an illness that seized him. On reaching his home he took to his bed and prepared for death, having had several visions foretokening his decease. He called his parents to his bedside and thus addressed them: "My days are counted and my life will soon be closed. O my parents! how badly have I returned the favor of your love to me; I shall never attain a name that shall reflect lustre on you." After uttering these words he shut his eyes and lost all strength and command over his body, and became unconscious of what was going on around him. His outward senses were inactive, his body appeared as dead, but his soul was acted upon by a peculiar energy, seeing and remembering things of a very extraordinary nature.

At first, when his eyes were closed he saw a dragon, a tiger, and a cock enter the room; a great number of men playing upon instruments then approached, bearing a beautiful sedan-chair in which they invited him to be seated. Not knowing what to make of this honor, he was carried away to a luminous and beautiful place wherein a multitude of fine men and women saluted him on arrival with expressions of joy. On leaving the sedan an old woman took him down to a river, saying: "Thou dirty man, why hast thou kept company with yonder people and defiled thyself? I must now wash thee clean." After the washing was over he entered a large building in company with a crowd of old and virtuous men, some of whom were the ancient sages. Here they opened his body, took out the heart and other organs, and replaced them by new ones of a red color; this done, the wound closed without leaving a scar. The whole assembly then went on to another larger hall, whose splendor was beyond description, in which an aged man, with a golden beard and dressed in black robes, sat on the highest place. Seeing Siu-tsuen, he began to shed tears and said: "All human beings in the world are produced and sustained by me; they eat my food and wear my clothing, but not one among them has a heart to remember and venerate me; what is worse, they take my gifts and therewith worship demons; they purposely rebel against me and arouse my anger. Do thou not imitate them." Hereupon he gave him a sword to destroy the demons, a seal to overcome the evil spirits, and a sweet yellow fruit to eat. Siu-tsuen received them, and straightway began to exhort his venerable companions to perform their duties to their master. After doing so even to tears, the high personage led him to a spot whence he could behold the world below, and discern the horrible depravity and vice of its inhabitants. The sight was too awful to be endured, and words were inadequate to describe it. So he awoke from his trance, and had vigor enough to rise and dress himself and go to his father. Making a bow, Siu-tsuen said: "The venerable old man above has commanded that all men shall turn to me, and that all treasures shall flow to me." This sickness continued about forty days, and the visions were multiplied. He often met with a man in them whom he called his elder brother, who instructed him how to act and assisted him in going after and killing evil spirits. He became more and more possessed with the idea, as his health returned, that he had been commissioned to be Emperor of China; and one day his father found a slip on which was written "The Heavenly King of Great Reason, the Sovereign King Tsuen." As time wore on, this lofty idea seems to have more and more developed his mind to a soberness and purity which overawed and attracted him. Nothing is said about his utterances while the war with England was progressing, but he must have known its progress and results. His cataleptic fits and visions seem not to have returned, and he pursued his avocation as a school-teacher until about 1843, having meanwhile failed in another trial to obtain his degree at Canton. In that year his wife's brother asked to take away the nine tracts of Liang A-fah to see what they contained; when he returned them to Siu-tsuen he urged him to read them too.

They consisted of sixty-eight short chapters upon common topics, selected from the Bible, and not exactly fitted to give him, in his excited state and total ignorance of western books and religion, a fair notion of Christianity. As he read them he saw, as he thought, the true meaning of his visions. The venerable old man was no other than God the Father, and his guide was Jesus Christ, who had assisted him in slaying the demons. "These books are certainly sent purposely by heaven to me to confirm the truth of my former experience. If I had received them without having gone through the sickness, I should not have dared to believe in them, and by myself to oppose the customs of the whole world. If I had merely been sick, but not also received the books, I should have had no further evidence as to the truth of my visions, which might also have been considered as mere products of a diseased imagination."

This sounds reasonable, and commends itself as wholly unlike the ravings of a madman. Nevertheless, while it would be unwise for us to closely criticise this narrative in its details, and assert that Siu-tsuen's pretensions were all hypocritical, we must bear in mind the fact that he had certainly, neither at this time nor ever afterward, a clear conception of the true nature of Christianity, judging from his writings and edicts. The nature of sin, and the dominion of God's law upon the sinner; the need of atonement from the stain and effects of sin; Christ's mediatorial sacrifice; were subjects on which he could not possibly have received full instruction from these fragmentary essays. In after days his conviction of his own divine calling to rule over China, seems to have blinded his understanding to the spiritual nature of the Christian church. His individual penchant was insufficient to resist or mould the subordinates who accepted his mission for their own ends. But he was not a tool in their hands at any time, and his personal influence permeated the ignorant mass of reckless men around him to an extraordinary degree, while his skill in turning some of the doctrines and requirements of the Bible as the ground and proofs of his own authority indicated original genius, since the results were far beyond the reach of a cunning impostor. From first to last, beginning with poverty, obscurity, and weakness in Hwa, continuing with distinction, power, and royalty at Nanking and throughout its five adjacent provinces, and ending with defeat, desertion, and death in his own palace, Hung never wavered or abated one jot of his claim to supreme rule on earth. When his end was reported at Peking in August, 1864, thirty-one years after his receiving Liang A-fah's tracts, the imperial rescript sadly said: "Words cannot convey any idea of the misery and desolation he caused; the measure of his iniquity was full, and the wrath of both gods and men was roused against him."

A career so full of exceptional interest and notable incidents cannot, of course, be minutely described in this sketch. After Hung's examination of the tracts which had lain unnoticed in his hands for ten years, followed by his conviction of the real meaning of his visions in 1837, he began to proclaim his mission and exhort those around him to accept Christianity. Hung Jin (who furnished Mr. Hamberg with his statements) and a fellow-student, Fung Yun-shan, were his first converts; they agreed to put away all idols and the Confucian tablet out of their schools, and then baptized or washed themselves in a brook near by, as a sign of their purification and faith in Jesus. As they had no portion of the Sacred Scriptures to guide them, they were at a loss to understand many things spoken of by Liang A-fah, but his expositions of the events and doctrines occurring in them were deeply pondered and accepted. The Mosaic account of creation and the flood, destruction of Sodom, sermon on the Mount, and nature of the final judgment, were given in them, as well as a full relation of Christ's life and death; and these prepared the neophytes to receive the Bible when they got it. But the same desire to find proof of his own calling led Siu-tsuen to fix on fanciful renderings of certain texts, and, after the manner of commentators in other lands, to extract meanings never intended. A favorite conceit, among others, was to assume that wherever the character *tsuen*, 全, meaning 'whole,' 'altogether,' occurred in a verse, it meant himself, and as it forms a part of the Chinese phrase for *almighty*, he thus had strong reasons (as he thought) for his course. The phrase *Tien kwoh*, denoting the 'Kingdom of Heaven' in Christ's preaching, they applied to China. With such preconceived views it is not wonderful that the brethren were all able to fortify themselves in their opinions by the strongest arguments. All those discourses in the series relating to repentance, faith, and man's depravity were apparently entirely overlooked by them.

The strange notions, unaffected earnestness, moral conduct, and new ideas about God and happiness of these men soon began to attract people to them, some to dispute and cavil, others to accept and worship with them. Their scholars, one and all, deserted them as soon as the Confucian tablet was removed from the schoolroom, and they were left penniless and unemployed, sometimes subjected to beatings and obloquy for embracing an outlandish religion, and other times ridiculed for forsaking their ancestral halls. The number of their adherents was too few to detain them at home, and in May, 1844, Siu-tsuen, Yun-shan, and two associates resolved to visit a distant relative who lived near the Miaotsz' in Kwangsí, and get their living along the road by peddling ink-stones and pencils. They reached the adjoining district, Tsingyuen, where they preached two months and baptized several persons; some time after Hung Jin took a school there, and remained several years, baptizing over fifty converts. Siu-tsuen and Yun-shan came to the confines of the Miaotsz' in Sinchau fu in three months, preaching the existence of the true God and of redemption by his Son, and after many vicissitudes reached their relative's house in Kwei hien among the mountains. Here they tarried all summer, and their earnest zeal in spreading the doctrines which they evidently had found so cheering to their own hearts, arrested the attention of these rude mountaineers, and many of them professed their faith in Christ. Siu-tsuen returned home in the winter, and was disappointed in not finding his colleague Yun-shan there as well as the other two, nor could he give any account of his course. It appeared afterward that Yun-shan had met some acquaintances on his road, and became so much interested in preaching to them at Thistle-mount that he remained there two years, teaching school and gathering churches.

Siu-tsuen continued to teach and preach the truth as he had learned it from the books in his hands. In 1846 he heard of I. J. Roberts, the American missionary, living at Canton, and the next spring received an invitation to come there and study. He and Hung Jin did so; the former remained with Mr. Roberts about two months, giving him a narrative of his own visions, conversion, and preaching, at the same time learning the nature and extent of foreign mission work in that city. He made a visit home with two native Christians, who had been sent to Hwa to learn more about him. They seem to have obtained good reports of his character; but others in Mr. Roberts' employ were afraid of his influence if he should enter their church, and therefore intrigued to have him refused admission just then. Mr. Roberts appears to have acted discreetly according to the light he had respecting the applicant's integrity, and would no doubt have baptized him had not the latter soon after left Canton, where he had no means of support. At this time the political disturbances in Kwangtung seem to have greatly influenced Siu-tsuen's course, and when he reached home he made a second visit to his relative, and thence went to Thistle-mount to rejoin Fung Yun-shan. Hung Jin states that before this date he had expressed disloyal sentiments against the Manchus, but these are so common among the Cantonese that they attracted no notice. On seeing Yun-shan and meeting the two thousand converts he had gathered, it is pretty certain that hopes of a successful resistance must have revived in his breast. A woman among them also began to relate some visions she had seen ten years before, foretelling the advent of a man who should teach them how to worship God. The number of converts rapidly increased in three prefectures adjacent to the River Yuh in the eastern part of Kwangsí, and no serious hindrance was met with from the officials, though there were not wanting enemies, by one of whom Yun-shan was accused and then thrown into prison. However, the prefect and district magistrate to whom the case was referred, finding no sufficient cause for punishment, liberated him; though the new sectaries had made themselves somewhat obnoxious to the idolaters by their iconoclasm—so hard is it to learn patience and toleration in any country. In very many villages in that region the *Shangtí hwui*, or 'Associations for worshipping God,' began to be recognized, but they do not seem to have quoted the toleration edict obtained in 1844 in favor of Christianity, as that only spoke of the *Tien-chu kiao*, or Catholics. The worship of Shangtí is a peculiar function of the Emperor, as has been already explained; and it is not surprising to be told by Hung Jin that the new sect was regarded as treasonable.

In 1848 Siu-tsuen's father died trusting in the new faith and directing that no Buddhist services be held at his funeral; the whole family had by this time become its followers, and when the son and Yun-shan met them soon after, they began to discuss their future. The believers in Kwangsí were left to take care of themselves during the whole winter, and appear to have gone on with their usual meetings without hindrance. In June, 1849, the two leaders left Hwa for Kwangsí, assisted by the faithful, and found much to encourage them in their secret plans in the general unity which pervaded the association. Some members had been favored with visions, others had become exhorters, denouncing those who behaved contrary to the doctrines; others essayed to cure diseases. Siu-tsuen was immediately acknowledged by all as their leader; he set himself to introduce and maintain a rigid discipline, forbade the use of opium and spirits, introduced the observance of the Sabbath, and regulated the worship of God. No hint of calling in the aid of a foreign teacher to direct them in their new services appears to have been suggested by any member, nor even of sending to Canton to engage the services of a native convert, though Liang A-fah was still living then. The whole year was thus passed at Thistle-mount, and the nucleus of the future force thoroughly imbued with the ideas of their leader, who had, by June, 1850, gathered around him his own relatives and chosen his lieutenants.[1]

The existence of such a large body of people, acting together under the orders of one man, whose aspirations and teachings had gradually filled their minds with new ideas, could not remain unnoticed by the authorities. The governor-general lived at Canton, and received his information through local magistrates and prefects, whose policy was rather to understate the truth. But Sü Kwang-tsin felt that he was not fitted for the coming struggle. His place was therefore filled by the appoint-

---

[1] The insurgents cut off the tail, allowed their hair to grow, and decided that all who joined the insurrectional movement should leave off the *chang* and the Tartar tunic, and should wear the robe open in the front, which their ancestors had worn in the time of the Mings.—Callery and Yvan, *History of the Insurrection in China*, translated by John Oxenford, p. 61. London, 1853.

ment of Lin, then living in Fuhchau, who started to fulfil his new charge, but died in October, as he entered the province. Governor Sü was obliged to leave Canton on duty, but he never met the enemy nor returned to his post. The populace of the city made themselves merry over his violent conduct toward a poor paper-image maker near the landing, who had just set out to dry some effigies dressed in high official costume, each one lacking a head. Sü chose to regard this proceeding as an intentional insult, as the artisan must have known that he was to pass by that way, and ordered him to be bambooed and his effigies destroyed to neutralize the bad omen. The Peking government had just sent three Manchus to superintend operations in Kwangsí; their predecessors, Lí and Chau, with the provincial governor, Ching, were all degraded, but these new imperial officials did no better, nor did those on the spot expect that they would succeed. Tahungah was the ruffian who had executed one hundred and eighty British prisoners in Formosa nine years before; and Saishangah was the prime minister of the young Emperor Hienfung, as worthless as he was depraved. Uruntai, who had long been in command of the Manchu garrison at Canton, was also sent, in May, 1851, to check the growing power of the insurgents. They were well posted in Wusiuen hien, near the junction of two rivers, and this chieftain naïvely expresses his surprise in his report to the Emperor that the rebels should occupy an important post which he had just decided to fortify. However, his official report[1] explains the reasons for the imperial reverses better than anything which had hitherto appeared. Corruption, venality, idleness, opium-smoking, and peculation had made the whole army a mass of rottenness; no one can wonder that the Tai-pings marched without danger through the land to their goal at Nanking.

A year previous to this date, however, the conflict had been begun by the followers of Siu-tsuen. In their zeal against idolatry they had destroyed temples and irritated the people, which ere long aroused a spirit of distrust and enmity; this was further increased by the long-standing feud and mutual hatred

---

[1] *Chinese Repository*, Vol. XX., p. 493.

between the *pun-tis* and *hakkas* (natives and squatters) which ran through society. Siu-tsuen and his chiefs were mostly of the latter class, and whenever villages were attacked and the hakkas worsted, they moved over to Thistle-mount and professed to worship Shangtí with Siu-tsuen. In this way the whole population had become more or less split up into parties. When a body of imperial soldiers sent to arrest him and Yunshan were driven off, they availed themselves of the enthusiasm of their followers to gather them and occupy Lienchu, a large market-town in Kwei hien. This proceeding attracted to their banner all the needy and discontented spirits in that region, but their own partisans were now able to regulate and employ all who came, requiring a close adherence to their religious tenets and worship. This town of Lienchu was soon fortified, and the order of a camp began to appear among its possessors, who, however, spared the townspeople. The drilling of the force, now increased to many thousands, commenced; its vitality was soon tested when it was deemed best to cross the river and advance on Taitsun in order to obtain more room. The imperialists were hoodwinked by a simple device, and when they found their enemy had marched off, their attack on the rear was repulsed with much loss. Like all their class, they turned their wrath on the peaceful inhabitants of Lienchu, killing and burning till almost nothing was left. This needless cruelty recoiled on themselves, and all the members of the *Shangtí hwui*, loyal and disaffected alike, felt that their very name carried sedition in it, and they must join Siu-tsuen's standard or give up their faith. He had induced some recent comers belonging to the Triad Society to put their money into the military chest and to submit to his rules. One of his religious teachers had been detected embezzling the funds while on their way to the commissariat, but the public trial and execution of the man had served both as a warning and an encouragement to the different classes who witnessed the affair. Most of the Triad chiefs, however, were afraid of such discipline, and drew off to the imperialists with the greater number of their followers. The defection furnished Siu-tsuen an opportunity to make known his settled opposition to this fraternity, and that every man joining his party must leave it. At this time the discipline and good order exhibited in the encampment at Taitsun must have struck the people around it with surprise and admiration, if the meagre accounts we have received are at all trustworthy.

About one year elapsed between the conflict near Lienchu and the capture of Yung-ngan chau, a city on the River Mei in Pingloh prefecture. During this period Siu-tsuen had become more and more possessed with the idea of his divine mission from the *Tien-fu*, or 'Heavenly Father,' as God was now commonly called, and the *Tien-hiung*, or 'Heavenly Elder Brother,' as he termed Jesus Christ. He began to seclude himself from the gaze of his followers, and deliver to them such revelations as he received for the management of the force committed to him to clear the land of all idolatry and oppression, and cheer the hearts of those pledged to the glorious cause. This course was destructive of all those peculiar tenets which Christianity teaches, and, so far as can be learned, neither he nor Yun-shan any longer prominently set forth the doctrines of salvation by repentance and faith in Christ, as they had done in their first journey among the Miaotsz', but held their followers together by fanaticism and the hope of final triumph. In its main features, his course was copied from that of Moses and Aaron when they withdrew into the tabernacle, and it was easy to impress upon his uninstructed followers the repetition in his person of the same mode of making known the will of Heaven. An adequate reason can also be found in this scheme why he never called in the aid of foreign missionaries to teach his followers the truth as it is in Christ Jesus, knowing full well that none of them would lend any countenance to such delusion. As early as April, 1849, when still in Kwei hien, he began to promulge his decrees in the form of revelations received from the Heavenly Father and Elder Brother, when one or the other came down into the world to tell him what course he should pursue. In March, 1853, just before capturing Nanking, he issued a book of "Celestial Decrees," containing a series of these revelations, from which the real nature of his character can be learned. Two extracts will be sufficient to quote:

The Heavenly Father addressed the multitude, saying, O my children! Do you know your Heavenly Father and your Celestial Elder Brother? To which they all replied, We know our Heavenly Father and Celestial Elder Brother. The Heavenly Father then said, Do you know your Lord, and truly? To which they all replied, We know our Lord right well. The Heavenly Father said, I have sent your Lord down into the world to become the Celestial King (*Tien-wang*); every word he utters is a celestial command; you must be obedient; you must truly assist your Lord and regard your King; you must not dare to act disorderly, nor to be disrespectful. If you do not regard your Lord and King, every one of you will be involved in difficulty.[1]

It is only from these official documents that we can learn the real political and religious tenets of the revolutionists now intrenched at Yung-ngan, and soon to burst forth in fury upon their country. It was in vain to expect gospel figs from such a bramble bush.

Another extract exhibits their jugglery still more clearly. It is dated December 9, 1851, and contains the proceedings and sentence in the case of Chau Sih-nang, who had been detected holding intercourse with General Saishangah at Taitsun. Four of the kings were that day consulting upon some weighty matters, when suddenly the Heavenly Father came down among them and secretly told them to instantly arrest Chau and two others and bring them to Yang, the Eastern King, while he returned to heaven. They did so, and reported the matter to the Tien-wang, but none of them had any evidence to proceed upon. "Happily, however, the Heavenly Father gave himself the trouble to appear once more," and ordered two of the royal cousins to go and inform the several princes of his presence. They all attended at court and entreated the Heavenly King to accompany them. Hereupon, his Majesty, guarded by the princes and body-guards, together with a host of officials, advanced into the presence of the Heavenly Father. They all kneeled down and asked, "Is the Heavenly Father come down?" He replied, addressing the Tien-wang, "Siu-tsuen, I am going to take this matter in hand to-day; a mere mortal would find it a hard task. One Chau has been holding collusive commu-

[1] This decree bears the date April 19, 1851, at Tung-hiang, a village near Wusiuen.

nication with the enemy yesterday, and has returned to court, intending to carry into effect a very serious revolt. Go and bring him here." The culprit soon came, and the examination is reported in full. In answer to the question, "Who is it that is now speaking to you?" he replied, "The Heavenly Father, the Supreme Lord and Great God (Shangtí) is addressing me." He said soon after, "I am aware that the Heavenly Father is omnipotent, omniscient, and omnipresent." By a series of questions his guilt was proved, and he and his accomplices, with his wife and son, were all put to death as a warning to traitors, in presence of a large concourse, to whom they confessed the justice of their fate.

When in possession of Nanking, Hung Siu-tsuen was formally proclaimed by his army to be Emperor of China, and assumed the style and insignia of royalty. Five leading chiefs were appointed to their several corps as South, East, West, North, and Assistant Kings; Fung Yun-shan was the Southern King. Who among them were the efficient disciplinarians and leading minds in carrying on their plan cannot be now ascertained, so complete was the secrecy which enveloped the whole movement from first to last as to the *personnel* of the force. Dr. Medhurst's translations of their orders, tenets, laws, revelations, and text-books furnish the most authentic sources for estimating its character, but they fail to describe its living agents. In so large an army, composed of the most heterogeneous elements, it cannot be expected that there would be at any time much knowledge of the sacred Scriptures, on which its leaders based their assumed powers derived from the 'Heavenly Father and Elder Brother;' but there certainly was a remarkable degree of sobriety and discipline among them during the first few years of their existence. A most perplexing question, which increased in its urgency and difficulty as soon as opposition drove the rebel general to intrench himself at Lienchu, was temporarily arranged by forming a separate encampment for the women, and placing over them officers of their own sex to see that discipline was maintained. In doing this he allowed the married people as great facilities for the care of their children as was possible under the conditions of army life; but during their progress through the land in 1852 and 1853, much suffering must have been endured.

In 1852 the state and size of the army in Yung-ngan fully authorized the leaders of the revolt to march northward. Several engagements had given their men confidence in each other as they saw the imperialists put to flight; defeats had furthermore shown that their persevering enemy entertained no idea of sparing even one of them if captured. The want of provisions during their five months' siege within its walls further trained them to a certain degree of patient endurance; when, therefore, they broke through the besieging force in three divisions on the night of April 7, 1852, they were animated by success and hope to possess themselves of the Empire. Marching north they now attacked Kweilin, the provincial capital, May 15th, but having no cannon fit to besiege a walled city of that size, crossed the border and captured Tau in Hunan, which gave them access to the River Siang and means of transportation. Their course was thenceforth an easy conquest of the towns along its valley. Kweiyang chau, Chin chau, Tunghing, Nganjin, and others were taken and evacuated, one after the other, until they reached the capital of this province, September 18th. Changsha and Siangtan together form one immense city, and its defenders fully understood their peril, and the probability of entire destruction if they allowed it to be captured. For eighty days the Tai-pings exerted themselves in vain to obtain possession, losing, however, very few men, and doing no great harm to their enemy, who kept beyond reach. December 1st they raised the siege, and by the 13th reached Yohchau on the Yangtsz', which was taken without a struggle. Ten days after, replenished and encouraged by the spoil found in Yohchau, they occupied Hanyang and Wuchang, the capital of Hupeh province, lying on the other side of the river. Its garrison was unable to escape, and many soldiers were destroyed. Hwangchau and Kiukiang, two prefect cities lower down, were captured January 12th and February 18th, while Nganking, the capital of Nganhwui, fell a week later. Nothing seemed able to resist the advance of the insurgents, and on March 8th they encamped before Nanking. It was garrisoned by

Manchus and Chinese, who, however, made no better defence than their comrades in other cities; in ten days its walls were breached, and all the defenders found inside put to death, including Luh, the governor-general of the province. Chinkiang and Yangchau soon were dragged to the same fate, thus depriving the imperialists of their control of the Grand Canal.

This rapid progress through the land since leaving Yung-ngan eleven months previously had spread consternation among the demoralized officers and soldiers of the Emperor, who, on his part, was as weak and ignorant as any of his subordinates. The march of the insurgents showed the utter hollowness of the imperial troops, the incapacity of their most trusted leaders, and the little interest taken by the great body of the nation in the conflict. Many causes which might adequately explain this extraordinary success cannot now be ascertained, but a national dislike of the Manchus on the part of the Chinese lay at the bottom of their coldness. They felt, too, that a government which could not protect them against a few thousand foreign troops might as well give place to a native one. The insurgents had perhaps not more than ten thousand adherents, including women and children, when they left Yung-ngan;[1] but these went forth in the full conviction of the heavenly commission of their leader to destroy idolatry, set up the worship of the true God, and inaugurate the kingdom of heaven in the person of the "Heavenly King." The term *Shangti* was known by every schoolboy to be the name of the God worshipped at Peking by the Emperor in his right as Son of Heaven, and the successor of the ancient sovereigns mentioned in the *Shu King;* accordingly, when the insurgents set up the worship of the true God as they had been able to learn it from Gutzlaff's revised version of the Bible, their countrymen immediately recognized the challenge. It was an attack on the religious as well as political position of Taukwang; whoever maintained his side in the gage of battle, with him were undoubtedly the powers above. The progress of the new banner

---

[1] Though one of their officers told Mr. Meadows, at Nanking, that the force was about three thousand.

from Yung-ngan to Nanking was like that of a fiery cross, and the sufferings of the people, except in a few large cities, were really more owing to the savage imperialists than to the Tai-pings. The latter grew in strength as they advanced, owing to indiscriminate slaughter on the part of their enemies of unoffending natives, and at last reached their goal with not much less than eighty thousand men.

Their position was now accessible to foreigners—who had been watching their rise and progress under great disadvantages in arriving at the truth—and they were soon visited by them in steamers. The first to do so was Governor Bonham in H. M. S. Hermes, accompanied by T. T. Meadows, one of the most competent linguists in China, who published the result of his inquiries. The visitors were at first received with incredulity, but this soon gave way to eager curiosity to learn the real nature of their religious views and practices. The insurgents themselves were even more ignorant of foreigners than were these of the rebels, so that the interest could not fail to be reciprocal, nor could either party desire to come into collision with the other.

About two months after the cities of Nanking, Chinkiang, and Yangchau had been taken, garrisoned, and put in a state of defence by their inhabitants, working under the direction of Tai-ping officers, the leaders felt so much confidence in their cause, their troops, and their ability, that they despatched a division to capture Peking. No particulars of its size or composition are given, but its course and achievements are recorded in the *Peking Gazette*. The force landed not far from Kwa-chau, where it defeated a body of Manchus, and then proceeded to Liuho and Fungyang fu without finding serious opposition. Crossing the province of Nganhwui, they entered that of Ho-nan, and in one month from landing the troops laid siege to Kai-fung, the provincial capital, June 19th. Three days later they were repulsed, and their leaders crossed the Yellow River to Hwaiking fu, about a hundred miles west of Kaifung. For two months they were baffled by an unusual resistance on the part of the imperialists, and were compelled to leave it and go west into Shansí, where they took Pingyang fu and flanked the enemy by turning east and north-east till they crossed the Liuming pass and got into Chihlí. It was their design to have gone down the River Wei to Lintsing chau on the Grand Canal, but they were compelled to make a detour of some hundreds of miles to reach this last place. In doing so they ascended the steep defiles leading from the basin of the Yellow River to the plateau in South Shansí. This march was accomplished in the month of September, and on October 9th the prefect city of Shinchau in Chihlí, only two hundred miles from Peking, was taken. Their army remained at Shinchau for a fortnight, when they marched across the plain north-easterly to Tsinghai hien, on the Grand Canal. Here they intrenched themselves on October 28th, but twenty miles south of Tientsin. A detachment sent to attack that city was repulsed, and the whole body were blockaded on November 3d by the Manchu force, which had followed it from Hwaiking, and other corps ordered from the north to intercept its progress toward the capital. In six months this insurgent force had traversed four provinces, taken twenty-six cities, subsisted themselves on the enemy, and defeated every body of imperialists sent against them. The men who performed this remarkable march of fully one thousand five hundred miles in the face of such odds, would have accomplished even greater deeds under better training. Considering all things, it is quite equal to General Sherman's march to the sea in 1864; yet so little is known of the details of this feat, that we are not even certain of its leader's name—whether Lin Fung-tsiang, spoken of by the *Gazette* as a 'Pretended Minister,' or some other general, was in command.

It is rather hard to understand why the Tai-pings intrenched themselves so near to Tientsin, but the officials of that city, in 1858, ascribed it to the fact that water covered the plain, preventing all operations against the town. Perhaps their want of siege guns, and the cavalry now brought from Mongolia, decided the leaders to intrench themselves at Tsinghai and send to Nanking for reinforcements. The Tai-ping Wang immediately despatched an auxiliary force, which also crossed Nganhwui to Funghien on the north bank of the Yellow River; this place was captured March 17, 1854, "after taking city after city," as the Emperor Hienfung expressed it. The ice was gone when the army reached Lintsing chau, April 12th, and that city was taken by a fierce assault against the combined resistance of its garrison and the imperialists outside, after the insurgent auxiliary was attacked in force. The other body had left Tsinghai in February, starved out rather than driven away, and gone to the district town of Hien, which they left March 10th for Fauching, and probably rejoined their comrades somewhere between that and Lintsing. They were about a hundred miles apart, and the intervening region was no doubt forcibly drained of its supplies. This joint army remained in possession of their depots as long as they saw fit, and treated the inhabitants reasonably well, among whom there were no Manchus. The inability to understand each other's speech kept the people of this district from mixing with the southerners, and, combined with the impossibility of keeping open the road to Nanking, decided the Tai-pings to return. This they did in March, 1855, by re-entering Nganhwui and rejoining the main body whereever ordered; but no details are known of their movements for nearly a year before that date. Peking and the Great Pure dynasty were saved, however; while the failure of Hung Siutsuen to risk all on such an enterprise proved his ignorance of the real point of this contest. He never was able to undertake a second campaign, and his followers soon degenerated into banditti.

The possession of Nanking, Chinkiang, and Kwachau, with the large flotilla along the Yangtsz' River west to Íchang in Hupeh, a distance of over six hundred miles, had entirely sundered the Emperor's authority over the seven south-eastern provinces. The country on each side for fifty or one hundred and fifty miles was visited by the insurgents' troops merely for supplies. Their boats penetrated to Nanchang in Kiangsí, went up the River Siang even beyond Changsha in Hunan, ravaged one town after another in quest of provisions and reinforcements, which were either taken to Nanking or used to support the crews; but nowhere did the leaders set up anything like a government, nowhere did they secure those who submitted or pursued their avocations quietly any protection against imperialist or other foes. As a revolution involving a reorganization of the Chinese nation on Christian principles, and a well-defined assertion of the rights and duties of rulers and subjects, it had failed entirely within a year after the possession of Nanking. There was no hope that any of the leaders in the movement would develop the ability to initiate the establishment of a consistent and suitable control, since not one of them was endowed either with the experience necessary to introduce provisional government over conquered communities, or with that tact calculated to impress their inhabitants with enduring confidence in them. All their prisoners were compelled to work or fight in their service, and were willing to earn their food and clothes; while in obeying such orders, and going through such religious ceremonies as were told them, they of course had not much to complain of; but this conduct did not imply hatred of the mandarins or an abjuration of Buddhism.

During the three years after Nanking had been occupied, the people in the Yangtsz' valley had suffered much from the conflict. Both armies lived on the land, and the danger of resisting the demands for food, clothes, and animals was nearly equalled by that of joining the contending forces; in either case beggary or loss of life was sure to be the end. As an instance of by no means unexampled suffering, the populous mart of Hankow and its environs was taken by assault six different times during the thirty months ending in May, 1855, and finally was left literally a heap of ruins. In country places the imperialists were, of the two parties, perhaps the more terrible scourge, but as the region became impoverished each side vied with the other in exhausting the people. The Tai-pings were gradually circumscribed to the region around Nanking and Nganking by the slow approaches of the government troops, and in 1860 seemed to be near their end. The interest which had been aroused at Shanghai in 1853, upon hearing of their Christian tenets and organization, had been satisfied in the various visits of foreign functionaries to Nanking, the intercourse with the leaders and men, perusal of their books, and observation of their policy.

One inherent defect in the enterprise, when viewed in its political bearing, ere long showed itself. Nothing could induce Hung Siu-tsuen to lead his men to the north and risk all in an attack on Peking. His own conviction of his divine mission had been most cordially received by his generals and the entire body of followers which left Yung-ngan in 1852; but their faith was not accepted by the enormous additions made to the Tai-pings as they advanced to Nanking, and gradually the original force became so diluted that it was inadequate to restrain and inspirit their auxiliaries. Moreover, the Tien-wang had never seriously worked out any conception of the radical changes in his system of government, which it would be absolutely necessary to inaugurate under a Christian code of laws. Having had no knowledge of any western kingdom, he probably regarded them all as conformed to the rules and examples given in the Bible; perhaps, too, he trusted that the "Heavenly Father and Elder Brother" would reveal the proper course of action when the time came. The great body of literati would naturally be indisposed to even examine the claims of a western religion which placed Shangtí above all other gods, and allowed no images in worship, no ritual in temples, and no adoration to ancestors, to Confucius, or to the heavenly bodies. But if this patriotic call to throw off the Manchu yoke had been fortified by a well-devised system of public examinations for office—modified to suit the new order of things by introducing more practical subjects than those found in the classics—and had been put into practice, it is hard to suppose that the intellectual classes would not gradually have ranged themselves on the side of this rising power. The unnecessary cruelty and slaughter practised toward the Manchu garrisons and troops carried more dread into the hearts of the population than stimulus to co-operate with such ruthless revolutionists. The latter had weakened their prospects by destroying confidence in their moderation, justice, and ability to carry out their aim to establish a new sway. There was a large foundation of national aspirations and real dislike to the present dynasty, on which the Tien-wang could have safely reckoned for help and sympathy. But he was far from equal to the exigency of his opportunity. The doubts of his countrymen as to his competency were proved by the satisfaction and relief felt when his movement collapsed.

When the remnants of the two corps which returned from the north in 1855 were incorporated into the forces holding the Grand Canal and the Liang Kiang province, their outposts hardly extended along the Great River beyond Chinkiang on the east and Nganking on the west. In that year dissensions sprung up among the leaders themselves inside of Nanking, which ended in the execution of Yang, the Eastern King, the next year; a fierce struggle maintained by Wei, the Northern King, on behalf of the Tien-wang, upheld his supremacy, but at a loss of his best general. Another man of note, Shih Ta-kai, the Assistant King, losing faith in the whole undertaking, managed to withdraw with a large following westward, and reached Sz'chuen. The early friend of Hung Siu-tsuen, Fung Yun-shan, known as the Southern King, disappeared about the same time. Rumors of these conflicts reached Shanghai in such a contradictory form that it was impossible to learn all their causes.

One source of strife arose by Yang assuming to be the Holy Ghost. Receiving communications from the Heavenly Father and Elder Brother, he thus placed himself above the Tien-wang, and, it is said by Wilson,[1] "required him to humble himself and receive forty lashes" for some misdemeanors complained of by the Comforter. The notices of this man which have reached us show that he early took a prominent part in the movement, and perhaps manipulated "descents of the Heavenly Father," like the one referred to above as mentioned in the "Book of Declarations" in the case of Chau Sih-nang.[2] Many proclamations were issued in his name on the progress to Nanking, which set forth the principles under which the Heavenly Dynasty were trying to conquer. Incentives addressed to the patriotic feelings of the Chinese were mixed up with their obligations to worship Shangtí, now made known to them as the Great God, our Heavenly Father, and security promised to all who submitted.

[1] *The "Ever-Victorious Army," Lt.-Col. Gordon's Chinese Campaign*, p. 43.

[2] J. Milton Mackie, *Life of Tai-ping-Wang, Chief of the Chinese Insurrection*, Chap. XXXIV., New York, 1857.

In one sent forth by him when nearing Nanking, he thus summarizes the rules which guided the Tai-pings:

> I, the General, in obedience to the royal commands, have put in motion the troops for the punishment of the oppressor, and in every place to which I have come the enemy, at the first report, have dispersed like scattered rubbish. As soon as a city has been captured, I have put to death the rapacious mandarins and corrupt magistrates therein, but have not injured a single individual of the people, so that all of you may take care of your families and attend to your business without alarm and trepidation. I have heard, however, that numbers of lawless vagabonds are in the villages, who previous to the arrival of our troops take advantage of the disturbed state of the country to defile mens' wives and daughters, and burn or plunder the property of honest people. . . . I have therefore especially sent a great officer, named Yuen, with some hundreds of soldiers, to go through the villages, and as soon as he finds these vagabonds he is commissioned forthwith to decapitate them; while if the honest inhabitants stick up the word *shun* ['obedient'] over their doors, they will have nothing to fear.[1]

Such manifestoes could not reassure the timid population of the valley of the Yangtsz', and the carnage of the unresisting Manchus in Nanking, Chinkiang, and elsewhere indicated a ruthless license among the followers of the Tien-wang, which made them feel that their success carried with it no promise of melioration. In addition, as the vast spoil obtained from these cities and towns up to 1856 was consumed, the outlook of the rebels was most discouraging. Among their forces, the disheartened, the sick, and the wounded, with the captived and desperate, soon died, deserted, or skulked, and their places were filled by forced levies. Under these circumstances the dissensions within the court at Nanking imperilled the whole cause, and showed the incapacity of its leaders in face of their great aim. Yang had sunk into a sensual, unscrupulous faction leader who could no longer be endured; by October, 1856, he and all his adherents, to the number of twenty thousand, were utterly cut off by Wei. But this latter king speedily met with a like fate. Shih, the Assistant King, was at this time in the province of Kiangsí. It had become a life struggle with Siu-tsuen, and his removal of the four kings resulted in leaving him without any real military chief on whose loyalty he could depend. The rumors which

[1] Lindley, *Tai-ping Tien-kwoh*, Vol. I., p. 94.

reached Shanghai in 1856 of the fierce conflict in the city were probably exaggerated by the desire prevalent in that region that the parties would go on, like the Midianites in Gideon's time, beating down each other till they ended the matter.

The success of the Tai-pings had encouraged discontented leaders in other parts of China to set up their standards of revolt. The progress of Shih Ta-kai in Sz'chuen and Kweichau engaged the utmost efforts of the provincial rulers to restore peace. In Kwangtung a powerful band invested the city, but the operations of Governor Yeh, after the departure of Sü Kwang-tsun in 1854, were well supported by the gentry. By the middle of 1855 the rising was quenched in blood. The destruction of Fatshan, Shauking, and other large towns, had shown that the sole object of the rebels was plunder, though it was thought at first that they were Tai-pings. The executions in Canton during fourteen months up to August, 1856, were nearly a hundred thousand men; but the loss of life on both sides must be reckoned by millions. A band of Cantonese desperadoes seized the city of Shanghai in September, 1853, killing the district magistrate and some other officials. They retained possession till the Chinese New Year, January 27, 1854, leaving the city amid flames and carnage, when many of the leaders escaped in foreign vessels.[1] None of these men were affiliated with the Tai-pings.

In Formosa and Hainan, as well as in Yunnan and Kansuh, the provincial authorities had hard work with their local contingents to maintain the Emperor's authority. This wretched prince was himself fast bound under the sway of Suhshun and his miserable coterie, devising means to replenish his coffers by issuing iron and paper money, and proposing counters cut out of jade stone to take the place of bullion. The national history, however, had many notices of precisely such disastrous epochs in former times, and the nation's faith in itself was not really weakened.

By 1857 the imperialists had begun to draw close lines about

---

[1] No foreigners here or elsewhere in China were injured designedly during all this insurrection.

the rebels, when they were nearly restricted to the river banks between Nganking and Nanking, both of which cities were blockaded. Two years later the insurgent capital was beleaguered, but in its siege the loyalists trusted almost wholly to the effects of want and disease, which at last reached such an extreme degree (up to 1860) that it was said human flesh was sold on the butchers' stalls of Nanking. Their ammunition was nearly expended, their numbers were reduced, and their men apparently desirous to disperse; but the indomitable spirit of the leader never quailed. He had appointed eleven other *wang*, or generals, called *Chung Wang* ('Loyal King'), *Ying Wang* ('Heroic King'), *Kan Wang* ('Shield King'), *Ting Wang* ('Listening King'), etc., whose abilities were quite equal to the old ones. As the siege progressed events assumed daily a more threatening aspect. Chang Kwo-liang and Ho Chun, two imperialist generals, invested the city more and more closely, driving the insurgents to extremity in every direction. The efforts of these men were, however, not aggressive in consequence of the war then waging with the British and French on the Pei ho. This encouraged the beleaguered garrison to a desperate effort to free themselves, and on May 6, 1860, a well-concerted attack on the armies which had for years been intrenched behind outworks about the city scattered them in utter disorder. A small body of Tai-pings managed to get out toward the north of Kiangsu, near the Yellow River. Another body had already (in March) carried Hangchau by assault by springing a mine; as many as seventy thousand inhabitants, including the Manchu garrison, perished here during the week the city remained in possession of the rebels. On their return to Nanking the joint force carried all before it, and the needed guns and ammunition fell into their hands. The loyalist soldiers also turned against their old officers, but the larger part had been killed or dispersed. Chinkiang and Changchau were captured, and Ho Kwei-tsing, the governor-general, fled in the most dastardly manner to Suchau, without an effort to retrieve his overthrow. Some resistance was made at Wusih on the Grand Canal, but Ho Chun was so paralyzed by the onslaught that he killed himself, and Suchau fell into the hands of Chung Wang with no resistance whatever.

It was, nevertheless, burned and pillaged by the cowardly imperialists before they left it, Ho Kwei-tsing setting the large suburbs on fire to uncover the solid walls. This destruction was so unnecessary that the citizens welcomed the Tai-pings, for they would at least leave them their houses. With Suchau and Hangchau in their hands, the Kan Wang and Chung Wang had control of the great watercourses in the two provinces, and their desire now was to obtain foreign steamers to use in regaining mastery of the Yangtsz' River. The loss of their first leaders was by this time admirably supplied to the insurgents by these two men, who had had a wider experience than the Tien wang himself, while their extraordinary success in dispersing their enemies had been to them all an assurance of divine protection and approval.

The populous and fertile region of Kiangnan and Chehkiang was wholly in their hands by June, 1860, so far as any organized Manchu force could resist them. The destruction of life, property, and industry within the three months since their sally from Nanking had been unparalleled probably since the Conquest, more than two centuries before, and revived the stories told of the ruthless acts of Attila and Tamerlane. Shanghai was threatened in August by a force of less than twenty thousand men led by the Chung Wang, and it would have been captured if it had not been protected by British and French troops. Many villages in the district were destroyed, but the flotilla approaching from Sungkiang recoiled from a collision with foreigners, and the insurgents all retired before September. They, however, could now be supplied with munitions of war, and even began to enlist foreigners to help them drill and fight. It was an anomalous condition of things, possible only in China, that while the allied force was marching upon Peking to extort a treaty, the same force was encircling the walls of Shanghai, burning its suburbs to destroy all cover, and aiding its rulers to preserve it to Hienfung—all in order to conquer a trade. It was then the moment for the Tai-pings to have moved rapidly upon Chihlí and tried the gage of battle before the metropolis, as soon as possible after Lord Elgin had withdrawn. But they had now very few left to them of the kind of troops which threatened the capital in 1853–54, and could not depend on recruits from Kiangnan in the hour of adversity.

At this juncture the imperialists began to look toward foreigners for aid in restoring their prestige and power by employing skill and weapons not to be found among themselves. An American adventurer, Frederick G. Ward, of Salem, Mass., proposed to the Intendant Wu to recapture Sungkiang from the Tai-pings; he was repulsed on his first attempt at the head of about a hundred foreigners, but succeeded on the second, and the imperialists straightway occupied the city. This success, added to the high pay, stimulated many others to join him, and General Ward ere long was able to organize a larger body of soldiers, to which the name of *Chang-shing kiun*, or 'Ever-victorious force,' was given by the Chinese; it ultimately proved to be well applied. Its composition was heterogeneous, but the energy, tact, and discipline of the leader, under the impulse of an actual struggle with a powerful foe, soon moulded it into something like a manageable corps, able to serve as a nucleus for training a native army. Foreigners generally looked down upon the undertaking, and many of the allied naval and military officers regarded it with doubt and dislike. It had to prove its character by works, but the successive defeats of the insurgents during the year 1862 in Kiangsu and Chehkiang, clearly demonstrated the might of its trained men over ten times their number of undisciplined braves.

But we must retrace our steps somewhat. In 1860 the possession of the best parts of Kiangsu and Chehkiang led the Tien Wang to plan the relief of Nganking by advancing on Hankow with four separate corps. They were under the leadership of the Chung Wang, and, so far as the details can be gathered, manifested a practical generalship hardly to be expected. The Ying Wang was to move through Nganhwui from Luchau westerly to Hwangchau; the Attendant King (Shih) was to leave Kiangsí and co-operate with the Chung Wang by reaching the Yangtsz' as near Hankow as possible, and a smaller force under the Tu Wang was to recover Hukau at the mouth of Poyang Lake and ascend the Great River in boats. The area through which this campaign was to be carried on may be understood when we learn that the Chung Wang's march of five hundred miles was over the two ranges of mountains on the frontiers of Kiangsí, and that of the Ying Wang two hundred miles through the plains of Nganhwui. This last king did actually take his force of about eighty thousand men two hundred miles to Hwangchau (fifty miles below Hankow) in eleven days, but none of his colleagues came to his aid. The experience of eight years had quite changed the elements of the contest.

The people now generally realized that neither life, property, nor government was secured under the Tai-pings; the imperialists had learned how to obtain the co-operation of the patriotic gentry, and the rank and file of the Tai-pings were by this date mostly conquered natives of the same region, as no recruits had ever come from Kwangsí. Moreover, the region was impoverished, and this involved greater privations to all parties. Yet the Chung Wang went from Wuhu south-west to Kwangsin, crossed the water-shed into Kiangsí, defeated a force at Kienchang, crossed the River Kan near Linkiang, and marched north-west to Wuning hien on the River Siu. Here he heard of the defeat of Tu Wang, and the non-arrival of Shih's force; and, lest he should be hemmed in himself, as the failure of the campaign was evident, he led his army back across the province to Kwangsin by September, 1861. The particulars of this last great exploit of the Tai-pings are so imperfectly known, that it is impossible to judge of it as a military movement accomplished under enormous difficulties; but the Loyal King must have been a strategist of no mean rank.

In November, 1861, Nganking succumbed to the imperialists. Its defenders and the citizens endured untold sufferings at the last, while its victors had an empty shell; but the river was theirs down to Nanking. On his return east, Chung Wang moved into Chehkiang and overran all the northern half of that province, his men inflicting untold horrors upon the inhabitants, whom they killed, burned, and robbed as they listed. Ningpo was taken December 9th and held till May 10th, when it was recaptured by the allies; foreign trade had not been interrupted during this period, and the city suffered less than many others. In September the Tai-pings were driven out of the valley of the Yung River, but the death of General Ward at Tsz'kí deprived the imperialists of an able leader. The career of this man had been a strange one, but his success in training his men was endorsed by honorable dealing with the mandarins, who had reported well of him at Peking. He was buried at Sungkiang, where a shrine was erected to his memory, and incense is burned before him to this day.

It was difficult to find a successor, but the command rather devolved on his second, an American named Burgevine, who was confirmed by the Chinese, but proved to be incapable. He was superseded by Holland and Cooke, Englishmen, and in April, 1863, the entire command was placed under Colonel Peter Gordon, of the British army. During the interval between May, 1860, when Ward took Sungkiang, and April 6, 1863, when Gordon took Fushan, the best manner of combining native and foreign troops was gradually developed as they became more and more acquainted with each other and learned to respect discipline as an earnest of success. Such a motley force has seldom if ever been seen, and the enormous preponderance of Chinese troops would have perhaps been an element of danger had they been left idle for a long time.

The bravery of the Ever-victorious force in the presence of the enemy had gradually won the confidence of the allies, as well as the Chinese officials, in whose pay it was; and when it operated in connection with the French and British contingent in driving the Tai-pings out of Ningpo prefecture, the real worth of Ward's drill was made manifest. The recapture of that city by Captain Dew's skilful and brave attack in reply to their unprovoked firing at H. M. S. Encounter, brought out the bravery of all nationalities, as well as restored the safety of the port. An extract from Captain Dew's report will exhibit the dreadful results to the common people of this civil war:

I had known Ningpo in its palmy days, when it boasted itself one of the first commercial cities of the Empire; but now, on this 11th of May, one might have fancied that an angel of destruction had been at work in the city as in the suburbs. All the latter, with their wealthy hongs and thousands of houses, lay levelled; while in the city itself, once the home of half a million of people, no trace or vestige of an inhabitant could be seen. Truly it was a city of the dead. The rich and beautiful furniture of the houses had become firewood, or was removed to the walls for the use of soldiers. The canals were filled with dead bodies and stagnant filth. The stonework of bridges and pavements had been uplifted to strengthen walls and form barricades in the streets; and in temples once the pride of their Buddhist priests, the chaotic remains of gorgeous idols and war gods lay strewn about—their lopped limbs showing that they had become the sport of those Christian Tai-pings whose chief, the Tien-wang, eight years before at Nanking, had asked Sir George Bonham if the Virgin Mary had a pretty sister for him, the King of Heaven, to marry! It has been my good fortune since to assist at the wresting of many cities from these Tai-pings, and in them all I found, as at Ningpo, that the same devilish hands had been at work—the people expelled from their houses and their cities ruined.[1]

Yet so speedy was the revival from the ruins, that we are told that in one month houses had been refurnished and shops opened; their owners had mostly fled across the river into the foreign settlement. A larger force was now organized—MM. Le Brethon and Giquel being in charge of a Franco-Chinese regiment—and an advance made on Yüyau, which was retaken, and one thousand drilled Chinese left to defend it. Tsz'kí, Funghwa, and Shangyü were also cleared of rebels, and during the month of March they evacuated the prefect city of Shauhing, never again to return to this fertile valley. Their inroad had been an unmitigated scourge, for they had now given up all pretense of Christianity, and had not the least idea of instituting a regular government; to plunder, kill, and destroy was their only business. Their sense of danger from the hatred of the people whom they had so grievously maltreated led them at this time to defend the walled cities with a reckless bravery that made their capture more difficult and dangerous. This was shown in the siege of Shauhing fu, within whose walls about forty thousand Tai-pings were well led by the Shí Wang. The possession of cannon enabled them to reply to the balls thrown by Captain Dew's artillery, while despair lent energy to their resistance; so that the attack turned into a regular siege of a month's duration, when, food and ammunition being exhausted, they retreated *en masse* to Hangchau.

While this success relieved the greater part of Chehkiang from the scourge, the failure of the Ever-victorious force to

---

[1] A. Wilson, *The "Ever-Victorious Army,"* p. 102, London, 1868.

retake Taitsang and Fushan, under Holland and Brennan, had discouraged Governor Lí, who had now come into power. He applied to General Stavely, who, with a full appreciation of the exigencies of the case, and concurrence of Sir Frederick Bruce, aided in reorganizing Ward's force and placing Colonel Gordon over it with adequate powers. There were five or six infantry regiments of about five hundred men each, and a battery of artillery; at times it numbered five thousand men. The commissioned officers were all foreigners, and their national rivalries were sometimes a source of trouble; the non-commissioned officers were Chinese, many of them repentant rebels or seafaring men from Canton and Fuhkien, promoted for good conduct. The uniform was a mixture of native and foreign dress, which at first led to the men being ridiculed as 'Imitation Foreign Devils;' after victory, however, had elevated their *esprit du corps*, they became quite proud of the costume. In respect to camp equipage, arms, commissariat and ordnance departments, and means of transport, the natives soon made themselves familiar with all details; while necessity helped their foreign officers rapidly to pick up their language. It is recorded, to the credit of this motley force, that "there was very little crime and consequently very little punishment; . . . as drunkenness was unknown, the services of the provost-marshal rarely came into use, except after a capture, when the desire for loot was a temptation to absence from the ranks."[1]

In addition, the force had a flotilla of four small steamers, aided by a variety of native boats to the number of fifty to seventy-five. The plain is so intersected by canals that the troops could be easier moved by water than land, and these boats enabled it to carry out surprises which disconcerted the rebels. Wilson well remarks concerning Gordon's force: "Its success was owing to its compactness, its completeness, the quickness of its movements, its possession of steamers and good artillery, the bravery of its officers, the confidence of its men, the inability of the rebels to move large bodies of troops with

[1] Wilson, *ibid.*, p. 132.

rapidity, the nature of the country, the almost intuitive perception of the leader in adapting his operations to the nature of the country, and his untiring energy in carrying them out."[1]

The details of this singular troop are worth telling with more minuteness than space here allows, for its management will no doubt form a precedent in the future; but the good its remarkable chief effected in restoring peace to Kiangsu calls for that recognition which skill, tact, and high moral purpose ever deserve. Being formally put in command on March 24, 1863, he promptly reinstated the foreign officers belonging to the force, paid their dues, and within a few days was in readiness to march upon Fushan, a town on the Yangtsz' above Paushan. The fall of this place on April 6th led to the capture of Chanzu, when preparations were made for besieging Taitsang fu, where an army of ten thousand rebels, aided by foreign adventurers, presented a formidable undertaking for his force of two thousand eight hundred men, although supported by a large body of imperialists. In its capture (May 2d) the killed and wounded numbered one hundred and sixty-two officers and men; the booty obtained was so large that Colonel Gordon led his men back to Sungkiang, in order to reorganize them after this experience of their conduct. Finding that their former license in appropriating the loot thus obtained tended to demoralize them all, he accepted the resignations of some of the discontented officers, and adopted stringent measures to bring the others to render military obedience. Consequently, when he started for Kiunshan with about three thousand men, he had his force in a much better condition. This city occupied an important position between Shanghai, Chanzu, Taitsang, and other large towns on the east, and Suchau on the west. The rebels had set up a cannon foundry within its walls, and from it obtained supplies for the last-named city, with which it was connected by a causeway. By means of the armed steamer Hyson, Colonel Gordon was able to bring up through one of the canals a company of three hundred and fifty men and field artillery, cutting the causeway and pursuing its defenders, some

---

[1] *Ibid.*, p. 138.

into the town and some toward Suchau, almost to its very gates. On the return of the steamer in the night, the commander found the imperialists engaged with the garrison in a sharp contest, in which the foreigners then aided, and completely routed the rebel body of nearly eight thousand men. Fully four thousand of them were killed outright, and others were drowned or cut off by the exasperated peasantry before the day was over. This was on May 30th. The captured town was made headquarters by its victors, as a more eligible location than Sungkiang, though against the wishes of the native officers, who desired to go back there with their booty. The loss of men, material, and position to the rebels was very great, and Colonel Gordon could now safely turn his whole thoughts to the capture of Suchau.

This city is like Venice in its approaches by canals; owing to its location it was deemed best, before attempting its capture, to reduce certain towns in the vicinity, from which it derived supplies, so that the Chung Wang should not be able to co-operate with its garrison. The district towns of Wukiang and Kahpu were both taken in July with comparatively little loss. This rapid reduction of many strong stockades, stone forts, and walled towns, with the panic exhibited by the men, proved how useless to the rebels the foreigners in their service had been in rendering them really formidable enemies, and how incapable the wangs had been to appreciate the nature and need of discipline. After these places had been occupied, Colonel Gordon found his position beset with so many unexpected annoyances, both from his rather turbulent and incongruous troops as well as from the Chinese authorities, that he went to Shanghai on August 8th for the purpose of resigning the command. Arriving here, however, he ascertained that Burgevine had just gone over to the Tai-pings with about three hundred foreigners, and was then in Suchau. The power of moral principle, which guided the career of the one, was then seen in luminous contrast to its lack as shown in the other of these soldiers of fortune. To his lasting credit Colonel Gordon decided to return at once to Kiunshan, and, in face of the ingratitude of the Chinese and jealousy of his officers, to stand by the imperialist cause. He gradually restored his influence over officers and men, ascertained that Burgevine's position in the Tai-ping army did not allow him freedom enough to render his presence dangerous to their foes, and began to act aggressively against Suchau by taking Patachiau on its southern side in September.

Emissaries from the foreigners in the city now reported considerable dissatisfaction with their position, and Colonel Gordon was able to arrange in a short time their withdrawal without much danger to themselves. It is said that Burgevine even then proposed to him to join their forces, seize Suchau, and as soon as possible march on Peking with a large army, and do to the Manchus what the Manchus had done, two hundred and twenty years before, to the Mings. Colonel Gordon's own loyalty was somewhat suspected by the imperialist leaders, but his integrity carried him safely through all these temptations to swerve from his duty.

As soon as these mercenaries among the rebels were out of the way, operations against Suchau were prosecuted with vigor, so that by November 19th the entire city was invested and carefully cut off from communication with the north. The city being now hard pushed, the besieging force prepared for a night attack upon a breach previously made in the stockade near the north-east gate. It was well planned, but the Muh Wang, *facile princeps* among the Tai-ping chiefs in courage and devotion, having been informed of it, opened such a destructive fire that the Ever-victorious force was defeated with a loss of about two hundred officers and men killed and wounded. On the next morning, however (November 28th), it was reported that the cowardly leaders in the city were plotting against the Muh Wang—the only loyal one among their number—and were talking of capitulating, using the British chief as their intermediary.

This rumor proved, indeed, to be so far true, that after some further successful operations on the part of Gordon's division, the Wangs made overtures to General Ching, himself a former rebel commander, but long since returned to the imperial cause and now the chief over its forces in Kiangsu. The Muh Wang was publicly assassinated on December 2d by his comrades, and on the 5th the negotiations had proceeded so far that interviews were held. Colonel Gordon had withdrawn his troops a short distance to save the city from pillage, but did not succeed in obtaining a donation of two months' pay for their late bravery from the parsimonious Lí. He therefore proposed to lay down his command at three o'clock P.M., and meanwhile went into the city to interview the Na Wang, who told him that everything was proceeding in a satisfactory manner. Upon learning this he repaired to the house of the murdered Muh Wang in order to get his corpse decently buried, but failed, as no one in the place would lend him the smallest assistance. While he was thus occupied, the rebel wangs and officers had settled as to the terms they would accept; and on reaching his own force, Gordon found General Ching there with a donation of one month's pay, which his men refused.

The next morning he returned into the city and was told by Ching that the rebel leaders had all been pardoned, and would deliver up the city at noon; they were preparing then to go out. Colonel Gordon shortly after started to return to his own camp and met the imperialists coming into the east gate in a tumultuous manner, prepared for slaughter and pillage. He therefore went back to the Na Wang's house to guard it, but found the establishment already quite gutted; he, however, met the Wang's uncle and went with him to protect the females of the family at the latter's residence. Here he was detained by several hundred armed rebels, who would neither let him go nor send a message by his interpreter till the next morning (December 7th), when they permitted him to leave for his boat, then waiting at the south gate; narrowly escaping, on his way thither, an attack from the imperialists, he reached his bodyguard at daybreak, and with them was able to prevent any more soldiers entering the city. His preservation amid such conflicting forces was providential, but his indignation was great when he learned that Governor Lí had beheaded the eight rebel leaders the day before. It seems that they had demanded conditions quite inadmissible in respect to the control of the thirty thousand men under their orders, and were cut off for their insolent contumacy. Another account, published at

Shanghai in 1871, states that nearly twenty chiefs were executed, and about two thousand privates.

As Colonel Gordon felt that his good name was compromised by this cruelty, he threw up his command until he could confer with his superiors. On the 29th a reply came to Lí Hung-chang from Prince Kung, highly praising all who had been engaged in taking Suchau, and ordering him to send the leader of the Ever-victorious force a medal and ten thousand taels—both of which he declined. The posture of affairs soon became embarrassing to all parties. The rebellion was not suppressed; the cities in rebel hands would soon gather the desperate men escaped from Suchau; Colonel Gordon alone could lead his troops to victory; and all his past bravery and skill might be lost. He therefore resumed his command, and presently recommenced operations by leading his men against Ĭhing hien, west of Suchau.

Concerning this wretched business of the Suchau slaughter, much was said both in the foreign communities in China and later in England. Mr. Wilson, in his book compiled largely from Colonel Gordon's notes on this campaign, discusses the question with as great fairness as precision, and concludes—as must every well-wisher of China with him—that it was in every way fortunate, both for his reputation and the cause to which he had lent himself, that this heroic man returned to his thankless task. Summing up the arguments of the Chinese and the various attendant circumstances that brought about this execution, Mr. Wilson points to Lí's not unnatural desire after revenge for his brother's murder by the rebels before Taitsang; to the army still under control of the wangs; to the almost absolute certainty of massacre of those imperialists who had already entered the city should he refuse compliance with their demands; as also to the impossibility of arresting these chiefs without an alarm of treachery spreading among their troops within the walls, and thus giving them time to close the gates, cutting off the imperial soldiers inside the city from those who were without. "Lí was in a very difficult and critical position," he says, "which imperatively demanded sudden, unpremeditated action; and though, no doubt, it would have been more honorable for him to have made the wangs prisoners, he cannot in the circumstances be with justice severely censured for having ordered the Tai-ping chiefs who were in his power, but who defied his authority, to be immediately killed. It is also certain that Colonel Gordon need not have been in a hurry to consider himself as at all responsible for this almost necessary act, because in a letter to him (among his correspondence relating to these affairs) from the Futai [Lí], dated November 2, 1863, I find the following noteworthy passage, which shows that the governor did not wish Gordon to interfere at all in regard to the capitulation of the Suchau chiefs: 'With respect to Moh Wang and other rebel leaders' proposal, I am quite satisfied that you have determined in no way to interfere. Let Ching look after their treacherous and cunning management.'"[1]

On reaching Íhing, the dreadful effects of the struggle going on around Gordon's force were seen, and more than reconciled him to do all he could to bring it to an end. Utter destitution prevailed in and out of the town; people were feeding on dead bodies, and ready to perish from exposure while waiting for a comrade to die. The town of Liyang was surrendered on his approach, and its inhabitants, twenty thousand in number, supplied with a little food. From this place to Kintan proved to be a slow and irksome march, owing to the shallow water in the canal and the bad weather. On March 21st an attack was made on this strong post by breaching the walls; but it resulted in a defeat, the loss of more than a hundred officers and men, and a severe wound which Colonel Gordon received in his leg—oddly enough the only injury he sustained, though frequently compelled to lead his men in person to a charge. Next day he retired, in order, to Liyang, but hearing that the son of the Chung Wang had retaken Fushan he started with a thousand men and some artillery for Wusih, which the rebels had left. The operations in this region during the next few weeks conclusively proved the desperate condition of the rebels, but a hopeless cause seemed often but to increase their bravery in defending what strongholds were left them. At the same time a

[1] Wilson, *The "Ever-Victorious Army,"* p. 204.

body of Franco-Chinese was operating, in connection with General Ching on the south of Suchau, against Kiahing fu, a large city on the Grand Canal, held by the Ting Wang. This position was taken and its defenders put to the sword on March 20th, but with the very serious loss of General Ching, one of the ablest generals in the Chinese army. Hangchau, the capital of Chehkiang, capitulated the next day, and this was soon followed by the reduction of the entire province and dispersion of the rebels among the hills.

Colonel Gordon had recovered from his wound so as to lead an attack on Waisu April 6th, which town fell on the 11th, when most of its defenders were killed by the peasantry as they attempted to escape. His force was also much weakened, and needed to be recruited. With about three thousand in all, he now went to aid Governor Lí in reducing Changchau fu, and invested it on the 25th. The entire besieging force numbered over ten thousand; and as the rebels were twice as many, on the whole well provided, and knew that no mercy would be shown, their resistance was stubborn. Several attacks were repulsed with no small loss to Gordon's force, so that slower methods of approach were resorted to till a general assault was planned on May 11th, when it succumbed. Only fifteen hundred rebels were slain, and the greater part of the prisoners were allowed to go home, the Kwangsí men alone being executed. With this capture ended the operations of the Ever-victorious force and its brave leader. Nanking was now the only strong place held by the Tai-pings, and there was nothing for that army to do there, as Tsăng Kwoh-fan, the generalissimo of the imperial armies, had ample means for its capture. Colonel Gordon, therefore, in conjunction with Governor Lí, dissolved this notable division; the latter rewarded its officers and men with liberal gratuities, and sent the natives home. During its existence of about four years down to June 1, 1864, nearly fifty places had been taken (twenty-three of them by Gordon), and its higher discipline had served to elevate the *morale* of the imperialists who operated with them. It perhaps owed its greatest triumph to the high-toned uprightness of its Christian chief, which impressed all who served with him. The

Emperor conferred on him the highest military rank of *ti-tuh*, or 'Captain-General,' and a yellow jacket (*ma-kwa*) and other uniforms, to indicate the sense of his achievements. Sir Frederick Bruce admirably summed up his character in a letter to Earl Russell when sending the imperial rescript:

HONGKONG, July 12, 1864.

MY LORD,

I enclose a translation of a despatch from Prince Kung containing the decree published by the Emperor, acknowledging the services of Lieutenant-Colonel Gordon, R. E., and requesting that her Majesty's government be pleased to recognize them. This step has been spontaneously taken. Lieutenant-Colonel Gordon well deserves her Majesty's favor; for, independently of the skill and courage he has shown, his disinterestedness has elevated our national character in the eyes of the Chinese. Not only has he refused any pecuniary reward, but he has spent more than his pay in contributing to the comfort of the officers who served under him, and in assuaging the distress of the starving population whom he relieved from the yoke of their oppressors. Indeed, the feeling that impelled him to resume operations after the fall of Suchow was one of the purest humanity. He sought to save the people of the districts that had been recovered from a repetition of the misery entailed upon them by this cruel civil war. I have, etc.,

F. W. A. BRUCE.

The foreign merchants at Shanghai expressed their sense of his conduct in a letter dated November 24th, written on the eve of his return to England, in which they truly remark: "In a position of unequalled difficulty, and surrounded by complications of every possible nature, you have succeeded in offering to the eyes of the Chinese nation, no less by your loyal and disinterested line of action than by your conspicuous gallantry and talent for organization and command, the example of a foreign officer serving the government of this country with honorable fidelity and undeviating self-respect." [1]

Such men are not only the choice jewels of their own nation (and England may justly be proud to reckon this son among

---

[1] "The rapidity with which the long-descended hostility of the Chinese government became exchanged for relations of at least outward friendship, must be ascribed altogether to the existence of the Tai-ping Rebellion, without whose pressure as an auxiliary we might have crushed, but never conciliated the distrustful statesmen at Peking."—*Fraser's Magazine*, Vol. LXXI., p. 145, February, 1865.

her worthies), but leave behind them an example, as in the case of Colonel Gordon, which elevates Christianity itself in the eyes of the Chinese, and will remain a legacy for good to them through coming years.[1]

After the dissolution of the Ever-victorious force, its leader visited Nganking and Nanking to see the governor-general, Tsăng Kwoh-fan, and his brother, who were directing operations against the rebels, in order to propose some improvements in their future employment of foreign soldiers and military appliances. They listened with respect, and took notes of important suggestions—knowing at the same time that their subordinates were unable to comprehend or adopt many such innovations. The work before Nanking indicated the industry of its besiegers in the miles of walls connecting one hundred and forty mud forts in their circumvallations, and in various mines leading under the city walls. The Tai-pings at that date seldom appeared on the walls, and had recently sent out three thousand women and children to be fed by their enemies, proof enough of their distressed condition. The only general capable of relieving the Tien Wang was the Chung Wang, whose army remained on the southern districts of Kiangsu, while he himself was in the city with the Kan Wang (Hung Jin), now the trusted agent of his half-brother. All egress from the doomed city was stopped by June 1st, when the explosion of mines and bursting of shells forewarned its deluded defenders of their fate. Of the last days of their leader no authentic account has been given, and the declaration of the Chung Wang in his autobiography, that he poisoned himself on June 30th, "owing to his anxiety and trouble of mind," is probably true. His body was buried behind his palace by one of his wives, and afterward dug up by the imperialists.

On July 19, 1864, the wall was breached by the explosion of forty thousand pounds of powder in a mine, and the Chung Wang, faithful to the last, defended until midnight the Tien Wang's family from the imperialists. He and the Kan Wang

---

[1] Compare further Col. C. C. Chesney's *Essays on Modern Military Biography* (from the *Edinburgh Review*), pp. 163–213, London, 1874.

then escorted Hung Fu-tien—a lad of sixteen, who had succeeded to the throne of Great Peace three weeks before—with a thousand followers, a short distance beyond the city. The three leaders now became separated, but all were ultimately captured and executed. The Chung Wang, during his captivity before death, wrote an account of his own life, which fully maintains the high estimate previously formed of his character from his public acts.[1] He was the solitary ornament of the whole movement during the fourteen years of its independent existence, and his enemies would have done well to have spared him. More than seven thousand Tai-pings were put to death in Nanking, the total number found there being hardly over twenty thousand, of whom probably very few were southern Chinese—this element having gradually disappeared.

After the recapture of Nanking, two small bodies of rebels remained in Chehkiang. The largest of them, under the Tow Wang, held Huchau fu, and made a desperate resistance until a large force, provided with artillery, compelled them to evacuate. During this siege the sanguinary conduct of the Tai-pings showed the natural result of their reckless course since their last escape from Nanking; the narrative of an escaped Irishman, who had been compelled to serve them in Huchau for some months, is terrible enough: "All offences received one punishment—death. I saw one hundred and sixty men beheaded, as I understood, for absence from parade; two boys were beheaded for smoking; all prisoners of war were executed; spies, or people accused as such, were tied with their hands behind their backs to a stake, brushwood put around them, and they burned to death." The rebel force numbered nearly a hundred thousand men, and their vigorous defence was continued for a fortnight, till on August 14th their last stockade was carried by the imperialists, and about half their number made good their escape to the neighboring hills, leaving the usual scene of desolation behind them. This body undertook to march south through the hilly regions between Kiangsí and

---

[1] *The Autobiography of the Chung-Wang, translated from the Chinese by* W. T. Lay, Shanghai, 1865.

Chehkiang. The best disciplined portion was led by the Shi Wang, who had joined it with his men from the former province, and arranged an attack on Kwangsin, near which they were defeated. The remainder managed to march across the intervening districts south-westerly to the city of Changchau, near Amoy, where they intrenched themselves till the next spring, subsisting on the supplies found in it and the neighborhood. The Shí Wang and Kan Wang then left it April 16th, in two bodies, unable to resist the disciplined force of eight thousand men brought from the north. Feeling that their days were numbered, they seem to have scrupled at nothing to show their savagery—as, for example, when they slaughtered sixteen hundred imperialists who had surrendered on a promise of safe-conduct. No mercy was therefore shown them by the inhabitants; at Chănping in Kwangtung they even cut down their growing rice in order to prevent the rebels using it. The last straggling relics of the Tai-ping Heavenly King's adherents were thus gradually destroyed, and his ill-advised enterprise brought to an end.

Fifteen years had elapsed since he had set up his standard of revolt in Kwangsí, and now there was nothing to show as a return for the awful carnage and misery that had ensued from his efforts. No new ideas concerning God or his redemption for mankind had been set forth or illustrated by the teachings or practices of the Tai-ping leader or any of his followers, nor did they ever take any practical measures to call in foreign aid to assist in developing even the Christianity they professed. True the Kan Wang called Mr. Roberts to Nanking, but instead of consulting with him as to the establishment of schools, opening chapels, preparing books, or organizing any kind of religious or benevolent work to further the welfare of his adherents, the Tien Wang did not even grant an interview to the missionary, who, on his part, was glad to escape with his life to Shanghai.

If this rebellion practically exhibited no religious truth to the educated mind of China, it was not for lack of publications setting forth the beliefs its leaders had drawn from the Bible, or for laws sanctioned by severe penalties, both of which were scattered through the land. Dr. Medhurst's careful translations of these tracts has preserved them, so that the entire disregard manifested by the new sect of their plainest injunctions may be at once seen.[1] The strong expectations of the friends of China for its regeneration through the success of Hung Siu-tsuen, would not have been indulged if they had better known the inner workings of his own mind and the flagitious conduct of his lieutenants.

In his political aspirations the Tien Wang entertained no new principle of government, for he knew nothing of other lands, their jurisprudence or their polity, and wisely enough held his followers to such legislation as they were familiar with. They all probably expected to alter affairs to their liking when they had settled in Peking. But if this mysterious iconoclast had really any ideas above those of an enthusiast like Thomas Münzer and the Anabaptists in the early days of the Reformation—whose course and end offers many parallels to his own—he must have lamented his folly as he reviewed its results to his country. The once peaceful and populous parts of the nine great provinces through which his hordes passed have hardly yet begun to be restored to their previous condition. Ruined cities, desolated towns, and heaps of rubbish still mark their course from Kwangsí to Tientsin, a distance of two thousand miles, the efforts at restoration only making the contrast more apparent. Their presence was an unmitigated scourge, attended by nothing but disaster from beginning to end, without the least effort on their part to rebuild what had been destroyed, to protect what was left, or to repay what had been stolen. Wild beasts roamed at large over the land after their departure, and made their dens in the deserted towns; the pheasant's whirr resounded where the hum of busy populations had ceased, and weeds or jungle covered the ground once tilled with patient industry. Besides millions upon millions of taels irrecoverably lost and destroyed, and the misery, sickness, and starvation

---

[1] *Pamphlets issued by the Chinese Insurgents at Nan-King; to which is added a history of the Kwangsî Rebellion*, etc., etc., compiled by W. H. Medhurst, Senr., Shanghai, 1853. Compare R. J. Forrest in *Journal N. C. Br. R. A. Soc.*, No. IV., December, 1867, pp. 187 ff. *The China Mail* for February 2, 1854.

which were endured by the survivors, it has been estimated by foreigners living at Shanghai that, during the whole period from 1851 to 1865, fully twenty millions of human beings were destroyed in connection with the Tai-ping Rebellion.[1]

---

[1] The most complete authorities on this conflict are files of the *North China Herald* (Shanghai) and the *China Mail* (Hongkong) during the years from 1853 to 1869; a careful summary of these has been made by M. Cordier in his *Bibliotheca Sinica*, pp. 273–281, which will be useful alone to those who can gain access to these newspapers. The number of articles on various phases of the rebellion contained in English and American magazines is exceedingly numerous, and can be readily found by reference to Poole's *Index*. Among these compare especially the *London Quarterly*, Vol. 112, for October, 1862; *Fraser's Magazine*, Vol. 71, February, 1865; *Blackwood's*, Vol. 100, pp. 604 and 683; W. Sargent in the *North American Review*, Vol. 79, July, 1854, p. 158. See also the various *Blue Books* relating to China; Capt. Fishbourne, *Impressions of China and the Present Revolution*, London, 1855; Callery and Yvan, *L'Insurrection en Chine*, Paris, 1853—translated into English, London, 1853; Charles Macfarlane, *The Chinese Revolution*, London, 1853; T. T. Meadows, *The Chinese and their Rebellions*, London, 1856; J. M. Mackie, *Life of Tai-ping Wang*, N. Y., 1857; Commander Lindesay Brine, *Narrative of the Rise and Progress of the Taeping Rebellion in China*, London, 1862; "Lin-le," *Ti-Ping Tien-kwoh, the History of the Ti-Ping Revolution*, London, 1866—a rather untrustworthy record; Sir T. F. Wade in the *Shanghai Miscellany*, No. I.; Richthofen, *Letter on the Province of Shensi*.

CHAPTER VI.

THE SECOND ANGLO-CHINESE WAR.

THE particulars given in the last chapter respecting the Taiping Rebellion did not include those details connected with foreign intercourse during the same period which have had such important results on the Chinese people and government. It is a notable index of the vigor and self-poise of both, that during those thirteen terrible years, the mass of inhabitants in the ten eastern provinces never lost confidence in their own government or its ability to subdue the rebels; while the leading officers at Peking and in all those provinces at no time expressed doubt as to the loyalty of their countrymen when left free to act. The narrative of foreign intercourse is now resumed from the year 1849, when the British authorities waived the right of insisting upon their admission into the city of Canton according to the terms of the convention with Kíying in 1847. The conduct of the Cantonese, in view of the forcible entrance of English troops into their city, is an interesting exhibition of their manner of arousing enthusiasm and raising funds and volunteers to cope with an emergency. The series of papers found in Vol. XVIII. of the *Chinese Repository* well illustrates the curious mixture of a sense of wrong and deep concern in public affairs, combined with profound ignorance and inaptitude as to the best means for attaining their object.

A candid examination of the real meaning of the Chinese texts of the four earlier treaties makes clear the fact that there were some grounds for their refusal; but more attractive than this appears the study of an address from the gentry of Canton, sent upon the same occasion, to Governor Bonham at Hongkong, dissuading him from attempting the entry. Their conduct was naturally regarded by the British as seditious, and of these many urged their authorities to vindicate the national honor and force a way over the walls into the city. The practice of an unwonted approach toward self-government which this popular movement in defence of their metropolis gave the citizens, was of real service to them in the year 1855, when it was beleaguered by the rebels, since they had learned how to use their powers and resources. One result of their fancied victory over the British at this time was the erection of six stone *pai-lau*, or honorary portals, in various parts of the city and suburbs, on each of which was engraved the sentence, "Reverently to commemorate glory conferred," together with a copy of the edict ordering their establishment, and a list of the wards and villages which furnished soldiers during their time of need.[1]

The outcome of the working of treaty provisions between foreigners and natives at the five opened ports during the ten years up to 1853, had been as satisfactory to both sides as could have been reasonably expected. The influx of foreigners had more than doubled their numbers; and as almost none of them could talk the Chinese language, it happened that natives of Canton became their brokers and compradores—rather more by reason of speaking *pigeon-English* than by their wealth or capacity. The vicious plan of marking off a separate plat of land for the residence of foreigners at each port was adopted, and their development tended to build up *concessions*, or settlements, which were to be governed by the various nationalities. In doing this the local authorities vacated their rights over their own territory, and these settlements have since become the germs of foreign cities, if not colonies.. The British and French consuls at Shanghai claimed territorial jurisdiction over all who settled within the limits of their allotted districts, and carried this assumption so far as to exercise authority over the natives against their own rulers. The British ere long gave up this pernicious system, which had no legal basis by treaty or conquest, and yielded the entire internal management

[1] The one placed near the southern gate became a target for the British gunners in October, 1856, its demolition, most unfortunately, involving the destruction and burning of millions of Chinese books in the shops on that street.

of all consular communities to those foreigners which composed them. There were not enough residents elsewhere to raise this question of local government to any importance, but the progress of the Tai-pings and the rapid growth of Shanghai as a centre of trade for the Yangtsz' basin, compelled the preparation and adoption of a set of land regulations in order to institute some means of governing the thousands of foreigners who had flocked thither. George Balfour, the first British consul in that port, had sanctioned a series of rules in 1845, which purported to be drawn up by the *tautai*, or intendant of circuit, and which worked well enough in peaceful times.

In the year 1853, however, the civil war altered the conditions, when certain Cantonese rebels captured Shanghai and killed some of its magistrates, driving others into the British settlement, to which ground the custom-house was shortly afterward removed. The collector of the port, Wu Kien-chang, had formerly been a hong merchant at Canton, and he willingly entered into an arrangement for putting the collection of foreign duties into the hands of a commission until order was restored. The presence there of the British, American, and French ministers facilitated this arrangement. Their respective consuls, R. Alcock, R. C. Murphy, and B. Edan, accordingly met Wu on June 29, 1854, and agreed to a set of custom-house rules which in reality transferred the collection of duties into the hands of foreigners. The first rule contains the reason for this remarkable step in advance of all former positions, and has served to perpetuate the employment of foreigners at all the open ports, and maintain the foreign inspectorate:

RULE I.—The chief difficulty experienced by the superintendent of customs having consisted in the impossibility of obtaining custom-house officials with the necessary qualifications as to probity, vigilance, and knowledge of foreign languages, required for the enforcement of a close observance of treaty and custom-house regulations, the only adequate remedy appears to be in the introduction of a foreign element into the custom-house establishment, in the persons of foreigners carefully selected and appointed by the *tautai*, who shall supply the deficiency complained of, and give him efficient and trustworthy instruments wherewith to work.[1]

---

[1] *McLane's Correspondence*, 1858. *Senate Ex. Doc.*, No. 28, p. 154.

In carrying out the new arrangement, each consul nominated one man to the intendant, viz., T. F. Wade for the British, L. Carr for the American, and Arthur Smith for the French member of the board of inspectors, who together were to take charge of the new department. The chief responsibility for its organization fell on Mr. Wade, inasmuch as he alone of this number was familiar with the Chinese language, and possessed other qualifications fitting him for the post. He, however, resigned within a year, and the intendant appointed H. N. Lay, a clerk in the British consulate, who completed the service organization. This proceeding shows the readiness with which the Chinese will shirk their own duties and functions in government employ, and illustrates as well many peculiar traits in their character.

The city of Shanghai had been in possession of a Cantonese chief, Liu Tsz'-tsai, and his rabble since September 7, 1853, and the position of foreigners at that port in the presence of such a body of outlaws developed new points of international law. If the foreigners had all been of one nationality the consul would probably have assumed temporary control of the city and port to assure their safety; but in this case a naval force under each flag lying in the river guaranteed ample protection of life and property. As soon as the city was occupied the difficulty of restraining the disorderly elements, as well among foreigners as natives, became painfully apparent to their rulers. Foreign rowdies eagerly purchased the plunder brought to them and supplied arms and other things in return—a line of conduct very naturally irritating to the officials in charge of the siege and inclining them at once toward coercive measures.

The fact that the French settlement adjoined the moat on the north side of the city made its authorities desirous to dislodge the brigands, which they essayed to do January 6, 1855, by joining the imperialists in breaking the walls; they were repulsed, however, with a loss of fifteen men killed and thirty-seven wounded, out of a rank and file numbering two hundred and fifty. Another joint attack, undertaken a month later, was likewise unsuccessful, though the attempt seems to have frightened the force within the walls, since on the night of February

16th they retired, leaving the place in ruins. A like cordiality was nevertheless not always maintained between native and foreign soldiers, for in the previous year (April 4, 1854) occurred a collision with the imperialists, in consequence of their near approach to the foreign quarter, in which over three hundred Chinese soldiers were killed by the foreigners who landed to resist them. This untoward rencontre did not, however, interrupt amicable relations with the intendant, and was followed by consular notifications that whoever entered the service of the combatants in or out of the city would forfeit all protection. These notices were nevertheless soon disregarded as the struggle went on, for the temptation to enjoy a lawless life was too strong for hundreds of sailors then found in that port. It was an anomalous state of affairs, and the exigency led to some acts of violence by consuls in control of men-of-war.

The city of Amoy had been captured by insurgents on May 18, 1852, but no contravention occurred; the number of foreigners residing at this port was small, while the opposite island of Kulang su afforded a refuge beyond the range of missiles. The city was regained by the imperialists before a year had passed. The districts north of Canton, whence Hung Siu-tsuen and many of his adherents originated, began the same year to send forth their bands of robbers to pillage the province. These gangs had really no affinity with the Tai-pings, either in doctrine or plans, and none of them succeeded in gaining even a temporary success. When the booty was expended they usually quarrelled, and the imperialists destroyed them in detail. Every part of the province was at one time or another the scene of savage conflict between these contestants, and it was soon shown that no regenerating principle was involved on either side. The confidence of the educated and wealthy classes in the just cause and final success of their rulers was shown in raising men and money for the public service and organizing bodies of local police; but the want of a sagacious leader to plan and execute, so that all this material and action should not be frittered away, was painfully apparent.

In the capture of Nanking by Tai-pings, the restless leaders of sedition in Kwangtung saw their opportunity, and gathered their bands of freebooters in the southern prefectures. In June, 1854, the district town of Tungkwan near the Bogue was taken, the rich manufacturing mart of Fuhshan (or Fat-shan) near Canton fell a month later, followed by that of Shunteh, Sanshui, and other lesser places, throwing the southern part of the province into a state of anarchy. The theory of the Chinese government, that if the capital is preserved the whole province is loyal, and its officers can use its revenue, enabled Governor-General Yeh to concert measures to repress these disorders. The City of Rams was environed during August by large bodies of insurgents, whose wants were supplied from Fuhshan. In this crisis about one thousand five hundred houses abutting outside the city walls were destroyed, and the ward police strengthened for the better protection of their neighborhoods against incendiaries. In all these proceedings the foreigners at Canton were never consulted or referred to by the officials, but their merchant steamers kept the Pearl River open to the sea, while their men-of-war lying off the factories proved a safeguard to the crowded city. The rebels had occupied a post near Whampoa, and their gunboats prowled through every creek in the delta, burning, destroying, capturing, and murdering without restraint. They would be followed by a band of imperialists, whose excesses were sometimes even more dreadful than those of their enemies. So terrible was the plight of the wretched countrymen that the headmen of ninety-six villages near Fuhshan formed a league and armed their people to keep soldiers from either side from entering their precincts.

In September, at a general meeting of the gentry of Canton, a proposal to save the city by asking foreign aid was approved by Yeh, but happily the project failed of fulfilment and only resulted in showing them how much better was a reliance upon their own resources. The news of this discussion led Chin Hienliang, the rebel leader near Whampoa, to circulate proposals among the foreigners asking them to help him in capturing the city and promising as reward a portion of the island of Honan. The condition of the people at this time was sad and desperate indeed, and their only remedy was to arm in self-defence, in doing which they found out how small a proportion of the inhabitants was disloyal. No quarter was given on either side, and the carnage was appalling whenever victory remained with the imperialists. During this year the emigration to California and Australia became larger than ever before, while the coolie trade waxed flourishing, owing to the multitudes thrown out of employment who were eager in accepting the offers of the brokers to depart from the country and escape the evils they saw everywhere about them. The terrors of famine, fighting, and plundering paralyzed all industry and trade, and enabled one to better understand similar scenes described by ancient historians as occurring in Western Asia.

The exhaustion and desperation consequent on these events had almost demoralized society in and around Canton, which was overcrowded with refugees, raising food to famine prices. It was creditable to these poor and sickly people that their influx produced no other fear than that of a higher rate of living—none of pestilence or plunder, even in the extremity of their sufferings. In Fuhshan, fifteen miles away, no one was safe. The rebels had depleted its resources, killed its gentry, and oppressed the townsfolk until a quarrel broke out in their camp, and they departed about the season of Christmas, leaving the whole a smoking ruin. One of the insurgent practices consisted in driving great numbers of people into squares and there shooting them down by cannon placed in the approaching streets, while the houses around them were burning. The flames could be seen for two or three days from Canton, and it was estimated that during this conflict fully two hundred thousand human beings perished. The town was the manufacturing centre for the foreign trade, where silks, satins, shawls, paper, fire-crackers, pottery, and other staples were made, and their workmen resided. After this dreadful act the insurgents grew more and more desperate, feeling that they could not hold out much longer for want of booty and supplies to keep their men together. By March the force of fifteen thousand men inside the city was ready, and on the 6th it went quietly down to attack the fort below Whampoa. The onset and resistance were most determined; before the position succumbed, some twenty-five thousand men must have perished by battle or flood; the rebel leader escaped toward Hiangshan. The insurrection was, however, scotched, and its victors celebrated their triumph three days later in the city to a grateful and applauding concourse. When the city of Shauking, west of Canton, was retaken in May, its victors boasted that thirty thousand rebels were drowned or beheaded.

Notwithstanding these reverses the insurgents did not yet disappear, but maintained themselves along the watercourses in large flotillas during many months. The Portuguese and British also fitted out expeditions to pursue the pirates, as the same men were now called, destroying them and their haunts at Kulan Lantao, and elsewhere. In rooting out these land and sea brigands, the merciless character of the people was made manifest; every one convicted of rebellion was straightway executed by the authorities. At Canton, where prisoners were received from all such districts, the executions were on a terribly huge scale, as many as seven or eight hundred persons being beheaded in a single day. A count taken at the city gate whence they all issued on their way to the field of blood near the river, revealed the fact that fully eighty thousand were thus executed in the year 1855. This did not include thousands who committed suicide in places provided for them near their homes, from which their relatives could take their bodies to the family tomb. As might be expected, other thousands left the province for the north, or escaped into distant lands as coolies and emigrants.

Public attention abroad was at this time so engrossed with the greater rebellion going on along the Yangtsz' River that the horrors of that in Kwangtung were overlooked. There were many foreigners at Whampoa and Hongkong who sided with the leading brigands, reported their successes in the newspapers, and supplied them with munitions of war. The inefficiency of a foreign consul to restrain his countrymen thus flagrantly violating all their treaty obligations toward China, showed most conclusively how easy it is for the stronger party in such cases to demand their rights, and shirk their duties if it suits their convenience.

During the year 1856 affairs between the Chinese government and foreign powers became more and more hampered, while all attempts to arrange difficulties as they arose were defeated by the obstinate refusal of Yeh Ming-chin, the governor-general at Canton, to meet any foreign minister. He intrenched himself behind the city gates, and would do nothing. Sir John Bowring, the British plenipotentiary and governor of Hongkong, had most reason to be dissatisfied with this conduct, inasmuch as there were many questions which could have been easily arranged in a personal interview. It was ascertained from some documents[1] afterward found in Yeh's office that this seclusion was a part of the system devised at Peking to maintain a complete isolation and keep the dreaded foreigners at a distance. No course could be more likely to bring upon the government the evils it feared, and at the same time show more conclusively the ignorant and inapt character of those who carried it on. This state of things could not long continue when such powerful agencies were at work along the coast to disorganize legal trade and thwart the utmost efforts of all officials to restrain the reckless conduct of their subjects. The ten years now elapsed since the opening of the five ports had involved the Chinese in more complications, miseries, and disasters than had been known since the Manchu conquest; nevertheless, neither rebellion nor foreign complications seem to have impressed their lessons upon the proud bureaucracy in Peking, which was as unwilling to remedy as unable to appreciate the real nature of the difficulties that beset the country.

In the struggle between nations, as between individuals, the agony and weakness of one side becomes the opportunity of the other; and these conditions were now open to the British, who speedily found their excuse for further demands. In order to develop the trade of the free port of Hongkong, its laws encouraged all classes of shipping to resort thither, by removing all charges on vessels and granting licenses, with but few and unimportant restrictions, to Chinese craft to carry on trade under the British flag. This freedom had developed an enormous smuggling trade, especially in opium, which the Chinese revenue service was unable to restrain or unwilling to legalize.

---

[1] *Blue Book*, 1857.

These boats cruised wherever they might find a trade to invite or reward them, wholly indifferent to their own government, which could exercise no adequate control over them, and kept from the last excesses only on account of the risk of losing their cargoes. To the evils of smuggling were added the worse acts and dangers of kidnapping natives to supply baracoons at Macao. The Portuguese had many of these lorchas to carry on their commerce, and gradually a set of desperate men had so far engrossed them in acts of daring and pillage that honest native trade about any part of the coast south of Shanghai became almost impossible except under their convoy. The two free ports of Macao and Hongkong naturally became their resorts, where they all took on the aspect of legitimate traders, which, indeed, most of them were—save under great temptations.

It was not surprising that Chinese rulers should confound these two classes of vessels, nor, from the traders' side, was it a wonder that their crews should use the flag which gave them the greatest protection when beyond foreign inspection and jurisdiction. Few nations have ever been subjected to such continuous and prolonged irritation in respect to its commercial regulations as was the Canton government from those two alien communities during the ten years ending with 1856; few nations, on the other hand, have acted more unwisely in exertions toward peace and the removal of such difficulties than did the unspeakable Governor-General Yeh. That the inevitable collision between the Chinese and British was now at hand, follows almost as a matter of course, when to our knowledge of the commissioner's character we add Mr. Justin McCarthy's very appropriate estimate of the two Englishmen in whose hands well-nigh all British affairs in China were vested: "Mr. Consul Parkes," says he, "was fussy. Sir John Bowring was a man of considerable ability, but . . . full of self-conceit, and without any very clear idea of political principles on the large scale."[1]

Early in the morning of October 8th, two boat-loads of

[1] *A History of Our Own Times*, Chap. XXX.

Chinese sailors, with their officers, put off from a large war-junk, boarded the lorcha Arrow lying at anchor in the river before Canton, pinioned and carried away twelve of the fourteen natives who composed her crew, and added to this unexpected "act of violence," as Mr. Parkes stated it, "the significant insult of hauling down the British ensign." One Kennedy, a young Irishman who is described as a very respectable man of his class, was master of the lorcha, but chanced at the time to be on another boat lying in the immediate neighborhood of his own, and could in consequence offer no resistance. It is probable, judging from testimony given at the British consulate, that the hauling down of the flag was a mere bit of wantonness on the part of the junk's officer upon his finding that no foreigner was on board, and the offence might readily have been followed by an apology had the command of negotiations been in any other hands than those of Yeh. The Arrow was owned by a Chinese, Fong A-ming, her nominal master being engaged by Mr. Block, the Danish consul at Hongkong; his vessel was not, however, entitled to protection, inasmuch as her British register had expired by its own limitation eleven days before the episode in Canton River, and the lorcha was already forfeited to the crown.[1] Her papers were then at the consulate, and it was contended by Mr. Parkes that under Clause X. of the ordinance she retained a right to protection; a mere quibble, since the cause refers to the vessel when upon a voyage, and the Arrow had confessedly remained about the ports of Macao and Canton during a month.

Consul Parkes, after ascertaining the facts connected with this high-handed outrage, pushed off to the war-junk—which remained the while quietly at anchor—to claim the captured sailors and "explain to the officers, if it were possible that they had acted in error, the gross insult and violation of national

---

[1] Sir John Bowring indeed conceded that "the Arrow had no right to hoist the British flag," but alleged that the Chinese had no knowledge of the expiry of the license, and that this ignorance deprived them of the legal value of the truth. He quoted, moreover, Article IX. of the Supplementary Treaty, requiring that "all Chinese malfaisants in British ships shall be claimed through the British authorities."

rights which they had committed."[1] This was in vain. Among the men was a notorious pirate, he was told, and their orders were that the suspected crew should be sent to the governor for examination. Yeh stoutly upheld the act of his subordinate, and affirmed that the lorcha had no right to fly the British flag, disclaiming, however, any intention of molesting lawful traders under the emblem. Naturally enough, he would not yield the right of jurisdiction over his own subjects, and in doing this was asserting precisely what Great Britain and every other nation on the globe knew to be the first privilege of an independent government. The case was not unlike that much-discussed affair of the American Commodore Wilkes, who boarded the Trent in 1863 and captured Mason and Slidell—performing a right-enough action, but in a wrong and hasty fashion.

In his reply to Mr. Parkes, Yeh declares that he has held an examination of the sailors and finds that three of them were implicated in a piracy of the preceding month on St. John's Island, that the officers had good reasons for seizing these men, that the remaining nine shall be sent back to their vessel; which he straightway does, but they are as promptly returned by the consul because the entire crew is not given up. Sir John Bowring now demands, through his representative at Canton (1), "an apology for what has taken place, and an assurance that the British flag shall in future be respected;" (2) "that all proceedings against Chinese offenders on board British vessels must take place according to the conditions of the treaty;"[2] in case of refusal the consul is to concert with the naval authorities the measures necessary for enforcing redress. This threat extracted from the governor-general a promise that "hereafter Chinese officers will on no account, without reason, seize and take into custody the people belonging to foreign lorchas;" adding very properly, "but when Chinese subjects build for themselves vessels, foreigners should not sell registers to them, for if this be done, it will occasion confusion between native and foreign ships, and render it difficult to distinguish

[1] *Blue Book: Papers relating to the Proceedings of her Majesty's Naval Forces at Canton*, p. 1.

[2] *Blue Book, Ibid.*, p. 12.

between them."[1] Twelve days afterward (October 22d) the entire crew were returned, but once more refused by Mr. Parkes, ostensibly because the apology was not sent with them —and this the commissioner could not offer either in justice to his government or to the cause of truth.

Ensconced behind the walls of Canton city, Yeh resolved to stand firm on his rights as he understood them, even should the doing so involve the lives and property of thousands of his countrymen. To all foreigners in China this affair was intimately connected with most important possibilities and consequences: the inviolability of national flags, protection to every one whom they covered, personal intercourse with Chinese officers, maintenance of treaty rights. In upholding these the British drew to their side the good wishes of all intelligent observers for their success in arms, however unhappy their excuse for a resort to such means might be. One more word from Mr. McCarthy before leaving the initial episode of this war. "The truth is," he sums up, "that there has seldom been so flagrant and so inexcusable an example of high-handed lawlessness in the dealings of a strong with a weak nation,"[2] but like many another conflict where strength and justice have been ranged on opposite sides, the latter was speedily pushed to the wall. The incident of the Arrow appeared a trifling one; nevertheless on so slight a hinge turned the future welfare and progress of the Chinese people in their intercourse with other nations, a hinge which, opening outward, unclosed the door for all parties to learn the truth respecting the countries of each, and, in the end, agree upon the only grounds on which a beneficial and intelligent intercourse could be maintained.

It is hardly necessary to recount in detail the steps by which Governor Bowring and Admiral Seymour vainly attempted to bring Yeh to their terms. "Acknowledge that you are in the wrong," was their ultimatum, "by merely sending the three

---

[1] *Ibid.*, p. 15.

[2] *History of Our Own Times*, Vol. III., Chap. XXX. Lord Elgin in his journal refers frankly enough to "that wretched question of the Arrow, which is a scandal to us, and is so considered, I have reason to know, by all except the few who are personally compromised."—*Letters and Journals of Lord Elgin*, edited by T. Walrond, p. 209.

suspects to the consulate, and ask that they be returned on charge of piracy." The long-continued national policy of exclusion could not, however, be so easily overthrown; its reduction must be by force. The seizure of a military junk was the first act of the British, then the capture of the Barrier forts, followed by that of all others on the south of Canton, and lastly breaching the city wall opposite Yeh's yamun. This was entered by Admiral Seymour with a small party of marines.

Sir John Bowring had already made the demand that the city gates should be opened to them in accordance with the agreement entered into ten years before between Governor Davis and Kíying, and expresses his gratification to the consul that now one great object of hostile action had been satisfactorily accomplished—an object which Mr. Parkes declares was clearly based on treaty rights. However, they did not see Yeh, who resorted to all manner of petty annoyances, the evils of which mostly fell on his own people, without in the least advancing his cause.

On November 15th, to the complications with the English was added a quarrel with the Americans, whose boats had been twice fired into and one man killed by the Chinese officers in command of the Barrier forts. Commodore J. Armstrong had under his command the San Jacinto, Portsmouth, and Levant, then lying at Whampoa. He ordered the two latter to go as near to these forts as possible, and directed Captain A. H. Foote of the Portsmouth to destroy them all. Foote accordingly organized a large force and attacked them on the 16th, 20th, and 21st, till they were reduced and occupied. The resistance of the Chinese on this occasion was unusually brave and prolonged, the admirable position of the forts enabling each of them to lend assistance to the others. On the part of the Americans, seven were killed and twenty-two wounded; perhaps three hundred Chinese were put *hors de combat;* the guns in the forts (one hundred and seventy-six in all) were destroyed, and the sea-walls demolished with powder found in the magazines.[1] This skirmish is the only passage of arms ever

[1] One brass gun of eight-inch calibre was twenty-two feet five inches long; the entire armament of these forts was superior in equipment to anything before seen in China.

engaged in by American and Chinese forces—one which Yeh seemed to regard as of slight moment, and for which he cared neither to apologize nor sympathize. His unexampled indifference in referring to the affair less than two days after the demolishment of his forts [1] was met by an equal frankness on the part of Dr. Parker, who at once resumed correspondence with the commissioner, and, content with the practical lesson just administered, said no more about "apologies and guarantees." This episode is interesting chiefly as an example of the American course regarding an insult to the national flag, as contrasted with the English dealing with an injury not very different either in nature or degree.

Relations between Great Britain and China continued in this constrained position until the opening of another year, the conflict now being almost wholly restricted to unimportant collisions with village braves on land and voluminous discussions with the governor-general on paper. In November the French minister withdrew his legation from Canton, there being by that time neither French citizens nor interests to watch over. Principal among the events during this interval was the burning of the foreign factories by order of Yeh, December 14th. They were fired in the night and were entirely consumed with all their contents, as well, too, as the contiguous portion of the suburbs. The offer of thirty taels head-money for every Englishman killed or captured resulted in a few endeavors on the part of natives, whereby they kidnapped or slew two or three seamen when separated from their ships. These attempts at guerilla warfare were so promptly met and rewarded on the part of the English, by wholesale punishment of offending villages, as to cause little annoyance after the lesson of certain retribution had been taken to heart by the Chinese. More important than all these was a dastardly attempt, on January 11,

[1] "There is no matter of strife between our respective nations. Henceforth let the fashion of the flag which American ships employ be clearly defined, and inform me what it is beforehand. This will be the verification of the friendly relations which exist between the two countries."—Hoppin, *Life of Admiral Foote*, pp. 110–140. *Correspondence of McLane and Parker*, *Senate Document* No. 22, December 20, 1858, pp. 1019 ff. *Blue Book*, p. 137.

1857, to poison the foreigners at Hongkong, by putting arsenic in the bread supplied from a Chinese baker. This, it was afterward ascertained, was at the instigation of certain officials on the mainland, but fortunately even here their villany was foiled, owing to the overdose contained in the dough. It ought to be stated, in passing, that such acts are not common in China, and, in this case, that the baker's employers were proven entirely innocent.

During much of this time Canton had been reminded of the presence of the British force by intermittent bombarding of the city from guns in Dutch Folly Fort. Sir John Bowring had demanded an interview with Yeh in November, but received a prompt refusal, followed by a still more vigorous carrying on of the war in his peculiar fashion, and by raising the price on English heads. Admiral Seymour had now less reason for remaining within the Bogue, as all trade was at an end. Hundreds of foreigners had already been thrown out of employment, their property destroyed, their plans broken up, and in a few instances their lives lost in consequence of this quarrel. After holding an intrenched position around the church and barracks of the factories for the space of a month, the uselessness of this effort when sustained by so paltry a force seems to have moved the admiral (January 14, 1857) to retire from Canton, falling back upon Macao Fort until reinforcements should arrive from India. Before leaving the site of the factories, however, he burned down the warehouses of those native merchants in the vicinity, their inmates having previously been warned to leave them. These buildings and their contents were private property, and the intrenched position in the factory garden was not endangered by their remaining. The leaders of the British operations had hitherto professed to spare private property; and even if the performance was meant as a parting menace to the governor-general—"to show him," as Mr. Parkes remarked, "that we can burn too"—it was one of the few acts, on their side, which has left a stigma upon the English name in China. The hostile proceedings of the Chinese authorities had been both petty and useless, but as Admiral Seymour's force was inadequate to take and hold Canton, a more serious cannonading of the imperial quarters might have been a more honorable method of taking retribution for outrages, and better calculated than this counter-incendiarism to increase respect for British arms and civilization.

The news of these operations in China excited great interest and speculation in Europe, inasmuch as all its nations were more or less interested in the China trade. Parliament was the scene of animated argument as to the policy of Sir John Bowring and his colleagues; the moral, commercial, and political features of British intercourse with China were discussed most thoroughly in all their bearings, the arguments of both parties in the debate being drawn from the same despatches. One remarkable series of papers was presented to the House of Lords in February, 1857, entitled *Correspondence respecting Insults in China*, "containing the particulars of twenty-eight outrages committed by the Chinese upon British and other foreigners between the years 1842 and 1856." This publication was intended apparently to show how impracticable the Chinese authorities were in all their intercourse with foreigners, and its contents became to members of the House so many arguments for placing this intercourse on a better basis at the imperial court. To those who had watched since 1842 the results of treaty stipulations upon the people of China and their rulers, it was plain that no satisfactory political intercourse could be hoped for so long as the governor-general at Canton had the power of concealing and misrepresenting to his government everything that happened between foreign representatives and himself. Nevertheless such a series of papers was but one side of the insults endured. As long as the British government upheld the opium trade, and did nothing to restrain smuggling and the awful atrocities of the coolie traffic at Macao, which were filling the ears of all the world with their shocking tales, these few "outrages" seem very petty if put forward as a defence of Lord Palmerston's going to war on account of the lorcha Arrow.

In the vote upon the question of employing force in China, the better sense of Parliament protested against the policy which had directed recent events; but the Premier knew his countrymen, and in forty days from the dissolution (March 21st) England returned him a House of Commons strongly in his favor. He now decided to complete what had been wanting in the treaty of Nanking, and obtain a residence for a British minister at Peking. The governments of France, Russia, and the United States were invited to co-operate with England so far as they deemed proper, and their united interests were those of Christendom. No well-wisher to China could patiently look forward to a continuation of the past tantalizing semblance of official intercourse at Canton, and the varied experience of twelve years at other ports proved that the Chinese people did not sympathize in this policy. The French Emperor had a special grievance against H. I. M. Hienfung, on account of the judicial murder of Père Chapdelaine, a missionary in Kwangsí province, who had been tortured and beheaded at Sí-lin hien on February 29, 1856, by order of the district magistrate. This outrage was in direct violation of the rescript of 1844, and some atonement and apology were justly demanded. How totally unconscious of all these discussions and plans were Hienfung and his counsellors at Peking, may be guessed from their blind fright during subsequent events, while their inability to devise a course of action corresponded to their childish ignorance of their position and duties.

A powerful though unspoken reflection among these rulers must not here be overlooked as a secret motive in deciding many of their short-sighted counsels. Remembering the way in which their ancestors had captured the Empire over two centuries before, they felt that great risk was run in admitting the barbarians to the capital now, since the same game would probably be played over again. The visits of foreign ministers to the insurgents at Nanking, and their readiness at Canton to quarrel about so trifling a point as pulling down a flag and carrying off a few natives under its protection, all indicated, in their opinion, nothing short of conquest and spoliation. With such tremendous power arrayed against so weak an adversary, they knew well enough what would ensue. Their miserable policy of isolation had left them more helpless in their ignorance than diminished in their resources, and they had to pay dearly for their instruction.

The appointments of Lord Elgin and Baron Gros as plenipotentiaries for Great Britain and France were most fortunate as a selection of eminent diplomatists and clear-headed men. The two ambassadors entered into most cordial relations as soon as the land and sea forces placed at their disposal arrived on the Chinese coast. Lord Elgin reached Hongkong in July, but learning the state of affairs in that region, and that no advances had been made from Peking to settle the dispute, concluded to take the Shannon to Calcutta, to the assistance of Lord Canning against the mutineers; from this place he proposed to proceed in the cold weather, when the force detailed for China would all be ready. Returning to Hongkong by September 20th, he was obliged to tarry yet another month before the last of his reinforcements, or those of the French, had joined him. By the end of November the American minister, W. B. Reed, in the frigate Minnesota, and the Russian admiral, Count Poutiatine, in the gunboat Amerika, had likewise come.

Early in December, after a refusal on the part of Yeh of their ultimatum, the allied forces advanced up the Canton River. An extract from one of Lord Elgin's private letters illustrates admirably the spirit in which he entered upon the work he had been chosen to do. "December 22d.—On the afternoon of the 20th I got into a gunboat with Commodore Elliot, and went a short way up toward the Barrier forts, which were last winter destroyed by the Americans. When we reached this point, all was so quiet that we determined to go on, and we actually steamed past the city of Canton, along the whole front, within pistol-shot of the town. A line of English men-of-war are now anchored there in front of the town. I never felt so ashamed of myself in my life, and Elliot remarked that the trip seemed to have made me sad. There we were, accumulating the means of destruction under the very eyes and within the reach of a population of about one million people, against whom these means of destruction were to be employed! 'Yes,' I said to Elliot, 'I am sad, because, when I look at that town, I feel that I am earning for myself a place in the Litany, immediately after "plague, pestilence, and famine."' I believe, however, that, as far as I am concerned, it was impossible for me to do otherwise than as I have done. . . . When we steamed up to Canton and saw the rich alluvial banks covered with the luxurious evidences of unrivalled industry and natural fertility combined—beyond them barren uplands sprinkled with a soil of reddish tint which gave them the appearance of heather slopes in the Highlands, and beyond these again the White Cloud mountain range standing out bold and blue in the clear sunshine—I thought bitterly of those who, for the most selfish objects, are trampling under foot this ancient civilization."[1]

On the 27th the British and French, about six thousand in all, landed on the east bank a short distance below the walls. During the whole of the following day a furious bombardment was opened upon the city from the ships, driving thousands of the frightened natives into the western suburbs and destroying considerable portions of the town. By three o'clock of the 29th the city was in the hands of the foreigners—almost exactly the two hundred and seventh anniversary of its capture and entire reduction by the Manchus (November, 1650). The victory was not a brilliant one, since scarcely any one could be found with whom to fight; three or four forts to be entered, the wall scaled, a loss of one hundred and ten in killed and wounded to the victors, perhaps five times as many to the vanquished—this was all. Immediately upon their entry within the hitherto forbidden city the chiefs were forced to turn their energy upon their own troops and prevent them from bullying and looting the helpless Chinese.

Governor-General Yeh was, after some little search, found and captured while attempting an escape from his yamun,[2] and within twenty-four hours the lieutenant-governor, Tartar general, and all others in high authority came into possession of the invaders. Yeh was carried forthwith on board H. B. M. S. Inflexible, a wise step which deprived him of further power of

---

[1] *Letters and Journals*, p. 212.

[2] Some very curious documents were found among his archives illustrating the character both of the man and his government. See Oliphant, *Elgin's Mission to China*, Vol. I., Chap. VIII. Reed's *Correspondence*, 1858, pp. 443–488.

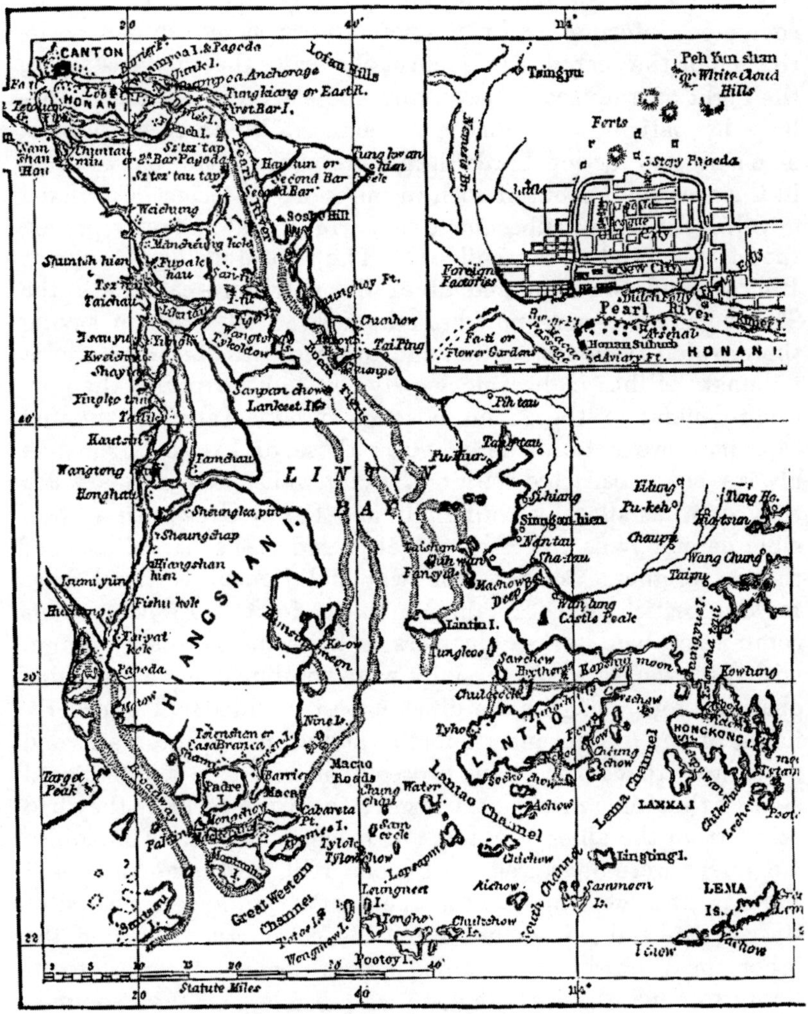

THE CITY OF CANTON AND ADJACENT ISLANDS.

resistance and misrepresentation, and left the plenipotentiaries free to arrange some method of temporary government for the city. This was a difficult problem, chiefly owing to the lack of competent interpreters, but rendered more so by the natural irritation of the conquered people at the losses they had sustained, the flight of the local officers, and the alarming extent of robbery by natives, somewhat countenanced by foreign soldiers. The skill and tact of Lord Elgin were never better shown than in the construction out of such incongruous materials of a mixed government whose subsequent easy working abundantly proved the master mind of the builder.[1] The two Manchus, Governor Pihkwei and the commandant of the garrison—called also the Tartar general—were now brought forward to assist in saving their capital from destruction and to form with the allies a joint tribunal. Pihkwei became legally (by Yeh's capture) the governor-general of the Liang Kwang, and his functions in that capacity were not interfered with; those of his colleague had always been restricted within the city walls. On January 9th they were installed by Lord Elgin and Baron Gros with all possible ceremony as rulers of the city, under the surveillance of three foreigners, Colonel Holloway and Consul Harry Parkes for the British, and Captain Martineau for the French. This commission had its headquarters in the same extensive yamun with Pihkwei, in whom happily were combined some estimable qualities for managing the difficult post he filled. The orderly habits of the literati and traders in and around Canton afforded a guaranty that no seditious proceedings would be countenanced against this joint authority if it gave them the security they had asked from the allies. A force of marines and the Fifty-ninth Regiment were quartered on Pagoda Hill, on the north side of the city, and ere long the commandant's yamun was cleared of its rubbish and put in order for the commission, leaving the other for Pihkwei. The allied chiefs deemed it wisest to attempt to govern as little in detail as possible, and their commissioners found enough to do in adjusting complaints brought by

[1] "You may imagine," he writes, "what it is to undertake to govern some millions of people when we have *in all* two or three people who understand the language! I never had so difficult a matter to arrange."

the Chinese against their own men. The Cantonese did not fail to contrast the considerate treatment they received from their foreign captors with the carnage and utter ruin which would have followed the occupation of the city by the Tai-pings or other insurgents, and during the whole period quietly submitted. The greater part of the responsible labor came upon Mr. Parkes, because of his ability to talk Chinese, but before many months he had taught many natives how to assist in carrying out the necessary details. He showed much skill in circumventing the designs of the discontented officials at Fuhshan, giving Pihkwei all the native criminals to judge, restraining the thievery or cruelty of the foreign police, and sending out proclamations for the guidance and admonition of the people.[1]

The kindness shown by Lord Elgin after the capture of Canton infused itself into the minds of those working with and under him, and the newly installed governor soon recovered his composure as he found himself in possession of his own dignities and power. The local and provincial officers under him kept themselves at Fuhshan, now recovering from its destruction of three years before. By the end of January affairs were put in order, the blockade was taken off the port, foreign merchants returned and settled in the warehouses still unharmed on Honam, while the native dealers reopened their shops in the vicinity.[2] Sixteen months had elapsed since the affair of the Arrow, and every one felt that a new day had begun to dawn on the relations of China with other lands.[3] Among the papers

---

[1] *Blue Book: Lord Elgin's Correspondence*, July 15, 1859, Despatches Nos. 88, 94, 108, and 128. Oliphant, *Elgin's Mission to China*, Vol. I., p. 170.

[2] Oddly enough, among the most earnest appeals for the restoration of commerce came one from Pihkwei himself, who wrote to Lord Elgin: "The eagerness with which merchants will devote themselves to gain, if the trade be now thrown well open, will increase manifold the good understanding between our nations, and the step will thus, at the same time, enhance your excellency's reputation."—*Blue Book*, January 24, 1858.

[3] The letters of G. W. Cooke, the *Times'* correspondent (London, Routledge, 1858), contain a fairly complete account of the proceedings of the allies at Canton; his conversations with Governor-General Yeh on the way to Calcutta are less valuable Compare an article in the *Revue des Deux Mondes* (1e juillet, 1859), by C. Lavallée, *Un Historiographe de la Presse anglaise dans la guerre de Chine.*

taken in Yeh's yamun were the ratified copies of the treaties between China and Great Britain, France, and the United States, carefully preserved there, it was said, by directions from Peking, in order to serve for reference in case of dispute as to the text. It was, however, one of the indexes proving the desire of the Emperor to keep himself aloof from personal contact with foreigners.

The allied chiefs, early in the month of February, proposed to their American and Russian coadjutors to join them in laying their demands before the Peking Court, and affording it one more opportunity to amicably settle the pending difficulties by sending an officer to Shanghai with full powers for that end. Both Russians and Americans were cordially in unison with the allies, and their several despatches addressed to Yü, the first member of the *Nui Koh*, or 'Inner Council,' at Peking, were taken up to Shanghai and thence to Suchau, where Ho Kwei-tsing received and forwarded them before the end of February. These four letters simultaneously sent to the secluded court at Peking contained nothing which could alarm its members; but such was the ignorance of the highest officers there, that they knew not what to do—ostrich-like, hiding their heads from the approaching danger, simply declining to answer any unpleasant communication, hoping thereby to put far off the evil day. Their isolation would remain if left to themselves, and to have sent Kiying again to the south would only have cherished their stupid pride and worked their subjects ultimate injury. Their old-time policy of absolute non-intercourse lay like some great frigate sunk athwart the mouth of a river; the obstacle once removed, nothing remained to prevent the vast and populous regions beyond the barrier from an active and profitable communion with the whole world. They could no longer be left *in statu quo*, and few can find fault with the plan proposed to solve their difficulties—a plan which brought the four most powerful nations of Christendom in joint consent to set themselves on a fair and advantageous footing with the most ancient and populous nation of Asia. To those who admit the direct government of the Almighty Ruler in ordering the policy of nations in accord with His wise plans, this simultaneous approach to Peking will always be deemed as one of the waymarks of human progress.

The letters presented to the Emperor[1] form in their topics and tone a pleasant contrast to the communications in past years. That of the Russian minister was peculiar in bringing forward the desirableness of allowing the profession of Christianity to all natives desirous of embracing it; but this point was made the subject of an address by the British missionaries at Ningpo and Shanghai to Lord Elgin, whose reply was a happy exposition of the dangers and difficulties connected with the toleration of Christianity by a government ignorant of its precepts. The imperial replies to these advances were, as every one expected, in the strain of *non possumus.* Lord Elgin returned his copy to Ho Kwei-tsing at Suchau, and enclosed therewith another despatch to Yü, in which he announced his intention to proceed to Taku, where he would await the arrival of a commissioner qualified to treat upon the points in dispute.

The force designed to accompany the allied chiefs was gathering at Shanghai, and by the middle of April most of the ships and transports had anchored off the Pei ho, together with the American frigates Minnesota and Mississippi and the Russian gunboat Amerika, having the legations of those nations on board. Nothing could be more dreary than the aspect of the rendezvous at this season. The ships were obliged to anchor about eight miles from shore, which was level, and would have been invisible if it had not been for the forts at the entrance of the river. The dim, hazy horizon was lurid with the rays of the sun shining through the dust that came in clouds from the plains of Mongolia and Chihlí. The turbid waters were often lashed into foam by the conflicting forces of tides and winds which acted on it from every quarter, and kept the gulf in a turmoil. No native boats ventured out to traffic, as would have been the case in the south, and the only signs of life were the gunboats and launches running in and out of the river, or the barges passing from ship to ship. Added to other discommodi-

---

[1] These are all given in the correspondence of Mr. Reed, printed by the Senate—Despatch No. 9, *Ex. Document* No. 30, March 13, 1860, pp. 122–183.

ties, were occasional blasts of hot air which swept over the water, charged with fine dust that settled on the decks and rigging, and insinuated itself into the dress and faces in an uncomfortable manner.

As usual the Chinese had done nothing. The increasing number and size of the ships which were anchored off the Pei ho had, however, been duly reported at Peking, and the Russian admiral had received a reply to his announcement of arrival. On April 23d communications were addressed by the four ministers to Yu-ching at Peking, and on the 26th replies came from Tan Ting-siang, governor-general of Chihlí, informing them that he, with Tsunglun and Wu, had been deputed to "receive their complaints and investigate and manage." The governor-general was not empowered to settle upon the terms of a treaty, but he desired to have a personal conference to learn what was demanded. Upon the day appointed the Russian and American ministers met Tan at the Taku forts (April 30th) at separate hours, when they learned that he had not been invested with "full powers," like those granted to Kíying and Ílipu in 1842, but had authority to discuss all matters preparatory to signing a treaty. The truth was that they were quite ignorant of the important questions raised at Canton; but while willing to discuss them, they were equally set on keeping the foreigners away from the capital. Here the allied chiefs and their two colleagues took issue. The former held out for commissioners to be sent with full powers; but the latter deeming that the governor-general had adequate authority, accordingly presented him with the main points of their demands and afterward with the drafts of their treaties. The negotiations were delayed by the difficulties of the entrance, but they afforded a needed instruction to these conceited and ignorant men, who were thus enabled at their leisure to prepare for the struggle. Not only were the officers themselves brought face to face with their dreaded visitors, and made to perceive the folly of resisting the armaments at their command, but with the democratic habits usual in Chinese courts, the hundreds of attendants present at the conferences heard all that passed.

Ere the non-belligerent powers had completed their negotiations, the allies turned over theirs into the hands of the two admirals, MM. Seymour and Rigault de Genouilly. These advanced up the river on May 20th, forcing the slight boom across the stream, and capturing all the forts on both banks, with all their stores. Comparatively few Chinese were killed, and their defence of the forts was creditable to their courage and skill. All the troops fled or were driven from their intrenched camps as far as Taku town, and the other defences, stockades, and fire-rafts having been destroyed, the gunboats proceeded to Tientsin. The losses by shot on the part of the Allies were unhappily doubled by the explosion of a powder magazine in a fort as a party of Frenchmen entered. The news that the foreigners had forced the defences at the mouth of the Pei ho was soon spread through the towns along its banks, and myriads of unarmed people flocked to the shore to see the gun boats, whose smoke and masts towering above the low land indicated their presence to the amazed inhabitants.

A house having been prepared at Tientsin for the allied chiefs, Lord Elgin and Baron Gros reached the city at daylight on May 30th, followed by the other two ministers, all of them having come up during the night without mishap or opposition. The inhabitants of the city were highly excited at the presence of the vessels and those of whom they had heard such dreadful stories, but their curiosity and fear kept them quiet and civil, and they were content with lining the shores in dense crowds, to gaze and talk. The general ignorance of each other's language did not prevent a constant intercourse with the citizens, all the more agreeable after the confinement on board ship. One old man was found managing a ferry-boat, who remembered Lord Amherst's visit in 1816. After his inquiries as to the meaning of the flags on board the ships had been answered, he exclaimed, "How easily you and we could get along if you but understood our language"—to which the crowd around reëchoed their hearty assent.

Two higher commissioners now appeared on the scene of action, Kweiliang and Hwashana, who superseded the discomfited Tan, Tsunglun, and Wu, and presented their cards as having been invested with full powers to treat. Negotiations were opened with them, and thus, after months of delay, the plan which Yeh had so foolishly adhered to at Canton in October, to refuse all personal discussion, was accomplished at Tientsin under far more promising circumstances. The Chinese were obliged to accept almost any terms offered them, for negotiations carried on under such conditions were hardly those of free agents. The high commissioners were ignorant beyond conception of the gravity of their position and the results which were to flow from these treaties, whose provisions, linked into one compact by the favored nation clause, were, in fact, to form the future magna charta between almost the two halves of the human race. It was true that the Chinese commissioners were not altogether their own masters in making them, but owing to their perverse seclusion, they had foolishly shut themselves out from the opportunity of learning their rights. They had, of course, no desire to learn what they knew nothing about, and there was no alternative other than the display of force to break down the barriers which pride alone made strong. They had some grounds for fear, from their recent occupation of Canton, that the British wished for more territory than Hongkong; and the frequent visits of the national vessels of Great Britain, the United States, and France to the insurgents at Nanking indicated serious results in the future, for the latter owed all their religious fanaticism to foreign inspiration. To the persistent smuggling of opium along the whole coast since the treaties negotiated by Kíying sixteen years before, and the many social and financial evils entailed thereby, were now added the atrocities of the coolie trade in Kwangtung province. Yet the reserve of the officials upon these and other topics on which they might be expected to have expressed their views or remonstrances, was only equalled by the politeness and freedom with which they met their enemies in consultation. Never again in the history of nations can functionaries to whom were confided the settlement of questions of so great moment, be brought together in such honest ignorance of the other's intentions, fears, and wishes. It was high time for each of the five powers, now face to face, to have the way opened for the removal of this ignorance and a better understanding substituted.

The despatches of Lord Elgin and Mr. Reed contain translations of many reports and memorials which were found in Yeh's yamun at Canton, and give one a good idea of the sort of information furnished to the Emperor by his highest officers. It is a wrong view of these papers to regard their extraordinary misstatements as altogether designed to deceive the court and screen the ill-success of the writers, for they had had no more facilities to investigate the real condition of foreign lands and the policy of their rulers than had the poor boy Caspar Hauser to learn about his neighbors.

One untoward event occurred during the negotiations. This was the sudden arrival of Kíying (June 8th) and his effort to force himself into the company of the plenipotentiaries. Since his departure from Canton in 1847 he had filled the premiership before the death of the late Emperor Taukwang, after which he had been deprived of all power and most of his honors. He seemed to have tried to recover them by making large promises at court respecting his influence over the *barbarians;* but when he reached Tientsin he was without credentials enabling him to participate, and acted as if his misfortunes had in a measure unsettled his reason. The British minister was suspicious of his designs, and sent his two secretaries, on the 9th, to learn what they could of or from him. These gentlemen plainly pointed out to the old man the difficulties in the way of settling the present troubles in any other manner than by acceding to the demands of Lord Elgin. Kíying had, however, put himself in a serious dilemma. Finding very soon that he was powerless to change the course of events and get the steamers away from Tientsin (as he no doubt had promised to do, and thus prove his influence), he returned to Peking on the 12th, though he had announced the reception of his full powers only the day before. His colleagues were not sorry to have him depart, but nothing definite was learned of his fate until at the end of three weeks, when the Emperor's rescript ordering him to commit suicide was received. His case was deemed of sufficient importance to call for a summation of the principal features in order to prove the righteousness of his sentence, and manifest the Emperor's extreme desire to be at once just and gracious in his decree. Kíying's case is rather an unusual one among Chinese officials, but the real reasons for his fall are probably not all stated; his prominence abroad, arising from his connection with the Nanking treaty, was no criterion of his influence at home or of the loss to the government by his death.[1]

Soon after his departure the impertinence of a native crowd to a party of British officers while walking through the city, lent some strength to the belief that Kíying's counsel had been warlike, and that a *coup*, similar to the one made at Canton in 1841 by Yihshan, had been suggested, and the destruction of all the foreigners in Tientsin was hoped for as its result. Their relations with the citizens thus far had been amicable on the whole, and the interruption in this desirable state of things was very brief. Negotiations continued, therefore, but with an undercurrent of doubt as to details on some important points among the foreign envoys. Lord Elgin had the greatest responsibility, indeed, and the task before him was difficult and delicate, but he failed in drawing to himself his colleagues and learning their views. They hardly knew what to do, for none of them wished to thwart his desires for complete and honorable intercourse with the central government, though the manner of reaching this end might admit of discussion. This he never invited. The position of the American and Russian envoys, pledged to their instructions not to fight, and having the feeling that their nations were to obtain the advantages resulting from the hostilities of the allies, was not a pleasant one; but it could have been made so, and he himself relieved of his main anxiety as to the result, by an interview. In contrast

[1] Oliphant's *Mission of Lord Elgin to China and Japan*, pp. 238–253 (American edition), N. Y., 1860. It is interesting to note, before leaving this episode, a Frenchman's opinion of the character of this statesman: "Kíying a été de 1842 à 1844 le grand négociateur de la Chine. Les ministres étrangers ont vanté son habileté, sa finesse, ses façons aimables et courtoises. . . . Son nom symbolisait une politique nouvelle, bienveillante pour les étrangers, tolérante, libérale; il représentait une sorte de jeune Chine."—M. C. Lavallée in the *Revue des Deux Mondes*, 15 Déc. 1859, p. 602. The same article contains an interesting account of the first expedition up the Pei ho and its results.

with Lord Elgin's general bearing toward those around him, as detailed in his correspondence, his biographer gives an extract from a private letter written the day after signing his treaty, which describes his perplexities :

> June 29th.—I have not written for some days, but they have been busy ones. We went on fighting and bullying, and getting the poor commissioners to concede one point after another, till Friday the 25th, when we had reason to believe that all was settled, and that the signature was to take place the following day. On Friday afternoon, however, Baron Gros came to me with a message from the Russian and American ministers to induce me to recede from two of my demands—1, a resident minister at Peking, and, 2, permission to our people to trade in the interior of China ; because, as they said, the Chinese plenipotentiaries had told them that they had received a decree from the Emperor stating that they should infallibly lose their heads if they gave way on these points.
>
> The resident minister at Peking I consider far the most important matter gained by the treaty; the power to trade in the interior hardly less so. I had at stake not only these important points in my treaty, for which I had fought so hard, but I know not what behind. For the Chinese are such fools that it was impossible to tell, if we gave way on one point, whether they would not raise difficulties on every other. I sent for the admiral ; gave him a hint that there was a great opportunity for England ; that all the powers were deserting me on a point which they had *all*, in their original applications to Peking, demanded, and which they all intended to claim if I got it ; that, therefore, we had it in our power to claim our place of priority in the East by obtaining this when others would not insist on it. Would he back me ? This was the forenoon of Saturday, 26th, and the treaty was to be signed in the evening.
>
> I may mention, as a proof of the state of people's minds, that Admiral Seymour told me that the French admiral had urged him to dine with him, assuring him that no treaty would be signed that day ! I sent Frederick to the imperial commissioners to tell them that I was indignant beyond all expression at their having attempted to communicate with me through third parties ; that I was ready to sign at once the treaty as it stood ; but that if they delayed or retreated, I should consider negotiations at an end, go to Peking and demand a great deal more, etc. Frederick executed this most difficult task admirably, and at six P.M. I signed the treaty of Tientsin. I am now anxiously awaiting some communication from Peking. Till the Emperor accepts the treaty I shall hardly feel safe. Please God he may ratify without delay ! I am sure that I express the wish just as much in the interest of China as in our own. Though I have been forced to act almost brutally, I am China's friend in all this.[1]

The importance of these two provisos was not exaggerated in his mind, but he might have seen that the difficulties with his colleagues were increased by his own reticence.

---

[1] Walrond's *Life and Letters of Lord Elgin*, p. 252.

However much a different course might have harmonized these discordant views, the pressure on the city of Tientsin was too near and severe upon the Chinese, and they yielded from fear of worse consequences when no other arguments could have induced them. It was not Lord Elgin alone who felt very sensibly, on that occasion, "the painfulness of the position of a negotiator who has to treat with persons who yield nothing to reason and everything to fear, and who are at the same time profoundly ignorant of the subjects under discussion and of their own real interests." Looked at in any point of view, this period of negotiation at Tientsin in 1858 was a remarkable epoch. The sole great power of paganism was being bound by the obligations of a treaty extorted from its monarch by a handful of men in possession of the entrance to its capital. As one of the British officers pithily stated it, two powers had China by the throat, while the other two stood by to egg them on, so that all could share the spoil. Yet the past sixteen years had proven most conclusively that, unless this pressure was exerted, the imperial government would make no advance, admit no opening for learning its real position among the nations of the world, but mulishly cherish its ignorance, its isolation, its conceit, and its folly, until these causes had worked out the ruin so fondly hoped to be avoided. Even the necessity of coming into personal official relations with the foreign consuls to promote the maintenance of good order between their subjects had been hampered or neutralized by the Chinese authorities at all the ports; and there was no hope of introducing a better state of things until foreign ministers were received at Peking. Happily, Lord Elgin then saw the question in all its bearings, and no one ever proved to be a truer friend to China than did he in forcing it upon her. He had little idea, probably, of one motive for their resistance, namely, the fear of the Manchu rulers, already referred to, that in admitting the enemy to the capital they would be as summarily ejected as had been their predecessors in 1644.

However, by the first week in July the four treaties had been signed and ratified by Hienfung, and all the vessels had left the Pei ho, which itself was no doubt the greatest proof to his Majesty that they were valid compacts; for if the tables had been turned he would not have let them off so easily, and perhaps wondered that Tientsin had not been ransomed at the same rate that Elliot had spared Canton in 1841. It is difficult to fully appreciate the crass ignorance and singular perversity of the men in whose hands the sway of the Chinese people were now lodged. He who is unwilling to acknowledge the overruling hand of God in this remarkable meeting of nations, would find it very difficult to acknowledge it anywhere in human history.

The revision of the tariff had been deferred for a future discussion among those qualified for the work. Five Chinese commissioners reached Shanghai early in October for this and other purposes, of whom Kweiliang and Hwashana were two. In this part of the negotiations the controlling power was properly left in the hands of the British, for their trade was worth more than all others combined. They used this power most selfishly, and fastened on the weak and distracted Empire a veritable remora, which has gone on sucking its resources without compunction or cessation. By making the tariff an integral part of the treaty, they theoretically made every infraction a *casus belli*, and as no provision was left for revision, it was virtually rendered impossible, since the original four powers could not again be brought to unite on its readjustment with a view to the rights of China. While particular provision was made in it for preventing the importation of salt and the implements and munitions of war, the trade in opium was legalized at a lower rate than was paid on tea and silk entering England, and the brand of immorality and smuggling was removed from its diffusion throughout China. The weakness and ignorance of the Chinese were such as laid them open to the power and craft of other nations, but the inherent wrong of the principle of ex-territoriality was never more unjustly applied than in breaking down the moral sense of a people by forcing them to legalize this drug. The evils of smuggling it were insufferable, but a heavy duty was desirable as a check and stigma upon the traffic. The solution to a statesman in Lord Elgin's position was exceedingly difficult in relation to this point, and he perhaps took the safest course under the existing circumstances, but it has proved to be fraught with evils to the Chinese. One who now reads his biography and learns his nice sense of right and equity in national affairs, will not be surprised to see his doubts as to the best course to take where all were so many moves in the dark.

The war which arose about the Arrow was now virtually closed, but many things remained to be enforced in carrying out the treaty stipulations or restraining the irritation they produced. The vastness of the Empire sundered its inhabitants so widely that each felt the troubles it endured only when they came near; but to all of them the obligations of treaty were of the most shadowy nature. It would require years of patient instruction to educate the mass of natives up to the idea that these obligations affected them as individuals. One means of this instruction, which subsequent years have shown to be both practical and profitable, was the extension and reorganization of the administration of the customs under foreign supervision. Its short service at Shanghai had proved it to be easy and safe of operation, and the increased fidelity everywhere in collecting the duties gratified the central and provincial governments exceedingly. It was a startling proof of the degrading effects of the opium and smuggling trade upon the honor of the foreign merchants that they generally resisted the transfer of collecting duties from native to foreign hands, and endeavored in a thousand ways to thwart and ridicule the altered system. This feeling, however, disappeared with the incoming of a new set of merchants, and the Chinese government has, since the first, found no difficulty in utilizing the skill, knowledge, and power of their employés, not only in fiscal departments, but whereever they felt the need of such qualifications. Beginning at Shanghai, when the local officers were helpless against their own subjects, mandarins and people alike desired the advantages of an honestly collected tariff to be extended to every port opened for foreign trade.

The changes formulated in the treaties of Tientsin could receive their accomplishment only after patient efforts on the part of ministers, consuls, and collectors to carry them into effect with due regard to the position of the native rulers. In order to open the way into the country, Lord Elgin visited Hankow in four ships in November, after he had signed the tariff. The rebels in possession of Nanking and other towns, being unapprised of his character, fired at him from some of their forts, for which "they were pounded pretty severely in return." But a few words afterward proved more effectual than many shots, and no further altercation occurred. The voyage to and return from Hankow occupied seven weeks, and inaugurated a commerce and intercourse which has resulted in much good to the natives by making them rapidly acquainted with foreigners. The right of China to the exclusive navigation of her internal waters was summarily set aside by making Hankow a seaport; on the other hand, the government derived many advantages in the moral assistance given her at the time against the rebels by having them restrained, and, up to the present day, in the stimulus given to internal trade and rapid intercourse between the peoples of remote districts.

The year 1858 was fraught with great events, involving the welfare of the people of China and Japan and their future position and progress. Much against their will they had been forced into political relations with Europe and America, and in a measure deprived of their independence under the guise of treaties which erected an *imperium in imperio* in their borders. Their rulers, ignorant of the real meaning of these principles of ex-territoriality, were tied down to observe them, and found themselves within a few years humbled before those of their own subjects who had begun to look to foreigners for protection. The perplexity of the Chinese commissioners at Shanghai in this new position was exhibited in a despatch addressed on November 1, 1858, to the three envoys. In it they discuss the right of foreigners who have no treaties to go into the interior, and insist upon the absolute necessity of restraining them, which their own mercantile consuls could not and would not do.

"Being unacquainted," they wrote, "with the usages of foreign nations in this respect, and unwilling of ourselves to lay down preventive regulations respecting issuing passports, we desire first to receive the result of your deliberations before we act in the premises." They then proceed to show how necessary it will be for the future peace between conflicting interests and nationalities that consuls should not be merchants, for "some of those of your respective nations have formerly and often acted in a manner calculated to impede and mar the harmony that existed between their nations and our own; wilfully disregarding everything but their own opinions, they have carried out their own high-handed measures to the ruin of all cordial feeling." The writers had no idea how this despatch was an argument and a proof of the need of strong measures to drag them out of their stupid ignorance and childish desires for isolation, and compel them to understand their duties. The education then begun was the only means through which to raise the Chinese rulers and people to a higher plane of civilization and liberty. One document like this carries in itself enough to show how ignorant were its writers and their colleagues of their own duties, and how hopeless was the prospect of their emerging voluntarily from their seclusion. The treaties bound them down to keep the peace, while they opened the channels through which the people could learn whatever was true and useful, without fear of punishment or reproach. The toleration of Christianity, the residence of foreign ministers at Peking, and the freedom to travel through the land were three avenues heretofore closed against the welfare and progress of China which the treaties opened, and through which she has already made more real advances than ever before in her history.[1]

[1] For full details on these important negotiations, see the Blue Book presented to Parliament July 15, 1859, containing Lord Elgin's correspondence; *U. S. Senate Executive Document* No. 30, read March 13, 1860, containing correspondence of Messrs. Reed, Williams, and Ward, from June, 1857, to September 17, 1859; Oliphant's *Mission of Lord Elgin to China and Japan*, London and New York, 1860; Lieutenant-Colonel Fisher, *Personal Narrative of Three Years' Service in China*, London, 1863; le Marquis de Moges, *Baron Gros's Embassy to China and Japan*, 1860; Walrond's *Letters and Journals of James, Earl of Elgin*, London, 1872; Lieut. J. D. Johnston, *China and Japan*, Philadelphia, 1860; *North American Review*, Vol. XC., p. 125; *Blackwood's Magazine*, Vols. LXXXVI., p. 647, LXXXVII., pp. 430, 535, and LXXXIX., p. 373.

By the end of December, 1858, the four envoys had left China, as well as most of the small force under their control. None of them had reached Peking, so that the Emperor was relieved of his fear that he would be carried off as was his commissioner, Yeh, from Canton; he had, moreover, another year of grace to learn what he ought to do to carry out the treaties. He was also relieved by the refusal of the allies to join their quarrel with the efforts of the Tai-pings and march together to the conquest of the Empire. In Canton the presence of the allies had been an irritation chiefly to the provincial officers, who busied themselves in stimulating large bodies of braves in its vicinity to assassinate and rob individual foreigners near or in the city, keeping up in this manner a lasting feeling of discontent. Several skirmishes took place, and a large district within the city near the British quarters on Kwanyin Shan was burned over to insure protection against sudden attacks. The new governor-general, Hwang, had formed a league of the gentry and braves, which chiefly exhibited their power in harassing their own countrymen. He was removed in disgrace at Lord Elgin's request, and all these puny and useless attacks brought to an end.

An incident which occurred near Canton about fifteen months after the city had been captured, strikingly shows the character of the people: "February 11th.—On the 8th a body of troops about one thousand strong started on an expedition which was to take three days. I accompanied, or rather preceded them on the first day's march, about twelve miles from Canton. We rode through a very pretty country, passing by the village of Shek-tsing, where there was a fight a fortnight ago. The people were very respectful, and apparently not alarmed by our visit. At the place where the troops were to encamp for the night a cattle fair was in progress, and our arrival did not seem to interrupt the proceedings. February 13th.—The military expedition was entirely successful. The troops were everywhere received as friends. Considering what has been of yore the state of feeling in this province toward us, I think this almost the most remarkable thing which has happened since I came here. Would it have happened if I had given way to those who wished me to carry fire and sword through all the country villages?"[1]

These same villages furnished thousands of volunteers in May, 1841, to attack Sir Hugh Gough's army, and had been engaged in a desperate struggle with their countrymen only three years before, so that this change was owing neither to cowardice nor sulkiness. It had been brought about chiefly through considerate treatment of the people by the British garrison in Canton, by honest payment for supplies, and by regard for the traffic and local government of the city; the citizens consequently had no complaint to make or revenge to satisfy. Those who from infancy had been brought up to call every foreigner a *fan-kwei*, or 'foreign devil,' now slowly appreciated the fact that they had been mistaken—nor were the misconceptions all on their side. During the three years the city was occupied, public opinion there underwent an entire change; and the Cantonese are now as courteous as they before were ill-mannered.

At this season of rebellion and foreign war under which China was now suffering, the province of Kwangtung had a special cause for just irritation against all foreigners in the coolie trade. The headquarters of this trade were at Macao, and by 1860 it had become nearly the only business carried on there. The population of the colony is perhaps seventy-odd thousand, of whom less than five thousand wear a foreign dress. Traffic and industry are mostly carried on by Chinese, who do all the work. When the trade of hiring Chinese as contract laborers to go to Cuba, Peru, and elsewhere began, there was no difficulty in obtaining men willing to try their fortunes abroad. As rumors of gold diggings open to their labors in California were spread abroad and confirmed by returning miners, the coolie ships were readily filled by men whose ignorance of outer lands made them easily believe that they were bound to El Dorado, whatever country they shipped for. The inducement for hiring them was the low rate of wages ($4 a month) at which they were willing to sell their labor, and the profits derived from introducing them into western tropical regions. The temptations

---

[1] Walrond's *Letters and Journals of Lord Elgin*, p. 308.

of this business became so great that within ten years the demand had far exceeded the supply. Seldom has the unscrupulous character of trade, where its operations are left free from the restraints either of competent authority or of morality, been more sadly exhibited than in the conduct of the agents who filled these coolie ships. The details of the manner in which natives of all classes, scholars, travellers, laborers, peddlers, and artisans, were kidnapped in town and country and sent to Macao, were seldom known, because the victims were unable to make themselves heard. When the rebels at Fuhshan were defeated in 1855, thousands of their followers were glad to save their lives by shipping as coolies, but this lasted only a short time.

The allied commissioners in charge of Canton took cognizance of these outrages, and upon the representations of Governor-General Lao took vigorous measures for breaking up the trade at Whampoa.[1] The United States minister, Hon. J. E. Ward, lent his aid in February, 1860, by allowing the Chinese authorities to take three hundred and seventeen men out of the American ship Messenger in order to ascertain whether any of them were detained on board against their will. Every one of them declined to go back to the ship, but it was not proved how many had been beguiled away on false pretences—the usual mode of kidnapping. The report of the commission sent to Cuba a dozen years later asserts, as the result of careful inquiries, that the majority of the coolies in Cuba "were decoyed abroad, not legitimately induced to emigrate."

The Portuguese rulers of Macao were unwilling to make thorough investigation into the facts about this business until after the return of the commission sent to Cuba in 1873, whose report disclosed the inevitable evils and wrongs inherent in the traffic. Urged by the British government, they finally (in 1875) closed the barracoons, and thus put an end to it. During the twenty-five years of its existence about five hundred thousand coolies were taken away.

---

[1] Compare Lieutenant-Colonel Fisher, *Personal Narrative of Three Years' Service in China*, pp. 260–342, where the matter is pretty thoroughly discussed and Lao's proclamations given in detail.

To return to the war: throughout the winter no event of note occurred in any part of China, but the imperial government was busily employed in fortifying the mouth of the Pei ho to prevent the entrance of the allies. They demolished the old forts to rebuild new ones of materials gathered on the spot, and constructed somewhat after the manner laid down in foreign authorities on fortification. These books had been translated for them by natives trained in mission schools. Notwithstanding all that Kweiliang and Hwashana may have assured them to the contrary, the Emperor and his officers could not divest themselves of their fears of serious reprisals, if not of conquest, should they permit the allied gunboats to anchor a second time at Tientsin and their embassies to enter the capital. The two commissioners awaited at Shanghai the arrival of the British, French, and American plenipotentiaries, for the purpose of urging them to exchange the ratifications in that city. Nevertheless, since Peking was expressly appointed in the first two treaties as the place for signing them, Mr. Bruce and M. Bourboulon, the English and French ministers, determined to insist upon this detail. The poor commissioners, on the other hand, knowing more than they dared to tell of the hostile preparations going on, steadily declined the offer of a passage to Taku. Mr. Ward was not tied down to any place or time for exchanging the American treaty, but decided to do so at the same place with his colleagues. The three ministers remained in the south to exchange views and allow the British gunboats to collect off Taku before their arrival, when they all joined them on June 20th. The appearance of the forts was entirely different from last year, and confirmed the reports of the great efforts making to prevent foreigners reaching the capital in large numbers. The river was found to be barred by an elaborate boom of timber and chains; but though no soldiers were in sight on the battlements, it was evident that a collision was intended. The reconnoissance had been carefully made from the 17th to the 24th, and the Chinese general, Săng-ko-lin-sin, felt confident of his ability to hold his own against the ships inside of the bar. All official intercourse was refused with Admiral Hope, though he had stated his purpose clearly, because, as was alleged, these forts and men were merely gathered by the common people to defend themselves against pirates.

In order to discover the real state of feeling toward a neutral, Commodore Tatnall took Mr. Ward, in the United States chartered steamer Toeywan, into the river on the 24th, and proceeded toward a jetty near the fort. The steamer ran aground when about half a mile short of it; the minister then sent his interpreters to the jetty, where they were met by a dozen or more miserably dressed fellows who had come from the fort for that purpose. On learning the errand of the foreigners, one or two of the men spoke up in a way which showed that they were officers—probably disguised as coolies—telling the deputation that the passage to Tientsin by the Pei ho had been barred, but that the governor-general, Hăngfuh, was then at Pehtang, a place about ten miles up the coast, where he was ready to receive the American minister. They added that they had no authority to take any letter or card for him; that they knew very well the nationality of the Toeywan, which would not be harmed if she did not attempt to break through the boom laid just above the jetty; and, lastly, that they were not at all empowered to aid or advise the Americans in getting up to Pehtang. The whole episode was a ridiculous ruse on the part of the Chinese to hide their design of forcibly preventing the ministers from ascending the river; but by so undignified a behavior the general commanding the works forfeited whatever moral advantage might otherwise have remained on his side. After Admiral Hope had commenced his operations against the barriers, Hăngfuh did indeed send a letter to the British minister—then lying nine miles off the shore—informing him of the arrangements made at Pehtang to take the allied envoys from thence to the capital. These arrangements certainly violated no article of the treaties, nor any promise made to the foreigners, though they neutralized entirely the journey to Peking upon which the British government had determined to send its plenipotentiary.

One may learn from the letters of Mr. Bruce to Lord Malmesbury (of July 5th and 13th) many details of the impertinent reception accorded to Admiral Hope's messengers by the rabble and soldiers near the Taku forts, all proving plainly enough their hostile intentions. But the minister overlooks what we, in retracing the history of these years, cannot too attentively keep in mind, namely, the ever-present fear of trickery and foul play with their unknown engines of war which the Emperor's counsellors momentarily dreaded from their foreign adversaries. On the other hand, what could be done with a government which would never condescend to appreciate its own weakness, would never speak or act the truth, would never treat any other nation as an equal? These and other despatches from the Blue Book afford a key to the policies of both parties in this remarkable contest, and convince the impartial student of the necessity of personal contact and acquaintance before it was possible to reach a lasting understanding between the holders of so widely separated views.

During the night of the 23d, after the Toeywan had floated at high water, the British advanced and blew up the first boom, leaving, however, the second and stronger obstruction untouched. The attempt to ascend the river in force was commenced by the allies in the following afternoon, when the forts opened fire upon them and by evening had sunk or silenced almost every vessel. In this fleet thirteen small gunboats were engaged, one of the largest among them, a French craft, carrying six hundred men; besides these were some six hundred marines and engineers designed to serve as an escort upon the journey to the capital. This guard was now landed in the mud before the forts and an attempt made to carry the works by escalade, but the effort failed, and by daylight the men were all once more afloat. From the gunboats twenty-five men were killed and ninety-three wounded; the loss among the marines was naturally heavier—sixty-four killed and two hundred and fifty-two wounded, while of the boats four were sunk.[1]

Throughout this action the American vessel Toeywan remained inside of the bar, being a non-combatant. The gallant energy of Commodore Tatnall, who in the thick of the fight passed through the fleet to visit the British admiral lying

[1] One of these afterward floated of itself and was preserved.

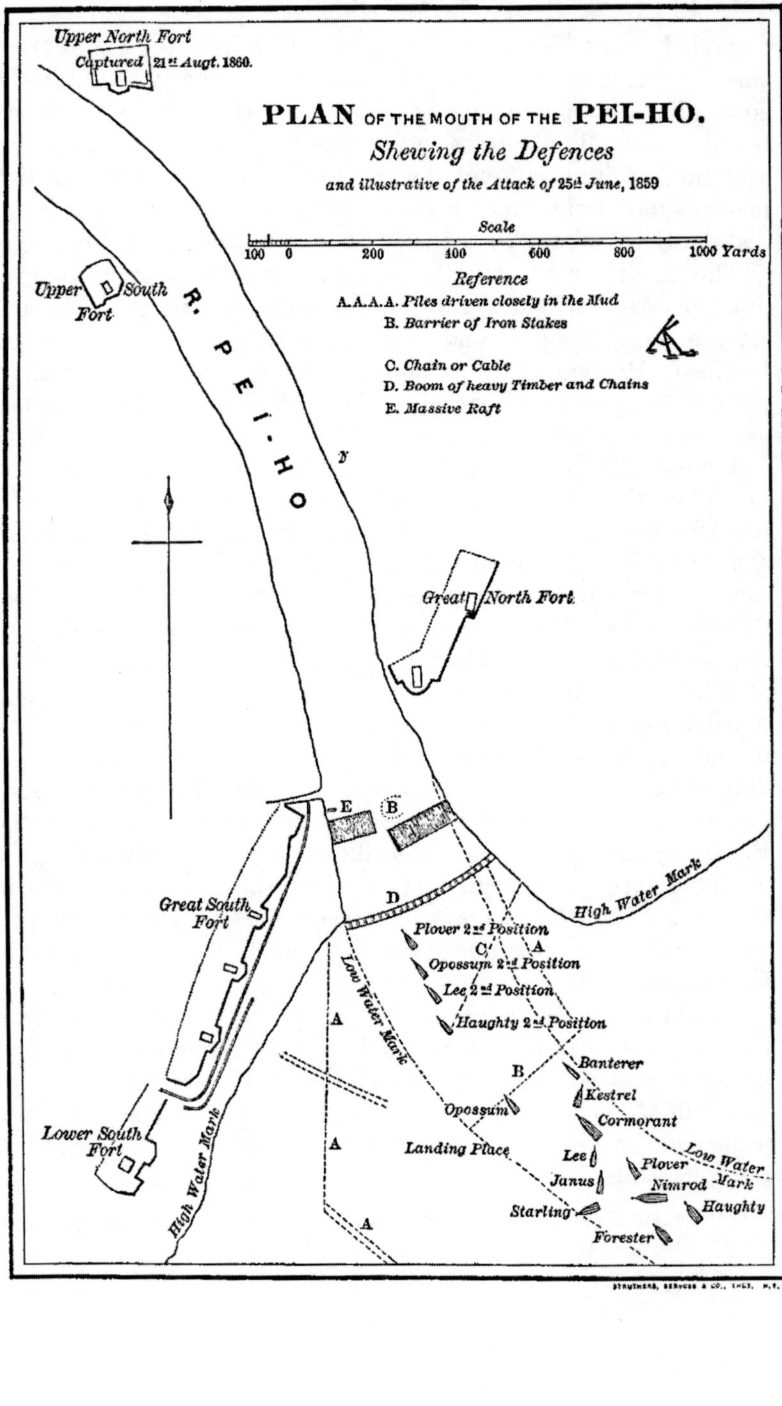

STRUTHERS, BERVOSS & CO., LHGY. N.Y.

wounded in the Plover, well-nigh cost him his life; a shot from the Chinese guns tore into the stern of his barge, killing the coxswain, and narrowly missed sinking the boat with all on board. Tatnall's declaration, in extenuation of his technical violation of international law by towing boat-loads of British marines into action, that "blood is thicker than water," has indissolubly associated his name with this battle of the Pei ho.[1]

The American minister was present as a spectator at this repulse before the Taku forts, but this could not be properly considered as a reason for not making further attempts to reach Peking. He accordingly, though not without some difficulty, notified the governor-general at Pehtang of his arrival, and four days later a pilot was sent off and the Toeywan taken up to Pehtang. Mr. Ward, in his report to Washington, expresses his belief that he would not be allowed to reach Peking, while the Chinese had no other intention than to escort him there and bring him safely back. On July 8th boats were sent to conduct his party to the place of meeting, which they reached through a line of soldiers in uniform placed along the sides of the streets, and were ushered into a large hall amid a crowd of officials. The recent encounter at Taku was discussed in a sensible manner, without apparent anxiety or bravado, and then the arrangements for taking the whole party of twenty to Peking were made known. Among other topics of inquiry brought forward was the cost of such vessels as had been sunk in the Pei ho by their guns—as if the officials had been estimating the probable expense of their victory when the English brought in their usual bill of damages. But the offer of Commodore Tatnall to place his surgeons at the disposal of the Chinese, to aid in treating the wounded men at the forts, was declined.

Everything being made ready by July 20th, the American minister set out under the escort of Chunghow, now first brought into contact with foreigners. About forty miles of flat, saltish plain was crossed, until the party reached Pehtsang, on the Pei ho, where were lying the boats prepared for

---

[1] Lieutenant-Colonel Fisher's *Personal Narrative of Three Years' Service in China*, Chaps. XIII. and XIV.

their reception. As they proceeded up the river the inhabitants flocked to the banks to behold the dreaded foreigners, but no expressions of vaunting or hostility were heard among the myriads who now gazed for the first time upon them. The vast crowd at Tungchau, when the twenty Americans landed, comprised apparently the whole population of that city; clad in white summer garments, and preserving a most remarkable stillness and decorum as they lined the river banks and highway, this silent, gazing multitude produced upon the strangers an effect incomparably weird. The day was oppressively hot, and many preferred the carts to the mules provided for the trip to Peking, where they all arrived on the 27th. A ridiculous rumor, illustrated by appropriate pictures, respecting this journey was circulated in Paris about a fortnight afterward, stating that Mr. Ward and his party were conducted from the coast in an immense "box or travelling chamber, drawn overland by oxen," and then put "on a raft to be towed up the river and Imperial Canal as far as the gate of the capital. They were well treated, and were taken back to the coast in the same manner." This *jeux d'esprit* probably expressed the popular sentiment in France of what was expected from the Chinese, and has ever since been associated with it.

On announcing his arrival, a meeting was arranged for the 30th between Mr. Ward and Kweiliang and Hwashana, at which all the time was occupied in discussing the question of the manner of audience. The minister had the advantage in this interesting colloquy, for he had come up at the invitation of the governor-general, had no directions from the President upon the matter, was quite indifferent as to the result of the conference, and had no presents to be rejected as Lord Amherst's were in 1816. The nature of the *kotow* and the reasons for requiring it of all who had audience of the Emperor were fully discussed at several interviews in the most amicable and courteous manner. The Chinese were anxious to bring about an audience, and went so far as to waive the *kotow*, or knocking head, from the first, and proposed instead that the envoy should bend one knee as he approached the sovereign. This was even less of an obeisance than English courtiers paid their Queen, and might have been accepted without difficulty—if any compromise were possible—had not one of the party previously declared the religious nature of the ceremony by saying, "If we do not kneel before the Emperor, we do not show him any respect; it is that or nothing, and is the same reverence which we pay the gods." Kweiliang further said that he himself would willingly burn incense before the President of the United States if asked to do so.[1]

During their whole national history the Chinese rulers and people had accepted this ceremony as the inseparable prerogative of the Son of Heaven; and as this discussion in their capital was in the hearing of a great crowd of officials, who, doubtless, were prompt enough in circulating among the populace a report of the disagreement, one may appreciate the feelings of the latter when the American embassy was allowed quietly to leave the city without entering into the "Great Interior" to behold the Dragon's Face. Foreigners have been so ready in China to ridicule or depreciate whatever partakes of resistance to their notions (unless it be backed up by force to make it respected), that this remarkable discussion on a vital point in Chinese etiquette and theology was generally regarded as silly verbiage on their part or ascribed to the effect of fear on the part of the Americans. As the time and place for exchanging ratifications were not mentioned in the treaty, there was no insuperable difficulty in adjourning the ceremony to another place; yet it seemed a grotesque ending to the four days' discussion for Kweiliang to seriously ask the minister for what purpose he had come to Peking, he himself being quite at a loss to understand the reason. Mr. Ward replied that it was to deliver the letter from the President, and to exchange the ratifications. It would have been better if he had held him to the promise made by the governor-general at Pehtang to do so in Peking. However, the return trip was concluded by the exchange of ratifications on August 15th at Pehtang, and the departure of the frigate for Shanghai soon after.

---

[1] See Ward's despatches, pp. 594–617, *U. S. Senate Executive Document* No. 30, read March 13, 1860; *American Eclectic Magazine*, New York, Vol. 51, April and May, 1861; *North China Br. R. A. Society*, Vol. I., No. 3, 1859.

The mortification of having been repulsed at Taku was not concealed by the British public or press, when they ascribed it to the too hasty landing at sunset on a mud flat over which there was no pathway or footing. There certainly was no treachery on the part of the Chinese, as Mr. Swinhoe declares in his *North China Campaign*, for they plainly told what they would do if the passage were attempted.[1] Yet it was a grievous disappointment to find that the exchange of ratifications had been interrupted from any cause; and though it will probably always be a debatable point whether it was right for the allied envoys to refuse the offered means of reaching Peking by way of Pehtang, there was no debate now as to the necessity of hastening to the capital at once.

The British and French governments moved immediately in the matter, and wisely decided to place the settlement of the question in the same hands that had carried it thus far. In April, 1860, Earl Russell wrote to Lord Elgin that "Her Majesty resolved to employ every means calculated to establish peace with the Emperor of China, and had determined to call upon him again to give his valuable services to promote this important object." The indispensable conditions were three, viz., an apology for the attack on the allied forces at the Pei ho; the ratification and execution of the treaty; and payment for the expenses incurred by the allies. Lord Elgin's colleague was Baron Gros, and the two were ready to leave Europe in April. They were supported in making their demands by an army of about ten thousand British troops of all arms, gathered from England, Cape Colony, and India, and nearly seven thousand French sent from France. Their respective naval forces were not largely added to, but the requisite transports increased the fleets to more than two hundred vessels in all, of which thirty-three

[1] Though they told many lies as well. These charges against the Chinese were reiterated until they were believed by all the world; but in the effort to find a good reason for proceeding to Peking in order to exchange the ratifications, it was not needful to say that the forts fired upon the British ships without notice. Mr. Bruce's despatches to Lord Malmesbury (of July 13th), together with the enclosures and translations of native documents, discuss this question with much good sense.

were French. The latter had small iron gunboats, fitted to carry one gun, brought from home in fifteen pieces each; when screwed together each boat had three compartments, made water-tight with layers of vulcanized rubber at the joinings. The British forces gathered at Talien-wan Bay on the south-eastern side of Prince Regent's Sword, and the French at Chifu on the coast of Shantung. The plenipotentiaries had arrived in July of this year and found the imperial government maintaining its old attitude of conciliation and undue assumption. On March 8th the foreigners' terms had been made known by Mr. Bruce, and a reply shortly afterward transmitted to him through Ho Kwei-tsing at Shanghai. In it the lurking fear of reprisals, so largely actuating its conduct, appears from the conclusion, when the council says: "If Mr. Bruce will come north without vessels of war and with but a moderate retinue, and will wait at Pehtang to exchange the treaties, China will not take him to task for what has gone by. But if he be resolved to bring up a number of war-vessels, and if he persist in proceeding by way of Taku, this will show that his true purpose is not the exchange of treaties."[1] After such a declaration there was but one way left by which to prove to the Emperor how thoroughly in earnest were the allies in their intention of exchanging the treaties. The last bulwark of Chinese seclusion was now to be broken down—never more, we may hope, to be erected against the advancing influences of a more enlightened civilization.

After the usual delays incident to moving large bodies of troops with their various equipages, the combined forces left their anchorages on July 26th, presenting with their long lines of ships a grand sight as they went up the smooth waters of the Gulf of Pechele toward the mouth of the Pehtang River. This assemblage was many times larger than the armaments sent to the same region in the two previous years, and the experiences of those years had prepared both parties to regard this third attempt to reach the Court of Cambaluc as decisive of their future relations. The forces found much inconvenience in ef-

---

[1] Wolseley's *Narrative*, p. 14. Fisher's *China*, Chap. XXIII.

fecting a landing at Pehtang, where the beach at low tide extends over miles of ooze and sticky mud, but met no forcible opposition. The towns in this region are among the most repulsive-looking on the whole Chinese coast. In consequence of the saline soil no trees or grass are to be seen on the wide plain; the only green things being a few fruit trees near the houses, or scattering patches of salsola and similar plants. The houses are built of mud and chopped straw; their walls rest on layers of sorghum stalks spread on the foundation to intercept the saline influences, while the thatched roofs also contain much mud. These soon present a scanty covering of grass, which, speedily withering in the hot sun, imparts to the dwelling a still more forlorn aspect. Cheerless enough on a bright day, the appearance of one of these hamlets in wet weather—with mud streaming from the roofs, the streets reeking with noisome filth, through which loaded carts and half-naked men wend dolefully their way—is certainly melancholy beyond any description.

The allies were on shore by the evening of August 2d, and in a most pitiable plight in their own eyes. The men had been obliged to wade through the mud left by the retiring tide to reach solid ground, and then cross a moat that received the drainings of the town, a reeking mass much worse, of course, than the other. No fresh water was to be had, and the time which elapsed before the men could be supplied from the boats was spent in putting themselves up for the night, wet, dirty, and hungry as they were. In the morning it was found that the few forts which they were to attack were merely for show, and soon the town was occupied by the troops, their generals taking the temples for quarters. In less than three days every house in it had been pillaged, and whatever was worthless for plunder was destroyed as useless, "the few natives that still lingered by their unusurped domiciles," adds Mr. Swinhoe, "quietly watching with the eye of despair the destruction of all the property they possessed in the world, and the ruin of their hopes perhaps forever." Even the poor wretches who were trying to carry off their goods in packs were stopped and stripped by the prowling soldiers.

In less than a fortnight the entire force had been brought ashore without accident or opposition. There were men, tents, guns, horses, provisions, animals, stores, ammunition, baggage, —everything, in short, which an army now needs and which steam easily brings to it. Besides these, two thousand five hundred Cantonese coolies, each of whom is estimated by Colonel Wolseley, with supreme candor, to have been of more general value than any three baggage animals. They were working constantly for ten days, carrying water, landing stores, and performing the toil devolving on camp followers, for which this author magnanimously praises them by saying: "They were easily fed, and when properly treated most manageable."

On August 12th the forces were ready to move on the Taku forts lying about five miles distant across the plain, now rendered miry by the constant rains. A single causeway three miles long, flanked by deep ditches, traversed it, and along this progress, especially for the heavy artillery, was exceedingly slow. Upon their passage of this road the Chinese general, Săngkolinsin, yielded the only vantage-ground where he could have encountered his enemy with hope of success. This ignorant blunder on the part of so energetic a commander seems all the more unaccountable, since a week previously the Chinese cavalry had been much emboldened by some slight successes over a reconnoitring party of the allies, and "approached our outposts with wonderful courage, a few even advancing to within a few hundred yards, brandishing the swords and making grotesque gesticulations."

At last the allies were ready to advance to the attack of the Chinese. The Mongol horsemen commenced the engagement by rushing fearlessly forward in several irregular lines of skirmishers, and bravely received the shot from the Armstrong guns, until they charged with a loud, wild yell the Sikh cavalry, with whom they engaged in close conflict. But "in less than a minute the Tartars had turned and were flying for their lives before our well-armed irregulars supported by two squadrons of the finest dragoons in the British army; the pursuit lasted for five miles, and was then only ended by our horses being pumped out. Had they been in good working order the results would have been far more satisfactory, and the worthy tax-payers at home would have had the pleasure of gloating over the account of an immense list of slain enemies." [1]

The allied infantry had already reached the intrenched camp, near the village of Sinho, and the "beautifully precise practice" of the Armstrongs, together with the accurate rifled guns of the French, were brilliantly successful in knocking over the Chinese who served their gingalls at the ranges of fourteen hundred or a thousand yards.

The reader cannot desire further particulars of this unequal contest as described by Colonel (now Lord) Garnet Wolseley. The various forces of the Chinese were entirely routed by the allies; the plain was speckled for miles by native corpses, while the care of wounded men called out the sympathies and skill of their conquerors. The village of Sinho was plundered, and its inhabitants fled, glad to escape with their lives.[2] The next morning an advance was made by the entire force upon the five forts and intrenched camps at Tangku, three miles off, from which the imperialists were dislodged with considerable loss on their part, the rest retreating across the Pei ho toward Taku. Tangku town was occupied by the foreigners, who took under their care everybody left in it, and relieved the wounded and starving while preparing for the intended attack on the forts. This kindness, and the consequent increased acquaintance arising between the contending parties in obtaining supplies, did much to remove their ignorance and contempt of each other—a result far more desirable and useful than the capture of forts and prisoners.

The French having already encamped on the further bank of the Pei ho, each army commenced the building of a bridge[3] across the stream, completing the structure so speedily that by the morning of August 21st the whole attacking force was in position. The twenty-three pieces of artillery now began to fire upon the north fort, from which the Chinese replied with

[1] Wolseley, *Narrative*, p. 103.

[2] A great collection of official documents disclosing the views of the court upon the struggle was found in the *yamun*.

[3] Lieutenant-Colonel Fisher, *Personal Narrative*, pp. 404–409.

all the alacrity they could, although taken thus in rear. About six o'clock, when the fire waxed hotter and hotter, and the troops were anxiously looking for the signal to advance, "a tall black pillar, as if by magic, shot up from the midst of the nearest fort, and then bursting like a rocket after it had obtained a great height, was soon lost in the vast shower of earth and wood into which it resolved itself—a loud, bursting, booming sound marking the moment of its short existence." But the fire from the fort only ceased for a minute or two, and the gunners served their pieces most manfully, though sometimes unprotected in any way from the crushing shell fire opposed to them. The attack began about seven o'clock, nearly four thousand men all told forming the advance. A gallant defence was made to a still braver onset, but the victory naturally fell to the disciplined forces of the allies, who had possessed themselves of all the defences before noon. A few guns taken from the ships destroyed June 25, 1859, were now recovered by the British, but otherwise the fort contained nothing of value. The loss of life on both sides was comparatively slight. The British had seventeen killed and one hundred and eighty-three wounded; the French, one hundred and thirty casualties in all: the Chinese lay dead in heaps in the fort, and their total loss probably exceeded two thousand. The interior testified in every part the noble manner in which it had been defended, even after the disastrous explosion had crippled the resources and discouraged the enthusiasm of its garrison. From this position the allies moved on the other northern fort with their artillery, under a continual fire from its walls; but before the guns could open upon it, many white flags appeared on the parapets; messengers were ere long seen to leave the great southern fort. They were all given up before sunset, and the famous Taku forts, which had last year witnessed the discomfiture of the allies, now saw them enter as conquerors[1]—"the tarnished honor of our arms was gloriously vindicated."

[1] When the allied generals came to carefully examine the construction of the walls, casemates, and internal arrangements, with the preparation made outside to hinder the enemy, they declared them to be absolutely impregnable from seaward if defended as well as the north fort had been.

Lord Elgin was quietly resting in Tangku, and refused to receive their surrender, or even to hold intercourse with Hangfuh, the governor-general of Chihlí, then in command, but turned him over to the commander of the forces. The path being now open for the troops to march upon Tientsin, the gunboats were sent forward to see that the river was clear. On the 25th the two plenipotentiaries were again housed at Tientsin, accompanied by naval and land forces amply strong to take them to Peking. No opposition was, however, experienced in reaching that city, while the pleasing contrast in the surface of this country with that of the dreary flats near Pehtang and Taku refreshed the men as much as the abundant supplies and peacefulness of the people aided them. Such remarkable contrasts in China illustrate the inert character of this extraordinary people; and further, also lead one to inquire what is the reason for their loyalty to a government which fails so completely in protecting them from their enemies. Mr. Swinhoe records[1] a conversation held with a well-to-do Chinese, in which this inquiry receives a partial answer in the peaceful education of a race which has no alternative.

His intrenchments at Sinho and Tangku being demolished, his vaunted defences upon the river razed, his enemies' ships in possession of Tientsin, nothing now remained for Săngkolinsin save to move his entire army nearer Peking, and there again meeting the invaders, endeavor to preserve the capital from capture. He would not there be able to shift the odium of defeat on the difficulties of the river defences, while the moral effect would be incomparably greater if he were vanquished near the palace.

The aged Kweiliang, the father-in-law of Prince Kung, was again directed to repair to Tientsin, where he arrived about August 28th. He and two others (all of them Manchus) endeavored to negotiate a peace so as to prevent the allies from advancing on Peking with their armies. Finding that they were trifling, Lord Elgin stopped the palaver, and started for Tungchau on September 8th, the British taking the left bank and

---

[1] *North China Campaign*, pp. 158–161.

the French keeping the southern. Near Yangtsun a new commission of higher rank reported itself, but it was rejected, and the army continued on its way. Further on, at Hosí-wu and Matau, signs of serious strife began to appear, but the commissioners assured their negotiators, Messrs. Wade and Parkes, that everything was or would be ready at Tungchau to conclude the convention. Affairs were becoming critical in the matter of supplies and transport, for Săngkolinsin's army prevented the people from safely bringing animals and making sales. The commissariat, therefore, was obliged to seize what could be found to feed the advancing force, and this involved ransacking most of the towns and hamlets lying near the river between Hosí-wu and Tungchau. The progress of the force was, therefore, much slower than below Tientsin, though the possession of sixty or eighty small boats helped to bring on the ammunition and other supplies.

On September 14th the interpreters, Messrs. Wade and Parkes, reached Tungchau, in order to meet Prince Í and his colleague to discuss the terms for stopping the army and exchanging the ratifications. This interview was marked with apparent sincerity, and resulted in an order for the army to move forward to a place designated near the town of Changkia-wan, about three leagues from Tungchau, where the troops were to encamp. The camp broke up from Hosí-wu early on the 17th to carry this arrangement into effect. Mr. Parkes was again sent forward to Tungchau (twenty-five miles), accompanied by an escort of twenty-six Sikh and other soldiers, to inform the imperial commissioners, and finally arrange terms. The ground pointed out was reached, and seemed to be well suited for the purpose. At Changkia-wan the party met an officer at the head of some cavalry, who challenged them, but allowed all to go on to Tungchau. Mr. Parkes soon met another high official in charge of a guard, who treated them with marked courtesy, informing them that he had been the general at Sinho, and let them proceed. They were received at Tungchau and conducted through the town to a temple by a messenger sent from the prince. At one o'clock the discussions began, but instead of entering into the details of carrying out the agreement, difficulties were made about Lord Elgin's delivering his letter of credence to the Emperor. The whole afternoon was consumed in this debate, which probably was grounded not a little on the recent decision of Hienfung to leave the capital for his summer palace at Jeh-ho while the way was yet clear. At eventide the commissioners waived the settlement of the audience, and soon agreed to all the other points relating to the encampment near Changkia-wan. In the morning Mr. Parkes, Colonel Walker, and eleven others, leaving the rest of their party in the temple to await the arrival of the plenipotentiaries the next day, departed to view the designated encampment. Their journey was somewhat eventful. As they reached Changkia-wan they met bodies of Chinese infantry going south, but no notice was taken of them, and the foreigners rode on to reach the appointed spot. In doing so they came across a body of a thousand dismounted horsemen concealed in a dry watercourse, or *nullah*, evidently placed there in ambush; while riding along in front no interruption was made to their progress. Further on, in a small village, they detected a large force hidden behind the houses and in gardens, but still no hindrance to their advance was interposed by these men. A short distance ahead they came upon a masked battery of twelve guns just placed in position, from which they were driven away. It was now plain that Săngkolinsin was preparing an ambushment for the allied forces to enter, feeling confident, no doubt, of his success.

Mr. Loch, who accompained Mr. Parkes thus far, was now designated to force his way through the Chinese troops, so as to meet the allied generals and tell them the state of things. Sir Hope Grant had already noticed some bodies of men on his flanks, and was preparing for them when he learned the truth; but in order to give Mr. Parkes and the others a chance to escape from Tungchau, he agreed to delay two hours before opening upon the enemy. Mr. Loch accordingly started, in company with Captain Brabazon and two horsemen, to return to Tungchau. They reached it in a few hours and found their friends, unconscious of the danger, wandering through the town. Mr. Parkes had learned something of it, and called on Prince Ĭ at his quarters to claim protection; this dignitary was in a state of much excitement, and said that "until the question of delivering the letter of credence was settled there could be no peace; there must be war." On returning to their temple the foreigners immediately started off in a body, but some of their horses were jaded, and the country was filled with moving bodies of troops.

When about five miles were gone over they came on a brigade of matchlock men, and ere long an officer of rank stopped them from going further, but offered to accompany two of them to obtain from the general a pass allowing the whole party to ride around the Chinese army on their way back. Mr. Parkes and Mr. Loch and a Sikh accordingly went with him, and he bravely looked after their safety. Meanwhile the battle had already begun, as the booming cannon intimated. They had advanced only a few rods when the trio found themselves in the midst of a large body of infantry, some of whom seized their bridles, but their guide rushed in, striking right and left, and thus cleared the way. Ten rods in the rear they met the Chinese general, to whom Mr. Parkes addressed himself, pointing to the flag of truce and asking for a pass for the whole party to return to the British army. Săngkolinsin "gave a derisive laugh, and broke out into a torrent of abuse. He accused Parkes of being the cause of all the troubles and difficulties that had arisen. Not content with attempting to impose conditions which would have been derogatory to the dignity of the Emperor to accept, he had now brought the allied armies down to attack the imperial forces." This is only a part of his excited conversation with Mr. Parkes, as reported by Mr. Loch. They were now imprisoned, and ordered to be taken in an open cart with two French prisoners to Tungchau, and delivered over to Prince Í. The others, twenty-three in all, had also been made prisoners where they were waiting, and ere long conducted to Tungchau in charge of a guard.

The five in the cart reached Tungchau after Prince Í had left his temple, and were therefore hurried on to Peking after him, but on the way were turned off near Pa-lí-kiau (*i.e.*, 'Eight *Lí* Bridge') and taken to the quarters of Jinlin, a general then in command of the Peking gendarmerie. He questioned Mr. Parkes upon the strength of the allied forces, until the latter ended this catechising under the torture of kneeling with the arms twisted behind him, by pretending to faint. In the afternoon, while again undergoing examination by some officials formerly with Prince I, they were suddenly interrupted by a commotion, and everybody ran off, leaving them alone. Soon a number of soldiers rushed in and bound their arms, while they were led away to be beheaded in an outer court. But just as they crossed the yard a mandarin hurried forward, and seizing hold of the soldier, then waving his sword over Mr. Loch, rescued them both and hurried them into a cart, where the other three prisoners lay, upon which they immediately started for Peking by the great stone road. The torture and jolting of this ride over the rough causeway were increased by their weariness, hunger, and cramped position, and when they got out of the cart at the *Hing Pu*, in Peking, they were utterly prostrated. Nevertheless, their misery during the ride of ten miles was transient and light compared with what awaited them inside of the Board of Punishments. They were there separated, heavily pinioned, and put with the native prisoners. Mr. Loch justly commends these wretched men for their sympathy, and mentions many little acts of kindness to him in dividing their cakes and giving him a special bench to sit on during the ten days he was quartered with them. He was then taken to the room with Mr. Parkes, and they were soon driven away to a temple in the northern part of the city, where rooms had been fitted up for them. As to the party of twenty-three English and thirteen Frenchmen left by Parkes at his capture, they had been taken to Yuen-ming Yuen under a strong guard.

Meanwhile the allied army had come up to the Chinese forces. These, about twenty thousand men in all, had been posted with considerable skill between Changkia-wan and the Pei ho, showing a front of nearly four miles, much of which was intrenched and presenting a succession of batteries. The battle on the 18th died away as the allies reached that town, having driven Săngkolinsin's troops toward Peking, captured eighty guns, and burned all his camps. The loss of life was much less among his men than at the Taku fort, for here none of them were chained to their guns, and were able to escape when their position was untenable. Changkia-wan was thoroughly pillaged that night by those who could get at it, especially the poor natives who followed the army.

On the 21st the Chinese forces made another stand near the Eight Lí Bridge over the Canal, from which the French dislodged them without much difficulty. The British came up on their flanks and drove them in upon their centre, which of course soon resulted in a general dispersion. The artillery opened up at long range; the cavalry riding in upon the Chinese horsemen, easily scattered them, often burning the separate camps before returning. The contest at the bridge was the most serious, and their loss here was estimated at three hundred; on the whole field it probably did not exceed five hundred, for neither their cavalry nor infantry often presented a solid front. The entire losses of the allies were less than fifty killed and wounded. Nothing interposed now between them and Peking, but they delayed to move until October 3d, when their entire force had come up, siege guns and commissary stores included. Full knowledge had been obtained of the environs of Peking, and negotiations had been going on respecting the return of the prisoners as a preliminary to the close of hostilities. These were now conducted with Prince Kung, the next younger brother of the Emperor, who was himself by this time safe at Jeh-ho.

On October 6th Lord Elgin and the generals were settled in the spacious quarters of the Hwang sz', a lamasary near the northwest gate of Peking, and their army occupied much of the open spaces between it and the city. On that day, the outposts of the French army and some of the British cavalry reached the great cantonment of Hai-tien (where the Manchu garrison of Peking was quartered) and the palace of Yuen-ming Yuen near by. This was soon pillaged under circumstances and in a barbarously wasteful manner which will reflect lasting obloquy upon General Montaubon, who, more than any other person, could have interposed to save the immense and precious collection of objects illustrating Chinese art, architecture, and literature. Lord Elgin's journal gives his view of this act in a few words:

October 7th, 5 o'clock P.M.—I have just returned from the Summer Palace. It is really a fine thing, like an English park—numberless buildings with handsome rooms, filled with Chinese *curios*, handsome clocks, bronzes, etc. But alas! such a scene of desolation. The French general came up, full of protestations. He had prevented looting in order that all the plunder might be divided between the armies, etc. There was not a room that I saw in which half the things had not been taken away or broken to pieces. I tried to get a regiment of ours sent to guard the place, and then sell the things by auction; but it is difficult to get things done by system in such a case, so some of the officers are left [there], who are to fill two or three carts with treasures, which are to be sold. Plundering and devastating a place like this is bad enough, but the waste and breakage are much worse. Out of a million pounds' worth of property, I daresay fifty thousand pounds will not be realized. French soldiers were destroying in every way the most beautiful silks, breaking the jade ornaments and porcelain, etc. War is a hateful business. The more one sees of it the more one detests it.[1]

Mr. Swinhoe's account of one room in this palace has now a historical interest—but his description must be condensed:

Facing the gate (he says) stood the grand reception hall, well adorned outside, and netted with copper wire under the fretted eaves to keep off the birds. Entering it we found ourselves on a marble floor in front of the Emperor's ebony throne; this was adorned with carved dragons in various attitudes; its floor was covered with light red cloth, and three low series of steps led up to it, on the central and widest of which his subjects made the kotow. The left side of the hall was adorned with a picture representing the grounds of the palace, and the side tables contained books in yellow binding and ornaments. There was somehow an air of reverence throughout this simple but neat hall. On an audience day the Emperor here seated himself attired in a yellow robe wrought with dragons in gold thread, his head surmounted with a spherical crown of gold and precious stones with pearl drops suspended around by light gold chains. Eunuchs and ministers in court costume kneel on each side in long lines, and the guard and musicians are arranged in the outer court. The name of the person to be introduced is called out, and as he approaches the band strikes up. He draws near the "Dragon's Seat" and kneels before the central step, removes his hat, placing it on the throne floor with the peacock's feather toward the imperial donor. His Majesty moves his hand and down goes the head, striking on the step three times three. The head is then raised, but with downcast eyes the man hears the behests of his great master. When

---

[1] *Elgin's Letters*, p. 361.

the voice ceases, again the head makes the nine knocks, thus acknowledging the sovereign right, and the man withdraws. How different the scene now, adds Mr. Swinhoe. The hall filled with crowds of a foreign soldiery, and the throne floor covered with the Celestial Emperor's choicest curios, destined as gifts for two far more worthy monarchs. "See here," said General Montaubon, pointing to them, "I have had a few of the most brilliant things selected to be divided between the Queen of Great Britain and the Emperor of the French." [1]

On the following day—October 8th—the commanders were greatly relieved by the return of Parkes, Loch, d'Escayrac de Lauture, and five soldiers; the first two of these gentlemen had been comparatively well treated after their terrible experiences within the Hing Pu. A few days later both armies were horrified by the appearance in camp of eleven wretched men—all who had survived from the party of French and English made prisoners near Tungchau; Anderson, Bowlby, de Norman, and others had succumbed to the dreadful tortures caused by the cords which bound them. The coffined bodies were all brought to camp within a few days, hardly recognizable from the effects of lime thrown upon them. On the 16th occurred the impressive ceremony of their interment in the Russian cemetery near Peking, Lord Elgin, Sir Hope Grant, Parkes, and Loch being chief mourners, while a deputation from every regiment in the allied armies followed in the train.

Two days after this Lord Elgin ordered the destruction of the palace of Yuen-ming Yuen; a sudden though deliberate act. Feeling probably that such a decision would be closely criticised by those who were far removed in time and place from the exciting scenes around him, he took occasion to review his position in a long despatch. It was impossible in his situation to learn whether the responsibility for the capture and savage treatment of these men rested with the same Chinese officials.[2] This

[1] Swinhoe, *North China Campaign*, pp. 294 ff.—the most detailed and interesting account of this palace and its destruction. Compare M. C. Lavallée in the *Revue des Deux Mondes* for August 1, 1865. Other French writers on this war are Lieutenant de vaisseau Pallu, *Relation de l'expédition de Chine*, Paris, 1863; le Comte d'Escayrac de Lauture, *Mémoires sur la Chine*, Paris, 1864; Sinnebaldo de Mas, *La Chine et les puissances chrétiennes*, 1861.

[2] Probably not. The prisoners were in the hands of lictors whose habit it was to torture in the hope of extorting money on their own account. The

much, nevertheless, was plain—that the Chinese were fully aware of the obligations of a flag of truce, inasmuch as they had already often availed themselves of its privileges. Lord Elgin makes the Emperor personally responsible for the crimes which had been committed, but specifies Săngkolinsin as the real culprit. He then says:

> I had reason to believe that it was an act which was calculated to produce a greater effect in China and on the Emperor than persons who look on from a distance may suppose. It was the Emperor's favorite residence, and its destruction could not fail to be a blow to his pride as well as to his feelings. To this place he brought our hapless countrymen, in order that they might undergo their severest tortures within its precincts. Here have been found the horses and accoutrements of the troopers seized, the decorations torn from the breast of a gallant French officer, and other effects belonging to the prisoners. As almost all the valuables had already been taken from the palace, the army would go there, not to pillage, but to mark, by a solemn act of retribution, the horror and indignation with which we were inspired by the perpetration of a great crime. The punishment was one which would fall, not on the people, who may be comparatively innocent, but exclusively on the Emperor, whose direct personal responsibility for the crime committed is established, not only by the treatment of the prisoners at Yuen-ming Yuen, but also by the edict in which he offered a pecuniary reward for the heads of the foreigners.[1]

The work of destruction left hardly a trace of the palace of the "Round-bright Garden;" indeed, the provocation for this act was great. The despatch refers only to the palace where Hienfung spent most of his time, and it is probable that Lord Elgin intended to burn that alone. He gave no orders for the destruction of the buildings on Wan-shao shan, Yuh-tsien shan, the Imperial Park near Pih-yun sz', and other places five to ten miles distant. All of these residences or villas had been erected or enlarged by former Emperors of the present dynasty; none have since been rebuilt. It is, nevertheless, easy to gather from Colonel Wolseley's record that his lordship's satisfaction in this

---

candid spirit of Loch's narrative is wanting in the more colored accounts of Wolseley and Swinhoe, written in the flush of victory. The charges they make against Prince Ĭ of treachery toward Mr. Parkes are not borne out; the deaths of Captain Brabazon and the Abbé de Luc seem to have been by order of Pao, and not from Săngkolinsin. Compare an article in the *Revue des Deux Mondes* (15 juillet, 1865) by C. Lavallée, *L'Expedition anglo-française en Chine.*

[1] *Elgin's Letters and Journals*, p. 366.

"retribution" was not greatly impaired by its over-zealous performance on the part of the troops. In addition to the loss of the palaces, the Chinese had to pay £100,000 as indemnity to be given to the prisoners and their families, before the victors would consent to sign the convocation.

On the 13th the ultimatum had been accepted by Prince Kung, who about two hours before noon opened the An-ting or northeast gate of Peking, which commanded the whole city. Arrangements were gradually completed for the grand entry of the plenipotentiaries into Peking. The *Lí Pu*, or Board of Rites, was selected as the place for exchanging the ratifications of the treaty of Tientsin and signing the convention, while the *fu*, or palace of Prince Í, had been chosen for Lord Elgin's residence in the city. On October 24th the latter was escorted to both these places by many officers, together with a body of four hundred infantry and one hundred cavalry, while in all the streets leading to them were guards placed. The whole city was out to witness the unusual parade. The procession passed slowly through the wide avenues, the music of the band heralding its approach to the dignitaries anxiously awaiting the arrival. The utmost care had been taken that no excuse should be ever after brought forward that the Emperor had not assented to the two documents signed that day; but much besides was done to show Prince Kung and his officers that they were in the presence of their conquerors.

The following day Baron Gros signed his convention and exchanged the ratifications of the French treaty under similar formalities. The principal points in the British convention of nine articles were—the payment of eight million taels; the permission given by imperial sanction for the emigration at will of Chinese subjects as contract laborers or otherwise; the cession of Kowlung to the crown as part of the colony of Hongkong.

Without delaying for additional comment, the insertion here of a portion of Lord John Russell's despatch to Lord Elgin will not be uninteresting in connection with these treaties. His lordship's document reads like the balance-sheet of a London merchant at the termination of some successful adventure: "The Convention is entirely satisfactory to Her Majesty's

Government. It records the reparation made by the Emperor of China for his disregard in the previous year of his treaty engagements; it sets Her Majesty's government free from an implied engagement not to insist in all particulars on the fulfilment of those engagements; it imposes upon China a fine in the shape of an augmented rate of indemnity; it affords an additional opening for British trade; it places on a recognized footing the emigration of Chinese coolies, whose services are so important to Her Majesty's colonial possessions; it relieves Her Majesty's colony of Hongkong from a source of previous annoyance."[1]

The French convention of ten articles contained like demands and rewards, but instead of a slice of territory, the sixth provided that Roman Catholic Christians should be indemnified for "all such churches, schools, cemeteries, lands, and buildings as were owned on former occasions by persecuted Christians, and the money handed to the French representative at Peking for transmission to the Christians in the localities concerned." The fulfilment of this article required over ten years; and as the injuries had been done in some cases as far back as the reign of Louis XIII., great irritation was aroused in the minds of the natives who had for generations been quietly in possession of lands which they had purchased.[2]

The great objects of the expedition were now attained, and foreign nations could congratulate themselves upon having settled their representatives in the Chinese capital on terms of equality. Two *fu*, or palaces, were immediately occupied by

---

[1] "The practical result was not very great," concludes Mr. McCarthy. "Perhaps the most important gain to Europe was the knowledge that Peking was by no means so large a city as we had all imagined it to be. . . . There is some comfort in knowing that so much blood was not spilt wholly in vain." —*A History of Our Own Times*, Chap. XLII., Vol. III.

[2] An instance is mentioned in No. IV. of the *Journal of the N. C. Br. R. A. Soc.*, 1867, pp. 21–33, where a Roman Catholic church at Hangchau, which had been confiscated by the Emperor Yungching (about 1730), was changed into a temple dedicated to *Tien Hao*, the Queen of Heaven, "to serve the double purpose of extirpating a religion of false gossip and obduracy, and of making an offering to a spirit who really has a beneficial influence over human destinies."

those from Great Britain and France. Subsequently, the ministers from other countries have grouped themselves around these, and a foreign quarter has gradually grown up in the south-eastern part of the city. The chief agents in this important opening, Lord Elgin and Baron Gros, were well fitted by their urbanity, philanthropy, and moderation for the delicate task assigned them. The terrified officials and citizens in Peking had expected the worst consequences on the capture of their city, but besides the destruction of Yuen-ming Yuen, their capital and national unity escaped uninjured.

It was probably a great aid to the policy adopted by Prince Kung and his colleagues that the Emperor and his court had fled to Jeh-ho, for their influence, as the sequel proved, would have opposed any pacification. It was still more important for all future co-operation that he never came back at all, and thus the real guidance of affairs fell into better hands.

The 24th day of October saw the ending of the seclusion of the Chinese from their fellow-men; the contest honestly enough begun in 1839 by Lin, to rescue his country from the curse of opium, was in a manner completed on that day by the admission of those regenerating influences which could alone effectually remove that evil. The intermediate twenty years had done much to prepare the Chinese for this concluding act; and the honorable manner in which they fulfilled their promises and payments will stand as a lasting monument to their national credit.

The retirement of the allies from Peking was accomplished without impediment from the Chinese army under Săngkolinsin; the money disbursed for boats, carts, supplies, fuel, etc., as the troops went down the river, compensating many natives for their losses. By the end of November all had embarked except the garrisons left at Tientsin and Taku, which latter were removed as soon as the portion of the indemnity involving their occupation was paid up. The effectual and salutary working of the treaty stipulations for the mutual welfare of all parties depended on the diplomatic and consular offices left in the capital and open ports. The British government alone was adequately supplied in this respect, and their consulates became the expositors to the local rulers of the manner in which the treaties were to be interpreted and enforced. The great mass of natives knew almost nothing of their provisions, and looked upon the struggle chiefly as one between their sovereign and the foreigners. The defeat of the latter was in remoter districts declared proven by their retirement from Peking; but along the coasts and up the Yangtsz' the actual sight of steamers and contact with foreigners who could talk with them and explain the new state of things, really did more than anything else to show them that these strangers were by no means overcome. What was thus achieved to enlighten the people near the trading marts only required time and contact to spread into distant regions of the interior. As for the citizens of Peking, they met only those foreigners who could talk with them, for that city was not open to trade; and thus one prolific source of misunderstanding was removed. The death of the Emperor Hienfung (August 17, 1861) relieved them, too, from any attempt he might have made, in his irritation on returning to the Forbidden City and seeing his ruined palaces, to vent his wrath on the few foreigners then living near him. Christian missionaries also began their work in 1861, and thus thousands, who had had only vague ideas about the "barbarians," could easily learn the truth concerning them. Most fortunately, then, circumstances were from the first favorable for forming an intelligent public opinion in the capital.

CHAPTER VII.

THE ADMINISTRATION OF THE EMPRESSES.

TWELVE months elapsed before the political atmosphere of China was disturbed by any break or change in its condition—a period of quiet which the government sorely needed for an appreciation of its relations with the foreigners who had forced their way into the capital. His Majesty Hienfung having ascended the Dragon Throne on high, left the Empire in the hands of his only son, a child six years old; whether through incapacity or disease, the debauched sovereign had long before his death allowed his courtiers to engross the reins of government, and these now formed a coterie which at Jeh-ho was all-powerful. At his death the administration rested in the hands of a council of eight, whose nominal head was Tsai-yuen, Prince Í, a member of the imperial family belonging to the same generation with the infant Emperor. The design of this cabal was to at once assume the absolute power of a regency, to retain possession of the young Emperor's person at Jeh-ho, to make way in secret with his mother and the Empress-dowager, and lastly to arrest and destroy his father's three brothers; these initiatory steps to sovereignty being accomplished, nothing would interrupt their complete mastery of the government.

But in Prince Kung,[1] the Emperor's oldest surviving brother,

---

[1] Kung Tsin-wang, 'Prince Respect'—called by the people Wu-ako, 'Fifth Elder Brother'—is the sixth son of Taukwang, and was born about 1831. Three older brothers died young; Hienfung, the fourth, succeeded his father, while the fifth, being adopted into a branch of the Emperor Kiaking's family, was dropped out of Taukwang's household, leaving Prince Kung in 1861 to be the first prince during the minority of Tungchí. His personal name, Yih-hü, is never employed by those outside his immediate family. He has a commendable record for an Asiatic statesman trained in habits of autocratic command. The background in the portrait on the opposite page is a bit of rock-work in the Foreign Office at Peking.

the conspirators found an opponent of no ordinary ability, to whose astuteness in outwitting their machinations (as may be safely affirmed in view of events which followed) is doubtless owing the continuance of the present reigning family. The prince was in concealment during the autumn of 1860, when his brother fled to Jeh-ho, but appearing when the capital was surrendered to the allies, he bore the brunt of that unpleasant task, signing the treaties, and undertook almost alone the management of affairs with foreigners while the government was recovering from its paralysis of defeat. It was a happy augury for the continuance of peace and friendly intercourse that to a man so well fitted by temperament for his difficult position should be joined the able and experienced statesman Kweiliang; though too old to take an active part in the settlement of the succession, this skilful diplomatist lent the greatest aid to his son-in-law by giving advice and a much needed support to the Empresses-dowager at this critical period.

Hastily quitting Jeh-ho with the boy—who had been proclaimed Emperor under the reign-name of Ki-tsiang, 'Lucky Omen'—the two Empresses availed themselves of their right to join the first prince, and repaired to Peking. Once settled in the Forbidden City they were able to impart to Prince Kung the magnitude of the plot against them, and concert measures with leading members of the imperial clan for the general safety. The arrest and trial of the traitors was promptly carried out; by a decree of December 2, 1861, Prince Ĭ and his principal coadjutor, Prince Chin, were allowed to commit suicide, while their powerful and clever colleague, Suhshun, was executed in the market-place, to the unfeigned delight of the populace. This conspirator in his machinations and gross assumptions had acted like a veritable Tigellinus, and earned for himself a hatred and contempt which even members of the war party could not conceal. Others of this unsuccessful clique were disgraced or banished, but the punishments were not numerous or barbarous. The reign-name was now changed from Ki-tsiang to *Tung-chi*, or 'Union Rule,' to mark the successful demolition of this conspiracy, while Prince Kung (now but thirty years old), the shrewd perpetrator of the *coup d'état*, was proclaimed *Í-ching-wang*, or 'Regent Prince,' and with the Empresses constituted the regency during the minority.[1]

Considering all the circumstances of this palace intrigue, the rank of its leading members, and its successful suppression by the operation of legal methods alone, it may well deserve the attention of those interested in the political and historical development of China as an admirable instance of both the strength and weakness of her paternal government. To the ordinary outlays of the Empire were superadded the immense burdens of a foreign invasion just concluded and a terrible struggle with domestic enemies; yet neither the Regent nor his colleagues appear during this period of stress to have lost a particle of their confidence in the loyalty of the people; through loss and gain, failure of material or resource, treachery in palace or camp, abuse or assistance from foreigners, this faith in one another failed not. The face of China in 1865 was perhaps as wretched as that of Central Europe after the peace of Westphalia; indeed a more general desolation could hardly be imagined. Nevertheless the rapidity with which its inhabitants not only resumed their occupations as best they could but rebuilt dwellings and reorganized trade, startled even their habitual disparagers into praise and testified to the marvellous recuperative powers of this much-despised civilization.

Pleased with the excellent results of the introduction of western drill and arms into their military service, as against the Tai-pings, certain of the mandarins at the south proposed utilizing foreign war-vessels to the same end. To this scheme as at first suggested there was not, perhaps, much to say either in its behalf or otherwise. Their purpose was to purchase three or four gun and despatch boats, man them with as many scores of native seamen, and impart to these the necessary instruction by placing them under foreign officers. Mr. Horatio N. Lay had in 1856 proposed the use of armed revenue vessels in the customs service, a very similar suggestion. But innocent as were these conceptions, they assumed the gravest proportions

[1] *Journal N. C. Br. R. A. S.*, December, 1864, pp. 110–114. Dr. Rennie, *Peking and the Pekingese*, Vol. II., passim—an interesting contemporary record of this event.

when in 1861 Mr. Lay was allowed to visit England and there contract for the construction of a steam fleet and secure a number of British naval officers for three years' service.[1] The Peking authorities were still laboring under the disadvantages of their ignorance, and nothing can illustrate better than this remarkable enterprise the good influence which Sir Frederick Bruce had acquired in their counsels, and their willingness to follow his suggestions. Their secluded life in Peking had prevented them from learning many things in respect to the conduct of affairs in their new relations, but they could hardly have had a better counsellor than he. The instructions from Prince Kung sent to Mr. Lay in England described the kind of officers and hands which the vessels were to carry; they were to be men able and willing to teach ignorant sailors the practice of navigation, the management of machinery, and the use of guns of every kind. Instead of these he contracted for eight gunboats of different sizes, one or two of them powerful vessels, able to carry two hundred and more men; they arrived in China early in 1863 under the command of Capt. Sherard Osborne, R. N. Mr. Lay's disappointment was great and undisguised when, on reaching Peking in June, he found that Prince Kung and his advisers were totally unprepared for such a fleet, and unwilling to endorse the engagements he had entered into with the Queen's officers; nor were the funds for their current expenses provided. His ideas of his own position were soon modified, for he found that the vessels must necessarily be placed under the direction of the provincial authorities in operations against the rebels. One of the articles in the agreement with Captain Osborne stipulated that he should receive all his orders on those matters from the Foreign Office through Mr. Lay, and would follow his own choice in obeying others. Mr. Lay says himself that he was "ambitious of obtaining the position of middle-man between China and the foreign powers, because I thought I saw a way of solving the problem of placing pacific relations with China upon a sure footing. . . . My position was that of a foreigner engaged by the Chinese government to perform certain work *for*

[1] *Blue Book*, China, No. 2 (1864), p. 7.

them, not *under* them. I need scarcely observe, in passing, that the notion of a gentleman acting *under* an Asiatic barbarian is preposterous."[1] Ideas like these quite unfitted him for working with the Chinese, either *under* or *for* them. He could not understand that the former days of coercion and bullying had passed away, and that time must be allowed for them to gradually learn in their own way how to rise in the scale of nations, and adopt such improvements as they pleased.

In his perplexity and chagrin, he began to blame the British minister for lukewarmness in supporting his schemes, and to weary the members of the Tsung-lí Yamun by his demands. The controversy continued to grow warmer after Captain Osborne's arrival at Peking in September, where he first learned its real nature. Finally, in October, Prince Kung refused to ratify Mr. Lay's agreement made in England, very properly remarking upon the obnoxious article which required the commander of the flotilla to act only under orders from Peking. Happily for China, the dissolution of the force was decided on. The ships were to be sent back, for it was impossible to prevent the native officials from selling them after they had full control, and persons were already looking at them for their own lawless designs. At this juncture Sir F. Bruce came to the relief of the Chinese, and took the ships off their hands on account of the British government, paying back from the indemnity fund due to England all claims for wages, salary, and other expenses to officers and men till their arrival in London. This settlement involved an outlay of about $525,000, but the total cost of the vessels, crews, and outfit from first to last was not much less than a million sterling. The Peking government had, therefore, by this arrangement escaped a serious imbroglio with the provincial governors and generals—one which would have soon neutralized all responsibility, and perchance, even at that late date, entailed the success of the Taï-pings.

Mr. Lay, blinded by his own egotism and ambition, ascribes his failure to the negligence, treachery, ignorance, and ill-will

[1] *Our Interests in China: A Letter to Earl Russell*, p. 19.

of Sir F. Bruce, whose performances in these lines are fully detailed in his *Letter to Earl Russell*[1] of November 26, 1864. This statement of what occurred in relation to the Lay-Osborne flotilla exhibits the difficulties in the progress of Asiatic nations in the path of what we call *civilization*, and the ideas which such men have as to the way in which they are to be forced into this desirable condition. This extraordinary paper is an instructive exhibition of British interference in the administration of Asiatic countries, and how totally alien "the spirit of trade and progress" is to the independence and elevation of a pagan people when it alone is the chief agency depended on. In no case, nor under the best control, could Mr. Lay's plan have worked real benefit to China; but carried out under the domineering leadership of such a man, the scheme would have not only been humiliating in the last degree to those whom it was designed to assist, but would have inevitably resulted in the restoration of the conservative party to power and another profitless struggle with the foreigners.

Upon the dismissal of Mr. Lay the management of the Imperial Maritime Customs was placed in the hands of Robert Hart, Esq., who for a period of two years had given proof of his discretion in this position, and (in the words of Mr. Burlingame) had "by his tact and ability won the regard of every one." Already the imperial officers began to appreciate the immense material advantages of a regular income from the open ports, especially in the practical help it furnished toward the expenses of the dying rebellion. The contact of native and foreign rule in the same territory necessarily involved much assumption of power and friction of authority growing out of the undefined limits of the laws of ex-territoriality; but the legitimate working of treaty provisions—the prompt reference of grievances from complainant to consul, from the consul to his minister at Peking—served to enlighten court and country as to the gen-

[1] *Our Interests in China*, by H. N. Lay, C.B., London, 1864, pp. 66. See also correspondence in *Blue Book*, and letter of Sir F. Bruce, of November 19, 1863. *U. S. Diplomatic Correspondence* for 1864, Part III., pp. 348–378; and for 1865, Part I., p. 670. A. Wilson, *The "Ever-Victorious Army,"* pp. 260–266. *Fraser's Magazine*, February, 1865, p. 147.

eral honesty of their quondam enemies, in a fashion which neither preaching nor fighting could ever have accomplished.[1] In the year 1866 the arsenals at Fuhchau, Nanking, and Shanghai were reorganized and made to include schools for naval and military instruction as well as engine and gun works; the value of such works was promptly understood by the Chinese, and has been already the source of a creditable navy.[2]

The retirement of the Hon. Anson Burlingame from the position of United States minister in November, 1867, furnished to the Chinese government both an admirable agent and opportunity for an initial step in establishing diplomatic intercourse with the treaty powers. Into the hands of this gentleman was placed the charge of a general mission to those governments, there being added two co-ordinate Chinese ministers, an English and French secretary, and six students from the Tung-wăn Kwan at Peking. The three ministers were appointed Imperial Envoys and furnished with a letter of credence to eleven governments. The party left Shanghai February 25, 1868, for San Francisco, which port they reached about a month later. Few persons can now appreciate the excitement and discussion in China and elsewhere caused by this first diplomatic effort of the imperial government to take its place among the family of nations. Mr. Burlingame, naturally hopeful and enthusiastic, described his mission as an earnest of future peaceful relations with the Middle Kingdom. Wherever he went he elevated the estimate held of that ancient land by his hearers, and urged the European courts to but wait in patience until its backward people might be prepared for the changes it wished to adopt. Those changes and improvements were only to be

---

[1] The trial and condemnation of an American, who was hung at Shanghai in 1864 for the murder of two Chinese, tended to repress lawlessness on the part of foreigners and assure the native rulers of their earnest co-operation in bringing the guilty to punishment. The enlightened and friendly action of Prince Kung in issuing a proclamation, at request of Mr. Burlingame, against allowing any American Confederate cruisers to enter Chinese waters, was warmly appreciated by this and the other treaty powers as an interesting testimonial of the genuine friendship which was already disarming fear.

[2] Compare Captain Bridge, *The Warlike Power of China*, in *Fraser's Magazine*, Vol. 99, pp. 778 ff.

adopted when China had become convinced of their need and practicability; but many of Mr. Burlingame's hearers were both more eager and more ambitious than he, regarding the introduction of railroads, telegraphs, and steamers as opening an enormous field for their own immediate activity and gain. The consequent indignation among foreign merchants in China and at home upon learning the extent of his exaggeration was universal; the British merchants especially representing in strong terms the evil consequences of such "baseless expectations." The different points of view of the two parties will account for their opposite opinions. On the one side, the merchants were vexed that their hopes of a general trade arising all over China, as a result of the treaties of Tientsin, were likely to be disappointed, owing to the increasing attention of native traders in their own internal and external commerce to the exclusion of foreigners; while on the other, Mr. Burlingame laid great stress on those things which the Chinese government desired and intended to do as they became more and more qualified to act for themselves, through the agencies and institutions which they were inaugurating. The merchants seemed to think that nothing had as yet been accomplished in the direction of "progress," inasmuch as their personal expectations of an instant and lucrative trade were not realized; in reply to Mr. Burlingame's "enthusiastic fictions," they called for "tangible evidence of the existence of this spirit which he celebrates so loudly—some tittle of proof to support his sweeping theory."[1]

Without dwelling further upon these discussions, it pertains to the present narrative to briefly point out the two salient features of China's initial attempt to knock at the doors of

---

[1] See the letters to the *Daily News* of J. Barr Robertson, of Shanghai, which have been taken as a fairly characteristic specimen of the mercantile and political view. An article by the same gentleman in the *Westminster Review* for January, 1870, is rather calmer in language. Other data and opinions may be gathered from a work filling 890 pages, by the late J. von Gumpach, entitled *The Burlingame Mission: A Political Disclosure*, etc., 1872. Compare also the English newspapers issued in Shanghai and Hongkong in 1867–70; *British Parliamentay Papers; U. S. Ex. Doc.*, *Foreign Relations*, 1868–71; *Harper's Monthly Magazine*, Vol. XXXVII., p. 592; *The Galaxy*, Vol. VI., p. 613.

other nations. Of these the first may be described as wholly sentimental; but it was the healthy sentiment of justice and good feeling toward a distant and unknown community, which Mr. Burlingame's tact and ability called forth in behalf of his clients' cause from their recent conquerors. During the years 1868 and 1869 he spoke for the right and privilege of the Chinese to manage their own affairs, and in America, England, France, Prussia, and other countries had already created a more healthy feeling of forbearance toward them, when his sudden death at St. Petersburg (February, 1870) cut short the complete achievement of his mission.[1]

In the United States the passage of this embassy might have made but a transient impression had it not negotiated a treaty of eight articles (July 28, 1868), regarded as an integral part of the Reed treaty of ten years previous. This, the second feature of the mission, has been attended with consequences whose influence does not yet appear to have ceased. Owing to the surprise of the Chinese government, which had given no express instructions as to treaty-making, the Foreign Office was somewhat tardy in ratifying this compact. This was, however, done in the following year. Its fifth article provides that the contracting powers "cordially recognize the inherent and inalienable right of man to change his home and allegiance, and also the mutual advantage of the free migration and emigration of their citizens and subjects respectively from the one country to the other for the purposes of curiosity, or trade, or as permanent residents. The high contracting parties therefore join in reprobating any other than an entirely voluntary emigration for these purposes." At this time the British and French ministers had recently agreed to a convention with Prince Kung respecting the conduct of the coolie trade in accordance with the stipulations made at Peking in October, 1860. The draft of those regulations had been submitted to the American as well as all other foreign legations, but only the Spanish treaty contained

[1] His colleagues, Chí-kang and Sun Kia-kü, afterward visited Italy, Spain, and other countries, returning to China within the same year. Neither of them was, however, brought forward at the capital as an adviser in relation to foreign affairs.

an article allowing the engagement of Chinese laborers in their own country for service abroad. This traffic had become so infamous from the cruelties and wrongs perpetrated on the coolies, both in China before they embarked and in Cuba and Peru after they had landed, that the American Congress had already passed laws against it; and this article was drawn up almost wholly with reference to that trade, and to show the abhorrence with which it was regarded. Chinese immigrants had come to San Francisco to the number of fifty-three thousand since 1855, and had been harshly treated by the miners and others in their common struggle for gold; the Burlingame treaty simply acknowledged their right to immigrate like other foreigners.[1]

Meantime at Peking the foreign ambassadors were in the way of learning that in their relations with the government to which they were accredited they had to deal with men of acute minds, whose prejudices and conservatism only needed enlightening to bring them quite upon a level with any other body of intelligent diplomatists. It was indeed a crucial period with Prince Kung and his coadjutors of the Tsung-lí Yamun—Wănsiang, Tung Siun, Tan Ting-siang, Hăng-kí—who were placed between the two great pressures of a warped and bigoted multitude of literati wedded to the old régime and the ministers of the outside powers, themselves dwelling complacently in the imperial city and representing armies and navies which had been found invincible. The pride of the "Celestial" was necessarily brought low, but the situation was accepted, on the whole, both wisely and cautiously; the good fortune of having men of the kindness and honor of Bruce, Vlangali, Berthémy, and Burlingame as heads of the four chief legations, can hardly be exaggerated in its encouraging and healthful effects upon the impression taking root in the minds of Chinese officers.

At this juncture occurred the massacre at Tientsin of twenty

---

[1] But notwithstanding its acceptance of their "inalienable right" to freely change their residence, the clamor against this admission was afterward so great among the people on the Pacific coast that a special embassy of three commissioners was sent to Peking in 1880, which relegated the right of admitting Chinese as immigrants into American territory entirely to Congress.

French and Russians and destruction of the French consulate, cathedral, and orphanage, by a mob on June 21, 1870, attended by circumstances of great atrocity. The event was a severe blow as well to the anxious mandarins at the capital as to every honest friend of the new order of things throughout the Empire. The Peking authorities were slow at first in opening an investigation, but testified to their earnestness and righteous indignation at the enormity in disposing troops about the capital and summarily examining the criminals, so that by the end of a month every fear of a general *émeute* had vanished.

The causes which led to this outbreak appear to have been almost wholly local, taking their rise in the year 1861, when the French occupied as their consulate a temple in Tientsin, where in former times the citizens used to promenade; this and other unpopular acts kept the natives at enmity with them. A more especial account of the most important of these is contained in Mr. Low's despatch of June 27th: "At many of the principal places in China open to foreign residence, the Sisters of Charity have established institutions, each of which appears to combine in itself a foundling hospital and orphan asylum. Finding that the Chinese were averse to placing children in their charge, the managers of these institutions offered a certain sum per head for all the children placed under their control given to them, it being understood that a child once in their asylum no parent, relative, or guardian could claim or exercise any control over it. It has been for some time asserted by the Chinese, and believed by most of the non-Catholic foreigners residing here, that the system of paying bounties induced the kidnapping of children for these institutions for the sake of the reward. It is also asserted that the priests or Sisters, or both, have been in the habit of holding out inducements to have children brought to them in the last stages of illness, for the purpose of being baptized *in articulo mortis*. In this way many children have been taken to these establishments in the last stages of disease, baptized there, and soon after taken away dead. All these acts, together with the secrecy and seclusion which appear to be a part and parcel of the regulations which govern institutions of this character everywhere, have created suspicions in the minds of the Chinese, and these suspicions have engendered an intense hatred against the Sisters on the part of all the common people who live anywhere near a mission; and any rumor concerning the Sisters or their acts, however improbable or absurd, found thousands of willing and honest believers among the ignorant and superstitious people. Some time about the end of May or beginning of June an epidemic prevailed at the Sisters' institution at Tientsin, and a considerable number of the children died. In some way the report got abroad that the Sisters were killing the children to get their eyes and hearts for the purpose of manufacturing some sort of a medical specific much sought after in Europe and commanding a fabulous price. This report spread from one to another, and soon the belief became general. Crowds of people assembled from time to time near the mission buildings, demanding the liberation of the children, and on one occasion they became so noisy that the Sisters, fearing violence from the mob, consented that an examination should be made by a committee of five. The consul, hearing of the disturbance, made his appearance about this time, and although the committee had been selected and were then in the building, he stopped the whole proceeding and drove away the committee with angry words. Subsequently the district magistrate took a man who had been industriously spreading the reports, who said he could point out the persons who were guilty of acts of sorcery and other crimes, to question him in the presence of the Sisters, and when confronted by them admitted that all his stories were without foundation and false. The day prior to the outbreak the district magistrate (*chihien*) called upon the French consul, and stated that unless permission be given for a thorough examination of the Sisters' establishment, it was difficult to foretell the result. The consul, construing the language into a threat, replied that the magistrate being inferior in rank to the consul, no negotiation could take place between them for the purpose indicated or any other."[1]

---

[1] *Foreign Relations of the United States*, 1870, p. 355. A private letter quoted in the *Westminster Review* for April, 1871, says: "Even then (on the 19th) I think the riot could have been prevented if the consul had earnestly joined

This very unwise answer turned the popular rage against the French consulate as well as the cathedral and orphanage, and the 21st saw a surging multitude assembled in their vicinity ready for any violence. M. Fontanier, the French consul, now thoroughly alarmed, hurried off to the yamun of Chunghow (the superintendent of customs), while stones flew about the building he was quitting. For the rest, this poor man's fate is involved in uncertainty. Reaching Chunghow's office in a "state of excitement bordering upon insanity," he failed, either by persuasion or menace, in getting that dignitary to promise the impossible—to quell at once the angry mob. The officials, indeed, by this time were as helpless as he, and could only urge his remaining in the compound until the streets were clear. But the Frenchman and his clerk heeded nothing; how they were cut down in the way, after firing into the angry mob, how the rampant populace now attacked and pillaged the three or four French buildings, how the defenceless Sisters were butchered in their orphanage after suffering nameless barbarities, and how the frenzied host left the burning ruins to glut their passions upon the neighboring houses, has come to the world solely on Chinese authority, and must remain always in the obscurity resulting from greatly conflicting testimony. The children of the orphanage, however, were taken off, and though attempts upon some of the Protestant buildings were made, nothing serious resulted. Among the saddest casualties of this bloody day was the death of a Russian, his young bride, and a friend, who in escaping toward the foreign settlement of Tsz'-chuh-lin, two miles away, were mistaken for Frenchmen and promptly hacked to pieces on the road. The total number of victims in the massacre amounted to twenty foreigners and as many more Chinese servants, acolytes, and others.

To the joint note of the seven foreign ministers in Peking, calling for immediate and vigorous measures in the face of this terrible news, Prince Kung replied (on the 25th) that in vindication of the honor and justice of the imperial government toward

---

with the local authorities in making a full inquiry, with a number of the gentry, inside of the infirmary and church, to show them again that the rumors of foul deeds therein were groundless."

foreigners, Tsăng Kwoh-fan (governor-general of the province) and Chunghow had already been directed to do everything in their power to suppress the spirit of riot and arrest lawless men. An imperial edict was issued for the apprehension of Chau, Chang, and Lin, the intendant, prefect, and magistrate of Tientsin, for their remissness and complicity in the riot. The fact that no foreign armed vessel was there on the 21st doubtless had its weight with these officials in carrying out their plans at the moment. They now saw that they had pursued their ill-will too far, and that retribution was sure to follow for their atrocities. Exaggerated reports of their doings had rapidly gone over the world, and as the extent and strength of the disaffection in other provinces could not be ascertained, the inference was made that all foreigners in China were in imminent jeopardy, and that the people had at last risen in their strength to aid their sovereign to drive them out of the land. When the storm had passed over, and those in authority had examined the criminals and given such justice as they could, the opinions of the best informed observers as to the immediate causes were found to be sustained.

In a few weeks the naval forces of the leading powers had assembled at Tientsin. The French chargé d'affairs, Count Rochechouart, took the lead and demanded the execution of the prefect and magistrate for having instigated the riot. The Chinese refused to do this until a trial had proved their guilt—having, perhaps, in some measure recovered their composure upon learning of the commencement of hostilities between France and Germany. The imperial government was unable itself to coerce the turbulent populace of Tientsin, for it had no troops who could be depended on to punish the rioters, with whom the soldiers sympathized. The extravagant statements and demands continually put forth in the Shanghai and Hongkong newspapers tended to irritate and disconcert those high officials, who were already at their wits' end and were anxious to prevent a worse disaster. The foreigners seemed to think that they could utter hard charges indiscriminately against the Chinese rulers and people, who on their part were not to say a word. Minister Low, in his despatch of August 24th, when speaking of the thousands of fans sold at Tientsin containing pictures of the riot and murdering of foreigners, says: "These fans are made to suit the taste of the people, and the fact that such engravings will cause a better sale for the fans is a conclusive argument that there is no sentiment of regret or sorrow among the people over the result of the riot. There is, undoubtedly, greater unanimity of opinion in Tientsin in favor of the rioters than in Ireland among the peasantry in favor of one of their number who shoots his landlord. If this feeling in Ireland is strong enough to baffle all attempts of the English government to bring to justice by the ordinary forms of law a peasant accused of injuring the person or property of his landlord, is it surprising that this feeble central government should find it difficult to ascertain and punish the rioters in a city of four hundred thousand inhabitants, all of whom either aided in the massacre or sympathized with the rioters?"[1]

The judicial investigations in Tientsin were conducted in a dilatory manner, but the above indicates some of the difficulties in the way of the presiding judges. However, on October 5th and 10th H. I. Majesty's decrees were made known to the foreign ministers, stating that the prefect and magistrate had been banished to Manchuria, twenty criminals who had killed the foreigners sentenced to death, and twenty-one others actively aiding in the riot banished. On the morning of October 18th sixteen were decapitated in the presence of the foreign consuls and others assembled as witnesses. This closing act of the tragedy, as a condign punishment of guilt, was, however, unfortunate; it was made rather an occasion of showing to the people that the sufferers had the sympathy of their rulers, while many foreigners looked upon the execution as a ghastly farce—"a cold-blooded murder." Many believed that the sixteen men were purchased victims; the proofs were ample, however, of the complicity of all; indeed, some of them gloried in what they had done, and were escorted by admiring friends to the block.[2]

---

[1] *Foreign Relations of the United States—China*, 1871, p. 380.

[2] As an instance of some of the bitter sentiment rampant upon this occasion, may be quoted the open proposition of a British missionary, who insisted that one-half of the city of Tientsin be razed by a detachment of foreign troops of

It is a palpable exaggeration of the power or desires of a Chinese official to affirm that he is capable of buying up candidates for immediate execution.

As to the remaining four condemned culprits, M. Vlangali, the Russian minister, judiciously refused to accept their deaths as a proper satisfaction for the murder of the three Russians until satisfied personally of their direct complicity in the deed. A careful examination of their case having been made before the consul-general of the Czar at Tientsin, revealed the fact that only two were guilty of the actual crime; the minister consented then that the punishment of the other two should be commuted to banishment. The sum of Tls. 400,000 was paid to the French for loss of life and property; in addition to this the loss done to Protestant mission premises was also made good. Chunghow was appointed imperial commissioner to proceed to France and present to that government a formal apology for the affair. This mission left Peking early in 1871 and returned the following year. The American missionaries who had in August been frightened away from their post in Tăngchau[1] by the warnings and threats of certain evil disposed persons, were taken back from their asylum in Chifu two months later in the U. S. S. Benicia, and publicly received by the prefect. This was the only instance throughout the Empire, connected with the riot of June, in which foreigners were interfered with, and here grave doubts exist as to the reality of danger and need of flight from Tăngchau.

In estimating the conduct of the Chinese in dealing with this eruption, the foreign press habitually spoke of them as if they were unwilling to grant any redress or take any measures for the future safety of those living among their subjects. Little consideration was made for the enormous difficulties of their position. They had been reared in ignorance of the multiplied questions and responsibilities involved in the recent treaties with other nations; and though the foreign ministers were

various nationalities, and that a pillar be erected upon the open space thus made, with a suitable inscription as to the occasion and authors of the monument.

[1] On the promontory of Shantung.

really acting most kindly toward them in forcing them to carry out every plain treaty obligation, the fair-minded observer can find small excuse for the harsh criticism, not to add abuse, which was hurled at everything said or done by Prince Kung and his colleagues in their peril and perplexity. The writers in newspapers seemed to look upon China as an appanage of Europe—one Englishman even going so far as to urge the most reckless employment of force to compel her rulers to give up the three odious officials to be dealt with and publicly executed. Another says that the execution of the sixteen criminals could "hardly be viewed as other than cold-blooded murder while those men are shielded from the demands of justice." Yet these writers forgot that all the treaties required that "Chinese subjects guilty of criminal acts toward foreigners shall be arrested and punished by the Chinese authorities according to the laws of China;" and each nation obliged itself to try and punish its own criminals. Chunghow was the object of much abuse because he had not prevented or put down the mob, though he was merely a revenue officer and had neither territorial nor military jurisdiction at Tientsin. Even the members of the Tsung-lí Yamun were freely charged with complicity in the tragedy, if not knowledge or approval. In short, the whole history of the riot—its causes, growth, culmination, results, and repression—combine as many of the serious obstacles in the way of harmonizing Chinese and European civilizations as anything which ever occurred.[1]

As a natural sequence to the judicial proceedings which ter-

[1] The records of this event are widely scattered in the local papers published in China and in diplomatic correspondence. See the *Missionary Recorder*, November, 1870, and January, 1871; *Journal of N. C. Branch of R. A. Soc.*, No. VI., pp. 186–196; *Edinburgh Review*, January, 1871; *Westminster Review*, April, 1871, Art. VI.; *The Tientsin Massacre*, &c., by Geo. Thin, M.D., Edinburgh, 1870; *Foreign Relations of the United States* for 1870 and 1871; *Legation to China; Parliamentary Blue Book*, 1871; H. Blerzy, *Les affaires de Chine en* 1871, *Revue des Deux Mondes*, 1 juillet, 1871; *North China Daily News* and *North China Herald* for 1870. One of the most carefully prepared and interesting accounts of the massacre is contained in Baron Hübner's *Ramble Round the World*, translated by Lady Herbert, New York, 1875, pp. 526–573.

minated the Tientsin tragedy, came the inquiry of the imperial counsel into what was briefly summed up as the "missionary question." More than ten years had now elapsed since the general repeal of all pre-existing edicts against Christianity in the Empire, and the officials were already concerned as to the movements and rumors respecting the new sect which had come to their ears since that time. Accordingly in February, 1871, after an earnest study of the matter from their stand-point, the Foreign Office sent to the various legations the following note and memorandum:

TUNGCHÍ, 9th year, 12th moon, 24th day.

SIR: In relation to the missionary question, the members of the Foreign Office are apprehensive lest in their efforts to manage the various points connected with it they shall interrupt the good relations existing between this and other governments, and have therefore drawn up several rules upon the subject. These are now enclosed, with an explanatory minute, for your examination, and we hope that you will take them into careful consideration.

With compliments, cards of WÄNSIANG.
SHÄN KWEI-FÄN.

The rules proposed (1) that only the children of native Christians be received into Romish asylums; (2) that "in order to exhibit the reserve and strict propriety of Christianity," no Chinese females should enter the chapels nor foreign women propagate the doctrines; (3) that missionaries should confine themselves to their proper calling, and that they "ought not to be permitted to set up an independent style and authority;" (4) that they should not interfere in trials of their native converts when brought into criminal courts; (5) that passports given to missionaries should not be transferred, but returned to the Chinese authorities when no longer required, "nor should they avail themselves of the passport to secretly go elsewhere," as the French ofttimes did; (6) that the missionaries should never receive men of bad character into the church, nor retain those of notoriously evil characters; moreover that quarterly reports of the converts be handed in to the provincial officers, as did the Buddhist and Taoist houses; (7) that missionaries should not use official seals, nor write official despatches to the local authorities, nor otherwise act as if they were officials instead of commoners. The last rule complained of the unreasonable demands of the Romish missionaries for lands and houses to be restored to them in accordance with the Peking convention; it proposed that no more be restored, and that lands bought for erecting churches be held in the name of the native church members.

This state paper was remarkable as being the first in which the Chinese government had expressed its desire for a satisfactory discussion and decision of the difficult questions involved in Christian missions, and the quasi independence allowed their foreign agents by the treaties. The public sentiment among foreigners in China was that these good people had a right to do everything not expressly prohibited by treaty until their own consular officers notified them to the contrary. The unauthorized conduct of Romish missionaries in two western provinces had already given rise to riots, in which Frenchmen had been killed. In such judicial proceedings as that described by Abbé Huc in his interesting travels are seen the high-handed perversion of justice denounced in the seventh section of this paper.[1] The writers of these rules were hardly aware of the serious import of the questions they had grappled, still less of the ignorance they exhibited in their handling of them. All the strictures referred exclusively to the Roman Catholics, for Protestant missionaries were hardly known to the Chinese magistrates, no complaints having been entered against them.

Most of the foreign ministers long delayed their answers to this minute, so that no personal discussion ever took place between the parties most interested. The straightforward and earnest reply of Mr. Low, the United States envoy (dated March 20th), carefully went over all the main points, and gave Wănsiang and Shăn Kwei-făn a clear idea of what they might expect from other ministers, together with many good suggestions as to their own duties. Nothing practical ever came of the paper, but the discussions it caused throughout the country showed the interest felt in the whole matter.[2] A few Protestant missionaries themselves indulged in harsh strictures on the native officials,

[1] *Travels in the Chinese Empire*, Vol. I., Chap. VI.

[2] *Foreign Relations of the United States*, 1871, pp. 99–111; also for 1872, pp. 118–130 and 137–138. *Missionary Recorder*, Vols. III. and IV. passim.

one going the length of saying that he "looked upon the document rather as an excuse offered beforehand for premeditated outrages than as an indication of measures being taken to prevent them." However, no evil results ever came to the converts or their teachers from the discussion of the minute, and its diffusion gave many readers their first information on the whole subject. Differences of opinion led to a comparison of facts, and the small number of grievances reported upheld the conclusion that the Chinese officials and literati had been, on the whole, extremely moderate, considering their limited opportunities to examine the question and the irritation aroused by the demands and hauteur of the Romish missionaries. The unjust manner in which they possessed themselves of the ground within the city of Canton on which the governor-general's yamun once stood had made a deep impression on the citizens; and when their cathedral, towering above all the temples and offices of the metropolis, was located upon this site, their indignation knew no bounds.

The year 1873 saw the conclusion of the Mohammedan insurrection in the north-western provinces, the exact extent of which has never been perfectly made known. The capture of Suhchau (near the Kiayü Pass in Kansuh) by the imperial troops under General Tso Tsung-tang brought to an end all organized rebellion in China Proper.[1] As is customary, the central government threw the responsibility of promoting the peace of the provinces upon their governors, and the well-disposed among the people were usually sure of protection. The foreign administration of the import customs turned a large and certain revenue into the hands of the Peking officials, and their development of the defences of the coast in building forts, launching war steamers, and making war material at the new arsenals, indicated their fears of foreign reprisals and their unwisdom in deeming such outlays effectual. The same money spent in making good wagon roads, working iron, coal, and other mines, deepening navigable watercourses, and intro-

---

[1] *Foreign Relations of the United States*, 1874, p. 250. *Peking Gazette*, December 28, 1873.

ducing small steamers on them, would have brought more substantial returns. But these were achievements which the future alone could accomplish, and the people must be somewhat taught and prepared for them before any permanent advances would ensue.[1]

On October 16, 1872, occurred the marriage of the Emperor Tungchí to Aluteh, a Manchu lady. The ceremonies attending her selection, betrothal, and espousal were elaborate and complete in every particular. Such an event had only once before taken place during the Manchu dynasty—when Kanghí was a minor, in 1674—all the other emperors having been married during their fathers' reigns. The occasion, therefore, excited great attention, while the attendant expenses were enormous; but all passed off without the least disturbance and apparently to general satisfaction. The two Empresses-dowager controlled the details, the most important of which were announced to the Empire in a series of edicts prepared by members of the *Lí Pu*, or Board of Rites, containing directions for every motion of the two principal actors, as well as for those who joined the ceremonies during the occasion till the 21st of the month.[2]

The young Emperor entered into the spirit of the preparations with great interest, and on the day before sending the bride her phœnix robes and diadem he ordered three princes to offer sacrifice and burn incense on the altar to heaven, "these informing heaven that he was about to marry Aluteh, the wise, virtuous, and accomplished daughter of Chung, duke and member of the Hanlin." Another prince informed mother earth, and a third announced it to the imperial ancestors, in their special temple. During the weeks preceding and following the happy day, all courts throughout the land were closed and a general jail delivery promulgated.

Many of the ceremonies and processions in Peking were not

---

[1] Compare a rather enthusiastic article by Captain A. G. Bridge, *The Revival of the Warlike Power of China*, *Fraser's Magazine* for June, 1879, p. 778.

[2] A translation of these papers was made at Shanghai, not long after, by Miss L. M. Fay, an American lady, and furnishes an interesting and authentic account of the whole wedding.

public, for considerations of state and security demanded great care.[1] On the 19th the wedding was thus announced to the foreign ministers by H. I. Majesty, through Prince Kung: "We having with pious veneration succeeded to the vast dominion founded by Our ancestors, and enjoying in its fulness the glorious lot to which We have been destined, have chosen one virtuous and modest to be the mistress of Our imperial home. Upon October 15th, We, by patent, installed Aluteh, daughter of Chung Chí, a *shí-tsiang* in the Hanlin College, as Empress. This from the Emperor." The court had not as yet outgrown its exclusiveness further than this step of announcing the marriage and its completion; and to those best acquainted with the etiquette observed for centuries, even this seemed to be a good deal in advance of former times. The great counsellors of state soon arranged for closing the regency which had existed since 1861. The Emperor Tungchí, though born on April 27, 1856, was called seventeen at his marriage. The Empresses-dowager accordingly announced on October 22d that he would attain his majority at the next Chinese new year, and be inaugurated with all the usual ceremonies. One of his special imperial functions, that of offering sacrifices to heaven at the winter solstice, would be performed by him in person—a ceremony which had been intermitted since December, 1859. Accordingly, on February 23, 1873, he issued a decree through the Board of Rites, as follows: "We are the humble recipient of a decree from their Majesties the two Empresses, declaring it to be their pleasure that We, being now of full age, should in person assume the superintendence of business, and in concert with Our officers in the capital and in the provinces, attend to the work of good government. In respectful obedience to the commands of their Majesties, We do in person enter upon the

---

[1] For a report of what could be watched of this ceremony, see William Simpson, *Meeting the Sun*, Chap. XV. The bridal procession came off during the night, when a bright moonlight enabled him to see it pass, without molestation, from the shop where he was hidden. This chiaroscuro sort of panorama rather suited the ideas of the people, and was submitted to by the Pekingese crowd without a murmur. Compare K. Bismark in the *Galaxy*, Vol. XIX., p. 182; *Cornhill Magazine*, Vol. XXVII., p. 82.

important duty assigned to Us on the 26th day of the 1st moon of the 12th year of the reign Tungchí."

This announcement was on the same day communicated to the ministers of Russia, Germany, the United States, Great Britain, and France. They returned a collective note the following morning, and asked Prince Kung to "take his Imperial Majesty's orders with reference to their reception." This intimation could not have been unexpected to him and his colleagues, but with their usual habit of putting off the inevitable, they began to make excuses. After deferring the consultation with the envoys a fortnight on the plea of Wănsiang's illness, they met at the Russian legation on March 11th. The question of the *kotow* was the crucial point, as it had been in 1859 between Kweiliang and Mr. Ward. Then the court was willing to accept a sort of curtsey instead of a prostration when the American minister approached the throne. Now the court had put the strongest argument into the hands of foreign ministers by sending the Burlingame mission to their courts, and the rights of independent nations could not be waived or implicated by the least sign of inferiority. The conference was amicable and the matter fully ventilated. The demands upon the Chinese were summarized by the ministers: That a personal audience with the Emperor was proper and needful; that it should not be unnecessarily delayed; and that they would not kneel before him, nor perform any other ceremony derogatory to their own dignity or that of their nationalities. These points were maintained as their united decision in the weary series of conferences, correspondence, and delays which ensued during the next four months in Peking. The prince and his colleagues, by their discussion of the point, had aroused the resistance of the great body of literati and conservative officials in the Empire, who had grown up in the belief that its unity and prosperity were involved in the performance of the kotow. The discussion in July, 1859, when the Emperor Hienfung could safely decline to admit Mr. Ward to an audience without it, had exhausted their arguments; but his son had come to the throne under the new influences, which were rapidly breaking down all those old ideas and safeguards. The prince had, moreover, learned that the foreign ministers were not very strongly supported by their own governments, none of whom intended to make the audience question a *casus belli*, or even a reason for withdrawing their legations from Peking. Perhaps the Yamun thought that the departure of the Russian and German ministers would leave the other three less inclined to persist in their demand, if serious consequences were likely to result.

The American minister clearly states the pith of the matter in his despatch of March 24th in his closing words: "I attach importance to the proper settlement of the audience question at the earliest time possible. To demand it, and urge compliance with the demand, is a duty every western nation owes to its own dignity and to the welfare of its citizens and subjects residing here; it is also a kindness to this government to try through this means to improve relations, and thus prevent, or at least postpone, what are now likely at any time to occur—hostile collisions, with their dreadful consequences."[1] This alternative was not a fanciful one, and this cause of chronic dispute and irritation between China and other nations during many centuries was removed chiefly through the patient persistance of Mr. Low in this discussion. His despatches contain every fact and argument of importance in perhaps the most serious controversy ever brought before China. One cannot but sympathize with Prince Kung and his colleagues in their dilemma, and to this embarrassment Mr. Low gives due weight.

The Chinese officials took a month to discuss the points among themselves, and signs of yielding were apparent both in the note of Prince Kung of April 16th and the memorandum of the 29th brought forward at an interview with the legations. Much of the same ground was gone over again; a vacation ensued, then another protocol on May 15th appeared, followed by notes on the 20th and 29th from both sides, all tending to the desired conclusion. At last the audience question was settled on June 29th by the Emperor first

---

[1] *Foreign Relations of the United States*, 1873, p. 169. See also the despatches of that year, and compare Pauthier's *Histoire des Relations Politique de la Chine*, Paris, 1858. Narrative of the American Embassy's visit to Peking, *N. C. Br. R. As. So.*, Vol. I, 1859.

receiving Soyeshima, the ambassador from Japan, by himself; and immediately afterward the five ministers of Russia, the United States, Great Britain, France, and Holland, accompanied only by Mr. Carl Bismarck, the German secretary, who interpreted for them.[1] Mr. Low's despatch of July 10th, giving the details of the ceremonies and the previous discussion in settling them, with the difficulty the prince and others had in swallowing the bitter pill, is very valuable as a description of the finale of this last struggle of Chinese seclusion to resist the incoming wave of western power. The wall of their separation was at last broken down. They were really stronger and wiser than ever, and every nation interested felt a relief that the days of proud assumption were ended. The young Emperor held only three more audiences during his short reign of nineteen months; and in all these discussions he seems to have taken no active part, nor did he oppose the conclusion. His ignorance of the whole question made his opinion a matter of small moment.

Among other advantages resulting to all parties by the settlement of this question was the right adjustment of the Chinese government in its relations with other courts. This acknowledgment of their equality as independent nations did not in anywise interfere with the obeisance of native officials when approaching their sovereign; but it smoothed the way for future diplomatic relations. No western power could maintain an envoy near the *Hwangti* at Peking with the least self-respect if he were not allowed to see this potentate unless by prostrating himself. While none of the great nations would deem a mere matter of ceremony a sufficient pretext for resorting to war—since war itself often fails to convince—a long continuance of this state of affairs must inevitably have led to complications the more unpleasant to diplomatists because sure to be oft-recurring. It was probably owing to the personal influence of Prince Kung and Wănsiang, the two most enlightened statesmen of this period, that a further insistance upon the kotow was not made, and preparations thus arranged for reciprocal courtesies when Chinese ambassadors appeared at foreign courts.

---

[1] Compare the *Illustrated London News* for June 23, 1873.

But against what tremendous odds of superstition and national prejudice these two officials were pitted in this curious contest those who have never lived in the Empire can hardly appreciate.[1]

The years 1873 and 1874 were marked by the abolition of the coolie trade at Macao, which since its rise in 1848 had been attended with many atrocities on land and sea. During these twenty-five years attempts had been made to conduct the trade with some regard for the rights of the laborers, but experience had shown that to do this was practically impossible if the business were to be made remunerative. Driven from Hongkong and Whampoa, the agents of this traffic had long found shelter in the Portuguese harbor of Macao, from which semi-independent port they could despatch Chinese crimps on kidnapping excursions for their nefarious trade. When at last the governor closed this haven to its continuance, the Spaniards and Peruvians were the only nationalities whom the action affected; but Spain, falling back on her treaty of 1864, insisted that the coolie trade be allowed. The Yamun was advised not to admit this privilege until the harsh treatment of the laborers in Cuba had been inquired into. This was done in 1873, by means of a commission composed of three foreigners and two Chinese, who made as thorough an inquiry as the Cuban authorities would permit and reported the results in 1874. Since the dreadful disclosures which transpired in their report the trade has never revived. Peru, indeed, sent M. Garcia as its envoy to Peking to negotiate a treaty and obtain the right of engaging laborers,

---

[1] Of Wănsiang's personal history little is known. He was a Manchu, and a man of uncommonly prepossessing manner, being perhaps most highly esteemed of all the officials who came in contact with the foreign legations. At the termination of hostilities and the organization of the Tsung-lí Yamun in 1861, he came prominently forward as a most efficient and sagacious adviser of the government. We have already in this narrative had occasion to note the influence of his name in the settlement of the Lay-Osborne flotilla and in the missionary question, the satisfactory conclusion of which was a meet tribute to his talents and judgment. He died at an advanced age in 1875, at the head of the administration. In his death the Chinese government lost an unselfish patriot and a keen observer of those things which were for the best interests of his country.

but this gentleman met with no success whatever. The Chinese negotiations on this occasion showed the good results of their freer intercourse with foreigners in the improved character of their arguments for maintaining their rights.[1] The lamentable condition of Chinese laborers in Peru was fully enough proved, inasmuch as their appeal for relief to their home government had been before the Yamun since 1868, but it could do nothing effectual to help them.

The Japanese government undertook in this year to try the issue of war with the Chinese in order to settle its demand of redress for the murder, in 1871, of some fifty-four Lewchewan sailors by savages on the eastern coast of Formosa. Japan had recently deposed the native authorities in Shudi, and being hard pressed for some employment of the feudal retainers of the retired daimios, undertook to redress Lewchewan grievances by occupying the southern part of Formosa, asserting that it did not belong to China because she either would not or could not govern its savage inhabitants. This view of the divided ownership of the island was promptly rejected by the foreign ministers resident at Tokio, but the officials were persuaded that all they had to do was to occupy the whole southern district, and the Chinese could not drive them out when once their intrenchments were completed.

The Mikado accordingly gathered his forces in Kiusiu during the years 1873–74, placing them under the command of General Saigo, and engaging qualified foreign military men to assist. The expedition was called a High Commission, accompanied by a force sufficient for its protection, sent to aboriginal Formosa to inquire into the murder of fifty-four Japanese subjects, and take steps to prevent the recurrence of such atrocities. A proclamation was issued April 17, 1874, and another May 19th, stating that General Saigo was directed to call to an account the persons guilty of outrages on Japanese subjects. As he knew that China was not prepared to resist his landing at Liang-kiao, his chief business was to provide means to house

---

[1] *Foreign Relations of the United States*, 1874, pp. 198–232. *Westminster Review*, Vol. 100, p. 75. *Customs Report on Cuban Coolie Trade*, 1876.

and feed the soldiers under his command. The Japanese authorities do not appear very creditably in this affair. No sooner did they discover the wild and barren nature of this unknown region than they seemed fain to beat an incontinent and hasty retreat, nor did the troops landed there stand upon the order of their going. They had in some measure been misled by the fallacious arguments of Gen. Charles Le Gendre, formerly United States consul at Amoy, who had travelled through these districts in 1865; the enormous cost which they had already incurred made them hesitate about proceeding further, though they had announced their intention of retaining possession of the territory. The aborigines having fled south after the first rencontre, the Japanese leader employed his men as best he could in opening roads through the jungle and erecting houses.

Meanwhile the Peking authorities were making preparations for the coming struggle, and though they moved slowly they were much in earnest to protect their territory. General Shin Pao-chin having been invested with full powers to direct operations against the Japanese forces, began at once to draw together men and vessels in Fuhchau and Amoy. The Japanese consuls at Amoy and Shanghai were allowed to remain at their posts; and during the year two envoys arrived at Peking to treat with the Court. Their discussions soon narrowed down to a demand on the Japanese ministers, Yanagiwara and Okubo, to withdraw from Formosa before treating with them upon the outrages there; which was met by a refusal on the ground that the Emperor had voided his sovereignty by having for three years taken no steps to punish his subjects, notwithstanding the repeated requests made to this end. The Chinese proved that the Japanese had violated their treaty, and acted in an underhand manner in certain negotiations with their envoy, Soyeshima, the preceding year; but this continued sparring was mere child's play. The probabilities were strong against any settlement, when the parties were induced to arrange their quarrel by the intervention and wise counsel of Sir T. F. Wade, the British minister. The Japanese accepted five hundred thousand taels for their outlays in Formosa for roads, houses, and defences; agreeing thereupon to retire and leave the further punishment of the aborigines to the Chinese authorities. The two envoys left Peking, and this attempt at war was happily frustrated.[1]

The history of this affair was exceedingly instructive to those who saw the risks to their best interests which both these nations were running in an unnecessary appeal to force. Never, perhaps, has the resort to arbitration been more happy, when to the difficulty of keeping out of a quarrel which so many fortune-seekers were ready to encourage was added the fact that both nations had been eagerly developing their land and marine forces by adopting foreign arms, drill, ships, and defences; every friend felt the uselessness of a disastrous conflict at this time and willingly strove to prevent any such result. The civilization of all parts of Formosa has since rapidly advanced by the extension of tea and sugar culture, the establishment of Christian missions, and the better treatment of the native tribes. A single incident at this time illustrated the undefined position of the parties in this dispute. This was the arrival in Peking, after Okubo's departure, of a large embassy of Lewchewans to make their homage to the Emperor Tungchí. The Japanese chargé d'affaires was denied admittance to the Lewchewan hotel, and the Yamun refused to dismiss the embassy, but gave it an audience, as was the usage in former days—probably the last in their history. The experience acquired by these three nations in their quarrel concerning Formosa has not prevented considerable bitterness about their rights to Lewchew.

No sooner had the Chinese government escaped from the Japanese imbroglio by the payment of half a million taels than it found itself involved in another and more troublesome question with the British. This arose from the persistent attempts of the latter to open a trade through Burmah, along the Irrawadi River, with Yunnan and other south-western parts of China. The Indian government had sent or encouraged explorers to go through the little known regions lying between

---

[1] *Is Aboriginal Formosa a part of the Chinese Empire?* with eight maps, folio, Shanghai, 1874, pp. 20. *Foreign Relations of the United States* for 1873 and 1874—China and Japan, passim. *The Japan Herald* and *North China Herald* for those years record all the leading events.

the Brahmaputra and Lantsang rivers, but no trade could be developed in so wild and thinly settled a region. During the Tai-ping Rebellion the Emperor's authority in Yunnan had been practically in abeyance, and over the western half of the province it had been superseded by a revolt of the Panthays, a Mohammedan tribe long settled in that region. These sectaries date their origin from the Tang dynasty, and had been generally unmolested by the Chinese so long as they obeyed the laws. During the Mongol sway their numbers increased so that they began to participate in the government, while ever since they have enjoyed more or less the control of affairs.[1] The differences in faith and practice, however, aided in keeping them distinct; and in Yunnan their numbers were recruited by settlers from Kansuh and Koko-nor, so that they were led to throw off the Chinese rule altogether.

They began about the year 1855 to defend themselves against the imperialists, captured Talí in 1857, pushing their arms as far eastward as the provincial capital Yunnan fu, which was seized and held for a brief period; but in 1867 they proclaimed Tu Win-siu as their Imam, and located their capital in Talí. With affairs in this condition law and order speedily vanished, life and property were sacrificed, and general misrule furnished the lawless with an opportunity to burn, kill, and destroy until the land became a desert. The Panthays, as the Burmese called the insurrectionists, turned their hopes westward for succor, and to this end endeavored to keep open the trade with Burmah and India, but under the circumstances it could not flourish. The British in those countries were, however, quite ready to countenance, if not aid, the new ruler at Talí, as soon as his power was sufficiently consolidated to keep open the roads and protect traders.

In 1868 a party was ordered to proceed to this city and "discover the cause of the cessation of trade formerly existing by these routes, the exact position held by the Kakhyens, Shans, and Panthays with reference to that traffic, and their disposition or

[1] Compare Dr. Anderson, *From Mandalay to Momien*, p. 223. Du Halde, *Histoire*, Tome I., p. 199. Grosier, *China*, Vol. IV., p. 270. Garnier, *Voyaye d'Exploration*, Tome I. Cooper, *Travels of a Pioneer of Commerce*.

otherwise to resuscitate it." This party, numbering a hundred in all, was in charge of Major Sladen, assisted by five qualified men, and guarded by an escort of fifty armed police; its object embraced diplomacy, engineering, natural science, and commerce. Their steamer reached Bhamo January 22, 1868, and the party began their travels early in March, arriving after much delay at Momein (or Tăng-yueh chau), a town on the Taping River, one hundred and thirty-five miles from Bhamo and about five thousand feet above the sea. Another forced delay of nearly two months convinced them of the impossibility of their getting to Talí (nearly as far again); in face of the determined opposition, therefore, both of the hill tribes and Chinese traders, Major Sladen was fain to retire in safety to Bhamo. The retreat of this anomalous expedition could be officially ascribed to the weakness of the Panthay rulers, the wild region traversed, and its yet wilder inhabitants. But to what principles of justice or equity can we attribute the action of the British in retaining their minister at the capital of an Empire while sending a peaceful mission to a rebel in arms at its boundaries? This impertinence seems thinly veiled by dubbing the expedition one of inquiry concerning trade; no trade did or could exist with an ill-assorted rabble of wild mountaineers; when these had been duly subjected an expedition for purposes of science would meet with as ready assistance from the authorities as did that of the Frenchman, Lieutenant Garnier, then exploring eastern Yunnan. This disregard of the courtesies and rights of independent nations reflects as little credit upon the powerful nation which used her strength thus unfairly as does her similar attempt of negotiating with another rebel, Yakub Beg in Îlí.

Major Sladen's mission, owing to the admirable qualities of its leader, made so fair an impression upon the natives along his route that upon his return in 1873 his progress was materially assisted, instead of retarded, by them as far as Momein. In the years intervening the Imam at Talí, with about forty thousand of his followers, had been hemmed in by the Chinese forces under the leadership of Lí Sieh-tai, or Brigadier Lí. The Mohammedans felt their weakness against such odds, and the so-called Sultan Suleiman sent his son Hassan to London to implore recognition and aid from the British government; but before he returned his father had killed himself and the victorious Chinese had massacred most of their opponents and regained possession of the whole province in 1873. Its western half had been virtually independent since 1855, during which period the wretchedness of the inhabitants had greatly reduced their numbers and resources.

Trade soon revived. The British appointed an agent to reside at Bhamo and learn its amount and character. In 1874 an expedition—this time provided with Chinese passports—was planned to make the trip across China from Burmah to Hankow, as Lieutenant Garnier had done from Saigon. The Chinese traders in Burmah set themselves to circumvent it, for its success boded disaster to them, as they better knew the resources of their competitors. The British plan was to send an accredited agent across the country from Hankow to Bhamo, there to meet a party under charge of Col. Horace Browne, which was to "thoroughly examine the capabilities of the country beyond Momein." As only six years had passed since Sladen's party had reached that town on its way to the Panthays at Talí, there had perhaps been hardly time to remove all suspicion among the local officials about the objects of this new move. One of the consular clerks, Augustus R. Margary, was furnished with necessary passports and instructions from her Majesty's legation to go to Bhamo and act as Colonel Browne's guide and interpreter. His journals testify that no better choice could have been made, and all who knew him were hopeful of the success of this young man.[1] He left Hankow September 2d and reached Bhamo January 17th without molestation or accident, having been received with respect by all Chinese officials, whom the governor-general of Yunnan had required thus to act. While the party in Bhamo prepared the equipment for its journey, Dr. Anderson observes that the Chinese "watched its movements with a secret feeling that the objects contemplated were somewhat beyond the peaceful pursuits of commerce and scientific inquiry."[2]

[1] *Journals of A. R. Margary*, edited by Sir R. Alcock, London, 1877.

[2] The report was also circulated that the party was going to lay down a railroad.

Mr. Margary intimated that he thought there were intrigues going on at Manwyne adverse to the advance of the mission ; but Brigadier Lí, who treated him there with great honor, did every thing to promote his journey to Bhamo.

The arrangements as to routes and escorts were at last completed so far as to allow the party finally to leave Bhamo February 3, 1875 ; it numbered nearly fifty persons in all, together with a Burmese guard of one hundred and fifty. The rivalries and deceptions of the Kakhyen tribes proved to be worse than in 1868, and progress was slower from the difficulty of providing animals for transport. By the 18th it had crossed the frontier, and the next morning Mr. Margary left, with five Chinese, for Manwyne, to arrange there for its reception by Brigadier Lí. Increased dissensions among the tribes as to escort, transport, and pay led Colonel Browne to push on after him with a guard so as to reach that town and find some competent authority to aid his expedition. Many signs of serious opposition had by this time manifested themselves; and when he was preparing to start from Seray on the 23d, large bodies of armed men were seen on the opposite hills coming to attack the British. A Burmese messenger also arrived from Manwyne with letters giving an account of the horrid murder of Mr. Margary and his attendants by the treacherous officials there on the 20th. The Chinese soldiers or robbers were in a manner repulsed by the bravery of Browne's escort and by firing the jungle, but the expedition was in face of too powerful an opposition to contemplate advancing after such disasters. The return to Bhamo was soon made, and the earnest efforts of the Burmese officers there to recover everything belonging to the British proved their honesty.

The disappointment at this rebuff was exceeded by the general indignation at the treachery which marked the murder. It was soon known that Lí Sieh-tai was not at Manwyne at the time, though the real actors in the tragedy belonged to his army, and must have made him cognizant of the deed.[1]

---

[1] *Mandalay to Momien: A Narrative of Two Expeditions to Western China*, by Dr John Anderson, contains a most satisfactory narrative of these attempts; the writer's opinion is of the highest value.

When news of this disaster reached London and Peking, the British minister was directed to demand an investigation of the facts connected with the outrage in presence of a British officer in Yunnan, the issue by the Yamun of fresh passports for a new mission, and an indemnity. After months of delay and correspondence with the Yamun Sir Thomas Wade, the British minister, was able to make up his commission and despatch it from Hankow, November 5th, for Yunnan fu. It consisted of the Hon. T. G. Grosvenor, second secretary of the legation, and Messrs. Davenport and Baber of the consular service, all of them well fitted by previous training for attaining the objects of their expedition. The journey was performed in company with a Chinese escort, without danger or interference, the city of Yunnan being reached in March. The gentlemen found the provinces through which they travelled perfectly at peace, and the Emperor's authority everywhere acknowledged—a fact extremely creditable to the Chinese after more than twenty years of civil war.

The Chinese appointed to conduct the inquiry into the murder, in connection with Mr. Grosvenor, was Lí Han-chang, governor-general at Wuchang and brother of Lí Hung-chang. He was long in making the journey, but the two began their proceedings, having Sieh Hwan, an old member of the Yamun in 1864, as aid. Those who had any experience or acquaintance with similar joint commissions in China anticipated but one result from it—an entire failure in proving or punishing the guilty parties; while those who wish to see their character should read Mr. Grosvenor's various reports [1] to learn how slow are the advances of the Chinese in truth-telling. Nevertheless, such an investigation had some prospective benefit in that the trouble which the British made on account of the taking of one life warned the officials to exercise the greatest caution in future. In this preventive aspect, the mission doubtless accomplished more than can be estimated. Mr. Baber is sure that Margary was killed (and his opinion is entitled to great respect) by the discontented Chinese train bands then around Manwyne—

[1] *Blue Book—China*, No. 1 (1876) and No. 3 (1877).

a lawless set, who were afterward hunted to death.[1] The weight of evidence obtained at Yunnan fu went to prove that the repulse of the British party was countenanced, if not planned, by the governor-general, and carried into effect with the cognizance of Brigadier Lí. Amid so much irreconcilable evidence, the inference that the officers, chiefly by so doing, intended to prevent the extension of trade by the British, offers the most adequate explanation. When the impoverished condition of Southwestern China is remembered, the question arises, Why should the Indian government strive to open a trade where industry and population have been so destroyed? But the expectation that thereby a greater market would be found for its opium in all Western China is a sufficient reason, perhaps, for undertaking so costly an experiment.

No sooner had Sir Thomas Wade learned of Margary's death than he impressed upon the Chinese government the necessity for unremitting and vigorous measures toward the arrest and punishment of the guilty. In addition to what has been already stated concerning this reparation, he brought forward some other matters affecting the intercourse between the two countries. They were long and painfully debated, and those agreed on were embodied in a convention which was signed by himself and Lí Hung-chang, on the part of Great Britain and China, September 13, 1876. The correspondence relating to this convention is given, with its text, in the Parliamentary Blue Books,[2] and is worth perusal by all who wish to learn the workings of the Chinese government.

The Yunnan case was settled by immediate payment of two hundred thousand taels ($280,000), which included all claims of British merchants on the Chinese government; by posting an imperial proclamation in the cities and towns throughout the Empire; by sending an envoy bearing a letter of regret to Queen Victoria for what had occurred in Yunnan; and by

---

[1] *Blue Book—China*, No. 3, 1878. *Report of Mr. Baber on the route followed by Mr. Grosvenor's mission between Talí fu and Momein.* Reprinted, with his other interesting travels and researches in Western China, in *Supplementary Papers*, Vol. I., Part 1, 1882, of *Roy. Geog. Soc.*, London.

[2] *Blue Book—China*, No. 1 (1876) and No. 3 (1877).

stationing British officers at Talí or elsewhere in that province to "observe the conditions of trade." The proclamation[1] was posted very widely (three thousand copies in Kiangsu province alone), and through it the people learned that the safety of all foreigners travelling through their country was guaranteed by the Emperor. Other matters agreed upon in this convention were the manner of official intercourse between native and foreign officers at Peking and the ports, so that perfect equality might be shown; the better administration of justice in criminal cases between their respective subjects, every such case being tried by the official of the defendant's nationality, while the plaintiff's official could always be present to watch proceedings; the extension of trade by opening four new ports as consular stations, and six on the Yangtsz' River for landing goods, with other regulations as to opium, transit, and *li-kin* taxes on goods; and lastly, the appointment of a joint commission to establish some system that should enable the Chinese government to protect its revenue without prejudice to the junk trade of Hongkong.

This final article might well have been omitted. The concessions and advantages in it accrued to the British, and through them also measurably to other nationalities. But while the Chinese under the circumstances had no right to complain of paying heavily for Margary's life, it was manifestly unfair to cripple their commerce by sheltering Hongkong smugglers under promise of a commission which could never honestly agree. In order to better understand the British minister's views regarding the political and commercial bearing of his convention, the reader is referred to his labored minute of July 14, 1877,[2] in which the fruits of thirty-five years of official experience in China impart much value to his opinions. The singular mixture of advice, patronizing decisions, and varied knowledge running through the whole render the paper extremely interesting. The Chinese historian of the next century will read with wonder the implied responsibility of the British minister for the conduct of the Empire in its foreign manage-

---

[1] *Blue Book—China*, No. 3 (1877). [2] *Ibid*, pp. 111–147.

ment, and the enormous development of the principle of ex-territoriality so as to cover almost every action of every British subject. He may also be instructed by this proof of the ignorance and fears of the former rulers, as well as their conceit and hesitation in view of their wants and backwardness to cope with the advancing age. He must acknowledge, too, that the sharp and prolonged discussion of eighteen months between Sir Thomas and the Yamun was one of the most profitable exercises in political science the high officers of Peking ever had allowed them.

Since the convention of Chifu the progress of China at home and abroad has been the best evidence of an improved administration. The reign of Hienfung ended in 1861, with the prestige, resources, and peace of the realm he had so miserably governed reduced to their lowest ebb. During the twelve years of his son's nominal régime, the face of affairs had quite changed for the better. Peace and regular government had been for the most part resumed throughout the Eighteen Provinces, and even to the extreme western frontier of Kashgar and Kuldja. The people were returning to their desolated villages, while their rulers did what they could to promote agriculture and trade. The young Emperor gave small promise of becoming a wise or efficient ruler; and when he died (January 12, 1875) it was felt that an effigy only had passed away, and no change would ensue in the administration. In the question of selecting his inheritor were involved some curious features of Chinese customs. It is a rule that the succession to the *Lung-wei*, or 'Dragon's Seat,' cannot pass to the preceding generation, since this would involve the worship of a lower or younger generation by an older one. The line of Hienfung died out in his childless son; the eldest of his brothers had, as we have seen, been made posthumous heir of an uncle in 1854, consequently his son, Pu-lun, was ineligible. The elevation of Prince Kung's son Tsai-ching to be Emperor was in the highest degree inexpedient, as this would necessitate the retirement of his father from active participation in the government, arising from their relationship of father and son. The next eligible candidate, Tsai-tien, a child of Prince Chun—the seventh son of Taukwang—born August 15,

1871, was unanimously chosen by the Empresses dowager and assembled princes of the Manchu Imperial Clan. His parents were brother and sister of those of his predecessors, while the same regency had been reappointed, so that his tender age involved neither difficulty nor alteration during the minority. He took the reign-name of *Kwang-sü*, or 'Illustrious Succession,' having reference to the disturbance in the regular descent. By this arrangement the same general set of officials was continued on the government, and the risk to its peaceful working from the freaks of Tungchí avoided.[1]

A most notable event during the last decade has been the recovery of the vast regions of the Tarim Valley to the imperial sway. Their loss took place during the early part of the Tai-ping Rebellion, beginning in Kansuh, where the discontented Moslem population, aided by the reckless and seditious of all clans, arose and drove out the governmental minions even to the eastern side of Shensí. Of this extended revolt little is known in the west save the name of its figure-head and leading character under whose mastery it culminated and succumbed.

The famous Yakub Beg, whom the jealous attentions of both England and Russia had united in raising to the rank of a hero, commenced his military career as lieutenant of Buzurg khan, a son of the notable Jehangír, kojeh of Kokand. By the year 1866 the energetic lieutenant had made way with his licentious and cowardly chief, and possessed himself of a large part of Western Kashgaria; then, turning his attention to the rebellious Dunganis north of him, a series of vigorous campaigns ended in leaving him undisputed ruler of all Tien-Shan Nan Lu. These conquests over, hordes of neighboring rebels must now be recognized as fatal errors in the policy of Yakub. The Atalik Ghazi, or 'Champion Father' as he was now called, had not only attracted the distrust of Russia—manifested in their taking of Kuldja from the Dunganis before his approach was possible—but in annihilating other Moslem insurrectionists,

---

[1] The Eastern Empress-dowager, the legal widow of Hienfung, whose only child, a daughter, died early in 1875, followed her to the grave in 1881, leaving the regency with her coadjutor, the Empress An, aided by Prince Kung.

had constituted himself an avenger of Chinese wrongs, and prepared the way of his own enemies whenever the terrible day of reckoning should come.

The attempt on the part of China to restore its prestige in a territory where every hand was turned against her seemed indeed hopeless. Her exhausted resources, her constant fear of the foreigners within her gates, her suspicions of Russia, the immense distances to be traversed, seemed to unite every factor against her success. Nevertheless, by 1871 symptoms of disorganization began already to appear among the rebels, while in the wishes of the common people for a strong power to insure order and encourage trade Tso Tsung-tang, the Chinese general, found both assistance and men.

A moment's attention to the relations between the Chinese and Mohammedans of this region will throw much light on their contest. Since their conquest by Kienlung, the inhabitants of Eastern Turkestan had enjoyed an unexampled period of tranquillity and prosperous trade. The Chinese, known as Kitai, settled in their cities and brought a degree of wealth and civilization far ahead of anything previously known, while the rulers, or ambans, joined to their duties as administrators of justice a fostering care of trade routes and methods for developing the country. They have at all times been celebrated for irrigating their provinces, and now reproduced their wonderful canals (says Boulger) "even in this outlying dependency. Eastern Turkestan is one of the worst-watered regions in the world. In fact there is only a belt of fertile country around the Yarkand River, stretching away eastward along the slopes of the Tien Shan as far as Hami. The few small rivers which are traced here and there across the map are during many months of the year dried up, and even the Yarkand then becomes an insignificant stream. To remedy this, and to husband the supply as much as possible, the Chinese sunk dikes in all directions. By this means the cultivated country was slowly but surely spread over a great extent of territory, and the vicinity of the three cities of Kashgar, Yangi Hissar, and Yarkand became known as the garden of Asia. Corn and fruit grew in abundance, and from Yarkand to the south of the Tien

Shan the traveller could pass through one endless orchard. On all sides he saw nothing but plenty and content, peaceful hamlets and smiling inhabitants. These were the outcome of a Chinese domination."[1]

In addition to the fields and rivers, mines were worked, mountain passes cut and kept in repair, and the internal government of tribes placed on an equable basis. As to the precise manner in which discontent and rebellion crept into this apparently happy territory, it must always remain a matter of conjecture. The customs of its inhabitants have for ages been based on the tribal principle to such an extent that they found it impossible to assimilate with the Chinese and their methodical government, even though for their advantage to do so. The repeated failures of the United States to introduce a certaindegree of civilization among the Indians present an analogous case. Uneasiness among the natives caused by agents from Kokand and Tashkend was speedily followed by larger demands from turbulent Mussulmans, who saw in Chinese moderation an evidence of weakness and decline. Jehangír's rebellion not unjustly incensed a government which had devoted more than half a century to the building up of a shattered State, and was punished with merciless rigor. Oppression from the Chinese met by resistance, equitable rule alternating with weakness and injustice, trade impeded by illegal imports, ambitious Usbeck chiefs exciting their tribes to rise against their conquerors—these and similar causes had been at work to prevent all permanent progress in Turkestan.

During the lowest ebb of Manchu authority in the Empire, when foreigners and Tai-pings were straining the utmost resources of the government in the East, a small village of Kansuh was the scene of a sudden riot. When after two days couriers brought word that the disturbance was quelled with some loss of life, the authorities began to suppose that the affair had already been forgotten; but it proved to be the fuse that lighted an outbreak scarcely smaller than the other civil war

---

[1] *Life of Yakoob Beg*, London, 1878. p. 59. See also R. B. Shaw, *Visits to High Tartary, Yarkand, and Kashgar*, London, 1871, Chaps. II. and III.

within the provinces.[1] The Dunganis had arisen and spread the infection of revolt wherever they existed—over large districts of Shensí, but principally toward the west, to Turfan, Kuche, and Aksu—continuing the weary story of surprise, slaughter, and barbarity even to the city of Kuldja.[2] Allying with themselves the Tarantchi, a sort of fellah class which the Chinese had imported into the regions from Kashgar, the victorious rebels established one of those ephemeral governments over the Tien Shan and its adjoining valleys that have so frequently arisen in the history of Central Asia. Under their rule travel beyond the Kiayü Pass was of course impossible, while trade diminished throughout the country, and Russia, as we have seen, wrested Kuldja from Abul Oghlan in order to secure her own borders. The first serious check received by this confederation was its virtual overthrow, when Yakub advanced upon Aksu and from thence cleared the great road eastward to Turfan.

Tso's first labor, then, was to clear Shensí and Kansuh of the rebels, in which his progress was marked by admirable foresight and energy in disposition of men, arrangement of courier service, and use of modern arms. Establishing himself by 1876 in Barkul and Hami as headquarters, by the following spring he was prepared for a concerted movement from the north (Gutchen and Urumtsi) and east (Pidshan) upon Yakub Beg at Turfan. The redoubtable chieftain was finally caught by the tardy but certain power which he had long despised with impunity, and driven backward through the towns of Toksun and Harashar to Korla, where he died or was murdered, May, 1877. During this and the following years the governor-general succeeded in reinstating the authority which had been in abeyance nearly a score of years. His army under two able generals advanced along the parallel roads north and south of the Tien Shan, punishing the rebels without mercy, while "the Moham-

[1] "It is impossible not to connect this event in some degree with that unaccountable revival among Mohammedans, which has produced so many important events during the last thirty years, and of which we are now witnessing some of the most striking results."—Boulger. *Life of Yakoob Beg*, p. 95.

[2] Which fell in January, 1866, after the Chinese governor had destroyed himself and his citadel by gunpowder.

medans who submitted themselves were permitted to revert to their peaceful avocations."[1] When upon the desert the troops were provisioned from Russian territory, but during the early years of the campaign it appears that the soldiers were made to till the ground as well as construct fortifications. The history of the advance of this "agricultural army" would, if thoroughly known, constitute one of the most remarkable military achievements in the annals of any modern country.[2]

With the fall of Kashgar (December 17, 1877) the reconquest was practically completed, though Yarkand and the neighboring towns held out some months longer, at the end of which the chiefs of the Moslem movement had either fled to Ferghana or succumbed in the fight. The Chinese now turned their attention to the occupation of Kuldja, and sent Chunghow in December, 1878, to St. Petersburg upon a mission relating to its restoration. The envoy needed, indeed, but to remind the Czar of Russian promises made in Peking in 1871 concerning the prompt retrocession of the occupied territory when China should have reasserted her authority in those regions; but neither European nor Oriental diplomats seemed to regard the city "held in trust for China by the Russian government" as in the least likely to return to the dominion of the Hwangtí, while many were persuaded that Russia would resort to arms before surrendering one of the most prosperous of her possessions in order to keep a rash promise.[3]

Chunghow—whose capacity had been in some degree tested in the Tientsin riot—was hardly the best choice for envoy even among the still ignorant officers at Peking, inasmuch as to the seemingly apparent defect of an unusually Bœotian temperament was added a profound ignorance of any European language, of modern methods of diplomacy, and of the topography of the territory in question. It is almost needless to add that

---

[1] *Peking Gazette.*

[2] *The Spectator*, April 13, 1878, *Pall Mall Gazette*, June, 1878, and *London Times*, November, 1878. Boulger, *Life of Yakoob Beg*, Chaps. XII.–XIV.

[3] For an excellent illustration of the prevailing sentiment on this question, even after Chunghow's embassy, see Mr. D. C. Boulger in *Fraser's Magazine* for August, 1880, p. 164.

such an embassy was ill-prepared to cope with the astute diplomatists of an eager court, or that it speedily fell a prey to the designs upon it. A treaty of eighteen articles was signed at Livadia yielding a portion of the Kuldja district to China, Russia retaining, however, the fruitful valley of the Tekes River, all the more important strategic strongholds and passes in the Tien Shan, and the city of Yarkand; China, moreover, to pay as indemnity five million rubles for the cost of occupying Kuldja. Other important concessions, such as a trade route from Hankow through Suhchau to Kuldja and Siberia, the opening to Russian caravans of thirty-six frontier stations, the modification of the Kashgarian frontier, the arming of Muscovite merchants, and the navigation of the Songari River, were apparently added to this compact according as the Russians increased their experience of the "gullability" of these remarkable ambassadors.

Even officers of the Czar's army, in referring afterward to this treaty, were prone to add to their remarks some measure of apology. When in January, 1880, Chunghow returned home with the unwise and humiliating document in his possession, he could not have felt wholly certain of a triumphant reception. Nevertheless it is not likely that the luckless ambassador contemplated being at once deprived by imperial edict of all his offices and turned over to a board for trial and punishment. Statesmen of both parties joined in denouncing him, Lí Hungchang and Tso alike presenting memorials to the same effect, while a flood of petitions more or less fierce poured upon the government from mandarins of all ranks. On the 28th the returned envoy was cashiered for having signed away territory and promised indemnity without special authorization, and in punishment was sentenced to decapitation. The actors in this movement, which upon the manifestation of such prompt and furious measures assumed the phase of an intrigue of the war party, were Tso and Prince Chung, who seized upon the popular wrath as an opportune moment for a master stroke against Prince Kung.

With the appearance of danger such as this the party in power recoiled at once from its angry position, depreciated the highly bellicose tone of court officials, and accepted the good offices of the foreign ministers who joined in protesting against the unworthy treatment of Chunghow and the monstrous barbarity of his sentence. Possibly the temperance of Russia's attitude in demanding the unconditional pardon of Chunghow before consenting to receive a second ambassador—the Marquis Tsăng, minister to England, already appointed—materially aided in quieting the storm. Fortunately, too, amid the rumors of a resort to arms and manifest preparations of the palace discontents to force an issue, Colonel Gordon visited the capital, and in a communication to Governor Lí pointed out the folly of attempting a foreign conflict and the peculiar dangers in overwhelming, by courting a certain defeat, the great benefits which must come to the Chinese army by its gradual reorganization upon modern methods. "Potentially," said this unpalatable but honest critic, "you are perhaps invincible, but the outcome of this premature war will show you to be vulnerable at a thousand points." Counsels such as these carried unusual weight as coming from a man whom all parties in China respected and admired; there can be little doubt that it sensibly decreased the war feeling, and possibly prevented the country from rushing to certain disaster.

Chunghow was accordingly reprieved, and in June of this year set free. The intelligence and experience of Tsăng[1] proved an acceptable contrast to his predecessor's unguarded conduct, and resulted in an agreement (May 15th) on the part of the Czar's negotiators to recede nearly the whole of the contested district, excepting a narrow strip upon its western edge for purposes of colonization or retreat for those inhabitants of Ílí who preferred to remain under Russian control.[2] In return

[1] Upon his return to China the marquis published his diary, some portions of which have found their way into the *China Review* (Vol. XI., p. 135) and are extremely interesting as the outspoken opinion of an appreciative and enlightened Chinese gentleman.

[2] Precisely the extent of this strip depends upon the exact definition of the boundary here under Taukwang. The present line is laid down in that portion of the new treaty quoted in Volume I., p. 218; the territory forms approximately a wedge whose apex is in the Ala Tau Mountains, and whose base, about three degrees south of this point, lies against the crest of the Tien Shan. It meets the old boundary at the Muzart (or Muz-daban) Pass. Since the treaty

"for military expenses incurred by Russia in holding and protecting Ílí on behalf of China since the year 1871, and in satisfaction of all claims by Russian merchants for losses previously suffered by pillage within Chinese territory, and by Russians who have suffered outrage," the Chinese agreed to pay nine million roubles. This appears to have been less repugnant to oriental diplomacy than five millions in acknowledgment of getting back their borrowed property. As for the other points, the treaty does not seem to have been greatly altered, save in the Songari River and other more vexatious clauses. This treaty was ratified August 19, 1881.

From domestic wars and political complications, the influences of which have hardly as yet disappeared from our morning newspapers, our attention must be turned to the yet sadder spectacle of famine and pestilence. The occasional notices of a great scarcity of food in Northwestern China which drifted into the news items of western countries may still remain within the memory of many; those, however, who live under the ascendancy of occidental institutions can with difficulty appreciate, from any mere description of this scourge, its immense influence as a factor in removing somewhat the suspicions of the ignorant and apathetic Chinese against their fellow-men in other lands. The sympathies and charities of the Christian world, as called forth by this terrible visitation, were more effectual in making acceptable the distasteful presence of foreigners within their cities than had been the united influence of two wars and a half-century of trade, diplomacy, and social intercourse.

The Great Famine of 1878 was in some measure foretold over Shansí and Shensí by the decreasing rainfall of the four previous years. The peculiar nature of this loess-covered region, and its absolute dependence for fertility upon a sufficient supply of moisture, has been pointed out in another chapter of this work. Here, then, and in Shantung the missionaries of all denominations were called upon to organize methods

---

strenuous efforts have been made by the officers of both nationalities stationed there to entice the Usbeck, Kirghis, and Dunganis of the region to settle permanently on their side of the boundary.

of relief as early as the summer of 1877. By the opening of the following spring a central committee in Shanghai and their agents in Chifu and Tientsin—all Protestant and Roman Catholic missionaries—had put forth so great energy in their well-directed efforts as to gain the zealous co-operation of Lí Hungchang, governor-general of Chihlí, and active countenance of the rulers and gentry in other provinces. "At the beginning of their labors," writes the secretary of the committee, "the distributors were received with a degree of prejudice and suspicion which utterly frustrated any attempt to prosecute the work. They were supposed to have sinister objects in view, and not only was their charity refused, but they were even in imminent danger of their lives. It required the utmost carefulness on their part to carry on their operations with any degree of success. They were urged to act in a way that contemplated the speedy exhaustion of their funds and their evacuation of the place. So far as we can ascertain, however, the distributors conducted themselves in a most commendable manner, and after a time at least bore down the ill-will and aspersions of all classes, changing their sentiments and feelings of doubt and distrust into those of the deepest gratitude and respect, so that they are now regarded as the very saviours of the people." [1]

After the experience of some weeks in the destitute regions, it was found that only the strictest adherence to a business system of distribution could be attended with any mitigation of the evil. Tickets representing certain amounts of money were given to the houses of each community which appeared on the catalogues of needy families furnished by village elders. Food being plenty in the south, the means of transportation and storage during distribution constituted the chief labor of those concerned in this work. When brought to the starving settlements, grain was promptly doled out in exchange for the tickets, and to the lasting credit of the Chinese character it must here be noticed that not a single raid upon the provisions or resort to force in any way has been recorded of these famished multitudes.

---

[1] Rev. W. Muirhead, in *Report of the China Famine Relief Fund*, Shanghai, 1879, p. 4.

That good-will, affection, and gratitude should take the place of the old mistrust under these conditions was most natural.[1] Nevertheless the terrors of their experiences in this awful time were hardly lightened by this cheering aspect of the curse. Misery and desolation such as this overwhelmed every other sentiment save that of compassion. The visitor was often met by the solitary remnant of a large household, to hear from him a harrowing recital of suffering and death, fitted to shock the most callous of humanity. Again, he would come upon the corpse of one recently fallen in the vain effort to walk to a neighboring town, and about it a lazy pack of wolves squatting —gorged and stupid from the fulness of many ghastly meals. At other times a silent dwelling might be found giving shelter only to the cadaverous bodies of its former inmates; or anon a ruined house would tell where the timbers had been plucked out and sold for a little bread. Of the last extreme of famine, cannibalism, which cropped out here and there, but which in most cases met with instant punishment when discovered, it is hardly necessary to add notice or description. The remarkable patience under suffering exhibited by the people made their relief comparatively easy, though the despair which had rendered them insensible to excitement or violence often prevented their recuperation from the fever and plague which laid hold upon their weakened bodies even after plenty had returned to the land.

In their report the committee at Shanghai acknowledge Tls. 204,560 as having passed through their hands, while about as much more may safely be said to have been otherwise expended by foreigners for the relief of the sufferers.[2] The Chinese government furnished food and supplies amounting to

---

[1] A notable exception to this universal sentiment of kindliness was exhibited among the officials and gentry of Kaifung, the capital of Honan, in which city foreigners were to the last forbidden to remain, or even to carry on their work in the environs.

[2] About $22,670 were subscribed in the United States—which does not include, however, the donation from the Pacific slope. An effort was made to induce Congress to return on this occasion the surplus of the Chinese indemnity fund, amounting to nearly $600,000, but upon this the Committee on Foreign Affairs reported adversely, alleging among other reasons that all the starving people would be dead before the machinery of both nations would admit of this money being exchanged for food!

more than Tls. 2,000,000, while rich natives contributed very largely in their own districts. Sixty-nine foreigners were personally engaged upon the work of distribution in the four afflicted provinces, of whom Messrs. Hall, Hodge, Barradale, and Whiting died in consequence of exposure and overwork.[1] Upon the mortality connected with this frightful visitation there exist but the vaguest figures. "The destruction as a whole is stated to be from nine and a half to thirteen millions," observes the *Report*[2] already quoted, and its proofs in support of this statement are as trustworthy as any that can be compiled. No famine is recorded in the history of any land which equalled this in death-rate. The area at the base of the Tibetan and Mongolian highlands will always be subject to great vicissitudes of heat and moisture,[3] and the future, like the past, cannot but suffer from these frightful droughts unless a careful attention to the climatic influence of trees and irrigation mitigate in some degree the dreadful comings of these plagues.

The Chinese plenipotentiary in London, Kwoh Sung-tao, gave utterance to the sincere sentiments of his government in saying:

> The noble philanthropy which heard, in a far-distant country, the cry of suffering and hastened to its assistance, is too signal a recognition of the common brotherhood of humanity ever to be forgotten, and is all the more worthy to be remembered because it is not a passing response to a generous emotion, but a continued effort, persevered in until, in sending the welcome rain, Heaven gave the assuring promise of returning plenty, and the sign that the brotherly succor was no longer required. Coming from Englishmen residing in all parts of the world, this spontaneous act of generosity made a deep impression on the government and people of China, which cannot but have the effect of more closely cementing the friendly relations which now so happily exist between China and Great Britain. But the hands that gave also assumed the arduous duty of administering the relief; and here I would not forget to offer my grateful thanks and condolence to the families of those, and they are not a few, who nobly fell in distributing the fund.[4]

---

[1] Mr. Whiting was honored by the governor of Shansí with a public funeral in Taiyuen, the provincial capital.

[2] P. 7.

[3] Mr. A. Hosie in the *N. C. Br. R. A. S. Journal*, Vol. XIII., 1878, has translated the native lists of more than eight hundred famines and droughts occurring in the Yangtsz' basin and northward on the Plateau during a thousand years ending A.D. 1643.

[4] Letter of October 14, 1878, to Lord Salisbury.

One who has been acquainted with Chinese affairs for the last fifty years can better than younger persons appreciate from this letter the vast stride which has been made by China since the withdrawal of the East India Company's factory in 1834. The Empire had then been closed for more than a century, and its inhabitants had been taught to believe that all mankind outside of its boundaries were little better than ignorant savages. Their rulers had maintained that "barbarians could only be ruled by misrule," and in their honest efforts to keep them from entering the gates of the Celestial Empire in order that the people might not become contaminated, had faithfully though ineffectually endeavored to fulfil the first duty of every government. We have seen how small was their success when dealing with the iniquitous opium traffic; no amount of moral or ethical principle in the cause which he represented could make up to Commissioner Lin for his ignorance and stiff-neckedness in pushing his injudicious methods of reforming this abuse. Had he succeeded as he and his imperial master had planned, they would have sealed their country against the only possible remedies for those evils they were striving to remove—free intercourse, commercial, intellectual, and political, with their fellow-men.

The story of China's rapid progress from semi-barbarism toward her appropriate position among nations is now fully known to any whose interests have directed their attention thither. It cannot be denied that the advance has been hampered by the mass of superstitions, assumptions, and weaknesses through which every such stride to reformation must push forward; nor is it strange that interested foreigners from their vantage-ground of a more perfect civilization should at times bemoan the wearisome course and manifold errors of this regeneration. Nevertheless, hopeful signs abound on every side; against a few errors may be balanced a multitude of genuine successes, and the fact that these latter have come about deliberately assures us that they are permanent. In the hands of statesmen as far-sighted and patriotic as those who now control the government, there is little cause to apprehend retrograde steps or a return to the exclusive policy of Commissioners Lin and Yeh. As for the conservative spirit which yet characterizes the present régime, in this will be found the safeguard against extravagant and premature adoption of western machines, institutions, methods, dress, and the thousand adjuncts of modern European life which, if too rapidly applied to an effete and backward civilization, push it rather into bankruptcy and overthrow than out into a new existence.

Before closing these volumes, and as an illustration of these observations, it remains to notice the so-called Chinese Education Commission—a highly lauded project which is still fresh in the minds of many Americans. Soon after the Tientsin riot and Chunghow's mission of apology, Yung Wing, a Chinese graduate of Yale College, proposed to Lí Hung-chang and others in authority a plan of utilizing certain surplus moneys remaining from the fund for military stores, to defray the expenses of educating a number of Chinese boys in the United States. The scheme found such favor with the governor-general and members of the Foreign Office, that early in the year 1872 thirty boys were selected by competitive examination at Shanghai, and took passage for San Francisco July 12th, Yung Wing having preceded them to make the necessary arrangements. This gentleman's acquaintance with the social life and educational methods in New England was so complete as to enable him readily to place the students—usually in pairs—in comfortable households, where they might learn English and become initiated into the manner of life among western peoples as agreeably as possible.

The commission established its headquarters in Hartford and easily disposed their boys in adjoining towns of Connecticut and Massachusetts, where numbers of families welcomed them with open arms. Prince Kung's satisfaction upon learning of this friendly reception was expressed in a personal note of thanks to Mr. Low at Peking, while the fair prospects of the scheme now tended to hasten other parties of students to these shores until their number was swelled to one hundred and twenty.[1] These lads proved themselves almost without excep-

[1] The original plan included the sending of one hundred and fifty boys, but the fund laid aside for the purpose was found to be insufficient to cover the cost of the full number.

tion capable and active in the studies set before them, and as their hold upon the language increased, began to outrank all but the brightest of their American classmates. As they advanced into the higher scientific schools or colleges, greater liberty was allowed them, each boy pursuing his inclination as to a special course or institution. With the appointment of Yung Wing to the Chinese legation at Washington and the arrival of one Wu Tsz'-tăng (who knew no English) as commissioner in his place at Hartford, the complexion of this enterprise seems to have changed. In the spring of 1881 a formal memorial, endorsed by Chin Lan-pin, the minister at Washington, was addressed to the home government, complaining of the course of study pursued by these youths as including Latin and Greek and other unnecessary subjects; of the disrespectful behavior of the boys when brought before their chiefs; of their deplorable lack of patriotism; of their forgetting their mother tongue, and other sins of omission and commission. The memorial seems to have fallen in with the desires of those momentarily in power at Peking; the commission and students were all recalled by the return mail, and arrived at Shanghai in the fall of the same year.

Although this action may have been in some degree prompted by a spirit of conservatism and distrust, the leading motive of the Chinese government cannot be far to seek. Had these boys of a dozen years each received his fifteen years' instruction in our common-school, classical, and professional courses, it is impossible to believe that they would not at the end of this time have been more American than Chinese. Their speedy recall was a matter of regret to the many friends these interesting lads had made in New England, but from a truly Chinese stand-point this foreign popularity would become as the flesh-pots of Egypt to them after their return to the arid intellectual life in China—and the event in one or two instances appears to have proved the shrewdness of this surmise. However, this experiment can in no wise be considered a failure, even if we consider only the knowledge of English and elements of a western education obtained by each student; how considerable has been its success will be seen when the young men—now engaged by their government in telegraph posts, arsenals, schools, etc.—shall have achieved sufficient distinction in their various professions to prove their fitness for the pains bestowed upon them. The organization of schools for other than Chinese methods of education is already begun in China—as, for example, the Tung-wăn Kwan, under charge of Dr. Martin, at Peking—and from these a much more rational advance to their proper position in scientific knowledge may be expected, than by hazardous schemes of foreign tuition.

CHAPTER VIII.

NARRATIVE OF RECENT EVENTS.

THREE occurrences of paramount importance constitute the main interest of the dozen years which followed those described in the preceding chapter. The first of these was a collision with France; the second, a great wave of anti-foreign feeling which carried terror to the hearts of every European and American resident of the Middle Kingdom; the third, a war with Japan, which, with incredible suddenness, swept China out of the list of the world's great powers, and set free all those elements of disaffection within the nation that have for a century threatened her political existence. Other happenings in this brief period are only important as intimations of progress, or the reverse, in her slow advance toward the ideals of modern statecraft. They are indications rather than achievements, while these great events comprehend consequences direct and indirect that are likely to affect permanently her national destiny. Taking them up in the order of their coming it is necessary first to consider the position and policy of France in Southeastern Asia, and the causes that involved the Republic in hostilities with China.

The beginning of French interest in Indo-China dates from the year 1787, when at the instigation of a patriotic missionary bishop, Monsignor Pigneaux de Behaine, the head of the exiled royal house of Annam, appealed to King Louis XVI. for assistance in regaining his throne. The outbreak of the French Revolution prevented the execution of the agreement then made, but the energetic missionary, fired by his ambition to recover for his country her lost foothold in Southern Asia, actually equipped two merchant ships at Pondicherry with war materials and officers sufficient to help King Gia Long defeat the rebels and reconquer his dominions. In return for this help the sovereign, who now assumed the dignity of Emperor, gave certain liberties to French and Spanish missionaries, and hired French engineers to fortify his chief cities. His successors, however, persecuted the fathers and their converts, and it was not until the reign of Louis Napoleon that France could conveniently insist upon a strict observance of the terms of the treaty of 1787. In August, 1858, a French fleet destroyed the forts at Tourane, the seaport of Hué, but finding an advance upon the capital impracticable, abandoned this attempt and captured the town of Saigon in the South.

Very little was then known about this portion of Asia, but it soon became manifest that the Annamese were disposed to resist to the uttermost this foreign occupation, and that in seizing Cochin-China, rather than Tongking, as a site for their colonial experiment, the French had miscalculated. It was hoped that the control of the Mekong delta would give them access to the whole inland district lying between Burma and the China Sea, besides tapping the trade of the populous provinces of Southern China. The publication of the results of an exploring expedition under Captain Doudart de Lagrée[1] showed, however, that the great river was unnavigable, but that a shorter waterway from Yunnan to the sea might be found in the Red River, or Song-koi (the Hong kiang or Yüan kiang of the Chinese), the chief stream of Tongking.

The Saigon authorities were enthusiastic about the development of a French colonial empire, and their representations to the home government became more insistent as the deficit in the Cochin-Chinese budget developed. It was not a difficult matter to send a vessel to the Red River delta to investigate the pirates, then to irritate and terrify the local officials at the provincial capital, and thereby to create an occasion for armed intervention. Admiral Dupré, the French Governor of Cochin-China, sent Lieutenant Garnier, in November, 1873, to Hanoi with a handful of soldiers to arbitrate in the matter. Garnier,

[1] *Voyage d'exploration en Indo-Chine effectué pendant les années*, 1866, 1867 *et* 1868, *par une commission française*, par Fr. Garnier. 2 vols. and atlas. Paris, 1873.

who was in unscrupulousness and daring a survival of the sixteenth-century adventurers, showed his conception of the word arbitration by at once demanding of the Governor of Hanoi a treaty giving the French free sway in the delta, and because the Governor demurred, pleading no authority for such negotiations, the impetuous Frenchman proclaimed the Red River open to foreign commerce, and five days later took the citadel of Hanoi by assault. This was followed by the capture of nearly all the strong places between Hanoi and the sea. Within a month after his arrival the whole of lower Tongking lay at the mercy of the young lieutenant and some two hundred Frenchmen.[1] The Annamese, in their plight, called upon the suzerain state of China for protection, an appeal that China had exceptional opportunity in this instance for complying with at once.

The French have repeatedly decried the pretensions of China with regard to Annam as a figment, but there is no proper reason to doubt the reality of the political relationship, or of Annam's recognition of her obligations to the court of Peking. The whole of this region was annexed (B.C. 214) by the great conqueror, Tsin Chi Hwangti, when feudal China was consolidated and expanded to about her present limits. In time the outlying territories of this vast empire regained some degree of autonomy under sovereigns of their own, receiving investiture from the Son of Heaven, but for the most part doing what they pleased at home. The settlement during many centuries of Chinese in the northern provinces of the Annamese empire has rendered this region quite Chinese as to population, with the result that its people have long looked rather to Peking than to Hué when protection or interference in their affairs is involved. The policy of China during the present century toward this, as toward other vassals, seems to have been to ex-

---

[1] *Histoire de l'intervention française au Tongking*, par F. Romanet du Caillaud, Paris, 1880. The narrative of the French adventurer, Dupuis, who was filibustering on the Song-koi at this time with a view to open the river to trade is found in the *Bulletin de la Société de Géographie* for July and August, 1877, and in the *Mémoires de la Société Académique Indo-Chinoise de Paris*, Tome II., 1879.

act as little as possible from her dependents in the hope that they would call upon her as seldom as possible for aid. Yet when the safety of a subject state is really menaced by a foreign power, she has not failed to fulfil in her mediæval fashion the duties of liege.[1]

Besides their dependence upon Chinese rather than Annamese authority in case of need, the civil officials in Tongking had for many years maintained a precarious tenure, amid frequent rebellions, solely upon the suffrance of organized bands of outlaws and pirates who went under the general name of "Black Flags." These were originally scattered remnants of the Tai-ping rebels who fled to the wild regions along the southern borders of China to escape the rigorous persecution which followed them wherever the arm of the Chinese official could reach. Owing to the physical character of this country, as well as to the lawlessness of its people, the Black Flags lived upon dakoity and piracy, retreating to the mountains, or out to sea when hard pressed, but for the most part secure in their infamous business because willing occasionally to share their plunder with the mandarins on both sides of the border.[2]

It also happened that during the Mohammedan rebellion in Yunnan a considerable number of Chinese troops had been moved into Tongking to prevent the escape of the insurgents in

---

[1] China's claims to suzerainty over Korea were analogous to these, and are discussed later. In 1875 she became involved in a dispute with the Japanese Minister to Peking, because Lewchewan tribute-bearers were received by the Emperor when Japan's authority over the Islands had been virtually conceded by China. On this occasion the French Minister made strenuous efforts to have the Japanese Envoy lay the matter before his colleagues, but the foreign representatives in Peking declined to co-operate.—*United States Foreign Relations*, 1875, Part I., p. 314.

[2] Tongking, or Dongkinh, "Capital of the North," is another name for Hanoi, applied by extension to the thirteen northern provinces of Annam; other names are Danghai, "Outside Kingdom;" Baktanh, or Bakki, "Kingdom of the North;" and Yuan, the term employed in Cantonese; *Tonquin* is a poor French effort to convey the sound Dongkinh. The province falls into three natural divisions, the delta, an isoseles triangle consisting of the low river basin—a fertile alluvial land covered with a network of rivers and canals—the plateaux north of this, rising steadily toward China and Laos to pine-clad mountains, and the forests in the northwest, mostly impenetrable jungle held by Laos and other aboriginal tribes.

this direction—a right pertaining to China's suzerainty—and these regulars under a Chinese commander were now occupying the towns of Bakninh and Sontai. There appears to have been some understanding between the Chinese garrisons and the Black Flags that enabled the latter to carry on their depredations with impunity, while the Chinese officers were not above acting in concert with them in face of the common enemy, the intruding French. The advantage of this arrangement was that the Imperial government could at its pleasure disavow any action which it was not convenient to acknowledge. Governor Dupré addressed requests to the Viceroys of Yunnan and the two Kwang to withdraw their troops from Annam on the beguiling ground that China ought not to bear the entire cost of policing the frontier,[1] while he advised the court at Hué that Garnier was sent to the Song-koi delta with no other object than "to convey to M. Dupuis [a French commercial adventurer entrenched with a small force above Hanoi] the order to withdraw, and to make him do so if he refused to obey with good grace." [2]

These preliminary explanations are of interest in view of the events that followed, and of the charge of treachery brought by the French against the Chinese. It is not surprising, when we recall the practically independent nature of a Viceroy's rule within his satrapy, that the Chinese governors paid no heed to Admiral Dupré's offer to share with him the responsibility of guarding the frontier, or that, when the Black Flags responded in large numbers to the Annamese appeal for aid, there were a good many Chinese braves among them. The new enemy swarmed down upon Garnier's garrison at Hanoi, now much depleted by detachments left to guard the various strongholds in the Delta, and after a succession of skirmishes lured the dash-

---

[1] "Il n'est pas juste que je laisse à votre Excellence tout le fardeau de la protection des intérêts du commerce dans une région, le Tonkin, aussi voisine de Saïgon."—Letter of Admiral Dupré to the Viceroy of the two Kwang, C. B. Norman, *Tonkin, or France in the Far East*, p. 102.

[2] Compare Paul Melon, *Le Tonking. Les événements de* 1873 *et* 1874, *etc.*, Paris, 1881; and P. de Villeneuve, *Les affaires du Tonkin et le traité français*, Paris, 1874.

ing lieutenant to his death in an ambush, driving the French back to the citadel in disorder (December 21st). Fortunately for the French, the negotiator appointed to repair the errors of Garnier, M. Philastre, was a man of honor and sense. He reached Hanoi a fortnight after the disaster, ordered the forts held by Garnier's troops to be evacuated, and arranged a treaty with Annam, providing for the free navigation of the Song-koi as far as Yunnan, the opening of Hanoi, Thinnai, and Ninhha to trade, and the establishment in them of consuls and their escorts to control Europeans, and if need were to refuse them permission to reside in the country; a French Resident was in the future to live in Hué, and France was, in general, to treat the country as her own preserve, where no other foreigners need apply for admission.[1]

By the treaty of 1874 France acquired a virtual protectorate over Tongking at the price of withdrawing her troops from the fortified towns, but owing to the disturbed condition of the country, the hatred of the Annamese, and the jealousy of the Chinese, this latter condition effectually vitiated the advantages which the French counted as already theirs. The contest became now one of diplomacy rather than of arms, since France was unable so soon after the prostration following upon her war with Germany to openly avow her intention of carving out by sheer force an Indo-Chinese empire. China neither withdrew her claim to suzerainty over Annam nor her troops from Tongking, and when in 1876 the usual tribute-bearing embassy left Annam for Peking under the eyes of a French consul, he was, for prudential reasons, obliged to refrain from protesting. An occasion occurred in 1879 for China to exercise still more effectively her historical right to protect Annam, when King Tu Duc called upon her, and not upon France, to suppress a rebellion in Tongking. Peace was restored by means of Chinese braves in January, 1880,[2] and French prestige further reduced in Southern Asia by the despatch of an-

---

[1] The text of the treaty, ratified in August, 1874, is to be found in C. B. Norman's *Tonkin*, pp. 148–156; the author's reflections upon the conduct of both Dupré and Garnier are severe but not unjust.

[2] Decree published in the *Peking Gazette* of January 25, 1880.

other mission of gratitude to the Emperor for his benevolence in a time of need.

The affairs of Indo-China did not seriously interest the French nation. This anomalous and uncomfortable condition might have continued indefinitely, in spite of representations made by Frenchmen in the East, had it not been for the selection of M. de Freycinet, a believer in an aggressive foreign policy, as Minister of Foreign Affairs. He initiated a plan, carried out subsequently by his successors, whereby the King of Annam should be made to understand by an adequate display of material force the real intent of the treaty of 1874. Early in 1882 the first instalment of French troops arrived in the China Sea, despatched under Commandant Henri Rivière to re-enforce the two companies of the consular guard which had been shut up in the provincial capital for more than a year. The new commander was bidden to avoid hostilities, but, like Garnier, he was a fighting man, and in a country where anarchy was rampant, a crisis was inevitable.[1] It was a melancholy repetition of the man and the events of 1873. Rivière could obtain nothing from the Annamites except by force, and these were encouraged in their aggressive attitude both by fresh troops sent from China and by strengthened defences in their strong places. After a year spent chiefly in Hanoi, waiting for reinforcements, during which time the Black Flags swarmed about the city, cutting off stragglers and harassing the garrison, the commander determined to make a demonstration, and on May 19, 1884, lost his life in a sortie, a victim to the same contempt of the enemy that had ended the career of Garnier.[2]

This disaster had the immediate effect of precipitating the conquest of Tongking. What had been sent out as an expedition to give France "an honorable situation" in Asia be-

---

[1] Mr. Henry Norman describes Rivière as being "an extremely gallant, but very nervous, man, ambitious of literary honors, who had said, 'Je m'en vais par le Tonkin à l'Académie.'"—*The Peoples and Politics of the Far East*, p. 88. Compare Jules Gros, *Origines de la conquête du Tonkin*, Paris, 1887.

[2] Hippolyte Gautier, *Les Français au Tonkin*, Paris, 1884, presents the French view of these events with the nearest approach to moderation.

came now the vanguard of an armed invasion. The Chamber at Paris voted credits for a sufficient army to accomplish its purpose, the capital of Annam itself was attacked and its sovereign, Tu Duc's successor, made to sign a peace recognizing the protectorate of France, and to destroy the seal of investiture which his predecessors had for centuries held as vassals of China. The court at Peking refused to recognize the validity of the treaty of 1883, as they had that of 1874, and after declaring that an attack by the French upon the imperial garrisons at Sontai or Bakninh would be considered as a *casus belli*, its minister, the Marquis Tsăng, was withdrawn from Paris. Both cities were taken (December, 1883, and March, 1884). A French army had met a Chinese army in open battle, and Tongking was reduced to subjection, yet war was not declared. The Imperial government was startled but not dismayed at the rapid successes of the French. It displayed considerable activity in forwarding troops and accumulating war material, but, conscious of its military weakness, it did not venture to invite a war.[1]

While the French legislature voted fresh sums to continue a war which was not acknowledged to be a war, the feeling in Peking culminated in a sudden change of ministers, when "the Empress Regent took personal action and of her own motion deprived Prince Kung and several other ministers of all their offices, and imposed condign punishment upon all who were responsible for the failure in Tongking."[2] Prince Kung was

[1] Three iron corvettes were ordered from Stettin, "but, though launched, the German government would not allow them to leave while the controversy between France and China continued unsettled. The observance of international duty was the more necessary as it was stated that the Chinese army had been brought to a state of high efficiency through the teaching of German officers, the French military instructors originally engaged having failed in their task."—*Annual Register*, 1883, p. 366. A few of the numerous French publications on this war are the *Livre jaune, Affaires du Tonkin*, two vols., 1883 ; ditto, *Exposé de la situation*, 1883 ; H. Cordier, *Le consulat de France à Hué sous la restauration*, 1884 ; Deschanel, *La question du Tonkin*, 1883 ; Dick de Lonlay, *L'Amiral Courbet et le "Bayard,"* 1885 ; L. Huard, *La guerre illustrée. Chine, Tonkin, Annam ;* G. Lafitte, *La verité sur le Tonkin, etc.*, 1888.

[2] S. Lane Poole, *Life of Sir Harry Parkes*, Vol. II., p. 375. The fall of

thus, after years of public service and in the prime of life, relegated to obscurity, and his place as head of foreign affairs taken by his brother, Prince Chun, the Seventh Prince, father of the reigning emperor.

Under these circumstances, at the suggestion of Mr. Detring of the Chinese Customs Service, the French Admiral was put in communication with the Viceroy Li Hung-chang, who secured a rather grudging consent from the Imperial court to discuss terms of peace.[1] Captain Fournier was sent to Tientsin with the proper powers from his government, and on May 11th the result of the negotiation was announced: France engaged to "protect the southern frontier of China" and to ask for no indemnity, in return for which China was to withdraw her troops from Tongking "immediately," to respect in the future treaties concluded between France and Annam, and allow trade along the whole extent of their conterminous frontiers in accordance with a tariff agreement to be subsequently made. This convention aroused extraordinary odium both in Paris and Peking. The Chinese objected because their suzerainty over Annam had been reduced to a fiction, and forty-seven memorials are said to have been addressed to the Throne demanding the impeachment of Li as a traitor; the French protested because the fiction of suzerainty was allowed to remain after eighteen months of hard campaigning; and, among those less directly involved but not less concerned, the English saw with anxiety the southern provinces of China opened up for the exclusive benefit of their French rivals.[2] It is impossible to avoid the conclusion that France was poorly served in her diplomatic efforts at this juncture. There seems to have been some discussion at Tientsin as to the time allowed the Chinese

---

Prince Kung was thought to mean the triumph of the war party in the palace, but the Empress, it appears on the authority of Sir Robert Hart, did not desire war with France, and dismissed her advisers for not informing her of the fall of Bakninh directly they received the news, while the mandarins were punished as a lesson to military men.

[1] R. K. Douglas, *Life of Li Hung-chang*, p. 208.

[2] *Blue Book—China*, No. 1 (1886). *Correspondence respecting the French Treaty with Annam, and Negotiations between France and China*, 56 pages.

to withdraw from Tongking. The Viceroy stipulated for three months, the Captain for three weeks. The latter is accused by the Chinese of having erased with his own hand the dates which he declares upon his honor were agreed to by Li and himself in a memorandum of May 17th. Before contradictions such as these, as a Frenchman once observed, "on salue et on passe;"[1] but it would seem an obvious precaution in a diplomatist to see that a paper was signed by both parties before undertaking to carry out its intent. On the date named by the French negotiator (June 21st) Colonel Dugenne appeared before Langson and demanded its evacuation. The Chinese general plead want of instructions for such withdrawal, and in a communication—which no one in the French camp at the time could read—asked for ten days in which to refer to Peking. Dugenne, with a very inadequate force, thereupon tried to capture the place, and was driven back with heavy loss.[2]

Hostilities, which both sides had been willing to conclude, were now renewed with vigor. The fighting in Tongking became increasingly difficult as the tropical climate told upon the European troops, and as they were compelled to leave the Delta and follow the elusive enemy among the mountains and forests. Langson, the principal fortress on the northern frontier of Tongking, was not occupied by the French until February 13, 1885. The Chinese in July again offered to renew negotiations, but the French, now thoroughly angry, only proposed impossible terms and closed their legation at Peking. Admiral Courbet, after announcing his orders to make reprisals for Langson, blockaded the coast of Formosa (August 1st), and two weeks later, taking advantage of the fact that no war was declared, passed the fortified estuary of the Min and assembled nine vessels of his fleet opposite the Chinese squadron and arsenal below Foochow. On August 23d Courbet, having demanded the immediate surrender of the fleet and forts and

[1] R. S. Gundry, *China and Her Neighbours*, p. 94.

[2] "It was only the desperate gallantry of the forty or fifty *chasseurs d'Afrique* that saved the whole column from annihilation."—J. G. Scott, *France and Tongking*, p. 150.

been refused, began firing upon the Chinese ships, numbering eleven, all of wood, and in seven minutes completed their destruction. The utter incapacity of the Chinese may have been due to their foolish conviction that the French would never execute their threat in earnest, and the paralysis of fear that ensued when their entire fleet seemed to be going up in one explosion ; but no excuse can be offered for their commander, who allowed such a trap to be closed about him. The defenceless arsenal was then burned with all its machinery and stores, and a few days later the Mingan and the Kinpai forts stormed and taken from the rear.[1] This first act of reprisal accomplished, the French, after some desultory raids along the coast, resumed operations against Formosa, captured Kelung (October 4th), and did their best with the ships at their command to make the blockade of the island effective.

The Chinese, despite their losses, showed a grim determination to continue the contest. Under the spur of necessity they rallied their forces, repaired the Foochow defences, and made Port Arthur impregnable; telegraph lines were rapidly stretched, connecting the capital with all parts of the Empire, and German officers were hired to drill the army. In Formosa, as well as Tongking, nature and numbers greatly assisted their efforts. The French found it impossible to penetrate far inland in either place without covering the country with garrisons, and this exhausted all their troops. After five vain attacks the Petao forts near Kelung were taken,[2] and in March, 1885, the French occupied the Pescadore group. Things were less satisfactory in Tongking. A guerilla war in such a country,

---

[1] This was the affair which Pierre Loti has called "la grande gloire de Fou-tchéou." An account of the attack appears in Deputy-Commissioner Carrall's *Report*, published by the Imperial Chinese Maritime Customs, Shanghai, 1885. The United States Minister, Mr. Young, was able to call the attention of the Tsung-li Yamun to the fact that about the only act of conspicuous gallantry in his Imperial Majesty's fleet was performed by some of the young Chinese students who had been educated in America and who had been ordered home on the plea that they had become "denationalized."—*United States Foreign Relations*, 1885, p. 144.

[2] A mutiny on board the *Bayard* during these operations is significant of the state of discipline and spirit in the French fleet.

where, with no roads and no cavalry, it was almost impossible to follow the enemy, proved more than sufficient to satisfy the appetites of the French soldiers for a little glory. Langson had hardly been occupied after hard fighting when the French had to evacuate it (April, 1885) and withdraw all their troops to the Delta awaiting further reinforcements. The total array of French forces in Tongking when hostilities with China ceased was 43,000 men, including sailors, marines, and drilled natives, together with 75 vessels of all kinds.

A contest which from lack of adequate motive had degenerated into a series of buccaneering expeditions disguised as acts of forfeit or reprisal could not but seriously affect the affairs of all foreigners in China. The customary law of nations would not apply to regulate their action, since where there was no formal state of war, there could of course be no neutrals. Trade at Shanghai was prostrated through no fault of the powers, for, as the British minister wrote in reply to a request for neutralizing that port, "if this is to be effected by the action of the neutral powers, the latter must be prepared to take Shanghai into their hands and *compel* both French and Chinese to observe strict neutrality."[1] Complaints by both China and France, however, of the use by each of Hongkong as a practical base of operations at length aroused the British authorities to consider the blockade of Formosa the equivalent of a declaration of war. The provisions of the Foreign Enlistment Act were made to apply to both belligerents, but this, it must be observed, was not so rigorously enforced as a stern and unbending neutrality would seem to require. The Chinese were altogether prohibited from repairing to the harbor, but, their own coasts being near, the inconvenience was not severe. The French, with no supply station of their own in these waters, were allowed to take sufficient coal and provisions to carry them to their nearest port, Saigon—all the difference to them between success and failure in their operations. The action of the Viceroy of Kwangtung in obstructing both river passages to Canton so as to prevent the entry of foreign vessels called forth the pro-

---

[1] *Life of Parkes*, Vol. II., p. 379.

tests of the legations in Peking, which eventually secured the partial removal of the barriers.[1]

Efforts to bring the contestants to discuss new terms were continued during the winter through the British legation with such success that by April 4, 1885, preliminaries of peace had been arranged at Peking between M. Billot and Sir Robert Hart, Inspector-General of the Chinese Customs Service. The embarrassments of the French were numerous. Tongking was theirs only so far as their soldiers occupied the ground; none of their intentions had been realized; China, indifferent to their troops in Formosa as in Annam, seemed impervious to anything short of an armed invasion; such an attempt would require at least a *corps d'armée*, perhaps two; but the military organization of France was such that to mobilize a corps meant putting the whole stress of a foreign war upon the few departments whence the corps came, and "Tonkin" Ferry had already heard a good deal about the sons of France lying dead in the jungle. On the other hand, without the definite and crushing effect of such an invasion could the French hope to hold their own in the tropical wilds south of China, where the dispirited troops were likely to be overcome by the mere multitude of the enemy? The situation was one calculated to check the jingoism of even the Ferry ministry, nor were the Chinese unaware of their antagonist's predicament. They were reaping now one of the advantages which they had only doubtfully anticipated in creating permanent legations abroad, and they needed no instruction as to making use of their knowledge of French domestic politics thus obtained. The French began negotiations firm in the conviction that the war ought to bring them a large indemnity and valuable concessions; but the Chinese, knowing the difficulties that would beset the path of a French cabinet which asked for more men and money, held fast to their terms and achieved a diplomatic victory. The treaty concluded at Tientsin by M. Patenôtre and Li Hung-chang, June 9th, on the basis of the preliminaries of April 4th, secured for France none of the great advantages she

---

[1] *United States Foreign Relations*, 1884, pp. 64, 66, 96.

had expected. It was substantially the same agreement that had been rejected twelve months before—Kelung and the Pescadores were to be evacuated, Annam was to have no diplomatic relations except through France,[1] the frontier was to be delimited by a commission, two towns in Southern China, one beyond Laokai, the other beyond Langson, were to be opened to foreign trade and the residence of consuls, while a special trade agreement regulating traffic and dues was provided for within three months. The trade arrangement was concluded and the treaty formally ratified at Paris in July, 1886. Its two most important articles gave merchandise passing across the border one-fifth less duty on imports, and one-third less on exports than was exacted at other open ports. Trade in opium was totally prohibited. In what the French tried especially to secure, an indemnity for the cost of the war, a Resident at Tali fu, or some centre of Yunnan, the right to collect a poll-tax on Chinese immigrants to Tongking, and to build whatever railways China intended to introduce, they failed entirely. Thus ended what was euphuistically called "the simultaneous intervention in the affairs of Annam." At the end of the year 1885 a special commission was sitting at Paris to consider whether, on the whole, Tongking was worth keeping; it had already cost the French nation some 250,000,000 francs.

So general was the dissatisfaction in France at the ostensible result of the war so far as commercial privileges were concerned, that M. Constans was sent to Peking in 1887 to renew the discussion with the Chinese. He was measurably successful. In an Additional Convention, signed June 26, 1887, the prohibition of trade in opium was withdrawn, the south of China was made more accessible to French trade by opening Manghao as a third place for traffic in addition to Măngtsz' and Lungchow,

---

[1] But "En ce qui concerne les rapports entre la Chine et l'Annam, il est entendu qu ils seront de nature à ne point porter atteinte à la dignité de l'Empire Chinois, et à ne donner lieu à aucune violation du présent traité." Thus China's "face was saved."—*Blue Book—China*, No. 1 (1886); A. Daniel, *L'Année politique*, 1885, p. 128; for Ferry's defence of the convention, *ib.*, 1884, p. 91.

already provided as treaty ports in Yunnan and Kwangsi, respectively, and import and export dues were slightly reduced on the schedule of 1886. But China retained her precious monopoly in salt, as well as a right to maintain consuls in certain Tongking towns, besides securing the Paklung Promontory on the coast frontier, claimed by both. The hope that Tongking opium might compete with that from India in Southern China has not been fulfilled, and opium seems now likely to go from Yunnan to Tongking instead of the other way. The two new ports of entry mentioned were occupied by their consular and customs staffs in July, 1889. A French railway from the Song-koi to Langson has been built, and small steamers are able to pass the rapids to Laokai; "but no trade of the kind expected has come"[1] thus far on the first route, indicating that there is more scope for developing traffic with Southwestern China than with the two Kwang provinces. On the other hand, the Red River commerce with Yunnan showed in 1895 an increase of thirty per cent. over the previous year, the total amount being 12,000,000 francs.

The Chinese government had now become convinced of the desirability of strengthening the country by the adoption of many Western economical devices, but it showed itself very reluctant to grant trading and financial concessions to foreigners. Still, signs of the long-expected "awakening" were not wanting. In 1882 it had given an intimation of a desire to conform to European customs by creating an Order of the Double Dragon, with insignia consisting of a jewelled star and ribbon, to be conferred only on distinguished foreigners. Much was also said about the construction of a system of railways, which, with the improvement of the navy and coast defence, scientific mining and manufactures, regulation of finances and encouragement of foreign studies, were part of the elaborate

[1] *C. I. M. Customs Decennial Reports*, 1882–91, pp. 653–680. The text of the Additional Convention is given in *United States Foreign Relations*, 1887, p. 232. Dr. L. Pichon in *Un voyage au Yunnan*, Paris, 1893, takes a much more optimistic view of the possibilities of the Red River route, though deploring the lack of enterprise shown by his countrymen in developing their opportunity here.

programme of reform outlined in the dying memorial of General Tso Tsung-tang to the Throne.[1] As though to prove to the world that these patriotic proposals were not to pass unheeded, Prince Chun, the head of the new Marine Board, emerged from the seclusion of the Palace and made, in the summer of 1886, a journey of inspection to the fleet and arsenals at Tientsin and Port Arthur, reviewing the troops of the new model organized by Li Hung-chang, and learning for himself what had been already accomplished. The appearance in public of the first Prince of the Imperial House, and his reception of foreign representatives, did not fail to create a profound impression wherever this departure from ancient custom was known. Captain Lang, an Englishman, was made admiral of the Peiyang, or northern fleet, and entrusted with the duty of providing and training an adequate naval force in five years. The Nanyang, or southern fleet, with head-quarters at Foochow, was kept distinct from the other squadron, in conformity with the established practice of dividing responsibility and checking, if possible, any tendency to sedition. This arrangement was but one of a thousand indications of the appalling prevalence of corruption everywhere in official circles, a cause of the slow improvement in Chinese affairs, and of the lack of success in exploiting the most obviously profitable measures to develop the resources of the country. The dry rot of dishonesty, having so long corrupted the body politic, was not to be eradicated by superficial and spasmodic efforts like these. Those best acquainted with Chinese character and institutions were least optimistic as to the regeneration that should spring from the adoption of modern armaments and the application of steam and electricity so long as these appliances were treated as costly toys by ignorant and prejudiced officials without the rudiments of technical education.[2]

---

[1] Printed in full in *United States Foreign Relations,* 1885, p. 176. The collected works of both Tso Tsung-tang and Tsăng Kwoh-fan have been published in China since their deaths. They are valuable for their information in regard to Chinese administration.

[2] A journey made in 1882 by Messrs. Colquhoun and Wahab from Canton across South China to Bahmo showed a sad condition of decay in a magnifi-

While the Imperial ministers were contesting the excessive demands of France in 1885 an agreement was reached by Lord Salisbury and the Marquis Tsăng, at London, amending the opium article of the Chifu convention of 1876, the terms of which had not been ratified. This compact, in a sense the last legacy of the Opium War, provided that the drug should pay besides the stipulated tariff (£30 per chest) a sum not higher than £80 per chest in lieu of *likin*, or internal transit dues. Though the additional tax appears enormous, the merchants were gainers by the bargain because of its fixed nature, the old system involving the indiscriminate levying of toll wherever a local mandarin was powerful or rapacious enough to erect a *likin* station. The practice of giving a voucher or transit pass to imported goods that had payed a fixed and recognized tax at their port of entry, commended itself to the government because the Imperial revenue thereby directly profited, while the old *likin* dues that escaped the clutch of dishonest officials went into provincial treasuries. This regulation of the opium trade was therefore only a belated application of a system that had for some time worked successfully in the case of other imports.[1] The solution of this problem was followed in 1886 by the appointment by both these nations of commissioners "to enable the Chinese to protect their revenue without prejudice to the interests of the colony of Hongkong." That colony had become a nest of smugglers almost from its origin, but of late years the Chinese having provided themselves with steam cruisers capable of effectively following pirates and smugglers, the Hongkong merchants complained that the revenue police unduly interfered with their legitimate junk trade. The commission, after declining the Chinese proposal to establish a Custom House in the colony, agreed to

---

cent region, once populous and flourishing, brought to ruin by a rebellion that was due to the shameless robbery and corruption of officials.—A. R. Colquhoun. *Across Chrysê.*, 2 vols., London, 1883. Compare also A. R. Agassiz's *From Haiphong to Canton Overland*, in *Proceedings* of the Roy. Geog. Soc., May, 1891.

[1] In 1890 the cultivation of the poppy in China, which had reached enormous proportions, was at length legalized—the final act in the long struggle against the inevitable.

forbid the import and export of raw opium there in quantities less than one chest, except by the person who farmed the prepared-opium privilege, who could, of course, be properly controlled. A customs station was placed at Kowlung under the Inspector-General to issue opium clearances at the new rate and investigate complaints.

The settlement of this business was conditional upon the consent of the authorities in Macao to an identical arrangement, and the co-operation of the two colonies in the same revenue district. This was effected in 1887 by a new treaty between China and Portugal that involved also the conclusion of an old controversy. Macao having been occupied by the Portuguese and their descendants since 1537, had never ceased to be technically Chinese soil. At first the customary tribute from dependents was exacted by the Emperor every third year, but in 1582 this was commuted for an annual rental of Tls. 500; this was paid until 1849, since which time the town had been tacitly treated as Portuguese soil by China, though no open retraction of her historical claims could be extorted. She succeeded, however, in selling her nominal rights of sovereignty and arrears of rent at a good price in the compact now made, the losses by smuggling in these waters having of late years reached alarming proportions.[1] Another change in political relationship about this time (1888) involved a complete alteration in the status of Roman Catholic missionaries in China. It had been the policy of Napoleon III. to consider all priests of the Propaganda of whatsoever nationality in the Far East as under the protection of France, a protection that, while never recognized by any treaty, was often extended to native converts. The war with France had lately shown what dangers lurked in this state of affairs. Priests from Italy, Spain, and Germany travelled under French passports, secured French intercession in complaints against mandarins, and were suspected of giving aid and information to French troops during their operations. It being impossible to obtain

---

[1] *Chinese Recorder*, April, 1889. The Portuguese appear to be steadily declining in wealth and numbers, the proportion of Chinese in Macao being as twelve to one.

a permanent legation from the Curia to control the whole body of Papist missionaries, the various European governments were requested to take charge of their Catholic priests, as has always been customary in the case of Protestants. Germany and Italy immediately complied in withdrawing their subjects from French consular authority; the other Catholic countries were less prompt in making this assertion of proper national dignity, but their ultimate compliance has materially simplified the missionary problem in at least one phase. It is not unlikely that the way was in some degree prepared for this consummation by the removal, after long negotiation, of the Peitang Cathedral, which stood in Peking on an eminence overlooking the Imperial palace. The site was one that the French had claimed in 1860 as part of the old Catholic possessions in the capital, and the erection there of a large building had wounded the sensibilities and superstitions of the Chinese court and people alike. The tardy consent of the Lazarists to accept another and less offensive location for their establishment was so gratefully appreciated by the government as to influence for a time its attitude toward all Christian bodies and their converts.

What might be called a temporary era of good feeling between European and Chinese diplomatists, following the rather fortunate outcome of China's difficulties with France, was further marked in this year by an Anglo-Chinese convention as to Burma. In this agreement, signed at Peking, July 24, 1886, Great Britain was given by China the same sort of administrative and official authority in Inner or "Independent" Burma that had recently been allowed France in Annam in consequence of a war. The Queen's Ministers thus obtained a practical advantage quite equal to that secured by a political and commercial rival in a vassal state where Chinese pretensions to suzerainty were precisely similar; and this advantage was the result of peaceful discussion instead of a costly and unsatisfactory war. This result was reached by two concessions on the part of Great Britain which are remarkable as being the first of the kind ever granted by a European power to China, and as an instance of the material benefit often to be acquired in Asiatic intercourse by yielding enough for the Oriental "to save his face." By one of these stipulations the Emperor's formal suzerainty over Burma was recognized in allowing a decennial mission to be sent from that country, bearing a small tribute of produce to the court of the Grand Khan; by the other, England consented to postpone until some convenient season a mission of exploration to the capital of Tibet, which was about to start from India. Both of these concessions were the objects of criticism and abuse on the part of advocates of a pushing policy in the East; but, apart from those extreme doctrines of international philanthropy which would condemn war under any circumstances, it is difficult to see wherein Great Britain lost by these concessions to Asiatic prejudice, or by exchanging the substance of practical control for the shadow of a suzerainty that is nothing more than a dignified withdrawal in lieu of a humiliation hard to bear.

Of somewhat the same character, as marking a new policy of conciliation toward China, were the negotiations which culminated this year in the restitution of Port Hamilton to Korea. This island, one of the Nan-how group, lying in latitude 34° off the south coast of Korea, was conveniently situated in the Straits of Korea so as to at once control the southern entrance to the Japan Sea and serve as a naval station for a fleet operating in the whole of the Hwang Hai, or Yellow Sea. Its position, therefore, concerned very intimately the interests of the three countries of Japan, Korea, and China, the latter as Korea's acknowledged suzerain—and it is improbable that the British Ministry telegraphed its order to Admiral Dowell in April, 1885, to "occupy Port Hamilton and report proceedings" without a previous understanding with these powers. Its object and theirs was to check Russia's suspected design of encroaching upon Korean territory, either on the south coast or at the roadstead in Broughton Bay, to which their navigators had already given the Russian name of Port Lazaref; the aggressive acts of Russian troops in seizing Pendjeh and other places on the Afghan frontier at this time made any suspicion of their intentions in Asia seem plausible to those who feared to be robbed or wronged. As a site for a fortress, Port Hamilton does not appear to have been approved by a majority of the British navy. Its harbor was too accessible from the sea to be secure without the presence of a squadron, while its fortification would involve heavy outlays. But while a discussion of these points was carried on in public, the secret purpose of this performance gradually transpired. During the year 1886 the Czar's ministers intimated with increasing warmth to the Tsung-li Yamun their impatience at England's continued occupation of this place, and at length declared their intention of seizing in their own behalf some place in Korea unless she withdrew. It only remained for the British cabinet through the Chinese representative at London to offer to retire from the island upon receiving a guarantee that it should not be occupied by any other European power. China, through these negotiations, was not displeased at having her pretensions to lordship over Korea treated seriously by Western statesmen; Japan was content to have her own freedom of action in these waters unhampered by the presence of any European; while England gained her ostensible object of keeping Russia out of the Korean Strait and extracting a promise that she would in future respect the integrity of Korea. The British flag was hauled down at Port Hamilton, February 27, 1887.[1]

The assumption by the young Emperor, Kwangsü, of the reins of government occurred at the beginning of the thirteenth year of his reign, February 7, 1887. In contrast to the precedent set in 1873, when Tungchi began to govern, the foreign legations received no formal notification of this event. A manifesto published in a Shanghai native paper, the *Shunpao*, of March 11th—but not in the official organ, the *Peking Gazette*—recorded the fact that the Empress had de-

---

[1] *Parliamentary Blue Book—China*, No. 1 (1887), containing the documentary evidence of the episode in full. In a despatch, on p. 37, Sir J. Walsham informs Lord Iddesleigh that the Russian Minister to Peking "had been empowered to offer the additional assurance that, in the event of the English occupation of Port Hamilton ceasing, Russia would undertake not to interfere with Corean territory under any circumstances"—a promise full of interesting possibilities for the future of this state. The story of Port Hamilton is told by Mr. R. S. Gundry in the *Westminster Review*, and republished in Chap. X. of his *China and Her Neighbours*, London, 1893.

clared his Imperial Majesty to be fit to rule. "When I heard of the decree," the document continues in customary Oriental phraseology, "I trembled as if I were in mid-ocean, not knowing where the land is. Her Majesty will, however, continue to advise me for a few years longer in important affairs of state. I shall not dare to be indolent, and, in obedience to the Empress's command, I have petitioned the Heaven and Earth and my Ancestors that I shall assume the administration of the government in person on the fifteenth day of the first moon, in the thirteenth year of my reign. Guided by the counsel of Her Majesty, everything will be done with care." The docility of the young sovereign's character may be inferred from his willingness to remain in a state of tutelage after the expiry of the legal term, but too much stress must not be laid upon the language he was made to employ in the rescript. In accordance with the policy outlined in this document the Empress Tsz' Hi continued in her regency until the month of March, 1889, when, having selected a bride for her Imperial Ward, she announced her intention of retiring from active participation in state affairs. These had been in her hands since the death of her husband, Hienfung, in 1861, and, considering the extraordinary difficulties of her position, powerless to emerge from the seclusion of a palace, and surrounded by ignorant and often interested counsellors, had been managed with great ability.

Since her formal retirement the Dowager Empress has no doubt exerted the influence due to a superior intellect and long experience, but to what extent she remains the power behind the throne is quite unknown.[1] The punishment of Li Hung-

[1] Colonel Charles Denby, United States Minister at Peking, sums up a resumé of her career in the following laudatory but not extravagant words: "To her own people she has been kind and merciful, and to foreigners she has been just. She leaves her country at peace with all the world, and destined by her influence to grasp the benefactions of foreign intercourse, and to assume a commanding place among the nations of the earth. While her own people will always venerate and bless her, history will rank her among the greatest rulers of mankind."—*United States Foreign Relations*, 1889, p. 100. She selected for the Emperor's first wife Yeh-ho-na-la, daughter of her brother, General Kwaisiang, and consequently the boy's own cousin, his

chang for visiting her without the imperial permission, at the Hai Tien Palace in the fall of 1896, indicates the existence of some jealousy of her continued influence in politics on the part of the Emperor.

The conventional exchange of compliments between the foreign representatives and the Foreign Office at Peking upon the double occasion of the Empress's retirement and the Emperor's nuptials calls for no comment except to note the banquet given by the Tsung-li Yamun to the ministers at command and in behalf of the Empress. This act of courtesy, which would be considered a matter of course in Europe, had especial significance here as indicating on the part of the Court a willingness to emerge from its old attitude of superiority and to enter into that spirit of comity which its rulers began to understand must exist among nations as well as among individuals. In December, 1890, in evident continuation of this amiable policy, there appeared an edict ordering an audience:

> In the first and second months of last year (it ran). when there were special reasons for expressing national joy, I received a gracious decree (from the Empress Dowager) ordering the Ministers of the Yamun for Foreign Affairs to entertain the Ministers of the foreign nations at a banquet. That occasion was a memorable and happy one. I have now been in charge of the Government for two years. The Ministers of foreign Powers ought to be received by me at an audience, and I hereby decree that the audience to be held be in accordance with that of the twelfth year of the reign of Tungchi (1873). It is also hereby decreed that a day be fixed every year for an audience, in order to show my desire to treat with honor all the Ministers of the foreign Powers resident in Peking, whether fully employed or temporarily in charge of the affairs of their governments. The Ministers of the Yamun for Foreign Affairs are hereby ordered to prepare in the first month of the ensuing New Year a memorial asking that a time for the audience may be fixed. On the

---

mother being a sister of the Dowager Empress. An account of the marriage appears in the *Asiatic Quarterly Review*, July, 1889. The consort of a Chinese emperor has no official name bestowed upon her until ten years after her marriage, unless she has in the meantime given birth to a son. Then and at subsequent solemn occasions titles of honor are given to her, Tsz' Hi having in her long career accumulated seven of these, expressed by two characters each. Their value derives from the fact that they entitle the recipient to Tls. 10,000 for each honorific character; thus the Dowager Empress secures an income of Tls. 140,000 for her long name.—Maurice Courant, *La cour de Péking*, p. 37, Paris, 1891.

next day the Foreign Ministers are to be received at a banquet at the Foreign Office. The same is to be done every year in the first month, and the rule will be the same on each occasion. New Ministers coming will be received at this annual audience.[1]

The foreign diplomatic body had wisely refrained from pressing the matter of an audience after the Emperor's formal accession, with the result of a free proffer instead of a reluctant assent to the ceremony, as in 1873. This much was gain; but there were some features in the case that left more to be desired. The foreigners had learned since their first memorable audience, what had before been suspected, that the Tsz' Kwang Koh, the hall of that ceremony, was objectionable as being the place where his Majesty received his vassals. Other points of detail requiring patient discussion related to the manner in which the envoys should deliver their letters of credence, the right of newly arrived Ministers to an audience without waiting until the following New Year day, the presence at the function of the entire staff of each Minister, etc. Trivial as such matters may appear to the Western mind, they possess in the East an importance that among Caucasians is monopolized by the logomachy of theology. It was a recurrence in a familiar form of the old dispute that had marked the whole intercourse of China with the West—the ever-present idea of superiority in the one party, which must be met and vanquished by the reasonable arguments of the other. The net result of the discussion, in which the foreign representatives acted as a unit, was a compromise with a tendency toward improvement in the future. The objectionable hall was accepted for the present, but was not to be again employed; the Ministers were to be attended by their suites; the letters were to be deposited near the Emperor, but not given into his own hand. The six foreign Ministers present at the capital were received separately and gave up their letters of credence at an audience, and immediately afterward they, with their staffs and the chargés d'affaires of Spain, Russia, France, and Belgium, returned in a body to the imperial presence (March

[1] *Peking Gazette*, December 12, 1890.

5, 1891). The Chinese were reluctant to fulfil all that their promise implied as to a change of hall when next year the Austrian Minister presented his letter. A new building was selected, but not one within the sacred precincts of the Palace proper. The French and Russian envoys refused to accept this half measure, which was, however, allowed by those from Great Britain and Germany in two audiences during 1893. But under stress of the military reverses in the following year the end was attained, sooner perhaps than might have been expected, and on November 12, 1894, the foreigners were honorably conducted to the Wăn-hwa-tien. It was the conclusion of a hundred years' struggle since the only other acceptable audience had occurred, that of the Emperor Kienlung and Lord McCartney, a period during which the rulers of China have often erred and been erred against, but in which they have fought sturdily for nothing as for this figment of supremacy represented in the audience dispute. The reluctant steps by which they have yielded point after point of etiquette are in a larger sense the stages of their advancement to modern political life; "a survey of these successive stages may help us to realize the magnitude of the change in Chinese conceptions since the Emperor ranked as the Solitary Man, and all the Princes of the world as tributaries and inferiors."[1]

Hopeful signs were not wanting in many parts that the Empire was at length really in control of those who realized that its political salvation depended upon its acceptance of certain Western institutions. The same year in which the Emperor attained his legal majority was signalized by the despatch of a dozen officials abroad to study European civilization, and by

---

[1] R. S. Gundry, *China, Present and Past*, p. 51, a volume containing much that is valuable and interesting about China's political circumstances. The documents in the audience question appear fully in the *United States Foreign Relations*, notably the volume for 1891. Mr. G. N. Curzon discusses the matter with his usual freedom from bias in his *Problems of the Far East*, pp. 285–296, and Dr. W. A. P. Martin touches it superficially, but with the authority of a long personal experience, in Chapter XIV. of his *Cycle of Cathay*, 1896. Other phases of the historic question are treated in the author's *Life of S. Wells Williams*, pp. 398 and 401, and *A Sketch of Russo-Chinese Intercourse*, printed in the *New Englander* for May, 1891.

the recognition of mathematics as a subject for study and competition in the civil service examinations. The effects of the first of these plans were obviously destined to be confined to the small circle of mandarins whose personal ambition led them to direct their attention to the diplomatic service of their country; of the second, however, much was reasonably expected, and it is but another indication of the enormous mass of inert ignorance needing to be quickened that from this leaven so little has yet come. To a memorial attributed to Prince Kung was due the Imperial Tungwăn College at Peking as a means to educate some portion of the literati class in Western learning. But this institution, the prototype of which has been so influential in the destinies of Japan, has proved only indirectly effectual in the work proposed in China, and inadequate to reach the great multitude of educated men away from the capital. Twenty years after the launching of this scheme of Prince Kung, his brother, Prince Chun, showed his appreciation of his country's needs by authorizing the introduction of some forms of Western studies as a preparation for official preferment. The prejudices of the old literati were considered in making these studies optional in the examinations, but there can be no doubt but that the change, timid and trivial though it appear to a European, is adapted, if honestly applied, to produce a general and permanent impression upon the minds of the present and coming generation. By this plan, moreover, the Tungwăn College was to be supplied with a class of students better fitted for its higher courses, successful mathematical graduates in the metropolitan examinations being entitled to appointments to the college. But thus far it must be confessed the promising scheme, though officially promulgated, has practically been of no avail.[1]

Even this modest encouragement is denied to those who have set their hearts upon the speedy introduction of railroads in the Empire. Many promises have been made to this end

[1] "Some mandarin more enlightened than the rest tries to get students in his neighborhood to take it up; but the practical effect upon the tone of the examinations has been next to null."—Gundry, *China, Past and Present*, p. 67. *United States Foreign Relations*, 1887, pp. 221 and 227.

by those in high places, and some fitful beginnings undertaken, but the magnitude of vested interests involved in this tremendous economic change has set the mandarins and people against it. Li Hung-chang has been, perhaps, the most powerful, as he has certainly been the most effective, advocate of a complete system of rail communication in China. A line covering part of the way to the Kaiping coal mines was quietly and rather slyly put through in 1883 by this energetic viceroy, and two years later he is credited with having won the boy-Emperor's heart by sending him a complete working model of a locomotive, passenger train, and rails to be laid down and run in the Palace garden. Schemes were outlined in this year and renewed in 1887 for four main lines—from Peking to Tientsin and the coast; from Tientsin to Chinkiang, or Nanking; from Nanking to Hangchow, or Shanghai; and from Canton to Nanning on the southern frontier. These projects were all abandoned, but in October, 1888, a road was opened from Tientsin past Taku to Kaiping, a distance of about ninety miles. This has been extended and successfully operated ever since. The war with Japan effectually converted many doubters in China, and lines from Tientsin to Hankow, to Peking, and to Manchuria are now ordered for strategic purposes, that in the latter direction, passing Shan-hai kwan, being at the end of the year 1896 completed for a distance of over two hundred miles.[1] In October, 1896, Russia was given permission to connect the trans-Siberian railway with the sea at Niuchwang or Port Arthur by constructing a line across Mongolia from Kiakhta, and also to join this road with Vladivostok via Kirin, the stations to be guarded by Russian troops. Such a compact, of course, involves a temporary protectorate exercised by Russia over all Manchuria. The roads operated at Tientsin are already profitable.

To the evidences of political and industrial improvement

---

[1] *United States Foreign Relations*, 1883. p. 199; 1885. p. 180; 1887, p. 208; 1889. p. 79, etc. *Annual Register*, 1887, and passim. The periodical publications are almost the only sources of information upon the subject thus far accessible. *Blackwood's Mag.*, March, 1894, p. 394; *Nineteenth Century*, Vol. 27, p. 225 (1890); *Le Correspondant*, 25 Mai, 1890, pp. 735–762.

which mark the year 1887 in China must be added some notice of an overflow of the Yellow River occurring in September, which for sheer destruction in life and property has perhaps hardly been equalled by any sudden cataclysm remembered in modern history. The waters of this great stream had found their way through the embankments raised along either side of its lower course and flooded the low-lying region of Western Shantung for a period of several years. It was evidently approaching one of its periodical climaxes when, having silted up its bed to the upper level of the embankments, and considerably above that of the surrounding country, the river sought a new outlet to the sea. Nor were the officials unmindful of the danger. They worked with energy upon the great dykes which rise in some places to a height of fifty feet above the plain, but these, by reason of the erosion of the current, of careless construction, and in certain spots of wilful cutting for the convenience of roads leading to fords and ferries across the stream, were inadequate to stand the strain of an unusual freshet. In the month of September the floods broke through their artificial bounds at a point where the river emerges from the loess hills west of Kaifung fu, and poured a torrent a mile wide and forty feet deep over the alluvial plain of Honan south of its course. The fertile country was first swept clean by the mighty rush and then turned into a vast lake. Every human habitation, and all vestiges of its former agricultural prosperity, in a district half the size of Scotland, disappeared in a few days. Nor was this all; for spreading gradually over the flat lands of Northern Nganhwui and Central Kiangsu the waters finally turned into the Ko and Hwai Rivers, flooding Lake Hung-tsih, and thence reached the sea at the old mouth of the Yellow River, or by small streams and canals poured south into the Yangtsz'. Only very general estimates can be made of the actual loss of life and property and of the area submerged. The entire region was immensely fertile and swarmed with villages. It is not improbable that it exceeded fifty thousand square miles in extent, all more or less affected, and that the number drowned was at least a million, while this figure must be multiplied by four or five to cover the diminution in the population of these provinces caused directly by the floods and their inevitable attendants, famine, destitution, and disease. With the poor means at their command the officials were powerless to deal with the disaster, though the government and many private individuals contributed liberally to support the starving survivors. Despite every effort on the part of mandarins, who knew that their political future depended upon their success, the breach could not be closed by the ensuing summer, and a fresh outburst of the flood in 1888 brought about a new and appalling catastrophe. The unsuccessful officials were disgraced, but nothing was allowed to interrupt the work of repair. At length, by throwing in stones to form a temporary breakwater above the breach, the main current of the stream was diverted and the dyke repaired.

On the 17th [January, 1889, says the *Peking Gazette*,] the embankment heads were united by cables stretched across, and on the 20th, after two days and nights of unremitting exertions, the narrow opening remaining was completely closed, all the waters of the river flowing away in the old channel. The Emperor feels that this speedy success is due to the unseen aid of Heaven and the gods. As a sign of his deep gratitude he sends ten sticks of Tibetan incense, which he desires Wu Ta-chăng to offer with prayers and thanks, on his behalf, at the temple of the river gods in the vicinity of the works.

But to all suggestions as to the desirability of allowing the river to retain its new course and providing for the future by a series of engineering works planned by foreign experts, the authorities remained indifferent and obdurate. Doubtless in addition to their natural conservatism they perceived the danger of an uprising on the part of the Honan land-holders, whose farms would thus be taken from them and whose suspicions would inevitably be aroused against the government by the application to this old source of danger of new remedies which they did not understand. In spite of herself, China must continue to nurse her old "sorrow."[1]

---

[1] The *Peking Gazette* for 1887–89 has many documents upon this subject highly interesting to the student of Chinese government. *The North China Herald*, published at Shanghai, contains the fullest accounts of eye-witnesses to the floods and relief measures. See also the *Chinese Recorder*, March, 1888. General J. H. Wilson's *China*, Chapter XVI. R. S. Gundry, *China, Present*

Those who were able to watch closely the course of events in China during this decade, discerned a distinct inclination, after the restoration of friendly intercourse with France, toward a policy of cordial relations with Western powers. This period was marked by the political ascendancy of such liberal statesmen as Li Hung-chang, Chang Chi-tung, and Liu Ming-chuan, supported at head-quarters by the resolute old Empress and Prince Chun, the Emperor's father, who indeed was converted to a more forward policy during the interval. But with the inevitable tendency to reaction after a term of activity that characterizes the careers of all nations alike, the conservatives of China erelong succeeded in checking the hopeful efforts of this progressive group, and by the year 1888 they had fully turned the tide of public opinion against the new programme of Western improvements and reform. In a country where the conduct of affairs is vested entirely in an intellectual aristocracy, as in the Middle Kingdom, it is easy to arouse this controlling element to vehement and united action by the cry that its interests are threatened, and, when once aroused, there is no other class in the community that possesses any capacity whatever for organized resistance. It is only necessary to show that a reform is liable to touch the prestige or personal profit of the literati to array against it the unanimous action of the whole body. And in some of the reforms now inaugurated the interests of the men of official standing were very materially affected. The Maritime Customs service had long taken a lucrative source of gain from their clutches, and now to this hardship was added that of compromising the *likin* dues by a lump sum paid to this service at the treaty ports. The projected railways moreover threatened to further curtail the transit dues on roads and rivers which enriched local officers, especially in the great business of transporting the tribute rice to the capital, a source of large illicit profit to those concerned. The conduct of the army and navy and the management of ship-yards and arsenals were also to be

---

and Past, Chapter XV. A valuable monograph on *Le canal impérial; étude historique et descriptive*, par le P. Domin. Gaudar, S. J., appears in *Variétés Sinologiques*, No. 4, Shanghai, 1894.

reorganized upon European principles. One by one their old privileges were being denied them, and in each case the origin of their grievance could be traced directly to this odious and un-Asiatic foreign influence.

Spurred on by their fears, the jealousy and hatred of the literati toward foreigners presently materialized into a policy of resistance to all measures that traced their origin to the outside world, and of concerted movement against any foreigners living in the country who could be safely and conveniently attacked. Their vengeance was wreaked chiefly upon missionaries living in the interior, and the disturbances that followed have, in consequence, been called the anti-missionary riots. It does not appear, however, that the missionaries were odious because of their creed, but on account of their race. They had to face the attack in its severest form, involving, in the aggregate, an enormous loss of property, but a comparatively small loss of life, because as a class they were more isolated and exposed than other foreigners.

A complete list of these casualties would be impossible here, but some notice of the more recent and notable among them is necessary before proceeding to a discussion of their probable motive. In 1883–84 a series of riots resulted in the destruction altogether of eighteen Christian chapels in Kwangtung province, the direct incentive to this work, as afterward learned, being an inflammatory proclamation issued by the governor-general and the admiral of the Southern fleet. Between the years 1885 and 1890 there were continual troubles in Shantung province, "where a German consul, sent to investigate, found the chief instigator to be a member of the Tsung-li Yamun itself." Other troubles arose in Kiangsi. In Sz'chuen province, where the antipathy of the mandrinate to foreigners has always been especially strong, a series of riots attended by looting occurred during the years 1886–90, when Catholic and Protestant missionary establishments in many places were destroyed and converts persecuted, while the rioters surged about the country side proclaiming that they had orders from the Emperor and the magistrates to root out and destroy Christianity. The government at Peking, when appealed to, compensated the missionaries for the loss of their houses, and acknowledged their right under their treaties to rebuild; but as the new chapels and schools were erected, angry gangs again sprang up to burn them, in one place the premises being destroyed three times within four years. An ominous feature in these events was not the violence but the pertinacity of the mobs, which seemed to be always on hand to execute, whenever occasion demanded, their threats of driving out the Christians. It also happened that the judicial investigations following these repeated outbursts were so grossly partial as to make legal redress a mockery. The wretched native converts, appealing to the commissioner for protection, were exhorted in full tribunal to apostatize, when they were promised all the protection they wished. It was palpably the purpose of the judges there to render the province too uncomfortable for foreigners, including all missionaries and converts, an object which, owing to its remoteness from the capital and the weakness of the central authority, they have temporarily at least, almost accomplished. In 1895–96 all Christian missionaries, after renewed persecutions, which will be considered later, were actually expelled from the capital and other towns of the province, though afterward reinstated by imperial command.

In Wuhu, a treaty port on the Yangtsz', about midway between Chingkiang and Kiukiang, a riot occurred in May, 1891, beginning the series which, spreading up and down the Great River during this and the following year, brought a feeling of insecurity to every foreigner in the Empire. Here the phenomena attending the uprising could be more closely observed. There seem to have been rumors of trouble floating about the community for some time before the outbreak, but nothing that seriously alarmed foreigners living there. On a Sunday two Chinese sisters of the Jesuit Mission were accosted in the street by some beggars asking alms in the usual way. They stopped to pat two urchins on the head and inquire what they wanted, when, with a cry that the foreign devils were bewitching them, a furious multitude that had apparently sprung up from nowhere in a moment, hurled themselves upon the women and carried them for punishment to the magistrate. He succeeded in appeasing the people for the nonce only. Two days later the mob broke down the gates and walls of the Jesuit Mission, and, digging up the bodies of some foundlings recently buried in the compound, declared that they saw evidence of their having been cut up for medicine. In an hour the whole pile of buildings was in flames, and by nightfall the crowd was attacking the British Consulate, the Imperial Customs buildings, and other houses occupied by foreigners; fortunately their inmates were rescued on board a steamer hulk. The Customs house was successfully defended against the mob until the fortunate arrival of three Chinese men-of-war steaming up the river on the following day drove the rioters off by firing a broadside or two, and quiet was restored.[1]

Here the notable features of the rising were, first, the especial virulence of the populace against the Roman Catholics, all of whose buildings, including a fine cathedral, were looted and destroyed, and second, the determined attack against the Consulate and Customs establishments, which had no connection with missionary work. The calumnies against the Catholics were a repetition of those heard in the Tientsin riot of 1870, and often elsewhere;[2] they received (and still receive throughout China) the same fanatical credence that was given to witch stories in Europe and America during the eighteenth century. A placard posted about the streets of Wuhu immediately after the emeute is worth quoting as embodying some of the crude conceptions rampant everywhere among the people.

The country is betrayed and the people are ruined! Human beings are trampled down and reduced to dust. Such being the state of affairs we humbly beg to state the following. Wuhu is a treaty port thickly populated with foreigners, who cause people injury to such an extent that it is impossible for the pen to fully describe. Lately the Roman Catholic Mission are building churches in every portion of the place. Every convert is paid a monthly sum of $6, and it is by such means that ignorant males and females are led to enter the churches where men and women congregate together without discrimination. This breach of morality and custom is in itself a

---

[1] The British acting consul-general, however, writes that these vessels, "by their mere presence and an occasional blank shot overawed the rioters." —*Parliamentary Blue Book—China*, No. 3 (1891), p. 4.

[2] *Middle Kingdom*, Vol. II., pp. 311 and 702 ff.

violation of the fixed laws of the State. Now women are procured from other places and are paid to abduct children whose eyes and intestines are taken out, and whose heart and kidneys are cut off. What crimes have these innocent children committed that they should suffer such horrible deaths? What makes it more lamentable is that when a child is stolen the child's family also perish. The loss of one's own flesh and blood is so deeply felt that the acute mental pain drives one to wish for death—quick apoplexy or suicide generally follows. But their [the Roman Catholics] sins have reached the limit, and the vengeance of Heaven is ready to burst forth. On the 3d of this moon two female child-thieves went to Honan and abducted a child by drugging him. The child's mother saw the act and called out to him, but he was unable to speak, looking stultified. The people, on apprehending the two abductresses, discovered on their persons two bottles containing drugs for stupefying children. They were taken to *Pao-chia-chu* [the street patrol's office] and thence to the magistrate's yamen. The Romanist priests hearing of the matter at once sent a bribe of 600 taels to the magistrate, who on receiving the money returned the two abductresses in sedan chairs to the church. The priests of the Roman Catholic Church steal and kill Chinese children, and their crimes should have been expiated with death punishment; but the god of wealth bought off their lives. Money is superior to law, the precious Code and Golden Rules are misapplied. It shows the [magistrates'] intention of exterminating our Chinese race, and of assisting barbarian thieves.

This manifesto, after detailing other incidents and reflecting upon the corrupt magistracy, urges the people to complete the destruction so well begun and drive the foreigners out of the district. From the tone of this and other documents, some of them grossly scurrilous, scattered broadcast through Central China, it was evident that a concerted movement against foreigners was afoot. The leaders of the mob, where they could be detected, seemed to be men of distinction who carried small red flags—as had been the case in a riot at Hankow in 1883—and who gave orders as though accustomed to command. That there was collusion with the mandarins, all the way up to the governor-general, was abundantly evident, though this was of course a matter difficult of proof in most instances.[1] There were few cases where the mob escaped from control, even when in the fury of robbery and destruction, a fact in itself as significant of official connivance in China as in Turkey.

[1] Copies of the most incendiary and indecent broadsides distributed among the people were found in numbers in the magistrates' yamens.

An outbreak of the same sort at Yangchow in Kiangsu was attempted on May 9th, but was promptly suppressed by Chinese troops. At Nanking, however, while the foreign women and children were leaving the city, in obedience to warnings received the day before, the missionaries' houses and hospital were set upon by a mob and only saved from destruction by the energy of an American who held the natives at bay until relieved by the arrival of troops. At Tanyang, on June 1st, the rioters succeeded in overpowering a military mandarin sent to preserve order at the Catholic Mission, and, after demolishing all the buildings, dug up the Christian cemetery and heaped the bones together "to the accompaniment of the usual calumnious and abusive shouts." Worse still were the events that occurred four days later at Wusueh, a flourishing trading town on the Yangtsz', thirty miles above Kiukiang. In this instance the blow seems to have fallen upon the foreigners quite unexpectedly, despite the rumors now everywhere current of a plan for their general massacre. "Here," we are told, "the Wesleyan Mission has been peaceably established for nearly twenty years, so peaceably that one is never called 'Foreign Devil' on the streets, and ladies go out without foreign escort, often even for thirty miles inland to Kwangchi hien, where also a married missionary lives." The disturbance began with the already familiar cry that a kidnapper was carrying dying babies to the Catholic foundling home at Kiukiang. A crowd collected with a rapidity which only those acquainted with Chinese town life can appreciate, smothered one of the hapless infants in the scuffle, and then turned upon the Wesleyan Mission establishment, which at the moment was occupied by only two English ladies and their children. These were terribly beaten and barely escaped with their lives. Two Englishmen, a newly arrived missionary and an employee of the Customs service, in attempting to rescue them, were murdered and horribly mutilated in the streets, while the buildings were, as usual, destroyed. A striking incident in this turmoil was the attempt of a Chinese subordinate official, having the title of *lung-ping-sz'*, to stop the mischief at its height by offering himself and his house as a vicarious sacrifice to the mob. They took him at his word, beat him nearly to death, burnt his dwelling, and continued their hunt for the foreigners.

Other convulsions of precisely similar character took place during this summer in Nganking, Kinkiang, Wusieh (on the Grand Canal), Yanking, Haimăn, and Tankao in Kiangsu, and other localities in the Yangtsz' valley, none of them, however, attended with loss of life. One at Ichang, a port on the river three hundred and sixty-five miles above Hankow, first opened to foreign trade in 1887, involved the complete demolishment of every missionary building in the city, while the British Consulate and Customs offices were spared. Here, too, the local authorities seemed strangely incompetent to cope with the rioters, though the number of these was small and the populace was only concerned in the disturbance in so far as the rabble were tempted by a share in the plunder. Here, too, as in several other places ununiformed Chinese soldiers were recognized among the most active incendiaries, and their methodical fashion of destruction indicated pretty clearly the presence of leaders whose orders were implicitly obeyed. It is to be noted in connection with the Ichang outbreak that Chungking, three hundred and sixty miles above Ichang, the head-quarters of traffic in the upper waters of the Yangtsz', was this summer, after years of negotiation, included among the treaty ports, to the dissatisfaction and alarm of all Western China.

An outrage which occurred near Kirin, the capital of Manchuria, in August of this year, though apparently unconnected with the riots along the Yangtsz', deserves mention here as an instance of anti-foreign feeling in other parts of the Empire. A missionary physician, Dr. J. A. Greig, while on his rounds in the country was seized and mercilessly beaten by some soldiers of the Tartar general's body-guard. The familiar charge of child-stealing was brought against him, and for three days he was kept captive, in imminent peril of his life; but here, again, as in many other instances, interference from higher authorities saved him and he was sent back to Kirin. This affair may perhaps have had some connection with an insurrection that broke out in Eastern Mongolia, when bands of brigands, in November, attacked several villages of Christian converts, destroying all their property and several hundred lives. The movement appears to have been started by some fanatical sects who aroused the Chinese population against the Christians—chiefly Mongols—by circulating the customary tales of kidnapping and heinous rites, but it soon attained the proportions of a rebellion that cost the government a serious effort to quell. At its suppression, in January, 1892, after the extermination of 20,000 insurgents, condign punishment was visited upon the three local magistrates responsible for the towns where the emeute began, on account of their remissness in checking the movement at its inception by publicly denying the baseless rumors against Christians.[1]

Though no year since 1891 has shown quite so distressing and widespread a series of overt acts against foreigners living in the interior of China, there has been none the less evidently a general reaction against them in all places where they did not enjoy the protection of their own men-of-war, or of armed volunteers sufficiently numerous to inspire respect. Anti-foreign publications continued to circulate, especially along the Yangtsz' towns, in spite of protests from the foreign representatives and the publication of imperial edicts forbidding their dissemination. In 1893, at Sungpu, sixty miles from Hankow, two Swedish missionaries were surrounded by a frantic mob and murdered under circumstances of peculiar atrocity. This time the government acted with promptness and energy, and, after a rigorous examination, ordered the punishment of such ringleaders as were apprehended. But the trial was hardly better than a mockery, and the results of this vigorous action were not altogether in keeping with the hopes of the foreigners; for, frightened by the terrible punishment visited upon them, the people of the vicinity boycotted all Europeans living there. Placards appeared now in many places, advocating a policy of absolute non-intercourse with foreigners, forbidding attendance at their chapels, and reading their books, and closing with the threat that, "if anyone in his greed for gain permits a foreigner

[1] Decree of punishment quoted in *United States Foreign Relations*, 1892, p. 96.

to build other houses, the headman is to inform us; we will destroy them and thus prevent future calamities." The murder of Rev. J. A. Wylie at Laoyang, near Manchuria, in August, 1894, by Manchu soldiers quartered in the city, was rather an act of lawlessness committed by insubordinate troops during the excitement of war than an item in the category of outrages upon Europeans domiciled in China.

What must be considered as the climax of Chinese anti-foreign feeling was attained in 1895 during two explosions in the widely separated provinces of Sz'chuen and Fuhkien. At Chingtu, the capital of the former province, a riot burst out on May 28th, the day of the *Twan-yang*, or Dragon-boat festival, ending the following day with the complete demolishment of every missionary establishment in the city. Here again the lives of the foreigners were spared, though some were badly maltreated, and several who fled to the magistrates for protection were denied admittance, while their prayers for official interference were refused point blank. The spirit of persecution spread like a prairie-fire through the province, and in the course of the following week some fourscore foreigners were driven pell-mell from their posts, where they had been earning golden reputations among the grateful natives, and forced to seek shelter in protected places. In none of the outbursts occurring within the past twenty years has there been such clear evidence of official connivance in the work of destruction.[1]

Thus far actual murder does not seem to have formed part of the programme, but on August 1st of this year the sudden descent of an armed party upon some English missionaries in a hill village of Fuhkien province, and the massacre of ten of their number, marks the most appalling disaster in the history of Protestant missions in China. The hamlet of Hwashan is located in Kutien (or Kuchăng) hien, about a hundred miles northwest of Foochow, and has been occupied as a sanitarium in times of excessive summer heat by Protestants of various denominations in that province. As has generally been the case,

---

[1] *History of the Szechuen Riots*, by Alfred Cunningham, sub-editor of the *Mercury*, Shanghai, 1895.

their personal popularity among the natives of the region seems to have been great, and, trusting to this and to their remoteness from the chief centres of anti-foreign sentiment, the occupants of this retreat—all but two of them women and children—were enjoying their well-earned vacation, serenely unconscious of the hideous plot brewing in a secret place among the hills hard by. The blow came from a local chapter of the *Tsai hwui*, or Vegetarian Society, about which much has been heard, but little is really known. Through the energy of one Liu Siangsing this society had been established in Kutien and the adjoining district in 1892, with the legitimate objects of mutual benefit, abstinence from opium, tobacco, wine, and flesh, and the less wholesome, but inevitable, secret signs, passwords, etc., of similar clubs everywhere. The secret propaganda in this particular district was successful in calling together the riffraff of the population, and when strong in numbers the policy was pursued of enforcing the selfish interests of their members by proceedings resembling those of the Ku-Klux in the United States, and the Mafia in Sicily—by terrorizing alike the officials and people of the region. Difficulties had arisen in the previous year between a Christian convert and certain followers of this sect, during which the local magistrate showed himself unable to punish a single one of them; the natural result of this was the establishment of the *Tsai hwui* in a position above the law, and the commission of frequent acts of robbery and murder. The prefect of the region shut the gates of Kutien town, and called for troops from the viceroy. They were not sent, owing to the secret influence of the society, and it was only after the indignant protests of the foreign consuls at Foochow that two hundred regulars were despatched to the disorderly district. The number sent was utterly inadequate to overawe a body of men that now counted many thousand adherents, but their arrival was the immediate cause of the tragedy of August. It was rumored that Mr. Stewart and other foreigners had contributed funds to bring the troops up. The Vegetarians immediately assembled their forces, organized a camp in the neighboring hills, and planned an attack upon Mr. Stewart, his family and associates, that should avenge the order and wipe out its dishonor in blood. Between two hundred and three hundred marched out of their fastness by night, falling upon the devoted band at dawn, murdering ten foreigners and wounding the others, destroying their houses, and disappearing as swiftly and silently as they had come.[1]

This account of ten years' riots does not even catalogue all the most notable disturbances in which foreigners were involved during this period. The evidence presented is, however, ample to justify the inference that there has existed in China a widespread feeling of unrest and discontent, which has culminated in outbreaks more or less severe at different times and places, but which has presented everywhere the common symptom of acute Chauvinism, of dislike to the presence and predominance of foreigners. It is too early to discuss impartially the motives of a movement which is not ended, and may perhaps have its most terrible manifestation yet in reserve, but some consideration must be given to its probable conditions. At the bottom of all, and equally effective in every portion of the Empire, lies the enmity of the literati, who imagine their old preponderance in the nation to be threatened by a new influence, the full meaning of which they cannot understand. It is not enough to say that this body of men are actuated by purely personal motives, fearing the loss of their offices in the event of a civil service reform, nor that they resent the attacks on Confucianism and the national cult of ancestors. Both of these considerations are mightily effective in extending the crusade against the "outsider," but neither accounts for its sudden recrudescence at irregular intervals during the past generation. To satisfactorily explain the explosions of hatred in regions where Christianity and foreigners are not only tolerated but welcomed by the masses, their recentness and their fitful and transitory nature in most places, some sources of apprehension or discontent must be sought which have moved only one element of Chinese society and developed within this element a policy of stubborn resistance to the treaty powers

---

[1] *Chinese Recorder*, September, 1895. *United States Foreign Relations*, 1895, p. 174 (Commander Newell's Report).

during the present generation. The opposition of the entire educated class in China to the coming of Europeans is too familiar to need emphasis here. It has been the leading idea in all her modern history. Their material strength, however, proved irresistible, and, after desperate antagonism, the nation has reluctantly yielded to the inevitable, contenting itself with the reflection that the Empire was large, and that foreigners were confined by their treaty stipulations to residence in a limited number of ports. But by a clause surreptitiously inserted in the French treaty of 1858, missionaries were admitted to travel and reside in the interior, and by the most-favored-nation clause this right passed to subjects of all the treaty powers. Their charitable work, and the fact that their presence did not affect the commercial and industrial life of the country, rendered them unobjectionable to the gentry and people, though it cannot be denied that they were looked upon with suspicion as unintelligible phenomena in communities where every action is supposed to be dictated by motives of self-interest.

A great light, however, broke upon the minds of thoughtful Chinese when, in discussing the revision of the Tientsin treaty of 1858, at the end of ten years, the British insisted upon a general extension of the right of residence in the country—involving, of course, the extraterritorial privilege in each case—supporting their demand by the argument that such right was already conceded to missionaries, and ought logically to be extended to merchants. The proposal was vigorously combated by Prince Kung and the Tsung-li Yamun, but no European knew at the time the consternation with which it was received in the country. It meant to the ruling class the invasion of their private preserves for squeezing and taxing the people, to the merchants the unrestricted competition of foreign rivals, to the multitudes of boatmen, carriers, and pedlers the extinction of their means of livelihood by the introduction of steamers, railroads, and Western inventions. The missionaries themselves had been regarded as comparatively harmless, but used as an argument for the invasion of China, they became a menace to the country. "Precedent, that *ultima ratio* of Chinese controversy, had been found, and was now being pressed into their teeth. Their own guns were being turned against themselves. By some means or other they must retake them. What else could they think of? Ponder a moment their dilemma. If they continued to allow one class of foreigners to enter, it would seem 'inconsistent and insidious' to deny a modified privilege of the same class to others. Plainly it had come to this—either all foreigners must be admitted freely into the interior, or all must be equally restricted to the open ports. The former they had resolved should be strenuously resisted; the latter alone remained, and how to accomplish it 'without hazarding the safety of the present situation' or 'giving these parties reason to suspect their plans' became now the absorbing topic of their councils. And now commence these 'disturbances,' inaugurated [by the Tientsin massacre of 1870] for the purpose of making the residence of missionaries inland no longer safe, and thus of crowding them back to the open ports." [1]

Such a conclusion as this is eminently characteristic of the Chinese mind, and, when once initiated, a policy of secret resistance based upon its premises would attract many opposing interests. The plan of campaign has been valiantly resisted by the more enlightened members of the government, who realize perfectly the dangers which beset the Empire and the dynasty in embroilments with Europeans. The conservatives or reactionaries, however, in the Palace and elsewhere, serve their private purposes by instigating the provinces to rise against the detested barbarians, by emphasizing all causes of ill-feeling, and by clandestinely protecting their secret agents whenever caught. However earnest its efforts, the Court is powerless to deal with this insidious and disloyal element in its bureaucracy; hence its failure to keep its pledges to foreigners, or to prevent the recurrence of outrages, or punish those that cause them. The most notable effort on the part of the government to arrest the movement in the provinces was the promulgation of a decree by the Emperor after the Wuhu and

---

[1] Rev. W. Ashmore's theory elaborated in the *Chinese Recorder* of July, 1896, the most satisfactory thus far suggested, and based upon indisputable historical evidence.

Wusueh uprisings. This edict of June 13, 1891, and the memorial of the Tsung-li Yamun that called it forth have not improperly been termed "the two most important state papers ever issued in China." In the rescript his Majesty solemnly declares that

> The propagation of Christianity by foreigners is provided for by treaty, and Imperial decrees have been issued to the provincial authorities to protect the missionaries from time to time. . . . The doctrine of Christianity has for its purpose the teaching of men to be good. Chinese converts are subjects of China and are amenable to the local authorities. Peace and quiet should reign among the Chinese and missionaries. But there are reckless fellows who fabricate stories that have no foundation in fact for the purpose of creating trouble. Villains of this class are not few in number and are to be found everywhere. . . . The local authorities must protect the lives and property of foreign merchants and missionaries and prevent bad characters from doing them injury. Should it transpire that the measures taken to protect them have not been adequate, and trouble in consequence ensues, the names of those officers that have been truly negligent are to be reported to us for degradation. . . . Let this decree be universally promulgated for the information of the people.

That this decree was honestly intended and faithfully proclaimed by the government is perfectly manifest, whatever complaints and assertions have been made to the contrary. It was obviously its only safe policy in view of the causes of disquiet prevailing throughout the Empire. It is also perfectly true that it was not made public in many places where infamous libels upon Christianity were scattered broadcast; but in these instances the imperial authority was impotent against the determined and rebellious action of local mandarins supported by the gentry. The enmity of these men had only to distort some trivial accident or exaggerate an idle rumor to transform the imperturbable and good-natured mass of a Chinese crowd into a mob of maniacs. In Chinkiang a Sepoy policeman slapped an impudent native; the result was a hurricane of riot. In 1895 a foreigner accidentally hit a petty mandarin with an air-gun at Ichang; it was enough to precipitate without further effort on their part the emeute which the literati had been preparing for months. Yet despite this persistent instigation a little sternness on the part of a local magistrate is always sufficient to quell any disorder that may arise among the people from sudden fright. They are accustomed to injustice and immorality; such when exhibited by foreigners do not greatly trouble them. But when told that the high walls of a Catholic convent protect the secret rites of witches within, that the charitable missionary going his rounds in town and country is clandestinely scattering fleas infected with the plague, that the tender touch of the foreign lady who lifts a fallen child in the street "hoodoos" all the brat's relations to the fourth degree, that a compound cathartic infallibly removes the queue of the taker—these are tales that sink deep into the superstitious mind already impressed with the marvels these foreigners perform, and bestir it to deeds of insane fury.

Nor can it be denied that the indiscreet actions of foreigners themselves give rise to great odium. Their proneness to employ their political influence to defend converts or protegés from just punishment is perhaps natural, but none the less inexcusable.[1] Their occasional pretensions to power, as seen in the case of a Roman Catholic bishop who assumed the port and trappings of a viceroy, and even issued "proclamations" to his diocese, stamped with a seal after the manner of the civil magistrate, are as dangerous as they are preposterous. Their physique, their dress and bearing, are all more or less disagreeable as well as strange to the ignorant people. It is not difficult to develop this inchoate unpopularity into active hatred.

Another factor in the matter is the habit, dear to every Chinese, of combination, and the enormous development thereby of secret societies. These associations for political purposes inevitably increase in strength and numbers in proportion as the imperial authority displays weakness. They have been especially numerous in China since the Opium War, and are now supposed to number as members a majority of all the civil servants in the Empire. The action of these secret clubs often changes from legitimate to illegitimate, according to the character and wishes of its leaders, the *Kolao hwui*, a Hunan soci-

---

[1] A recent instance of this is given at length by Dr. W. Ashmore in a series of articles on "Outrages on the American Baptist Mission at Kho-khoi," in the *Chinese Recorder*, August, September, October, and November, 1896.

ety,[1] having degenerated from a loyal political club founded by Tsăng Kwo-fan during the Tai-ping rebellion into an organization to overthrow the reigning dynasty. It is palpably the object of at least some members of this society to create anti-foreign riots by stirring up the people, and thus embroil the government with the great powers.

These centres of incipient revolt exist everywhere in China, but chiefly in the province of Hunan, which contains the least mixed and most conservative descendants of the ancient dominant race. This province furnishes the army with its bravest soldiers, and the administration with some of its most capable officers. It has preserved its territory thus far intact from the detested foreigner, and has been the source whence all the most virulent and injurious lies about him come. The strength of bigotry concentrated in this province has been so intense as to prevent the government from punishing the notorious Chu Han, the proud author of many infamous publications that brought about the riots of 1891. These riots have always been most formidable in the Yangtsz' valley, as much because directed from this central province as because fear of foreign rivalry in the river trade renders the people living in its towns especially sensitive.

There are plenty of theories ascribing these outbreaks to other sources, or emphasizing a subordinate motive as a leading cause. With rebellion a chronic malady of the body politic, it is not difficult to attribute them all to disaffection. So with other factors, as official turpitude and incapacity, the superstitions of the people, the indiscretions and narrowness of missionaries, etc. Each of these is supremely effective somewhere, but the phenomenon is too varied and extensive to have been directly caused by any but the most deliberate plans employing a vast army of willing instruments and ignorant dupes.[2]

---

[1] *China Review*, Vol. XV., p. 129; J. D. Ball, *Things Chinese*, second edition, New York, 1893, p. 430.

[2] The literature on the anti-foreign riots is already considerable and promises to become voluminous. The best authorities on the events themselves are the *United States Foreign Relations* series from 1887 to 1896, two or three *Parliamentary Blue Books* devoted to the riots (1891, 1892, etc.), and files of

Whatever the causes of these risings, it was manifestly the policy of the foreign representatives at Peking to act together in demanding reparation from the Foreign Office and to base their demands upon the rights enjoyed by the injured, not as missionaries but as foreign subjects, to protection under the treaties. Doubtless if more firmness had been shown after the first great riot at Tientsin in 1870, the imperial government might have made a more desperate effort to suppress these disorders, though it is improbable that it could have altogether prevented them.[1] The acceptance of a money compensation for such acts of violence became a matter of course, and the Chinese not unnaturally began to suppose that Europeans thought only of pecuniary indemnity as expiation for each horrible attack. If more were necessary it was always easy to produce victims for the headsman as a sop to very conscientious foreigners. When, however, they began to insist upon the presence of their representatives at the trials, and demanded the public punishment of guilty officials as an indispensable

---

the Shanghai and Tientsin papers. From the Shanghai press a volume entitled *The Anti-Foreign Riots in China in* 1891, was compiled in 1892. The *Chinese Recorder*, though curiously lax and irregular in printing reliable accounts of the riots which chiefly concerned the body it represents in China, has a few valuable articles (1891, 1892, 1895, etc.) by men of experience and ability like Rev. J. Ross, Dr. W. Ashmore, and others. Discussion of the problem in its various phases forms the subject of two notable pamphlets entitled *Missionaries in China*, and *China and Christianity*, by Alexander Michie, Tientsin, 1892–93 (republished in London); *Sources of the Anti-Foreign Disturbances in China*, by Rev. Gilbert Reid. Shanghai, 1893; also in "Correspondance sur les émutes de Ou-hou, etc., *Toung Pao*, Vol. II., January, 1892, pp. 447–558; "The Riots in China," *Blackwood's Magazine*, November and December, 1891; Gundry's *China, Present and Past*, 1895; Curzon's *Problems of the Far East*, 1894; Dr. W. A. P. Martin's *Cycle of Cathay*, 1896; H. Norman's *Peoples and Politics*, 1895 (which states the extreme anti-missionary argument): J. D. Ball's *Things Chinese*, 1893, pp. 389, 419, etc.

[1] A former missionary, Dr. W. A. P. Martin, declares that "if, in 1870, the French *chargé*, declining the offer of money and heads, had waited until he could have a fleet of gun-boats in the Peiho, if then the whole suburb where the riot occurred had been laid in ashes, and the ground confiscated for a French concession, the government would have taken care that there should not be a second riot. Being let off cheap, the anti-foreign mandarins felt that they could afford to continue the process of fanning the flame of patriotism." —*A Cycle of Cathay*, p. 445.

condition, the indifference of the government disappeared. A great change in spirit was brought about in 1895 by the determined effort of the American Minister to send a commission to Sz'chuen and determine, if possible, the guilt of the ex-Viceroy, Liu Ping-chang. "China fought this commission for some days," writes Colonel Denby, "but was finally forced to consent to its going overland to Chengtu. China also fought with unparalleled obstinacy the proposition to punish the Viceroy Liu, partly on account of his influence with the Dowager Empress, and partly because there was no precedent for this action. The entering wedge in overcoming this obstinacy was the action of the [United States State] Department in ordering the going of an American commission. After China had accepted this proposition as inevitable the British Minister stepped in with an ultimatum that the officials should be punished. A fleet was ordered to these waters as a menace. The Minister of France then intervened to explain to China that to avoid trouble she must punish the officials."[1] The Viceroy was degraded from office, "never to be employed again, as a warning to others," and the taotais, prefects, and other officers concerned,

---

[1] *United States Foreign Relations*, 1895, Vol. I., p. 150. In a letter to the department, dated March 22, 1895, Colonel Denby declares his views of missionary work in China in a document which has already become famous in the East as one of the ablest defences of foreign missions from the secular side ever formulated. In it he touches upon the patent fact that natives of all classes are benefited by the labors of missionaries in hospitals, schools, translations, charitable relief, and sanitary reforms. "As far as my knowledge extends," he continues, "I can and do say that the missionaries in China are self-sacrificing; that their lives are pure; that they are devoted to their work; that their influence is beneficial to the natives; that the arts and sciences and civilization are greatly spread by their efforts; and that many useful Western books are translated by them into Chinese; that they are the leaders in all charitable work, giving largely themselves, and personally disbursing the funds with which they are entrusted; that they do make converts, and such converts are mentally benefited by conversion. In answer to these statements, which are usually acknowledged to be true, it does not do to say, as if the answer were conclusive, that the literati and gentry are usually opposed to missionaries. This antagonism was to have been expected. . . . In the interests, therefore, of civilization, missionaries ought not only to be tolerated, but ought to receive protection, to which they are entitled from officials, and encouragement from other classes of people."

punished in various ways. This act of justice is not improperly said to constitute an era in the treatment of foreigners in China.

The revival of anti-foreign fanaticism in China during 1894 and 1895 was more particularly due to the invasion of her territory by Japan, the third and most important event remaining to be chronicled in this chapter. It was not a sense of defeat—the majority of the lower classes in China being probably to this day unaware of the disasters to their arms—but of indignation at the reported intrusion of another foreign race upon their soil which helped to stir up the old fury once more and proved the direct cause (as in the murder of Mr. Wylie) of several recent riots.

The contention of China and Japan over Korea may be considered as having originated in the sixteenth century, when Hideyoshi's formidable invasion (1592–98) established Japan's shadowy pretensions to suzerainty in the peninsula. China being appealed to at that time, succeeded in expelling the invaders, though the Korean King was compelled to send tribute to both Shogun and Grand Khan until the year 1832, when, becoming tired of the expense involved in entertaining the embassy, the Court of Yedo ordered its discontinuance. This was, perhaps, a mistake from the stand-point of Asiatic diplomacy, as was Japan's action when she refused a renewal of the old connection with her quandam vassal upon a threatened invasion by France in 1866. Both of these errors she had later occasion to regret; nor is she less likely in future to regret the legacy of hatred toward her which exists wherever the Korean people remember the period of their oppression during the invasion.

China's intermixture in the affairs of the peninsula represents a more natural affiliation than that of her rival as regards civilization, letters, and territorial connection. Tribute embassies were sent to Peking as well as to Japan, but with greater regularity and continuity, and with a far deeper sense of obligation; for, though the tribute itself was nominal, the Korean monarch received his reign-name from the Chinese Emperor, accepted the calendar—a mark of vassalage—from his hands, and had to personally welcome the Chinese ambassador at a spot outside of his capital, Seoul. Such formalities imply much in oriental relations. Some aspects of China's supremacy in Continental Asia have already been considered in the case of Annam. It is difficult to reconcile the docility of such imperial fiefs as Annam, Burma, Korea, and even Tibet, with the contumacy of her rebellious subjects in Central Asia and elsewhere. "The real reason," explains a profound student of her history, "is that Chinese nominal over-lordship leaves to the vassal populations the maximum of liberty with the minimum of injury to the pocket. China has always been willing to grant the kernel of home-rule, including taxation, if only her imperial pride were fully gratified with the gilded shell of tribute and nominal subordination. . . . Another reason why China—at a distance—is held in profound respect by her vassal nations is because her splendid literature, equally readable in Korean, Annamese, Japanese, or Lewchewan, appeals to the 'barbarian' mind in the same way that degenerate Rome still exercises a semi-religious fascination over the 'barbarians' of Europe. . . . In a word, China, like Rome, is morally indestructible."[1]

There was no question, then, as to the reality of the dependence of the lesser upon the greater state. China, however, like Japan, vitiated the logic of her position by discreditable diplomatic oscillations when, upon the demand of France for reparation after the murder of some missionaries in Korea in 1866, she weakly denied responsibility for acts committed by subjects of an avowedly vassal state. Again, in 1871, when the United States presented a similar claim after the murder of a whaling crew on the Korean coast, the Americans were requested to chastise the Koreans and force a treaty upon them if they could. They both could and did.[2] Lastly, in 1876, the Japanese were given the same answer under like circum-

---

[1] E. H. Parker in the *Asiatic Quarterly Review* for October, 1896, p. 291.

[2] *United States Diplomatic Correspondence*, 1867, Vol. I., pp. 420–428, etc. *Foreign Relations*, 1871, pp. 73, 115–149, etc. *Shanghai Budget*, March, June, and July, 1871. W. E. Griffis, *Corea, the Hermit Nation*, 1882. A treaty negotiated by Japan, February 26, 1876, first "opened" Korea; foreign trade was allowed at Gensan, Fusan, and Chemulpo.

stances, and China carelessly threw away the winning cards in her hand. Realizing her mistake as soon as the foreigners began to make their treaties, she afterward tried to recoup by compelling the King to accompany each compact with an incongruous confession of fealty to China. But if he was a vassal he had no business to be negotiating treaties and sending representatives abroad; and this, of course, the nations recognized when, ignoring the paradox altogether, they treated Korea as an autonomous state.

Despite a curious inability to pursue a consistent policy, China managed, nevertheless, to retain all the practical advantages of lordship over the administration in Korea, where until July, 1894, her minister resident was the real power behind the throne. The immediate causes of the conflict that was the culmination of her rivalry with Japan may be traced directly to the rebellions which had become a chronic malady of Korea, and to the quarrels of two Court factions which involved murderous attacks upon the Japanese embassy at Seoul and the assassination of a liberal leader friendly to Japan. The dreadful misgovernment of the country long ago brought its miserable peasantry to regard any change as likely to be for their betterment. One manifestation of their desperate condition was the organization, about 1859, of a sect upholding certain doctrines of the three religions of China with a few Christian ideas added. Any connection with the despised and persecuted followers of the Jesuits was, however, disavowed by calling this sect the *Tong Hak*, or "Eastern Doctrine," to distinguish it from the "Western," or Roman Catholic, doctrine. The association presently became more political than religious in its purposes, and after subverting government authority in the southern provinces, marched in 1893 upon the Palace at Seoul to demand redress for grievances. The petitioners were sent away with promises, but these being stultified the following spring, they reassembled in such force as to threaten the very existence of the Throne. When in May the government troops sent against them were overwhelmingly defeated, the Court turned in alarm to its ancient protector and asked aid from China to put down the rebels.

If misery pushed to the extreme of insurrecticn indicates anything, the state of Korea at this time would seem of itself adequate cause for the cataclysm of 1894. Added to this, however, was the plotting of rival factions at the capital and the jealous interference of both China and Japan in the administration of a helpless and degraded country which both alike claimed to protect. The two Court parties were the Mins, mostly members of the clan to which the Queen belonged, and the anti-Mins, headed by the King's father, the Tai Wen Kun, or regent, who had practically usurped the sovereignty during his son's minority, ruling with great severity and a marked anti-foreign bias. It was this particular prejudice that had brought him to intrigue with the Min clique in 1882, and excite a mob which murdered several Japanese and drove their entire legation out of the country. The idle plot cost both him and his country dear. The government was made not only to pay and apologize for the outrage, but to admit Japanese and Chinese troops in Seoul, while to simplify the complexity of palace politics the Tai Wen Kun, the arch-plotter, was kidnapped by Chinese officers and made to spend two years of ignominious captivity in China. Another emeute, two years later, involving the assassination of the conservative Min leaders and the formation of a government under one Kim Ok-kiun, a liberal with Japanese proclivities, was more serious. It was followed by the return to power of the Mins, who with the aid of Chinese troops ousted their opponents and once more burned the Japanese legation, driving its members and body-guard to the coast. The part played in this political revolution by Chinese soldiers was fatuous in the extreme. It gave abundant cause for a declaration of war, which Japan had all but made, when the Viceroy Li promptly and sensibly averted a crisis, and Korea had once again to pay for her folly. In consequence of this grave peril, and to establish a more satisfactory *entente* respecting this bone of contention, a covenant between Count Ito and Li Hung-chang was concluded at Tientsin in April, 1885, in which Japan and China agreed to withdraw all their troops from Korea, to advise the King to engage officers from some third power to drill and equip his army, and, thirdly, to inform the other country whenever either party should find it necessary, to send an armed force to Korea.

Kim Ok-kiun had escaped from Seoul and spent the ten following years in Europe and Japan. Early in 1894 he was inveigled by a compatriot to leave the latter country and visit Shanghai. There he was assassinated by his treacherous friend, undoubtedly at the instigation of the reactionary party in Seoul. Though the crime was committed in the foreign concession, the consular body rather weakly turned the murderer and the corpse of his victim over to the Chinese authorities, who promptly forwarded them both to Korea. The former was landed and rewarded as the first patriot in his country; the body was quartered and exposed during several weeks in sightly places about the capital. It would be unjust to complain of Korean politics as lacking in excitement or picturesqueness of a certain sort.

This tragedy occurring at the moment when the Tong Haks were threatening Seoul, brought matters to extremities. Japan being herself aflame with the social and political renascence at home, had posed successfully as the friend of progress and reform in the little kingdom, while one motive of her policy there was palpably that of thwarting China. That Empire, on the other hand, won from Europeans a great deal of gratuitous odium by seeming to discourage these reform schemes. She did so because under the existing conditions of a grossly corrupt official class, and an ignorant and apathetic populace, these plans were simply chimerical. The Japanese Court may, moreover, have been influenced by the Jingo party at home, who rendered the conduct of parliamentary government extremely difficult for the ministry unless it played a little now and then to the gallery by a brave show of bullying Korea and insulting China. Japan had, it must be remembered, an army and fleet of which she was pardonably proud, and she was too near a neighbor of China not to perceive, what Europeans only dimly understood, that an almost unconquerable aversion to the profession of arms on the part of her governing class had rendered all Chinese attempts at military rehabilitation practically valueless. Japan was ready, her old rival was not; she knew also that a place among nations would not be allowed her until she had conquered an enemy in a fight. The Korean imbroglio was but the pretext for consummating a carefully matured project.

Upon the appeal of Korea for help against the Tong Haks, already alluded to, China forwarded a small body of troops to the disturbed region, duly informing her rival according to agreement. Japan, alleging—not without excuse—that her subjects were insecure in that country, landed in the month of June seven or eight thousand soldiers, securing and occupying the approaches to Seoul with military precision. It was, as the terrified Koreans began to realize, an invasion. Then began a diplomatic campaign, short and sharp. The Japanese Minister, Otori, demanded from the King a clear definition of his relationship to China, advised him of the impossibility of shielding in future the abuses of his administration behind the ægis of Chinese suzerainty, and proposed a sweeping scheme of reform, including the laws, educational system, army, finances, all to be intrusted to Japanese hands. The poor monarch had to submit to the humiliation of being made the shuttlecock between his more powerful neighbors; his compliance, which involved the ejection of the conservatives and establishment of a ministry that formally requested Japan to take care of them, was utterly insincere, but his attempts at obstruction were futile. From this moment, while China and Japan delayed yet a little to collect their forces for a direct blow, the ruler of the miserable country over which they were fighting sinks back into pathetic obscurity.

China, indeed, conscious of her unpreparedness, tried hard to avoid hostilities, and even asked Russia, the arch-terror of the Far East, to interfere. She continued to despatch reinforcements to her troops in Korea, but as this was within her technical, not to say traditional, rights, she still hoped for some amicable settlement when there occurred a tragedy which rendered all thought of compromise impossible. On July 23d, the political farce having been played out at Seoul, three fast cruisers were sent from Japan to intercept any additional Chinese troops on their way to Korea. Two days later they encountered opposite Asan two small Chinese men-of-war, the *Kwang yi* and *Tsi yuen*, which, instead of saluting, cleared for action. The action that followed was brief, and speaks better for the pluck than the intelligence of the Chinese in attacking three vessels, any one of which was a match for them both. Within an hour the *Kwang yi* was disabled and beached, the other running for Wei hai wei riddled with shot. The transport which these two vessels had come out to convoy, a British steamer, the *Kowshing*, was met by the victorious Japanese while chasing the *Tsi yuen* an hour later. An officer of the *Naniwa* upon boarding her found that she was carrying 1,200 troops and a few foreign officers under the British flag. He bade the steamer follow him, but when the Europeans signalled back that the Chinese would not let them go, preferring to sink the ship rather than be taken prisoners, the answer came back, "quit the ship at once." Therewith the *Naniwa*, placing herself at a convenient distance, fired a broadside and launched a torpedo at the defenceless steamer, which sank immediately with most of those on board.

The act was a critical one, for war had not been declared, and the British flag in Asiatic waters enjoys a quite fearful prestige. But at a moment when both sides were pouring all the soldiers they could mobilize into the disputed territory, and on the very morning when the Japanese had fought two Chinese vessels, it was natural that they should consider hostilities actually begun. The technical correctness of their decision was afterward sustained by two English authorities in international law;[1] but the annihilation of more than a thousand ignorant and defenceless men cooped up in an unarmed steamer cannot be reconciled with the usage of civilized nations.

This incident led to declarations of war by both parties. The two documents are characteristic; the Japanese, calm and firm in tone, protesting a desire for peace, and rehearsing—

---

[1] Professors J. Westlake and T. E. Holland in the *London Times* of August 3 and 7, 1894.

not always with irrefutable accuracy—their statement of the case; the Chinese, true to the tradition of centuries, reasserting sovereignty over Korea, and exhorting their officers "to root the *Wojin* out of their lairs," and "to refrain from the least laxity in obeying our commands."[1] The contrast is suggestive.

Though superior in numbers the situation of the Japanese in Korea was still precarious, so long as the capital was threatened on the south by the Chinese force at Asan, and upon the other side by an army rapidly hurrying to Ping yang, or Phyöng yang, on the Tai tong River, one hundred and thirty miles, or thereabouts, north of Seoul. After a little sharp fighting at the hamlet of Söng hwan, near Asan, where the enemy were entrenched, they drove them from their position (July 28th), thus removing the first danger. Some fifteen hundred of this garrison, under General Yeh, made their way to Ping yang, a performance sufficiently suggestive of the sympathies of the peasantry, for such a force, without provisions or knowledge of the country, would have perished in a hostile community. The Japanese pressed after them, but not hurriedly, for they had to await reinforcements. With admirable discretion Marshal Yamagata moved his forces in four detachments, two under Generals Oshima and Nodzu by the highway from Seoul, another under General Tadzumi, by a detour to the right through the towns of Sak riöng and Sin gé; the fourth, assembling at the port of Gensan on the northeast coast, under Colonel Sato, and advancing across the mountains upon the flank of the Chinese position. Meantime a Chinese army had been pouring from Manchuria across the Amnok, or Yalu, River, and concentrating at Ping yang, the key of Northern Korea; their total is estimated at four armies, comprising about 13,000 men, occupying twenty-seven forts, a very strong position. The Japanese numbered altogether some 14,000 effective

[1] Both documents are given in full in Appendix D of "Vladimir's" *China-Japan War*, London, 1896. The text of the Chinese declaration in the *Translation of the Peking Gazette*, 1894, has "attack the enemy" instead of "root the *Wojin* out." *Wojin* is the common but contemptuous Chinese term for Japanese.

troops. Quite six weeks had elapsed before, on September 15th, the first great blow of the war was struck. The joint attack was then delivered with precision and effect. While the right wing of Oshima's detachment, the so-called Mixed Brigade, threatened the forts defending a bridge of boats leading to the city across the Tai tong, its left wing attended to those commanding the Chung hwa road south of the city, and the main body under Nodzu, having crossed the stream the day previous, opened upon the southwestern angle of the town. The Sak riöng detachment, at the same time, faced the four forts north of the Chinese, while the Gensan troops controlled their northwestern defences on the Wiju road, cutting off the main avenue of retreat. The engagement was not without some severe fighting, but the Chinese were surprised and disheartened at the unexpected appearance of the enemy on all sides at once; they had no courage left for a hopeless defence. Only one of their generals, Tso Pao-kwei, showed a proper spirit, and he alone prevented an evacuation of all the works on the night of the 14th. His death in the midst of the carnage was the end of all real resistance; there was no thought in the garrison except of flight, and all through the night after the battle the Chinese fled along the Wiju road, suffering fearfully at the hands of the Japanese of the Main and Gensan detachments, but preferring, as usual, risk of death to capture. By morning not a Chinese soldier was to be found in Ping yang. The Japanese loss may be reckoned at about 350 officers and men, including (as it is safe to do) all the missing among the slain; the Chinese are supposed to have had 2,000 killed, 1,500 of these in the fatal flight by night. About 600 were taken alive.[1]

The Japanese victory at Ping yang was the China-Japan war in epitome. The contest was, in fact, despite some instances of individual bravery, one between children and men; an array of undisciplined and listless "braves" under hopelessly

[1] These figures are interesting when compared with the accounts telegraphed to Europe after the battle, which placed the Chinese losses at 4.000 killed and 16,000 taken prisoners. The story about the Chinese fighting under oiled-paper umbrellas at Ping yang is a fable.

benighted officers against troops trained and eager for the encounter under capable leaders. Beyond seizing upon a strong defensive position the Chinese showed no conception whatever of strategy. In a country where every inhabitant was willing to give them information of the enemy's movements they remained cooped up in a fortress, quite unmindful of his approach on three sides and of his menace to their base line. The utter inefficiency of the Chinese generalship must not be forgotten as affording favorable conditions that furnish no real test of the Japanese evolutions. Perhaps the lesson of chief interest to be derived from this campaign was its conclusive demonstration of the theory of sea-power recently formulated by Captain Mahan, United States Navy. Japan's correct use of her fleet and transports in conveying troops simultaneously to Chemulpo and Gensan, and detaching a few vessels and torpedo-boats to secure the Tai tong estuary against surprise, both insured the success of her army in Korea and determined at the first blow the issue of the military campaign there.

Immediately after the battle the Japanese pushed a strong column along the route leading to the Amnok gang, or Yalu, River and Manchuria, less than one hundred and fifty miles by road from Ping yang. Here at Wiju, on the southern bank, the whole of the First Army had assembled by October 20th, having encountered on the march only such difficulties as the physical character of the country presented. The Chinese, demoralized by their reverses, had not tried to make a stand until safely across the river, where they were now re-enforced by troops sent to this point both by land and sea. As for Korea, the ground was swept clear of Chinese; not a single "brave" lingered anywhere in the peninsula except in hiding. The completeness of this result was due, however, not alone to the victory of Ping yang, but to the naval battle fought one day later in the Bay of Korea.

A policy of masterly inactivity had been maintained by the Chinese fleet after the brush with the Japanese cruisers off Asan. It is difficult to account for this except upon the general ground of Chinese ignorance and ineptness in the art of war. During the month of August there occurred a series of palace upheavals, about which little is known, but the secret influences of which told lamentably upon the conduct of the war. Now the war party, and again the peace-at-any-price party, would secure the Emperor's ear, and with each obscure success the policy of the nation and the generals at the front must be changed. Habit and custom also inclined the Court to land rather than sea campaigns, and it is probable that they trusted to saving Korea by the historic route through Manchuria, preferring to retain the fleet as a secondary defence against the contingency of a direct invasion of China by Japan. This policy, whatever its motive, was altered when they observed that Japan was pouring troops into Korea faster than China, and that they already outnumbered them in the Tai tong valley. This induced them early in September to despatch transports from Talien Bay, on Regent's Sword, to the Yalu, under convoy of Admiral Ting's squadron. The trip was made and the troops landed with success. As the ships were returning they met, on the morning of September 17th, the Japanese fleet under Admiral Ito, which, having been employed on the same business at Chemulpo, was reconnoitring the coast in search of the enemy. The two fleets were nearly equal in effective strength, with twelve vessels on either side; the advantage of tonnage (about 38,400 to 33,300) and quick-firing guns was with the Japanese, and that of protective armor and heavy guns with the Chinese, conditions which might have rendered the contest pretty equal, except that skill, mutual support, and efficiency were almost wholly on the Japanese side. It should be added, however, that the latter was seriously hampered in its evolutions by the presence of an armed transport and a gun-boat which ought not to have been allowed to remain after the enemy was sighted. The Chinese strength was not materially increased by the arrival of two gun-boats and six torpedo-boats during the action, though it is supposed that the presence of the latter[1] influenced the Japanese admiral in

---

[1] Only two of these, according to Captain McGiffin, went into the action at all.—*The Century*, August, 1895.

withdrawing his ships before dark, thus allowing the escape of Ting to Port Arthur.

This most important sea-fight since the engagement of the *Monitor* and *Merrimac* lasted about five hours. Coming upon the enemy near the island of Hai yang (Hai yun tau), about half-way between Port Arthur and Ta tung kau, on the Yalu, the Japanese were able by their superior speed to circle around their adversary, keeping at safe distance from the two armored battle-ships and concentrating their fire with deadly effect upon the weaker vessels of his squadron. The Chinese formed in a line with the iron-clads *Chen yuen* and *Ting yuen* in the centre; they were met by the Japanese advancing in column at an acute angle across the front of this line, but in two divisions, one made up of their four fastest vessels, the other of the slower craft. Admiral Ito probably had some motive in executing this manœuvre, which does not transpire; it was only possible to avoid the risk of ramming thus incurred by crossing the enemy's bows at double his speed and at a distance that diminished the efficacy of his own fire. One vessel, the *Hiyei*, indeed, failing to get across, turned and passed between the two Chinese iron-clads, preferring punishment from them to the risk of annihilation from the concentrated fire of their entire line. After this first movement the order of the Chinese was soon broken, and four of their ships were in turn singled out and destroyed by the quicker moving Japanese.[1] The Front, or Flying, Squadron of the latter was deflected for a short time from its intention of wheeling round the Chinese by the appearance of the *Kwang ping* and the *Ping yuen* with the torpedo-boats from the Yalu estuary. These being chased away, they returned to protect the *Akagi* and *Saiko Maru*, and the now shattered *Hiyei*, their three weak vessels, which were thus able to effect their escape from the battle. The fiercest fighting of the day now occurred between the Main Japanese squadron of five and the Chinese centre of two armored vessels, the two flagships *Matsushima* and *Ting yuen* being closely engaged. The

---

[1] A fifth ran aground while retreating near Talien Bay, and was blown up to prevent her capture by the Japanese.

Chinese ship was once in flames, that might have got beyond control had not her sister ship, the *Chen yuen*, come to her aid. To the successful resistance of these two armored vessels against the whole fighting strength of the Japanese is due the rescue of the Chinese fleet from extermination. The iron-clads were less effective than might have been the case had they been adequately supplied with shells; having for the most part to use solid shot in their great guns, they were able only to injure where they might have destroyed. A single 30.5-centimetre shell from the *Chen yuen* bursting on the *Matsushima* killed or wounded eighty of her crew, disabled her 13-inch Canet gun, and set her on fire. With a larger stock of such ammunition these two iron-clads might have withstood for an indefinite time any force the Japanese could bring within range. Their weakness in this respect, and the demoralization of the rest of the fleet, however, made them anxious to retire, and at 5.30 P.M., with their last shot in their cannon, they thankfully observed their enemy turn from the pursuit, and with their shattered fleet crept back to Port Arthur.

The naval power of China, so far as it affected this campaign, had been destroyed at a blow; her best ships were greatly damaged, her prestige gone. While her actual losses in men and material were not irreparable,[1] this defeat opened the sea to the enemy as effectually as Ping yang had left him full control of Korea. She had been dazed by the suddenness of the first disaster, she was paralyzed by this. Her collapse was so

---

[1] They are estimated at about 700 killed—600 of these in the sinking of three vessels—and 200 or 300 wounded. The Japanese loss was only 115 killed and 103 wounded. The literature on this engagement, which is commonly, though erroneously, known in English as the Yalu battle, is already copious, but in few instances authoritative or instructive. Besides technical treatises in the military and naval journals of various nations may be mentioned Lieutenant von Müller, *Der Krieg zwischen China und Japan*, Part I., Berlin, 1895; P. N. McGiffin, *The Battle of the Yalu; personal recollections by the Commander of the "Chen yuen,"* *The Century*, August, 1895, and Captain Mahan's instructive comments on the article in the same magazine; W. L. Clowes. *The Naval War in the East*, *Blackwood's Magazine*, February, 1895; S. M. Eardley-Wilmot. *The Collapse of China at Sea*. *Fortnightly Review*, January, 1895: and H. A. Herbert, *The Fight off the Yalu River*, *North American Review*, November, 1894.

complete, and the exhibition of Japan's superiority so overwhelming, as to benumb the senses of her few capable military leaders and statesmen during the remainder of the war. Without attempting here to discuss the military and tactical features of this great battle, which is likely to occupy the attention of experts for some time to come, it would be difficult to exaggerate its transcendent importance in deciding the issue of this conflict. It not only dispirited the Chinese liberal and progressive leaders, but gave the anti-war cabal in the Palace renewed vigor in their opposition to the conduct of an energetic campaign and the employment of costly modern armaments. The reactionary policy was strong enough to forbid the purchase of new war material and to insist upon forwarding to the frontier recruits from the interior armed for the most part with matchlocks and bows. It was with such futile measures that unregenerate China a generation after Yuen ming yuen sought to oppose one of the best equipped and most skilfully conducted military invasions of modern times.

Having command of the sea, the first objective point of the Japanese was one of the two fortresses which had been built within recent years upon the promontories forming the entrance to the Gulf of Pechele. The point selected was Lü shun kau, called by Europeans Port Arthur, on the southeastern point of the Regent's Sword, or Liau tung Promontory, a harbor and arsenal that had been rendered practically impregnable at enormous cost under the superintendence of German and French engineers. With this stronghold and the sister fortress of Wei hai wei on the opposite promontory of Shantung untaken, the Japanese could not safely venture against Taku, however complete their mastery of the coasts and waters of the Yellow Sea. Their determination to reduce each of these places in turn while their army was working its way across Shingking shows at once their mastery of the military problem confronting them and their sense of the necessity of striking at the capital rather than at any of the great trading centres of China in order to secure permanent results from their victories. A second army was organized for this important work and placed under command of Marshal Oyama, Minister of war. Owing to the shoal water a landing-place was only found at the mouth of a little stream, the Hwa yuan, a hundred miles distant from Port Arthur. On October 24th the army disembarked from their transports without interference from a single Chinese ship, though several, if not all, of the Pei yang squadron must by this time have been in condition to considerably annoy the enemy in the dangerous operation of landing his troops, artillery, and stores. It was a costly mistake on the part of the Chinese. Like the Russians in the Crimea in 1854, their doom was sealed when, the invader once ashore, they had no better use for their ships than to sequester them uselessly under fortresses and behind a barrier of sunken torpedoes. The Japanese, sure of the water behind them, could ignore the sea approach to Port Arthur, and by occupying the neck of the peninsula could then cut off the hope of succor and reduce the forts at leisure. Their progress was rapid. Chin chow (or Kin chau) and the Talien Bay forts protecting this narrow isthmus fell on November 5th and 6th, after almost no fighting, and the Japanese held not only the formidable land defences of Port Arthur but a convenient landing-place for their siege-train and heavy artillery.

There remained only the march upon the Port with its formidable array of twenty-two supporting forts. With their customary precautions the invaders marched down the converging roads of the peninsula in two divisions, expecting opposition but meeting none, until, on November 20th, the Right Division after a slight skirmish drove the garrison out of the first fort reached. It was the same story with each in succession; by noon of the 21st the whole land defences had succumbed, and in the evening of that day the Japanese, at the absurdly small cost of eighteen men actually killed in battle,[1] were possessors of one of the strongest places and best

---

[1] About two hundred and seventy were wounded, of whom a number died subsequently. The Chinese casualties can only be roughly estimated at about a thousand, not including the villagers subsequently massacred. Besides the cannon and small arms an immense amount of stores, ammunition, and war material fell into the hands of the visitors. The docks, machinery, and buildings at Port Arthur are supposed to have cost China over $30,000,000.

equipped dock-yards in Eastern Asia. "A first-class fortress," observes an English writer in China, "splendidly armed and garrisoned by 20,000 troops, is stormed and taken in a few hours by an inferior force. It is a pitiable spectacle. In 1860 one of the Taku forts was cannonaded by a park of 11 siege guns, 36 field cannon, and a battery of rockets, which succeeded in blowing up the principal magazine, an incident calculated to demoralize the stoutest troops. When assaulted, and finally captured by nearly 3,000 French and English, the garrison were found to number but 500, of whom but 100 escaped alive, while the attacking party had 22 killed and 179 wounded. That was a sample of the kind of defence the Chinese could make a generation ago against the best troops in the world. Every one of the Port Arthur forts might have done as well. They were proportionally better armed, better disposed for defence, better fortified, more numerously garrisoned. Yet the total loss inflicted by them upon their assailants did not greatly exceed the loss suffered by the allies in capturing a single fort guarded by five hundred Chinamen. How such an extraordinary discrepancy of results is to be explained it is impossible to say. The Chinese appear to have been totally demoralized. The cruel lesson they received may be for their nation's ultimate good, but it is difficult not to be moved to some sentiment of compassion by the spectacle of a great nation put to such signal shame." [1]

To the shame of the Chinese on this occasion was added a disgrace of another sort acquired at Port Arthur, which is likely long to affect the reputation of the Japanese in the eyes of Christian peoples. It was here that the victors repaid savagery with savagery, and gave some credit to the sneer of their detractors that their civilization is only veneer. What happened after the fall of the stronghold has been vigorously denied by those chiefly implicated, but the witnesses to their conduct are too numerous and too reputable to be disbelieved. Upon entering the town the Japanese found the heads and mutilated corpses of a few of their captured comrades sus-

[1] *China Gazette* (Shanghai), December 1, 1894.

pended near the gates, and moved by the sight to a common impulse of fury, the soldiers broke at once into a disorderly pursuit of every living thing to be found in the place. Under the circumstances this might be considered a pardonable outburst of feeling; but the slaughter of non-combatants thus begun continued apparently without interference from their officers during four or five days in the town and outlying villages, and, not content with shooting their victims wherever found, the rampant soldiery hacked at their bodies and insulted them in unimaginable ways. It was a gratuitous ebullition of barbarism, a revolting repudiation of pretended humanity. "More of these piteous deaths we saw," says a correspondent on the spot,[1] "unable to stay the hands of the murderers, until sick and saddened beyond the power of words to tell we slowly made our way in the gathering gloom to headquarters. There at the Chinese general's pavilion, facing the spacious parade-ground, Field-Marshal Oyama and all his officers assembled amid strains of strange music from military bands, now weird, now lively, and ending with the impressive national anthem, 'Kimi gayo,' and a huge roar from 20,000 throats of *Banzai Nippon*. The contrast was horrible, insufferable." It must be added, moreover, that the Japanese had posted notices written in Chinese all over the place that the natives would be kindly treated who surrendered their arms and did not attempt escape. This had also been done after Ping yang, and the conquerors there had lived up to their word. Now the wretched inhabitants who believed and remained found no mercy, because their countrymen had known none when, in accordance with Asiatic usage, they butchered their prisoners. And the officers made no effort to stay their men. It was perhaps not altogether unnatural, but Western nations will not soon forget this quick relapse to the level of their despised antagonists.[2]

---

[1] *London Times*, January 9 and February 1, 1894.

[2] The foreign witnesses to this incident were the newspaper correspondents, military attachés, and members of the Red Cross Society, who attended one or both armies. The severest indictments against the Japanese were published by the New York *World* correspondent, Mr. J. Creelman, in his news-

Port Arthur and Talien at once became the naval base for the further operations of the Japanese, while the second army, after the intoxication of victory had passed, addressed itself composedly to the task of driving the enemy's few remaining troops out of Liautung and advancing in force to the mouth of the Liau at the head of the gulf. Meantime the first army, having crossed the Yalu, October 24th, the same day on which a landing was effected at Hwa yuan, occupied the important positions of Chiu lien (Kiu len tsz'), Antung, and Ta tung kau, and began the advance across Southern Manchuria in three divisions. With the approach of winter, campaigning in this country, which is similar in climate and many physical features to the Province of Quebec, became increasingly difficult.[1] The Chinese resistance, though ineffective, was more persistent, while the Japanese army was too small to both conquer and hold a difficult region without severe exertion that might, had the enemy understood his advantage, have fatally strained their strength. But other motives were at work which made Marshal Yamagata willing to delay. First of these was the necessity of waiting until Port Arthur fell and the second army could secure its left flank from attack by advancing to the line of the Liau River; this conjunction was not effected until the middle of January. Secondly, there appears on the part of the Japanese ministry from this time an increasing disinclination to push the Chinese government too hard, lest in sheer despair it would sacrifice its future and invite the intervention of some European power, or lest its military disasters, by arousing a rebellion, should suddenly sweep the reigning dynasty from the Throne, leaving no power with whom peace might be made and the country itself a prey to ravening foreigners. How greatly apprehensions like these influenced

---

paper, and by Mr. Frederic Villiers in the *North American Review* for March, 1895; both perhaps unduly emphasized the horrors of the affair. Compare Mr. Dun's despatches (88 and 90) in *United States Foreign Relations*, 1894, *Appendix* I. The number killed after the surrender is variously estimated at between two thousand and three thousand.

[1] The region is described in Williamson's *Journeys*, H. E. M. James's *Long White Mountain*, and F. E. Younghusband's *Heart of a Continent*.

Japanese policy will not soon be known, but it is interesting to note from this time onward their circumspection, their patience with the vacillating and undignified Chinese efforts to secure a suspension of hostilities, and the moderation of their terms when peace was ultimately concluded. The fall of Mukden, the old home of the reigning dynasty, and the burial-place of its earlier sovereigns, would have been a paralyzing blow to Manchu pride, involving a loss of prestige among their Chinese subjects quite incommensurate with its strategic importance. It is possible with this in mind to account for the feverish though futile efforts of the Chinese to protect the provincial capital, and the evident reluctance of the Japanese to incur the grave political embarrassments which its downfall might involve. Their troops after the capture of Ying tsz' (Ying kow, one of the treaty ports known as Niuchwang) and Haiching held the country effectually in their grasp, but they never advanced beyond the River Liau.

Before considering the tentative efforts of the Chinese Court toward arranging a truce with its adversary, it remains to describe the capture of Wei hai wei, which was important as a feat of arms rather than for its ultimate effect upon the course of the war. The village which gives its name to this fortress stands upon a deep bay in Shantung Promontory, the sea approach to which is defended by the large island of Liu kung, and a smaller one called Jih tau. About the circuit of the bay the ground rises abruptly from the water's edge to fine hills or bluffs between five hundred and fifteen hundred feet in height, which have been crowned by twelve forts of modern type, while three forts on the islands protect the entrance. These batteries were armed with fifty-seven guns, many of them quick-firing, and several mounted on disappearing carriages. In the harbor, which has anchor room for a whole navy, lay the poor residue of Admiral Ting's defeated squadron and such others as were left to China in her emergency—nine war-ships, six small gun-boats, and eleven torpedo-boats. These vessels could co-operate with the land batteries for the defence of the station, but they were imprisoned in the bay by two torpedo-booms stretched across the entrances to protect them from the Japanese fleet. The troops manning forts and ships together appear to have amounted to less than 10,000, a very inadequate number.[1] Such was the formidable place which the Japanese had determined to reduce, both to insure complete control of the Gulf of Pechele and to remove the danger from the remnant of the Pei yang squadron sheltered there. Like Port Arthur, the fortress might, under spirited leadership, have held out almost indefinitely against anything the enemy could bring against it, but the fighting spirit was as deplorably lacking here as there. The whole line of Chinese fortifications at Wei hai wei was, moreover, much too long to be held without the active aid of a field army, well organized and well handled; this, of course, they did not have, and the comparative uselessness of forts without soldiers to support them was clearly demonstrated by the Japanese success in this campaign.

Operations were begun about the middle of January by a feigned attack of the Japanese squadron upon Tăngchau and the destruction of the telegraph line near Yung ching. The invading army of 27,000 men, under Marshal Oyama, sailed from Talien Bay in fifty transports, accompanied by the entire available Japanese fleet, and landed, January 23d, in the Bay of Yung ching, immediately south of the extreme promontory of Shantung, and thirty-seven miles by land from Wei hai wei. The advance was made, as usual, in two columns. There was some show of fighting at the outset, but when first one fort fell, and then another, the remainder were evacuated without even the precaution of rendering their guns useless. Taking advantage of a storm of such severity as to compel the Japanese to suspend operations on February 1st, Admiral Ting landed a few sailors, who destroyed all the guns in the western forts before they could be taken, thus saving his ships and the islands from bombardment. So long as these remained intact the conquered town was an unpleasant resting-place for the invader, whose heaviest cannon in the eastern batteries were too far away to reach the anchorage, and whose fleet could not

---

[1] The Japanese gave the total strength of the Chinese at the time of the capitulation at 3,084 navy, and 2,040 army.

cross the torpedo-booms, covered as they were by the island forts. His dilemma was presently solved by one of the most remarkable and effective torpedo attacks attempted in modern warfare. On the night of February 4th–5th a flotilla of ten torpedo-boats succeeded in removing one end of the booms, and, stealing into the harbor, sank the battle-ship *Ting yuen.* Instantly the whole bay was a pandemonium of noise, while a hail of bullets fell upon the little craft as they sought to escape in the darkness. Two were lost and two disabled, but the rest escaped, and only fourteen men in all were killed or drowned. On the following night the attack was renewed with five boats, three of which succeeded in getting to the anchorge and destroying the *Lai yuen* and the *Wei yuen*, together with a transport, the *Pao hwa*, with no casualties. This appalling loss sealed the doom of the Chinese. Their torpedo-boats and two steam-launches dashed out from cover on the morning of the 8th, and made what shift they could to escape into the gulf. It is a significant testimony to the far-reaching nature of Chinese ineptitude and mal-administration that all this craft failed even in running away. If a torpedo-boat is good for anything it ought to be for speed, but these badly kept little vessels were in no condition to distance the fleet *Yoshino* which pursued them, and all were in time either sunk or captured or run ashore. In the combined action of the Japanese on shore and water against the islands the day following, the cruiser *Ching yuen* was sunk by two well-placed shells fired from the forts held by the enemy.

All that was left now was the brave old Admiral Ting with four fighting vessels and the Liu kung forts. To the credit of Admiral Ito and Marshal Oyama it must be recorded that they showed a humanity quite unusual in Asiatics, having invited him at the commencement of these operations to surrender to the inevitable and take refuge in Japan until peace was concluded, when he might be allowed to return and effect the necessary military reforms in his country. In his remarkable letter to him Admiral Ito makes an observation that deserves especial notice for its historical interest. He attributes the real cause of Chinese disaster to the literary class.

"It is not the fault of one man," he writes, "that has brought China into the position she now occupies; the blame rests with the errors of a Government that has long administered affairs. She selects her servants by competitive examination, and literary attainments are the test. Thus it results that her officers, the repositories of administrative power, are all literati, and literature is honored above everything. Her practice in this respect is as uniform as it was a thousand years ago. It is not necessarily a defective system, nor does it necessarily produce a bad government. But a country can never preserve its independence in practise by such means. For you know well what troubles Japan had to encounter thirty years ago, what perils she had to surmount. She owes her preservation and her integrity to-day wholly to the fact that she then broke away from the old and attached herself to the new. In the case of your country also that must be the cardinal course at present; if you adopt it I venture to say that you are safe; if you reject it you cannot escape destruction. In a contest with Japan it has long been fated that you should witness results such as are now before you. Can it be the duty of faithful subjects of the Empire, men really solicitous for its welfare, to swim idly with the tide now sweeping over the country by the decree of an ancient fate, making no effort to stem it? . . . To hand over squadrons to the foe, to surrender a whole army to the enemy, these are mere bagatelles compared with the fate of a country."[1]

It was the voice of the present addressing the dead past; there was no response. Admiral Ting, who is almost alone as an example of high honor in high command on his side during this war, was loyal only as a Chinaman understands loyalty. He knew the fate that awaits the defeated general in China; he also knew his duty as he had been taught. Making no reply to Ito's communication until the fall of the fortress was imminent, he then surrendered the helpless remnant of the fleet and forts (February 12th) and, together with three or four naval and military officers, committed suicide. It is pleasant to add that the enemy showed their appreciation of the defeated, but not dishonored, leader by returning his body to Chifu in the *Kwang tsi*, one of the surrendered steamers. The four men-of-war and six gun-boats delivered up were estimated as being worth 30,000,000 yen to the Japanese. All the land forts at Wei hai wei were destroyed by its captors, but Liu kung island and anchorage were held by a garrison until the conclusion of hostilities. Within a month of the day on which they landed at Yung ching the remainder of the army were

---

[1] Translated from the *Nichi Nichi Shimbun.*

re-embarked for Talien, where they joined the troops in Manchuria.

With the fall of Wei hai wei and the further successes in Manchuria, culminating in the capture of Old Niuchwang, Japan had secured all the prestige and possessions necessary to dictate her own terms of peace. An expedition to the Pescadores in March, which effected the reduction of the forts on Pang hu, the principal island of the group, a convenient base for operations against Formosa, was the only other military movement of importance undertaken during the war. By this time, however, both sides were devoting their best energies, not to the continuance of the conflict, but to arranging a peace. Some ineffectual efforts to this end had already been made by China. Soon after the fall of Port Arthur, Mr. Detring, an American employee of the government as Customs Commissioner at Tientsin, had been sent to Japan with propositions of peace, but either through sheer fatuousness or ignorance of diplomatic usage the envoy was furnished with a letter from Li Hung-chang in lieu of suitable credentials, and the Japanese prime-minister refused to see him. He was promptly recalled, but when a second mission was sent in January to Japan with two plenipotentiaries and a considerable retinue, together with General John W. Foster, ex-secretary of state of the United States, as adviser, and the credentials again proved to be insufficient, the Court at Peking laid itself open to the charge of trifling or something worse in a very serious national predicament. It is hardly probable, however, that this apparent tergiversation arose from anything but the pitiable incapacity of a palace council distraught with apprehension and as helpless in this emergency as it had been in 1861. An attempt was first made to amend the instructions given to the Ministers Chang and Shao, but a person of greater reputation and authority was manifestly needed in the exigency. Through the masterful influence of the Empress Dowager the Viceroy Li Hung-chang was restored to the honors that had been taken from him after the early disasters of the war and ordered to Shimonoseki with plenary powers. This astute statesman was able to forestall the criticisms of his personal enemies by inviting every official of the first rank to send a memorial on the advisability of concluding the war, and, since the necessity of so doing was obvious, he had no difficulty in thus securing for his mission the moral support of the literati, besides the expressed command of his sovereign. The viceroy, with a respectable suite numbering one hundred and thirty-two persons, again including General Foster as confidential adviser, landed at Shimonoseki on March 20th, and at once began negotiations. With no possible chance left to defend herself on land or on sea, China, so soon as she gave over her shuffling policy and consented to sue in earnest for peace, was let off with only the abandonment of her old pretensions as to Korea, the cession of Formosa, the Pescadores, and Liau tung Promontory, and the payment of an indemnity. While these terms were under consideration occurred a savage attempt on the part of a fanatic to assassinate the aged Chinese envoy. Fortunately the wound inflicted was slight; the incident caused, however, a feeling of profound mortification in the breasts of the sensitive Japanese. It had the beneficent effect for Li's country of inducing the Japanese Emperor to assent immediately to an armistice (March 30th), which was made perpetual by the signature of a treaty on April 17th.[1]

---

[1] The treaty, which was ratified at Chifu, May 8th, ceded to Japan the promontory of Liau tung, Formosa, and the Pescadores, provided for the independence of Korea, an indemnity of Tls. 2,000,000, to be paid in instalments within seven years, the opening to foreign trade of Shashi in Hupeh, Chungking, in Sz'chuen, Suchau, in Kiangsu, and Hangchau, in Chekiang, navigation of the Woosung and upper Yangtsz', the right to erect warehouses in the interior and to engage in manufacturing in China, and the gradual withdrawal of the Japanese troops. The Liau tung clause was subsequently omitted, for which China paid an additional sum of Tls. 50,000,000. The indemnity was reduced from Tls. 3,000 000 to Tls. 2,000,000, the new treaty ports from seven to four, and the navigation of the Siang and West Rivers, at first demanded, withdrawn during the negotiations. The commercial treaty also provided for in the compact was not concluded until the fall of 1896. Its most important provision allows the right of manufacture by Japan within China, "the taxation on such undertakings to be governed entirely by the Shimonoseki Treaty," which leaves the privilege rather obscure. The commercial provisions of the treaty are likely to embody the most important results of the war in case China remains

No more significant indication of the increasing importance of Eastern Asia in the world's politics has appeared in recent years than the concern with which this war was watched by European governments. It had been a revelation of the enormous value of scientific training and modern military methods over mere numbers in antique array; more than this, it demolished China's pretensions to rank among political powers of the first magnitude and proclaimed Japan as likely to become the foremost factor in Asiatic politics. Without pausing in this concluding paragraph to discuss the historical consequence of the appearance of a new military power in the family of nations, its full gravity must be understood in order to comprehend the attitude of those European states that have within a century accustomed themselves to regard Asia as a territory wholly at their disposal. Japan's victory introduced a power naturally at variance with any division of the spoil that would be suggested by Europeans, a rival claimant for supremacy in the Far East that, politically speaking, was born but yesterday. Her military successes were so rapid and overwhelming as to offer no opportunity for armed interference during the eight months of the war; there occurred no long sieges like those of Sevastapol and Plevna, when an outsider might call a halt. But at the conclusion of peace it was feared that the pride of Japan if unopposed might be liable in future to commit any excess. Two plans remained open to interested European statesmen: to proceed at once to the partition of China between themselves and Japan, or to compel the victorious nation to surrender some part of its spoil, and preserve for China at least the form and outward show of her independence. A coalition of Russia, France, and Germany decided upon the latter programme; Great Britain, either through dislike or indifference, declined to join them, thereby gaining from Japan whatever feeling of gratitude she might lose in China. Japan was advised to withdraw the demand for Liau tung, in-

---

an autonomous state. The periodical literature upon the political and trading aspects of China as affected by the war and its concluding treaty is too recent and accessible to call for specification.

cluding the fortress of Port Arthur; in view of the armed forces representing these three military nations she consented, but the bitterness of the humiliation thus inflicted upon a sensitive and impetuous people is something that, though bravely concealed, remains to be reckoned with in the future.

INDEX.

ABEL, Clarke, 106.
Abu Zaid's work on China, 34, 62, 73.
Adams, J. Quincy, mistaken idea of Chinese War, 117.
Aksu, in Ili, Yakub Beg captures, 378.
Alcock, Sir R., 275.
Almanac, given by China to Korean King, 437.
Amherst, Lord, embassy to Peking, 106.
American, trade with China, 108; and Governor-General Lin at Canton, 172; embassy concludes treaty of Wanghia, 215; homicide of a Chinese in Canton, 216; Chinese favorably disposed to, 218; fleet destroy the Barrier forts, 286; government asked to co-operate with Great Britain, 290; Minister Reed, arrives, 291; Minister Ward assists in checking coolie trade, 311; negotiations at Taku forts, 313; embassy escorted to Peking, 317; minister declines to kotow, 318; sailor hung for murder at Shanghai, 344; treaty with China negotiates by Burlingame, 346; missionaries flee from Tăngchau, 353; commission of inquiry to Sz'chuen, 436; treaty with Korea, 438.
Amoy, Chinese and Dutch take, 86; trade of East India Company at, 93, 96; captured by the British, 172, 176; not hostile to foreigners, 221; during Tai-ping Rebellion, 277.
Anderson, Dr. J., 377, 379, 380.
Annam, and France, 390; Chinese suzerainty over, 392, 395, 438; French protectorate over, 403.
Anti-foreign riots in China, 348, 419–436.
An-ting măn, Peking gate opened to the allied troops, 334.
Arab travellers in China, 62, 79.
Army of China, condition at outbreak of Tai-ping Rebellion, 138; in war with Japan, 450.
Arrow, case of the lorcha, 283–286.
Ashmore, Rev. W., 431, 433, 435.
Asan, Korea, fighting near, 443, 444.
Auber, on foreign trade, 98, 101.
Audience, before Chinese Emperor, Dutch, 83; Lord Macartney's, 103; question not raised by Minister Cushing, 118; discussed by Minister Ward, at the capital, 317; description of, at Yuen-ming yuen, 331; first, granted to all foreign ministers, 362; renewed discussion and settlement, 413.

BABER, E. C., with Grosvenor mission, 371, 372.
Bakninh, in Tongking, 394, 397.
Ball, J. Dyer, 434, 435.
Bamboo books, the, their authenticity, 15, 21.
Barrier forts, Canton River, destroyed by Americans, 286.
Barrow, J., 103.
Behaine, Bishop Pigneaux de, in Annam, 390.
Bell, John, residence in Peking, 90.
Bible, mention of China in, 56; revision and J. R. Morrison, 108.
Black flags in Tongking, 393, 396.
Bogue, or Bocca Tigris, Canton River, negotiations with Kishen at, 165; forts taken, 168; destroyed again, 176; supplementary treaty signed at, 209; Governor Davis retakes the forts, 221.
Bonham, Governor, visits Tai-pings at Nanking, 225; advised by Canton gentry not to enter the city, 273.
Book of Records (*Shu King*), 12 ff., 35.
Books, burned by Tsin, 27; destroyed at Canton, 274.
Boulger, D. C., 3; on Turkestan, 376; on Mohammedan revolt, 378, 379.
Boundary disputes, on the Amur, 89; at Kuldja, 381.
Bowring, Sir J., and Viceroy Yeh, 281; his character, 282; and the *Arrow* case, 283; opens hostilities, 285; his conduct discussed in Parliament, 289.
Braam, A. van, Dutch Ambassador to China, 87.
Bremer, Sir G., attacks Tinghai, 162;

captures Bogue forts, 165, 168; sails for Calcutta. 169.
Bretschneider, Dr. E., 61.
Bruce, Sir F. A., and the Ever-Victorious force, 259; endorses Gorden's conduct, 267; sent by Lord Elgin to Tientsin, 303; repairs to Taku with allies, 312, 313, 319, 320; and the Lay-Osborne flotilla affair, 341, 342; his influence in China, 347.
Buddha's relics sought by Chinese embassy, 62.
Buddhism, introduced into China, 29; in the fourth century, 31; and the Emperor Wuti, 32.
Buddhist, pilgrims between China and India, 61; notions of cosmogony, 5; charm cut in Kü-yung kwan, 42.
Burgevine, Henry, commands the Ever-Victorious force, 257; joins the Tai-pings, 261; proposal to Gordon, 262.
Burlingame, Anson, 343; represents China to foreign powers, 344; his death, 346; personal influence in China, 347.
Burma, becomes British, 408; as a fief of China, 408, 438.
Bushell, Dr. S. W., 26, 40.

CAILLAUD, F. R. DE, 392.
Canfu (Kanpu), 52; Abu Zaid on, 63.
Cannon found at Tinghai, 173; at Shanghai, 184; at the Barrier Forts, 286.
Canton, taken by Manchus in 1650, 45; Roman Embassy reaches, 58; East India Company at, 94; homicides among foreigners at, 99; Lord Napier at, 115–21; Lin detains foreigners in, 146; Elliot leaves, 151; fortified, 161, 169; Elliot accepts ransom for, 171; dislike of foreigners in, 203; Kiying sent to, 205; troubles with foreigners at, 216; admission of foreigners to, 221; lawlessness at. 228; sentiment in, 273; rebels about, 278; their wholesale execution. 280; Admiral Seymour enters, 286; French legation withdraws from, 287; captured by Franco-British forces, 292; Elgin's tact at, 295. 309; coolies serve British at Taku, 322; French missionary aggressions at. 357; river obstructed during hostilities with France, 401.
Cathay, signification in Middle Ages, 56.
Ceylon, Yungloh's expedition against, 62.
Chang-an, in Shensi. See Si-ngan.
Changchau, in Fuhkien, captured by Tai-pings, 253.
Chang Chi-tung, 419.
Changsha stormed by Tai-pings, 243.
Chapu, 62; captured by the British, 181.
Chau Dynasty, 23–26, 28; After Chau, 38.
Chau-sin, Emperor of the Shang, 22.
Chen-yuen, battleship, 448, 449.
Chifu, in Shantung, French at, 320; Convention, 372, 406; during war with Japan, 458; treaty ratified at, 460.
Children, in Romanist asylum at Tientsin, 348; rumors as to Catholics kidnapping, 423.
Chin Dynasty, 32.
China, probable origin from *Tsin*, 27; early history, 1; earliest notices of, 56; condition of, after Opium War, 221; forcibly opened, 304; condition in 1865, 340; hopeful prospects for, 386; policy toward vassals, 392, 437; attitude in Port Hamilton affair, 410; and foreign powers in compensation for riots, 456; and Korea, 437; appeals to Russia, 442; naval power shattered, 449; concludes peace with Japan, 460.
Chinchew, or Tsiuenchau, the ancient Zayton, 70, 76.
Chinese, chronology and cosmogony, 2–10; their origin, 10; adopt the queue, 45; isolation and suspicion of foreigners, 54; ideas of foreigners influenced by Portuguese, 75; maltreated by Spanish in Manila, 80; terms for "foreigner," 109; view of the Opium War, 156; feeling during Tai-ping troubles, 252, 273; abused by foreigners, 354; character exhibited during the great famine, 383, 384; Education Commission to the United States, 387, 388; suzerainty over Annam, 392; tendency to combine, 433; declare war with Japan. 444; ineptness in war, 446; demoralization at Port Arthur, 452; corruption evident everywhere, 405, 457.
Chinhai, in Chehkiang, captured, 174.
Chin Hwa-ching, Chinese General at Wusung, 182, 183.
Chinkiang, in Kiangsu, taken by British. 188; by Tai-pings, 244; recaptured by rebels, 253; riot at, 432.
Christianity, in Formosa 82; Hung Siutsuen converted to, 234, 236; in Tai-ping movement, 248; Elgin to missionaries upon, 297; an official opinion of, 355; persecuted in Sz'chuen, 420, 421; imperial edict endorsing, 432.
Chronology, Chinese, 1; its claim to belief, 9.
Chu Han, author of anti-foreign libels, 434.
Chu Hi, commentator of Confucius, on cosmogony. 7; on the tablets of Yu, 16; the scholar in politics, 40.
Chun, the Seventh Prince, 374; made prime minister, 398; emerges from the Palace and visits arsenals, etc., 405; and Western science, 415, 419.
Chunghow, escorts American embassy to Peking, 316; and the Tientsin riot, 350, 351; sent to France, 353; abused by

foreign press, 354; in Russia, 379; his punishment, 380.
Chungking, in Sz'chuen, opened to trade, 425.
Chusan Archipelago, British in, 163; restored, 228.
Cochin-China seized by France, 391.
Colquhoun, A. R., 405, 406.
Commerce. See Trade.
Confucius, temple to, at Peking, 25; and the early emperors, 12; writings burned, 27.
Coolie trade, and Kwangtung rebellion, 279; its atrocities, 310; laborers employed by British at Taku, 332; convention respecting, 346; finally abolished, 363.
Cooper, T. T., 367.
Cordier, Henri, 272, 397.
Corea. See Korea.
Cosmogony, Chinese, 3; Chu Hi's, 7.
Courbet, Admiral, 397; at Fuhchau, 399, and Formosa, 400.
Creelman, J., 453.
Cunningham, A., 427.
Curzon, G. N., 414, 435.
Cushing, Caleb, United States Minister to China, 213; concludes a treaty at Wanghia, 215; correspondence in homicide case, 216.
Customs, Chinese Imperial, management by foreigners, 275, 306; under Sir R. Hart, 343; disliked by literati, 419; house at Wuhu attacked, 422.
Cycle adopted by Hwangti, 12.

D'AVEZAC, 64, 66.
Davis, Sir J., meets Kiying, 215; takes the Bogue forts, 221, 222; his *China during the War*, 224.
De Guignes, 58, 87.
Deluge of Yao, probably an inundation, 13.
Denby, Colonel Charles, 411; his defence of missions, 436.
Dent, Thomas, invited to meet Lin, 147; conducted to the consulate by Elliot, 148; desired as a hostage, 156.
Detring, Commissioner, 398, 459.
Dew, Captain, captures Ningpo, 257; before Shauhing, 258.
Douglas, R. K., 398.
Dudgeon, Dr. J., 91.
Du Halde, J. B., 91, 367.
Dunganis, Mohammedan tribe, and Yakub Beg, 375; their revolt, 378.
Dupré, Admiral, 394.
Dupuis, T., filibusterer in Tongking, 392, 394.
Dutch, driven from Formosa by Koxinga, 46; in the Pescadores, 101; Chinese notice of the, 75; trade and embassies to China, 82.
Dutch Folly Fort, at Canton, British bombard from, 288.
Dynasties, table of Chinese, 52.

EAST INDIA COMPANY, influence and character in China, 91; monopoly ceases, 107, 111; attempts to trade at Fuhchau, 93; controls British in China, 101; its responsibility, 106; its cessation, 107, 386.
Eclipses, noticed in the *Shu King*, 15.
Elgin, Lord, on the *Arrow* case, 285; reaches China, 291; before Canton, 292; forms a provisional government there, 294; replies to Shanghai missionaries, 297; at Tientsin, 299, 303; visits Taipings at Hankow, 305; among natives near Canton, 309; reappointed plenipotentiary, 319; refuses surrender of Taku forts, 325; view of the pillage of Yuen-ming Yuen, 331; orders its destruction, 332; signs treaty of Peking, 334; his character, 336.
Elliot, Charles, British superintendent of trade, 129; his opinion of opium trade, 130; ordered to drive away the opium ships, 139; exertions against smuggling, 144; offers co-operation with Lin, 147; circular on surrender of opium, 150; leaves Canton, 151; retires to ships, 154; effect upon Lin of his protecting Mr. Dent, 157; returns as plenipotentiary, 163; interview with Kishen, 164; at the Bogue, 166; his humane policy, 167; reward offered for, 168; ransoms Canton, 171; superseded by Sir H. Pottinger, 172.
Elliot, G., British admiral, 163.
Ellis, Henry, 106.
Embassy, received by Kienlung, 48; from Rome to China, 58; Ibn Batuta, 70; under the Mings, 74; Portuguese, 76; Spanish, 80; Dutch, 86, 87; Lord Macartney's, 102; Lord Amherst's, 106; Pottinger inquires as to reception of, 200; Chinese, under Burlingame, 345; tribute, from Annam, 395; from Korea, 437.
Emigration of Chinese to America, 347.
Emperor of China, in Chinese annals, 20; Ming and Tsing dynasties, 52; succession of the present, 374; his accession to throne, 410; audiences, 414.
Empress-regent, during Tungchi, 50; critical position of, at death of Hienfung, 339; and marriage of Tungchi, 358; of Kwangsü, 411; death of Tsz' An, the "Eastern," 375; Tsz' Hi dismisses Prince Kung, 397; and Liu Pingchang, 436; retires, 411; and Li Hungchang, 412, 459.
England, attitude at commencement of opium war, 158; observations upon, 220; China and Japan, 409, 461.

English, attempt trade in 1635 and 1664, 92; and French sailors quarrel, 99; troops at Macao, 104; and Chinese expectations of Napier, 114; petition to king from, at Canton, 124; losses in opium war, 204; murder of, near Canton, 226; consuls at Chinese ports, 227; waive right to enter Canton, 221, 273; attack pirates, 280; flag insulted, 283; open hostilities at Canton, 286; opinion at home supports Palmerston, 289; influence of consular body in China, 337; explorers in Yunnan, 366–370; jealousy of French in Tongking, 398; concessions as to Chinese suzerainty over Burma, 408; seizure of Port Hamilton, 409.

Escayrac-de-Lauture, Comte de, imprisoned at Peking, 332.

Ever-Victorious Force (*Chang-shing Kiun*), organized by General Ward, 255; under Colonel Gordon, 257; uniform and character, 259; captures Fushan, etc., 260; before Suchau, 261; last operations, 265; dissolved, June, 1864, 266.

Exports, duties on, in the eighteenth century, 95.

Ex-territoriality, its inherent wrong, 305; Chinese inquire concerning, 307; indirect influence of, 343; assumption of, by British Minister, 374; proposed extension, 430.

FACTORIES, the, Canton, 122; attacked by Chinese mob, 143; Lin shuts foreigners in, 148; occupied by British troops, 169; brawl and fire at, 204; burned by Gov. Yeh, 287.

Famine, of 1878, extent, 382; relieved by foreigners, 384; follows Yellow River flood, 418.

Fan kwei, "foreign devil," use and influence of epithet, 109; its gradual disappearance, 310; in Wusueh, 424.

Fisher, Col. G. B., 308, 311, 315, 316, 323.

Five Sovereigns, the, of Chinese legendary history, 8–14.

Flint tries to establish trade, 96; is imprisoned, 97.

Foochow. See Fuhchau.

Foreigners in China, Chinese contempt for, 98–102; terms for, 109; kept like animals in Canton, 125; imprisoned in the factories, 148; disliked by natives, 156; comprehended in treaty of Nanking, 209; hated by Cantonese, 226, 228; and the Tai-pings at Nanking, 245; none injured by rebels, 252; enlisted by rebels, 254; and by imperialists, 255; in the Ever-Victorious force, 259; collect duties for government at Shanghai, 275; Chinese opinion of, after war of 1860, 337; on Chinese war vessels, 340; abuse China, 354; admitted to imperial audience, 362, 413; assist in relieving famine of 1878, 383; and Franco-Chinese hostilities in 1884, 401; an Order of the Double Dragon instituted for, 404; concerted movement of the literati against, 420; their indiscretions, 433; treatment of, improved by Sz'chuen commission, 437.

Formosa, or Taiwan, Dutch driven from, 46, 81–86; massacre of shipwrecked crews on, 202; during Tai-ping rebellion, 252; Japanese raid on, 364; development of, 366; attacked by the French, 400; ceded to Japan, 459–460.

Forts, at the Bogue, 168; at Taku, 324; at Port Arthur, 451; at Wei hai wei, 455–457.

Foster, Gen. J. W., 459.

Fournier convention, 398.

French, relations with China, 89; and English brawls at Canton, 99; treaty of Whampoa, 219; attack rebels at Shanghai, 276; legation leaves Canton, 287; grievance against China, 290; convention of Peking, 335; massacred at Tientsin, 348; action in consequence, 351, 435; interest in Indo-China, 390; acquire protectorate over Tongking, 395; destroy Fuhchau arsenal, 899; unwilling to invade China, 402; protect all Roman Catholics in China, 407; and Korea, 437; coalition with Russia and Germany to check Japan, 461.

Fuhchau (Foochow), van Hoorn reaches, 86; East India Company tries trade at, 93; treatment of foreigners at, 228; arsenal established at, 344; arsenal destroyed by French, 399; head-quarters of Nanyang, 405.

Fuh-hi, the first monarch of China, 8.

Fuhshau (Fat-shau) captured by rebels, 278, 279.

Fung Yun-shan, an early follower of Hung Siu-tsuen, 234; made the 'Southern King,' 244; disappears, 250.

GARNIER, Lieut. Fr., 391; in Tongking, 394.

Gaudar, Père, 419.

Gautier, Hippolyte, 396.

Gensan (Wŏnsan), in Korea, 444.

Gerbillon, Père, 47, 89.

German, representative sent to China, 1843, 213; neutrality and officers in 1883, 397, 400; Catholic missionaries, 407, 408; in coalition to check Japan, 461.

Genghis Khan takes Peking, 410.

God perhaps worshipped by Chingtang as Shangti, 20.

Goës, Benedict, journey to Cathay, 72.

Gordon, Charles George, commands the Ever-Victorious force, 257, 259; during

the Tai-ping rebellion, 260-267; advice to Peking officials in case of war, 381.
Gough, Sir Hugh, reaches China and assumes command, 169; invests Canton, 170; at Ningpo, 177; force at Chapu, 181; at Chinkiang, 189, 190; before Nanking, 193; rewarded, 204.
Grand Canal, deepened by Kublai, 42; Tai-pings control, 244; Gaudar on, 419.
Great Wall of China, built by Tsin, 26; Mongol arch in, 42.
Greece, China known as Θῖν in, 56: communication with China in dark ages, 60.
Greig, Dr. J. A., outrage on, near Kirin, 425.
Griffis, W. E., 438.
Gros, Baron, reaches China, 291; at fall of Canton, 294; reaches Tientsin, 299; leaves China, 309; reappointed envoy, 319; signs treaty of Peking, 334; his ability, 336.
Gros, Jules, 396.
Grosier, Abbé, 367.
Grosvenor, T. G., commissioner sent to Yunnan, 371.
Gully, Robert, shipwrecked and murdered on Formosa, 202.
Gundry, R. S., 399, 410, 414, 415, 418.
Gutzlaff, Charles, 3, 46; at Chusan during war, 163; at Shanghai, 184; at Chinkiang, 190; services unrecognized, 204.

HAILING, General, at Chinkiang, his devotion, 188; posthumous honors to, 205.
Hai-tien, near Peking, Allies at, 331; Dowager-Empress at, 412.
Hai yang tau, naval battle of, 448.
Hakkas and the Tai-pings, 230; quarrels with natives, 239.
Hamburg, T., *Life of Hung Siu-tsuen*, 230.
Han Dynasty, its historians, 25; its founder, 28; and Eastern Han, 30; the After Han, 38.
Hangchau, capital of Chehkiang, Abu Zaid on, 63; retaken by imperialists, 266; Romanist church confiscated, 335.
Hankow, in Hupeh, during rebellion, 248, 255.
Hanoi, in Tongking, captured by Garnier, 392; Rivière at, 396.
Hart, Sir R., takes management of Chinese Customs service, 343; on Dowager-Empress, 398; arranges preliminaries of peace, 402.
Hayton of Armenia visits Mangu khan, 68.
Heeren, A. H. L., 58-60.
Hi, Empress-Dowager, Regent, 50, 339, 358, 411; dismisses Prince Kung, 397; defends Viceroy Liu, 436; retires, 411; and Li, 412, 459.
Hia Dynasty, founded, 14; early annals, 18; its period, 24.
Hia, a Tartar tribe, 39, 40.
Hideyoshi's invasion of Korea, 437.
Hienfung, Emperor, 50; attitude toward foreigners, 223; his imbecility during Tai-ping revolt, 252; ignorance during war with England, 290; signs Tientsin treaty, 304; escapes to Jeh-ho, 327; his death, 337.
History and chronology in China, 2; period of fable, 3; of legend, 9; of the twenty-six dynasties, 14-53; work of Chinese, 61.
Hobson, B. H. E., 46.
Ho Kwei-tsing, viceroy of Kiangsu, cowardice, 253; receives letters of the allies, 296; replies to Mr. Bruce, 320.
Holland, T. E., 443.
Homicides, foreign, at Canton, 99-103; of Lin at Hongkong, 153; of Sü A-mun at Canton, 216; of English near Canton, 226.
Honan landholders and the Yellow River, 418.
Hong merchants, monopoly established, 95; relations with foreign traders, 98; placed between Governor Lu and Napier, 117, 121; and native shopkeepers, 125; protest against opium smuggling, 141, 142; a last effort to squeeze, 207.
Hongkong, homicide at, 153; seized by the British, 205; smuggling at, 281; foreigners poisoned at, 288; British encouragement to smuggling, 373; during Franco-Chinese hostilities, 401; smuggling checked by convention, 406.
Hoorn, Pieter van, Dutch ambassador, 86.
Hoppin, J. M., 287.
Howqua, a Canton merchant, 207.
Huc, Père, E. R., 71, 356.
Hué, in Annam, escapes capture, 391; a French Resident in, 395.
Hunan province, inscription of Yu in, 15; hatred of foreigners in, 434.
Hung Jin, brother of the Tien Wang, 230; converted, 234, 235; at capture of Nanking, 268; subsequent efforts, 270.
Hung Siu-tsuen, the Tien Wang or Taiping leader, 230; his vision, 231; belief in divine calling, 233; applies to Roberts, 236; begins military operations, 238; opposes Triad Society, 239; proclaimed Emperor at Nanking, 242; climax of his movement, 247; indomitable spirit, 253; death, 268; character of his ambitions, 271.
Hungwu, Emperor, founds the Ming dynasty, 43.
Huns, driven back by Tsin, 27; repeated inroads, 31; their kingdom of Wei, 321.
Hunter, W. C., 208.
Hwang ho. See Yellow River.
Hwangti, an appellation of the Emperor, 12, 362.

Hwashan, Fuhkien, massacre at, 427.
Hwashana, Commissioner, at Tientsin, 299; at Shanghai, 305, 312; discussions with Ward at Peking, 317.

I, "BARBARIAN," a term for foreigners in China, 109.
I, Prince, at Tungchau, 326, 327; prisoners sent to, 328; his palace assigned to Elgin, 334; his conspiracy, 338; death, 339.
Ibn Batuta, travels in Cathay, 69.
Ibn Wahab, Arab traveller, 62, 73.
Ichang on the Yangtsz' reception of British at, 192; riot, 425, 452.
Ides, E. Ysbrandt, Russian envoy to Peking, 90.
Ilipu, Commissioner, 165; banishment, 177; thanks English, 182; associated with Kiying, 185; concludes treaty, 195, 201; his death, 205.
Isolation of the Chinese, causes and results, 290, 296, 308.
Ito Hirobumi, Count, 440.
Ito Yuko, Admiral, 447; correspondence with Ting, 458.

JAMES, H. E. M., 454.
Japan, raid on Formosa, 364; interest of, in Port Hamilton, 409; relations with Korea, 437; convention of 1885, 440; declares against with China, 443; European jealousy of, 461.
Japanese, embassy at Seoul attacked, 439; savagery at Port Arthur, 453; policy in Manchuria, 455; humiliation by Europe, 461.
Jehangir, Kojeh of Kashgar, 50, 375, 377.
Jeh-ho, or Chingtih, Hienfung retires to, 330; palace conspiracy at, 338.
Jesuit missionaries, disliked by Yungching, 91; mission at Wuhu wrecked, 422.

KAIFUNG (Pien-liang), capital of Honan, stormed by Tai-pings, 245; surly spirit in during famine, 384; Yellow River flood at, 417.
Kanghi, Emperor, and Koxinga, 46; Portuguese embassy to, 77; Louis XIV. to, 89; sends Tulishen to the Czar, 90; his prophecy quoted, 132.
Kansuh, province, Mohammedan rebellion in, 378.
Kara-korum Mountains, Carpini's visit to Kuyuk at, 64.
Kashgar, government and town, 376; its reconquest, 379.
Kautsu, or Lin Pang, founder of Han Dynasty, 28.
Kautsung, Emperor of Tang Dynasty, 36.
Kelung (or Kilung), Formosa, taken by the French, 400, 403.
Kiakhta, on Russian frontier, 91.
Kiaking, Emperor, 48.
Kiayü kwan, on Great Wall, in Kansuh, 11.
Kieh Kwei, last Emperor of Hia Dynasty, 19.
Kienlung, Emperor, 47; Van Braam's embassy to, 87; and Mr. Flint, 97.
Kim Ok-kiun, a Korean patriot, 440.
Kin, or Niu-chih (Nu-chih), Tartars in Peking, 40; inscription in Kü-yung kwan, 42; overthrow the Mings, 44.
Kingsmill, T. W., 25, 54.
Kirin in Manchuria, outrage at, 425.
Kishen, Viceroy of Chihli, 164; apologizes, 165; negotiates with Captain Elliot at the Bogue, 166; ordered to Peking, 169; associated with Yihking, 177.
Kitan, or Liautung Tartars, harass the After Tsin, 38.
Kiukiang, on the Yangtsz', captured by rebels, 243.
Kiying, Commissioner, 78; associated with Ilipu, 185; writes to Pottinger, 194; signs Nanking treaty, 197; exchanges ratifications, 205; his proclamation, 206; includes all foreigners, 209; and other foreign representatives, 213; meets Minister Cushing, 214; on homicide case, 216; treaty with France, 219; on opium question, 225; on murder of Englishman, 226; disbands braves about Canton, 228; appears unexpectedly at Tientsin, 301; his fate, 302.
Klaproth, J., 13, 26, 28, 59, 69, 90.
Kolao hwui, a secret society, 433.
Korea, conquered by the Tang, 35; Port Hamilton restored to, 409; relations with China and Japan, 437-439; invaded, 442; cleared of Chinese, 446; declared autonomous, 460.
Kowlung, opposite Hongkong, 154; ceded to the British, 206, 334; customs house located at, 407.
Kowshing sunk off Asan, 443.
Koxinga takes Formosa, 46, 83.
Kublai khan, 41; receives the Polos, 68.
Kuche, in Ili, 378.
Kuchăng (or Kutien) massacre, 427.
Kuldja (Gouldja, Kulja, Kuren or Hwuiyuen ching) and Russia, 375, 378; negotiations respecting, 379-382.
Kung, Sixth Prince (*Kung tsin-wang*), appointed regent, 50; rewards Colonel Gordon, 264; negotiates with Elgin at Peking, 330; signs treaty, 334; his *coup d'état*, 339; refuses to ratify Lay's agreement, 342; and coolie trade, 346; and Tientsin riot, 350; and audience question, 360, 363; his son in the succession, 374, 387; dismissed by Empress-Dowager, 397; and education, 415; and extension of foreign residence, 430.
Kuyuk khan, Plano Carpini's visit to, 63.
Kü-yung kwan, gateway at, 42.

Kwangsü province and Tai-ping rebellion, 238–243.
Kwangsü, Emperor, 51, 52; his accession, 374; marriage and reign, 410.
Kwangtung province, resists Manchu conquest, 45; rebels in, 252, 278; anti-foreign riots in, 420.
Kweiliang, Commissioner, 299; sent to Shanghai, 305; refuses to accompany allies to Taku, 312; discusses audience question with Minister Ward, 317; sent to intercept Elgin at Tientsin, 325; supports Prince Kung, 339.
Kweilin, capital of Kwangsi, attacked by Tai-pings, 243.

LAGRÉE, Captain Doudart de, 391.
Lagrené, French envoy to China, 89; concludes treaty at Whampoa, 219.
Lang, Captain, 405.
Lange, Laurent, in Peking, 90.
Langson, in Tongking, French repulse at, 399; evacuated, 401; mentioned, 403, 404.
Laokai, on Yunnan frontier, 404.
Lavallée, C., 295, 302, 332, 383.
Lay, H. N., appointed intendent of customs, 276; his flotilla, 340.
Lay, W. T., 269.
Le Gendre, C. W., 365.
Legge, J., 9, 10, 13.
Lew Chew Islands and China's suzerainty, 393.
Li Hung-chang, 259; executes surrendered Tai-pings, 263, 264; dissolves the Ever-Victorious force, 266; and Wade in Chifu convention, 372; denounces treaty of Livadia, 380; during the famine, 383; and the Fournier convention, 398; concludes a treaty with Patenôtre, 402; and the military improvements, 405; punished, 411, 459; and railroads, 416; 419; concludes treaties with Japan, 440, 460.
Liang Dynasty, 32; After Liang, 37.
Liang A-fah's tracts reach Hung Siu-tsuen, 230, 237.
Liau, Tartar tribe, 39, 40.
Liau tung Promontory, 459, 454; retrocession of, 460.
Li-kin, tax on opium compromised, 406, 419.
Lin Tseh-sü, Commissioner, 50; reaches Canton, 145; demands surrender of opium, 146; proceedings at Canton, 146–164; memorial to Emperor, 166; recalled from banishment, 177; his death, 238.
Lintin, opium smugglers at, 127; and Captain Elliot, 139.
Literati, or literary aristocracy of China, persecuted by Tsin, 28; prejudiced against Western learning, 415; cause of anti-foreign outrages, 419, 429.
Liu Ming-chuan, 410.
Liu Ping-chang, Viceroy, punished, 436.
Ljungstedt, Sir A., History of Macao, 78.
Loch, Captain G. G., 184, 189, 191, 195, 198.
Loch, Henry, at Tungchau, 326; imprisoned at Peking, 328, 329; returned to the English, 332, 333.
Lohyang, ancient capital, 25, 28, 30, 34, 40, 59.
Low, F. F., United States Minister, 348; on sentiment toward foreigners at Tientsin, 352; reply to Wănsiang, 356; on the audience question, 361, 362; thanked by Prince Kung, 387.
Lu, Governor of Kwangtung, 112; rejects Napier's letter, 115; stops the trade, 119, 120; is superceded, 129.
Lungchow, Kwangsi, opened to trade, 404.

MACAO, Governor of Canton, escapes from pirates to, 49; origin of name and settlement, 76; recent history, 78; Dutch repulsed before, 81; British warship at, 96; troops occupy, 104; Lord Napier reaches, 112; retires to, 154; Lin's soldiers repulsed at, 164; Kiying goes to, 215; becomes a hive of smugglers, 282, 407; and of Coolie traders, 310; coolie iniquity stopped, 363; ceded to Portugal and smuggling checked, 407.
Macartney, Lord, embassy to Peking, 102.
McCarthy, Justin, 213; on "Arrow War," 282, 285, 335.
McClatchie, Canon T., 8.
McGiffin, Captain P. N., 447, 449.
Mackie, J. Milton, 250, 272.
Magaillans (Magalhaens), Père Gabriel, his embassy, 77.
Mahan, Captain A. T., 446, 449.
Mailla, J. A. M. de M., 3, 18, 61.
Maimai chin, frontier trading post, 91.
Manchu Dynasty, dreads invasion, 290; pride in Mukden, 455.
Manchuria, railroads in, 416; anti-foreign outrage in, 427; Chinese troops in, 444, 454.
Manchus, spring from the Kins, 40; overthrow the Mings; 44; their government better than their predecessors, 51; close China to foreign trade, 74; terrible destruction of, at Chinkiang, 190; as rulers of China, 228; Chinese dislike of and Tai-ping revolt, 244.
Manghao, in Yunnan, 403.
Mangtsz', in Yunnan, treaty town, 403.
Mangu khan, Kuyuk's successor, and Rubruquis, 66; visited by King Hayton, 68.
Marco Polo. See Polo.
Margary, A. R., sent from Hankow to Bhamo, 369; his murder, 370; investigated, 371, 372.

Martin, R. M., 54, 91, 210; proposition as to Chusan, 228.
Martin, W. A. P., 389, 414; on Tientsin riot, 435.
Meadows, T. T., 244, 245, 272.
Medhurst, W. H., 17; Tai-ping translations, 242, 272.
Mekong River, explored, 391.
Miaotsz', Hung Siu-tsuen among the, 235.
Michie, Alex., 435.
Ming Dynasty, 43–45; table of emperors, 52.
Mingti, Emperor, 29.
Missionaries, in Kanghi's reign, 47; information derived from French, 88; French beheaded in Kwangsi, 290; British, address Lord Elgin, 297; influence in Peking, 337; French, killed in Tientsin, 348; American, leave Tăngchau, 353; Chinese grievances against, 357; devotion during the great famine, 384; Roman Catholic, and French protection, 407; chief sufferers from anti-foreign outbreaks, 420; residing in the interior, 430.
Missions, Russian, established at Peking, 91; rules suggested for regulating Christian, in China, 355; destroyed during riots, 348, 420–430.
Mobs, attack British troops before Canton, 171; attack factories, 143, 204, 206; at Wusueh, 424.
Mohammedan, insurrection in Kansuh, 357; in Yunnan, 367; in Eastern Turkestan, 375–379; refugees from Yunnan in Tongking, 393.
Mohammedans found in China by Ibn Batuta, 70; general uprising of, 378.
Mongols, their dynasty, the Yuen, 41, 43; their conquests in Europe, 63; Christian converts persecuted, 426.
Montecorvino, John of, in Cathay, 69; found by Oderic in Peking, 71.
Morrison, J. R., 168; his services, 195, 196, 204; his death, 208.
Morrison, Dr. Robert, 101, 106, 107.
Mukden, capital of Shingking, 455.
Murray, Hugh, 3, 18, 54, 58.
Myths, Chinese cosmic, 4–9.

NANKING, a feudal capital, 30; pillaged by the Kin, 41; capital of the Ming Dynasty, 43; the British before, 193; treaty of, 197; capital of the Tai-pings, 232; rebel capture of, 244; their distress in, 253; its fall, 268.
Napier, Lord, superintendent of British trade, 112; letter to Governor Lu rejected, 115; contest with the Governor, 119; death, 122.
Navy, Chinese, Lay's flotilla fiasco, 340; developed in 1865, 405; paralyzed at Hai yang tau, 449; remnant at Wei hai wei, 455; surrendered there, 458.
Nestorian, missionaries at Taitsung's court, 35; with traders, 59; priest and Rubruquis, 66.
Nganking (Anking), in Nganhwui, captured by Tai-pings, 243; their march to relieve, 255; taken by imperialists, 256.
Ningpo, Portuguese at, 76; captured by British, 175; attempted recapture, 179; during Tai-ping revolt, 256, 257.
Nieuwhof (Nieuhoff), J., 76; account of fall of Fort Zelandia, 84.
Niu Kien, Viceroy, at Wusung, 183, 185; and ransom of Nanking, 192; joint letter to Pottinger, 194.
Niu-chih (Nu-chih) or Kin Tartars, 40.
Niuchwang (Yingtsz'), 455; captured by Japanese, 459.
Nodzu, General, 444, 445.
Norman, C. B., 394, 395.
Norman, Henry, 396, 435.

ODORIC, Friar, journeys to Cathay, 70.
Officers in China, their methods, 205; and foreigners at close of the Opium War, 223; sent to Europe to study, 415; energy in repairing Yellow River dykes, 418; suicides after Wei hai wei, 458.
Oliphant, Lawrence, 292, 295, 302, 308.
Opium, smuggling under Taukwang, 50; value of trade, 78; Robinson's paper on, smuggling, 127; proposal to legalize, 130; referred to Canton, 134; prohibition enforced, 138; smuggling increases, 140; demanded by Lin, 146; surrendered, 150; and destroyed, 152; sales recommence, 154; Pottinger as to, 186; discusses, with commissioners, 198; smuggling at Hongkong, 206, 407; policy of Chinese and English after 1842, 209, 225; increased smuggling of, 281; legalized in revised tariff, 305; trade with Tongking, 403; *likin* on compounded and cultivation of legalized, 406.
Order of the Double Dragon, 404.
Osbeck, Peter, voyage to China, 109.
Oshima, General, 444, 445.
Ouchterlony, J., 199, 222.
Oyama, Marshal, 450, 453, 457.

PAI-LAU erected to commemorate British retirement from Canton, 274.
Panthay insurrection in Yunnan, 367.
Paper money, during Yuen Dynasty, 43; mentioned by Ibn Batuta, 70.
Parker, E. H., 438.
Parker, Dr. Peter, 215, 287.
Parker, Sir W., British Admiral, arrives, 172.
Parkes, Sir Harry, McCarthy's estimate of, 282; in *Arrow* affair, 283–285; in temporary government of Canton, 294; his ability, 295; at Tungchau, 326; capture

and imprisonment, 328; on "neutralizing Shanghai," 401.
Pascal, Spanish friar, at Kuldja, 72.
Pauthier, G., 61, 67, 351.
Pearl River (Chu kiang, or West River), Kwangtung, pirates on, 49; kept open by foreigners, 278; blocked below Canton, 401; navigation of withdrawn from Shimonoseki treaty, 460.
Pehtang, in Chihli, 313; Americans land at, 316; Ho desires ratifications exchanged at, 320; captured by Allies, 321.
Pei ho, Allies reach, 297; battle of the, 314.
Peking, captured by the Mongols, 41; by the Mings, 43, 44; Friar Odoric visits, 71; Van Hoorn's embassy at, 86; Russian mission at, 91; Tai-ping advance against, 245; Minister Ward's visits to, 317; Allies at, 330, 334; foreign quarter in, 336; removal of Catholic cathedral in, 408.
Penal Code framed by Yungloh, 43.
Pescadore Islands (Panghu), Dutch in, 81; French capture, 400; and evacuate, 403; Japanese seize, 459; and retain, 460.
Pichon, Dr. L., 404.
Pigeon-English, 274.
Pihkwei, made Governor of Canton, 294; wants trade reopened, 295.
Pilgrims, travels of Buddhist, 61.
Ping yang (or Phyöng yang), battle of, 445.
Pirates, infest Kwangtung, 49; chased by British and Portuguese, 280; in Tongking, 393.
Plano Carpini, John of, visits Kuyuk, 65.
Polo, Marco, 42, 63; journeys in China, 68, 73.
Poole, S. Lane, 397.
Pope of Rome, sends Plano Carpini to Kuyuk, 63; declines to establish a legation in China, 408.
Population, of China under the Tang, 37; of Peking, 335.
Port Arthur, or Lü shun kau, 400, 405, 449; captured, 450–453.
Port Hamilton seized, 409.
Port Lazaref, Korea, 409.
Portuguese, under the Mings, 43; and pirates in China, 49; their conduct in China, 74; misrepresent the English, 92; keep them from Canton, 94; homicide at Canton, 99; attack pirates, 280; smuggling lorchas, 282; abolish coolie trade at Macao, 311; Macao ceded to, 407.
Pottinger, Sir H., 172; takes Chinhai and Ningpo, 175; proclamation before Chinkiang, 185; and the opium trade, 187; Kiying writes to, 194; exchanges civilities, 195; discusses the opium problem, 198; signs treaty, 201; after Formosa massacres, 203; exchanges ratifications, 205; on J. R. Morrison, 209; and opium smuggling, 210.
Poutiatine, Admiral Count, 291.
Protestants in China. See Missionaries.
Ptolemy the geographer, mentions China, 56; his "Stone Tower," 57.
Pwanku, the first man, 4–7.

RAILROADS in China, 403, 404, 416; French in Tongking, 404.
Reed, W. B., U. S. Minister, 291, 297.
Reid, Gilbert, 435.
Reinaud, J. T., 34, 62, 73, 74.
Rémusat, Abel, 5, 33, 42, 89.
Rennie, Dr. D. F., 340.
Ricci, Père Matteo, 73.
Richthofen, F. von, 55, 59, 272.
Rivière, Henri, 396.
Roberts, I. J., and Hung Siu-tsuen, 235, 271.
Robinson, Sir G. B., and Napier, 112; succeeds him, 127.
Rome, Chinese knowledge of, under the Hans, 29; intercourse with, 58.
Roman Catholics, indemnified in treaty of Peking, 335; mission in Tientsin destroyed, 348; and French protection, 407; attacked at Wuhu, 422; pretensions of, 433.
Ross, John, 435.
Rubruquis, Friar W., visits Mangu khan, 66, 73.
Russia, seizes Kuldja, 375; in the Port Hamilton incident, 409–410; appealed to by China in 1894, 442; interferes to check Japan, 461.
Russian, boundary disputes, trade, and treaties with China, 89; Admiral joins Allies in China, 291; and American Ministers in Tientsin, 302; diplomacy and the Kuldja question, 380; railroad across Manchuria, 416.

SĂNGKOLINSIN, Tartar general, 312, 314; blunders before Taku, 322; retires toward Peking, 325; deception, 327; talks with Parkes, 328; responsibility for treatment of English prisoners, 333; allows the return of allied troops, 336.
Scott, J. G., 399.
Secret societies, in Hwashan massacre, 428; instigate anti-foreign fanaticism, 433.
Seoul, capital of Korea, 438, 440; politics at, 441; Japanese gain, 444.
Seres, Latin designation distinguished from *Sinæ*, 56.
Seymour, Admiral, 285; in South China, 286–288; takes Taku forts, 299.
Shang Dynasty, its annals, 20–24.
Shanghai, taken and ransomed by British,

284; at close of opium war, 221; captured by rebels, 252; protected by foreigners, 254; thanks Gordon, 267; customs duties at, collected by foreigners, 275; trouble with Cantonese rebels, 276; arsenal established at, 344; trade at, prostrated by Franco-Chinese hostilities, 401.

Shangti, perhaps worshipped as God, 20, 233; worship of, by the Tai-pings, 236, 244.

Shan-hai, kwan, railroad to, 416.

Shauking, in Kwangtung, Ricci at, 79; rebel slaughter at, 280.

Shaw, R. B., 377.

Shaw, Samuel, voyage to China, 108.

Shensi province, the Huns in, 31.

Shimonoseki, treaty of, 460.

Shu King, or "Book of Records," on Deluge of Yao, 13; its credibility, 18, 21; and House of Chau, 23, 25; and Shangti, 244.

Shun, Emperor, 11, 12, 14.

Shunchi, Emperor, 89.

Si-ngan (Hao-king, Chang-an), ancient capital, 18, 24, 34, 37; under the Tang Dynasty, 340.

Smuggling, at Hongkong, 281, 406; British encouragement of, 373; convention of 1887 to check, 407.

Songari River, in treaty of Livadia, 380.

Song-koi, or Red River, in Tongking, 391, 395; as a trade route, 404.

Sontai, in Tongking, 397.

Spanish trade and relations with China, 79; Don S. de Mas, Minister, 213; government and the coolie trade, 363.

Staunton, Sir G. L., 92, 102.

Staunton, Sir G. T., 100, 106, 108.

Stewart, Rev. R. W., murdered, 428.

Sü Kwang-tsin, Viceroy, keeps foreigners out of Canton, 221; his folly, 238, 252.

Suchau, in Kiangsu, captured by Tai-pings, 254; recaptured, 261.

Sushun, favorite of Hienfung, 252; his conspiracy and fate, 339.

Sui Dynasty, 33.

Sung Dynasty, Northern, 32; period of Sung, 39; Southern, 40.

Sungkiang, captured by Ward, 255; Gordon at, 260.

Sungpu, riot at, 426.

Suzerainty, China's claims over Annam, 393, 395, 398. 403; over Burma recognized, 409; over Korea, 437, 438.

Swedish missionaries killed, 426.

Swinhoe, Robert, 319, 321, 325, 331, 332, 333.

Sz'chuen province, under Tang generals, 39; missionary troubles in, 420, 427; Viceroy of, punished, 436.

Sz'ma Kwang, a historian, 40.

Sz'ma Tsien, a historian, 12, 15.

TAI-PING, 50; origin of term, 229; insurrection, 237-270; authorities on the movement, 272; rebels visited by Elgin, 307.

Taitsung, Emperor, 34-36.

Tai Wen Kun, Regent of Korea, 440.

Taku, on the Pei ho, Elliot and Kishen at, 163; allied fleet at, 297; Russians and Americans interview Tan at, 298; forts taken, 299; foreign Ministers repair to, 312; Americans negotiate at, 313; repulse of British at, 314; second capture of, 324; Chinese bravery at, and at Port Arthur, 452.

Talien Bay, 448; captured by Japanese, 451, 456.

Tang Dynasty, 33-37; After Tang, 38; official history, 61; travelling regulations under, 73.

Tăng Ting-ching, governor at Canton, 129; his son in opium trade, 141; position toward foreigners, 143; answer to Captain Elliot, 144; visits Macao, 154.

Tăngchau, missionaries leave, 353; Japanese before, 456.

Tan Ting-siang, Viceroy of Chihli, at Taku, 298; superseded by Kweiliang, 299.

Tanyang, riot at, 424.

Tariff, after Opium War, 206; after second war, 305; Franco-Chinese on Tongking border, 463, 464.

Tarim (or Ergu) River, reconquest of valley, 375.

Tatnall, Commodore Josiah, at Taku, 313, 316.

Taukwang, Emperor, 49; efforts to stop opium trade, 140, 145; rejects Bogue treaty, 167; his spirit in pushing the war, 175; proclamation on its causes, 187; his death, 223.

Tea, duty on in 1689, 94.

Telegraphs in China, 389, 400.

Tennent, Sir T. E., 61.

Terranova, an American sailor, 101; his judicial murder, 108.

Thom, R., interpreter to Pottinger, 196, 204, 205.

Tientsin, Flint at, 87; Tai-pings repulsed at, 246; Allies reach, 299; negotiations at, 302; allied armies return to, 325; riot at, 348; feeling in the city, 351; railroads built from, 416; foreign policy after riot ineffective, 435.

Timur (Ching-tsung), Kublai's successor, 42.

Ting Ju-chang, Admiral, 447, 455, 457; his suicide, 459.

Tinghai, Chusan Archipelago, first capture, 162; second, 173.

Ting yuen, battleship, 448; sunk, 457.

Timkowski, E. F., 90, 91.

Tong hak, or "Eastern Doctrine" rebellion in Korea, 439, 441.

Tongking, occupied by Garnier, 392, 395; conquered by French, 397; guerilla war in, 399, 490.
Tourgouths, Tulishen's mission respecting the, 90.
Touraue, in Annam, 391.
Trade, ancient with Roman Empire, 59, 63; restricted by Manchus to Canton, 74; Portuguese, 78; Spanish, 79; Dutch, 81; Russian, 89; English, 91–107; peculiarities of early Chinese, 98; American, 108; Napier, superintendent of British, 112; during his control, 121–125; Lin stops the British, 155; during the opium war, 165, 169, 172; regulations after the war, 205; with Tongking under treaty, 403, 404; Hongkong junk, and customs agreement, 406.
Travel, ancient and mediæval, to China, 60–74; regulated under the Tangs, 73.
Treaty, Russian, 89; failure of negotiations at Bogue, 166; of Nanking, 197; ratified, 207; British supplementary signed at Bogue, 209; of Wanghai between China and the United States, 215; French, at Whampoa, 219; how regarded by Chinese, 226; of Tientsin signed, 304; difficulty of enforcing, 306; American, ratified at Pehtang, 318; English and French signed at Peking, 334; the Burlingame, 346; of 1880, 347; of Livadia, 380; of Marquis Tsăng settling the Kuldja question, 382; of 1874 between Annam and France, 395; China's refusal to recognize it, 397; the Fournier, 398; concluding Franco-Chinese hostilities, 402; between China and Portugal, 407; proposed revision of Tientsin, 430; American, with Korea, 438; concluded by Li and Ito respecting Korea, 440; of Shimonoseki, 460.
Triad Society opposed by Hung Siutsuen, 239.
Trigautius (Trigault), French missionary, 73, 76.
Tsăng Kwoh-fan, generalissimo against Tai-pings, 266; visited by Gordon, 268; investigates Tientsin riot, 351; his son sent to Europe, 381; collected works published, 405; founds a loyalist society, 434.
Tsăng Chi-tsz', Marquis, 381; withdraws from Paris, 397; arranges opium agreement of 1885 with Lord Salisbury, 406.
Tsi Dynasty, 32.
Tsin Dynasty, 29, 31; after Tsin, 38.
Tsin, name China perhaps derived from, 27; *Ta-tsin*, ancient term for Rome, 58.
Tsin Chi Hwangti, "Emperor First," 26; subjugates Annam, 392.
Tsing Dynasty, 45–52.
Tsiuenchau (Chinchew), the ancient Zayton, 79.
Tso Tsung-tang, campaign against Mohammedan rebels, 357; successful, 378; leader of the war faction, 380; his dying memorial favors progress, 405.
Tsung-li Yamun, 342; parties in the, 347; accused of complicity in Tientsin riot, 354; discusses audience, 360; and Lewchewan envoys, 366; and Sir T. Wade, 374; entertains foreign ministers, 412; anti-foreign member, 420; and foreign residence in the interior, 430.
Tsz'ki, near Ningpo, visited by British, 178; camp near, 179; Ward's death at, 257; taken from the Tai-pings, 258.
Tu Duc, King of Annam, 395.
Tungchau, Ward's embassy at, 317; Parke's experiences in, 326–329.
Tungchi, Emperor, 50; palace intrigue upon accession of, 339; his marriage, 358; audience to foreign ministers, 362; his death, and the succession, 374.
Tung-wăn Kwan, Imperial College at Peking, 344, 389, 415.
Turkestan, Chinese, Tien-shan Nan Lu, 374.

UNITED STATES of America, begins a trade with China, 108; first minister sent, 213; treaty of Wanghia, 215; joins the Allies in Second War, 291; Minister Ward at Peking, 317; concludes Burlingame treaty, 346; and indemnity surplus, 384; Chinese sent to, for education, 387; forces Korea to make a treaty, 438. [See also under American.]

VEGETARIAN Society (*Tsai hwui*), in Fuhkien, 428.
Villiers, Frederic, 454.
Vlangali, Russian Minister to Peking, 347; action at trial of Tientsin rioters, 353.

WADE, Sir T. F., 272; intendant of customs at Shanghai, 274; experiences at Tungchau, 326; good offices between Japan and China, 365; action upon Margary's murder, 372; his minute on the Chifu Convention, 373.
Walrond, T., 285, 303, 308, 310.
Wanghia, treaty of between the U. S. and China, 215; taken as basis for subsequent French treaty, 219.
Wănsiang, Minister of the Tsung-li Yamun, 347; letter to foreign Ministers, 355; Minister Low's reply, 356; and the *kowtow*, 362; character and influence, 363.
War, with Great Britain, the Opium, 111; England's reasons for declaring, 158; debate upon, 160; its progress, 162–198; a wholesome infliction, 220; authorities

upon, 222; the Tai-ping Rebellion, 213-2?2; Second English, 283-307; renewed by repulse at Taku, 314; the Allies recommence, 321; and conclude. 330; authorities on, 332; objects attained, 335, 336; with France over Annam, not declared, 397; its progress and conclusion, 398-404; with Japan, averted, 365, 440; declared, 443; its course, 443-459.
Ward, Fred'k. G., organizes the "Ever-Victorious Force," 255; his death at Tsz'ki, 257.
Ward, Minister J. E., 308; and coolie trade, 311; with Allies at Taku, 312; interviews Chinese, 313; goes to Peking, 316; refuses to kotow and returns, 318.
Wei hai wei, Shantung, 450; Japanese attack, 455; capture, 457.
Westlake, J., 443.
Whampoa, on Canton River, homicide at, 101; Franco-Chinese treaty of, 219.
Wiju, on the Yalu River, 446.
Williamson, Alexander, 454.
Wilson, Andrew, 250, 258, 259, 264, 265, 343.
Wilson, General J. H., 418.
Wolseley, Garnet, 320, 323; on coolies, 322; his narrative, 333.
Wu Tsih-tien, Empress Wu of the Tang Dynasty, 36.
Wuchang, in Hupeh, captured by Taipings, 243.
Wuhu, riot at, 421.
Wusueh, riot at, 424.
Wusung, near Shanghai, captured by the British, 182.
Wylie, Alexander, 42.
Wylie, J. A., murder of, 427, 437.

YAKUB BEG, Atalik Ghazi, of Turkestan, 375; defeat and death, 378.
Yalu River, Amnok gang, 444, 454; so-called Battle of the, 448.
Yamagata, Marshal, in Korea, 444, 454.
Yang and *Yin*, the two principles in creation, 3, 7.
Yangi Hissar, Kashgar, 376.
Yangtsz', or Ta kiang, British fleet upon, 182; ravages of Tai-pings in valley of, 251; their control of, 254; ports on, opened to foreign trade, 373, 425; anti-foreign feeling in, valley, 434; ports opened by Japanese treaty of 1895, 460.
Yao the Great, his place in history, 10; and the deluge, 13.
Yarkand, or Yerkiang, 376; its reconquest, 379.
Yeh Ming-chin, Commissioner and Governor General, 252, 278; his policy of seclusion, 281, 282; action in *Arrow* case, 284-286; burns the foreign factories in Canton, 287; refuses British ultimatum, 291; captured, 292; sent to India, 295.
Yeh-ho-na-la, consort of Kwangsü, 411.
Yellow River (Hwang ho), early migration to, 10; ancient record of its overflow, 13; terrible inundation of 1887, 417.
Yihking, the "majesty-bearing generalissimo," 177; his terror and flight to Suchau, 179.
Yihshau, nephew of Taukwang, general of Canton forces, 169; his defensive measures there, 275, 302.
Yingtsz' or Yingkow, Niuchwang port, 455, 459.
Younghusband, F. E., 454.
Yu the Great, Emperor, drains the flood, 13, 14; inscription of, 15; his acts and successors, 19.
Yuen, or Mongol Dynasty, 41-43.
Yuen-ming Yuen, palace, destroyed by Allies, 330.
Yukien, Commissioner, despair and suicide at fall of Chinhai, 174.
Yule, Sir H., 34, 42, 56, 57, 58, 60, 61, 62, 63, 64, 65, 66, 67, 68, 69, 71, 72, 73, 89.
Yung Wing, and Chinese education commission, 387, 388.
Yungching, Emperor, 47; receives Magaillans, 76; and Russian mission, 91.
Yungching, Shantung Promontory, 456.
Yungloh, Emperor, 43; expedition against Ceylon, 62.
Yunnan province, Sladen's expedition to, 367; the Grosvenor mission to, 371; Black Flags come from, 393; trade with Tongking after French treaty, 404; ruin in, 405.

ZAYTON (Chinchew) visited by Friar Odoric, 70, 76.